Pro ASP.NET Web API

HTTP Web Services in ASP.NET

Tugberk Ugurlu
Alexander Zeitler
Ali Kheyrollahi

Apress

Pro ASP.NET Web API: HTTP Web Services in ASP.NET

ISBN-13 (pbk): 978-1-4302-4725-8

ISBN-13 (electronic): 978-1-4302-4726-5

President and Publisher: Paul Manning
Lead Editor: Gwenan Spearing
Development Editor: Chris Nelson
Technical Reviewer: Robert Swafford
Editorial Board: Steve Anglin, Mark Beckner, Ewan Buckingham, Gary Cornell, Louise Corrigan, Morgan Ertel,
    Jonathan Gennick, Jonathan Hassell, Robert Hutchinson, Michelle Lowman, James Markham,
    Matthew Moodie, Jeff Olson, Jeffrey Pepper, Douglas Pundick, Ben Renow-Clarke, Dominic Shakeshaft,
    Gwenan Spearing, Matt Wade, Tom Welsh
Coordinating Editor: Anamika Panchoo
Copy Editors: Tom McCarthy, Mary Bearden
Compositor: SPi Global
Indexer: SPi Global
Artist: SPi Global
Cover Designer: Anna Ishchenko

Distributed to the book trade worldwide by Springer Science+Business Media New York, 233 Spring Street, 6th Floor, New York, NY 10013. Phone 1-800-SPRINGER, fax (201) 348-4505, e-mail orders-ny@springer-sbm.com, or visit www.springeronline.com. Apress Media, LLC is a California LLC and the sole member (owner) is Springer Science+Business Media Finance Inc. (SSBM Finance Inc.). SSBM Finance Inc. is a Delaware corporation.

For information on translations, please e-mail rights@apress.com, or visit www.apress.com.

Apress and friends of ED books may be purchased in bulk for academic, corporate, or promotional use. eBook versions and licenses are also available for most titles. For more information, reference our Special Bulk Sales–eBook Licensing web page at www.apress.com/bulk-sales.

Any source code or other supplementary materials referenced by the author in this text is available to readers at www.apress.com. For detailed information about how to locate your book's source code, go to www.apress.com/source-code/.

Contents at a Glance

Contents

About the Authors

Tugberk Ugurlu is a software developer and a Microsoft MVP who specializes in software for the tourism industry, where he has worked for the past 10 years. He works mostly with ASP.NET and its different frameworks such as ASP.NET MVC, ASP.NET Web API, and ASP.NET SignalR. After studying travel management at college, he was dragged into programming and has been passionate about .NET and its siblings ever since. Although he gets paid for building software applications for tourism services and products, he is also a very involved member of the community and likes to share his knowledge with others through his blog (http://tugberkugurlu.com) and webcasts, by authoring books, and giving talks on various topics. He currently lives in Istanbul, Turkey, and is married to his lovely wife, Nihan.

Alexander Zeitler is a self-employed developer at PDMLab. He has spent over 17 years developing software and web applications, mainly for the tool industry, as well as machinery and plant engineering, where he works mainly with ASP.NET Web API and ASP.NET MVC on the server side and HTML5, CSS3, and JavaScript on the client side. He has been rewarded repeatedly with the Microsoft MVP award in ASP.NET for his engagement with the German .NET community, and he maintains a blog at http://blog.alexonasp.net.

Ali Kheyrollahi left medicine for his love of programming after years of study and five years of practicing. Thirteen years later, he is a solutions architect for a blue chip company, yet at heart he is the same kid in the toy shop enjoying coding and discovering new shiny technologies. Ali loves HTTP, API design, and business modeling DDD style. In his spare time, he is a blogger and open source author and contributor, working on a few popular projects such as CacheCow, an HTTP-caching solution for ASP.NET Web API. He also has a passion for computer vision and has published a few papers on the subject in scientific journals, including *Machine Vision and Applications*. He has a taste for avant-garde films and music and enjoys watching films with his lovely wife, Khatereh.

About the Technical Reviewer

Rob Swafford is a senior developer at Sonoma Partners, LLC, specializing in .NET web application development. He has been working with ASP.NET and related technologies for nearly a decade. His industry experience has spanned a wide range of companies from small startup shops to government and multinational corporations.

Acknowledgments

I especially thank my beautiful wife, Nihan, for her support to make the possibility of this book a reality. I also thank everyone at Apress who dedicated his or her time for this book.

—*Tugberk Ugurlu*

I thank my wonderful wife for her patience and for always being there. I also thank the folks at Apress for the opportunity to contribute to this book.

—*Alexander Zeitler*

I thank my lovely wife for putting up with a couch potato staring at a laptop, occasionally typing a few words, and then pressing the backspace button. And needless to say, thanks to the amazing people at Apress for making this possible.

—*Ali Kheyrollahi*

Introduction

If you would like to discover the possibilities offered by HTTP on the .NET Framework, ASP.NET Web API is the technology for you. This book will get you up to speed on how it works and how to use it at both high and low levels.

We have structured this book to make it really easy to use. If you would like to get your hands dirty quickly, we recommend that you work through Chapters 1 to 7 in order, because Chapters 5, 6, and 7 are all about building a sample multitier application using ASP.NET Web API. This sample application is intended as a guide on how to structure an ASP.NET Web API application in a hosting-agnostic way (from both API and client perspectives). We recommend you download the source code and run the application locally to begin with. You can download the source code from www.apress.com/9781430247258 along with all the other code related to this book. Alternatively, you can get it from GitHub (https://github.com/tugberkugurlu/PingYourPackage) through a Git client (make sure to check out the "Edition-1" branch). No matter which method you choose, be sure to read the "Run the Application" section inside the README.md file (https://github.com/tugberkugurlu/PingYourPackage/blob/Edition-1/README.md) to get the sample application running smoothly.

If you prefer to get into the core of the ASP.NET Web API framework, you can choose to skip the sample application chapters and go straight to the feature-specific chapters on routing, controllers, message handlers, filters, and so on. These chapters really dive into the details of the specific parts of the ASP.NET Web API request pipeline and will give you a deep understanding of how the framework is processing your request.

Required Software

To use this book, you will need:

- .NET Framework 4.5 or higher
- Visual Studio 2012 or later
- Visual Studio Extension: NuGet Package Manager
- Visual Studio Extension: xUnit.net runner for Visual Studio
- SQL Server Express (for sample applications and some other samples)

Any other software we make use of in the book is available through NuGet.

CHAPTER 1

■ ■ ■

Introduction to ASP.NET Web API

The fact that you are reading this means you are interested in learning *something* about ASP.NET Web API (application programming interface). Perhaps you are relatively new to web services and want an expansive view. You may already be familiar with the technology and just need to swim a bit deeper into the Web API waters; hence, you need a beacon to guide you through unfamiliar places. Or maybe you are already a pro and just want to fill those few gaps in your knowledge. Wherever you are in this journey, stay tight as we are about to start our ride, and it is going to be fun!

ASP.NET Web API is the new cool kid on the block that gets us all excited. It is the new shiny tool that we love to use and it would be great to claim experience in it on our CV. But that is not why you should learn about it.

We believe ASP.NET Web API is a technology that is going to change the way we think about and develop our server applications. It will change how we approach designing and implementing services. It will also affect our decisions in writing client code. ASP.NET Web API already has a rich and active community around it that is adding useful building blocks on top of its extensible model. And it is here to stay, as it *talks web*. So these are some of reasons why it is necessary to learn about it.

This chapter won't deal with much code, but not to worry, there will be plenty of opportunities in the upcoming chapters. But first it is essential to see how ASP.NET Web API is going to fit into the overall picture of modern web-based architecture as well as middle tier services.

This chapter will start by defining what the ASP.NET Web API is and then move on to the background and architecture before giving the reasons why you would choose (or not choose) ASP.NET Web API for solving business solutions.

ASP.NET Web API

This section will briefly explain what ASP.NET Web API is, the libraries that comprised it, and where its source came from. We keep the more detailed discussion until after we have covered its background in the following section.

The Basics

ASP.NET Web API is a web framework that is built on top of Microsoft .NET 4.0 and above, implements the HTTP (HyperText Transfer Protocol) specification, and can be used to build or consume HTTP service, as opposed to SOAP (Simple Object Application Protocol) or WCF (Windows Communication Foundation) services. As we will see later, ASP.NET Web API started its life as WCF Web API, but as the team started building the framework, it became more and more evident that it was best suited as a web framework rather than a service framework. As such, the team became part of the ASP.NET team and started working with them to build the rest.

The first version of the project was released in August 2012 along with Visual Studio 2012, .NET 4.5, and ASP.NET MVC (Model-View-Controller). The next version of the framework is due to be released in late 2013.

As Glenn Block, one of the key ASP.NET Web API project leaders puts it, ASP.NET Web API embraces HTTP as a first-class citizen and makes it extremely easy to build RESTful services. So ASP.NET Web API implements RFC 2616 (HTTP 1.1 specification) while staying nonopinionated toward REST. (REST or REpresentational State Transfer is covered as part of Chapter 3.) This was a key decision by the team, which kept ASP.NET Web API from getting entangled in the endless controversies surrounding REST and enabled it to stay practical, pragmatic, and focused on delivering value through implementing HTTP. As such, in the rest of this book we usually avoid the common phrase REST API (unless we actually mean RESTful) and instead use the phrase HTTP API.

ASP.NET Web API can be used to turn a traditional ASP.NET web project into a powerful HTTP API capable of taking advantage of all the richness of HTTP including content negotiation, caching, concurrency validation, and so forth. The client part of the framework can be used by desktop or Windows phone applications (as well as server applications and middleware) to consume any HTTP API written in any framework as long as it stays compliant with the HTTP specification.

ASP.NET Web API is revolutionary in many aspects not limited to the promise it delivers. It was one of the first Microsoft projects to run completely as an open source project that accepts contributions and fixes from the community. It has fully engaged with the community, constantly receiving feedback, and the team has been listening carefully to what the community has been saying.

ASP.NET Web API was inspired by the ASP.NET MVC concepts and design, and it was built with similar abstractions. If you are familiar with ASP.NET MVC, you will see many parallel implementations (such as controllers, actions, filters, etc.). Yet as you will see, it improved on the modularity of its components and is an *independent implementation* from ASP.NET MVC and can be used on its own.

■ **Note**   ASP.NET Web API was released with ASP.NET MVC 4 and its implementation has many similarities with ASP.NET MVC. A common mistake is to think of ASP.NET Web API as an extension to ASP.NET MVC partly because Web API Visual Studio templates can only be accessed by choosing an ASP.NET MVC 4 project type. This notion is incorrect and unhelpful as these two frameworks are completely independent. Although they can be used together, they do not have to be. ASP.NET MVC is ideal for serving server-side–rendered views, while ASP.NET Web API is best used as a web service exposing a service API.

ASP.NET Web API Libraries

ASP.NET Web API can be downloaded or used as NuGet packages. Also in order to get Visual Studio project templates, you need to download and install ASP.NET MVC 4.

To download ASP.NET MVC 4, you can go straight to the Microsoft Download Center and look for the ASP.NET MVC 4 bundle, or you can use the Web Platform Installer and choose ASP.NET MVC 4, which will contain the essential libraries for building ASP.NET Web API as well as Web API project templates as part of the ASP.NET MVC 4 templates.

If you would like to add NuGet reference to your project, depending on your scenario, you need to select from the different NuGet packages available. Each of these NuGet packages contains a subset of the framework tailored for a particular use case. It is important to note that some of these libraries are additions to the .NET Framework and are now standard DLLs (Dynamic Link Library) of .NET 4.5. Table 1-1 lists the ASP.NET Web API NuGet packages and their use cases.

Table 1-1. *ASP.NET Web API NuGet Packages and Their Dependent Packages*

NuGet Package	NuGet Dependency (Contains)	Use Case
`Microsoft.AspNet.WebApi.Core`	`Microsoft.AspNet.WebApi.Client` (`System.Web.Http.dll`)	Library development
`Microsoft.AspNet.WebApi.Client`	`Microsoft.Net.Http` `Newtonsoft.Json` (`System.Net.Http.Formatting.dll`)	Consuming HTTP endpoints using `HttpClient`; capable of consuming different formats
`Microsoft.AspNet.WebApi.HelpPage`	`Microsoft.AspNet.WebApi.WebHost` `Microsoft.AspNet.Mvc` `Microsoft.AspNet.Razor` (templates, views, and assets required for displaying help page)	Creating help pages for your APIs implemented in ASP.NET Web API
`Microsoft.AspNet.WebApi.OData`	`Microsoft.Net.Http` `Microsoft.AspNet.WebApi.Client` `Microsoft.AspNet.WebApi.Core` `Microsoft.Data.OData` (`System.Web.Http.OData.dll`)	Exposing your data as an OData HTTP service
`Microsoft.AspNet.WebApi.SelfHost`	`Microsoft.AspNet.WebApi.Core` (`System.Web.Http.SelfHost.dll`)	Creating a Web API service and exposing it inside a non-web application as a self-hosted service
`Microsoft.AspNet.WebApi.Tracing`	`Microsoft.AspNet.WebApi.Core` (`System.Web.Http.Tracing.dll`)	Allows the ASP.NET Web API framework to trace to `System.Diagnostics.Trace`
`Microsoft.AspNet.WebApi.WebHost`	`Microsoft.AspNet.WebApi.Core` `Microsoft.Web.Infrastructure` (`System.Web.Http.WebHost.dll`)	Hosting Web API in a web application
`Microsoft.Net.Http`	(`System.Net.Http` `System.Net.Http.WebRequest`)	Provides a programming interface for modern HTTP applications; contains `HttpClient`
`Newtonsoft.Json`	(`Newtonsoft.Json.dll`)	JSON serialization and deserialization

One of the interesting aspects of ASP.NET Web API is that Microsoft decided to have a dependency on `Newtonsoft.Json`, which is an open source library. Although this had happened before with jQuery in previous versions of MVC, this is the first time Microsoft has had an open source .NET library dependency. `Newtonsoft.Json` is an excellent JSON (JavaScript Object Notation) implementation widely adopted in the community.

Because work on the ASP.NET Web API is ongoing, there are also prerelease NuGet packages available for some of the libraries listed above.

ASP.NET Web API Source Code

As part of the Microsoft initiative to embrace open source software (OSS), ASP.NET Web API (along with some other projects such as Entity Framework 5.0) started its life as an open source project. The project was (and is) hosted on the CodePlex web site as a Git repository and run under agile methodology with the complete visibility of the whole backlog. You can download the source code from `http://aspnetwebstack.codeplex.com/SourceControl/latest`. Alternatively, you can clone the Git repository hosted on the CodePlex web site. Complete instructions on how to set up Git and then clone the repository can also be found on the CodePlex web site (`http://aspnetwebstack.codeplex.com/`).

After downloading the source code, you can run the `build.cmd` file in the command prompt. Before doing that, you might have to open the solution and enable the NuGet package restore on the solution so the NuGet dependencies can be downloaded. We highly recommend to download the source code, review the code, and get a feel for the extent of the framework.

You can also download the nightly build libraries containing prerelease features of the ASP.NET Web API from the same web site.

ASP.NET Web API Background

Now that you know what ASP.NET Web API is and how to get its libraries and source code, let's look at the context in which ASP.NET Web API was formed.

As stated earlier, ASP.NET Web API is an implementation of the HTTP specification that enables you to build an HTTP API on top of the .NET Framework. Considering the HTTP 1.1 specification (which is the latest HTTP spec, although work on HTTP 2.0 has started) was ratified in 1999, why did it take 13 years for Microsoft to finally provide a first-class framework to expose the true power of HTTP? We are going to find out with a journey back in time.

HTTP

In the early 1990s, a few talented engineers in the CERN laboratory, led by Tim Berners-Lee, were working on a concept called the World Wide Web (originally one word, "WorldWideWeb"), which was meant to provide document exchange over the network. World Wide Web, also known as WWW or W3, was initially targeted at scientific organizations over the world to be able to author, publish, and exchange research materials. By the end of 1990, Tim Berners-Lee already had a working prototype of a web server and a browser capable of rendering documents and traversing links.

In 1993, CERN decided that WWW would no longer be a proprietary body of work and it would be free for everyone to use. This led the way for an international body created by the end of 1994, which was known as the World Wide Web Consortium or W3C.

W3C started to formalize the work that had been done in CERN, and as a result, drafts of a few key protocols were created. These protocols were later known as HTTP, HTML, and URI based on the earlier work by Tim Berners-Lee. These three protocols were the building blocks of the revolutionary phenomenon that we know now as the Internet. A timeline of these events is provided in Table 1-2.

Table 1-2. *World Wide Web and HTTP Timeline*

Year	Event
1945	Vannevar Bush described Memex, the first proto-hypertext system in the article "As We May Think."
1960s	Systems are built around the hypertext concepts such as Hypertext Editing System (HES), Project Xanadu, and oN-Line System NLS.
1970	Arthur C. Clarke predicted that satellites would someday "bring the accumulated knowledge of the world to your fingertips" using a console that would combine the functionality of the photocopier, telephone, television, and a small computer, allowing data transfer and video conferencing around the globe.
1980	Tim Berners-Lee built the first system based on hypertext.
1984	Tim Berners-Lee joined CERN to enable collaboration of scientists over the network in a heterogenous platform environment.
1989	Tim Berners-Lee wrote a proposal on a large hypertext system with typed hyperlinks.
1990	Robert Cailliau formalized Tim's proposal and suggested the name "WorldWideWeb" or W3 for the hypertext project.
1990	Tim Berners-Lee finished building the first working prototype of a web server and a browser.
1993	Mosaic, the first graphical web browser, is built.
1993	CERN decided WWW will be free.
1994	World Wide Web Consortium is formed at MIT.
1996	HTTP 1.0 specification ratified by W3C as RFC 1945.
1999	HTTP 1.1 specification ratified by W3C as RFC 2616.
2006	Amazon uses RESTful API to expose its public cloud.
2012	Microsoft publishes ASP.NET Web API framework.

Source: Wikipedia `http://en.wikipedia.org/wiki/World_Wide_Web`

W3C published the HTTP 1.0 specification in 1996 as part of RFC 1945. This specification listed three authors: Tim Berners-Lee, Roy Fielding, and Henrik Frystyk Nielsen. By the time HTTP 1.1 was published in 1999 by the same authors (and a couple more), *HTTP was not merely a document exchange protocol, it was the engine of distributed computing for many years to come.*

Roy Fielding, best known for proposing the REST architectural style, was seminal in bringing distributed computing concepts such as caching and concurrency to the heart of HTTP. At the time of writing HTTP 1.1 spec, he was studying toward his PhD in information and computer science, and as part of his thesis, he was working on an optimal architectural style for distributed computing. Chapter 5 of his dissertation is on REST, which was later popularized (and even idolized) by the community in the latter half of 2000. We will discuss and review REST in Chapter 3, but here it is important to note that a lot of REST is already considered (or even fulfilled) part of HTTP 1.1.

HTTP PROTOCOL

HTTP is a text-based protocol. In this book, we will be dealing with requests and responses in their raw format, so you need to be familiar with how HTTP requests and responses look. It is likely that you are already familiar with this, however, if you are not, no need to panic because it is very easy to pick up and get started with.

An HTTP request starts with a first line containing the HTTP verb, URL, and HTTP version (separated by a space) and then each header in each line (\r\n ends a line). The HTTP header is a name-value field separated by a colon (:). After all of the headers, there is a blank line and then the payload (or body or entity) appears if there is one. For example:

```
POST /api/v1/person HTTP/1.1
host: example.com
Content-Type: x-www-form-urlencoded

name=joe&surname=blogg
```

An HTTP response starts with the first line containing the status code and description and subsequently with headers, each in one line. Then there is a blank line followed by the payload, if there is one. For example:

```
201 Created
Content-Type: text/plain
Location: /api/v1/person/123

Person was successfully created
```

Throughout this book, we have used the Fiddler tool to examine raw requests and responses, so it would be useful to familiarize yourself with this tool if you have not used it before (download at `http://fiddler2.com/`).

Henrik Frystyk Nielsen was also a key part of the WWW success as he was working with Tim Berners-Lee in the early years of CERN and is a contributor to both HTTP 1.0 and 1.1 specifications. It is very interesting to know that Henrik is actually the architect of the ASP.NET Web API project and has ensured that all the goodness of the RFC 2616 is exposed in this project. After publication of HTTP 1.1, he joined Microsoft to work on a new protocol named SOAP, which ironically delayed the adoption of HTTP as the programming model of the distributed computing.

SOAP

SOAP was proposed by Dave Winer and Don Box in 1998. SOAP was designed to solve the problem of hybrid platform enterprises where each system used a proprietary means of communication and was unable to connect to other systems. SOAP proposed the use of HTTP as the transport mechanism for sending and receiving XML (Extensive Markup Language) data. At that time, XML was seen as the text-based data language that would "save the world," so it was inevitable that XML and web (HTTP) should be combined to form a protocol.

In 1998, creating objects in many programming languages was deemed expensive. As such, many technologies such as COM/DCOM (Distributed Component Object Model) and CORBA (Common Object Request Broker Architecture) had been created to share the business logic through the objects hosted on a central server. Microsoft was working on Microsoft Transaction Server (MTS), which later turned into COM+, which was designed to create and pool business objects on a server that could be accessed by various clients. This is being mentioned because the naming of SOAP probably had a lot to do with the time and company context in which SOAP was formed. As later was experienced, SOAP did not have a lot to do with accessing objects because the underlying systems were being abstracted behind a contract. Also, as many learned, it was not necessarily simple either, especially with the WS-* extensions, as we will see.

The SOAP programming model embodies the Remote Procedure Call (RPC) paradigm where a client does what can be modeled as calling a method or procedure on the remote system by sending input parameters and receiving the return parameter over the network. This RPC paradigm was already implemented in DCOM and CORBA, but they were not compatible. SOAP was solving the cross-platform communication problem by using a widely adopted high-level transfer protocol (HTTP), which was built on top of TCP/IP (Transmission Control Protocol/Internet Protocol) and used a text-based messaging format (XML), which was very promising. HTTP is normally served over port 80, which is usually an open port. On the other hand, all systems were capable of processing text, hence processing XML was not a technical challenge in itself.

SOAP was used to build web services connecting different platforms and systems. It brought the opportunity to build real B2B (business-to-business) systems, allowing companies to generate more revenue through more reach and broader wholesale markets. On the other hand, SOAP was the enabler to build web services to implement Service-Oriented Architecture (SOA), where each service exposes its boundary.

Different software and platform vendors jumped on the SOAP bandwagon and soon built the necessary software development kit (SDK) for building and running SOAP web services. Microsoft introduced ASP.NET Web services (sometimes also referred to as ASMX Web services because file extensions ended in .asmx rather than .aspx), and it was relatively easy to add web services to an existing ASP.NET application.

The contract definition for web services was formalized as Web Service Definition Language (WSDL), which used XML schema for defining the input and output schemas. WSDL allowed client proxy generation to be automated, helping developers to quickly build an application capable of consuming a web service.

The world was good again, until it was not.

Web Services Extensions

Web services lacked many aspects required by scalable distributed computing. The design of SOAP was rushed due to the pressure caused by its own buzz, which led to inconsistent versions 1.1 and 1.2 being adopted by some yet rejected by others, which made cross-platform communication (which was the promise of the SOAP) more challenging.

One of the aspects seriously neglected in all of this was security. In 2004, an effort was made by the Organization for the Advancement of Structured Information Standards (OASIS) to formalize a protocol to secure web service communication by the means of username/password tokens. This protocol was later known as WS-I Basic Profile 1.0, and it became a very popular implementation among enterprises. Listing 1-1 shows an example of the protocol.

Listing 1-1. A Sample WS-I Basic Profile SOAP Security Header

```
<wsse:Security xmlns:wsse='http://docs.oasis-open.org/wss/2004/01/oasis-200401-wss-wssecurity-
secext-1.0.xsd'
                xmlns:wsu='http://docs.oasis-open.org/wss/2004/01/oasis-200401-wss-wssecurity-
                utility-1.0.xsd'
                xmlns:xenc='http://www.w3.org/2001/04/xmlenc#'
                xmlns:ds='http://www.w3.org/2000/09/xmldsig#' >
    <wsse:BinarySecurityToken wsu:Id='SomeCert'
                        ValueType="http://docs.oasis-open.org/wss/2004/01/oasis-200401-wss-
                        x509-token-profile-1.0#X509v3"
                        EncodingType="http://docs.oasis-open.org/wss/2004/01/oasis-200401-
                        wss-soap-message-security-1.0#Base64Binary">
lui+Jy4WYKGJW5xM3aHnLxOpGVIpzSg4V486hHFe7sHET/uxxVBovT7JV1A2RnWSWkXm9jAEdsm/hs+f3NwvK23bh46mNmn
CQVsUYHbYAREZpykrd/+ByeFhmSviW77n6yTcI7XU7xZT54S9hTSyBLN2Sce1dEQpQXh5ssZK9aZTMrsFT1NBvNHC
3Qq7wO0tr5V4axH3MXffsuI9WzxPCfHdalN4rLRfNY318pc6bn00zAMwOomUWwBEJZxxBGGUc9QY3VjwNALgGDaEAT7gpURk
CI85HjdnSA5SM4cY7jAsYX/CIpEkRJcBULlTEFrBZIBYDPzRWlSdsJRJngF7yCoGWJ+/HY0yP8P4OM59FDiOkM8GwOEOWgYr
JHH92qaVhoiPTLi7
    </wsse:BinarySecurityToken>
</wsse:Security>
```

(Taken from the specification at www.ws-i.org/profiles/basicsecurityprofile-1.0-2004-05-12.html.)

Around this time, a body of work was initiated by working groups and contributed to by the big software vendors (such as Microsoft, Oracle, IBM, etc.) to create extensions to the web services (or rather SOAP). These were known as WS-*, and this led to a very diverse set of specifications, some of which never saw the light of day. During rapid turnaround of the draft specifications, vendors were publishing frameworks only to be broken by the next update. Microsoft Web Services Extension (WSE) had up to three different versions, each with several service packs. For example, Basic Profile 1.0 was first implemented in WSE 2.0 SP3.

The work on these drafts continued, but as we will see, by the time they were finalized, they were so complex no one could understand or implement them. *Web services extensions meant to enhance SOAP, but as we will see later, instead they seemed to kill it.*

WCF

WCF (codenamed Indigo) was one of the three "foundations" released as part of .NET 3.0. The others were Windows Presentation Foundation (WPF) and Windows Workflow Foundation (WF), with the latter having a lackluster start and, at the time of this writing, is still being redesigned.

WCF was a bold and ambitious move to abstract RPC once and for all. It took the SOAP schema as its internal implementation but completely abstracted the transport so that, unlike SOAP, it was not tied to HTTP. It was designed to be able to use TCP, named pipes, and even asynchronous MSMQ (Microsoft Message Queuing) as well as HTTP, and in terms of WS-*, it supported many of the new and shiny protocols coming out of the WS-* factory (such as `wsHttpBinding` and `wsFederationHttpBinding`). It used the pipe and filter pattern to implement a message processing pipeline in both the client and server. These pipes and filters sequentially process the message with respect to encoding, transport, security, reliable messaging, and transactions. WCF also had many extensibility and aspect-oriented points at which one could step in and customize the implementation. The classic SOAP web service was also supported, as it became just one binding out of a dozen (`basicHttpBinding`). It came with error logging, tracing, debugging, and diagnostics tools and functionalities built in to the framework. It could be hosted on an Internet Information Server (IIS), a Windows service, or any plain old .exe process (such as Windows Forms, WPF, or a console app) and could be consumed equally by servers, ASP.NET Web applications, and desktop applications.

But there were problems. First, abstracting the transport means that only the least common denominator of the transport features will be available. Considering such a diverse range of transports (TCP, HTTP, MSMQ, named pipes), this common denominator is actually small. In this respect, Nicholas Allen from the WCF team wrote back in 2007:

> *Can I get the IP address of a client connecting to my service?*
>
> *No. Sorry. In most cases this information is not available. Exposing such functionality is left to the transport to be done in an implementation-specific manner. The most popular transports we supply out of the box do not offer this. You can ask the client to supply that information as part of its identity, although you need a way of making sure that the client isn't lying before taking action based on the IP address. However, it is possible under some circumstances for the client to lie about its address even when you can directly query the socket.*

—Nicholas Allen blog,
`http://blogs.msdn.com/b/drnick/archive/2007/05/16/client-ip-address.aspx`

It was not surprising to see comments from unhappy developers who expected that such features (e.g., getting the IP address of the client) were just very basic and had to be in the framework.

Finally, and after some initial resistance, these features were added to WCF. But this means that *abstractions started to leak.* To accommodate all possible cases, WCF started to build and expose many aspects of the underlying transports, and this led to very complex configurations. Configuring a WCF endpoint almost always required consulting the documentation and possibly copying and pasting some configuration from the documentation. At times, configuring a WCF endpoint resembled the switches and knobs of an airplane's cockpit, where only the exact combination of switches works; otherwise, the plane would crash!

Another consequence of transports leaking back to WCF was that the disposal of the transport-specific system resources got more complicated and resulted in a broken IDisposable implementation where instead of a standard using block to dispose the disposable WCF channels, Microsoft recommended the model shown in Listing 1-2 (source: http://msdn.microsoft.com/en-us/library/aa355056.aspx).

Listing 1-2. Recommened Disposal Method for WCF Channels

```
try
{
    ...
    client.Close();
}
catch (CommunicationException e)
{
    ...
    client.Abort();
}
catch (TimeoutException e)
{
    ...
    client.Abort();
}
catch (Exception e)
{
    ...
    client.Abort();
    throw;
}
```

Having said this, WCF is still used by many teams and is a useful tool when it comes to exposing an RPC or when a WS-* implementation is required. It is now a mature product and has been widely used in the industry. However, Microsoft has not updated it since .NET 4.0 and does not seem to have any plans to add features.

Rage Against the SOAP: HTTP Makes a Comeback

Although SOAP was using HTTP basically apart from the raw transport, it was ignoring it. It used only the POST method, which is not cacheable in any circumstance; hence, systems using SOAP (including WCF) had to build their own caching layer and logic. So in a way it was a waste of a protocol to use only a handful of the features.

Also WS-* made SOAP very bloated and hard to work with. Implementing these standards (there were more than 20 different WS-* standards) was out of reach for all but a few very large vendors. Using these implementations was difficult and required a lot of configuration. So it led to a lot of frustration in the community. Simple was good and Simple Object Access Protocol was anything but simple!

So the industry looked for an alternative for the verbose and full of ceremony SOAP. The answer came in Roy Fielding's thesis and the RESTful API. Inspired by his writings, a new breed of APIs surfaced that did not have any of the SOAP baggage and were light and extensible. Although initial APIs were not fully RESTful, they were successful attempts to build a system on top of HTTP richness. The community also started to distance itself from SOAP by replacing the term *web services* with Web API, referring to the fact that this new breed of APIs was web-friendly. As can be seen in Figure 1-1, the interest in Web API started in 2005 and it has recently grown exponentially.

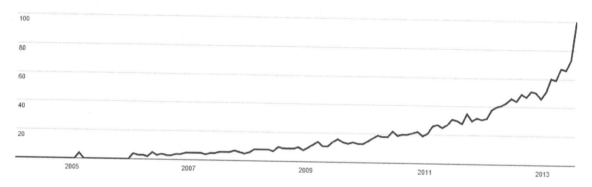

Figure 1-1. *Google search trend for the phrase "Web API" since 2005. As can be seen, search trend—which is roughly correlated with the interest—has taken a parabolic form.*
(Source: Google, `http://tinyurl.com/lymkkf5`*)*

The Flickr API is probably one of the first public non-SOAP HTTP APIs, dating back to 2004. However, arguably the most groundbreaking API was Amazon S3, which was launched on March 1, 2006. This was a commercialization of Amazon's internal IT infrastructure as a cloud platform exposing the services via a RESTful API. By 2008, REST was a hot topic among HTTP enthusiasts and, at the time of writing this book, it has gained a wide adoption and is no longer a novelty.

During the past few years, Web API, and particularly REST/HTTP API, has been a very hot topic in the computer community, leading to heated debates on what a RESTful implementation means in practice. Regardless of all the debates and controversies on the edge cases, HTTP has been delivering a premium value in the new Web and cloud-based systems. Emergence of powerful smartphones and advances in HTML5/JavaScript/CSS3 programming techniques have led to the introduction of premium experience in web applications consuming HTTP APIs.

Another area that helped the adoption of HTTP API was the emergence of identity protocols that were fully based on the HTTP programming paradigm and free of any SOAP or WS-* ceremony. The work on OAuth and OpenID started around 2006, but it took a few years for them to mature. Explosion of the social media (Facebook, Twitter, etc.) meant that many web users already had a login with one of the social media sites, and they could authenticate or interact with other sites or applications.

HTTP, which was designed for distributed computing, returned fully to the picture of interoperable APIs.

WCF REST

In the meantime, Microsoft, which had invested heavily in WCF, could not ignore what was happening in the community. Many were moving away from RPC and joining the REST movement. In an attempt to appease the REST enthusiasts among the WCF adopters, the WCF team developed WCF REST in 2008. This was released as the WCF Starter Kit, which worked with .NET 3.5.

WCF REST, by mixing RPC and REST, which were two different and opposing paradigms, inherently could not be successful because it was built on a paradox (see Table 1-3). As a result, it did not succeed in practice, and many adopters soon found themselves fighting against the framework to satisfy REST.

Table 1-3. *Impedance Mismatch Between SOAP (RPC/WCF) and HTTP (REST): Comparison of Available Axes of Conveying Intent or Data*

Axis	SOAP	HTTP
URL fragments	Yes, contains endpoint and method (action)	Yes, contains resource information and can include many pieces of data
Payload	Yes, contains envelope that has a header and body	Yes
Contract	Yes	No
URL query string	No	Yes
Verb	No, SOAP header is part of payload	Yes
Status code	No	Yes
Formatting and content negotiation	No	Yes, implemented in Accept header*
Caching	No	Yes, implemented in headers
Concurrency	No	Yes, implemented in headers†
Authentication	No, implemented in the payload	Yes
Encoding	No, although WCF has an encoding axis	Yes
Partial response	No	Yes
Hypermedia	No	Yes, can be implemented in the payload or header

In some cases, resource is modified to denote the formatting. For example, a URL ending with .json to denote JSON formatting.
†This is used in conditional PUT requests using an if-match header.

webHttpBinding in WCF

.NET 3.5 included a binding that was not talking SOAP: `webHttpBinding`. It was capable of sending or receiving plain old XML over HTTP (POX) or JSON.

Although this was not RESTful and similar to SOAP, only the POST verb was supported, and it allowed for consumption of WCF API by JavaScript-enabled devices.

WCF Web APIs

After finishing his work in the Microsoft Extensibility Framework (MEF), Glenn Block joined the WCF Web API team to create success from the failure of WCF REST. Initial Community Technical Preview (CTP) versions of WCF Web API received a lot of positive feedback from the community and encouraged the team to move forward. The first preview was released in October 2010 and the latest one was version 6, which was released in November 2011.

As the work progressed, it became evident that fitting a pure HTTP model into the constraints of WCF/RPC is very hard, if not impossible. On the other hand, the work involved to make HTTP a first-class citizen of the framework and exposing all the power as type-safe classes, properties, and methods had a lot more to do with the Web than WCF. As such, it was decided to rename the framework as ASP.NET Web API and move the work to the ASP.NET team. This coincided with the release of version 6 in November 2011.

Birth of ASP.NET Web API

After the integration of Web API into the ASP.NET team, the framework gained even more popularity. The team worked closely with the community and nightly builds were available. The team released a single beta version followed by the RTM (release to manufacturing) in August 2012.

In HTTP/REST, we have resources, and each resource is identified by a Unique Resource Identifier (URI). ASP.NET Web API uses the familiar programming model of ASP.NET MVC and implemented resources as methods, or more specifically, actions within controllers. As stated earlier, there is an impedance mismatch between RPC and HTTP/REST. Although ASP.NET Web API internalizes the richness of the HTTP and treats it as a first-class citizen, there was still bound to be a clash of the RPC paradigm because resources are implemented as methods (see Figure 1-2).

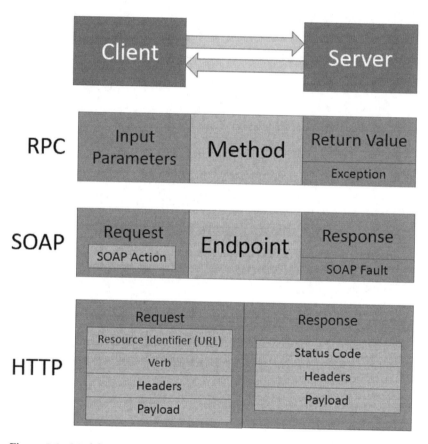

Figure 1-2. *Modeling client-server communication in RPC, SOAP, and HTTP. Note how SOAP is built on the RPC logical model*

■ **Note**   In SOAP 1.1, SOAP Action was sent in the HTTP request header, but in SOAP 1.2, it became part of the SOAP header. In SOAP, the "method" was the combination of the endpoint and the SOAP header.

So let's have a look at the task at hand. The team had to turn this pair (this is just a random HTTP request/response pair example with the site name anonymized):

```
POST /ajax/bz HTTP/1.1
Host: www.example.com
Connection: keep-alive
Content-Length: 477
Origin: https://www.example.com
User-Agent: Mozilla/5.0 (Windows NT 6.2; WOW64) AppleWebKit/537.36 (KHTML, like Gecko) _
Chrome/27.0.1453.116 Safari/537.36
Content-Type: application/x-www-form-urlencoded
Accept: */*
Referer: https://www.example.com/messages/...
Accept-Encoding: gzip,deflate,sdch
Accept-Language: en-GB,en;q=0.8,en-US;q=0.6
Cookie: datr=...


HTTP/1.1 200 OK
Cache-Control: private, no-cache, no-store, must-revalidate
Content-Type: application/x-javascript; charset=utf-8
Expires: Sat, 01 Jan 2000 00:00:00 GMT
Pragma: no-cache
Strict-Transport-Security: max-age=60
Content-Encoding: gzip
Date: Sun, 30 Jun 2013 11:28:31 GMT
Transfer-Encoding: chunked
Connection: keep-alive
...
```

into some form of this:

```
public Baaz Foo(Bar bar)
{
    ...
}
```

This clearly demonstrates the impedance mismatch between RPC and HTTP and the big task at hand. The initial approach used to solve this problem was to wrap the input parameter and return value into a generic "envelope:"

```
public HttpResponseMessage<Baaz> Foo(HttpRequestMessage<Bar> request)
{
    ...
}
```

These envelopes would be able to support and supply additional aspects of HTTP request and response while staying loyal to the type safety of the method parameters.

This in fact was the original approach even after the release of the ASP.NET Web API beta. However, after a while, it became apparent that maintaining the same generic type for the response through the chain of the HTTP processing pipeline was impractical. In other words, the content of the response could change while the response was passing through the HTTP pipeline; hence, having a generic request and response would both pose technical challenges with the async model as well as not being logically correct.

So the team decided to remove the generic parameter from the request and response and allow the generic type to be expressed in the Content property (which models the request and response payload or in HTTP jargon the "entity"). So our example of the action method could be rewritten (we have used the async pattern, which will be covered in Chapter 2):

```
public async Task<HttpResponseMessage> FooAsync(HttpRequestMessage request)
{
        var bar = await request.Content.ReadAsAsync<Bar>();
        ...
        var  response = request.CreateResponse();
        response.Content = new ObjectContent<Baaz>(new Baaz());
        return response;
}
```

This model solves the impedance mismatch. But that is not the only solution. ASP.NET Web API uses other techniques to model other axes not available in an action method. Also it is important to note that unlike ASP.NET MVC actions, ASP.NET Web API actions can return any type and they do not have to inherit from the ActionResult type. Let's examine the ASP.NET Web API architecture to understand those techniques.

ASP.NET Web API Architecture

ASP.NET Web API has a very modern design and takes advantage of the latest features of the .NET Framework. But at the core, it is built on a simple pipe and filter design pattern and, as we know, simplicity is power. This section will review the design and architecture of the ASP.NET Web API.

Architectural Features

The ASP.NET Web API team made some key decisions that have led to the framework's robustness, modularity, and testability. Some of these decisions include:

- *Async all the way:* The ASP.NET Web API framework has been designed using the task-based asynchronous programming model from the top to the bottom. As we'll see in Chapter 2, this leads to increased scalability.

- *No more HttpContext.Current:* Although ASP.NET MVC has wrapped HttpContext inside HttpContextBase for better testability, ASP.NET Web API takes this even further and stores all contextual properties of the request in the Request.Properties dictionary. Although accessing HttpContext in ASP.NET Web API could still work, use of HttpContext.Current is strongly discouraged due to the possible loss of context in task-based async thread switching.

- *Replicating the same HTTP pipeline in client library as well as server library:* This helps with unifying the programming model as well as ease of integration testing because you can short circuit the client–server communication and bypass the network by connecting the client pipeline directly to the server pipeline (this will be covered in Chapter 15).

- *Ability to host both in IIS (or development server) and in any nonweb server process (called self-hosted):* Future versions of ASP.NET Web API will have the ability to be hosted in custom web servers. We'll look into this in Chapter 17.

- *Built-in support for dependency injection:* ASP.NET Web API supports any custom dependency injection framework through a simple service location interface. We cover dependency injection in Chapter 14.

- *Service location even for components of the framework itself:* You can customize many elements of ASP.NET Web API by supplying your own custom implementation. We cover this feature in Chapter 14.

- *Ultimate testability:* ASP.NET Web API has been designed with testing in mind. Almost all parts of the framework are testable, and we'll cover unit testing in Chapter 15.

- *HttpConfiguration:* The ASP.NET Web API runtime context is abstracted and represented in the HttpConfiguration class. HttpConfiguration is a central place for defining different aspects of the runtime and does not have static properties, making it more testable. Important contextual properties include:

    - Routes

    - Message handlers

    - Global filters

    - Formatters

    - Dependency resolver

    - Parameter binding providers

ASP.NET Web API Elements

ASP.NET Web API has been built to map the web/HTTP programming model to the .NET Framework programming model. For solving these problems, it sometimes uses familiar constructs introduced in ASP.NET MVC, such as Controller, Action, Filter, and so forth. In other cases, it creates its own abstractions, which we'll mention here but fully discuss in the upcoming chapters.

Figure 1-3 shows an example request and the mapping of HTTP constructs to the ASP.NET Web API abstractions. We'll look into some of the key ASP.NET Web API abstractions so that we can see the big picture.

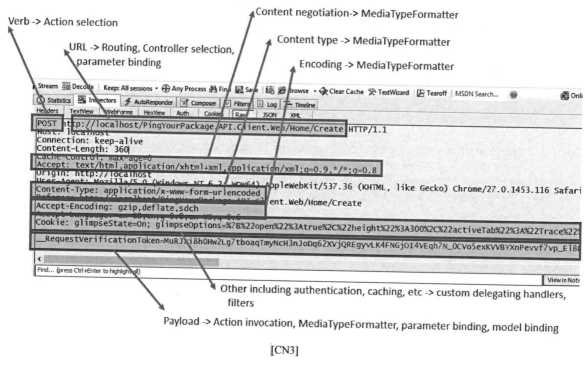

[CN3]

Figure 1-3. *Mapping HTTP concepts in HTTP to ASP.NET Web API elements*

Routing

The ASP.NET Web API has been built on top of the ASP.NET routing, although it has not been coupled to it. As we'll see in the HTTP processing pipeline, HttpControllerDispatcher is the engine for dispatching the requests to controllers and is routing aware.

ASP.NET Web API uses a similar (but not the same) approach for route set up and resolution. The route data are then further used by IHttpControllerSelector and HttpActionSelector to find the right controller and action. Routing is discussed in Chapter 8.

Parameter Binding, Model Binding, and Validation

Parameter binding and model binding are used to bind the URL fragments and query string parameters and pieces of data from the request payload to action parameters and model properties.

If you have already used ASP.NET MVC, you are familiar with binding concepts. Parameter and model binding in ASP.NET Web API is inspired by ASP.NET MVC but has some additional functionality. We'll cover these two topics throughout the book but mainly in Chapters 6 and 11.

Validation is a related subject, which is discussed in Chapter 13.

Controllers and Actions

Controllers and actions are familiar concepts borrowed from ASP.NET MVC, although there are several differences. ASP.NET Web API controllers must be derived from the ApiController class. This topic is covered in Chapter 9.

Formatting and Content Negotiation

Formatting and content negotiation are integral parts of HTTP specification. ASP.NET Web API provides the MediaTypeFormatter abstract type and its concrete implementations to look after formatting of the request and response payload.

MediaTypeFormatter is similar to a serializer that can serialize and deserialize types to and from a stream. However, it has a responsibility overlap with the model binder and bridges the gap between the HTTP world of payload and media type to the .NET world of actions, parameters, and types. We'll cover formatting in Chapter 12.

Filters

ASP.NET Web API filters are similar to ASP.NET MVC filters and, in the same way, define a temporal logic related to a single action that runs before and after the action. Filters are implemented as attributes and declared on actions, while global filters are added to the configuration. Filters are discussed in Chapter 11.

Message Handlers

Message handlers are probably the most important abstraction in ASP.NET Web API because a lot of the internal classes are based on this pipeline processing paradigm. We'll look at this pipeline in the next section. Message handlers themselves are covered in Chapter 10.

HTTP Processing Pipeline

The ASP.NET Web API processing pipeline is based on a simple pipe-and-filter abstraction. Pipe-and-filter or simply pipeline is a design pattern where components will process the incoming request sequentially and each component's output is the next component's input. Figure 1-4 demonstrates a request/response pipeline; this model is shown in two different representations.

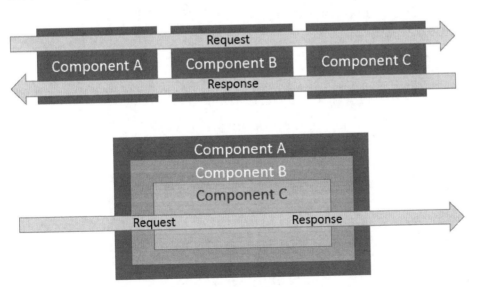

Figure 1-4. *Modeling a pipe-and-filter (pipeline) design pattern in a request/response (two-way) pipe. These two models are equivalent, but the lower one (the Russian doll model) is a better representation of the ASP.NET Web API HTTP processing pipeline*

17

Because each component passes the pipeline once for the request and again for the response (in the reverse order), the ASP.NET Web API team chose the *Russian doll* model as a more descriptive and fitting analogy. Russian dolls, or Matryoshka dolls, are wooden figurine dolls of decreasing size where each doll fits inside the doll next in size (see further discussion in Chapter 10).

Every component, upon receiving the request, has two choices: to pass it on to the next component in the chain and receive the response when it passes back, or to cut off the chain and return the response. The last component does not have a choice and has to do the latter. This concept is similar to the concept of HTTP modules and HTTP handlers, but here these two have been combined. This has been modeled in the abstract class HttpMessageHandler. The magic of the message handler is in its single async method, which receives the request and returns a Task<HttpResponseMessage>:

```
protected override Task<HttpResponseMessage> SendAsync(HttpRequestMessage request,
CancellationToken cancellationToken)
{
    ...
}
```

In any hosting scenario, an implementation of HttpServer (a class inherited from HttpMessageHandler) will receive the request. HttpServer will pass the request through a series of message handlers defined in the runtime (against HttpConfiguration) and then normally would pass it to the HttpControllerDispatcher. At the end, the HttpServer will receive the response and send it back to the user.

ASP.NET Web API in Modern Architecture

Now that we know something about ASP.NET Web API, let's see how it can be used to solve business problems. ASP.NET Web API is fit to be used in a diverse set of scenarios and opens the door to new possibilities (see Figure 1-5).

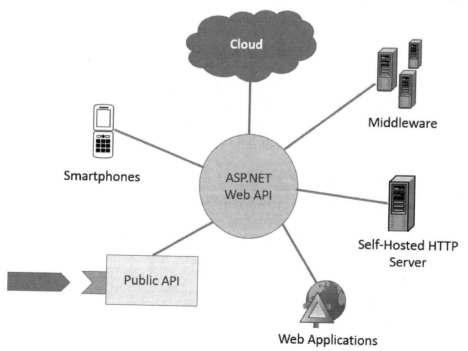

Figure 1-5. ASP.NET Web API can be used in a wide variety of scenarios

On the one hand, by using pure HTTP, it is very lightweight and can be easily consumed by low-power devices. On the other hand, because it talks web, it is browser ready and can be used in serving data to web applications. And above all, because it is built on top of HTTP, it is ready for distributed computing in both the cloud and in enterprises.

Public API

With the growing popularity of REST API, companies are quickly moving toward making their services available through a pure HTTP API. In these cases, HTTP API is usually used in conjunction with SOAP API and sometimes only HTTP API is supported.

In recent years, the biggest public APIs have been mainly implemented in pure HTTP. Twitter, Facebook, Amazon, Google, Flickr, Netflix, and many more have the REST API as their main public API. Most of these APIs implement OAuth or OAuth 2.0 rather than the heavy WS-* protocols over SOAP. As mentioned earlier, the OAuth protocol helped with the adoption of HTTP API over SOAP.

The ProgrammableWeb web site (`www.programmableweb.com/`) is dedicated to registering public APIs (mainly RESTful), and since its launch in 2005, it has registered around 10,000 APIs and 7,000 mashups (see Figure 1-6).

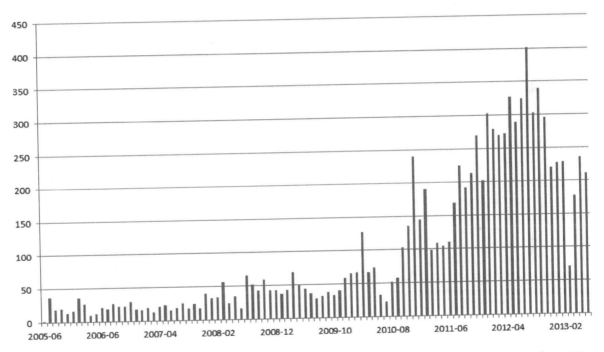

Figure 1-6. *Number of public APIs registered every month on the ProgrammableWeb web site since its launch in 2005. A rise in registration the past three years is evident.*
(Source: `www.programmableweb.com/apis/directory`)

■ **Note** Mashup in API jargon refers to a web site or a web application that "mashes up" two or more sources of data (where at least one is a public API) to build a new functionality. For example, you can mix the Twitter firehose status data with Google Maps to show points in real time where the tweets are coming from. The web site `www.geochirp.com` is one site implementing such a mashup.

Nowadays companies with existing SOAP public APIs are adding REST endpoints to their systems. If your company has a public API, using ASP.NET Web API for exposing your services is a very wise investment.

Middleware and Internal API

As Daniel Jacobson, Greg Brail, and Dan Woods explain in their excellent book *API: A Strategy Guide* (O'Reilly 2011), public APIs are only the tip of the iceberg of all APIs. They firmly believe the real benefits of APIs are materialized in the private and internal APIs within enterprises and organizations.

As explained earlier, HTTP was designed with distributed computing in mind. A lot of enterprises had to reinvent the wheel when it comes to caching, concurrency, security, compression, and encryption, while HTTP has all of those to offer out of the box. We strongly believe that ASP.NET Web API will gradually replace most of the existing WCF (and ASMX) services in the next three to five years.

Modern Web Application API

Web programming is in a much different place that it had been five years ago. Emergence of smart devices and adoption of better JavaScript techniques and libraries have opened the avenue for heavy client-side programming, relying less and less on the server for driving application logic.

A type of web application called Single Page Application (SPA) has gained a lot of popularity (Gmail is a famous example of SPA). In this type of application, the server only provides static HTML views and templates and JavaScript and then the application starts to load the data by calling the server API using Ajax. All navigation and subsequent loading of different views are handled without a single full post back to the server. SPA is usually used with a Model-View-Controller JavaScript library/framework such as Backbone.js, AngularJS, or Knockout.js (the latter known as a Model-View-ViewModel library).

■ **Note** The sample application in Chapter 15 is an SPA. Although the focus of this book is not SPA or JavaScript, because of its popularity, we found it useful to add an SPA sample here.

ASP.NET Web API in its short lifespan has become a popular data provider for these types of applications. Because views are rendered on the client using JavaScript templating rather than on the server, ASP.NET Web API is a perfect fit for providing raw data.

On closer examination, we will find that in many cases a nicely designed public API can be equally used as a data provider for SPAs. Such an API can provide a lot of value by serving B2B customers as well as various customer devices and desktop applications.

Cloud Services

As pointed out earlier, the release of Amazon Web Services (AWS) was an important milestone in the adoption of REST. Microsoft's Windows Azure platform provides its services through both a RESTful API and client SDKs (AWS also has client SDKs), where the client SDK is just a wrapper around the API call.

ASP.NET Web API has been a popular framework for exposing Azure cloud applications, and Microsoft is working toward better integration between these two frameworks. For a tutorial on the subject, visit the Windows Azure web site at `www.windowsazure.com/en-us/develop/net/tutorials/rest-service-using-web-api/`.

Services for Native Apps

As stated earlier, smartphones had an important part in the trend toward simpler pure HTTP API and away from SOAP. Many of the native apps can be likened to dumb terminals connected to a big mainframe, with the mainframe being the cloud. In these apps, the cloud provides storage and server-side processing and the app is mainly used for the consumption of the services exposed by an API.

If you are thinking of building an app for smartphones, you should seriously consider exposing your backend services through a REST API using ASP.NET Web API.

Self-Hosted HTTP Server

Before ASP.NET Web API, there was no easy way to host a simple web server in your Windows service or desktop application. If you needed to host a service, you had to use WCF, which was not ideal.

ASP.NET Web API has made it extremely easy to host your API in a nonweb server process. Most of the code you need to write is exactly the same as the code you would write in a web-hosted scenario. You can also use the self-hosted Web API server to serve static resources or even a server-rendered view (e.g., Razor) so you can serve web pages. A common scenario is when you have a process running as a Windows service and you need a web-based administration console for it, in which case the self-hosted Web API is all you need.

ASP.NET Web API and Other Architectural Aspects

In the past few years, the software world has experienced a massive change and a huge influx of ideas and practices (cloud, devops, BDD, SPA, Big Data, etc.). ASP.NET Web API was born in a landscape of very heterogenous architectural patterns. There are emerging trends in the community that, whether we like it or not, are going to affect how we will be using ASP.NET Web API.

This by itself is a big subject, and we are only going to scratch the surface here, but it is important to provide pointers relevant to the rest of this book!

ASP.NET Web API and ASP.NET MVC

As stated earlier, there is a considerable similarity between ASP.NET Web API and ASP.NET MVC. Having said that, there is not a great deal of functional overlap between them, but a question that crops up time and time again is the choice between these two independent frameworks.

If you have tried the ASP.NET Web API template in the Visual Studio, you have probably noticed that this template combines ASP.NET Web API and ASP.NET MVC. In fact, nothing stops you from using both of these frameworks in the same project. But you need to be clear about what the main value of each framework is.

ASP.NET MVC is ideal for generating server-side views (Razor or Web Forms). And in terms of processing client-side data, it is mainly geared toward x-www-form-urlencoded data (form post data). Although ASP.NET Web API can process x-www-form-urlencoded data and can generate Razor views, it is best for exposing an API.

If you have both these requirements in a project, use both frameworks in conjunction.

ASP.NET Web API and DDD

Since its formalization in 2003, Domain-Driven Design (DDD) has provided the vocabulary, semantics, and conceptual tools for designing and architecting modern software. Eric Evans introduced DDD in his book *Domain-Driven Design: Tackling Complexity in the Heart of Software* (Addison-Wesley 2003), which has earned classic status among computer software books along with the Gang of Four design patterns book (*Design Patterns: Elements of Reusable Object-Oriented Software*, by Erich Gamma et al., Addison-Wesley 1994) and Martin Fowler's *Patterns of Enterprise Application Architecture* (Addison-Wesley 2002).

21

DDD introduced strategic design, which is a collection of patterns and practices important in designing SOA. According to DDD, each of the bounded contexts in your enterprise would be mapped to a service in your domain, and the service would be exposed through its API.

If you are using ASP.NET Web API to build exposure to your domain, you should seriously consider designing your API in such a way that it completely hides the complexity of your bounded context. Client-Server Domain Separation (CSDS) is an architectural style inspired by REST and DDD that advocates that the client and server should live in their own bounded context.

The server is responsible for defining and maintaining its state and hides its complexity behind its API (see Figure 1-7). The client can interact with (query or modify) the state only through the public API. The server does not know the nature of the client, as the client could be a browser, native mobile application, or another server. This separation leads to better decoupling and a more maintainable system.

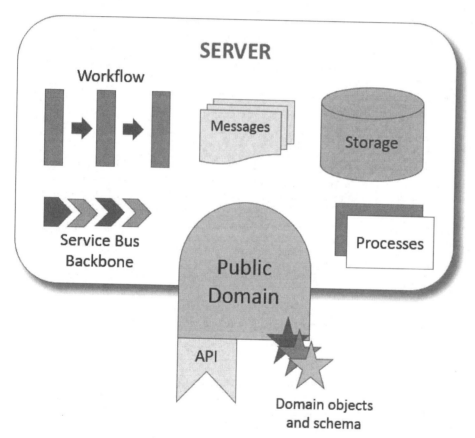

Figure 1-7. *The server is inherently very complex, containing many different elements, but it hides the internal complexity of its bounded context behind its API. It exposes a public domain, which includes the API and public messages (domian objects and schemata). In Client-Server Domain Separation (CSDS), the server and client live in their separate bounded contexts*

ASP.NET Web API and CQRS

Command Query Responsibility Segregation (CQRS) is a pattern in software design and architecture that advocates separation of reads from writes and claims this leads to more scalable software. So the change in the state is carried out by the commands, while reads are carried out by the queries.

CQRS is also associated with other design practices. For example, reads are usually served by a denormalized data store separate from the write store and in a different format.

Historically, CQRS systems have used the service bus to deliver messages. Although this can be the case in a closed enterprise, a public API would need open connectivity where HTTP is a superior choice. In fact, HTTP already has the semantics for a CQRS design.

On the one hand, HTTP has GET as a safe verb for queries and unsafe verbs (PUT, POST, and DELETE) for commands. In HTTP, a safe verb is a verb that does not result in a change in state (see Chapter 3 for a more detailed discussion).

On the other hand, *idempotency* is an important aspect of designing messages in CQRS. An operation is considered idempotent where its execution once or multiple times has the same effect. So in a CQRS system, you can use POST for a nonidempotent command and PUT for an idempotent command.

Even HTTP status codes are suitable for expressing CQRS results. For example, a successful GET operation would normally return the denormalized data with a 200 (OK) status code, while a command would return no data and send back status code 202 (Accepted), which signifies an asynchronous operation.

So if you are designing a CQRS system and you need to expose your commands and queries outside your internal network, consider using ASP.NET Web API. By doing that, you can take advantage of caching your queries (GET) and concurrency-aware commands (PUT) for free.

ASP.NET Web API and Transactions

Databases have traditionally supported transactions over the past three decades. Transactions in classic systems are defined by the acronym ACID (*A*tomicity, *C*onsistency, *I*solation, and *D*urability). This is how they have ensured that when you make a payment, your balance is not deducted unless your payee receives your payment.

With the rise of distributed systems, maintaining ACID across the boundaries has posed challenges that are hard to solve. A service is normally dependent on other services, and in its traditional form, a transaction between two services will involve a cascade of systems and lock resources, reducing scalability. However, transactions are a fact of life, so systems have to support transactions, although in a looser form. As such, the acronym BASE (*B*asic *A*vailability, *S*oft state, and *E*ventual consistency) describes a looser form of transactions, and BASE implementations have been widely used across many big SOA systems, such as the Amazon web site.

HTTP/REST (and hence ASP.NET Web API) can be used to interface transactions in an SOA. Cesare Pautasso and Guy Pardon have proposed an implementation that involves a state machine moving through states using HTTP calls. This proposal involves a mediator where you can obtain a token when using POST, confirm the transaction using PUT, or cancel it using DELETE. For more information, visit his presentation at `www.inf.usi.ch/faculty/pautasso/talks/2012/soa-cloud-rest-tcc/rest-tcc.html#/title`.

ASP.NET Web API and API Governance

As stated earlier, ASP.NET Web API is a disruptive technology: it is going to change the way we design software. With any change comes challenges. So while embracing the change and taking advantage of all the benefits, we need to be careful about the challenges.

The rest of the chapter highlights those areas that you need to focus on and invest time in to ensure the transition to ASP.NET Web API will be smooth. You need to be aware of what we call the "client burden of REST," which means that with the extended semantics and extra client-server axes data and intent comes the requirement for clients to accommodate and consume them.

Provide Top-Notch Documentation

Most .NET developers have gotten used to the ease of consuming WCF and web services by adding a service reference to the project or consuming contract libraries. As discussed earlier, WCF is an implementation of RPC that makes it very similar to consuming a library. As such, documentation is normally concerned only with the input and output schemas and possible exceptions or faults.

With the extra flexibility, there are many aspects of a REST service that need to be documented. The good news is that Microsoft has realized the need and the ASP.NET Web API team has been working on making API documentation easier. This feature is covered in Chapter 18.

Just bear in mind that API documentation is the responsibility of the team working on the API. Good documentation is the key for the adoption of a public API.

Publish Schemas

In SOAP, WSDL would normally publish the schema along with the service definition. This is possible because web services assume XML, and XML supports schema. In a REST service, you could be exposing other formats, some of which might not support schema. For example, although there have been efforts to propose a schema for JSON, this has not yet been widely accepted and adopted.

In any case, it is important to publish schema of your API messages. Some APIs would use examples or plain text documentation for publishing the schema. Make sure you have supplied users of your API with enough information on how to use it.

Plan Your Versioning Strategy

As they say, the only thing that does not change in a system is change itself. With changes come requirements for versioning.

On the one hand, versioning an API is similar to versioning a library. With RPC in mind, calling an API can be very similar to calling a method in a library. On the other hand, publishing and rolling out a library is nothing like publishing an API.

First, avoid changing the version just for the sake of changing it. Commonly, frequent version changes can be a sign of poor domain analysis. If you have to change your version soon after going live, no versioning strategy can help you. What you need is a thorough review of your domain analysis. For example, Amazon S3 API version has stayed the same since its launch in 2006.

Avoid microversioning your API. Granularity of API should be much coarser than you would have in the case of a library. Although this is a very controversial subject, we believe that the top level version needs to be placed in the resource URL itself, especially with a public API, as it is with many APIs such as Google or Twitter.

Consider not upgrading the version if the changes are nonbreaking. As such, prefer nonbreaking changes over breaking ones. If the changes are breaking, change the version but keep running both versions. By providing more functionality in the new versions, you can gradually wean clients off the older versions and then decommission them (see Figure 1-8).

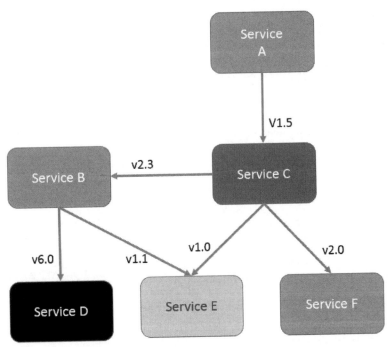

Figure 1-8. Example of the dependency chain in an SOA. Services B and C are dependent on different versions of service E, which means versions 1.0 and 1.1 of service E need to be running. Practically, you need to consider upgrading the dependency of service C to v1.1 of service E as soon as possible

Provide Test Services, Logging, and Tracing Facilities for Consumers

"Treat others as you would like to be treated yourself." This is certainly true if you have an API used by other teams or other companies! Consider a situation where you are trying to consume an API and having to use the live endpoint for your tests or where you have gone live and you suddenly get errors and do not know what is happening.

Consider providing a test service with a reasonable number of scenarios for the developers integrating your API into their system. Your error information should be descriptive enough and provide as much information as needed for the integrators to be able to trace their issue. A key approach is a *thorough validation of the input* so you can report the issue in a descriptive manner, although a good API has to validate the input anyway.

Even if your API is free, you should require an API key from the users of your API so you can control the usage and provide logging and tracing per API key.

Heavily Instrument, Benchmark, and Monitor Your API

The API is your application—as far as the server is concerned—so the quality of service (QoS) is really important. Scalability and performance requirements of your API need to be defined and various performances of your API benchmarked and recorded for comparison after any release.

On the other hand, when something goes wrong with the system, you need to be able to respond quickly. This is almost impossible without proper instrumentation of your API implementation. Consider instrumenting your API and storing traces and activity logs. These are your best friends if something goes wrong, which sooner or later it will.

Avoid Publishing Client Libraries if You Can

Exposing a full-blown REST API means a lot more cross-cutting features for the consumers of your API. But as stated earlier, this creates a burden in order for clients to consume all of the features. If you have a public API, this could translate into a slow adoption and integration. A common solution is to provide an RPC client library on top of a RESTful API. This is exactly what many vendors such as Amazon or Microsoft are doing for their cloud services' APIs.

Providing a client library can improve the uptake on your API but it reduces your agility to update and improve the API. Remember the diagrams about the RPC-REST impedance mismatch and the fact that exposing on top of RPC has to compromise either the simplicity of the RPC API or reduced the set of features. So avoid publishing a client if it is at all possible.

Summary

This chapter defined what ASP.NET Web API is and how to get it. We believe ASP.NET Web API is a disruptive technology that is going to change our server-side codes and will affect our client-side decisions.

We reviewed the history of HTTP and then moved on to the SOAP and how this journey gradually resulted in ASP.NET Web API. We explained the differences of RPC and REST and the impedance mismatch between them.

We covered the architectural features of ASP.NET and how these help with writing scalable and flexible applications. We listed possible use cases of ASP.NET Web API, and at the end, we identified areas you need to focus on in terms of governing your API. Now we are ready to jump in and show you some code!

CHAPTER 2

■ ■ ■

Introduction to Asynchronous Programming in .NET

Asynchronous programming is generally one of the hardest programming concepts to grasp. It is even harder to understand what it means when it comes to dealing with server applications, notably web applications. Besides the general concept, the asynchronous programming model in the .NET Framework was also hard to grasp in the early days of the framework. With the introduction of Task Parallel Library (TPL) in .NET version 4.0, it became easier, but the programming model was still not ideal. With the new asynchronous programming language features of C# in .NET 4.5, it got easier still. It now may be said to offer the ideal programming model as well.

In terms of both infrastructure and extensibility points, ASP.NET Web API framework is asynchronous from top to bottom by design. In addition, it leverages the Task-based Asynchronous Pattern (or TAP) introduced in .NET 4.0 to enable this. As we will be dealing with asynchrony throughout the book, it would be helpful to ensure up front that there is a good understanding of asynchronous programming and TAP. So this chapter will focus on asynchronous programming in .NET and, especially at the server level, with IIS Web Server, which is the most commonly used hosting platform for ASP.NET Web API applications.

What Is It All About?

Put very simply, "asynchronous code" refers to code in an operation (which the code executes) where that code won't wait till the operation completes; therefore, it doesn't block the thread it is running on. The need for asynchronous programming comes from the fact that a long-running operation blocks the thread that is executing it until the operation completes. If such an operation is performed synchronously, the result will be an unresponsive software application—one that might risk the health of your entire application. This may sound a little abstract, so let's use a scenario from daily life to make sense of it.

Assume that a few days ago, after I bought a product from Company A, I began having a problem with it. I called the company's support center to explain and sort out the problem. After listening to my explanation, the customer service representative asked me to wait a few minutes. While he tried to solve the problem, I was left hanging on the telephone. The important part here is that I couldn't do anything else until the representative got back to me. Any other tasks I needed to perform were, like me, left on hold while I waited for my call to end.

My situation in this scenario can be related to **synchronous** processing of a long-running operation (Figure 2-1).

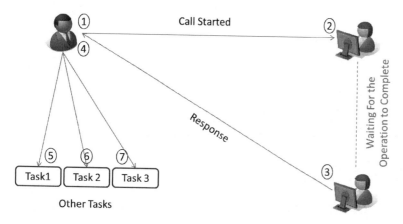

Figure 2-1. *A synchronous phone call between me and Company A's customer service representative*

Let's construct another scenario. This time I bought a product from Company B; again, there was a problem. I called Company B's support center and explained the problem to a customer service representative. This time, however, since the representative said she would call me back as soon as the problem got sorted out, I could hang up the phone. This allowed me to see to other tasks while Company B's people worked on my problem. Later, the representative called me back and informed me of the problem's resolution. This scenario resembles how an **asynchronous** operation works (see Figure 2-2).

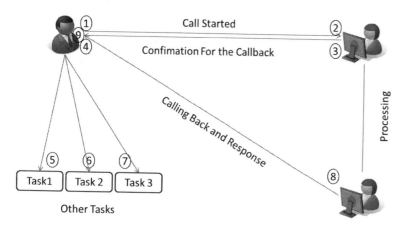

Figure 2-2. *An asynchronous phone call between me and Company B's customer service representative*

It is pretty easy to get confused about asynchronous programming, but it is even easier to get confused about leveraging asynchrony on server applications. The advantage of asynchronous programming is easily recognizable on client applications such as WPF, Windows Forms or Windows Store applications. Let's look at an example. In a WPF application, for instance, we want to download a web page (let's say www.apress.com) and insert its HTML code as text somewhere in our window. If we try to do this synchronously (in other words, on the same thread with the UI), the UI will stay unresponsive until the download operation is completed. It's certain that all of us have seen "(Not Responding)" at the top of the window at least a couple of times. The same situation will occur in this example if we try to move the window around because the UI thread is busy and cannot do anything else. On the other hand, if we try to perform the same operation asynchronously, our UI thread will be freed up and stay responsive.

There's one important thing to keep in mind in our sample here. No matter whether the operation is performed asynchronously or not, the user has to wait for the same amount of time to see the result. Though you may well think that this makes asynchrony undesirable for server applications, you would be wrong. Keep the phone conversation example in mind as we consider how requests are processed in IIS web server and how we can take advantage of asynchrony.

IIS Web Server and Asynchronous Processing

IIS Web Server offers a flexible, secure, and easy-to-manage Web server for hosting anything on the Web. When an ASP.NET application is hosted under IIS, it uses a CLR thread pool to manage requests and sends HTTP responses back one at a time because a thread cannot serve multiple requests simultaneously.

This section will show how asynchronous processing improves scaling and helps several IIS configurations get the best out of IIS.

IIS Web Server Processing Architecture in a Nutshell

IIS reserves a collection of free threads inside CLR's thread pool. These threads serve by responding to requests made to the IIS web server. By nature, a thread from the thread pool can respond to only one request at a time. This is not an issue most of the time, but it may well be if you start to get more traffic over time.

This structure will also cause problems with scaling if there is an application processing multiple long-running operations. This type of application will block the thread the operation is running on. As the number of requests increases, the number of free threads to handle requests inside the CLR's thread pool will decrease. This problem, also known as *Thread Starvation,* can affect the responsiveness of the application drastically.

In an asynchronous processing structure, threads are not blocked while waiting for operations to complete. When an operation starts (a network call, a file system operation, etc.), the web server hands the request to a free thread inside the thread pool. If this operation is long running and is processed asynchronously, the action informs the thread that the operation will take time and that it will inform the IIS when it is completed. Then the thread will return to the thread pool, where it will be able to handle other requests while the operation is waiting for a response. As soon as the running operation is completed and the data are ready, the action will inform the IIS about the operation's status. From that point, IIS will grasp a free thread from the thread pool and assign it to this operation. Note that the thread assigned to complete the processing of that request might or might not be the thread that started processing the request. This situation is processed by IIS, and the application itself is not concerned about it. In other words the application does not concern itself about which thread the operation runs on. It cares only about the result.

Another important point, one not to be overlooked, is that no matter how the operation is being processed, the amount of time the operation needs for completion will be approximately the same. One of the common misconceptions of asynchrony in .NET is that it allows an individual asynchronous operation to complete faster than the synchronous version. The positive side of asynchronous processing is that asynchronous operations will not block the thread they run on, whereas normal synchronous operations will. What's more, you may run two asynchronous operations at the same time in parallel; doing so will cut the time the two operations need to complete. We will see how this benefits us in our ASP.NET Web API applications.

IIS and Server Configuration for High Concurrency

For asynchronous processing in IIS 7.5 and 8.0, running with default configuration works best in general, but in some cases you might need to make some changes to your default server and IIS settings in order to get the most out of it.

With .NET Framework 4.0, the default configuration settings are suitable for most scenarios. For example, in ASP.NET 4.0 and 4.5, the **MaxConcurrentRequestsPerCPU** value is set to 5000 by default (it had been a very low number in earlier versions of .NET). According to team members of IIS, there's nothing special about the value 5000. It was set because it is a very large number and will allow plenty of async requests to execute concurrently. This setting should be fine, so there is no need to change it.

■ **Tip**   Windows 7, Windows Vista, and all other Windows client operating systems handle a maximum of 10 concurrent requests. You need to have a Windows Server operating system or use IIS Express to see the benefits of asynchronous methods under high load.

Even if a large number of concurrent requests per CPU are allowed, other factors can still limit effective asynchronous processing. There is an attribute named queueLength that indicates to HTTP.sys how many requests to queue for an application pool before rejecting future requests. **HTTP.sys (hypertext transfer protocol stack)** is the HTTP listener that is implemented as a kernel-mode device driver in order to listen for HTTP requests from the network, pass the requests onto IIS for processing, and then return processed responses to client browsers. The default value for the HTTP.sys queue limit is 1000. If this setting is too low for the application pool, HTTP.sys will reject requests with an HTTP 503 status, which indicates that the server is unavailable for any request to process. The HTTP.sys kernel queue limit is controlled by IIS and can be configured per application pool. To configure the HTTP.sys kernel queue limit for a particular application pool, open the IIS Manager and navigate to the Application Pools node (see Figure 2-3).

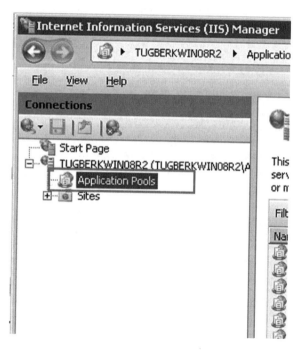

Figure 2-3. *The Application Pools node in the IIS Manager*

Inside the middle section of the IIS Manager window that shows the application pools, right-click on the application pool you would like to configure and select Advanced Settings (see Figure 2-4).

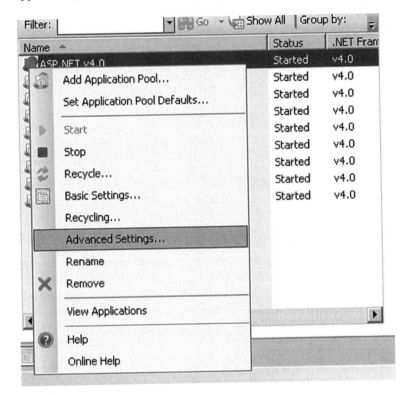

Figure 2-4. The Advanced Settings option of an IIS application pool

In the Advanced Settings dialog box (see Figure 2-5), find the Queue Length option under General node. This should be set to 1000 as default. Changing **Queue Length** from 1000 to 5000 should be fine.

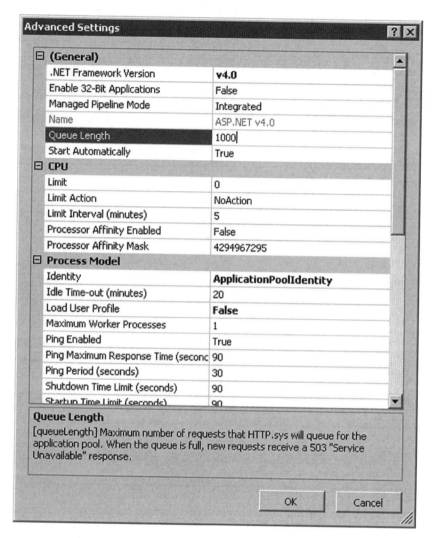

Figure 2-5. *The Queue Length option in the Advanced Settings dialog box*

These IIS and server settings are general, but some other settings are specific to the asynchronous operation type. You will see some of them later in Chapter 16 when use cases and scenarios are discussed.

Where to Favor Asynchronous Programming

Although operations performed asynchronously *can* make applications much more responsive, this isn't the case for every scenario. Because asynchronous programming is much more complex than normal synchronous programming, even if C# 5.0 language features make it easier to implement, the processing logic is still complex and thus hard to get right.

A specific case where asynchrony doesn't provide a performance benefit is where operations are primarily CPU operations. These shouldn't be performed asynchronously because asynchrony provides no advantages and results in more overhead by incurring more resource usage and an expensive thread switch.

> ■ **Tip** Task Parallel Library (TPL) also allows for parallel processing. If you have a scenario in which you need to kick off a CPU-bound task and this operation can be split into discrete tasks, TPL lets you run them in parallel and thus allows you to benefit from modern multicore CPUs.

Favor asynchrony over synchrony where operations are network-bound or I/O-bound instead of CPU-bound. Database operations, web service calls, and extensive file system operations are prime candidates for asynchrony.

In general, these situations are applicable for all server applications, but the choice of asynchronous or synchronous programming depends on the application itself. It should be tested to determine whether asynchrony provides a performance benefit or not.

Old Asynchronous Programming Models in .NET

An asynchronous programming paradigm is something that the .NET Framework has provided support for since version 1.1, and the .NET Framework has introduced three different types of asynchronous programming models since then. With .NET Framework 1.1, the Asynchronous Programming Model (APM) was introduced. In version 2.0, the .NET Framework provided Evented Asynchronous Programming (EAP). The most important step ahead in APM terms was the introduction of Task-based Asynchronous Pattern (TAP), along with Task Parallel Library (TPL), in .NET Framework 4.0. Each new programming model was slightly better than the previous one, but still not the most desirable programming experience.

This book's main concern will be Task-based Asynchronous Pattern, along with new C# 5.0 asynchronous language features, but in this section, we'll start by going through each model. We'll see how we can use asynchrony with these patterns and how the patterns differ from each other.

Asynchronous Programming Model (APM)

In *Asynchronous Programming Model (APM)*, asynchronous operations are represented by a pair of Begin/End methods such as FileStream.BeginRead and FileStream.EndRead.

The .NET Framework has various types of Begin/End methods designed to perform asynchronous operations. For example, System.IO.FileStream class has Read, BeginRead, and EndRead methods. Read method reads the number of bytes from a file stream synchronously and blocks the thread it runs on till the operation is completed. However, BeginRead and EndRead method pairs enable execution of the same operation asynchronously in a very complex manner.

When the BeginRead method is called, the asynchronous operation is started, and the method returns immediately while the operation is still running. When the operation is completed, the CLR gets notified by the Windows kernel about the status of the operation, and then the delegate that's been specified as a parameter to BeginRead method gets invoked. Inside this delegate, the EndRead method needs to be executed by passing the IAsyncResult object (which has been passed to the delegate by the BeginRead method) as a parameter in order to access the bytes read from the file stream.

Listing 2-1 shows the code that performs the action just explained.

Listing 2-1. Reading a File from the File System Asynchronously with APM Methods

```
static byte[] buffer = new byte[100];

static void Main(string[] args) {

    const string filePath = @"C:\Apps\Foo.txt";
```

```
        FileStream fileStream = new FileStream(filePath,
            FileMode.Open, FileAccess.Read, FileShare.Read, 1024,
            FileOptions.Asynchronous);

        IAsyncResult result = fileStream.BeginRead(buffer, 0, buffer.Length,
                new AsyncCallback(CompleteRead), fileStream);

        Console.ReadLine();
}

static void CompleteRead(IAsyncResult result) {

    Console.WriteLine("Read Completed");

    FileStream strm = (FileStream)result.AsyncState;

    // Finished, so we can call EndRead and it will return without blocking
    int numBytes = strm.EndRead(result);

    strm.Close();

    Console.WriteLine("Read {0} Bytes", numBytes);
    Console.WriteLine(BitConverter.ToString(buffer));
}
```

This code is only for one operation. Imagine the complexity if nested asynchronous operations had to be performed! Also, figuring out how to perform exception handling isn't as obvious as it might be. The next model looks slightly better than this one, but it, too, has its cons.

Event-based Asynchronous Pattern (EAP)

In *Event-based Asynchronous Pattern (EAP)*, asynchronous operations are represented by a method/event pair named OperationNameAsync and OperationNameCompleted; for example, WebClient.DownloadStringAsync and WebClient. DownloadStringCompleted. In the .NET Framework, some types support EAP as well. For example, the System.Net. WebClient class defines the DownloadStringAsync method and a DownloadStringCompleted event, to be called by the DownloadStringAsync method when the downloading operation is completed. DownloadStringAsync method also passes the argument e, a type of System.Net.DownloadStringCompletedEventArgs that contains the results of the operation and additional information about it.

USING THE SYSTEM.NET.WEBCLIENT ASYNCHRONOUS METHODS

In this section, we use the System.Net.WebClient class and its different types of asynchronous operations to demonstrate the usage of old asynchronous patterns. However, WebClient uses HttpWebRequest, which does a lot of setup work synchronously (proxy, DNS, connection pooling, etc.) and unfortunately is not therefore very asynchronous, even if "asynchronous" methods are used. This issue is not present with the HttpClient API, which is introduced in .NET 4.5. We don't therefore recommend using WebClient for HTTP request calls. In Chapter 4, we'll show how to use HttpClient asynchronous methods.

Listing 2-2 shows how to download a web page as string with WebClient EAP methods and events.

Listing 2-2. Downloading a Web Page as String with WebClient EAP Methods and Events

```
static void Main(string[] args) {

    WebClient client = new WebClient();

    client.DownloadStringCompleted += (sender, eventArgs) => {

        Console.WriteLine(eventArgs.Result);
    };

    client.DownloadStringAsync(new Uri("http://example.com"));

    Console.ReadLine();
}
```

As this pattern is also not the desired pattern for asynchronous programming in .NET, let's look at Task-based Asynchronous Pattern (TAP), which we'll be working with throughout the rest of this book.

Task-Based Asynchronous Pattern (TAP)

TAP is a pattern for asynchrony in the .NET Framework. It is based on the Task and Task<TResult> types in the System.Threading.Tasks namespace, which are used to represent arbitrary asynchronous operations introduced inside the Task Parallel Library (TPL). TPL is a set of public types and APIs in the System.Threading and System.Threading.Tasks namespaces in the .NET Framework.

In TAP, the asynchronous methods do not represent the real result as a returning object. Instead, they represent an ongoing task which will only eventually be completed at some later point. Understand from this expression that the asynchronous methods may be returned before the operation is completed. Those methods may, in addition, complete synchronously.

The System.Threading.Tasks.Task class is the one that represents asynchronous operations in TAP. An asynchronous method can return either Task or Task<T> for some T, based on whether the corresponding synchronous method would return void or a type T. If the method returns Task, there is not going to be an end result for the operation—except for the operation status that the Task class instance will carry. If the returning result of the asynchronous method is Task<T> for some T, the result will also have the end result (which is of type T) along with the Task class instance; it can be reached through the Result property of the Task class instance. Listing 2-3 shows how to retrieve the result of an asynchronous method directly from the Result property of the Task class.

Listing 2-3. Retrieving the Result from an Asynchronous Method Directly from the Result Property of the Task Instance

```
static void Main(string[] args) {

    var result = DoWorkAsync().Result;
    Console.WriteLine(result);
    Console.ReadLine();
}

static Task<string> DoWorkAsync() {

    return Task<string>.Factory.StartNew(() => {
        Thread.Sleep(3000);
        return "Hello world...";
    });
}
```

Inside the sample, we used the StartNew method of the TaskFactory class through Task.Factory to create and start a Task. This is not the optimal way of doing what needs to be done here (this topic is covered in a later subsection, "TaskCompletionSource<TResult>"). The StartNew method accepts a delegate to schedule the Task for execution. Inside the lambda function we are passing as a delegate, we wait for three seconds and then return the result.

■ **Tip** Asynchronous methods in TAP are usually named with an "Async" suffix attached to the operation's name; for example, MethodNameAsync. If adding a TAP method to a class that already contains a method MethodNameAsync, the suffix "TaskAsync" may be used instead, resulting in MethodNameTaskAsync.

However, invoking an asynchronous method, as shown in Listing 2-3, is not good practice with methods whose return type is Task<T>. Trying to get the result directly from the Result property of the Task class instance will block the thread until the operation is completed. That makes no sense for what we are trying achieve here. The next subsection shows how to address this problem.

■ **Note** A bit later in this chapter, you will see that most of the work we are trying to do is actually done by the new C# 5.0 asynchronous language features, but it is useful to learn a few of TAP's important points before diving into async/await features.

Continuations, Errors, and Task Status

In addition to retrieving the result out of a Task object through its Result property, we can work with the ContinueWith method of the Task class. The ContinueWith method creates a continuation that executes when the target Task completes. Listing 2-4 shows how to provide continuations to a task that represents an ongoing operation.

Listing 2-4. Retrieving a Result from an Asynchronous Method Inside the ContinueWith Method of a Task Instance

```
static void Main(string[] args) {

    DoWorkAsync().ContinueWith(task => {

        Console.WriteLine(task.Result);
    });
    Console.ReadLine();
}

static Task<string> DoWorkAsync() {

    return Task<string>.Factory.StartNew(() => {
        Thread.Sleep(3000);
        return "Hello world...";
    });
}
```

Listing 2-4 still retrieves the result through the Result property, but this time the operation is sure to have been completed. So reaching out to the Result property gets an immediate return because the result is already available. Although this way of retrieving results won't block the main thread, it's still not the optimal way of working with asynchronous methods in TAP.

Calling the ContinueWith method this way without checking the status of the operation will cause the continuation to run in every case, regardless of the task's final state. To handle this situation, use one of the overloads of the ContinueWith method that accepts a parameter of the type System.Threading.Tasks.TaskContinuationOptions. Passing a TaskContinuationOptions instance as a parameter to the ContinueWith method let you specify where to run the delegate function. Listing 2-5 shows how to set TaskContinuationOptions.

Listing 2-5. Using TaskContinuationOptions to Specify Where to Run the delegate Function

```
static void Main(string[] args) {

    DoWorkAsync().ContinueWith(task => {

        Console.WriteLine(task.Result);
    }, TaskContinuationOptions.NotOnFaulted);

    DoWorkAsync().ContinueWith(task => {

        Console.WriteLine(task.Exception.InnerException.Message);
    }, TaskContinuationOptions.OnlyOnFaulted);

    Console.ReadLine();
}

static Task<string> DoWorkAsync() {

    return Task<string>.Factory.StartNew(() => {
        Thread.Sleep(3000);
        return "Hello world...";
    });
}
```

On the other hand, there might be some asynchronous methods which complete synchronously. So check the status of the calls to see whether they completed asynchronously or not. Based on the result, unnecessary calls to ContinueWith methods can be avoided. Listing 2-6 shows an example of such use.

Listing 2-6. Detecting Whether the Task Has Completed Synchronously

```
static void Main(string[] args) {

    var doWorkTask = DoWorkAsync();

    if (doWorkTask.IsCompleted) {

        Console.WriteLine(doWorkTask.Result);

    } else {

        doWorkTask.ContinueWith(task => {

            Console.WriteLine(task.Result);
        }, TaskContinuationOptions.NotOnFaulted);
```

```
    doWorkTask.ContinueWith(task => {

        Console.WriteLine(task.Exception.InnerException.Message);
    }, TaskContinuationOptions.OnlyOnFaulted);

    Console.ReadLine();
    }
}

static Task<string> DoWorkAsync() {

    return Task<string>.Factory.StartNew(() => {
        Thread.Sleep(3000);
        return "Hello world...";
    });
}
```

In the sample shown in Listing 2-6, we check whether the task is completed. If it is, then we draw the result directly from the Result property of the Task class instance. Doing so is safe in this case because we know the task is completed and we won't block any thread.

Finally, we have a chance to see the status of the Task inside the continuation provided. The Task class holds a property, Status, which is a type of the TaskStatus enumeration. As soon as a Task object is initiated, the Status property is set to a value and the value of the Status property changes throughout its life cycle. A Task object can be in any one of the seven different states listed in Table 2-1.

Table 2-1. *The TaskStatus Enumeration Values and Their Descriptions*

TaskStatus Enumeration Value	Description
Created	The starting state of the Task object created through its constructor.
WaitingForActivation	The starting state of a Task object created through such methods as ContinueWith, ContinueWhenAll, ContinueWhenAny, and FromAsync, as well as from a TaskCompletionSource<TResult>.
WaitingToRun	This state has been set when the Task object is scheduled for execution but has not yet begun executing.
Running	This state indicates that the Task is running but is not yet completed.
WaitingForChildrenToComplete	This state indicates that the Task has finished executing and is implicitly waiting for attached child tasks to complete.
RanToCompletion	One of the three final states. It indicates that the Task has completed its execution successfully.
Canceled	One of the three final states. It indicates that the Task object in this state has completed its execution but has been canceled.
Faulted	One of the three final states. It indicates that the Task has been completed due to an unhandled exception.

The next section shows how to determine the status of a Task through a TaskStatus enumeration object.

Composition

It's sometimes helpful to execute multiple asynchronous operations in concert to perform more complex operations. Compared with previous asynchronous patterns in the .NET Framework, combining asynchronous operations with TPL is fairly straightforward. Still, it requires effort, and there are various ways of achieving it.

The Task class has two static methods: WaitAll and WaitAny. The WaitAll method accepts a collection of tasks and waits for all of them to complete. WaitAny, on the other hand, accepts a collection of tasks but waits until at least one of them is completed. You can start a bunch of related asynchronous operations you would like to execute in combination and then pass them all to WaitAll or WaitAny. Then you can collect the results once all are complete. Since these two methods will block the current thread, it is not the best way to achieve what you are after.

On the other hand, the TaskFactory class offers the ContinueWhenAll method, which invokes a continuation only once all of the asynchronous operations are completed. There is another method, ContinueWhenAny, and it invokes the continuation as soon as at least one task is completed. Neither of these two methods block the current thread, and they invoke the continuation by passing the completed task or tasks if the method in question is ContinueWhenAny. Listing 2-7 shows how the ContinueWhenAll method can be used.

Listing 2-7. An Example of TaskFactory.ContinueWhenAll in Use

```
static void Main(string[] args) {

    //First async operation
    var httpClient = new HttpClient();
    Task<string> twitterTask =
        httpClient.GetStringAsync("http://twitter.com");

    //Second async operation
    var httpClient2 = new HttpClient();
    Task<string> googleTask =
        httpClient2.GetStringAsync("http://www.google.com");

    Task.Factory.ContinueWhenAll(new[] { twitterTask, googleTask }, (tasks) => {

        //all of the tasks have been completed.
        //Reaching out to the Result property will not block.

        foreach (var task in tasks) {

            if (task.Status == TaskStatus.RanToCompletion) {

                Console.WriteLine(task.Result.Substring(0, 100));
            }
            else if (task.Status == TaskStatus.Canceled) {

                Console.WriteLine("The task has been canceled. ID: {0}", task.Id);
            }
```

```
            else {
                Console.WriteLine("An error has been occurred. Details:");
                Console.WriteLine(task.Exception.InnerException.Message);
            }
        }
    });

    Console.ReadLine();
}
```

To demonstrate how our example works, we used the new HttpClient API, which is introduced with .NET 4.5 to download web pages of two different web sites. We kicked off the operations and passed the two of them as parameters into the Task.Factory.ContinueWhenAll method. We also provided a continuation, which will be invoked when all these two tasks are completed. Inside the continuation, we have all the completed tasks in our hands. The first thing we do is put them inside a foreach loop. Notice that we are checking the status of each completed task before doing anything else (cf. the previous subsection, where the task statuses were explained). When the application is run, we see the first 100 characters of each web page's source code on the console if each web call completes successfully (see Figure 2-6).

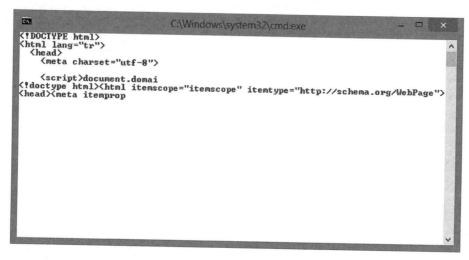

Figure 2-6. *The console window showing the result of our ContinueWhenAll example*

Although the ContinueWhenAll helper method allows the asynchronous operations to be run together, it actually doesn't compose them together. At the end of the operations, you'll have a reference for each completed task. In order to actually compose them together, you'll need to work with Task.WhenAll. This static class was introduced only in .NET 4.5 and was therefore not available in prior versions of .NET. There is another static method, WhenAny, which is equivalent to ContinueWhenAny.

Unlike TaskFactory.ContinueWhenAll, Task.WhenAll returns a Task or Task<T[]> that represents the completion of all of the supplied tasks. Listing 2-8 shows an approach for our little sample different from the one in Listing 2-7.

Listing 2-8. Another Example of Task.WhenAll in Use

```csharp
static void Main(string[] args) {

    //First async operation
    var httpClient = new HttpClient();
    Task<string> twitterTask =
        httpClient.GetStringAsync("http://twitter.com");

    //Second async operation
    var httpClient2 = new HttpClient();
    Task<string> googleTask =
        httpClient2.GetStringAsync("http://google.com");

    Task<string[]> task = Task.WhenAll(twitterTask, googleTask);

    task.ContinueWith(stringArray => {

        //all of the tasks have been completed.
        //Reaching out to the Result property will not block.

        if (task.Status == TaskStatus.RanToCompletion) {

            for (int i = 0; i < stringArray.Result.Length; i++) {

                Console.WriteLine(stringArray.Result[i].Substring(0, 100));
            }
        }
        else if (task.Status == TaskStatus.Canceled) {

            Console.WriteLine("The task has been canceled. ID: {0}", task.Id);
        }
        else {
            Console.WriteLine("An error has been occurred. Details:");
            foreach (var ex in task.Exception.InnerExceptions) {
                Console.WriteLine(ex.Message);
            }
        }
    });

    Console.ReadLine();
}
```

In the case here, when the two tasks are passed into Task.WhenAll, we know that we will get back a Task<string[]>, representing an ongoing operation. So we provide a continuation to allow processing to go on when all tasks are completed. Look inside the continuation delegate; you will see that the implementation is nearly the same as that shown in Listing 2-7. However, we are looping through the InnerExceptions property of the AggregateException instance to retrieve the exceptions when the task state is known to be faulted—that is, when at least one exception is thrown—because Task.WhenAll performs multiple ongoing operations and returns only one Task object. So if there are multiple errors, we want to reach all of them, not just one.

It is also very important to know how the returned Task or Task<T[]> object's status is set.

- If any of the supplied tasks completes in a Faulted state, the returned task will also complete in a Faulted state, where its exceptions will contain the aggregation of the set of unwrapped exceptions from each of the supplied tasks.

- If none of the supplied tasks faulted but at least one of them was canceled, the returned task will end in the Canceled state.

- If none of the tasks faulted and none of the tasks were canceled, the resulting task will end in the RanToCompletion state.

- If the supplied array and/or enumerable contains no tasks, the returned task will immediately transition to a RanToCompletion state before it's returned to the caller.

As you've seen, the composition of multiple asynchronous operations is fairly straightforward with TPL. However, there is still a lot of work to do inside the continuation to figure out the returned operation's completion state. Inside the "C# 5.0 Asynchronous Language Features" section in this chapter, these issues are addressed.

TaskCompletionSource<TResult>

You've probably noticed that in an ongoing operation, Task.Factory.StartNew has been used to create new Task objects. As you've seen, StartNew accepts a delegate to schedule the Task for execution. On the other hand, no work's been done so far that requires a thread switch inside the delegate provided. However, Task.Factory.StartNew runs our code in another thread, and as you know, thread switching has its own cost. Besides, using Task.Factory.StartNew to represent an ongoing operation runs counter to the title of this chapter, because Task.Factory.StartNew doesn't produce an asynchronous operation; instead, it introduces multithreading. Even if an asynchronous code is run inside the delegate passed into Task.Factory.StartNew, we'll still be doing multithreading. That's not a good idea for a server application in most scenarios.

In the ASP.NET Web API framework, you'll see that there are lots of extensibility points which require a return to a Task or Task<T> for some T. You won't always need a new thread for our code to run because our code might not have any risk of blocking the current thread or producing an asynchronous operation. Having said all of this, we shouldn't be using Task.Factory.StartNew to create new Task objects if code doesn't need to run in another thread. Instead, we should work with the System.Threading.Tasks.TaskCompletionSource generic class to return new Task objects.

TaskCompletionSource<TResult> is not just about the scenario just explained. One of TPL's primary developers, Stephen Toub, has defined TaskCompletionSource as follows:

The TaskCompletionSource<TResult> type serves two related purposes, both alluded to by its name: it is a source for creating a task, and the source for that task's completion. In essence, a TaskCompletionSource<TResult> acts as the producer for a Task<TResult> and its completion.

http://blogs.msdn.com/b/pfxteam/archive/2009/06/02/9685804.aspx

The TaskCompletionSource<TResult> object provides methods for controlling the lifetime and completion of the associated Task, such as SetResult, SetCanceled, and SetException methods. Those methods have their TrySet* variants as well, and they return Booleans as a result. TrySet* variants of those methods exist because a Task can be completed only once. So trying to complete a Task multiple times with TrySet* variants of those methods will return false.

To illustrate how TaskCompletionSource is used, Listing 2-9 creates a very naive example.

Listing 2-9. An Example of TaskCompletionSource in Use

```
public class AsyncFactory {

    public static Task<int> GetIntAsync() {

        var tcs = new TaskCompletionSource<int>();

        var timer = new System.Timers.Timer(2000);
        timer.AutoReset = false;
        timer.Elapsed += (s, e) => {
            tcs.SetResult(10);
            timer.Dispose();
        };

        timer.Start();
        return tcs.Task;
    }
}
```

What is here is an internally bogus asynchronous method; it fakes an operation that takes two seconds as a parameter and enables the client to consume this method in an unblocking fashion. We have created a TaskCompletionSource<int> instance inside the method, as well as a Timer object with a two-second interval, but the delegate is run just once and then the Timer object is disposed of.

For consuming this static method, the implementation won't be any different than it is for the others (see Listing 2-10).

Listing 2-10. Consuming Our AsyncFactory.GetIntAsync Method

```
static void Main(string[] args) {

    AsyncFactory.GetIntAsync().ContinueWith((task) => {

        if (task.Status == TaskStatus.RanToCompletion) {

            Console.WriteLine(task.Result);
        }
        else if (task.Status == TaskStatus.Canceled) {

            Console.WriteLine("The task has been canceled.");
        }
        else {

            Console.WriteLine("An error has been occurred. Details:");
            Console.WriteLine(task.Exception.InnerException.Message);
        }
    });

    Console.ReadLine();
}
```

43

Though it's a matter not entirely related to TaskCompletionSource, it is worth mentioning here that with .NET 4.5, there is a new static method, FromResult, that takes a T object and returns a Task<T> that is already completed without consuming any other threads. This returned Task<T> has the RanToCompletion status set. Listing 2-11 shows a simple example for use of the FromResult method.

Listing 2-11. An Example of the Task.FromResult Method in Use

```
static void Main(string[] args) {

    var intTask = GetIntAsync();

    if (intTask.IsCompleted) {

        Console.WriteLine("Completed Instantly: {0}", intTask.Result);
    }
    else {

        intTask.ContinueWith((task) => {

            if (task.Status == TaskStatus.RanToCompletion) {

                Console.WriteLine(task.Result);
            }
            else if (task.Status == TaskStatus.Canceled) {

                Console.WriteLine("The task has been canceled.");
            }
            else {
                Console.WriteLine("An error has been occurred. Details:");
                Console.WriteLine(task.Exception.InnerException.Message);
            }
        });
    }

    Console.ReadLine();
}
static Task<int> GetIntAsync() {

    return Task.FromResult(10);
}
```

Without having to employ the TaskCompletionSource object, we were able to create a new completed Task<int> object. We also didn't introduce a thread switch. The Task.FromResult method is one of those we'll use a lot in samples throughout this book.

Cancellation

In an asynchronous operation, you sometimes need to control its state to cancel the operation. With .NET 4.0, a new model for cancellation of asynchronous or long-running synchronous operations has been introduced. This model is based on an object called cancellation token.

The object that invokes the cancelable operation passes the cancellation token to the operation. At some point, the object that created the token can signal it to request a cancellation to get the operation to stop processing. The object receiving the token can then pass it to other operations; in this way it supports the cancellation chain. However, only the issuer of the cancellation token can issue the cancellation request, and the request can be done only once. On the other hand, there's no way to get the requested cancellation back. The cancellation, so to speak, can't be canceled.

This cancellation model is embraced by the .NET Framework, and as you will see, the ASP.NET Web API framework leverages the same model. There are three types of objects that you need to be aware for this cancellation model (see Table 2-1):

- *CancellationTokenSource*: The object that creates a cancellation token and manages its state, such as by issuing the cancellation request for all copies of that token.

- *CancellationToken*: A value type passed to one or more listeners, who then can observe this object to figure out whether the cancellation is requested or not by polling, callback, or wait handle.

- *OperationCanceledException*: Listeners have the option to throw this exception to verify the source of the cancellation and notify others that it has responded to a cancellation request.

Listing 2-9 shows a bogus asynchronous method over whose completion we have no control. The operation may complete instantly, or it may take ten minutes. However, nothing prevents the implementation of such functionality. Listing 2-12 shows a sample implementation for it.

Listing 2-12. An Example of a Cancellation Token in Use

```
public class AsyncFactory {

    public static Task<int> GetIntAsync(
        CancellationToken token = default(CancellationToken)) {

        var tcs = new TaskCompletionSource<int>();

        if (token.IsCancellationRequested) {
            tcs.SetCanceled();
            return tcs.Task;
        }

        var timer = new System.Timers.Timer(2000);
        timer.AutoReset = false;
        timer.Elapsed += (s, e) => {
            tcs.TrySetResult(10);
            timer.Dispose();
        };

        if (token.CanBeCanceled) {

            token.Register(() => {
                tcs.TrySetCanceled();
                timer.Dispose();
            });
        }

        timer.Start();
        return tcs.Task;
    }
}
```

For the GetIntAsync method, a CancellationToken value is now accepted as a parameter, but passing a CancellationToken isn't mandatory. The first thing to do is check whether the cancellation is requested. This information is found through the IsCancellationRequested property of the CancellationToken. If the cancellation is requested, then set the status of the Task object to Cancelled and return from there immediately. If the condition is false, continue to implement the logic in Listing 2-9. However, there is another piece of code there, one that handles the actual cancellation logic.

First of all, we check whether the token can be canceled at all. For example, if the caller of this method doesn't provide a cancellation token, the token will be set to its default value, and there is then no way for it to be canceled. If the token is cancelable, we use the Register method of the token to register a callback when the cancellation request is signaled. Also, notice that the Try* variants of the set methods have been used for TaskCompletionSource because when the timer has elapsed, the cancellation can be requested at the same time. So it isn't known for sure which one has set the status.

Let's see how to call this method by providing a cancellation token (see Listing 2-13).

Listing 2-13. Consuming GetIntAsync by Providing a Cancellation Token

```
static void Main(string[] args) {

    CancellationTokenSource cts = new CancellationTokenSource();
    cts.CancelAfter(1000);

    AsyncFactory.GetIntAsync(cts.Token).ContinueWith((task) => {

        //We get the response.
        //So dispose the CancellationTokenSource
        //so that it is not going to signal.
        cts.Dispose();

        if (task.Status == TaskStatus.RanToCompletion) {

            Console.WriteLine(task.Result);
        }
        else if (task.Status == TaskStatus.Canceled) {

            Console.WriteLine(
                "The task has been canceled.");
        }
        else {
            Console.WriteLine(
                "An error has been occurred. Details:");
            Console.WriteLine(
                task.Exception.InnerException.Message);
        }
    });

    Console.ReadLine();
}
```

First of all, a CancellationTokenSource object has been created to handle the cancellation token. Then, the CancelAfter method of the CancellationTokenSource has been used to tell it to request a cancellation after one second has elapsed. Finally, the Token property of the CancellationTokenSource object has been used to retrieve a CancellationToken value and has fired up the GetIntAsync method by passing that token. As the

CancellationTokenSource is unaware of the state of our ongoing task, dispose of the CancellationTokenSource object as soon as our continuation method is fired, because it will still try to cancel the request even if the task is completed in less than one second. The rest of the method is same as before. When this application is run, you should be able to see that the cancellation occurs (see Figure 2-7).

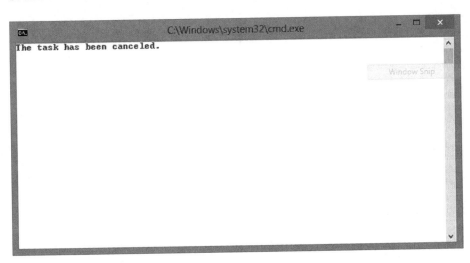

Figure 2-7. *Console window showing the result of the canceled operation*

Linked Cancellation Tokens

Some scenarios require listening to multiple cancellation tokens at once. For example, a cancelable object may accept a cancellation token as a parameter and also have an internal cancellation token. In order to handle such a scenario, create a so-called linked token, one that can join two or more tokens into one.

The CancellationTokenSource class provides a static method named CreateLinkedTokenSource to create a new CancellationTokenSource instance, which consists of the provided cancellation tokens. You can pass as many cancellation tokens as you like into CreateLinkedTokenSource method. The created CancellationTokenSource will signal the cancellation as soon as any one of the individually provided cancellation tokens is canceled.

Listing 2-14 provides an example.

Listing 2-14. InternalGetIntAsync Method and Linked Cancellation Token Sample

```
class Program {

    static void Main(string[] args) {

        CancellationTokenSource cts =
            new CancellationTokenSource();
        cts.CancelAfter(1000);

        Stopwatch watch = new Stopwatch();
        watch.Start();

        InternalGetIntAsync (cts.Token).ContinueWith((task) => {
```

```
            Console.WriteLine(
                "Elapsed time: {0}ms",
                watch.Elapsed.TotalMilliseconds);
            watch.Stop();

            //We get the response.
            //Dispose of the CancellationTokenSource
            //so that it is not going to signal.
            cts.Dispose();

            if (task.Status == TaskStatus.RanToCompletion) {

                Console.WriteLine(task.Result);
            }
            else if (task.Status == TaskStatus.Canceled) {

                Console.WriteLine("The task has been canceled.");
            }
            else {
                Console.WriteLine(
                    "An error has been occurred. Details:");
                Console.WriteLine(
                    task.Exception.InnerException.Message);
            }
        });

        Console.ReadLine();
    }

    static Task<int> InternalGetIntAsync(
        CancellationToken token) {

        var cts = new CancellationTokenSource(500);
        var linkedTokenSource =
            CancellationTokenSource.CreateLinkedTokenSource(
                cts.Token, token);

        return AsyncFactory.GetIntAsync(linkedTokenSource.Token);
    }
}
```

This example still uses the implementation of the AsyncFactory.GetIntAsync method used in Listing 2-12, but this time a proxy method is in between. This proxy method, the InternalGetIntAsync method, has its own internal cancellation token and also accepts another cancellation token as a parameter. The two tokens can be combined into one through the CreateLinkedTokenSource method, and the generated token can be passed into the AsyncFactory.GetIntAsync method.

Now this new token source signals the cancellation after 500 milliseconds, and our cancellation token requests a cancellation after a second. Also, since AsyncFactory.GetIntAsync takes two seconds to complete the request, this operation should be canceled after 500 milliseconds. For this sample, unlike the others, we also use a Stopwatch to see how long completing the operation takes. As you will see, it will take approximately half a second; then the status of the completed task will be canceled (see Figure 2-8).

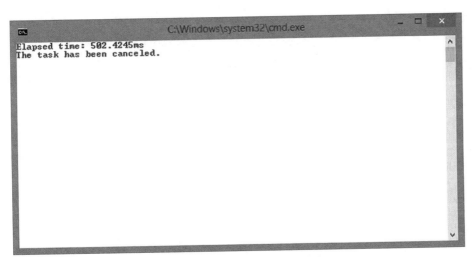

Figure 2-8. *The console window showing the result of the canceled operation and its completion time*

C# 5.0 Asynchronous Language Features

C# 5.0 has two new keywords: async and await. They provide a whole new asynchronous programming experience, one that .NET stack hasn't had so far. These features, also known as *Asynchronous Functions*, move most of the work from developer to compiler.

Asynchronous Functions in C# 5.0 constitute a new feature and provide a much easier way of dealing with asynchronous operations. Inside asynchronous functions, *await expressions* await ongoing tasks and suspend the logical execution flow of the code. This capacity will cause the rest of the function to be transparently signed up as a continuation of the awaited task and allows you to write code as though it was synchronous, even though the compiler turns it into an asynchronous function. As a result, asynchronous code retains its logical structure from the developer's perspective, while the code structure is dramatically changed by the compiler. With these new asynchronous language features, the compiler is not just generating the code that we would have written on our own, but it also does it in a virtually optimum way. Going into detail on how this is enabled is beyond this book's scope. Here, what we really want to achieve is to familiarize ourselves with these new features.

ASYNC/AWAIT IN .NET V4.0

We are targeting .NET 4.5 in order to leverage C# 5.0's asynchronous language features—new features that are not compatible with .NET 4.0. If you would like to work with the async and await keywords in .NET 4.0, you'll need additional pieces, depending on the Visual Studio version you use.

If you are working with Visual Studio 2010, you'll need to install Visual Studio Async CTP, which will change the C# and Visual Basic compilers, and install necessary libraries and samples. If the installation completes successfully, you'll find the necessary libraries in the **%userprofile%\Documents\Microsoft Visual Studio Async CTP\Samples** directory. For ASP.NET Web API, you'll need to add AsyncCtpLibrary.dll as a reference to your project. However, keep in mind that this solution works less optimally than .NET 4.5 and C# 5.0 compilers, nor do we know how long it is going to be supported.

If you are using Visual Studio 2012 and would like to work with async/await keywords in .NET Framework 4.0, you can install the Microsoft.Bcl.Async NuGet package. By the time of this writing, the Microsoft.Bcl.Async NuGet package is a pre-release NuGet package. So, you need to add the -pre switch to install this package through the NuGet Package Manager Console inside Visual Studio. You can find more information about this package from the BCL team's blog post: http://blogs.msdn.com/b/bclteam/archive/2012/10/22/using-async-await-without-net-framework-4-5.aspx.

In both scenarios, the compilers will work with these two keywords. On the other hand, there will be an additional class, TaskEx, which will hold WhenAll, WhenAny, and some other utility methods. So you'll need to modify the code explained here accordingly. All code other than these utility methods will work as in .NET 4.5.

Previous sections have shown how to use the DownloadStringTaskAsync method in WebClient API. Listing 2-15 shows the same operation with the new language features.

Listing 2-15. Using WebClient with async and await Keywords

```
public async Task<string> DowloadPage(string uri) {

    using (WebClient client = new WebClient()) {

        string htmlString = await client.DownloadStringTaskAsync(uri);
        return htmlString;
    }
}
```

There are a few specific things about this method to notice. First of all, the method is marked with the async modifier. Without this modifier, you'll get a compile-time error if you try to work with await expressions inside the method since the await operator can be used only within an async method. The second thing to note is the return type of this method. It is indicated that the method will return Task<string>, but inside the method the object returned is a type of string. This is perfectly valid because the await expression takes care of this situation, and the compiler generates the necessary code to make this work. If an asynchronous function's return type is either void or Task, the return statement must not have an expression. If the return type of the asynchronous function is Task<T> for some T, the return statement must have an expression implicitly convertible to T. Also notice that we were able to use the await keyword inside the using statement. At first glance, it might seem that the WebClient instance will be disposed before it completes it work, but the reality is that the compiler will also inspect this and ensure that the WebClient instance is disposed at the right time.

Chaining multiple asynchronous methods with the await pattern is extremely easier and cleaner compared with a pure TAP model. Listing 2-16 shows this in action.

Listing 2-16. Multiple Asynchronous Operation Chaining Cample

```
private async void Button_Click_1(object sender, RoutedEventArgs e) {

    using (Stream stream = await GetWebPageAsync())
    using (var fileStream = new FileStream(@"c:\apps\msg.bin", FileMode.Create)) {
        await stream.CopyToAsync(fileStream);
        StatusLabel.Content = "Done...";
    }
}

private async Task<Stream> GetWebPageAsync() {

    using (var httpClient = new HttpClient()) {
```

```
        var stream = await httpClient.GetStreamAsync("http://www.apress.com");
        return stream;
    }
}
```

This little WPF application downloads the Apress home page and saves it to the disk. The GetWebPageAsync method downloads the web page and returns it as a stream but does it asynchronously. Again, we used new HttpClient here to download the web page asynchronously. Also, notice that we make the asynchronous call inside the using block, and we didn't hesitate to use it because, as mentioned before, the compiler does all the heavy lifting here and makes sure that HttpClient won't be disposed of until the operation is completed.

There is also an event handler named Button_Click_1 for the button. The async and await keywords can be used inside a method whose return type is void, but it is better to avoid that as much as possible and return at least Task, because the caller of the asynchronous method probably wants to know the details and status of the operation even if the method isn't returning anything. However, as this is an event handler, there's no other choice here. Inside the Button_Click_1 method, you can consume the GetWebPageAsync method and await it as well. As soon as you get the Stream from the GetWebPageAsync method, go ahead and save it to the disk. This is done using the CopyToAsync method of the Stream class. The CopyToAsync method returns Task, and therefore you can await that as well. After every operation is completed, the message on the UI indicating that the operation is completed is displayed.

When the application is fired up and the button pressed, you won't lose any UI responsiveness because every operation is performed asynchronously (see Figure 2-9).

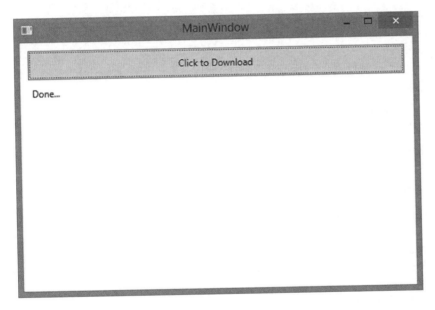

Figure 2-9. *Our application UI*

In the .NET Framework, the recommended pattern for asynchrony is TAP, and the Task class has the main role in this pattern. When you call a method that returns Task or Task<T> for some T and "await" that, the compiler does the heavy lifting: assigning continuations, handling exceptions, and so on. As we mentioned and saw in action, Task or Task<T> for some T can be awaited by the await keyword to suspend the execution of an asynchronous function. Besides, any type that satisfies the await pattern can be awaited. This chapter won't go into the details of this pattern since its main concern is to provide the infrastructure to work with asynchrony.

On the other hand, we will go through some of the important concepts of this new pattern to make the most out of it when working in an ASP.NET Web API application.

Exception Handling

Listing 2-16's code didn't perform any exception handling, but it's possible that an operation may crash for any of several reasons. Exception handling is not an easy task in general, and it is certainly not easy when dealing with asynchrony. However, when using async and await keywords, exception handling is easier than with the pure TAP implementation. As we usually do when writing synchronous code, we need to put our awaited method inside a try/catch block. The compiler then understands our intention and generates the code that will enable us to catch the exception.

Also, as was seen in earlier sections, the status of the Task is set to Faulted, and the actual exception is wrapped inside the AggregateException if an exception occurs during an asynchronous operation. The main reason for this is that it was not possible to rethrow exceptions without losing the actual stack trace, which is vitally important for examining the exception. However, with .NET v4.5, it's now possible to rethrow the exception without losing any actual stack trace information.

Listing 2-17 shows a modified version of the code inside Listing 2-16.

Listing 2-17. Multiple Asynchronous Operation Chaining Sample with Exception Handling

```
private async void Button_Click_1(object sender, RoutedEventArgs e) {

    try {

        using (Stream stream = await GetWebPageAsync())
        using (var fileStream = new FileStream(@"c:\apps\msg.bin", FileMode.Create)) {
            await stream.CopyToAsync(fileStream);
            StatusLabel.Content = "Done...";
        }
    }
    catch (Exception ex) {

        StatusLabel.Content = string.Format(
            "An exception occurred: {0}{1}Stack Trace:{1}{2}",
            ex.Message,
            Environment.NewLine,
            ex.StackTrace
        );
        StatusLabel.Foreground = Brushes.Red;
    }
}

private async Task<Stream> GetWebPageAsync() {

    using (var httpClient = new HttpClient()) {
        var stream = await httpClient.GetStreamAsync("http://localhost:9999");
        return stream;
    }
}
```

We've exchanged the URI for a broken URI to get an exception to demonstrate our example. When the application is run and the button is pressed, the exception details should be displayed on the UI (see Figure 2-10).

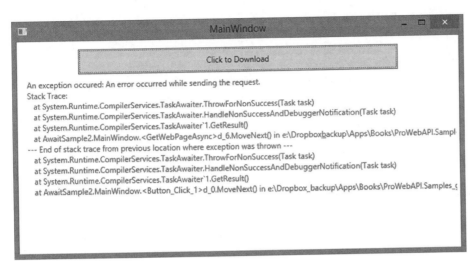

Figure 2-10. *Our application UI displaying the exception details*

The exception handling with `async` and/or `await` is an extensive topic as well. As it's outside this book's scope, it's not looked at in detail.

SynchronizationContext

There's another important feature of the `async` and `await` keywords: support for `SynchronizationContext`. When you await an asynchronous method, the compiler hooks up the continuation, if there is any, and the resulting code is context-aware. Thus, if a `SynchronizationContext` is available, the `await` expression will capture it and use it to invoke the continuation. This is why we were able to work with the UI controls directly right after the await expressions, as a SynchronizationContext is available in WPF applications.

The `SynchronizationContext` is not just about the TPL, and it's been inside the framework since .NET 2.0. If you are working with the `async` and `await` keywords, however, all the code that you would be writing to work with the `SynchronizationContext` will already be written for you by the compiler. Your code will always execute along with the right context.

However, unless enough care is taken, this feature may lead to some problems. If you consume a method in a blocking fashion and that method has been implemented by using the new asynchronous language features, you will end up with a deadlock if you have an available `SynchronizationContext`. When, for instance, you wait on the `Task` with the `Wait` method or take the result directly from the `Result` property of the `Task`, you block the main thread at the same time. When eventually the `Task` completes inside that method in the thread pool, it is going to invoke the continuation to post back to the main thread (as we never left it), because `SynchronizationContext.Current` is available and captured. But there's a problem: the UI (or main) thread is blocked. You have a deadlock!

Having created a simple .NET client for an HTTP API (Listing 2-18), we consume the HTTP API by using the `HttpClient`'s asynchronous methods along with the `async`/`await` keywords.

Listing 2-18. Simple HTTP API .NET Client

```
public class Car {

    public int Id { get; set; }
    public string Make { get; set; }
    public string Model { get; set; }
```

```
        public int Year { get; set; }
        public float Price { get; set; }
}

public class SampleAPIClient {

    private const string ApiUri = "http://localhost:17257/api/cars";

    public async Task<IEnumerable<Car>> GetCarsAsync() {

        using (HttpClient client = new HttpClient()) {

            var response = await client.GetAsync(ApiUri);

            response.EnsureSuccessStatusCode();
            return await response.Content.ReadAsAsync<IEnumerable<Car>>();
        }
    }
}
```

As you saw earlier, if there is a SynchronizationContext available, the code that the compiler generates will capture it and post the continuation back to that context to be executed. Keep this part in mind. This little class has been put inside a separate project, SampleAPI.Client, and referenced from our web clients. An ASP.NET MVC application has also been created, and it has a controller that has two actions: one calls the API asynchronously, and the other does the same in a blocking fashion (see Listing 2-19).

Listing 2-19. An ASP.NET MVC Controller That Consumes the HTTP API Through the .NET Client

```
public class HomeController : Controller {

    public async Task<ViewResult> CarsAsync() {

        SampleAPIClient client = new SampleAPIClient();
        var cars = await client.GetCarsAsync();

        return View("Index", model: cars);
    }

    public ViewResult CarsSync() {

        SampleAPIClient client = new SampleAPIClient();
        var cars = client.GetCarsAsync().Result;

        return View("Index", model: cars);
    }
}
```

Listing 2-20 shows the cars on the web page displayed in a simple Razor view.

Listing 2-20. The Razor View Display of the Cars on the Web Page

```
@model IEnumerable<SampleAPI.Client.Car>
@{
    ViewBag.Title = "Home Page";
}

<h3>Cars List</h3>

<ul>
    @foreach (var car in Model) {
        <li>
            @car.Make, @car.Model (@car.Year) - @car.Price.ToString("C")
        </li>
    }
</ul>
```

Navigating to /home/CarsAsync should get the result to return smoothly (see Figure 2-11).

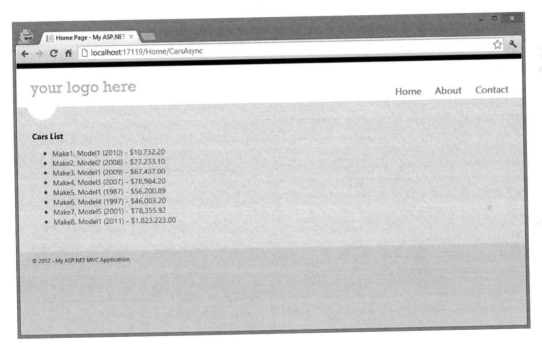

Figure 2-11. The web page display of the cars list

However, if you navigate to /home/CarsSync to invoke the CarsSync method, you will see that the page never comes back because a deadlock was just introduced for the reasons explained earlier.

Taking a look at our GetCarsAsync method implementation inside our .NET client for the HTTP API will show that it is completely unnecessary to get back to the current SynchronizationContext because nothing is needed from the current context. This is actually a good sign because it is not our .NET client's concern to do anything under the current SynchronizationContext. It is, on the other hand, our consumer's responsibility.

In the case here, the default SynchronizationContext behavior that the compiler is generating needs to be suppressed. This can be achieved with the ConfigureAwait method of the Task class, which was introduced with .NET 4.5. The ConfigureAwait method accepts a Boolean parameter named continueOnCapturedContext. By passing false into this method so as not to marshal the continuation back to the original context captured, our problem will be solved. Listing 2-21 shows the new look of our .NET client for the HTTP API.

Listing 2-21. The New Look of Our Simple HTTP API .NET Client

```
public class SampleAPIClient {

    private const string ApiUri = "http://localhost:17257/api/cars";

    public async Task<IEnumerable<Car>> GetCarsAsync() {

        using (HttpClient client = new HttpClient()) {

            var response = await client.GetAsync(ApiUri)
                .ConfigureAwait(continueOnCapturedContext: false);

            response.EnsureSuccessStatusCode();
            return await response.Content.ReadAsAsync<IEnumerable<Car>>()
                .ConfigureAwait(continueOnCapturedContext: false);
        }
    }
}
```

As you'll be creating HTTP APIs with the ASP.NET Web API framework, you'll probably also create .NET client libraries to make it easy to consume the API. If you write a .NET client for your HTTP API using the new asynchronous language features, you might want to consider these facts before moving on. Otherwise, your consumers will have a hard time understanding what is really going wrong. As a general rule, if you are developing a library, the default behavior that await gives in terms of synchronization context is nearly never what you want. However, if you are developing an application such as ASP.NET MVC or ASP.NET Web API, the default behavior will nearly always be what you want.

Summary

Asynchrony is very important if you are aiming for scalability in your application when you are consuming long-running I/O intensive operations. This chapter has shown what asynchrony is in theory, where it makes sense, and how the .NET Framework and C# language features help along the way. Considering the fact that the ASP.NET Web API framework deals with asynchrony at a very high level, this chapter will give a better understanding of how to manage asynchronous methods and operations in Web API, especially with many of the extensibility points ASP.NET Web API introduces.

■ ■ ■

CHAPTER 3

HTTP, REST, and Hypermedia

Before speaking about ASP.NET Web API itself, we need to provide some fundamentals to get a better understanding of why ASP.NET Web API works as it does. The very basic goal of ASP.NET Web API was to make HTTP a first-class citizen in .NET and provide a foundation for RESTful applications based on the .NET Framework. So in order to understand the Web API framework better, we will explain the fundamentals of HTTP, REST and hypermedia, starting with HTTP basics.

HTTP Basics

As just mentioned, ASP.NET Web API primarily is about handling the HTTP protocol in an efficient and fluent manner using .NET, so we need a good understanding of HTTP.

Consider a scenario now happening billions of times a day. A user types www.google.com into a web browser, and within a few milliseconds she gets the Google search start page rendered in her browser. This is a simple request and response technique which is displayed simplified in Figure 3-1.

Figure 3-1. *Simplified request response model between browser and server*

As you can imagine, this doesn't happen without some technical stuff under the hood, and that's where HTTP enters the room.

HTTP is the abbreviation for "hypertext transfer protocol," which handles the communication (through the requests and responses) between the user's web browser and web servers (in this case Google's). To speak in a more generalized manner, the web browser is an HTTP client and the web server is just an HTTP server.

As HTTP is a communication protocol, it has a set of standardized elements, both of which the server and the client need to be able to deal with. We'll explain each of them in the following sections in detail.

Resources and URIs

Basically, all pages in web sites in the World Wide Web (WWW) are regarded as resources, and that's exactly what they're called in HTTP language. But resources in HTTP are not just files in the form of HTML web pages. In general, a resource is any piece of information that can be unambiguously identified by a Uniform Resource Identifier (URI), such as `http://microsoft.com/windows`. (In nontechnical contexts and on the World Wide Web, the term URL—uniform resource locator—is also used.)

A URI consists of a URI scheme name such as "http" or "ftp" followed by a colon character and then by a scheme-specific part. The scheme-specific part's syntax and semantics are defined in scheme specifications, where they share a general syntax that reserves certain characters for special purposes. The general syntax is as follows, according to RFC 3986:

```
<scheme name> : <hierarchical part> [ ? <query> ] [ # <fragment> ]
```

The HTTP protocol uses the generic syntax, as the following URI shows:

```
http://www.apress.com/web-development/web-api?dir=asc&order=name
```

In that sample URI, the *scheme name* is "http"; it is followed by the *hierarchical part*, "`www.apress.com/web-development/web-api`", which is also referred to as *path*. The hierarchical part usually starts with "`//`", as shown in the sample URI. It also contains an optional *query*, which is "dir=asc&order=name" here.

An example of a URI containing the optional *fragment* part would be the following:

```
http://localhost/wiki/rest#hypermedia
```

In this example, "hypermedia" is the fragment part.

In order to provide consistency, the syntax of the URI also enforces restrictions on the scheme-specific part.

HTTP Methods

To handle actions on URIs (i.e., our resources), HTTP uses so-called HTTP request methods—also referred as to "verbs." There are a few of them, and we'll take a look at the most important ones now.

- GET
- POST
- PUT
- DELETE

One of the HTTP request methods frequently used in web browsers is GET. GET is always used when requesting a URL like `microsoft.com`.

With that in mind, Figure 3-2 takes a more technical look at the previous request/response model.

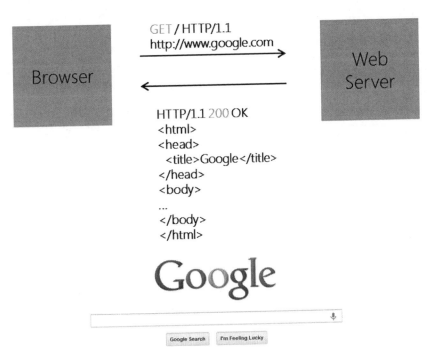

Figure 3-2. *A request/response model between browser and server using the HTTP protocol*

You can see now what's happening at the level of HTTP: the client sends a request to the server, with the first line of the request looking like this:

```
GET / HTTP/1.1 http://www.google.com
```

Just as it sounds, GET is telling the server that we want to get a resource from it. *Which* resource is told here by the slash, "/", following GET, which in this case is the resource at the root of the server. This often (not to say always) is mapped to a default document such as "index.htm" or "default.htm" in the case of Microsoft Internet Information Services (IIS). If you want to receive another resource, you need to specify the resource's identifier after the slash, for example, "/search".

Another important verb is POST, which allows you to send data to the server. If you have a web development background, you may have seen POST when submitting HTML forms to the server, as shown in Listing 3-1.

Listing 3-1. An HTML 5 Form That Is Sent Using the POST Method

```
<form action="http://www.example.org/feedback" method="post">
        <input name="firstname" type="text" />
        <input name="lastname" type="text" />
        <input name="email" type="email" />
        <textarea name="feedback" />
        <button type="submit">Send Feedback</button>
</form>
```

Very similar to POST is PUT, but PUT is used for updating a resource. As surprising as it may seem, the HTTP specification was written with that in mind; also, you won't be able to invoke it from within your browser.

Once this is understood, it seems quite logical that HTTP also provides a DELETE method.

To get a deeper understanding of which method should be used and when to use it, let's inspect the HTTP methods under the aspects of *safety* and *idempotency*.

Safe Methods

Some methods (e.g., GET and OPTIONS) are defined as safe. That means they should not have side effects. Exceptions to that are effects such as logging, caching, and incrementing an access counter. Issuing arbitrary GET requests should therefore be considered safe if they're not changing the application's state.

In contrast, methods such as POST, PUT, and DELETE are used for actions that do create side effects on the server; also included are subsequent external effects, such as a sent e-mail.

When it comes to implementation, you should be aware that although GET requests are called safe, their handling by the server is not technically limited in any way. As a consequence, you can write code that can very well lead to side effects on the server. In a RESTful application, you should absolutely avoid that, because it can cause problems for web caching, search engines and other automated agents, all of which rely on the safety of GET.

Idempotent Methods

The methods PUT and DELETE are defined as idempotent. That means that multiple identical requests should have the same effect as a single request. As HTTP is a stateless protocol, the methods being prescribed as safe (namely, GET, HEAD, OPTIONS and TRACE) should also be idempotent.

■ **Note** Idempotence refers to the state of the system after the request has completed. That means that the action the server takes (e.g., deleting a customer) or the response code it returns may differ for subsequent requests, but the system state will be the same every time.

In contrast, the POST method is not necessarily idempotent. Thus, sending the same POST request multiple times may further affect state or cause further side effects (such as sending e-mails). There may be some cases where this is wanted. But there may also be cases where it happens by accident, such as when the user, having failed to receive adequate feedback that the first request was successful, sends another request. Also, most web browsers warn users in cases where reloading a page may reissue a POST request; generally the web application is responsible for handling when a POST request should only be submitted once.

As with safety, whether a method is idempotent is not enforced by the protocol or handling on the server. For example, it is easily possible to write a web application in which a database insert or other non-idempotent action is invoked by a GET or some other HTTP method. If you ignore this, your requests may have undesirable consequences. Remember that clients assume the correct behavior when repeating a request.

HTTP Status Codes

HTTP Status codes are another important part of the HTTP protocol. Look again at Figure 3-2; you will see that the server returns not only an HTML page but also this:

```
HTTP/1.1 200 OK
```

200 is a status code; it means "everything is OK"—that is, the server found the requested resource and has been able to send it to the client.

This status code is always returned when you browse the Web and everything works fine; you won't see the status code itself, however.

A status code you might have already seen in your browser is the 404 status code; it means that the requested resource identified by the URI you sent to the server could not be found.

There are other status codes, including 303, which stands for "see other"—that is, the resource of the initial request can be found under a different URI and should be retrieved using the GET method on that URI.

If you have tried to access a web server that has been under heavy load, you might have also seen a 503 status code—for "Service Unavailable"—in your browser. That message means that the server is overloaded or under maintenance.

If you compare the preceding status codes, you will notice that not only do they have different values as a whole but they also start with different digits. That is so because they are divided into five classes.

- 1xx—Informational—indicates a provisional response, which consists only of the status line and optional headers. The status code line is terminated by an empty line. This class of status code does not require any headers.

- 2xx—Successful—indicates that the client's request was successfully received, understood, and accepted.

- 3xx—Redirection—indicates that the client needs to take further action in order to complete the request. The action required may be carried out by the client without user interaction when the second request method is GET or HEAD. In addition, a client should detect infinite redirection loops.

- 4xx—Client Error—should be used if the client seems to have done something wrong. For all requests other than HEAD, the server should include a response body explaining the error, whether the error is temporary or permanent, and whether the response body should be shown to the user. The 4xx status can be applied to any request method.

- 5xx—Server Error—indicates cases where the server is aware that it is responsible for an error or is not able to perform the request For all requests other than HEAD, the server should include a response body explaining the error, whether the error is temporary or permanent, and whether the response body should be shown to the user. The 5xx status can be applied to any request method.

The HTTP protocol defines many more status codes besides, but we'll stick with these.

HTTP in Action

To see how URIs, resources, verbs, and status codes play together within requests and responses, let's take a closer look at the Apress web site.

Figure 3-3 shows how the site looks in the browser of your choice.

Figure 3-3. *The Apress web site inside the browser*

As there's nothing uncommon to see (besides great books), let's dig a little bit deeper using Fiddler, which was introduced in the "Know Your Tools" section in Chapter 1.

First, let's issue a new request inside the Composer tab to the URI http://apress.com, as shown in Figure 3-4.

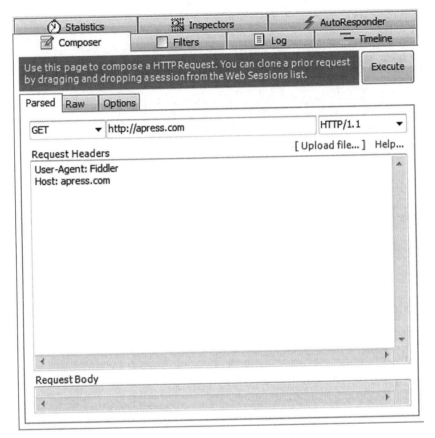

Figure 3-4. Issuing a new request to apress.com using Fiddler

Now let's take a look at the left section of Fiddler, as shown in Figure 3-5, where the list of issued requests contains two new entries.

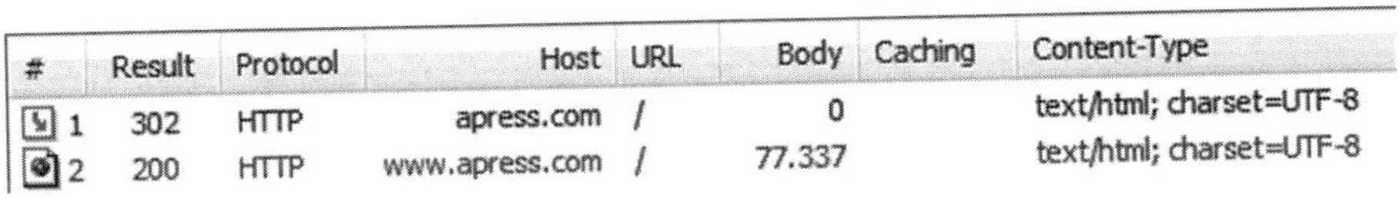

#	Result	Protocol	Host	URL	Body	Caching	Content-Type
1	302	HTTP	apress.com	/	0		text/html; charset=UTF-8
2	200	HTTP	www.apress.com	/	77.337		text/html; charset=UTF-8

Figure 3-5. The left section of the Fiddler request to apress.com

You might wonder why there are two requests. That's because we issued `http://apress.com`, which sent a 302 status code response to the client. The 302 status code tells the client that the requested resource is temporarily available under another URI. If you select the 302 response from the left list, you can inspect it in the lower right window by clicking the Raw tab, as shown in Figure 3-6.

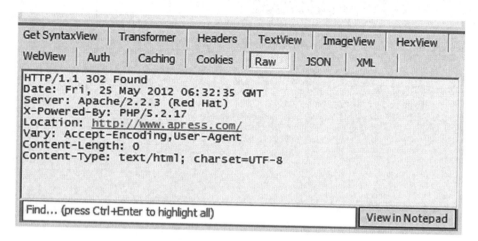

Figure 3-6. *A 302 response in Fiddler*

Please take note of the line containing

```
Location: http://www.apress.com/
```

That information tells the client where to find the temporary new location of the requested resource specified by `http://apress.com/`. The new location is `http://www.apress.com/`; that's where the second request is issued automatically by the browser itself.

Notice the response for that request inside the WebView tab of Fiddler, as shown in Figure 3-7; it looks totally different from the browser view of Figure 3-3.

Figure 3-7. Apress web site in Fiddler WebView

The reason for that is that the returned HTML code does not contain any style sheets, scripts, or pictures.

The style sheets in particular are referenced by `<link />` HTML tags, which tell the browser (more generally, the client) to follow them, fetch their resources (i.e., the style sheet), and use them to render the HTML representation of the web page according to the format definitions inside the style sheet. We'll take a closer look at the `<link />` tags later in this chapter.

HTTP Header Fields

In Figure 3-6 we saw the following line:

```
Location: http://www.apress.com/
```

Around that line are `Content-Type`, `Content-Length`, and a few others. Each of them is a so-called HTTP Header Field. These fields exist in both requests and responses. Most of them differ for requests and responses, but some, such as content-type, exist on both sides of the HTTP protocol.

HTTP Header Fields define parameters for the HTTP operation; we'll be using some of them throughout the book.

One of the most important HTTP Header Fields is the aforementioned content-type header, which tells the other side (request or response) which type the transmitted content is. In the case of web pages, the content-type is text/html, and the complete header definition looks like this:

```
content-type: text/html
```

The phrase "text/html" is an identifier for a file format on the Internet and is called an Internet media type.

Internet Media Types

Internet media types were originally called MIME types (Multipurpose Internet Mail Extensions), but their use has expanded from e-mails sent using the SMTP protocol to HTTP and other Internet protocols.

As was seen in the text/html media type definition, it consists of (at least) two parts, where the first is a type and the second is a subtype. Either can be followed by one or more parameters.

We'll get deeper insight into Internet media types (or just content-types, as they are also referred to) in "Shifting to a RESTful Architecture" and sections that follow it in this chapter.

If you need more detailed information about the HTTP protocol and its elements, read RFC 2616, the specification of the HTTP protocol; it can be found at https://www.ietf.org/rfc/rfc2616.txt.

Now that you have a very basic understanding of the HTTP protocol and its most important concepts—resources, URIs, HTTP methods, status codes, headers and media types—let's head over to Service Oriented Architectures to see how they have been created within the last decade.

REST

In this section, we will first consider Service Oriented Architectures (SOA) using a SOAP example, as this has become a familiar solution nowadays. With that context in mind, we will look at REST, which is an architectural style for distributed applications introduced first by Roy T. Fielding in his doctoral dissertation in the year 2000. Throughout the section, we'll see how we can improve SOA by moving toward a RESTful architecture.

Service Oriented Architectures and HTTP

If you've heard about Service Oriented Architectures, you might also have heard about or even used SOAP in a distributed application—as in the .NET ecosystem, represented by ASMX web services, or Windows Communication Foundation (WCF).

The original meaning of SOAP was "Simple Object Access Protocol"; it was a specification for exchanging structured data (i.e., XML) using web services built on top of the HTTP protocol.

As it relies on HTTP, it also follows the request/response model, where both request and response are represented by XML documents, called messages.

A typical SOAP request message representing a request to a customer service that returns a customer named Microsoft might look like Listing 3-2.

Listing 3-2. A Typical SOAP Request Message

```
<?xml version="1.0"?>
<soap:Envelope
xmlns:soap="http://www.w3.org/2001/12/soap-envelope"
soap:encodingStyle="http://www.w3.org/2001/12/soap-encoding">
```

```
<soap:Body xmlns:m="http://www.example.org/customer">
  <m:GetCustomer>
    <m:CustomerName>Microsoft</m:CustomerName>
  </m:GetCustomer>
</soap:Body>

</soap:Envelope>
```

The message consists of some header information and a so-called envelope, which contains the message body.

The method of the addressed customer service that should be invoked is the GetCustomer method, and the required parameter is CustomerName, where the value is Microsoft.

In SOAP the message above (to get a customer resource) is POSTed to the server via HTTP protocol, because according to the HTTP specification, the method to send (new) content from the client to the server is POST, as you can see in Listing 3-3.

Listing 3-3. HTTP POST Request in SOAP

```
POST /customerservice HTTP/1.1
Host: www.example.org
Content-Type: application/soap+xml; charset=utf-8
Content-Length: 332
```

After some operations involving the database, the service might return the customer wrapped in a response message such as the one shown in Listing 3-4.

Listing 3-4. SOAP Response Message

```
<?xml version="1.0"?>
<soap:Envelope
xmlns:soap="http://www.w3.org/2001/12/soap-envelope"
soap:encodingStyle="http://www.w3.org/2001/12/soap-encoding">

<soap:Body xmlns:m="http://www.example.org/customer">
  <m:GetCustomerResponse>
    <m:CustomerId>123</m:CustomerId >
    <m:CustomerName>Microsoft</m:CustomerName>
  </m:GetCustomerResponse>
</soap:Body>

</soap:Envelope>
```

As everything went fine during request and response, the response header will look like Listing 3-5.

Listing 3-5. Response Headers of a SOAP Response

```
HTTP/1.1 200 OK
Content-Type: application/soap+xml
charset=utf-8
Content-Length: 390
```

Now let's try that again, but this time let's imagine that we mistyped the customer name and our new request is the one from Listing 3-6.

Listing 3-6. SOAP Request with Mistyped Customer Name

```
POST /customerservice HTTP/1.1
Host: www.example.org
Content-Type: application/soap+xml; charset=utf-8
Content-Length: 332
<?xml version="1.0"?>
<soap:Envelope
xmlns:soap="http://www.w3.org/2001/12/soap-envelope"
soap:encodingStyle="http://www.w3.org/2001/12/soap-encoding">

<soap:Body xmlns:m="http://www.example.org/customer">
  <m:GetCustomer>
    <m:CustomerName>Microsft</m:CustomerName>
  </m:GetCustomer>
</soap:Body>

</soap:Envelope>
```

The response generated by the server might easily be the one in Listing 3-7.

Listing 3-7. SOAP Response to Request with Mistyped Customer Name

```
HTTP/1.1 200 OK
Content-Type: application/soap+xml
charset=utf-8
Content-Length: 390

<?xml version="1.0"?>
<soap:Envelope
xmlns:soap="http://www.w3.org/2001/12/soap-envelope"
soap:encodingStyle="http://www.w3.org/2001/12/soap-encoding">

<soap:Body xmlns:m="http://www.example.org/customer">
  <soap:Fault>
    <faultcode>soap:Server</faultcode>
    <faultstring>Customer could not be found.</faultstring>
    <detail />
  </soap:Fault></soap:Body>

</soap:Envelope>
```

As you can see, the server tells you that it couldn't find a customer with the name Microsft—well, you *are* to blame!

That's how we've handled SOA many times for many years. More or less we have been happy with it—but does that mean it's been the best way? We'll try to answer that question within the next section.

Shifting to a RESTful Architecture

Now let's inspect the two requests and responses again; this time let's focus on the HTTP headers, status codes, and methods being used.

First things first, we POST the requests to get data from the server. Again, we send data to get data. At the very beginning of this chapter, we mentioned two things that contrast with that behavior:

> HTTP uses URIs to unambiguously identify resources.

> HTTP uses GET to retrieve representations of resources from the server.

With that in mind, wouldn't it be more natural to get (or at least try to get) the customer named Microsoft that way?

```
GET /customer/Microsoft HTTP/1.1 http://www.example.org
```

That request lets us get exactly the same result as the first SOAP request got, but with three improvements:

> The URI identifying the resource for the customer named Microsoft is unique now.

> GET is the semantically right method to request the customer data.

> We don't need to send a request body that consumes bandwidth unnecessarily and is potentially slower.

■ **Note** ASP.NET Web API makes it quite easy for you to embrace REST and create a RESTful application, but it doesn't force you to do so.

After tweaking the client side, let's head over to the server. When comparing both responses shown before, there's one commonality—the responses start with the following line:

```
HTTP/1.1 200 OK
```

Well, what's wrong with that? In the SOAP world, that's totally fine, as both responses are able to ship their response message: the XML containing the SOAP envelope containing a representation of the requested customer. Really? Remember that the second response contained an error code and no customer. So not everything has been OK, as the status code 200 indicates; instead, the customer requested has not been found. What would be a better and a more obvious solution? Earlier in this chapter we learned that there are far more status codes than the 200 OK. To be honest, we have already seen the solution to our problem above: it's status code 404 Not Found, which should be thrown when the server has not found anything matching the requested parameter in the URI. So if we return

```
HTTP/1.1 404 NOT FOUND
```

we're telling the client exactly the same thing we did with our full-blown XML response message before. The shift from SOAP to a more HTTP-oriented approach did work well for GET and thus for getting data from the server. But will it also work if we want to create data on the server? Of course, it does; that's how our request and response look, as shown in Listings 3-8 and 3-9.

Listing 3-8. Request for Creating a New Customer Using HTTP

```
POST /customers/ HTTP/1.1
Content-Type: application/vnd.247app.customer+xml
Accept: application/vnd.247app.customer+xml
```

```
<customer xmlns:xsd="http://www.w3.org/2001/XMLSchema"
xmlns:xsi="http://www.w3.org/2001/XMLSchema-instance"
xmlns="http://www.example.org">
    <name>Apress</name>
    <address>233 Spring Street</address>
    <city>New York</city>
</customer>
```

Listing 3-9. Response After Creating a Customer Using HTTP

```
HTTP/1.1 201 CREATED
Location: http://www.example.org/customer/42

<customer xmlns:xsd="http://www.w3.org/2001/XMLSchema"
xmlns:xsi="http://www.w3.org/2001/XMLSchema-instance"
xmlns="http://www.example.org">
    <id>42</id>
    <name>Apress</name>
    <address>233 Spring Street</address>
    <city>New York</city>
    <link rel="self" href="http://www.expample.org/customer/42" />
    <link rel="previous" href="http://www.example.org/customer/41" />
</customer>
```

Now let's inspect the request first. Since we're aiming to create a new customer, the request is a POST operation. The POST is addressed to the /customers URI. That's because we're adding another customer to an already existing list of customers.

By specifying the content-type header with its value application/vnd.247app.customer+xml, we tell the server that we're sending the customer data for our application to it. The format application/vnd.247app.customer+xml is not a definition made or registered by an official organization like IANA; it's a definition we made to describe the format of our request or response content being sent around. What application/vnd says is that the Internet media type defined by it is vendor specific (i.e., us); 247app is the name of our application, and customer+xml indicates that it represents a customer resource based on the XML format.

If you prefer the JSON (JavaScript Object Notation) format to XML, your media type definition would look like this: application/vnd.247app.customer+json. That's the only thing you'd have to modify to tell the server or client which format you want to get or send your customer representation. You don't have to attach /xml or /json to your URI—it's tied into HTTP from the very beginning.

■ **Note** Don't worry if you don't know exactly what JSON is. It'll be explained in Chapter 12.

So if you'd like to provide a PNG image of your customers logo, you could still use the URI http://www.example.org/customer/{id}/; by specifying the content-type application/png or, being even more specific, application/vnd.247app.customerlogo+png, you tell the server that it should stream a PNG image.

Now let's get back to the request we're sending our server using POST. There's a second HTTP header, Accept, and its value is application/vnd.247app.customer+xml. By providing the Accept header, we tell the server which media type we're expecting to get within the response for our current request. That's what we're inspecting next.

The head line of the response is

```
HTTP/1.1 201 CREATED
```

which introduces another HTTP status code to us. Instead of just telling us that our request has been processed and everything is OK (200), that response is more specific; it says that the customer has been CREATED (201) based on the input POSTed to the server.

The next response header is one we saw earlier in this chapter.

```
Location: http://www.expample.org/customer/42
```

It tells the client where to find the newly created customer so that the client can store that information for later use.

Listing 3-10 shows the response body, consisting of the requested application/vnd.247app.customer+xml media type.

Listing 3-10. Response body for application/vnd.247app.customer+xml media type

```
<customer xmlns:xsd="http://www.w3.org/2001/XMLSchema"
xmlns:xsi="http://www.w3.org/2001/XMLSchema-instance"
xmlns="http://www.example.org">
    <id>42</id>
    <name>Apress</name>
    <address>233 Spring Street</address>
    <city>New York</city>
    <link rel="self" href=" http://www.expample.org/customer/42" type="
application/vnd.247app.customer+xml" />
    <link rel="previous" href=" http://www.example.org/customer/41" type="
application/vnd.247app.customer+xml"/>
</customer>
```

But what happened to our customer? He got assigned an ID on the server side, and there are two <link /> tags inside, as the application now uses hypermedia as the Engine of Application State (HATEOAS). A client can follow the links to navigate through an application by entering a single fixed URI. This contrasts with the strongly coupled interface that SOAP has. The contrasts grow greater as the links above are generated dynamically at runtime, whereas the strongly coupled interface of SOAP is a contract being defined at the development time of the server and client.

Further operations are discovered by the media types and their provided links.

The application-specific Internet media types using links are called hypermedia. This concept allows server and client to evolve independently without each breaking functionality on the other's side.

Now that we've moved very far from the SOAP messages at the beginning of this section, let's sum up the changes with some theory behind REST and hypermedia.

REST in Theory

The architectural style which uses HTTP as an application protocol and hypermedia, as shown in the last section, is called REST (representational state transfer). The term was introduced by Roy T. Fielding in his doctoral dissertation in the year 2000.

REST is constraint driven, whereas other approaches are requirements driven. That means that REST is aware of the eight fallacies of distributed computing; the constraints of REST exist to protect an application from the effects of those fallacies.

The eight fallacies of distributed computing are

- The network is reliable.

- Latency is zero.

- Bandwidth is infinite.

- The network is secure.

- Topology doesn't change.

- There is one administrator.

- Transport cost is zero.

- The network is homogeneous.

By ignoring them you may add harmful effects to your application.

REST defines six constraints a RESTful architecture needs to apply to deal with the eight fallacies of distributed computing. Table 3-1 shows the six constraints and the benefits a RESTful application gains from them.

Table 3-1. *The Six REST Constraints and Their Benefits*

Constraint	Benefits
Client/server	Evolvability, portability of clients, scalability
Stateless	Reliability, visibility, scalability
Cacheable	Performance, efficiency, scalability
Layered system	Manageability, scalability
Code on demand (optional)	Managing complexity, extensibility
Uniform interface	Evolvability, visibility

Now let's see how these six constraints achieve the benefits.

Client/Server

The client/server constraint improves separation of concerns by separating servers from clients. That means, the client doesn't have to deal with data storage, and so the client is allowed to evolve independent of the server. Moreover it allows the client's software to be ported to other platforms or programming languages. On the other hand, servers don't need to care about user interfaces to let them evolve independently. Due to the lack of complicated UI code (besides other client-side aspects), the server-side code is more simple and scalable.

Stateless

The stateless constraint ensures that no client context is stored on the server. This constraint requires every request from any client to contain all the information necessary to process the request. All session states need to be stored on the client. The constraint embraces reliability, visibility, and scalability.

Cacheable

As is known from web browsers, clients can cache responses they receive from the servers. To prevent clients from reusing stale or inappropriate data in response to further requests, servers, implicitly or explicitly, must declare responses cacheable or not. When done right, caching may completely (certainly at least partially) make a lot of client/server interaction obsolete, with improved performance and scalability of the application being the result.

Layered System

Adding intermediary servers, load balancers, or shared caches to the system improves overall scalability. Security might be improved by enforcing security policies. That way clients won't be able to determine whether they are communicating with the end server.

Code on Demand (Optional)

The server is able to send executable code to the client to modify or add functionality on the client side. The coding, introduced with Java applets in mind, is now mainly achieved by using client-side JavaScripts.

Uniform Interface

The uniform interface was partially dealt with in the "Shifting to a RESTful Architecture" section in this chapter. In theory it consists of four concepts:

- identification of resources
- manipulation of resources through these representations
- self-descriptive messages
- Hypermedia as the engine of application state

Identification of resources means that the resources of your application can be identified by URIs. The resources are separated from their representations, which are sent to the client. This means that the servers sends, for example, an XML or JSON fragment that represents a resource, such as a customer, with its properties.

Manipulation of resources through these representations means that if a client holds a representation of a customer including, for example, the metadata and has the appropriate permission, it is able to modify or delete the resource for that representation on the server.

Self-descriptive messages means that each message includes enough information to describe how to process the message. For example, the Internet media type tells the client or server how to parse the message. Another example is the indication of cacheability in server-side response (as also shown in the Cacheable constraint).

Hypermedia as the engine of application state (HATEOAS) means that after hitting a fixed entry point URI, the client navigates through the application by dynamically generated hypermedia (hypertext with hyperlinks), which the client receives within the representations of the resources from the server.

Richardson Maturity Model

As was seen in the "Shifting to a RESTful Architecture" section, we continuously improved the application from a classical service-oriented architecture using SOAP (also referred to as "plain old XML," or POX) toward a RESTful one.

The path from POX to the use of hypermedia inside the application has been described in a three-step model by Leonard Richardson, the Richardson Maturity Model, shown in Figure 3-8.

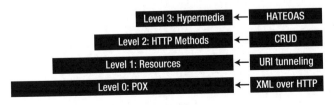

Figure 3-8. *The Richardson Maturity Model*

The Richardson Maturity Model describes the levels leading to a RESTful architecture, beginning at level 0, which is XML over HTTP (SOAP). Using the example from the preceding sections, it's at level 0 because it was the base camp from which we started; it messed up HTTP methods and status codes and made no use of any improvement shown later. Each of the other three levels accounts for a step in the Richardson Maturity Model.

1. Level 1 embraces the use of Resources, by introducing unambiguous URIs for "customer" and "customers".

2. Level 2 makes proper use of HTTP methods and status codes, both on the client and server.

3. By adding hypermedia (links and custom Internet media types) to the application, the peak of REST at level 3 is finally reached.

There are a few more aspects to be seen to when planning or implementing a RESTful architecture. Some of them we'll discover during the implementation of our sample application, as well as the implementations of ASP.NET Web API extensions in the upcoming chapters.

As has already been said, ASP.NET Web API allows you to easily embrace REST and hypermedia, but it doesn't force you to. So if a piece of code shown in this book helps you to move toward a RESTful architecture in your application, it is marked appropriately.

Now you might ask, why should I care about REST at all?

If you're developing a distributed application that deals with a huge number of platforms and programming languages, you should regard REST as a valid option. It is even more of a good choice if you want to support different client deployment cycles and if you're planning to host your application in the cloud. If your application needs to deal with eventual available connectivity (think of all those mobile devices which have already entered or will someday enter the market), a RESTful implementation will lend you a hand in dealing with those issues.

Consider a RESTful application to have a network-based API instead of a library-based API.

Summary

ASP.NET Web API, in our opinion, is a great piece of software. It allows easy creation of HTTP-based applications. In this chapter we laid out the foundation for a proper understanding of what HTTP is and how to use it in an evolvable, scalable, and well-performing application.

As ASP.NET Web API was developed with those concepts as a major goal, it should be quite easy now to understand the hows and whys of ASP.NET Web API in the coming chapters.

CHAPTER 4

HttpClient

During the previous two chapters we've learned some important basics about asynchronous programming in .NET and the HTTP protocol. This is the first chapter that makes use of both foundations by introducing the HttpClient class; this class provides a way to handle HTTP requests and responses in .NET asynchronously on the client side (a server could also be a client). Before using HttpClient itself, let's look at some new classes being used within both the HttpClient class and the ASP.NET Web API framework.

Commonalities: HTTP in ASP.NET Web API and HttpClient

You learned in Chapter 3 that HTTP, a network transfer protocol, handles the communication between servers and clients. As was said above, the HttpClient class represents the client-side implementation in .NET, and ASP.NET Web API represents the server-side implementation. But as shown in Chapter 3, HTTP mostly is not about servers or clients—it's about both sides' exchange of requests and responses. So regardless of whether you're implementing an HTTP client or an ASP.NET Web API service (hence, the server), you need to be able to access the content of HTTP requests. In the client side case, you need to set the URI relative to the server root, the HTTP headers, and so on, in order to get data from the server or modify data on the server. On the server side, you need to access incoming requests to be able to understand what the client wants done—that is, creating, delivering, or modifying existing data or starting subsequent processes, like sending e-mails. As no one wants to deal with requests using native objects, Microsoft has introduced a .NET class that draws away that complexity. This class is named HttpRequestMessage, and its implementation and usage are examined in the next section.

HttpRequestMessage

In an HTTP-based scenario, everything starts with an HTTP request being sent from the client to the server; so let's start there . HTTP requests in HttpClient and ASP.NET Web API are represented by the HttpRequestMessage class, which resides in the System.Net.Http namespace in .NET 4.5. If you're using .NET 4.0, you won't have access to that namespace. To use HttpRequestMessage anyway, you can install the NuGet package Microsoft.Net.Http, the backported version of the System.Net.Http namespace for .NET 4.0. The implementation of HttpRequestMessage (Listing 4-1 shows its public signature) conforms to HTTP messages, as defined in RFC 2616 by the IETF.

Listing 4-1. The Public Signature of the HttpRequestMessage Class in the System.Net.Http Namespace

```
public class HttpRequestMessage : IDisposable {

    public HttpContent Content { get; set; }
    public HttpRequestHeaders Headers { get; }
    public HttpMethod Method { get; set; }
    public IDictionary<string,object> Properties { get; }
```

```
        public Uri RequestUri { get; set; }
        public Version Version { get; set; }

        public HttpRequestMessage();
        public HttpRequestMessage(HttpMethod method, String requestUri);
        public HttpRequestMessage(HttpMethod method, Uri requestUri);

        protected virtual void Dispose(Boolean disposing);
        public override string ToString();
        public void Dispose();
}
```

Let's break this signature down to its components. HttpRequestMessage has six properties:

- The first one is Content, which is of type HttpContent. This property represents the body content of the incoming request. The HttpContent type is an abstract class; we'll discuss it in detail later in this chapter.

- The HttpRequestHeaders collection type of the Headers property is a typed collection of the request header; we'll come back to it a bit later.

- The Method property is of type HttpMethod. It contains the HTTP method, like GET or POST, that the request should use (on the client side) or has been using (on the server side).

- IDictionary<string,object> Properties allows storage of contextual state information that can be used during the request lifetime in your Web API application or HttpClient instance. There is more on this property in Chapter 14.

- The RequestUri property allows setting or getting the URI of the request.

- The Version property of type Version refers to the HTTP version; by default it is 1.1. The only reasonable nondefault value is 1.0 at this time.

HttpRequestMessage has three constructors:

- The first is parameterless. When creating an instance using this constructor, the Method property of the request is set to HttpMethod.Get. The Uri property remains unset; it has to be set after the HttpRequestMessage instance is created.

- The second constructor accepts two parameters, method and requestUri, which are the HTTP method and the URI of the request as a string.

- The third constructor is quite similar to the second one, but the requestUri parameter now is of type Uri instead of String; this allows access to the parts of the URI in a typed way.

HttpRequestMessage also exposes three methods. Both Dispose methods concern disposing the HttpRequestMessage instance. The ToString method is overridden and produces some useful information that can be used for debugging or tracing purposes. Listing 4-2 shows the instantiation of an HttpRequestMessage writing the ToString output to the console window, as can be seen in Figure 4-1.

Listing 4-2. Instantiation of an HttpRequestMessage

```
private static void Main(string[] args) {
    var request =
        new HttpRequestMessage(HttpMethod.Get,
                                new Uri("http://apress.com"));
```

```
request.Headers.Accept.Add(new MediaTypeWithQualityHeaderValue("text/html"));
Console.WriteLine(request.ToString());
Console.ReadLine();
}
```

```
┌─────────────────────────────────────────────────────────────┐ _ □ ✕
│ C\.           HttpRequestMessageSample.exe                    │
├───────────────────────────────────────────────────────────────┤
│ Method: GET, RequestUri: 'http://apress.com/', Version: 1.1, Content: <null>, ▲
│ Headers:                                                          │
│ {                                                                 │
│   Accept: text/html                                               │
│ }                                                                 ▼
└───────────────────────────────────────────────────────────────┘
```

Figure 4-1. *Output of the ToString method of the HttpRequestMessage class*

After creating the request instance pointing to http://apress.com to get the content of the Apress web site, the Accept header is set in a strongly typed manner to text/html. After that, the string representation of the request is written to the console, as shown in Figure 4-1.

As HttpRequestMessage has no complex dependencies, it can be unit-tested easily (see Chapter 14 for more).

In Listing 4-2, besides setting the request's Method property to HTTP GET and pointing it to the URI http://apress.com, the HTTP Accept request header is set to text/html in a typed manner. As was already said, the Headers property of the HttpRequestMessage class is of type HttpRequestHeaders. This class encapsulates the HTTP request headers according to RFC 2616. Listing 4-3 shows the public signature of the HttpRequestHeaders class.

Listing 4-3. Signature of the HttpRequestHeaders Class

```
public sealed class HttpRequestHeaders : HttpHeaders {
    public HttpHeaderValueCollection<MediaTypeWithQualityHeaderValue> Accept { get; }
    public HttpHeaderValueCollection<StringWithQualityHeaderValue> AcceptCharset { get; }
    public HttpHeaderValueCollection<StringWithQualityHeaderValue> AcceptEncoding { get; }
    public HttpHeaderValueCollection<StringWithQualityHeaderValue> AcceptLanguage { get; }
    public AuthenticationHeaderValue Authorization { get; set; }
    public CacheControlHeaderValue CacheControl { get; set; }
    public HttpHeaderValueCollection<string> Connection { get; }
    public bool? ConnectionClose { get; set; }
    public DateTimeOffset? Date { get; set; }
    public HttpHeaderValueCollection<NameValueWithParametersHeaderValue> Expect { get; }
    public bool? ExpectContinue { get; set; }
    public string From { get; set; }
    public string Host { get; set; }
    public HttpHeaderValueCollection<EntityTagHeaderValue> IfMatch { get; }
    public DateTimeOffset? IfModifiedSince { get; set; }
    public HttpHeaderValueCollection<EntityTagHeaderValue> IfNoneMatch { get; }
    public RangeConditionHeaderValue IfRange { get; set; }
    public DateTimeOffset? IfUnmodifiedSince { get; set; }
    public int? MaxForwards { get; set; }
    public HttpHeaderValueCollection<NameValueHeaderValue> Pragma { get; }
    public AuthenticationHeaderValue ProxyAuthorization { get; set; }
    public RangeHeaderValue Range { get; set; }
    public Uri Referrer { get; set; }
    public HttpHeaderValueCollection<TransferCodingWithQualityHeaderValue> TE { get; }
```

```
    public HttpHeaderValueCollection<string> Trailer { get; }
    public HttpHeaderValueCollection<TransferCodingHeaderValue> TransferEncoding { get; }
    public bool? TransferEncodingChunked { get; set; }
    public HttpHeaderValueCollection<ProductHeaderValue> Upgrade { get; }
    public HttpHeaderValueCollection<ProductInfoHeaderValue> UserAgent { get; }
    public HttpHeaderValueCollection<ViaHeaderValue> Via { get; }
    public HttpHeaderValueCollection<WarningHeaderValue> Warning { get; }
}
```

The HttpRequestHeaders class derives from the HttpHeaders class, which mainly implements logic to handle HTTP headers easily from within a derived class such as HttpRequestHeaders. The properties of HttpRequestMessage shown in Listing 4-3 represent the HTTP request headers defined in RFC 2616. As can be seen, certain headers, like Accept, allow multiple values using collections, whereas others, like Host, allow string and other simple value types.

Besides the HTTP header properties in Listing 4-3, HttpRequestHeaders exposes a few methods derived from the underlying HttpHeaders class. Methods like Add, Remove, and Clear allow you to modify the list of HTTP headers in the HttpRequestHeaders instance. Listing 4-4, which shows a modified version of Listing 4-2, sets a custom request header not defined in RFC 2616.

Listing 4-4. Adding a Custom Header to a Request

```
private static void Main(string[] args) {
    var request =
        new HttpRequestMessage(HttpMethod.Get,
                                new Uri("http://apress.com"));
    request.Headers.Accept.Add(new MediaTypeWithQualityHeaderValue("text/html"));
    request.Headers.Add("X-Name", "Microsoft");
    Console.WriteLine(request.ToString());
    Console.ReadLine();
}
```

Figure 4-2 confirms that the custom header has been added to the headers collection.

Figure 4-2. Custom HTTP header in a HttpRequestMessage instance

Having now learned the most important details about the HTTP request abstraction for HttpClient and ASP.NET Web API, let's go to its counterpart and dig into the HttpResponseMessage that represents the HTTP request.

HttpResponseMessage

After receiving a request on the server side from the client, you can process the request and return its results to the client. The means of transportation for these results is, according to RFC 2616, an HTTP response. Along with HTTP requests, HTTP responses are abstracted for easier use with the .NET CLR. The implementation can be found in the HttpResponseMessage class, a neighbor of the HttpRequestMessage in the System.Net.Http namespace.

As can be seen in Listing 4-5, its public signature is comparable with the one of HttpRequestMessage.

Listing 4-5. HttpResponseMessage Signature

```
public class HttpResponseMessage : IDisposable {

    public HttpContent Content { get; set; }
    public HttpResponseHeaders Headers { get; }
    public bool IsSuccessStatusCode { get; }
    public string ReasonPhrase { get; set; }
    public HttpRequestMessage RequestMessage { get; set; }
    public HttpStatusCode StatusCode { get; set; }
    public Version Version { get; set; }

    public HttpResponseMessage();
    public HttpResponseMessage(HttpStatusCode statusCode);

    protected virtual void Dispose(Boolean disposing);
    public void Dispose();
    public override string ToString();
    public HttpResponseMessage EnsureSuccessStatusCode();
}
```

HttpResponseMessage has seven public properties:

- As responses, like requests, have a content body, HttpResponseMessage owns an HttpContent property similar to HttpRequestMessage; HttpContent will be dissected later in this chapter.

- The Headers property of HttpResponseMessage provides a collection of HTTP response headers of the type HttpResponseHeaders; we'll look at them shortly.

- The Boolean IsSuccessStatusCode indicates whether the request has been successful. We'll come back to that detail in the section on HttpClient.

- The ReasonPhrase property corresponds to the reason phrase element of the HTTP specification and represents the human-readable part of the status line. A reason phrase example is "Not Found" for the HTTP status code 404.

- The RequestMessage property contains the HttpRequestMessage that caused the initial response.

- The StatusCode property contains the HTTP status code in a typed manner.

- The Version property is the same as for HttpRequestMessage; it permits specifying the HTTP version, which by default is 1.1.

HttpResponseMessage has two constructors. The first, parameterless constructor creates an instance whose StatusCode is set to 200 OK. The second constructor expects an HttpStatusCode instance as a parameter.

HttpResponseMessage also exposes four methods, where both Dispose methods concern disposal of the HttpResponseMessage instance. As with HttpRequestMessage, the ToString method is overloaded and produces useful debugging information. The EnsureSuccessStatusCode method, related to the IsSuccessStatusCode, will be explained in detail in the "HttpClient" section.

This section has shown how HTTP responses are represented in ASP.NET Web API and HttpClient. The HttpResponseMessage class is an HTTP response message implementation according to RFC 2616 and allows typed access to the properties of an HTTP response. As was seen in the sections on HttpRequestMessage and HttpResponseMessage, they have a common property, one that represents the request or response body: HttpContent. Let's explore that next.

HttpContent

In Chapter 3, you learned that content sent from the server to the client, such as an HTML page or a representation of a customer object, is contained in the body part of the HTTP response. Furthermore, when sending data from the client to the server (for example, when sending a file using HTTP POST or updating a customer using HTTP PUT), the data are also contained in the body part of the HTTP request. The sections on HttpRequestMessage and HttpResponseMessage have shown that the body part of the HTTP requests and responses are represented by a class named HttpContent. First, let's look at the HttpContent class and then consider a custom implementation.

The HttpContent Class

HttpContent is an abstract base class in the System.Net.Http namespace. Its signature is shown in Listing 4-6.

Listing 4-6. Abstract Base Class HttpContent

```
public abstract class HttpContent : IDisposable {

    protected HttpContent();

    public HttpContentHeaders Headers { get; }

    public Task CopyToAsync(Stream stream, TransportContext context);
    public Task CopyToAsync(Stream stream);
    protected virtual Task CreateContentReadStreamAsync();
    public Task LoadIntoBufferAsync();
    public Task LoadIntoBufferAsync(long maxBufferSize);
    protected abstract Task SerializeToStreamAsync(Stream stream, TransportContext context);
    protected internal abstract bool TryComputeLength(out long length);
    public Task<byte[]> ReadAsByteArrayAsync();
    public Task<Stream> ReadAsStreamAsync();
    public Task<string> ReadAsStringAsync();

    public void Dispose();
    protected virtual void Dispose(bool disposing);
}
```

Besides a parameterless default constructor, HttpContent exposes a public property, Headers, which is of type HttpContentHeaders. Regarding the request and response headers, this also conforms with RFC 2616. HttpContentHeaders implements an abstraction of the so-called entity header fields, which define metainformation about the entity body (that is, the request or response body) or, if no body is present, about the resource identified by the request.

Listing 4-7 shows the public interface of the HttpContentHeaders class.

Listing 4-7. HttpContentHeaders Class

```
public sealed class HttpContentHeaders : HttpHeaders {

    public ICollection<string> Allow { get; }
    public ContentDispositionHeaderValue ContentDisposition { get; set; }
    public ICollection<string> ContentEncoding { get; }
    public ICollection<string> ContentLanguage { get; }
    public long? ContentLength { get; set; }
    public Uri ContentLocation { get; set; }
    public byte[] ContentMD5 { get; set; }
    public ContentRangeHeaderValue ContentRange { get; set; }
    public MediaTypeHeaderValue ContentType { get; set; }
    public DateTimeOffset? Expires { get; set; }
    public DateTimeOffset? LastModified { get; set; }
}
```

The HttpContentHeaders class includes a number of properties:

- The Allow property contains a collection listing the methods supported by the resource identified by the initial request URI.

- The ContentEncoding property allows provision of additional information about the media type of the content. Common content encodings used are gzip and Deflate (you'll see a sample later).

- ContentLanguage allows you to set the intended audience's natural language in the representation of the resource returned in the response body.

- The ContentLength property describes the length of the content in bytes.

- The next property, ContentLocation, may contain an alternative URI to the one by which the content has been requested. This can be useful if your server provides specific URIs for different media types for the same resource. For an example of a request, see Listing 4-8.

Listing 4-8. Requesting a Customer Representation

```
GET http://localhost/api/customer/1
Accept: application/json
```

A possible response to the request from Listing 4-8, with the Content-Location header set, is shown in Listing 4-9.

Listing 4-9. Response Containing a Content-Location Header

```
200 OK
Content-Type: application/json
Content-Location: http://localhost/api/customer/1.json

{ "id" : 1, "name" : "Microsoft" }
```

- Be aware that Content-Location should not be used for linking when a restful API using hypermedia is being created.

- The ContentMD5 property, which provides an MD5 digest for the content, can be used for integrity checks.

- Another property exposed by the HttpContentHeaders class is ContentRange, which is set if the content of the body represents only a part of an entity. ContentRange defines the position where the content of the body should be placed in the complete entity.

- The ContentType property defines the content-type header already seen in Chapter 3; it specifies the type of the content in the body. An example of a content type is text/html.

- The Expires property returns either the date or time (or both) after which the response is considered stale.

- The last property of the HttpContentHeader class is LastModified, which indicates the date and time at which the sender claims the entity was last modified.

With this little excursion into HTTP entity headers and their representation in .NET now done, let's go back to the HttpContent class in Listing 4-6. All methods exposed by the HttpContent base class—along with the inherited methods for disposing, as well as the TryComputeLength method—are asynchronous.

The CopyToAsync methods of the HttpContent class serialize the HttpContent into a stream and then copy it to a stream passed in as a parameter. Besides that stream parameter, the second CopyToAsync method expects a parameter of type TransportContext, which provides support for authentication scenarios. The TransportContext instance can be retrieved from the GetRequestStream method of the HttpWebRequest class, for example.

The virtual CreateContentReadStreamAsync method can be overridden by a concrete implementation of HttpContent; it serializes the HTTP content into a memory stream asynchronously. Both LoadIntoBufferAsync methods serialize the HTTP content to a memory buffer as an asynchronous operation; the second one expects a long value as maximum buffer size.

The abstract SerializeToStreamAsync method has to be overridden in a derived class, and it has to serialize the HTTP content into a stream being passed in as a parameter. The TransportContext parameter of the SerializeToStreamAsync method is the same as the one for the CopyToAsync method already described.

The last three methods allow you to return the data of the HttpContent as a byte array, stream, or string. Listing 4-10 shows the use of StringContent deriving from HttpContent.

Listing 4-10. Use of StringContent

```
class Program
{
    static void Main(string[] args)
    {
        var stringContent = new StringContent("Hello World");
        stringContent.ReadAsStringAsync().ContinueWith(
            (t) => Console.WriteLine(t.Result)
            );
        Console.ReadLine();
    }
}
```

The result of Listing 4-10 is shown in Figure 4-3.

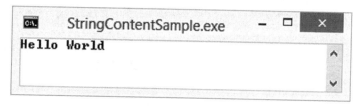

Figure 4-3. *The output of a StringContent instance*

As was said, HttpContent is an abstract base class. System.Net.Http provides five concrete implementations of HttpContent out of the box; see Figure 4-4.

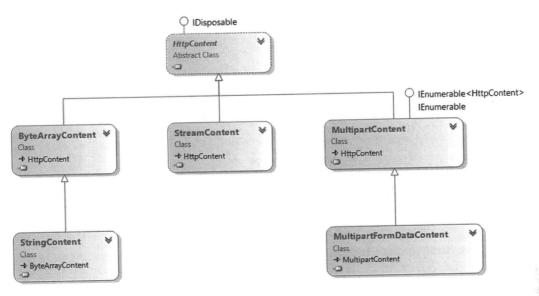

Figure 4-4. *Classes deriving from HttpContent base class*

We have already used one implementation of HttpContent in Listing 4-10: StringContent. The StringContent class derives, not from HttpContent, but from ByteArrayContent instead. ByteArrayContent provides HTTP content based on a byte array. Another class deriving directly from HttpContent is StreamContent, which provides HTTP content based on a stream. The last two implementations of HttpContent are MultipartContent, which is derived by MultitpartFormatDataContent. MultipartContent (shown in Figure 4-4) not only derives from HttpContent but also implements the IEnumerable<HttpContent> interface, as well as the IEnumerable interface. That way, it is possible to send or receive multipart content. Multipart messages have multiple body parts split by a boundary. An example of a multipart message is multipart/form-data, which allows you to send the input of an HTML form and several files within a single request.

As with almost all frameworks, most of the time the default implementations work well. But sometimes there are scenarios where you need to add functionality that is not contained in the box. That's what we will do next: create a custom HttpContent implementation.

Custom HttpContent Implementation: CompressedContent

Though we live in a world of high-speed Internet connections, the connection always feels too slow. One way to reduce the amount of data transferred, thus increasing your Web API application's speed and responsiveness, is to compress your response body before sending it to the client. In HTTP two compression standards have been established: gzip and Deflate.

A client able to read gzip- or Deflate-compressed content can communicate that to the server by setting the Accept-Encoding header to gzip or deflate or both separated by a comma. If a server is serving gzip- or Deflate-compressed content, it communicates that to the client, setting the Content-Encoding header accordingly. Note that Microsoft's Internet Information Services (IIS) supports HTTP compression; you might want to implement your own compression, as it isn't available out of the box when using the self-hosting option of ASP.NET Web API.

A viable way to support HTTP compression is to implement an HttpContent class that can create compressed content from an existing HttpContext instance. Listing 4-11 shows the implementation of the CompressedContent class.

Listing 4-11. An Example Console App Using the CompressedContent Class

```
class Program
{
    static void Main(string[] args)
    {
        var httpContent = new StringContent(@"
Lorem ipsum dolor sit amet, consetetur sadipscing elitr, sed diam nonumy eirmod tempor invidunt ut
labore et dolore magna aliquyam erat, sed diam voluptua. At vero eos et accusam et justo duo dolores
et ea rebum. Stet clita kasd gubergren, no sea takimata sanctus est Lorem ipsum dolor sit amet.
Lorem ipsum dolor sit amet, consetetur sadipscing elitr, sed diam nonumy eirmod tempor invidunt ut
labore et dolore magna aliquyam erat, sed diam voluptua. At vero eos et accusam et justo duo dolores
et ea rebum. Stet clita kasd gubergren, no sea takimata sanctus est Lorem ipsum dolor sit amet.
");
        httpContent.ReadAsStringAsync().ContinueWith(
            t =>
                {
                    Console.WriteLine(t.Result);
                    Console.WriteLine("Initial size: {0} bytes",
                        httpContent.Headers.ContentLength);
                }
        );

        var compressedContent = new CompressedContent(httpContent, "gzip");
        compressedContent.ReadAsStringAsync().ContinueWith(
            t =>
                {
                    var result = t.Result
                    Console.WriteLine("Compressed size: {0} bytes",
                    compressedContent.Headers.ContentLength);
                }
        );

        Console.ReadLine();
    }
}
```

The CompressedContent class has a constructor that expects an HttpContent parameter and a string parameter called contentEncoding. After two null value checks, the content parameter is copied to a private field, _initialContent. The contentEncoding parameter is copied to a private field, _contentEncoding. If a Content-Encoding header setting other than gzip or Deflate has been passed as a contentEncoding parameter, an exception with a meaningful description is thrown. If everything went fine until now, all HTTP headers except the Content-Length header from the initial content are copied to the headers collection of the CompressedContent instance. When the SerializeToStreamAsync method is called, a GZipStream or DeflateStream, depending on the _contentEncoding field value, is created. The initial content is copied to the compressedStream instance and gets compressed that way. The continuation of the CopyToAsync task disposes the compressed stream (if any) in the end. Listing 4-12 shows an example to prove the function of the CompressedContent class.

Listing 4-12. Sample Usage of the CompressedContent Class

```
class Program {
    static void Main(string[] args) {
        var httpContent = new StringContent(@"
Lorem ipsum dolor sit amet, consetetur sadipscing elitr, sed diam nonumy eirmod tempor invidunt ut
labore et dolore magna aliquyam erat, sed diam voluptua. At vero eos et accusam et justo duo dolores
et ea rebum. Stet clita kasd gubergren, no sea takimata sanctus est Lorem ipsum dolor sit amet.
Lorem ipsum dolor sit amet, consetetur sadipscing elitr, sed diam nonumy eirmod tempor invidunt ut
labore et dolore magna aliquyam erat, sed diam voluptua. At vero eos et accusam et justo duo dolores
et ea rebum. Stet clita kasd gubergren, no sea takimata sanctus est Lorem ipsum dolor sit amet.
");
        Console.WriteLine(httpContent.ReadAsStringAsync().Result);
        Console.WriteLine("Initial size: {0} bytes", httpContent.Headers.ContentLength);

        var compressedContent = new CompressedContent(httpContent, "gzip");
        var result = compressedContent.ReadAsStringAsync().Result;

        Console.WriteLine("Compressed size: {0} bytes",
            compressedContent.Headers.ContentLength);
        Console.ReadLine();
    }
}
```

In Listing 4-12, an instance of StringContent is first created. That content, as well as its size in bytes, is written to the console output. After that, a CompressedContent instance is created with the StringContent and gzip encoding as parameters. The size of the compressed content then is also written to the console output.

When running that program at the console, what is output is similar to Figure 4-5.

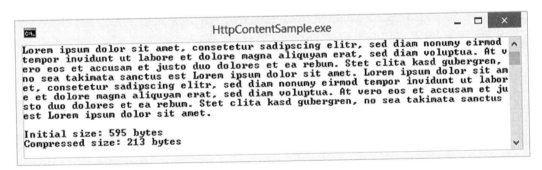

Figure 4-5. Regular content size versus compressed content size

In order to make the CompressedContent work in your ASP.NET Web API application, you need to register the HttpCompressionHandler shown in Listing 4-13. Don't worry if you don't understand it now; message handlers will be explained in depth in Chapter 10.

Listing 4-13. HttpCompressionHandler for Use with ASP.NET Web API and CompressedContent

```
public class CompressHandler : DelegatingHandler {
    protected override Task<HttpResponseMessage> SendAsync(HttpRequestMessage request,
        CancellationToken cancellationToken) {
        return base.SendAsync(request, cancellationToken)
```

```
            .ContinueWith<HttpResponseMessage>((responseToCompleteTask) => {
                var response = responseToCompleteTask.Result;

                if (response.RequestMessage != null &&
                    response.RequestMessage.Headers.AcceptEncoding.Any()) {

                    var contentEncoding =
                        response.RequestMessage.Headers.AcceptEncoding
                            .First().Value;

                    if (null != response.Content) {
                        response.Content =
                            new CompressedContent(response.Content,
                                contentEncoding);
                    }
                }
                return response;
            },
            TaskContinuationOptions.OnlyOnRanToCompletion);
    }
}
```

The `HttpCompressionHandler` implementation checks the requests for Accept-Encoding headers for values. If it contains at least one value, an instance of `CompressedContent` is created with the initial content of the response. The updated response with the compressed content is then returned.

With some necessary foundations—including `HttpRequestMessage`, `HttpResponseMessage`, their HTTP headers, and the `HttpContent` class—explained, we can finally start using `HttpClient` itself.

HttpClient

You've already seen that `HttpClient` is a class that allows you to handle HTTP requests and responses in .NET. `HttpClient` has been introduced in a rewritten version with .NET 4.5 and resides in the `System.Net.Http` namespace. It is also available in the NuGet package `Microsoft.Net.Http` for .NET 4.0. A previous version (2009) of `HttpClient` was introduced by Microsoft when it released the REST Starter Kit, but it never became part of the core .NET Framework before .NET 4.5. Before `HttpClient`, handling HTTP requests and responses in .NET was sort of an awkward task. Since .NET Framework 1.1, the choice was to use the `HttpWebRequest` and `HttpWebResponse` classes or the `WebClient` class, but none of these provided the streamlined concept that `HttpClient` does. Furthermore, there was no easy way to handle HTTP content or headers, as previous sections have shown. But enough of the advance praise for `HttpClient`! Let's see how to work with HTTP on the client side in .NET.

Introducing HttpClient

To start, take a look at the public signature of `HttpClient` in Listing 4-14.

Listing 4-14. HttpClient Public Signature

```
public class HttpClient : HttpMessageInvoker {
    public HttpRequestHeaders DefaultRequestHeaders { get; }
    public Uri BaseAddress { get; set; }
    public TimeSpan Timeout { get; set; }
    public long MaxResponseContentBufferSize { get; set; }
```

```
public HttpClient();
public HttpClient(HttpMessageHandler handler);
public HttpClient(HttpMessageHandler handler, bool disposeHandler);

public Task<HttpResponseMessage> SendAsync(HttpRequestMessage request);
public override Task<HttpResponseMessage> SendAsync(HttpRequestMessage request,
    CancellationToken cancellationToken);
public Task<HttpResponseMessage> SendAsync(HttpRequestMessage request,
    HttpCompletionOption completionOption);
public Task<HttpResponseMessage> SendAsync(HttpRequestMessage request,
    HttpCompletionOption completionOption, CancellationToken cancellationToken);

public Task<HttpResponseMessage> GetAsync(string requestUri);
public Task<HttpResponseMessage> GetAsync(Uri requestUri);
public Task<HttpResponseMessage> GetAsync(string requestUri,
    HttpCompletionOption completionOption);
public Task<HttpResponseMessage> GetAsync(Uri requestUri,
    HttpCompletionOption completionOption)
public Task<HttpResponseMessage> GetAsync(string requestUri,
    CancellationToken cancellationToken);
public Task<HttpResponseMessage> GetAsync(Uri requestUri,
    CancellationToken cancellationToken);
public Task<HttpResponseMessage> GetAsync(string requestUri,
    HttpCompletionOption completionOption, CancellationToken cancellationToken);
public Task<HttpResponseMessage> GetAsync(Uri requestUri,
    HttpCompletionOption completionOption,
    CancellationToken cancellationToken)

public Task<string> GetStringAsync(string requestUri);
public Task<string> GetStringAsync(Uri requestUri);

public Task<byte[]> GetByteArrayAsync(string requestUri);
public Task<byte[]> GetByteArrayAsync(Uri requestUri);

public Task<Stream> GetStreamAsync(string requestUri);
public Task<Stream> GetStreamAsync(Uri requestUri);

public Task<HttpResponseMessage> PostAsync(string requestUri,
    HttpContent content);
public Task<HttpResponseMessage> PostAsync(Uri requestUri,
    HttpContent content);
public Task<HttpResponseMessage> PostAsync(string requestUri,
    HttpContent content, CancellationToken cancellationToken);
public Task<HttpResponseMessage> PostAsync(Uri requestUri,
    HttpContent content, CancellationToken cancellationToken);

public Task<HttpResponseMessage> PutAsync(string requestUri,
    HttpContent content);
public Task<HttpResponseMessage> PutAsync(Uri requestUri,
    HttpContent content);
```

```
    public Task<HttpResponseMessage> PutAsync(string requestUri,
        HttpContent content, CancellationToken cancellationToken);
    public Task<HttpResponseMessage> PutAsync(Uri requestUri,
        HttpContent content, CancellationToken cancellationToken);

    public Task<HttpResponseMessage> DeleteAsync(string requestUri);
    public Task<HttpResponseMessage> DeleteAsync(Uri requestUri);
    public Task<HttpResponseMessage> DeleteAsync(string requestUri,
        CancellationToken cancellationToken);
    public Task<HttpResponseMessage> DeleteAsync(Uri requestUri,
        CancellationToken cancellationToken)

    public void CancelPendingRequests();

    protected override void Dispose(bool disposing);
}
```

At first sight, the HttpClient signature seems huge. Don't worry; it will feel small and handy once we've dissected it.

HttpClient contains four properties:

- DefaultRequestHeaders of type HttpRequestHeaders. We inspected them earlier in this chapter.

- BaseAddress. This property is self-explanatory: it contains a common URI to which all request URIs are relative. An example of a BaseAddress is http://localhost/api.

- Timeout. This property defines a TimeSpan in milliseconds, after which the request times out.

- HttpClient. This last property is the MaxResponseContentBufferSize, which defines the maximum number of bytes to buffer when reading the response content. It defaults to 64 kilobytes.

The simplest way to create an instance of HttpClient is to call its parameterless default constructor. To provide some context for the next two constructors of HttpClient, we'll look at the implementation of the parameterless constructor in Listing 4-15.

Listing 4-15. Parameterless Constructor Implementation of HttpClient

```
public HttpClient() : this((HttpMessageHandler) new HttpClientHandler()) {
}
```

The only thing that happens in this constructor is that it creates an instance of HttpClient, with a new instance of HttpClientHandler as a parameter. HttpClientHandler itself derives from HttpMessageHandler. So calling the parameterless constructor of HttpClient is similar to calling its second constructor in the way shown in Listing 4-16.

Listing 4-16. Creating an Instance of HttpClient Using the Second Constructor

```
var httpClient = new HttpClient(new HttpClientHandler());
```

Digging deeper into the implementation details of HttpClient reveals that HttpClient itself contains no code that can handle requests or responses. Instead, it delegates the complete workload to the HttpMessageHandler implementation, which is by default HttpClientHandler (message handlers will be covered in depth in Chapter 10). The HttpMessageHandler base class contains only one method, called SendAsync. Its implementation in the HttpClientHandler class under the hood uses HttpWebRequest and HttpWebResponse classes. Thanks to the shown abstractions of HTTP requests and HTTP responses, there is no longer a need to work with them directly. You don't have to touch HttpClient itself to change its implementation; instead, just implement a new HttpMessageHandler and pass it to the constructor of HttpClient as a parameter.

The third constructor of HttpClient expects another parameter, called disposeHandler of type bool. This parameter's background is as follows: if you create an HttpMessageHandler instance and pass it into the HttpClient as a parameter when HttpClient is disposed, the passed-in HttpMessageHandler instance will be disposed, too. If the disposeHandler parameter of HttpClient is set to false, the passed-in HttpMessageHandler instance won't be disposed.

With respect to the constructors in Listing 4-14, there are four variations of the SendAsync method. SendAsync overrides the SendAsync method of the HttpMessageInvoker class from which HttpClient derives. The SendAsync method of the HttpMessageInvoker is the one responsible for calling the SendAsync method on the HttpMessageHandler used in the HttpClient implementation. Basically, all variations of the SendAsync method of HttpClient expect a HttpRequestMessage as the first parameter. The second parameter, HttpCompletionOption, of some overloads of SendAsync allows the decision whether to receive the complete response, including all headers and the complete content, before doing further processing or to just read the headers without reading the complete content. This can be useful when the server content received is huge.

The methods after the SendAsync methods in Listing 4-14—including GetAsync, PostAsync, PutAsync, and DeleteAsync (as well as their overloads)—are helper methods; they wrap the SendAsync method to abstract the details of creating instances of HttpRequestMessage, HttpResponseMessage, and HttpContent when sending requests. Basically, all these helper methods expect a URI to which the request should be addressed. With the PostAsync and PutAsync methods, it is also mandatory to pass in an instance of HttpContent according to RFC 2616.

The last method of HttpClient worth mentioning is CancelPendingRequests, which allows cancellation of all pending requests independent of their current processing state.

Now that we have handled the theory of HttpClient, it's time to fire some requests and see what happens.

Getting Data Using HttpClient

When using an HTTP client, you'll mostly want to get data as a string from a server. As you may have noticed, three methods—GetStringAsync, GetByteArrayAsync, and GetStreamAsync (and their overloads)—were kept back when the methods of HttpClient were explained. These methods are helper methods around the GetAsync method of HttpClient. With these methods, getting data from a server using the HttpClient class is a no-brainer, as Listing 4-17 verifies.

Listing 4-17. Getting Data from a URI as a String

```
var uri = "https://raw.github.com/AlexZeitler/HttpClient/master/README.md";
var httpClient = new HttpClient();
httpClient.GetStringAsync(uri).ContinueWith(
    t => Console.WriteLine(t.Result));
Console.ReadLine();
```

After creating an instance of HttpClient, the uri instance defined before is passed as a parameter to the GetStringAsync method of the HttpClient instance. The result of this Task (which is a string) can be written directly to the console output. The result of Listing 4-14 is seen in Figure 4-6.

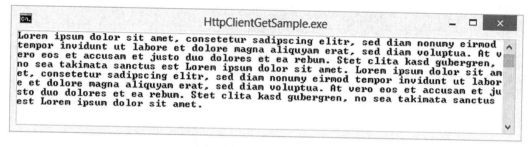

Figure 4-6. *Output of the GetStringAsync method of HttpClient*

The GetByteArrayAsync and GetStreamAsync methods are akin in use. To get data from a Web API instead of a web site, you might want to pass it into a local variable, like an instance of a Customer class. Thanks to some extension methods for the HttpClient class, this can be done almost effortlessly. First let's take a look at the customer representation we'll receive from our Web API (see Listing 4-18).

Listing 4-18. Customer Representation in JSON

```
{
    "id" : 1,
    "name" : "Apress"
}
```

As Listing 4-19 shows, the Customer class implementation on the client side is pretty straightforward.

Listing 4-19. Customer Class Implementation

```
public class Customer {
    public int Id { get; set; }
    public string Name { get; set; }
}
```

To deserialize a Customer instance from the JSON shown in Listing 4-18, you would have to access the response content, determine the type you want to deserialize it to, and find an appropriate MediaTypeFormatter. (This topic, a huge one, is handled in Chapter 12.) After that, you have to invoke the ReadFromStreamAsync method of the MediaTypeFormatter—and keep your fingers crossed. Thanks to the HttpContentExtensions class in the System.Net.Http namespace, you don't have to do any of this work. Instead, simply use the code shown in Listing 4-20.

Listing 4-20. Deserializing HttpContent into CLR Types

```
var client = new HttpClient();
client.GetAsync("http://localhost:3739/api/customer/1").ContinueWith(
    tr => tr.Result.Content.ReadAsAsync<Customer>()
        .ContinueWith(
            tc => Console.WriteLine("Id: {0}, Name: {1}", tc.Result.Id, tc.Result.Name)
        )
    );
Console.ReadLine();
```

The result of Listing 4-20 is shown in Figure 4-7.

Figure 4-7. The output of the ReadAsAsync<T> extension method

In order to use the `HttpContentExtensions`, you'll need to reference `System.Net.Http.Formatting` in .NET 4.5, or else you'll need to install the NuGet package `Microsoft.AspNet.WebApi.Client` when using .NET 4.0.

Now that requests have been sent using `HttpClient` to GET data from a Web API and a web site, we're ready to do something more difficult. Let's try to POST some data to a Web API now.

Sending Data Using HttpClient

As you saw during the overview of the members that `HttpClient` exposes, there are several `PostAsync` methods that allow you to send data to a Web API. Besides these methods, the Content-Type header has to be set to tell the server side which media type is being used to send the new entity over the wire. Normally you'd have to create an instance of `HttpRequestMessage`, assign its content with a new instance of the appropriate `HttpContent` implementation, and set the contents request headers accordingly. The signature of the `PostAsync` methods shows that there is no overload of `PostAsync`, which allows a parameter of type `HttpRequestMessage`. This is not a mistake; the `PostAsync` method provides a much nicer way to get the work done. Listing 4-21 shows the solution's implementation.

Listing 4-21. Posting Data Using PostAsync

```
var customer = new Customer()
{
    Name = "Microsoft"
};

var client = new HttpClient();
client.PostAsync(
    "http://localhost:3739/api/customer",
    customer,
    new JsonMediaTypeFormatter())
        .ContinueWith(
        t =>
            {
            if (t.Result.StatusCode == HttpStatusCode.Created)
            {
                t.Result.Content.ReadAsAsync<Customer>().ContinueWith(
                    tc => Console.WriteLine("Id: {0}, Name: {1}",
                        tc.Result.Id, tc.Result.Name)
                );
            }
            });
```

First, let's create a new instance of the Customer class without assigning an ID, as this is the responsibility of the server side. After instantiating a new HttpClient, call its PostAsync method with the URI of the Web API that creates the new instance, the Customer instance, on the server side. The last parameter is an instance of JsonMediaTypeFormatter; it handles serialization of the Customer instance into JSON. After getting the response as a result, you can evaluate the HTTP status code, which should be "201 Created". If this is the case, deserialize the entity returned as JSON into the Customer instance again. The console output is similar to the one in Figure 4-7. If you don't want to mess around with media-type formatters, you can use another extension method, one that simplifies use of PostAsync even more (see Listing 4-22).

Listing 4-22. Using PostAsJsonAsync Instead of PostAsync

```
var response = client.PostAsJsonAsync("http://localhost:3739/api/customer", customer).Result;
```

As sending data using the HTTP POST method has not been much more difficult than receiving data, let's now try using the SendAsync method of HttpClient directly to achieve a more difficult goal.

Using ASP.NET Forms Authentication from HttpClient

As a last sample for HttpClient, consider the following: authenticate a request against a Web API that has been implemented using ASP.NET MVC. This API is protected using Forms Authentication. Forms Authentication works as follows: in a POST request you send username and password using application/x-www-form-urlencoded media type. If your credentials can be authenticated at the server side, you get a response containing a Set-Cookie header with the authentication cookie. This string value has to be sent as the Cookie header during subsequent requests to authenticate yourself against the Web API. Listing 4-23 shows the complete implementation of the client side.

Listing 4-23. Using Forms Authentication with HttpClient

```
private static void Main(string[] args) {

    Console.WriteLine("Username:");
    var username = Console.ReadLine();
    Console.WriteLine("Password:");
    var password = Console.ReadLine();

    var client = new HttpClient();

    // setup initial authentication request
    var authRequest = new HttpRequestMessage() {
        Method = HttpMethod.Post,
        RequestUri = new Uri("http://localhost:3915/Account/Login"),
        Content = new FormUrlEncodedContent(
            new List<KeyValuePair<string, string>> {
                new KeyValuePair<string, string>("Username", username),
                new KeyValuePair<string, string>("Password", password)
            })
    };

    // try to authenticate
    var authResponse = client.SendAsync(authRequest).Result;
    IEnumerable<string> values;
    authResponse.Headers.TryGetValues("Set-Cookie", out values);
```

```
    if (null == values || string.IsNullOrEmpty(values.First())) {
        Console.WriteLine("Username and password must equal.");
        Console.ReadLine();
        return;
    }

    var cookie = values.First();

    // setup request to retrieve data from the server
    var request = new HttpRequestMessage() {
        RequestUri = new Uri("http://localhost:3915/customer/get/1")
    };

    // assign cookie
    request.Headers.Add("Cookie", cookie);
    request.Headers.Accept.Add(new MediaTypeWithQualityHeaderValue("application/json"));

    var response = client.SendAsync(request).Result;
    Console.WriteLine("Customer: {0}", response.Content.ReadAsAsync<Customer>().Result.Name);
    Console.ReadLine();
}
```

After requesting username and password from the console and wiring up a new HttpClient instance, a new HttpRequestMessage is created. According to the Forms Authentication requirements, the method of the request is set to POST, and the credentials are assigned to a FormUrlEncodedContent instance. The request is POSTed against the login URI of the Web API. If authentication has been successful on the server side, the cookie is returned, parsed from the response, and reassigned to the request header of the subsequent request, which then retrieves the required data. The output is written to the console again. Figure 4-8 shows the workflow with valid credentials in the console window, whereas Figure 4-9 shows a failing scenario.

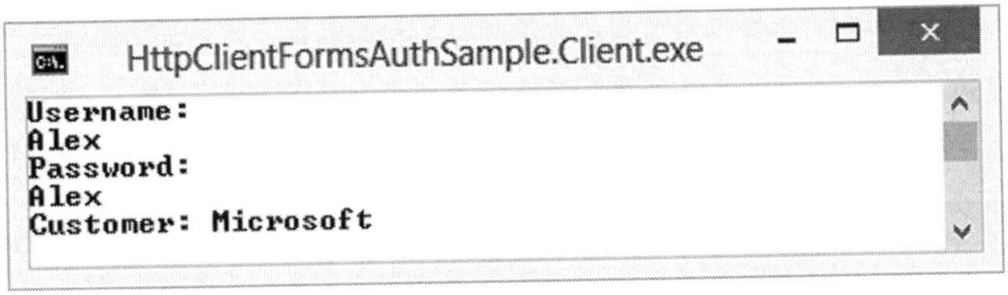

Figure 4-8. Successful login

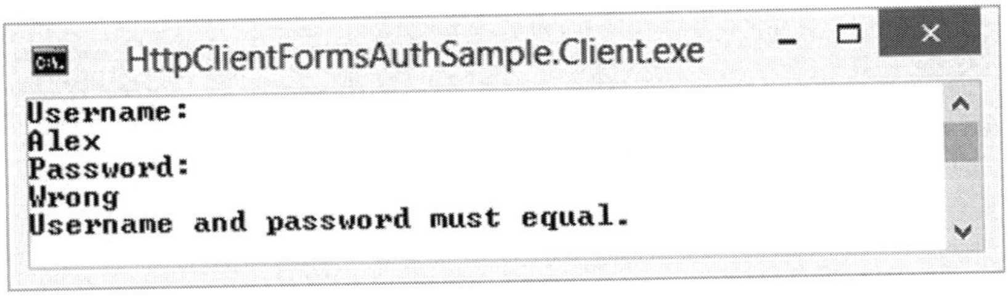

Figure 4-9. Login failed

Also, note that the last sample made no use of any helper or extensions methods; it's been quite easy to implement the requirements using the SendAsync method of HttpClient. There might be more complex scenarios, but in the end the use of HttpClient, the requests and responses, and the content sent or retrieved remains mostly the same.

Summary

With the introduction of the System.Net.Http namespace in .NET framework 4.5 and its backport to 4.0, available via NuGet, handling HTTP in .NET became handier and more straightforward to use. Thanks to the abstractions of HTTP requests, responses, and body content, they can be accessed in a typed manner. HttpClient itself provides a modern and robust handler for HTTP in the .NET framework, which additionally provides useful extensibility points.

CHAPTER 5

◼◼◼

Sample Application: Application Structure and Domain Model

There are two main approaches to learning new stuff: learning by practicing or learning the theory first. If the first one is your preferred option, the next three chapters are for you. If you prefer knowing theory first, you might want to skip to Chapter 8 and continue reading to Chapter 18 before coming back here. In the next three chapters I'll help you build a sample application using ASP.NET Web API. Also, Chapter 7 will cover implementing a .NET wrapper around our HTTP API to make its consumption easy from .NET applications. We'll then use this wrapper to build a client application based on ASP.NET MVC. However, the client application doesn't have to be an ASP.NET MVC application. It could be an HTML5 application that makes AJAX calls to the HTTP API, a Windows Store application, or an iOS application. Any platform that knows how to talk HTTP can consume our HTTP API.

PingYourPackage: An Overview

The application to be implemented during the next three chapters is called **PingYourPackage**; it covers a few scenarios you may already be familiar with. Let's say you're ordering some printed books at Amazon.com or a similar site; if the books you ordered are in stock, you'll receive an e-mail indicating that they will be shipped soon. Once they're shipped, you'll receive an e-mail notifying you of the fact. Furthermore, you'll get a tracking number for that shipment. Using that tracking ID, you can trace your package. At every stage of shipment, you'll have information about where your package is at that moment.

To simplify the domain model a bit, we added some constraints:

- We, the company running the PingYourPackage application, have affiliates that can assign shipment orders to us using the HTTP API.

- Each shipment contains one package.

Of course, in implementing the PingYourPackage application in the next chapters and sections, we won't cover the entire process described above. We'll look at the most important aspects from the business perspective, as well as from that of implementing a Web API using ASP.NET Web API.

In this section, to understand more clearly what will be implemented and to set up some context before starting the implementation, I'll describe the above scenario in more detail. I'll first define our application features and extract a domain language. After that, I'll define the resources for our API and how to identify them using URIs.

■ **Note** You can download the entire application's source code, along with the other samples, from the Apress web site. In addition, the application source code is hosted on GitHub (`https://github.com/tugberkugurlu/PingYourPackage`). Go to the ReadMe section for more information (`https://github.com/tugberkugurlu/PingYourPackage#readme`).

Application Features and Domain Language

There are several ways to start implementing an application. I've chosen to specify the requirements first before writing any lines of code. As the main goal here is to put forward the ASP.NET Web API, we won't go into many details of the application features. I'll touch on just the most specific ones.

As mentioned above, the PingYourPackage project allows companies to delegate shipment to another delivery company by consuming the public HTTP API. This API requires authentication via the HTTP Basic Authentication mechanism (you'll see how to implement it in Chapter 6). So each allowed request arriving at our HTTP API will be attached to a user, and each user record has a specified role. For our application, the roles required to distinguish borders for security reasons are these:

- Admin
- Affiliate
- Employee

Each part of the API allows access to users associated with specific roles (more about this in Chapter 6). With the roles identified, let's try to extract the domain language and define the key words in it. The domain language consists of substantives naming objects, processes, or conditions. By extracting them from the user stories, we get the following list of objects, which become the domain entities at the PingYourPackage application:

- `Affiliate`. An affiliate is a customer. Affiliates can assign shipments to us to get packages sent to their customers.
- `PackageReceiver`. Under `PackageReceiver` are listed the customers of an affiliate. They order goods, which we ship to them. Customers can track shipments until they reach them.
- `Shipment`. A shipment consists of a package, assigned by the affiliate to us, to be sent to the `PackageReceiver` customer.
- `ShipmentType`. The `ShipmentType` declares which type the package being shipped is. Values include parcel, envelope, and sachet.

In addition to the domain entities, there are two more necessary entities.

- User. Everyone interacting with the PingYourPackage API is a user.
- Role. A role defines a group of users with specific permissions.

The overall scope of PingYourPackage can also be visualized as a work flow chart, as shown in Figure 5-1.

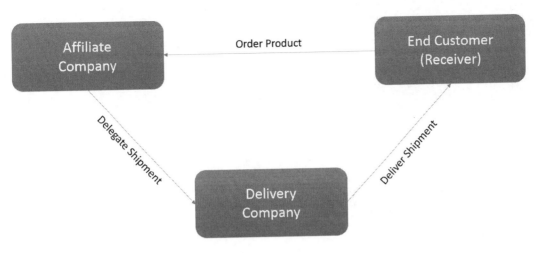

Figure 5-1. *Simple real-world workflow of the delivery company*

Now that the business scope of the sample application, its entities, and the user stories have been defined, let's dig into some technical concepts and the architecture of the application.

Project Structure and Architecture

Based on the goals and cases specified in the previous sections, we can create an architectural overview of the application and set up a new Visual Studio solution containing all the application's parts. Let's start with the architecture.

Architecture

The architecture of the PingYourPackage sample application to be created in the next three chapters consists of a database and several other elements, including .NET class libraries and web applications. Figure 5-2 shows the high-level structure of the application.

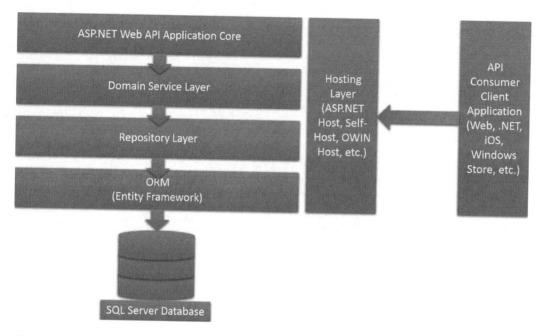

Figure 5-2. *Architecture of the PingYourPackage application*

The entire project is based on the SQL Server database. However, since our API will not talk directly to the database itself with raw .NET SQL-client APIs, we will separate it into several layers. Let's use an ORM (object-relational mapping) library to communicate with the database (I've chosen Entity Framework as the ORM library). Also, let's leverage the "code-first" feature of the Entity Framework to create the schema of our SQL Server database through .NET objects. Let's also create a generic repository (more on this in upcoming sections) to abstract away the Entity Framework DbContext object. Some operations will require talking to two different repositories or maybe performing a few validations that requires a trip to the database. Since such things will get messy if we try to perform them inside the controller action itself, let's introduce a layer, called a service layer, between the ASP.NET Web API core application and the repositories.

Project Structure

The next subsections will guide you through the process of adding the appropriate projects to that solution and including the dependencies for Data Access, Unit Testing, IoC, and the like. They'll also explain the purpose of each project inside the solution. The only additions will be the projects for the server part of our applications; new projects will be added as needed in the next two chapters. At the end, our solution will look like Figure 5-3.

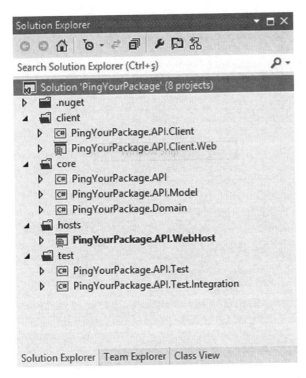

Figure 5-3. *How the complete solution will look at the end*

To achieve the structure shown in Figure 5-3, we first need to create a new, empty Visual Studio solution by clicking the File entry on the menu bar, then New, followed by Project... in the Visual Studio 2012 start page, as shown in Figure 5-4.

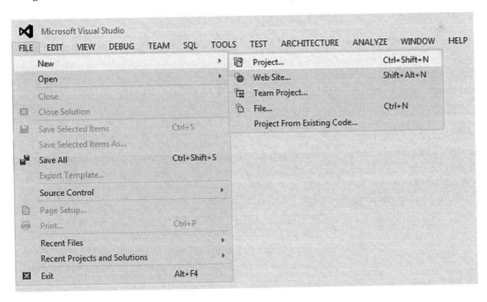

Figure 5-4. *Starting a new project inside Visual Studio 2012*

Clicking New ➤ Project… will cause a dialog to pop up; in it you can choose the type of project to create. Figure 5-5 shows Blank Solution and the name PingYourPackage as the choices made.

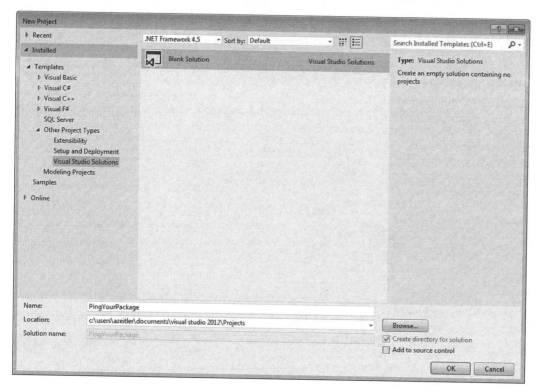

Figure 5-5. *Creating a blank solution in Visual Studio 2012*

Visual Studio 2012 now creates the new, blank solution name PingYourPackage and displays it in the Solution Explorer. That solution is the container for all projects needed to implement the PingYourPackage sample application. In the next sections we'll add Visual Studio projects of different types, according to the technical need they have to fulfill. We are splitting the application into several logical projects so that we can create reusable components from them and deploy the Web API in different hosting environments, if necessary.

PingYourPackage.Domain Project

The first project, which we now take a closer look at, is the project containing the domain entities, data access logic (repositories), and application logic (service layer). So let's add **Class Library** project for our domain-entity objects. To do this, right-click the PingYourPackage solution entry in the Solution Explorer window and choose Add, followed by New Project… in the context menu shown. Figure 5-6 shows that click sequence.

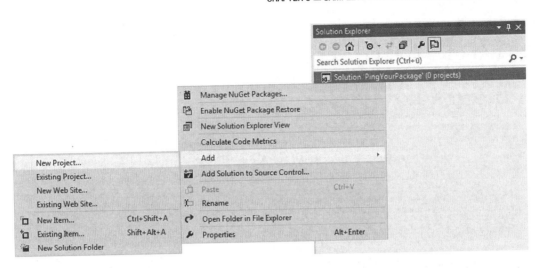

Figure 5-6. *Starting to add a new project to the PingYourPackage solution in Visual Studio 2012*

As was said, we want to add a new Class Library project; select it from the upcoming dialog and name it **PingYourPackage.Domain**, as shown in Figure 5-7.

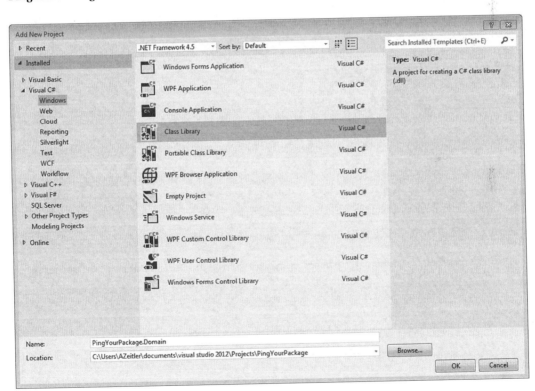

Figure 5-7. *Adding the PingYourPackage.Domain Class Library project to the solution*

After Visual Studio has added the PingYourPackage.Domain project, delete the file `Class1.cs`, which has also been created by default but makes no sense here. The necessary references and entities will be added to this project later on, when we describe the database schema and how to use `EntityFramework` with the Code First approach.

PingYourPackage.API Project

The PingYourPackage.API project will hold the ASP.NET Web API components for building the HTTP API logic itself. These components contain controllers, message handlers, filters, custom parameter bindings, and other tools to maintain the project over time by separating the concerns. The PingYourPackage.API will hold the authentication and authorization logic, too.

The PingYourPackage.API project will be a class library project, too; it contains no host-specific information. First, much as in the process shown in the previous section, we here add a class library project to the solution. This one is called **PingYourPackage.API**. The `Class1.cs` file can safely be deleted. Now our solution should look similar to the one in Figure 5-8.

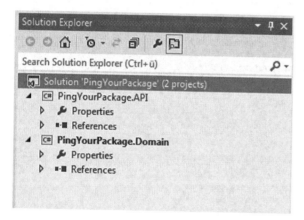

Figure 5-8. *PingYourPackage solution after adding the PingYourPackage.API project*

The next step is to add ASP.NET Web API components to the PingYourPackage.API project. Thanks to Microsoft NuGet, this is done easily and without worry about where to store the dependent DLL files. In the NuGet Package Manager Console, just type the following:

```
Install-Package Microsoft.AspNet.WebApi.Core -ProjectName PingYourPackage.API
```

After Visual Studio resolves all dependencies correctly, downloads it from the NuGet server, and references the core ASP.NET Web API DLLs, your NuGet Package Manager Console should look like the one shown in Figure 5-9.

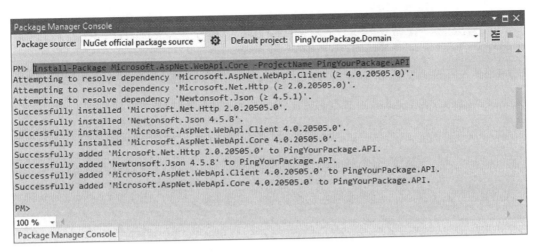

Figure 5-9. *Referencing ASP.NET Web API package using NuGet Package Manager Console*

Another dependency that should be added is the Autofac IoC Container. It is used to inject required dependencies, like repositories, into our controllers. The Autofac container neatly integrates with ASP.NET Web API and the appropriate NuGet package, for this is **Autofac.WebApi**, which refers to the core Autofac container. Type the following in the NuGet Package Manager Console:

```
Install-Package Autofac.WebApi -ProjectName PingYourPackage.API
```

Now let's add folders and classes to the PingYourPackage.API project. Start with the folders for the overall structure. Folders are added by right-clicking the project file or the folder under which the new one is to be created.

One of the folders to be added is the Config folder; it will hold the ASP.NET Web API configuration files, such as the general ASP.NET Web API configuration (`WebAPIConfig.cs`), Web API routes configuration (`RouteConfig.cs`), and IoC container configuration (`AutofacConfig.cs`). See Figure 5-10.

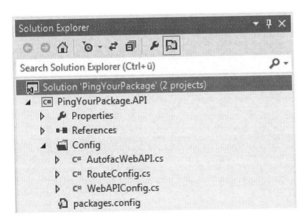

Figure 5-10. *The temporary structure of the PingYourPackage.API project*

The reason why we have separated these into different files and classes is to make them more maintainable. Each static class will have static methods to get their job done, and they will be called through the hosting layer once per application life cycle. We'll invoke these static methods during integration testing.

Now that a coarse structure of the PingYourPackage.API project is in place, we can add some infrastructural code to it. First, we'll add code baseframe to the AutofacWebAPI.cs class file, which is shown in Listing 5-1.

Listing 5-1. Code Baseframe for Autofac Used in the PingYourPackage.API Project

```
public class AutofacWebAPI {

    public static void Initialize(HttpConfiguration config) {

        Initialize(config,
            RegisterServices(new ContainerBuilder()));
    }

    public static void Initialize(
        HttpConfiguration config, IContainer container) {

        config.DependencyResolver =
            new AutofacWebApiDependencyResolver(container);
    }

    private static IContainer RegisterServices(ContainerBuilder builder) {

        builder.RegisterApiControllers(Assembly.GetExecutingAssembly());

        // registration goes here

        return builder.Build();
    }
}
```

As Listing 5-1 shows, there are two Initialize methods: Initialize(HttpConfiguration config), which will be called by the hosting layer, and Initialize(HttpConfiguration config, IContainer container), which will be called through the integration tests by providing an IContainer instance. The first Initialize method calls the second one by providing an IContainer instance through the RegisterServices private method, which is where our dependencies are registered. Inside the second Initialize method a new AutofacWebApiDependencyResolver instance, which accepts an implementation of IContainer through its constructor, is assigned to the passed-in HttpConfiguration instance DependencyResolver property.

The WebAPIConfig and RouteConfig classes will be touched on in Chapter 6, when the core Web API logic is being built.

PingYourPackage.API.Test

Not only is ASP.NET Web API a great framework, in the sense of implementing the HTTP specification, but it also promotes easy testing. To test Web API–specific elements like controllers for our PingYourPackage implementation, add another class library project to the PingYourPackage solution, one named PingYourPackage.API.Test, and as before, also remove the Class1.cs file. As you learned in Chapter 1, we're writing tests for ASP.NET Web API using the xUnit.net test framework. As xUnit.net is a state-of-the-art unit-testing framework, it may be easily added to your projects via NuGet packages. To reference xUnit.net in our PingYourPacakage.API.Test project, execute the following command in the NuGet Package Manager Console:

```
Install-Package xunit -ProjectName PingYourPackage.API.Test
```

When it comes to unit testing, the need may arise to mock dependent objects or, to be more specific, their behavior and properties. You can write mock objects or stubs by hand, but you can also choose a mocking framework. The latter has been my choice; we use the mocking framework called Moq, which was touched upon in Chapter 1, as well as xUnit.net. Moq also provides NuGet packages; the command to reference it is quite similar to the one for xUnit.net:

```
Install-Package Moq -ProjectName PingYourPackage.API.Test
```

As we're going to test the parts of our Web API core application which depend on ASP.NET Web API itself, we need to reference ASP.NET Web API in the PingYourPackage.API.Test project:

```
Install-Package Microsoft.AspNet.WebApi.Core -ProjectName PingYourPackage.API.Test
```

To check whether PingYourPackage.API.Test contains all required NuGet package references, execute the following command:

```
Get-Package -ProjectName PingYourPackage.API.Test
```

The output should contain the NuGet packages shown in Figure 5-11 (note that the versions shown may differ as the projects are in continuous development).

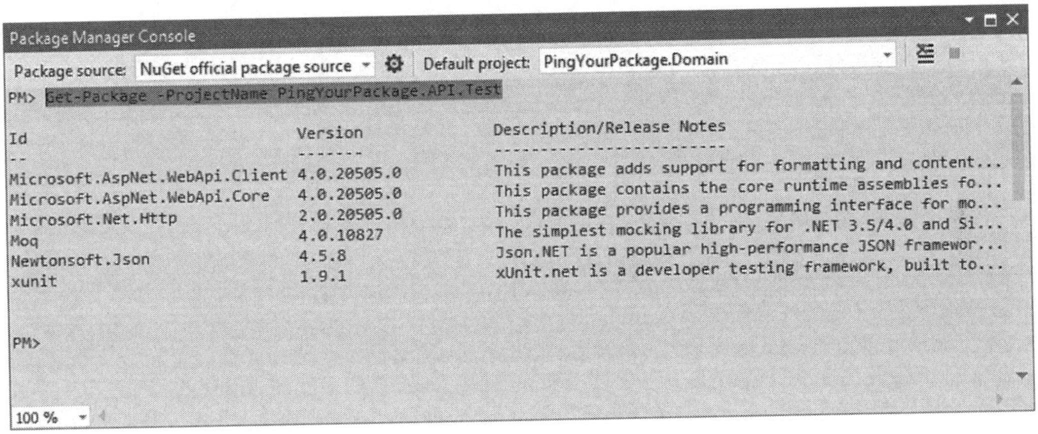

Figure 5-11. Installed NuGet packages for PingYourPackage.API.Test

As we implement the controllers for PingYourPackage in the next chapter, we'll also write the test for them at that time. For now, we're done with the PingYourPackage.API.Test project.

PingYourPackage.WebHost Project

Look back at Figure 5-2, and you'll see that the next step up in the PingYourPackage architecture is the web hosting environment for the PingYourPackage HTTP API. This is accomplished by adding another project to the PingYourPackage solution. This time, you'll add a new project type of ASP.NET Empty Web Application named PingYourPackage.API.WebHost (see Figure 5-12).

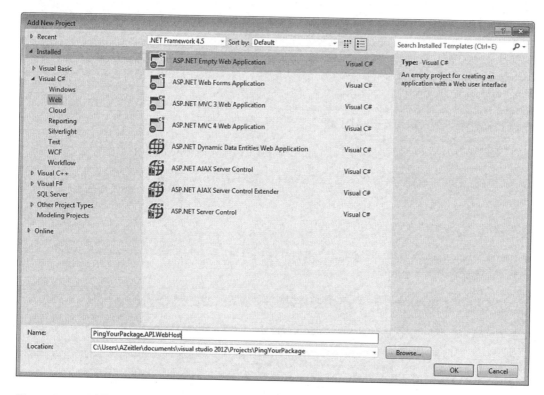

Figure 5-12. Adding an empty ASP.NET Web application project to PingYourPackage

The first NuGet package to add is **Microsoft.AspNet.WebApi.WebHost**, which resolves all necessary ASP.NET Web API dependencies and also references them. The Microsoft.AspNet.WebApi.WebHost NuGet package depends on the Microsoft.AspNet.WebApi.Core package and brings a specific hosting component for ASP.NET.

In order to wire up the PingYourPackage API implementation with our ASP.NET web hosting environment, we need to add a so-called **Global Application Class** to our PingYourPackage.API.WebHost project. This is done by right-clicking the PingYourPackage.API.WebHost project entry in the Solution Explorer, followed by a click to the Add entry and then another on the New Item . . . entry, as shown in Figure 5-13. In the following dialog, you have to choose the Global Application Class entry and keep the Global.asax name, according to Figure 5-14.

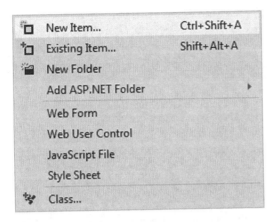

Figure 5-13. *Adding a new item to the PingYourPackage.API.WebHost project*

Figure 5-14. *Selecting the Global Application Class*

After the Global Application Class is added, replace the autogenerated `Application_Start` method stub with the implementation from Listing 5-2.

Listing 5-2. *Wiring Up the Parts of the PingYourPackage Application*

```
protected void Application_Start(object sender, EventArgs e) {

    var config = GlobalConfiguration.Configuration;

    RouteConfig.RegisterRoutes(config);
    WebAPIConfig.Configure(config);
    AutofacWebAPI.Initialize(config);
}
```

The code shown in Listing 5-2 initializes the configuration for the PingYourPackage application by calling the static configuration methods created previously. Every part of that configuration and the objects being configured will be covered in the next sections and chapters.

These projects needed to be added to our solution, but they are enough for now. We will add a few more projects along the way.

Building the Domain Model

Before going further with our API design and implementation, it would be a good idea to build the domain model, because knowing what we are working with in our API application is desirable.

■ **Note** Opinions differ as to whether starting a project this way is a good idea or not, but we favor this approach. Remember, this book focuses on ASP.NET Web API; the tools used and the approach followed are just for our sample application. In fact, each tool used in this project can be replaced by your own favorite relevant tool. These chapters only explain our sample application; they aren't intended to give guidance on how you should design your application. Design needs vary with the application in question and are outside this book's scope. The main purpose here is to explain how to create a maintainable application, one where advantage can be taken of the ASP.NET Web API framework and of how pieces fit together for our specific scenario.

For our sample application, we decided to use an object-relational mapping (ORM) framework to access our data on the SQL Server; the Microsoft Entity Framework is the one that we've chosen.

Brief Introduction to Entity Framework

Entity Framework (commonly abbreviated EF) is an ORM framework that enables us to work with relational data using domain-specific objects. It is one of the most frequently used data access technologies in .NET applications.

■ **Note** Entity Framework is also an open source project at ASP.NET Web API and accepts contributions from the community.

With Entity Framework, we can issue queries against our database using LINQ and then retrieve and manipulate data as strongly typed objects. EF also eliminates the need for focusing on the data access fundamentals; this enables us to focus more on the business logic of our application. On the other hand, EF provides Code First experience to create entity models using code; this will be the approach we take. Along with the Code First model, EF has a few more advantages as a data access technology.

- It is compatible with multiple database technologies, including Microsoft SQL Server, Microsoft SQL Server Compact, and Oracle.

- It has high-level integration with Visual Studio for a better experience.

- It has language-integrated query (LINQ) support.

- It provides several models to work with the database: Code First, Database First, Model First.

- When using the Code First model, EF provides the migrations feature to update the database schema during the development or at runtime.

To include Entity Framework in our project, we'll use NuGet and install the Entity Framework package in the domain application (PingYourPackage.Domain), as shown in Figure 5-15. We also need to include this package in our core API application (PingYourPackage.API), API host application (PingYourPackage.API.WebHost) and API test project (PingYourPackage.API.Test).

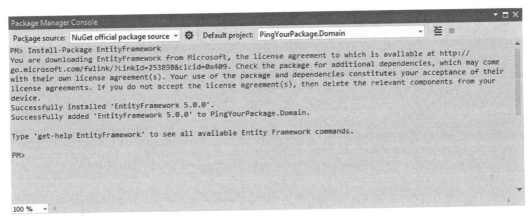

Figure 5-15. *Installation of the Entity Framework NuGet package through the Package Manager Console*

Installation of the Entity Framework NuGet package will get all the necessary components we need, such as `EntityFramework.dll` and the migration parts. We'll talk about them later in the chapter.

Building Entity Objects and DbContext

If you know your business needs, it won't be hard to structure the database in your mind. However, our SQL Server database won't be created through SQL Server Management Studio or an SQL script code, but it could be if it had to. Instead, let's work directly with the C# code to build our database structure.

It was briefly mentioned earlier that the Code First with Entity Framework enables the creation of CLR classes that define our models and generate a database based on these classes. The beauty here is that these classes are noting but plain old CLR objects, commonly known as POCO classes.

The most desirable database schema is the one shown in Figure 5-16.

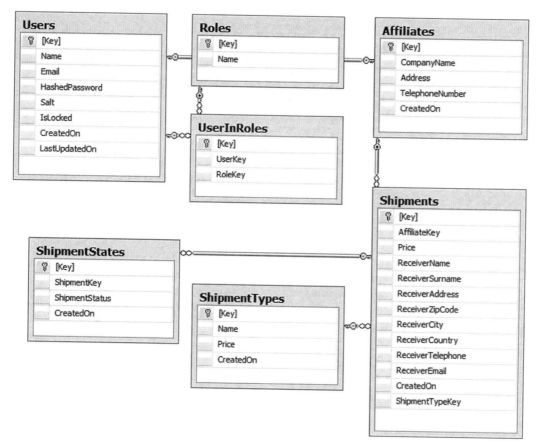

Figure 5-16. *PingYourPackage application database schema*

Working with Entity Framework Code First

First off, let's create an interface to use as a common construct for our entity classes. It doesn't *have to* be done to work with Entity Framework Code First, but it will help create a better repository structure, as you'll soon see. This simple interface is shown in Listing 5-3.

Listing 5-3. IEntity Interface for the Entity Classes

```
public interface IEntity {

    Guid Key { get; set; }
}
```

As you see, the interface contains only the Key property, a type of Guid; it will be mapped to the primary key for all our tables. We decided to use Guid, which is equivalent to uniqueidentifier in SQL Server, as the primary key type but it's not necessary to do so.

Our API application requires authentication and role-based authorization; so we need some sort of membership system. To get this type of system, we don't want to use ASP.NET's built-in membership system; we need a simpler approach, and so we'll implement our own. We don't encourage you to use this system for your own application, because security is very hard to get right. You need to consider all the facts of your application and build security accordingly. For our sample application, this membership system, which we'll now explain, is good enough.

We have three classes for our membership system: the User class, which will hold user information such as Name, Email, and so on (Listing 5-4); the Role class, which contains the roles (Listing 5-5), and the UserInRole class, which will log which user is in which role (Listing 5-6).

Listing 5-4. User Class

```
public class User : IEntity {

    [Key]
    public Guid Key { get; set; }

    [Required]
    public string Name { get; set; }

    public string Email { get; set; }

    [Required]
    public string HashedPassword { get; set; }

    [Required]
    public string Salt { get; set; }

    public bool IsLocked { get; set; }
    public DateTime CreatedOn { get; set; }
    public DateTime? LastUpdatedOn { get; set; }

    public virtual ICollection<UserInRole> UserInRoles { get; set; }

    public User() {

        UserInRoles = new HashSet<UserInRole>();
    }
}
```

Listing 5-5. Role Class

```
public class Role : IEntity {

    [Key]
    public Guid Key { get; set; }

    [Required]
    public string Name { get; set; }

    public virtual ICollection<UserInRole> UserInRoles { get; set; }
```

```
    public Role() {

        UserInRoles = new HashSet<UserInRole>();
    }
}
```

Listing 5-6. UserInRole Class

```
public class UserInRole : IEntity {

    [Key]
    public Guid Key { get; set; }
    public Guid UserKey { get; set; }
    public Guid RoleKey { get; set; }

    public User User { get; set; }
    public Role Role { get; set; }
}
```

There are a few important things to mention here regarding Entity Framework Code First. We use IEntity interface for these three classes and implement the Key property for them. Each Key property also has a KeyAttribute (located under the System.ComponentModel.DataAnnotations namespace) applied to it. This attribute indicates that the property serves as the primary key for the entity. Another attribute used here is the RequiredAttribute; it marks the column Not Null at the corresponding SQL Server database table. We don't need to put the RequiredAttribute for other types, except for string, because they will be already marked Not Null. If we need those types of properties to be marked Null, we need to make them Nullable properties with either the ? operator at the end or by using the Nullable generic type.

There is also a UserInRoles property in both User and Role classes; that property is a type of ICollection<UserInRole>. It's also a virtual property, because Entity Framework will generate proxy classes for those behind the scenes. We also need to initialize those collection properties inside the parameterless constructor. For the UserInRole class, we have two properties, UserKey and RoleKey, besides the Key property. They are types of User and Role. These properties—UserKey and RoleKey—will serve as "foreign keys," because Entity Framework will pick them up from the structure we have just put in place.

Now with three classes in our hands, let's move forward and generate the database based on them. But to build up that database, we'll need to create our DbContext class first. We'll talk about that next.

Creating the DbContext Class

The Entity Framework DbContext class is the main class we'll draw from for our database context class. This class will represent the unit of work, so that it can be used to query from a database and group changes together. They in turn will be written back to the database as a unit. Listing 5-7 shows the initial structure of EntitiesContext, a derived class from the DbContext class.

Listing 5-7. EntitiesContext Class

```
public class EntitiesContext : DbContext {

    public EntitiesContext() : base("PingYourPackage") {
    }
}
```

By convention, if we use the parameterless constructor of the base DbContext class, the class name will also be the database name on creation. However, we want the database name to be PingYourPackage. One of the constructors of the DbContext class allows passage of this information, just as we do in our sample. As for the database type, Entity Framework will use conventions to figure out which type you specify. However, let's specify a connection string inside the PingYourPackage.API.WebHost project configuration file. We will name this connection string "PingYourPackage", as shown in Listing 5-8.

Listing 5-8. "PingYourPackage" Connection String

```
<add name="PingYourPackage"
     connectionString="Data Source=.\SQLEXPRESS;Initial Catalog=PingYourPackage;Integrated Security=True"
     providerName="System.Data.SqlClient" />
```

We specified that the connection string use SQL Express here; when we are ready for production, we can change the connection string on the fly (e.g., with a build script) to target the production database.

Currently, we have three classes to represent our membership system; we can add those to the EntitiesContext class, as shown in Listing 5-9.

Listing 5-9. EntitiesContext Class with Properties

```
public class EntitiesContext : DbContext {

    public EntitiesContext() : base("PingYourPackage") {
    }

    public IDbSet<User> Users { get; set; }
    public IDbSet<Role> Roles { get; set; }
    public IDbSet<UserInRole> UserInRoles { get; set; }
}
```

Being now completely set, we can create the database. We'll use **Entity Framework Code First Migrations** to create the database; we'll also set up the infrastructure we need to automate this process.

Working with Entity Framework Migrations

Code First Migrations allows you to implement database changes all through the code. Database migrations through the code itself have been around for a while; they aren't a feature specific to Entity Framework. Installing the Entity Framework through NuGet yields the Code First Migrations components as well. When you open up the packages folder inside the root solution directory and navigate to the EntityFramework.5.0.0\tools folder from there, you'll find some files—most of them for the Code First Migrations feature (see Figure 5-17).

Name	Date modified	Type	Size
about_EntityFramework.help.txt	10/4/2012 6:14 PM	TXT File	1 KB
EntityFramework.PowerShell.dll	10/4/2012 6:14 PM	Application extens...	132 KB
EntityFramework.PowerShell.Utility.dll	10/4/2012 6:14 PM	Application extens...	16 KB
EntityFramework.PS3.psd1	10/4/2012 6:14 PM	Windows PowerS...	24 KB
EntityFramework.psd1	10/4/2012 6:14 PM	Windows PowerS...	24 KB
EntityFramework.psm1	10/4/2012 6:14 PM	Windows PowerS...	30 KB
init.ps1	10/4/2012 6:14 PM	Windows PowerS...	11 KB
install.ps1	10/4/2012 6:14 PM	Windows PowerS...	11 KB
migrate.exe	10/4/2012 6:14 PM	Application	128 KB
Redirect.config	10/4/2012 6:14 PM	XML Configuratio...	1 KB
Redirect.VS11.config	10/4/2012 6:14 PM	XML Configuratio...	1 KB

Figure 5-17. *Entity Framework NuGet package tools folder*

Migrations can be worked with in different ways, such as directly with the `migration.exe` file and using the **NuGet Package Manager Console (PMC)** commands, which are installed when the Entity Framework NuGet package is installed. For our sample application, we'll work with PMC to scaffold migrations. Let's see this in action.

■ **Note**   The Entity Framework Code First Migrations feature is straightforward, but depending on your scenario, it may not be your best choice. As this book is not about Entity Framework, it won't explore the migrations feature in depth. Its main focus is to create a fully functioning application with ASP.NET Web API.

First, we need to enable migrations. To do so, we've opened the PMC and set the **Default project** to `PingYourPackage.Domain`. This is the project where our `DbContext` instance, which is `EntitiesContext` class, lives (see Figure 5-18).

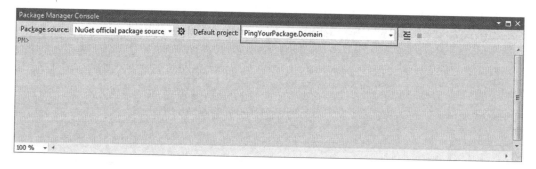

Figure 5-18. *Setting the Default project in Package Manager Console*

Now we can run the `Enable-Migrations` command to enable EF Code First Migrations. We'll pass `StartUpProjectName` as PingYourPackage.API.WebHost, because this is where the connection string of our database lives (see Figure 5-19).

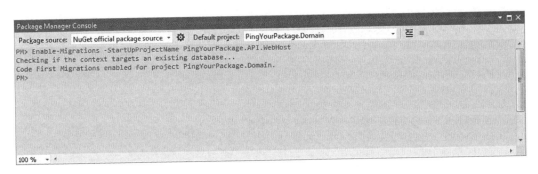

Figure 5-19. *Enabling EF Code First migrations*

After running this command, you'll see that a folder named Migrations has been created inside our target project (see Figure 5-20).

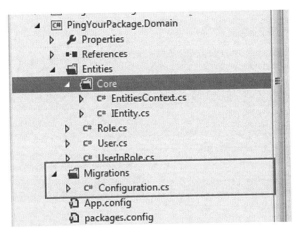

Figure 5-20. *Migrations folder has been added to the specified project automaticaly when EF Code First Migrations is enabled*

The Configuration.cs file, which is also generated automatically in the Migrations folder, includes the code shown in Listing 5-10.

Listing 5-10. Configuration.cs File Content

```
namespace PingYourPackage.Domain.Migrations
{
    using System;
    using System.Data.Entity;
    using System.Data.Entity.Migrations;
    using System.Linq;
    using PingYourPackage.Domain.Entities;
```

```
internal sealed class Configuration : DbMigrationsConfiguration<EntitiesContext>
{
    public Configuration()
    {
        AutomaticMigrationsEnabled = false;
    }

    protected override void Seed(EntitiesContext context)
    {
        //  This method will be called after migrating to the latest version.

        //  You can use the DbSet<T>.AddOrUpdate() helper extension method
        //  to avoid creating duplicate seed data. E.g.
        //
        //     context.People.AddOrUpdate(
        //       p => p.FullName,
        //       new Person { FullName = "Andrew Peters" },
        //       new Person { FullName = "Brice Lambson" },
        //       new Person { FullName = "Rowan Miller" }
        //     );
        //
    }
}
}
```

This class is `internal`, but it should be made a `public` class, as it will be used from our WebHost project. To avoid using automatic migrations, leave the `AutomaticMigrationsEnabled` property set to `false`.

Inside the Seed method, we can provide seed data, which will be inserted as soon as the database has been created. Use the `AddOrUpdate` method to ensure that each record is added only once between migrations. For this scenario, we need three roles for our membership system: Admin, Employee, and Affiliate. These roles will be included inside the Seed method when we initialize the database (see Listing 5-11).

Listing 5-11. Overriden Seed Method of DbMigrationsConfiguration

```
protected override void Seed(EntitiesContext context) {

    context.Roles.AddOrUpdate(role => role.Name,
        new Role { Key = Guid.NewGuid(), Name = "Admin" },
        new Role { Key = Guid.NewGuid(), Name = "Employee" },
        new Role { Key = Guid.NewGuid(), Name = "Affiliate" }
    );
}
```

The next thing to do is add the initial migration to define the initial database schema. To apply a migration, run the `Add-Migration` command inside the PMC. Specify the `StartUpProjectName` parameter as `PingYourPackage.API.WebHost`. We also need to give this migration a name (see Figure 5-21).

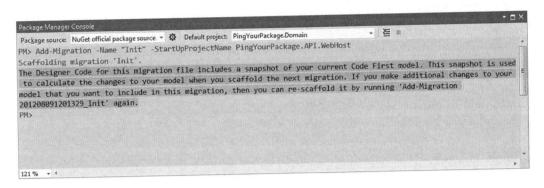

Figure 5-21. *Add-Migration command use*

After running the Add-Migration command, a file is added to the Migrations folder (see Figure 5-22). It contains the database schema information based on our EntitiesContext class.

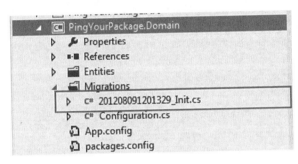

Figure 5-22. *Migration file added after the Add-Migration command has run*

When a change is made to the EntitiesContext class itself or to any related classes in EntitiesContext (User, Role, etc.), we can add another migration, as we did here. The migration will drop another file inside the Migrations folder, but it will contain only differences, not the whole database definition.

We can finally create the database! In doing so, we have a few options. We could use the PMC, as we did in creating our migrations, but instead we could kick this off when our Web API application starts. Let's add a class to the WebHost project, as shown in Listing 5-12.

Listing 5-12. The EFConfig Class That Runs the Migrations

```
public class EFConfig {

    public static void Initialize() {

        RunMigrations();
    }

    private static void RunMigrations() {

        var efMigrationSettings = new PingYourPackage.Domain.Migrations.Configuration();
        var efMigrator = new DbMigrator(efMigrationSettings);
```

```
        efMigrator.Update();
    }
}
```

Then we register the migrations to run at the application startup (see Listing 5-13).

Listing 5-13. Registering the Entity Framework Migrations to Run at the Application Startup

```
protected void Application_Start(object sender, EventArgs e) {

    //Lines omitted for brevity

    EFConfig.Initialize();
}
```

When we now start the WebHost application, the database will be created as expected (see Figure 5-23).

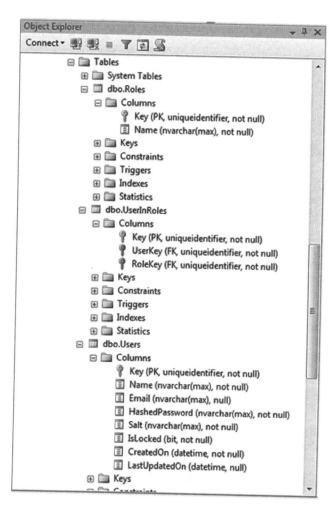

Figure 5-23. *The database created on the basis of our initial migration*

Notice that relationships between tables are also set, and the properties set as Required inside the classes are reflected as not null columns. We have our initial structure here, but there are things we'd like to modify in it. For example, string properties have been created as a NVARCHAR(MAX) column inside the database, but we'd like to restrict the number, and the Email column inside the Users table is set as a null column, though it shouldn't be.

Applying the Validation Attributes

Entity Framework permits use of several data annotations attributes for validation; some of them are reflected directly to the database.

So far, we have used the RequiredAttribute, which specifies that a data field value is required. We'll also be using one more attribute extensively: StringLengthAttribute. This attribute specifies the minimum and maximum length of characters allowed in a data field.

We can change the User class by adding StringLengthAttribute for several properties and RequiredAttribute for the Email property (see Listing 5-14).

Listing 5-14. The User Class with Validation Attribute Changes

```
public class User : IEntity {

    [Key]
    public Guid Key { get; set; }

    [Required]
    [StringLength(50)]
    public string Name { get; set; }

    [Required]
    [StringLength(320)]
    public string Email { get; set; }

    [Required]
    public string HashedPassword { get; set; }

    [Required]
    public string Salt { get; set; }

    public bool IsLocked { get; set; }
    public DateTime CreatedOn { get; set; }
    public DateTime? LastUpdatedOn { get; set; }

    public virtual ICollection<UserInRole> UserInRoles { get; set; }

    public User() {

        UserInRoles = new HashSet<UserInRole>();
    }
}
```

Also, we add the StringLengthAttribute for the Name property of Role class (see Listing 5-15).

Listing 5-15. The Role Class with Validation Attribute Changes

```
public class Role : IEntity {

    [Key]
    public Guid Key { get; set; }

    [Required]
    [StringLength(50)]
    public string Name { get; set; }

    public virtual ICollection<UserInRole> UserInRoles { get; set; }

    public Role() {

        UserInRoles = new HashSet<UserInRole>();
    }
}
```

We need to reflect these changes to our database. To do so, we create another migration (see Figure 5-24). This one will include only changes; it will modify the database accordingly when the WebHost application is run.

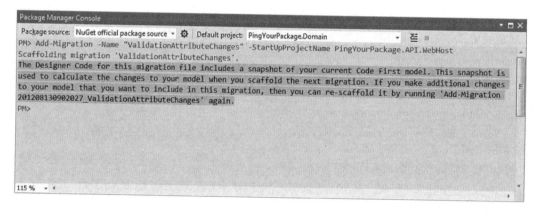

Figure 5-24. Adding a new migration to reflect the latest changes to the database

With the database updated based on our latest migration, we should be able to see the changes applied (see Figure 5-25).

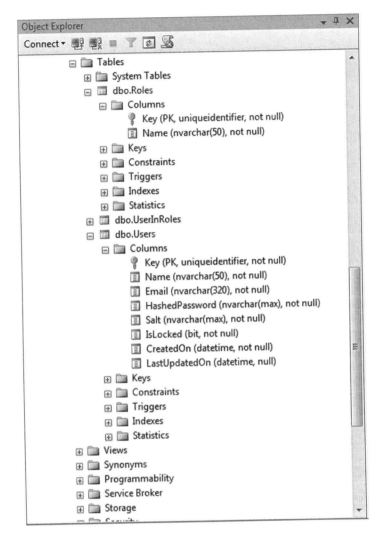

Figure 5-25. *The database as changed after our latest migration was applied*

So far, we have set up the initial structure of the database only for our membership system, modified the entity classes after the initial creation by applying several validation attributes, and reflected the changes to the database through Entity Framework migrations. The next step involves completing our entities and reflecting those changes to the database, as well.

Completing the Entities and DbContext Implementation

First of all, we create the Affiliate class, which will hold the affiliate information and have a one-to-one relationship with the Users table. Listing 5-16 shows the Affiliate class and that one-to-one relationship configuration.

Listing 5-16. The Affiliate Class

```
public class Affiliate : IEntity {

    [Key]
    public Guid Key { get; set; }

    [Required]
    [StringLength(50)]
    public string CompanyName { get; set; }

    [Required]
    [StringLength(50)]
    public string Address { get; set; }

    [StringLength(50)]
    public string TelephoneNumber { get; set; }

    [Required]
    public DateTime CreatedOn { get; set; }

    [Required]
    public User User { get; set; }
}
```

We applied the RequiredAttribute on the User property; it is a type of User created as shown in Listing 5-14; it will configure the one-to-one relationship along with the modifications we will make to the User class (see Listing 5-17).

Listing 5-17. The Modified User Class

```
public class User : IEntity {

    //Lines omitted for brevity

    public virtual Affiliate Affiliate { get; set; }

    public User() {

        UserInRoles = new HashSet<UserInRole>();
        Affiliate = new Affiliate();
    }
}
```

Now let's create the ShipmentType class, which will provide the price information according to the shipment type (see Listing 5-18).

Listing 5-18. The ShipmentType Class

```
public class ShipmentType : IEntity {

    [Key]
    public Guid Key { get; set; }

    [Required]
    [StringLength(50)]
    public string Name { get; set; }

    public decimal Price { get; set; }

    public DateTime CreatedOn { get; set; }
}
```

We have created the necessary classes around the Shipment class. The Shipment class will hold such information as the type of the shipment, the price, and the receiver information (see Listing 5-19).

Listing 5-19. The Shipment Class

```
public class Shipment : IEntity {

    [Key]
    public Guid Key { get; set; }
    public Guid AffiliateKey { get; set; }
    public Guid ShipmentTypeKey { get; set; }

    public decimal Price { get; set; }

    [Required]
    [StringLength(50)]
    public string ReceiverName { get; set; }

    [Required]
    [StringLength(50)]
    public string ReceiverSurname { get; set; }

    [Required]
    [StringLength(50)]
    public string ReceiverAddress { get; set; }

    [Required]
    [StringLength(50)]
    public string ReceiverZipCode { get; set; }

    [Required]
    [StringLength(50)]
    public string ReceiverCity { get; set; }

    [Required]
    [StringLength(50)]
    public string ReceiverCountry { get; set; }
```

```
    [Required]
    [StringLength(50)]
    public string ReceiverTelephone { get; set; }

    [Required]
    [StringLength(320)]
    public string ReceiverEmail { get; set; }

    public DateTime CreatedOn { get; set; }

    public Affiliate Affiliate { get; set; }
    public ShipmentType ShipmentType { get; set; }
}
```

As you can see, the Shipment class's properties are types of the Affiliate and PackageType classes. Two other properties, AffiliateKey and ShipmentTypeKey, will serve as a foreign key inside the database. A shipment entry always has a reference to one Affiliate and one ShipmentType entry, but an Affiliate and a ShipmentType entry can have references to one or multiple Shipment entries. In order to represent those collections, we need to modify the Affiliate and ShipmentType classes, as Listings 5-20 and 5-21 show.

Listing 5-20. Modified Affiliate Class

```
public class Affiliate : IEntity {

    //Lines omitted for brevity

    public virtual ICollection<Shipment> Shipments { get; set; }

    public Affiliate() {

        Shipments = new HashSet<Shipment>();
    }
}
```

Listing 5-21. Modified ShipmentType Class

```
public class ShipmentType : IEntity {

    //Lines omitted for brevity

    public virtual ICollection<Shipment> Shipments { get; set; }

    public ShipmentType() {

        Shipments = new HashSet<Shipment>();
    }
}
```

Another useful feature is being able to track the shipment state. For this feature, we will create another class, ShipmentState. The ShipmentState class will appear as the ShipmentStates table inside our database and hold the shipment state entries. Listing 5-22 shows the ShipmentState class.

Listing 5-22. The ShipmentState Class

```
public class ShipmentState : IEntity {

    [Key]
    public Guid Key { get; set; }
    public Guid ShipmentKey { get; set; }

    [Required]
    public ShipmentStatus ShipmentStatus { get; set; }
    public DateTime CreatedOn { get; set; }

    public Shipment Shipment { get; set; }
}
```

The ShipmentState class also has a property, named ShipmentStatus, which is a type of ShipmentStatus enumeration, as shown in Listing 5-23.

Listing 5-23. The ShipmentStatus Enumeration

```
public enum ShipmentStatus {

    Ordered = 1,
    Scheduled = 2,
    InTransit = 3,
    Delivered = 4
}
```

The ShipmentStatus data field represents the status of the shipment as an integer value inside the database. With the addition of the ShipmentState class, the Shipment class needs to be modified (see Listing 5-24).

Listing 5-24. The Modified Shipment Class

```
public class Shipment : IEntity {

    //Lines omitted for brevity

    public virtual ICollection<ShipmentState> ShipmentStates { get; set; }

    public Shipment() {

        ShipmentStates = new HashSet<ShipmentState>();
    }
}
```

The last step for our domain model structure involves modifying the EntitiesContext class accordingly, as shown in Listing 5-25.

Listing 5-25. The Modified EntitiesContext Class

```
public class EntitiesContext : DbContext {

    public EntitiesContext() : base("PingYourPackage") {
    }

    public IDbSet<ShipmentType> PackageTypes { get; set; }
    public IDbSet<Affiliate> Affiliates { get; set; }
    public IDbSet<Shipment> Shipments { get; set; }
    public IDbSet<ShipmentState> ShipmentStates { get; set; }

    public IDbSet<User> Users { get; set; }
    public IDbSet<Role> Roles { get; set; }
    public IDbSet<UserInRole> UserInRoles { get; set; }
}
```

To end, we should reflect the changes to the database by adding another migration (see Figure 5-26) and apply it by running our WebHost application.

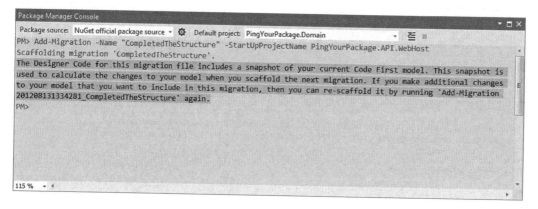

Figure 5-26. Adding a new migration to reflect the latest changes to the database

When this migration is applied, the database should be modified accordingly, as shown in Figure 5-27.

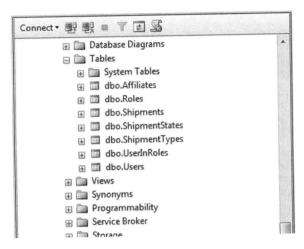

Figure 5-27. *The complete look of the database as modified*

Working with the Repository Pattern

With our DbContext implementation, we can work with data directly through EntitiesContext. However, doing so would make testing harder, since it is not possible to completely mock or fake the DbContext instance. We might easily extract an interface for EntitiesContext and work with a fake DbContext, but still, some parts are hard or impossible to fake. Besides, maintaining our application would be hard if we allowed arbitrary data access through our DbContext instance. Finally, we should also encapsulate the repetitive data access code.

To solve these problems, we can work with a specific pattern, known as Repository Pattern, and centralize data access logic. However, instead of implementing a separate repository for each entity, we create a generic repository to be used for all our entities without repeating ourselves.

Listing 5-26 shows the IEntityRepository<T> interface for our generic repository.

Listing 5-26. The IEntityRepository Interface

```
public interface IEntityRepository<T> where T : class, IEntity, new() {

    IQueryable<T> AllIncluding(
        params Expression<Func<T, object>>[] includeProperties);
    IQueryable<T> All { get; }
    IQueryable<T> GetAll();
    T GetSingle(Guid key);
    IQueryable<T> FindBy(Expression<Func<T, bool>> predicate);

    PaginatedList<T> Paginate<TKey>(
        int pageIndex, int pageSize,
        Expression<Func<T, TKey>> keySelector);

    PaginatedList<T> Paginate<TKey>(
        int pageIndex, int pageSize,
        Expression<Func<T, TKey>> keySelector,
        Expression<Func<T, bool>> predicate,
        params Expression<Func<T, object>>[] includeProperties);
```

```
    void Add(T entity);
    void Delete(T entity);
    void Edit(T entity);
    void Save();
}
```

This structure holds all the basic and generic functionality for our data access. When we need to work with the data—for example, inside a controller—we will be working with IEntityRepository<T> (e.g., IEntityRepository<User>), and the implementation will be injected through an IoC container, which is the Autofac for our application.

Notice, too, that we require the entity classes to implement IEntity; in that way we can have a generic GetSingle method based on the Key property. Besides, we have a custom type named PaginatedList. This is a class that is derived from List<T> and makes paginating the collection of items easy. Listing 5-27 shows the implementation of the PaginatedList<T> class.

Listing 5-27. The PaginatedList Class

```
public class PaginatedList<T> : List<T> {

    public int PageIndex { get; private set; }
    public int PageSize { get; private set; }
    public int TotalCount { get; private set; }
    public int TotalPageCount { get; private set; }

    public PaginatedList(
        int pageIndex, int pageSize,
        int totalCount, IQueryable<T> source) {

        AddRange(source);

        PageIndex = pageIndex;
        PageSize = pageSize;
        TotalCount = totalCount;
        TotalPageCount = (int)Math.Ceiling(totalCount / (double)pageSize);
    }

    public bool HasPreviousPage {

        get {
            return (PageIndex > 1);
        }
    }

    public bool HasNextPage {

        get {
            return (PageIndex < TotalPageCount);
        }
    }
}
```

The generic `PaginatedList<T>` class has one constructor and accepts four parameters: current page index, the size of the objects per page, the total collection, and the collection itself. The `PaginatedList<T>` class doesn't provide pagination logic. This class represents only a paginated collection of objects. To perform pagination logic, there is an extension method for the `IQueryable` interface; it converts a collection of objects to a `PaginatedList` object, as shown in Listing 5-28.

Listing 5-28. ToPaginatedList Extension Method for the IQueryable Interface

```
public static class IQueryableExtensions {

    public static PaginatedList<T> ToPaginatedList<T>(
        this IQueryable<T> query, int pageIndex, int pageSize) {

        var totalCount = query.Count();
        var collection = query.Skip((pageIndex - 1) * pageSize).Take(pageSize);

        return new PaginatedList<T>(
            pageIndex, pageSize,
            totalCount, collection);
    }
}
```

The `ToPaginatedList<T>` extension method first performs the pagination logic with the Skip and Take LINQ methods. Then it goes to the database to retrieve the total count of the collection. Finally, it constructs a new `PaginatedList<T>` instance and returns it. The pagination logic inside the `ToPaginatedList<T>` extension method generates the optimum T-SQL query to execute at the SQL Server. So what will be retrieved is only the number of rows, just as was indicated. It is also the effect desired here.

With these extensions in place, we can now implement our generic repository.

Implementing the Generic Repository

The implementation of the `IEntityRepository<T>` is very straightforward. The implementation class will be the `EntityRepository<T>` class; it will use the DbContext class directly to perform such data access operations as retrieving, inserting, editing, and deleting data. So we'll have no direct dependency on `EntitiesContext`, even inside the repository implementation. Instead, there will be only one constructor for this class; it accepts a parameter that is a type of DbContext class. We will pass an instance of `EntitiesContext` here. Thus, we won't be decoupling our specific context class and repository implementation. Also, we'll be able to use a per-request DbContext (more on this in Chapter 6) when we hook up our IoC container to the ASP.NET Web API infrastructure.

Listing 5-29 shows the `EntityRepository<T>` implementation.

Listing 5-29. The EntityRepository<T> Class Implementation

```
public class EntityRepository<T> : IEntityRepository<T>
    where T : class, IEntity, new() {

    readonly DbContext _entitiesContext;
```

```
    public EntityRepository(DbContext entitiesContext) {

        if (entitiesContext == null) {

            throw new ArgumentNullException("entitiesContext");
        }

        _entitiesContext = entitiesContext;
    }

    public virtual IQueryable<T> GetAll() {

        return _entitiesContext.Set<T>();
    }

    public virtual IQueryable<T> All {

        get {
            return GetAll();
        }
    }

    public virtual IQueryable<T> AllIncluding(
        params Expression<Func<T, object>>[] includeProperties) {

        IQueryable<T> query = _entitiesContext.Set<T>();
        foreach (var includeProperty in includeProperties) {

            query = query.Include(includeProperty);
        }

        return query;
    }

    public T GetSingle(Guid key) {

        return GetAll().FirstOrDefault(x => x.Key == key);
    }

    public virtual IQueryable<T> FindBy(Expression<Func<T, bool>> predicate) {

        return _entitiesContext.Set<T>().Where(predicate);
    }

    public virtual PaginatedList<T> Paginate<TKey>(
                int pageIndex, int pageSize,
                Expression<Func<T, TKey>> keySelector) {

        return Paginate(pageIndex, pageSize, keySelector, null);
    }
```

```
public virtual PaginatedList<T> Paginate<TKey>(
    int pageIndex, int pageSize,
    Expression<Func<T, TKey>> keySelector,
    Expression<Func<T, bool>> predicate,
    params Expression<Func<T, object>>[] includeProperties) {

    IQueryable<T> query =
        AllIncluding(includeProperties).OrderBy(keySelector);

    query = (predicate == null)
        ? query
        : query.Where(predicate);

    return query.ToPaginatedList(pageIndex, pageSize);
}

public virtual void Add(T entity) {

    DbEntityEntry dbEntityEntry = _entitiesContext.Entry<T>(entity);
    _entitiesContext.Set<T>().Add(entity);
}

public virtual void Edit(T entity) {

    DbEntityEntry dbEntityEntry = _entitiesContext.Entry<T>(entity);
    dbEntityEntry.State = EntityState.Modified;
}

public virtual void Delete(T entity) {

    DbEntityEntry dbEntityEntry = _entitiesContext.Entry<T>(entity);
    dbEntityEntry.State = EntityState.Deleted;
}

public virtual void Save() {

    _entitiesContext.SaveChanges();
}
}
```

This will be the only repository class used throughout the application. For example, we can construct an EntityRepository<User> object by simply passing the EntitiesContext instance and can work with User data through this repository class.

Repository Extension Methods

At some point, we'll need more than our generic repository offers. For example, we have the EntityRepository<User> class instance and can get a single user based on the primary key value through the GetSingle method. However, if we want to get a single user based on the user name, we'd need to use the FindBy method and provide a lambda expression.

If this is something you do often, consider centralizing to reduce code redundancy. You might create a separate repository class for a User entity derived from EntityRepository<User>—but this is not a clean solution. Instead, consider creating extension methods for repositories. Listing 5-30 shows an example that allows you to get a single User entity based on the user name.

Listing 5-30. The UserRepositoryExtensions Static Class

```
public static class UserRepositoryExtensions {

    public static User GetSingleByUsername(
        this IEntityRepository<User> userRepository, string username) {

        return userRepository.GetAll().FirstOrDefault(x => x.Name == username);
    }
}
```

An extension method named GetSingleByUsername has been added for the IEntityRepository<User> type. It allows extension of each repository's specific type. Listing 5-31 has a similar example for the IEntityRepository<Role> type.

Listing 5-31. The RoleRepositoryExtensions Class

```
public static class RoleRepositoryExtensions {

    public static Role GetSingleByRoleName(
        this IEntityRepository<Role> roleRepository, string roleName) {

        return roleRepository.GetAll().FirstOrDefault(x => x.Name == roleName);
    }
}
```

In the coming pages, you will see how to take advantage of these extensions when the MembershipService class is built.

Creating the Service Layer

We've just created our repository infrastructure for the data access logic. Yet we also have our business logic, which we intend to process inside our controller. But as our business logic matures and grows, maintaining the application will be difficult if we try to handle business logic inside the controller directly. The controller should be the place where the data access logic and the business logic are glued together. A main goal in the design of our ASP.NET Web API application is to keep the controllers as thin as possible.

To get this type of application design, we'll work with the service layer model. A service layer is a layer added to our ASP.NET Web API application that is responsible for communication between a controller and the repository layer. A service class at the service layer can work with multiple repositories at once if it needs to. However, there are some service classes that don't need to work with any repositories.

This section will cover two of our services: the CryptoService and the MembershipService. Additional services will be covered in Chapter 6.

CryptoService

The CryptoService is a stand-alone service that doesn't deal with data; it provides method for password encryption. Instead of creating a utility class for encrypting passwords, we decided to create a service to do this. The signature of the ICryptoService interface is shown in Listing 5-32.

Listing 5-32. The ICryptoService Interface

```
public interface ICryptoService {

    string GenerateSalt();
    string EncryptPassword(string password, string salt);
}
```

Basically, there are two responsibilities here: generating the salt for the password and encrypting the password. Implementation of this service is shown in Listing 5-33.

Listing 5-33. The CryptoService Class

```
public class CryptoService : ICryptoService {

    public string GenerateSalt() {

        var data = new byte[0x10];
        using (var cryptoServiceProvider = new RNGCryptoServiceProvider()) {

            cryptoServiceProvider.GetBytes(data);
            return Convert.ToBase64String(data);
        }
    }

    public string EncryptPassword(string password, string salt) {

        if (string.IsNullOrEmpty(password)) {

            throw new ArgumentNullException("password");
        }

        if (string.IsNullOrEmpty(salt)) {

            throw new ArgumentNullException("salt");
        }

        using (var sha256 = SHA256.Create()) {

            var saltedPassword = string.Format(
                "{0}{1}", salt, password);

            byte[] saltedPasswordAsBytes =
                Encoding.UTF8.GetBytes(saltedPassword);
```

```
            return Convert.ToBase64String(
                sha256.ComputeHash(saltedPasswordAsBytes));
        }
    }
}
```

For the salt generation, we used .NET cryptography features; we used SHA256 hashing algorithm for the password hashing. This service will mainly be used by the MembershipService.

MembershipService

As we mentioned, we won't be using the built-in ASP.NET membership system. Instead, we have created a lightweight infrastructure in our database. In order to process the membership logic involved in creating the user, changing the user password, and adding a user to a role, we create a service layer.

The IMembershipService interface signature is shown in Listing 5-34.

Listing 5-34. The IMembershipService Interface

```
public interface IMembershipService {

    ValidUserContext ValidateUser(string username, string password);

    OperationResult<UserWithRoles> CreateUser(
        string username, string email, string password);

    OperationResult<UserWithRoles> CreateUser(
        string username, string email,
        string password, string role);

    OperationResult<UserWithRoles> CreateUser(
        string username, string email,
        string password, string[] roles);

    UserWithRoles UpdateUser(
        User user, string username, string email);

    bool ChangePassword(
        string username, string oldPassword, string newPassword);

    bool AddToRole(Guid userKey, string role);
    bool AddToRole(string username, string role);
    bool RemoveFromRole(string username, string role);

    IEnumerable<Role> GetRoles();
    Role GetRole(Guid key);
    Role GetRole(string name);

    PaginatedList<UserWithRoles> GetUsers(int pageIndex, int pageSize);
    UserWithRoles GetUser(Guid key);
    UserWithRoles GetUser(string name);
}
```

Notice that a few methods of IMembershipService return an OperationResult or OperationResult<T> object. These are the classes that were created in order to let a caller know about operation status. For example, we don't want to create the user if the picked user name is already present inside the database. The OperationResult and OperationResult<T> classes can be seen in Listing 5-35.

Listing 5-35. OperationResult and OperationResult<T> Classes

```
public class OperationResult {

    public OperationResult(bool isSuccess) {
        IsSuccess = isSuccess;
    }

    public bool IsSuccess { get; private set; }
}

public class OperationResult<TEntity> : OperationResult {

    public OperationResult(bool isSuccess)
        : base(isSuccess) { }

    public TEntity Entity { get; set; }
}
```

The MembershipService itself has dependencies on a few repositories and on the CryptoService. Instead of referencing them directly, MembershipService accepts them as parameters through its only constructor. The constructor of the MembershipService is shown in Listing 5-36.

Listing 5-36. The Constructor of the MembershipService

```
public class MembershipService : IMembershipService {

    private readonly IEntityRepository<User> _userRepository;
    private readonly IEntityRepository<Role> _roleRepository;
    private readonly IEntityRepository<UserInRole> _userInRoleRepository;
    private readonly ICryptoService _cryptoService;

    public MembershipService(
        IEntityRepository<User> userRepository,
        IEntityRepository<Role> roleRepository,
        IEntityRepository<UserInRole> userInRoleRepository,
        ICryptoService cryptoService) {

        _userRepository = userRepository;
        _roleRepository = roleRepository;
        _userInRoleRepository = userInRoleRepository;
        _cryptoService = cryptoService;

    }
}
```

Also notice that we are working with interfaces; this will make it easier to test the MembershipService. The IoC container will handle the dependencies and inject the provided implementations of these interfaces.

Let's look at the ValidateUser method implementation first (see Listing 5-37).

Listing 5-37. The ValidateUser Method Implementation

```
public class MembershipService : IMembershipService {

    //Lines omitted for brevity

    public ValidUserContext ValidateUser(string username, string password) {

        var userCtx = new ValidUserContext();
        var user = _userRepository.GetSingleByUsername(username);
        if (user != null && isUserValid(user, password)) {

            var userRoles = GetUserRoles(user.Key);
            userCtx.User = new UserWithRoles() {
                User = user, Roles = userRoles
            };

            var identity = new GenericIdentity(user.Name);
            userCtx.Principal = new GenericPrincipal(
                identity,
                userRoles.Select(x => x.Name).ToArray());
        }

        return userCtx;
    }

    //Lines omitted for brevity

    private bool isUserValid(User user, string password) {

        if (isPasswordValid(user, password)) {

            return !user.IsLocked;
        }

        return false;
    }

    private IEnumerable<Role> GetUserRoles(Guid userKey) {

        var userInRoles = _userInRoleRepository
            .FindBy(x => x.UserKey == userKey).ToList();

        if (userInRoles != null && userInRoles.Count > 0) {

            var userRoleKeys = userInRoles.Select(
                x => x.RoleKey).ToArray();
```

```
            var userRoles = _roleRepository
                .FindBy(x => userRoleKeys.Contains(x.Key));

            return userRoles;
        }

        return Enumerable.Empty<Role>();
    }

    private bool isPasswordValid(User user, string password) {

        return string.Equals(
                _cryptoService.EncryptPassword(
                    password, user.Salt), user.HashedPassword);
    }
}
```

The ValidateUser method returns a value that is a type of IPrincipal, which defines the basic functionality of a principal object. If the return value is not null, the user is validated, and the user information will be returned. The validation logic is also straightforward. First of all, we try to get the user from the database based on the username parameter. An extension method named GetSingleByUsername is used; it was implemented earlier to perform this query on the database. If the User object is null, we will return null. If it is not null, we move to the next step: checking the password's validity. If it is valid, we then create the identity using the GenericIdentity class of the .NET Framework. Finally, we retrieve the roles the user is currently on and create the GenericPrincipal object based on these roles and the GenericIdentity.

Like the user validation logic, the CreateUser logic is straightforward. We have three overloads for the CreateUser method, but only one of them implements the actual logic, which is shown in Listing 5-38.

Listing 5-38. Implementation of the CreateUser Method and Its Overloads

```
public class MembershipService : IMembershipService {

    //Lines omitted for brevity

    public OperationResult<UserWithRoles> CreateUser(
        string username, string email, string password) {

        return CreateUser(username, password, email, roles: null);
    }

    public OperationResult<UserWithRoles> CreateUser(
        string username, string email, string password, string role) {

        return CreateUser(username, password, email, roles: new[] { role });
    }

    public OperationResult<UserWithRoles> CreateUser(
        string username, string email, string password, string[] roles) {

        var existingUser = _userRepository.GetAll().Any(
            x => x.Name == username);
```

```csharp
        if (existingUser) {

            return new OperationResult<UserWithRoles>(false);
        }

        var passwordSalt = _cryptoService.GenerateSalt();

        var user = new User() {
            Name = username,
            Salt = passwordSalt,
            Email = email,
            IsLocked = false,
            HashedPassword =
                _cryptoService.EncryptPassword(password, passwordSalt),
            CreatedOn = DateTime.Now
        };

        _userRepository.Add(user);
        _userRepository.Save();

        if (roles != null || roles.Length > 0) {

            foreach (var roleName in roles) {

                addUserToRole(user, roleName);
            }
        }

        return new OperationResult<UserWithRoles>(true) {
            Entity = GetUserWithRoles(user)
        };
    }

    //Lines omitted for brevity

    private void addUserToRole(User user, string roleName) {

        var role = _roleRepository.GetSingleByRoleName(roleName);
        if (role == null) {

            var tempRole = new Role() {
                Name = roleName
            };

            _roleRepository.Add(tempRole);
            _roleRepository.Save();
            role = tempRole;
        }
```

```
        var userInRole = new UserInRole() {
            RoleKey = role.Key,
            UserKey = user.Key
        };

        _userInRoleRepository.Add(userInRole);
        _userInRoleRepository.Save();
    }
}
```

The CreateUser methods return UserWithRoles instances wrapped inside the OperationResult. If the user has been created successfully, the return value indicates the unsuccessful operation. This is not the best way of handling this situation—we might want to show the actual cause of the failure—but for our sample application, we didn't want to expand this logic.

Implementation of other MembershipService methods aren't shown here, as they aren't used in our sample application. However, we have implemented them anyway, and you can have a look at them from the source code.

This section has shown how to implement a service layer that talks to one or many repositories to perform the specified operation. There is one more service interface, IShipmentService, and its implementation, ShipmentService. However, the processing of creating it won't be elaborated in this book. You'll find the implementation under PingYourPackage.Domain project, along with other service classes.

Summary

We believe that the best way to show the capabilities of a framework is by providing a real-world sample application; that's why we dedicated three chapters to explaining every step of an application creation process with ASP.NET Web API. This chapter explained the main idea of the application, set up the fundamental parts by implementing the domain layer with Entity Framework, and utilized some patterns, including the Repository Pattern and Service Layer Pattern. In the next chapter, we will start building our ASP.NET Web API application to create the HTTP API for our application.

CHAPTER 6

■ ■ ■

Sample Application: Building the Web API

In Chapter 5, you set up the infrastructure of the HTTP API application. You created your database models by leveraging the Entity Framework code–first approach and created a generic repository to gain access to the data. You also introduced the service layer by implementing the membership and crypto services.

This chapter will leverage the infrastructure you have built and use it to build the HTTP API application. From typical configuration to extending the Web API infrastructure, you'll experience how it feels to build a real-world HTTP API with ASP.NET Web API. Throughout this chapter, unless otherwise stated, we will be working with the PingYourPackage.API project that was created earlier.

We'll show how to write unit and integration tests against several parts of ASP.NET Web API throughout this chapter. We'll be using xUnit as our testing framework and Moq as the mocking framework.

Infrastructure of Our Web API Application

Before jumping into building the core components of our application, we'll lay out its infrastructure such as routes, configuration, and setting up the Inversion of Control (IoC) container.

Creating Routes

First, you must register the routes to reflect what you need for the HTTP API resources. In Chapter 5, we explained the URI structure that we want to provide, and in many cases, our default route will cover your needs; but you still need a few extra routes to produce a better-structured HTTP API.

To register the routes, you'll use the RouteConfig class inside the PingYourPackage.API project, created earlier during our initial set up (see Figure 6-1).

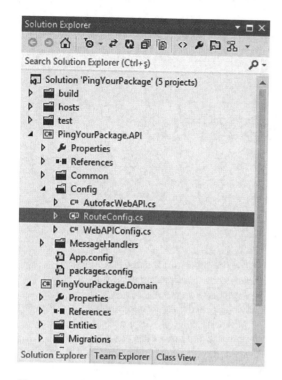

Figure 6-1. *RouteConfig.cs file inside PingYourPackage.API project*

Inside the RouteConfig class, you'll only have one static method that returns void: RegisterRoutes. The RegisterRoutes method accepts one parameter, which is of type HttpRouteCollection. By separating route registration like this, you'll be able to pass the configuration of the ASP.NET Web API host into RegisterRoutes method and register the routes easily.

■ **Note**   If you would like to learn more about ASP.NET Web API routing, you can look at Chapter 8, which is entirely dedicated to routing. Also, you will find detailed information about action selection and the effect of routing during this process in Chapter 9.

First, you'll register the default route, which will accommodate most of your needs (see Listing 6-1).

Listing 6-1. RegisterRoutes Static Method of RouteConfig Class

```
public static void RegisterRoutes(HttpRouteCollection routes) {

    routes.MapHttpRoute(
        "DefaultHttpRoute",
        "api/{controller}/{key}",
        defaults: new { key = RouteParameter.Optional },
        constraints: new { key = new GuidRouteConstraint() });
}
```

As you can see, a static segment was used at the beginning of the route: `api`. You'll use this convention with each route.

With this registered route in place, you can map a URI to any controller you want. For example, we'll implement a `ShipmentTypesController` later in this chapter and the request will go through this route to get to that controller; for example, through a GET request against `/api/shipmenttypes`. Notice also that the key parameter's default value is set as `RouteParameter.Optional`, which indicates this parameter is optional.

Also, a constraint has been set for the key parameter in order to only allow values that can be parsed as `Guid`. The implementation of the `GuidRouteConstraint` is shown in Listing 6-2.

Listing 6-2. The GuidRouteConstraint Implementation

```
public class GuidRouteConstraint : IHttpRouteConstraint {

    private const string _format = "D";

    public bool Match(
        HttpRequestMessage request,
        IHttpRoute route,
        string parameterName,
        IDictionary<string, object> values,
        HttpRouteDirection routeDirection) {

        if (values[parameterName] != RouteParameter.Optional) {

            object value;
            values.TryGetValue(parameterName, out value);
            string input = Convert.ToString(
                value, CultureInfo.InvariantCulture);

            Guid guidValue;
            return Guid.TryParseExact(
                input, _format, out guidValue);
        }

        return true;
    }
}
```

The `GuidRouteConstraint` looks at its associated value and determines if it is in the desired `Guid` format. Chapter 8 will cover route constraints more in depth, so we won't go into details here.

Initial Configuration

You'll configure the API application through the `WebAPIConfig`, which was created inside the `PingYourPackage.API` project in Chapter 5. You haven't started developing the Web API application yet, but there are a few configuration changes that need to be done for the API up front.

The `WebAPIConfig` has only one method, named `Configure`, and this method accepts one parameter, which is a type of `HttpConfiguration`. The configuration was separated by putting it inside another class for the same reason this was done for the `RouteConfig` class.

The initial look of the `Configure` method is shown in Listing 6-3.

Listing 6-3. Static Configure Method of the WebAPIConfig Class

```
public class WebAPIConfig {

    public static void Configure(HttpConfiguration config) {

        //Formatters
        var jqueryFormatter = config.Formatters.FirstOrDefault(
            x => x.GetType() ==
                typeof(JQueryMvcFormUrlEncodedFormatter));

        config.Formatters.Remove(
            config.Formatters.FormUrlEncodedFormatter);

        config.Formatters.Remove(jqueryFormatter);

        foreach (var formatter in config.Formatters) {

            formatter.RequiredMemberSelector =
                new SuppressedRequiredMemberSelector();
        }

        //Default Services
        config.Services.Replace(
            typeof(IContentNegotiator),
            new DefaultContentNegotiator(
                excludeMatchOnTypeOnly: true));

        config.Services.RemoveAll(
            typeof(ModelValidatorProvider),
            validator => !(validator
                is DataAnnotationsModelValidatorProvider));
    }
}
```

First, we removed the unnecessary formatters that won't be needed: JQueryMvcFormUrlEncodedFormatter and FormUrlEncodedFormatter, which only have reading ability for the application/x-www-form-urlencoded media type.

Second, we replaced the default implementation of the IContentNegotiator service. By default, the DefaultContentNegotiator class is registered as a content negotiator, but its ExcludeMatchOnTypeOnly property is set to false. If the ExcludeMatchOnTypeOnly property of the DefaultContentNegotiator is set to false, it will find the best possible media type match and negotiate on it. For example, if there is no support for application/xml media type but only for application/json and a request accepts responses in XML format, the negotiator will send back the response as application/json format. This may be the desired functionality for your application, but we decided to be strict with our API and set the ExcludeMatchOnTypeOnly property of the DefaultContentNegotiator to true. If ExcludeMatchOnTypeOnly is set to true, then it doesn't match on type only. This means that the Negotiate method of the DefaultContentNegotiator will return null if it can't match anything in the request. This is useful for generating 406 (Not Acceptable) status codes if there is no media type match, and this is the exact behavior desired here.

The RequiredMemberSelector properties of all the formatters have been set, and you will have to do your own implementation to prevent generating duplicate error messages for required members, as explained in Chapter 13 in detail. The IRequiredMemberSelector implementation is shown in Listing 6-4.

Listing 6-4. The SuppressedRequiredMemberSelector Class

```
public class SuppressedRequiredMemberSelector
    : IRequiredMemberSelector {

    public bool IsRequiredMember(MemberInfo member) {

        return false;
    }
}
```

Finally, we removed every validation provider except for the `DataAnnotationsModelValidatorProvider` because only Data Annotations validation functionality is needed. You can check Chapter 13 for more information about validation providers.

A few parts the application have been configured, but later you'll tweak the `Configure` method of the `WebAPIConfig` class.

Registering Dependencies

In Chapter 5, you created a class named `AutofacWebAPI` inside the `PingYourPackage.API` application. Inside this class, you also set up the infrastructure to register dependencies for this application through the Autofac IoC container.

The `RegisterServices` private method is the place to register the dependencies, and there are three kinds of dependency you need to be concerned with for now (see Listing 6-5).

Listing 6-5. The RegisterServices Method of the AutofacWebAPI Class

```
public class AutofacWebAPI {

    // Lines removed for brevity

    private static IContainer RegisterServices(
        ContainerBuilder builder) {

        builder.RegisterAssemblyTypes(
            Assembly.GetExecutingAssembly())
            .PropertiesAutowired();

        //EF DbContext

        //Repositories

        //Services

        return builder.Build();
    }
}
```

As you can see in Listing 6-5, the repositories and the services will be registered through the IoC container. You'll register the DbContext instance through the IoC container, too. Let's register our DbContext instance, the EntitiesContext class, first and explain the benefits of doing this (see Listing 6-6).

Listing 6-6. Registering the DbContext Instance Through the IoC Container

```
private static IContainer RegisterServices(
    ContainerBuilder builder) {

    // Lines removed for brevity

    //EF DbContext
    builder.RegisterType<EntitiesContext>()
        .As<DbContext>().InstancePerApiRequest();

    // Lines removed for brevity
}
```

The Autofac ASP.NET Web API integration package has support for instance per-request dependency registration. By registering the EntitiesContext instance through the IoC container, as shown in Listing 6-6, you will be able to use only one instance of DbContext per request. Autofac also will inject the registered DbContext instance through the only constructor of our repositories.

As you learned in Chapter 5, there is only one repository implementation, which is the generic EntityRepository class. You can register a separate EntityRepository instance through the IoC container for every entity class there is. The code for registering the repositories is nearly the same as for the DbContext with a different method for registering generic methods (see Listing 6-7).

Listing 6-7. Registering the Repositories Through the IoC Container

```
private static IContainer RegisterServices(
    ContainerBuilder builder) {

    // Lines removed for brevity

    // Register repositories by using Autofac's OpenGenerics feature
    // More info: http://code.google.com/p/autofac/wiki/OpenGenerics
    builder.RegisterGeneric(typeof(EntityRepository<>))
        .As(typeof(IEntityRepository<>))
        .InstancePerApiRequest();

    // Lines removed for brevity
}
```

Notice that we didn't indicate anything about the constructor of the EntityRepository and which DbContext type it should be injected into. The Autofac ContainerBuilder has a registration for a DbContext instance and it will use that instance to construct the repositories. If you need to use more than one type of repository for a request, only one instance of DbContext will be used to create repositories, which is a desirable approach here.

Lastly, there are two services that were created in Chapter 5 to register through the IoC container: the MembershipService and the CryptoService. The CryptoService has only a parameterless constructor, but the MembershipService class has a constructor that accepts a few repositories and the ICryptoService implementation (see Listing 6-8).

Listing 6-8. The MembershipService Constructor

```
public class MembershipService : IMembershipService {

    private readonly IEntityRepository<User> _userRepository;
    private readonly IEntityRepository<Role> _roleRepository;
    private readonly IEntityRepository<UserInRole>
        _userInRoleRepository;
    private readonly ICryptoService _cryptoService;

    public MembershipService(
        IEntityRepository<User> userRepository,
        IEntityRepository<Role> roleRepository,
        IEntityRepository<UserInRole> userInRoleRepository,
        ICryptoService cryptoService) {

        _userRepository = userRepository;
        _roleRepository = roleRepository;
        _userInRoleRepository = userInRoleRepository;
        _cryptoService = cryptoService;

    }

    // Lines removed for brevity
}
```

Let's register the services (see Listing 6-9) and then explain what would happen when the IMembershipService implementation is requested from the IoC container.

Listing 6-9. Registering the Services Through the IoC Container

```
private static IContainer RegisterServices(
    ContainerBuilder builder) {

    // Lines removed for brevity

    // Services
    builder.RegisterType<CryptoService>()
        .As<ICryptoService>()
        .InstancePerApiRequest();

    builder.RegisterType<MembershipService>()
        .As<IMembershipService>()
        .InstancePerApiRequest();

    builder.RegisterType<ShipmentService>()
        .As<IShipmentService>()
        .InstancePerApiRequest();

    // Lines removed for brevity
}
```

Now when you request an IMembershipService implementation from the IoC container, it will first resolve the constructor parameters. Each repository also has a constructor that accepts a DbContext implementation. Because the DbContext was registered through the IoC container, the container will pull that down and construct the required repositories. Finally, the container will use the constructed repositories and the crypto service to construct the MembershipService class.

■ **Tip**   If you register a type through the Autofac IoC container and that type has multiple constructors, you can always use the UsingConstructor extension method for the IRegistrationBuilder instance (the As<TService> method returns an IRegistrationBuilder instance and you can use the UsingConstructor extension method on that). The UsingConstructor method has two overloads. One of them allows you to specify the signature of the constructor by indicating the types of the parameters in order. The other accepts an IConstructorSelector instance, which allows you to specify the policy to be used when selecting a constructor.

Implementing the Security

Before moving forward and implementing the controllers of the Web API application, let's set up the security fundamentals to have the following authentication and authorization requirements for the Web API application:

- Force the client to communicate over HTTPS
- Implement Basic Authentication through a message handler
- Implement the authorization for the resources

This section will complete the first two items of this list, and you'll apply authorization to the resources (in a case of an ASP.NET Web API application, the resources are the controller actions) later.

First, you'll simply separate the authentication and authorization by delegating them to different components of the framework.

Implementing the Message Handler for Forcing HTTPS

In order to force the communication over HTTPS, you need to intercept the request on its way in and check whether it is being communicated over HTTPS. A message handler is the best place to perform such actions. So, let's create the RequireHttpsMessageHandler, as shown in Listing 6-10.

Listing 6-10. The RequireHttpsMessageHandler Implementation

```
public class RequireHttpsMessageHandler : DelegatingHandler {

    protected override Task<HttpResponseMessage> SendAsync(
        HttpRequestMessage request,
        CancellationToken cancellationToken) {

        if (request.RequestUri.Scheme != Uri.UriSchemeHttps) {

            HttpResponseMessage forbiddenResponse =
                request.CreateResponse(HttpStatusCode.Forbidden);

            forbiddenResponse.ReasonPhrase = "SSL Required";
            return Task.FromResult<HttpResponseMessage>(
                forbiddenResponse);
        }

        return base.SendAsync(request, cancellationToken);
    }
}
```

Here, if the request is communicated over HTTPS, no further action is required, and it is simply executed by the inner handler by calling the SendAsync method of the base class. As you'll see in Chapter 10, the Web API framework infrastructure will create the so-called Russian doll effect by chaining the message handlers together. So, calling the SendAsync method of the base DelegatingHandler class will allow us to invoke the next message handler inside the pipeline. This basically means "Keep going!" for the Web API pipeline.

If the communication is not over HTTPS, the request will terminate immediately and stop processing further. This is achieved by retuning a new Task<HttpResponseMessage> object instead of calling the SendAsync method of the base class. The response message indicates that the request is forbidden and the reason is included as a reason phrase. Also, as you learned in Chapter 2, you use the FromResult<T> method of the Task class to return a precompleted Task object instead of spinning up another thread unnecessarily just to return the HttpResponseMessage instance.

Finally, you'll register this message handler as the first handler inside the static WebAPIConfig.Configure method because you want this message handler to see the request first before other handlers (see Listing 6-11).

Listing 6-11. Registering the RequireHttpsMessageHandler

```
public class WebAPIConfig {

    public static void Configure(HttpConfiguration config) {

        // Message Handlers
        config.MessageHandlers.Add(
            new RequireHttpsMessageHandler());

        // Lines removed for brevity
    }
}
```

Testing the RequireHttpsMessageHandler

You have created the RequireHttpsMessageHandler and now you'll write some unit tests to see its behaviors. It is trivial to write unit tests against the RequireHttpsMessageHandler because it contains a simple logic, but this will give you a solid idea on how to write tests against the message handlers. You'll put these tests under the PingYourPackage.API.Test project and run them using the xUnit.net Runner for Visual Studio 2012.

Before creating the test methods, you'll create a fairly simple helper class, which will allow you to invoke a message handler independently (see Listing 6-12).

Listing 6-12. The Static DelegatingHandlerExtensions Class

```
internal static class DelegatingHandlerExtensions {

    internal static Task<HttpResponseMessage> InvokeAsync(
        this DelegatingHandler handler,
        HttpRequestMessage request,
        CancellationToken cancellationToken =
            default(CancellationToken)) {

        handler.InnerHandler = new DummyHandler();
        var invoker = new HttpMessageInvoker(handler);
        return invoker.SendAsync(request, cancellationToken);
    }

    private class DummyHandler : HttpMessageHandler {

        protected override Task<HttpResponseMessage> SendAsync(
            HttpRequestMessage request,
            CancellationToken cancellationToken) {

            var response =
                new HttpResponseMessage(HttpStatusCode.OK);

            return Task.FromResult(response);
        }
    }
}
```

The InvokeAsync extension method for DelegatingHandler type will allow you to invoke a DelegatingHandler without any problems. Because you have set a dummy HttpMessageHandler as the inner handler of the DelegatingHandler, it will not throw any exceptions if the DelegatingHandler implementation calls the base.SendAsync method, which requires an inner handler to be attached.

There are two test methods for RequireHttpsMessageHandler. One of them will test the behavior that is performed when the request is made over HTTP and the other will test the reverse behavior (see Listing 6-13).

Listing 6-13. The RequireHttpsMessageHandlerTest Class

```
public class RequireHttpsMessageHandlerTest {

    [Fact]
    public async Task Returns_Forbidden_If_Request_Is_Not_Over_HTTPS() {

        // Arange
        var request = new HttpRequestMessage(
            HttpMethod.Get, "http://localhost:8080");

        var requireHtttpsMessageHandler =
            new RequireHttpsMessageHandler();

        // Act
        var response = await
            requireHtttpsMessageHandler.InvokeAsync(request);

        // Assert
        Assert.Equal(
            HttpStatusCode.Forbidden,
            response.StatusCode);
    }

    [Fact]
    public async Task Returns_Delegated_StatusCode_When_Request_Is_Over_HTTPS() {

        // Arange
        var request = new HttpRequestMessage(
            HttpMethod.Get, "https://localhost:8080");

        var requireHtttpsMessageHandler =
            new RequireHttpsMessageHandler();

        // Act
        var response = await
            requireHtttpsMessageHandler.InvokeAsync(request);

        // Assert
        Assert.Equal(
            HttpStatusCode.OK,
            response.StatusCode);
    }
}
```

The xUnit can handle Task returning methods as well. So, here you'll make use of C# 5.0 language features inside the unit test methods, too. There are a few ways to run these tests. You can navigate to Test ➤ Windows ➤ Test Explorer from the main Visual Studio menu and bring up the Text Explorer window (see Figure 6-2). Then you can select the test you would like to run.

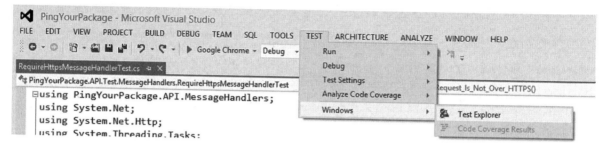

Figure 6-2. *Bringing up the Test Explorer window*

The other way to run tests is to right-click inside the test class and click Run Tests, as shown in Figure 6-3.

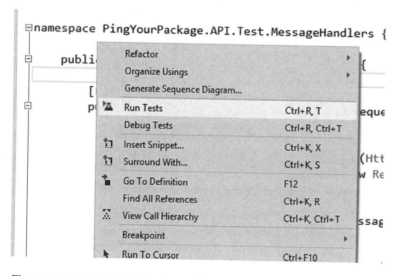

Figure 6-3. *Right-click inside the test class and click Run Tests to run all the tests inside that class*

When you run these tests, you should see them passed inside the Test Explorer (see Figure 6-4).

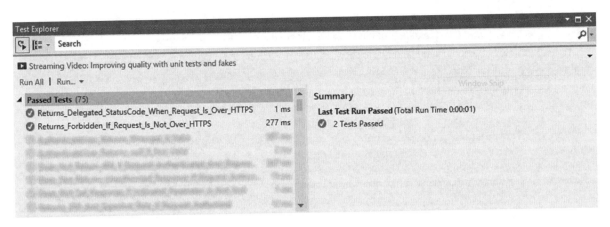

Figure 6-4. *Test Explorer shows the status of the tests after they were run*

This was a simple message handler and, thus, the tests were simple. You'll create one more message handler, but we won't go through creating tests against that in this chapter because it is fairly similar. You will find those tests under the PingYourPackage.API.Test project.

Implementing the Message Handler for Basic Authentication

For this application, you'll authenticate requests with basic authentication, which you'll implement through a message handler. This may not be the best option for your own application, but this will give you an idea about the authentication and authorization separation inside an ASP.NET Web API project.

Before you start implementing the basic authentication message handler, you must install a NuGet package for an open source library named WebAPIDoodle (see Figure 6-5). The WebAPIDoodle is an ASP.NET Web API extension library that contains several useful components such as filters, message handlers, and so forth, and you'll use a few of them for this application.

```
Package Manager Console
Package source: NuGet official package source ▾  ⚙  Default project: PingYourPackage.API                ▾  🔳 ■
PM> Install-Package WebAPIDoodle
Attempting to resolve dependency 'WebAPIDoodle.Meta (≥ 1.2.3)'.
Attempting to resolve dependency 'WebAPIDoodle.Formatting (≥ 1.2.3)'.
Attempting to resolve dependency 'WebAPIDoodle.Http (≥ 1.2.3)'.
Attempting to resolve dependency 'Microsoft.Net.Http (≥ 2.0.20710.0)'.
Attempting to resolve dependency 'Microsoft.AspNet.WebApi.Client (≥ 4.0.20505.0)'.
Attempting to resolve dependency 'Newtonsoft.Json (≥ 4.5.6)'.
Attempting to resolve dependency 'Microsoft.AspNet.WebApi.Core (≥ 4.0.20710.0)'.
Successfully installed 'WebAPIDoodle.Meta 1.2.3'.
Successfully installed 'WebAPIDoodle.Http 1.2.3'.
Successfully installed 'WebAPIDoodle.Formatting 1.2.3'.
Successfully installed 'WebAPIDoodle 1.2.3'.
Successfully added 'WebAPIDoodle.Meta 1.2.3' to PingYourPackage.API.
Successfully added 'WebAPIDoodle.Http 1.2.3' to PingYourPackage.API.
Successfully added 'WebAPIDoodle.Formatting 1.2.3' to PingYourPackage.API.
Successfully added 'WebAPIDoodle 1.2.3' to PingYourPackage.API.

PM>
100 % ▾ ◀
```

Figure 6-5. *Installing WebAPIDoodle NuGet package*

The WebAPIDoodle contains an abstract message handler called BasicAuthenticationHandler and you can use this as the base class for our handler. By using this abstract class, you'll get all the standard operations out of the box, such as extracting the username and password from the WWW-Authenticate header and decoding the password.

■ **Note** This chapter won't go into details of how you can create the base `BasicAuthenticationHandler`. Also, we don't recommend the use of Basic authentication for every application. Security is a tough topic and should be considered carefully for your specific type of scenario. Apress has a book by Badrinarayanan Lakshmiraghavan, called *Pro ASP.NET Web API Security*, which covers this topic in considerable detail (Apress, 2013).

Here you'll create a message handler named PingYourPackageAuthHandler based on the BasicAuthenticationHandler, as shown in Listing 6-14.

Listing 6-14. The PingYourPackageAuthHandler Implementation

```
public class PingYourPackageAuthHandler :
    BasicAuthenticationHandler {

    protected override Task<IPrincipal> AuthenticateUserAsync(
        HttpRequestMessage request,
        string username,
        string password,
        CancellationToken cancellationToken) {

        var membershipService = request.GetMembershipService();

        var validUserCtx = membershipService
            .ValidateUser(username, password);

        return Task.FromResult(validUserCtx.Principal);
    }
}

internal static class HttpRequestMessageExtensions {

    internal static IMembershipService GetMembershipService(
        this HttpRequestMessage request) {

        return request.GetService<IMembershipService>();
    }

    private static TService GetService<TService>(
        this HttpRequestMessage request) {

        IDependencyScope dependencyScope =
            request.GetDependencyScope();

        TService service =
            (TService)dependencyScope
            .GetService(typeof(TService));

        return service;
    }
}
```

The `BasicAuthenticationHandler` will invoke the `AuthenticateUserAsync` method if the basic authentication credentials are sent in a correct format. Inside the `AuthenticateUserAsync` method, it is supposed to return back an `Task<IPrincipal>` instance if the user is authenticated. As you can see, you delegate that work to the `IMembershipService` implementation, which was obtained through the dependency resolver and returns the result as a precompleted `Task` object.

If the request is not authenticated, the `ValidateUser` method of `IMembershipService` implementation returns null, which is what is desired here. The default behavior when the request is not authenticated is that the `BasicAuthenticationHandler` terminates the request and sends back the unauthorized response with the WWW-Authenticate header. This is a fine approach for your needs here because you won't allow any unauthenticated requests at all, but depending on your situation, you may want to override the `HandleUnauthenticatedRequest` method of the `BasicAuthenticationHandler` to handle the unauthenticated requests with your own behavior.

However, if the request is successfully authenticated, an `IPrincipal` implementation is returned from the `ValidateUser` method of `IMembershipService` implementation. The `BasicAuthenticationHandler` uses this object to set the current authenticated user.

■ **Note** It is obvious that you don't perform any kind of authorization here. You'll perform authorization at the controller level, as each controller has its own authorization requirements. We'll discuss this in the upcoming section.

Lastly, you'll register this handler as the second handler inside the pipeline (see Listing 6-15).

Listing 6-15. Registering the PingYourPackageAuthHandler

```
public class WebAPIConfig {

    public static void Configure(HttpConfiguration config) {

        // Message Handlers
        config.MessageHandlers.Add(
            new RequireHttpsMessageHandler());

        config.MessageHandlers.Add(
            new PingYourPackageAuthHandler());

        // Lines removed for brevity
    }
}
```

If the HTTPS requirements that have been established with `RequireHttpsMessageHandler` are fulfilled by the request, the `PingYourPackageAuthHandler` will be invoked. At that point, if the request is successfully authenticated, the request will go up one level inside the pipeline and the associated dispatcher will take over from there, which we'll talk about in the "Per-Route Message Handler for AffiliateShipmentsController" section.

AuthorizeAttribute

Web API framework has a concept of filters that allows you to execute a piece of code to take action at different levels of the controller pipeline. Chapter 11 goes through filters in depth and you'll leverage filters with the sample application, too.

155

There are three types of filters, one of which is the authorization filter, and the framework provides a default implementation for this filter type—AuthorizeAttribute—which you'll use to authorize the requests. The AuthorizeAttribute checks against the System.Threading.Thread.CurrentPrincipal to see whether the user associated with the current request is authenticated. You can also pass usernames and roles through the AuthorizeAttribute properties to authorize against those.

You haven't implemented the controllers yet, but you'll have a controller named AffiliatesController, which only users in admin and employee roles can have access to. You'll apply the AuthorizeAttribute to the AffiliatesController and apply the necessary authorization to each controller, as shown in Listing 6-16.

Listing 6-16. The AffiliatesController with AuthorizeAttribute

```
[Authorize(Roles = "Admin,Employee")]
public class AffiliatesController : ApiController {

    // Lines removed for brevity
}
```

Implementing Controllers

You might think of controllers inside an ASP.NET Web API application as converters for our business data. A controller will consist of actions, and each action should be tiny and shouldn't perform too many operations. For example, a controller action can perform the necessary operation through another layer based on the input it received. Then, it can convert the output of that operation into a data transfer object and return it back. Chapter 9 is specifically dedicated to controllers and actions. So, we won't dive deep into their behavior here. Instead, you'll see how you'll structure them to meet the needs of our application, as described in Chapter 5.

To be able to employ the requirements explained in Chapter 5, you'll have seven different controllers, as shown in Figure 6-6.

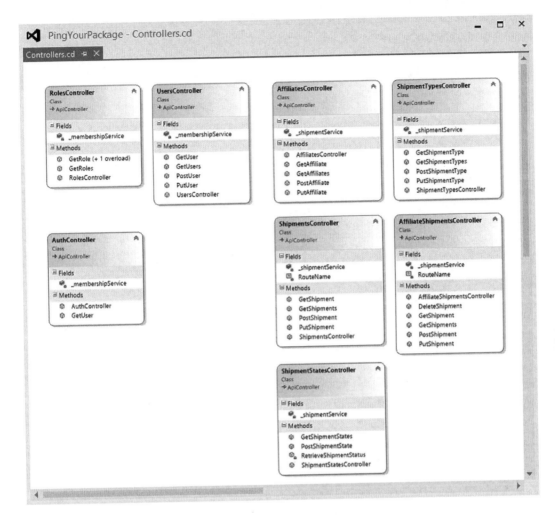

Figure 6-6. `PingYourPackage.API` *project's controller structure*

In general, we took a hierarchical approach for our API design and tried to reflect that structure to the controllers. For example, all shipment records can be retrieved by an admin or employee by sending an HTTP GET request against /api/shipments. Besides that, each affiliate needs to view their shipment records. We could have designed our API so that an affiliate would retrieve its shipment records by sending an HTTP GET request against /api/shipments?affiliateKey={key}. Although there is nothing wrong with this approach, it doesn't look good hierarchically.

As an alternative approach to this, an affiliate can send an HTTP GET request against /api/affiliates/ {affiliateKey}/shipments to retrieve the associated shipment records. In order to retrieve the single shipment record, an affiliate needs to send an HTTP GET request against /api/affiliates/{affiliateKey}/shipments/ {shipmentKey}.

To be able to cleanly handle the above scenarios, there are two controllers to serve shipment records: ShipmentsController and AffiliateShipmentsController. By separating these into two controllers, you'll cleanly handle the authorization, record ownership and record existence, as you'll see in upcoming sections.

This chapter won't go through all the controllers to show how they were implemented because they are fairly similar. Instead, we have picked ShipmentsController and AffiliateShipmentsController as case examples. These two controllers have different structures. So, we'll be describing a new approach with each one.

Before moving further, let's create another project named `PingYourPackage.API.Model` to hold the data transfer objects (DTOs), input validation logic, request commands, and request models. The next section will explain why another project is needed for these.

PingYourPackage.API.Model Project

In Chapter 5, you created the domain model and domain entities. Those entity classes will represent our data, but we don't want to send everything through the wire by our HTTP API. In order to represent the data that will be sent through the API, you will create DTOs. Besides DTO classes, there will be request commands and request models. Those classes will represent the data and metadata that our API is going to receive as input.

These type of objects are the ones that both our HTTP API application and the .NET client of that HTTP API (this could also be called the .NET wrapper of the HTTP API) need. You don't want to repeat yourself by creating these objects twice. So, you'll put those in a separate project and have a reference to that project from the `PingYourPackage.API` project and the `PingYourPackage.API.Client` project, which we'll explain in Chapter 7.

When you open the complete solution, you should see the `PingYourPackage.API.Model` project structure, as shown in Figure 6-7.

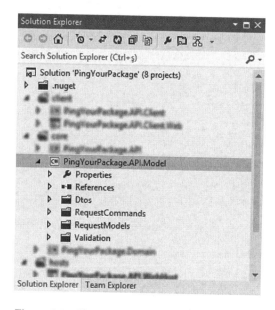

Figure 6-7. `PingYourPackage.API.Model` *project structure*

Data Transfer Objects

DTO classes are the .NET POCO (Plain Old CLR Object) entities that will represent our outbound data. Any DTO class under our model project should either implement the `IDto` (see Listing 6-17) or `IPaginatedDto` (see Listing 6-18) interface.

Listing 6-17. IDto Interface

```
public interface IDto {

    Guid Key { get; set; }
}
```

Listing 6-18. IPaginatedDto Interface

```
public interface IPaginatedDto<out TDto> where TDto : IDto {

    int PageIndex { get; set; }
    int PageSize { get; set; }
    int TotalCount { get; set; }
    int TotalPageCount { get; set; }

    bool HasNextPage { get; set; }
    bool HasPreviousPage { get; set; }

    IEnumerable<TDto> Items { get; }
}
```

The IDto interface contains only one property and is fairly simple, whereas the IPaginatedDto interface has a few properties to represent paginated data.

You'll only have one implementation of the IPaginatedDto interface, as shown in Listing 6-19.

Listing 6-19. The PaginatedDto Class

```
public class PaginatedDto<TDto> :
    IPaginatedDto<TDto> where TDto : IDto {

    public int PageIndex { get; set; }
    public int PageSize { get; set; }
    public int TotalCount { get; set; }
    public int TotalPageCount { get; set; }

    public bool HasNextPage { get; set; }
    public bool HasPreviousPage { get; set; }

    public IEnumerable<TDto> Items { get; set; }
}
```

You'll be able to cleanly represent the paginated data using this PaginatedDto<TDto> generic class. You'll also create the individual DTO classes by implementing the IDto interface. Listing 6-20 shows the ShipmentDto class implementation as a sample.

Listing 6-20. The ShipmentDto Class

```
public class ShipmentDto : IDto {

    public Guid Key { get; set; }
    public Guid AffiliateKey { get; set; }

    public decimal Price { get; set; }
    public string ReceiverName { get; set; }
    public string ReceiverSurname { get; set; }
    public string ReceiverAddress { get; set; }
    public string ReceiverZipCode { get; set; }
    public string ReceiverCity { get; set; }
    public string ReceiverCountry { get; set; }
```

```
    public string ReceiverTelephone { get; set; }
    public string ReceiverEmail { get; set; }
    public DateTime CreatedOn { get; set; }

    public ShipmentTypeDto ShipmentType { get; set; }
    public IEnumerable<ShipmentStateDto>
        ShipmentStates { get; set; }
}
```

The ShipmentDto class has a property named ShipmentStates, which represents a collection of ShipmentStateDto, which is another DTO class (see Listing 6-21).

Listing 6-21. The ShipmentStateDto Class

```
public class ShipmentStateDto : IDto {

    public Guid Key { get; set; }
    public Guid ShipmentKey { get; set; }
    public string ShipmentStatus { get; set; }
    public DateTime CreatedOn { get; set; }
}
```

We don't cover all DTO classes here. You can always check them from the project. They are all similar to the ShipmentDto class.

Request Commands

Request commands are .NET classes that will represent the data obtained from the request URI. You could use separate simple-type objects to represent URI data, but with request commands, you can employ desired input validation.

Each request command class needs to implement the IRequestCommand interface, as shown in Listing 6-22.

Listing 6-22. The IRequestCommand Interface

```
public interface IRequestCommand {

}
```

This is an empty interface, but you'll use this interface as a reference while registering the parameter binding rule for request commands.

For this application, you only need one request command class to represent the pagination information. The PaginatedRequestCommand class is shown in Listing 6-23.

Listing 6-23. The PaginatedRequestCommand Class

```
public class PaginatedRequestCommand : IRequestCommand {

    [Minimum(1)]
    public int Page { get; set; }

    [Minimum(1)]
    [Maximum(50)]
    public int Take { get; set; }
}
```

As you can see, there are some validation attributes associated with each property. The `MinimumAttribute` and `MaximumAttribute` are not validation attributes provided by the .NET Framework itself. We have implemented these custom validation attributes, which we'll explain later in this chapter.

By default, ASP.NET Web API isn't going to bind URI data to complex type action parameters (see Chapter 9 for more information), but you can apply the `FromUriAttribute` to complex type parameters where you want them to be bound from the URI. This attribute is provided by the framework and gives the parameter binding layer a hint about where to get the data from (request body, from URI parts, etc.). You can also register global parameter binding rules, and we'll follow this approach for our request commands (see Listing 6-24).

Listing 6-24. Registering the Paramater Binding Rule for IRequestCommand

```
public class WebAPIConfig {

    public static void Configure(HttpConfiguration config) {

        // Lines removed for brevity

        config.ParameterBindingRules.Insert(0,
            descriptor => typeof(IRequestCommand)
                        .IsAssignableFrom(
                            descriptor.ParameterType)
                    ? new FromUriAttribute()
                        .GetBinding(descriptor) : null);

        // Lines removed for brevity

    }
}
```

With this configuration code, you can now get the request command object through the action method as a parameter without any additional configuration.

■ **Note**   Complex type action parameters that are bound from the URI may cause action selection problems if you have multiple action methods that accept these types of parameters inside one controller. This depends on the case you have. However, the `WebAPIDoodle` NuGet package contains a custom action selector that can be used to support complex types for action selection. You will find more information about this from www.tugberkugurlu.com/archive/complex-type-action-parameters-with-complextypeawareactionselector-in-asp-net-web-api-part-1 and www.tugberkugurlu.com/archive/complex-type-action-parameters-with-complextypeawareactionselector-in-asp-net-web-api-part-2.

Request Models

Request models will represent the message body of the HTTP request, which our controller action receives as an object. In our application, HTTP POST and PUT requests will contain a message body, and this input should also be validated. We'll discuss validation in the next section. Listing 6-25 shows a sample request model class: `ShipmentRequestModel`.

Listing 6-25. The ShipmentRequestModel Class

```
public class ShipmentRequestModel : ShipmentBaseRequestModel {

    [Required]
    public Guid? AffiliateKey { get; set; }

    [Required]
    public Guid? ShipmentTypeKey { get; set; }
}
```

Notice that the ShipmentRequestModel class inherits from the ShipmentBaseRequestModel class. The ShipmentBaseRequestModel class holds the properties that are needed on both POST and PUT requests (see Listing 6-26).

Listing 6-26. The ShipmentBaseRequestModel Class

```
public abstract class ShipmentBaseRequestModel {

    [Required]
    public decimal? Price { get; set; }

    [Required]
    [StringLength(50)]
    public string ReceiverName { get; set; }

    [Required]
    [StringLength(50)]
    public string ReceiverSurname { get; set; }

    [Required]
    [StringLength(50)]
    public string ReceiverAddress { get; set; }

    [Required]
    [StringLength(50)]
    public string ReceiverZipCode { get; set; }

    [Required]
    [StringLength(50)]
    public string ReceiverCity { get; set; }

    [Required]
    [StringLength(50)]
    public string ReceiverCountry { get; set; }

    [Required]
    [StringLength(50)]
    public string ReceiverTelephone { get; set; }

    [Required]
    [EmailAddress]
    [StringLength(320)]
    public string ReceiverEmail { get; set; }
}
```

Listing 6-27 also shows the ShipmentUpdateRequestModel class, which inherits from the ShipmentBaseRequestModel class and doesn't have any other properties.

Listing 6-27. The ShipmentUpdateRequestModel Class

```
public class ShipmentUpdateRequestModel
    : ShipmentBaseRequestModel {

}
```

When you start building your controllers, use of the request model classes will become clearer.

Validation

ASP.NET Web API has a built-in validation mechanism, and Chapter 13 explains this topic in depth. Briefly, you can annotate the properties of the request model class with the desired validation attributes, and you can detect their validation state at certain points such as before the action method is executed.

The .NET Framework provides some useful validation attributes out of the box, which are explained in Chapter 13. However, you can create your custom validation attributes, too. For example, our PaginatedRequestCommand class, seen earlier in Listing 6-23, uses two custom validation attributes to restrict the page size per request: MinimumAttribute and MaximumAttribute. The implementation of the MinimumAttribute is shown in Listing 6-28.

Listing 6-28. The MinimumAttribute Class

```
[AttributeUsage(AttributeTargets.Property, AllowMultiple = false)]
public class MinimumAttribute : ValidationAttribute {

    private readonly int _minimumValue;

    public MinimumAttribute(int minimum) :
        base(errorMessage: "The {0} field value must be minimum {1}.") {

        _minimumValue = minimum;
    }

    public override string FormatErrorMessage(string name) {

        return string.Format(
            CultureInfo.CurrentCulture,
            base.ErrorMessageString,
            name,
            _minimumValue);
    }

    public override bool IsValid(object value) {

        int intValue;
        if (value != null && int.TryParse(value.ToString(),
            out intValue)) {
```

```
            return (intValue >= _minimumValue);
        }

        return false;
    }
}
```

■ **Note**   You need to add the framework reference of `System.ComponentModel.DataAnnotations` for the `PingYourPackage.API.Model` project in order to get access to .NET Framework's data annotations infrastructure.

Each validation attribute needs to inherit from the `ValidationAttribute` class, which is under the `System.ComponentModel.DataAnnotations` namespace. You have also overridden the `IsValid` method of the `ValidationAttribute` inside the `MinimumAttribute` class to check the validity of the value. The `MaximumAttribute` attribute has the reverse functionality of the `MinimumAttribute` and nearly the same implementation (see Listing 6-29).

Listing 6-29. The MaximumAttribute Class

```
[AttributeUsage(AttributeTargets.Property, AllowMultiple = false)]
public class MaximumAttribute : ValidationAttribute {

    private readonly int _maximumValue;

    public MaximumAttribute(int maximum) :
        base(errorMessage: "The {0} field value must be maximum {1}.") {

        _maximumValue = maximum;
    }

    public override string FormatErrorMessage(string name) {

        return string.Format(
            CultureInfo.CurrentCulture,
            base.ErrorMessageString,
            name,
            _maximumValue);
    }

    public override bool IsValid(object value) {

        int intValue;
        if (value != null && int.TryParse(value.ToString(),
            out intValue)) {

            return (intValue <= _maximumValue);
        }

        return false;
    }
}
```

As indicated earlier, ASP.NET Web API has a built-in mechanism to check against validation attributes after the parameter binding process and provides the result of that action through a `ModelStateDictionary` instance. You can inspect this object instance through an action filter before the controller action is executed and returns the *400 Bad Request* HTTP response. The `WebAPIDoodle` NuGet package provides a built-in action filter for this functionality: `InvalidModelStateFilterAttribute`. You'll register this action filter globally through the `WebAPIConfig.Configure` method under the `PingYourPackage.API` project, as shown in Listing 6-30.

Listing 6-30. Globally Registering the InvalidModelStateFilterAttribute

```
public class WebAPIConfig {

    public static void Configure(HttpConfiguration config) {

        // Lines removed for brevity

        // Filters
        config.Filters.Add(
            new InvalidModelStateFilterAttribute());

        // Lines removed for brevity
    }
}
```

We have explained each piece of the `API.Model` project, so we can now move on to implement the controllers. However, this is not the complete view of the `API.Model` project. We didn't go through every class inside the project for brevity. You can see the complete view of the project inside this sample application's source code.

Implementing the ShipmentsController

The `ShipmentsController` is responsible for retrieving, updating, and inserting new shipment records. However, you only want to allow users under the admin or employee role to have access to this controller. So, you will applied the `AuthorizeAttribute`, as shown in Listing 6-31.

Listing 6-31. The ShipmentsController with the AuthorizeAttribute

```
[Authorize(Roles = "Admin,Employee")]
public class ShipmentsController : ApiController {

    // Lines removed for brevity
}
```

The shipment controller will interact with the `IShipmentService` implementation. Because our dependency resolver has been registered, you can now just pass the `IShipmentService` as a constructor parameter through the controller's constructor (see Listing 6-32).

Listing 6-32. Passing the IShipmentService Implementtaion as a Constructor Parameter

```
[Authorize(Roles = "Admin,Employee")]
public class ShipmentsController : ApiController {

    private readonly IShipmentService _shipmentService;
```

165

```
    public ShipmentsController(IShipmentService shipmentService) {

        _shipmentService = shipmentService;
    }

    // Lines removed for brevity
}
```

Now our controller is ready to implement the action methods.

Creating the First Action Method

With this controller, you'll allow four simple operations through the following URIs:

```
GET /api/shipments

GET /api/shipments/{key}

POST /api/shipments

PUT /api/shipments/{key}
```

First, let's implement the GetShipments action method, which will return the shipment records within the specific range (see Listing 6-33).

Listing 6-33. GetShipments Action Method of the ShipmentsController

```
public PaginatedDto<ShipmentDto>
    GetShipments(PaginatedRequestCommand cmd) {

    var shipments = _shipmentService
        .GetShipments(cmd.Page, cmd.Take);

    return shipments.ToPaginatedDto(
        shipments.Select(sh => sh.ToShipmentDto()));
}
```

One of our aims was to keep the controller actions as few as possible, and by separating the concerns, this was achieved through the GetShipments action method. The GetShipments action accepts a parameter that is of type PaginatedRequestCommand. As seen earlier, the PaginatedRequestCommand class implements IRequestCommand and any type is registered that implements the IRequestCommand to use FromUriAttribute by default. For example, the client can now send a request against /api/shipments?page=1&take=20 to receive the first 20 shipment records.

Also, properties of the PaginatedRequestCommand class carry some validation attributes. So, if the model state is not valid, the globally registered action filter will terminate the request and return the *400 Bad Request* response. If the model state is valid, the request will eventually arrive at the action method and the requested data can be retrieved through the IShipmentService.GetShipments method. At that point, that controller action method doesn't care where the data are coming from or how. It only knows that IShipmentService.GetShipments will be returning the PaginatedList<Shipment> object, which will represent the collection of shipment records along with the pagination information.

After receiving the PaginatedList<Shipment> object, it is best not to return the database entity as it is because not all the data are appropriate to transfer over the wire. Here is the place where the entity objects map into DTOs. There are some great open source projects to make this mapping easier (such as AutoMapper), but we have created some extension methods in the PingYourPackage.API project to achieve this action. First, you need to map the PaginatedList<T> to PaginatedDto<T> (see Listing 6-34).

Listing 6-34. ToPaginatedDto<TDto> Extension Method for PaginatedList<TEntity>

```
internal static class PaginatedListExtensions {

    internal static PaginatedDto<TDto>
        ToPaginatedDto<TDto, TEntity>(
        this PaginatedList<TEntity> source,
        IEnumerable<TDto> items) where TDto : IDto {

        return new PaginatedDto<TDto> {
            PageIndex = source.PageIndex,
            PageSize = source.PageSize,
            TotalCount = source.TotalCount,
            TotalPageCount = source.TotalPageCount,
            HasNextPage = source.HasNextPage,
            HasPreviousPage = source.HasPreviousPage,
            Items = items
        };
    }
}
```

You also needed to map the shipment objects to ShipmentDto objects. For this reason, we created the ToShipmentDto extension method, as shown in Listing 6-35.

Listing 6-35. ToShipmentDto Extension Method for Shipment Class

```
internal static class ShipmentExtensions {

    internal static ShipmentDto ToShipmentDto(
        this Shipment shipment) {

        return new ShipmentDto {
            Key = shipment.Key,
            AffiliateKey = shipment.AffiliateKey,
            Price = shipment.Price,
            ReceiverName = shipment.ReceiverName,
            ReceiverSurname = shipment.ReceiverSurname,
            ReceiverAddress = shipment.ReceiverAddress,
            ReceiverZipCode = shipment.ReceiverZipCode,
            ReceiverCity = shipment.ReceiverCity,
            ReceiverCountry = shipment.ReceiverCountry,
            ReceiverTelephone = shipment.ReceiverTelephone,
            ReceiverEmail = shipment.ReceiverEmail,
            CreatedOn = shipment.CreatedOn,
            ShipmentType =
                shipment.ShipmentType.ToShipmentTypeDto(),
            ShipmentStates =
                shipment.ShipmentStates.Select(
                    ss => ss.ToShipmentStateDto())
        };
    }
}
```

The first controller action is now complete, so let's look at our options on how to write tests for this action method. Because we used the service interface instead of its direct implementation, it is easy to provide a fake or mock of that service. As for the testing itself, there are two options here:

- Directly write unit tests against the controller action method as you did with the message handler in Listing 6-13.

- Write integration tests against the endpoints because it is easy to host the application in memory with the HttpClient. To do is, you would initialize an System.Web.Http.HttpServer instance and set this as the inner handler of the HttpClient.

Getting Ready for Integration Testing

There are a few helper methods that can be used while writing the integration tests. Some of them are for the HttpConfiguration object, as shown in Listing 6-36.

Listing 6-36. IntegrationTestHelper Class for Configuration and DependencyResolver Helper Methods

```
internal static class IntegrationTestHelper {

    internal static Guid[] GetKeys(int count) {

        var array = new Guid[count];
        for (int i = 0; i < count; i++) {
            array[i] = Guid.NewGuid();
        }

        return array;
    }

    internal static HttpConfiguration
        GetInitialIntegrationTestConfig() {

        var config = new HttpConfiguration();
        RouteConfig.RegisterRoutes(config);
        WebAPIConfig.Configure(config);

        return config;
    }

    internal static HttpConfiguration
        GetInitialIntegrationTestConfig(IContainer container) {

        var config = GetInitialIntegrationTestConfig();
        AutofacWebAPI.Initialize(config, container);

        return config;
    }
}
```

```
internal static ContainerBuilder
    GetEmptyContainerBuilder() {

    var builder = new ContainerBuilder();

    builder.RegisterAssemblyTypes(
        Assembly.GetAssembly(typeof(WebAPIConfig)));

    return builder;
}

// Lines removed for brevity
}
```

For these integration tests, you won't be directly invoking the Web API application's methods. Hence, it's not possible to provide mocked version of these services. However, they are provided through the dependency resolver. You can achieve this by providing an IContainer implementation to the AutofacWebAPI.Initialize method inside the GetInitialIntegrationTestConfig method, as shown in Listing 6-36.

■ **Note**   Testing and dependency injection will be covered in detail in Chapter 14 and 15.

There is another class named IntegrationTestHelper that has a few static methods to set up the in-memory host to send a request through the HttpClient (see Listing 6-37).

Listing 6-37. IntegrationTestHelper Class for HttpRequestMessage Helper Methods

```
internal static class IntegrationTestHelper {

    // Lines removed for brevity

    internal static async Task<PaginatedDto<TDto>>
        TestForPaginatedDtoAsync<TDto>(
            HttpConfiguration config,
            HttpRequestMessage request,
            int expectedPageIndex,
            int expectedTotalPageCount,
            int expectedCurrentItemsCount,
            int expectedTotalItemsCount,
            bool expectedHasNextPageResult,
            bool expectedHasPreviousPageResult)
                where TDto : IDto {

        // Act
        var userPaginatedDto = await
            GetResponseMessageBodyAsync<PaginatedDto<TDto>>(
                config, request, HttpStatusCode.OK);

        // Assert
        Assert.Equal(
            expectedPageIndex, userPaginatedDto.PageIndex);
```

169

```csharp
        Assert.Equal(
            expectedTotalPageCount,
            userPaginatedDto.TotalPageCount);

        Assert.Equal(
            expectedCurrentItemsCount,
            userPaginatedDto.Items.Count());

        Assert.Equal(
            expectedTotalItemsCount,
            userPaginatedDto.TotalCount);

        Assert.Equal(
            expectedHasNextPageResult,
            userPaginatedDto.HasNextPage);

        Assert.Equal(
            expectedHasPreviousPageResult,
            userPaginatedDto.HasPreviousPage);

        return userPaginatedDto;
    }

    internal static async Task<TResult>
        GetResponseMessageBodyAsync<TResult>(
            HttpConfiguration config,
            HttpRequestMessage request,
            HttpStatusCode expectedHttpStatusCode) {

        var response = await GetResponseAsync(config, request);
        Assert.Equal(expectedHttpStatusCode, response.StatusCode);
        var result = await
            response.Content.ReadAsAsync<TResult>();

        return result;
    }

    internal static async Task<HttpResponseMessage>
        GetResponseAsync(
            HttpConfiguration config, HttpRequestMessage request) {

        using (var httpServer = new HttpServer(config))
        using (var client =
            HttpClientFactory.Create(innerHandler: httpServer)) {

            return await client.SendAsync(request);
        }
    }
}
}
```

The GetResponseAsync in Listing 6-34 is the base method that all the other helpers are using. It initializes the HttpClient with an HttpServer instance. Now when you call the SendAsync method of the HttpClient instance, you won't be actually making an HTTP call because you have swapped the HttpClientHandler with the HttpServer as an inner handler.

As discussed in previous sections, there is a message handler registered to provide the HTTP basic authentication check and to act on the request accordingly. So you will be using that message handler during the integration tests, too. Listing 6-14 shows how to authenticate the request, and you'll see that you get the IMembershipService implementation through the dependency resolver. You will invoke its ValidateUser method to indicate whether the request is authenticated. There is another helper class named ServicesMockHelper that has a static method named GetInitialMembershipServiceMock, which will provide a IMembershipService mock that can be used to register through the dependency resolver (see Listing 6-38).

Listing 6-38. The ServicesMockHelper Class

```
internal static class ServicesMockHelper {

    internal static Mock<IMembershipService>
        GetInitialMembershipServiceMock() {

        var membershipServiceMock =
            new Mock<IMembershipService>();

        var users = new[] {
            new {
                Name = Constants.ValidAdminUserName,
                Password = Constants.ValidAdminPassword,
                Roles = new[] { "Admin" }
            },
            new {
                Name = Constants.ValidEmployeeUserName,
                Password = Constants.ValidEmployeePassword,
                Roles = new[] { "Employee" }
            },
            new {
                Name = Constants.ValidAffiliateUserName,
                Password = Constants.ValidAffiliatePassword,
                Roles = new[] { "Affiliate" }
            }
        }.ToDictionary(
            user => user.Name, user => user
        );

        membershipServiceMock.Setup(ms => ms.ValidateUser(
            It.IsAny<string>(), It.IsAny<string>())
        ).Returns<string, string>(
            (username, password) => {

                var user = users.FirstOrDefault(x => x.Key.Equals(
                    username,
                    StringComparison.OrdinalIgnoreCase)).Value;
```

```
                    var validUserContext = (user != null)
                        ? new ValidUserContext {
                            Principal = new GenericPrincipal(
                                new GenericIdentity(user.Name),
                                user.Roles
                            )
                        } : new ValidUserContext();

                    return validUserContext;
                }
            );

            return membershipServiceMock;
        }
    }
```

The GetInitialMembershipServiceMock method obtains the users from the Constants class, as shown in Listing 6-39. The Constants class stores the valid and invalid users and these credentials are used when the request messages are constructed with the HTTP authorization header.

Listing 6-39. The Constants Class

```
internal static class Constants {

    internal const string ValidAffiliateUserName = "tugberkAff";
    internal const string ValidAffiliatePassword = "86421";
    internal const string ValidEmployeeUserName = "tugberkEmp";
    internal const string ValidEmployeePassword = "13579";
    internal const string ValidAdminUserName = "tugberkAdmin";
    internal const string ValidAdminPassword = "12345678";
    internal const string InvalidUserName = "tgbrk";
    internal const string InvalidPassword = "87654321";
}
```

In order to make constructing HttpRequestMessage instances easier, you'll use another helper class named HttpRequestMessageHelper, as shown in Listing 6-40.

Listing 6-40. The HttpRequestMessageHelper Class for HttpRequestMessage Helper Methods

```
internal static class HttpRequestMessageHelper {

    internal static HttpRequestMessage ConstructRequest(
        HttpMethod httpMethod, string uri) {

        return new HttpRequestMessage(httpMethod, uri);
    }

    internal static HttpRequestMessage ConstructRequest(
        HttpMethod httpMethod, string uri, string mediaType) {
```

```csharp
        return ConstructRequest(
            httpMethod,
            uri,
            new MediaTypeWithQualityHeaderValue(mediaType));
    }

    internal static HttpRequestMessage ConstructRequest(
        HttpMethod httpMethod, string uri,
        IEnumerable<string> mediaTypes) {

        return ConstructRequest(
            httpMethod,
            uri,
            mediaTypes.ToMediaTypeWithQualityHeaderValues());
    }

    internal static HttpRequestMessage ConstructRequest(
        HttpMethod httpMethod, string uri, string mediaType,
        string username, string password) {

        return ConstructRequest(
            httpMethod, uri,
            new[] { mediaType }, username, password);
    }

    internal static HttpRequestMessage ConstructRequest(
        HttpMethod httpMethod, string uri,
        IEnumerable<string> mediaTypes,
        string username, string password) {

        var request = ConstructRequest(
            httpMethod, uri, mediaTypes);

        request.Headers.Authorization =
            new AuthenticationHeaderValue(
                "Basic",
                EncodeToBase64(
                    string.Format(
                        "{0}:{1}", username, password)));

        return request;
    }

    // Private helpers
    private static HttpRequestMessage ConstructRequest(
        HttpMethod httpMethod, string uri,
        MediaTypeWithQualityHeaderValue mediaType) {

        return ConstructRequest(
            httpMethod,
            uri,
            new[] { mediaType });
    }
```

```
    private static HttpRequestMessage ConstructRequest(
        HttpMethod httpMethod, string uri,
        IEnumerable<MediaTypeWithQualityHeaderValue> mediaTypes) {

        var request = ConstructRequest(httpMethod, uri);
        request.Headers.Accept.AddTo(mediaTypes);

        return request;
    }

    private static string EncodeToBase64(string value) {

        byte[] toEncodeAsBytes = Encoding.UTF8.GetBytes(value);
        return Convert.ToBase64String(toEncodeAsBytes);
    }
}
```

In one extension method, you can use an extension method for the ICollection interface: AddTo (see Listing 6-41).

Listing 6-41. AddTo Extension method for ICollection Interface

```
internal static class ICollectionExtensions {

    internal static void AddTo<T>(
        this ICollection<T> destination,
        IEnumerable<T> source) {

        foreach (T item in source) {
            destination.Add(item);
        }
    }
}
```

Now you're ready to write the actual integration tests against the HTTP API application.

Integration Tests for the First Action Method

After setting up the global helper methods for integration testing, you can now implement the tests themselves. You'll create a class for each controller and have subclasses under it for controller actions. To be able to mock the dependent services, you'll also have a few helper methods for this class and the GetShipments class (see Listing 6-42).

Listing 6-42. The ShipmentsControllerIntegrationTest Class

```
public class ShipmentsControllerIntegrationTest {

    private static readonly string ApiBaseRequestPath =
        "api/shipments";

    public class GetShipments {

        // Lines removed for brevity
        // Tests for GetShipments action method will come here
```

```
    private static IContainer GetContainer() {

        var shipments = GetDummyShipments(new[] {
            Guid.NewGuid(), Guid.NewGuid(), Guid.NewGuid()
        });

        Mock<IShipmentService> shipmentSrvMock =
        new Mock<IShipmentService>();
        shipmentSrvMock.Setup(ss =>
            ss.GetShipments(
                It.IsAny<int>(), It.IsAny<int>()
            )
        ).Returns<int, int>(
            (pageIndex, pageSize) =>
                shipments.AsQueryable()
                    .ToPaginatedList(pageIndex, pageSize)
        );

        return GetContainerThroughMock(shipmentSrvMock);
    }
}

// Lines removed for brevity

private static IEnumerable<Shipment>
    GetDummyShipments(Guid[] keys) {

    var shipmentTypeKeys = new Guid[] {
        Guid.NewGuid(), Guid.NewGuid(), Guid.NewGuid()
    };

    for (int i = 0; i < 3; i++) {

        yield return new Shipment {
            Key = keys[i],
            AffiliateKey = Guid.NewGuid(),
            ShipmentTypeKey = shipmentTypeKeys[i],
            Price = 12.23M * (i + 1),
            ReceiverName =
                string.Format("Receiver {0} Name", i),
            ReceiverSurname =
                string.Format("Receiver {0} Surname", i),
            ReceiverAddress =
                string.Format("Receiver {0} Address", i),
            ReceiverCity =
                string.Format("Receiver {0} City", i),
            ReceiverCountry =
                string.Format("Receiver {0} Country", i),
            ReceiverTelephone =
                string.Format("Receiver {0} Country", i),
            ReceiverZipCode = "12345",
            ReceiverEmail = "foo@example.com",
```

```
                    CreatedOn = DateTime.Now,
                    ShipmentType = new ShipmentType {
                        Key = shipmentTypeKeys[i],
                        Name = "Small",
                        Price = 4.19M,
                        CreatedOn = DateTime.Now,
                    },
                    ShipmentStates = new List<ShipmentState> {
                        new ShipmentState {
                            Key = Guid.NewGuid(),
                            ShipmentKey = keys[i],
                            ShipmentStatus = ShipmentStatus.Ordered
                        },
                        new ShipmentState {
                            Key = Guid.NewGuid(),
                            ShipmentKey = keys[i],
                            ShipmentStatus = ShipmentStatus.Scheduled
                        }
                    }
                }
            };
        }
    }

    private static ContainerBuilder GetInitialContainerBuilder() {

        var builder = IntegrationTestHelper
            .GetEmptyContainerBuilder();

        var mockMemSrv = ServicesMockHelper
            .GetInitialMembershipServiceMock();

        builder.Register(c => mockMemSrv.Object)
            .As<IMembershipService>()
            .InstancePerApiRequest();

        return builder;
    }

    private static IContainer GetContainerThroughMock(
        Mock<IShipmentService> shipmentSrvMock) {

        var containerBuilder = GetInitialContainerBuilder();

        containerBuilder.Register(c => shipmentSrvMock.Object)
            .As<IShipmentService>()
            .InstancePerApiRequest();

        return containerBuilder.Build();
    }
}
```

Most of these methods initialize the IoC container and create mocks, but the GetDummyShipments static method provides the fake data that are needed. The GetContainer method under the GetShipments class creates the mock object for IShipmentService and uses the GetDummyShipments method to provide the fake data. After all this set up, you can now write the first integration test to check if you get expected shipments when the request is authenticated and authorized (see Listing 6-43).

Listing 6-43. The GetShipments Integration Test

```
public class ShipmentsControllerIntegrationTest {

    // Lines removed for brevity

    public class GetShipments {

        [Fact, NullCurrentPrincipal]
        public Task
            Returns_200_And_Shipments_If_Request_Authorized() {

            // Arrange
            var config = IntegrationTestHelper
                .GetInitialIntegrationTestConfig(GetContainer());

            var request = HttpRequestMessageHelper
                .ConstructRequest(
                    httpMethod: HttpMethod.Get,
                    uri: string.Format(
                        "https://localhost/{0}?page={1}&take={2}",
                        ApiBaseRequestPath, 1, 2),
                    mediaType: "application/json",
                    username: Constants.ValidAdminUserName,
                    password: Constants.ValidAdminPassword);

            return IntegrationTestHelper
                .TestForPaginatedDtoAsync<ShipmentDto>(
                    config,
                    request,
                    expectedPageIndex: 1,
                    expectedTotalPageCount: 2,
                    expectedCurrentItemsCount: 2,
                    expectedTotalItemsCount: 3,
                    expectedHasNextPageResult: true,
                    expectedHasPreviousPageResult: false);
        }

        // Lines removed for brevity
    }

    // Lines removed for brevity
}
```

Thanks to the helper methods that were put in place, you have an unobtrusive test method. First, you initialized an HttpConfiguration object by passing the IoC container. Then, you constructed an HttpRequestMessage instance. Finally, you used these two objects to invoke the IntegrationTestHelper.TestForPaginatedDtoAsync method to actually run the assertions. Also notice that you have applied an attribute named NullCurrentPrincipalAttribute to this test method. This is an xUnit BeforeAfterTestAttribute implementation to set the Thread.CurrentPrincipal to null (see Listing 6-44).

Listing 6-44. The NullCurrentPrincipalAttribute Class

```
public class NullCurrentPrincipalAttribute :
    BeforeAfterTestAttribute {

    public override void Before(MethodInfo methodUnderTest) {

        Thread.CurrentPrincipal = null;
    }
}
```

Now when you run this test, you should see the results passed as shown in Figure 6-8.

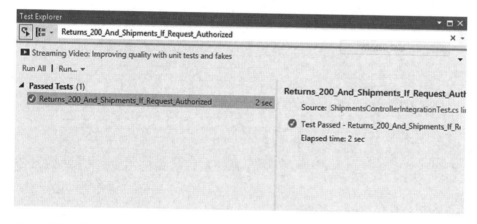

Figure 6-8. The Returns_200_And_Shipments_If_Request_Authorized test results

Other Action Methods for ShipmentsController

Let's implement some other action methods to complete the ShipmentsController. With this controller, you can process one other HTTP GET request to retrieve a single entity. The GetShipment action method will enable this feature and it returns the ShipmentDto instance (see Listing 6-45).

Listing 6-45. GetShipment Action Method of the ShipmentsController

```
public ShipmentDto GetShipment(Guid key) {

    var shipment = _shipmentService.GetShipment(key);
    if (shipment == null) {
```

```
        throw new HttpResponseException(HttpStatusCode.NotFound);
    }

    return shipment.ToShipmentDto();
}
```

Inside the GetShipment action method, you want to get the Shipment object first based on the key value that you received as an action parameter. If the shipment record based on the received key doesn't exist, it will throw an HttpResponseException to return a *404 Not Found* HTTP response.

■ **Note**　We don't cover all the integration tests in this chapter but we implemented nearly all of them for our application. For example, you can find integration tests for ShipmentsController inside the ShipmentsControllerIntegrationTest.cs file in the PingYourPackage.API.Test.Integration project.

To be able to add new shipment records through this API, we added the PostShipment method, which accepts a ShipmentRequestModel instance, as was implemented in Listing 6-25, as an action parameter. Then, you can try to add the shipment though the IShipmentService instance. If the operation is a success, it will return the *201 Created* HTTP response message with the created shipment record in the message body. If the operations fails, it will simply return the *409 Conflict* HTTP response message. The PostShipment action method is shown in Listing 6-46.

Listing 6-46. PostShipment Action Method of the ShipmentController

```
public HttpResponseMessage PostShipment(
    ShipmentRequestModel requestModel) {

    var createdShipmentResult =
        _shipmentService.AddShipment(requestModel.ToShipment());

    if (!createdShipmentResult.IsSuccess) {

        return new HttpResponseMessage(HttpStatusCode.Conflict);
    }

    var response = Request.CreateResponse(HttpStatusCode.Created,
        createdShipmentResult.Entity.ToShipmentDto());

    response.Headers.Location = new Uri(
        Url.Link(RouteName, new {
            key = createdShipmentResult.Entity.Key
        })
    );

    return response;
}
```

However, there is a small issue with the PostShipment action method here. The consumer of our API can send a POST request with an empty message body against a URI, which will eventually correspond to the PostShipment action method. Validation attributes were applied to members of the ShipmentRequestModel class, but if the message body is empty, the validation attributes won't get executed and the ShipmentRequestModel parameter for the action method will be passed as null. There are a few ways to handle this behavior, but we created an action filter that is going to check against the parameter whose name is supplied through the constructor of the action filter object. Look inside the HttpActionContext.ActionArgumenets collection to retrieve the action parameter value and then check it to see whether it's null. If so, the HttpActionContext.Response is set to return a *400 Bad Request* response with the validation error message (see Listing 6-47).

Listing 6-47. The EmptyParameterFilterAttribute Class

```
[AttributeUsage(AttributeTargets.Method, AllowMultiple = true)]
public class EmptyParameterFilterAttribute
    : ActionFilterAttribute {

    public string ParameterName { get; private set; }

    public EmptyParameterFilterAttribute(string parameterName) {

        if (string.IsNullOrEmpty(parameterName)) {

            throw new ArgumentNullException("parameterName");
        }

        ParameterName = parameterName;
    }

    public override void OnActionExecuting(
        HttpActionContext actionContext) {

        object parameterValue;
        if (actionContext.ActionArguments.TryGetValue(
            ParameterName, out parameterValue)) {

            if (parameterValue == null) {

                actionContext.ModelState.AddModelError(
                    ParameterName, FormatErrorMessage(
                                    ParameterName));

                actionContext.Response = actionContext
                    .Request.CreateErrorResponse(
                        HttpStatusCode.BadRequest,
                        actionContext.ModelState);
            }
        }
    }

    private string FormatErrorMessage(string parameterName) {

        return string.Format(
            "The {0} cannot be null.", parameterName);
    }
}
```

You can now apply the `EmptyParameterFilterAttribute` to the `PostShipment` method (see Listing 6-48).

Listing 6-48. EmptyParameterFilterAttribute Applied PostShipment Method

```
[EmptyParameterFilter("requestModel")]
public HttpResponseMessage PostShipment(
    ShipmentRequestModel requestModel) {

    // Lines omitted for brevity
}
```

If you send a request to invoke the `PostShipment` method with an empty message body, you should now get the *400 Bad Request* HTTP response (see Figure 6-9).

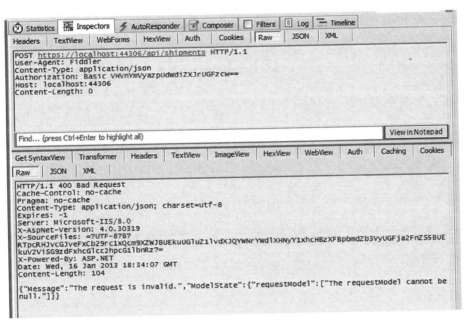

Figure 6-9. POST Request against /api/shipments with empty message body

You also need to cover the update operations for a shipment record. In the HTTP world, update operations are usually performed through the PUT HTTP method. When there is an HTTP PUT request to a resource, the message body content is supposed to replace the existing record on the server. Listing 6-49 shows the implementation to respond to a PUT request for `ShipmentsController`.

Listing 6-49. The PutShipment Action Method

```
[EmptyParameterFilter("requestModel")]
public ShipmentDto PutShipment(
    Guid key,
    ShipmentUpdateRequestModel requestModel) {
```

```
    var shipment = _shipmentService.GetShipment(key);
    if (shipment == null) {

        throw new HttpResponseException(HttpStatusCode.NotFound);
    }

    var updatedShipment = _shipmentService.UpdateShipment(
        requestModel.ToShipment(shipment));

    return updatedShipment.ToShipmentDto();
}
```

You first try to get the shipment record whose key has been supplied. If the shipment record doesn't exist, you throw an HttpResponseException to return a *404 Not Found* HTTP response message. If the shipment record exists, you continue, update the shipment record, and return back the updated shipment record.

■ **Note** In some cases, you may want to replace only certain properties of a record instead of replacing it entirely. Semantically, doing this type operation through the HTTP PATCH method is the right way. There is a great blog by Filip Wojcieszyn that explains how to handle PATCH operations in ASP.NET Web API:

http://www.strathweb.com/2013/01/easy-asp-net-web-api-resource-updates-with-delta.

Also, notice that the EmptyParameterFilterAttribute was applied to the PutShipment action method, too. So, if you send a PUT request with an empty message body to this resource, you'll get the *400 Bad Request* response.

Lastly, you must provide an endpoint to remove a shipment record. You can enable this operation through the HTTP DELETE request. However, some shipment records cannot be deleted. As explained in Chapter 5, a shipment record has states that indicate the movement of a shipment. If the shipment's current state is InTransit or beyond, the shipment cannot be deleted. The IShipmentService.RemoveShipment method will handle this operation. Let's look at the DeleteShipment action method (see Listing 6-50).

Listing 6-50. The DeleteShipment Action Method

```
public HttpResponseMessage DeleteShipment(Guid key) {

    var shipment = _shipmentService.GetShipment(key);
    if (shipment == null) {

        throw new HttpResponseException(HttpStatusCode.NotFound);
    }

    var shipmentRemoveResult =
        _shipmentService.RemoveShipment(shipment);

    if (!shipmentRemoveResult.IsSuccess) {

        return new HttpResponseMessage(HttpStatusCode.Conflict);
    }

    return new HttpResponseMessage(HttpStatusCode.NoContent);
}
```

If the shipment is removed successfully, it will return the *204 No Content* response. If not, the response status code will state *409 Conflict*.

Implementing the AffiliateShipmentsController

At this point, you might be wondering how an affiliate would be able to add shipment records through the HTTP API. There are a few concerns you need to consider before moving on for this:

- The affiliate should indicate its key through the URI.
- The existence of the affiliate should be ensured before moving forward.
- If the existence of the affiliate is checked, the currently authenticated user needs to be related to that affiliate.
- If a single shipment record is requested at the further level inside the pipeline, that shipment should belong to the currently authenticated affiliate.

To be able to cleanly handle these scenarios, you won't allow affiliates to access the ShipmentController. In other words, affiliate requests against the /api/shipments URI won't be authorized. You'll have a separate controller to handle shipment records of affiliates: the AffiliateShipmentsController. There is also a different approach that can be followed by leveraging the per-route message handler feature.

Per-Route Message Handler for AffiliateShipmentsController

Previously you created a few message handlers to handle operations such as authentication and placed them into the HttpConfiguration.MessageHandlers collection. These handlers are applied globally and are run for every single request. The ASP.NET Web API also has a notion of applying message handlers per route. By providing a per-route message handler, you are completely suppressing the controller pipeline, which includes filters, parameter bindings, and validation. In other words, you are telling the framework to replace the HttpControllerDispatcher message handler with your own supplied message handler for any request that matches that route. Figure 6-10 shows the high-level view of the message handler pipeline of the ASP.NET Web API framework.

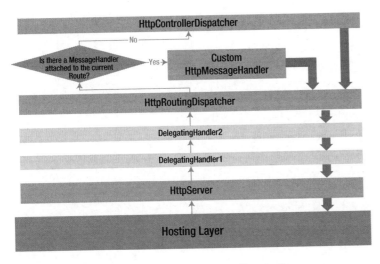

Figure 6-10. ASP.NET Web API message handler pipeline

However, in order to get inside the controller pipeline, you only need to hand off the request to HttpControllerDispatcher at the right place. As the message handler pipeline applies the chain of responsibility pattern, and you can simply chain the custom message handler and HttpControllerDispatcher together. In order to do that, you need to create a custom message handler by taking DelegatingHandler as the base class.

So, why would you want to create a custom per-route message handler here for this case? You can understand this by looking at the URI templates for possible HTTP requests for this controller:

```
GET api/affiliates/{key}/shipments

GET api/affiliates/{key}/shipments/{shipmentKey}

POST api/affiliates/{key}/shipments

PUT api/affiliates/{key}/shipments/{shipmentKey}

DELETE api/affiliates/{key}/shipments/{shipmentKey}
```

As you can see, the affiliate key needs to be supplied for every request that an affiliate will make. So, you should be confident about the fact that the supplied affiliate key really corresponds to an affiliate in the database. This is where our custom per-route message handler enters the scene. Let's look at the complete implementation of our per-route message handler, the AffiliateShipmentsDispatcher (see Listing 6-51).

Listing 6-51. The AffiliateShipmentsDispatcher Message Handler

```
public class AffiliateShipmentsDispatcher : DelegatingHandler {

    protected override Task<HttpResponseMessage> SendAsync(
        HttpRequestMessage request,
        CancellationToken cancellationToken) {

        // We know at this point that the {key}
        // route variable has been supplied.
        // Otherwise, we wouldn't be here.
        // So, just get it.
        IHttpRouteData routeData = request.GetRouteData();
        Guid affiliateKey =
            Guid.ParseExact(
                routeData.Values["key"].ToString(), "D");

        IShipmentService shipmentService =
            request.GetShipmentService();

        if (shipmentService.GetAffiliate(affiliateKey) == null) {

            return Task.FromResult(
                request.CreateResponse(HttpStatusCode.NotFound));
        }

        return base.SendAsync(request, cancellationToken);
    }
}
```

```
internal static class HttpRequestMessageExtensions {

    internal static IShipmentService GetShipmentService(
        this HttpRequestMessage request) {

        return request.GetService<IShipmentService>();
    }

    // Line omitted for brevity
}
```

This is a fairly simple implementation that can be digested easily. At this point inside the SendAsync method, you know that the affiliate key has been supplied and you can just grab it through the match route data object. Then, you get the IShipmentService implementation through the dependency resolver. The GetShipmentService extension method uses the GetService extension method for HttpRequestMessage, as you saw in Listing 6-14, to get the IShipmentService implementation. Lastly, you check if the affiliate exists or not. If it doesn't exist, it will terminating the chain and returning a *404 Not Found* response. Otherwise, you call the base SendAsync method, which will eventually call the inner handler's SendAsync method and that inner handler will be HttpControllerDispatcher.

Before moving on, you should register this message handler for the route. You do that by chaining AffiliateShipmentsDispatcher and HttpControllerDispatcher together, then setting the created pipeline as the handler for the route. Use the static HttpClientFactory.CreatePipeline method to chain these handlers together (see Listing 6-52).

Listing 6-52. Registering Per-Route Message Handler for AffiliateShipmentsHttpRoute

```
public static void RegisterRoutes(HttpConfiguration config) {

    var routes = config.Routes;

    // Pipelines
    HttpMessageHandler affiliateShipmentsPipeline =
        HttpClientFactory.CreatePipeline(
            new HttpControllerDispatcher(config),
            new[] { new AffiliateShipmentsDispatcher() });

    // Routes
    routes.MapHttpRoute(
        "AffiliateShipmentsHttpRoute",
        "api/affiliates/{key}/shipments/{shipmentKey}",
        defaults: new {
            controller = "AffiliateShipments",
            shipmentKey = RouteParameter.Optional
        },
        constraints: new {
            key = new GuidRouteConstraint(),
            shipmentKey = new GuidRouteConstraint()
        },
        handler: affiliateShipmentsPipeline
    );
```

```
routes.MapHttpRoute(
    "DefaultHttpRoute",
    "api/{controller}/{key}",
    defaults: new { key = RouteParameter.Optional },
    constraints: new { key = new GuidRouteConstraint() });
}
```

This setup will give you the confidence that the affiliate really exists. So, you can now move on to solve the next problem.

Creating a Custom AuthorizeAttribute for AffiliateShipmentsController

When the request arrives inside the controller pipeline, you need to ensure that the affiliate, whose key has been supplied and existence has been checked, and the authenticated user are related to each other. You can make this check through an authorization filer, which will be applied at the controller level. Because you also need to check if the authenticated user is in the Affiliate role, you can take the AuthorizeAttribute as the base class for the custom authorization filter and run its logic before your own because you don't need to perform any further checks if the user is not inside the Affiliate role.

Let's have a look at the complete implementation of the AffiliateShipmentsAuthorizeAttribute (see Listing 6-53).

Listing 6-53. The AffiliateShipmentsAuthorizeAttribute

```
[AttributeUsage(AttributeTargets.Class, AllowMultiple = false)]
public class AffiliateShipmentsAuthorizeAttribute :
    AuthorizeAttribute {

    public AffiliateShipmentsAuthorizeAttribute() {

        base.Roles = "Affiliate";
    }

    public override void OnAuthorization(
        HttpActionContext actionContext) {

        base.OnAuthorization(actionContext);

        // If not authorized at all, don't bother
        // checking for the user - affiliate relation
        if (actionContext.Response == null) {

            // We are here sure that the request
            // has been authorized and the user is
            // in the Affiliate role. We also don't need
            // to check the existence of the affiliate
            // as it has been also already done
            // by AffiliateShipmentsDispatcher.

            HttpRequestMessage request = actionContext.Request;
            Guid affiliateKey =
                GetAffiliateKey(request.GetRouteData());
```

```
        IPrincipal principal = Thread.CurrentPrincipal;
        IShipmentService shipmentService =
            request.GetShipmentService();

        bool isAffiliateRelatedToUser =
            shipmentService.IsAffiliateRelatedToUser(
                affiliateKey, principal.Identity.Name);

        if (!isAffiliateRelatedToUser) {

            // Set Unauthorized response
            // as the user and  affiliate isn't
            // related to each other. You might want to
            // return "404 NotFound" response here
            // if you don't want to expose the existence
            // of the affiliate.
            actionContext.Response =
                request.CreateResponse(
                    HttpStatusCode.Unauthorized);
        }
    }
}

private static Guid GetAffiliateKey(
    IHttpRouteData routeData) {

    var affiliateKey = routeData.Values["key"].ToString();
    return Guid.ParseExact(affiliateKey, "D");
}
}
```

Because the authorization filter is derived from the AuthorizeAttribute, the OnAuthorization method will be called to authorize the request. So, you have overridden it and run its own logic before yours. Then, you check if the HttpActionContext.Response is set or not. If it's not set, it means that the request is authorized and the user is in the Affiliate role because you have set the Roles property to Affiliate inside the constructor. Then, you check whether the authenticated user is related to the affiliate. If it is, you do nothing and let the request flow through the pipeline. If the user is not related to the affiliate record, you construct a new *401 Unauthorized* response and set it to HttpActionContext.Response property to terminate the request. You may want to return the *404 Not Found* response instead if you don't want to expose the existence of the affiliate for security reasons.

You can now apply this to your AffiliateShipmentsController and for every request that is eventually routed to AffiliateShipmentsController, this authorization filter will be invoked (see Listing 6-54).

Listing 6-54. The AffiliateShipmentsController's Initial Look

```
[AffiliateShipmentsAuthorize]
public class AffiliateShipmentsController : ApiController {

    private readonly IShipmentService _shipmentService;
    private const string RouteName =
        "AffiliateShipmentsHttpRoute";
```

```
    public AffiliateShipmentsController(
        IShipmentService shipmentService) {

        _shipmentService = shipmentService;
    }

    // Lines omitted for brevity
}
```

From now on, you can be sure through the action methods of AffiliateShipmentsController that the affiliate exists and is related to the currently authenticated user.

Creating the GetShipment and GetShipments Action Methods

Inside the GetShipments action method, you will receive the PaginatedRequestCommand as usual and you will also have the affiliate key that you can use to filter the shipment records (see Listing 6-55).

Listing 6-55. GetShipments Action Method

```
public PaginatedDto<ShipmentDto> GetShipments(
    Guid key, PaginatedRequestCommand cmd) {

    var shipments = _shipmentService
        .GetShipments(cmd.Page, cmd.Take, affiliateKey: key);

    return shipments.ToPaginatedDto(
        shipments.Select(sh => sh.ToShipmentDto()));
}
```

The GetShipment method, which will return the single shipment record, is a little different for this controller. Let's look at the implementation first, then we'll discuss it more (see Listing 6-56).

Listing 6-56. GetShipment Action Method

```
[EnsureShipmentOwnership]
public ShipmentDto GetShipment(
    Guid key,
    Guid shipmentKey,
    [BindShipment]Shipment shipment) {

    return shipment.ToShipmentDto();
}
```

There are two parts here that we haven't touched on yet. The method is marked with the EnsureShipmentOwnership attribute and it is receiving a parameter that is of the type Shipment and it is applying the BindShipmentAttribute to this parameter. Let's see what these indicate and why they are needed here.

Ensuring Shipment Ownership

The resource URI for the GET request, which corresponds to the GetShipment method, will look like this:

```
/api/affiliates/041f765a-1019-4956-b610-370d05be95ac/shipments
/6527CA96-9491-4755-A89D-3FA2A01A2D1C
```

Here, the affiliate key and the shipment key are expressed to retrieve the shipment record that belongs to the affiliate in question. So, you need to be sure that the affiliate really owns this shipment record before returning the result. The EnsureShipmentOwnershipAttribute enables this. This could be handled inside the action method itself, but keeping the action methods as thin as possible is one of our intents with this application. Also, this behavior will also be needed for PUT and DELETE requests, too. The EnsureShipmentOwnershipAttribute implementation is shown in Listing 6-57.

Listing 6-57. The EnsureShipmentOwnershipAttribute Implementation

```
[AttributeUsage(AttributeTargets.Method, AllowMultiple = false)]
public class EnsureShipmentOwnershipAttribute
    : Attribute, IAuthorizationFilter {

    private const string ShipmentDictionaryKey =
        "_AffiliateShipmentsController_Shipment";

    public Task<HttpResponseMessage>
        ExecuteAuthorizationFilterAsync(
        HttpActionContext actionContext,
        CancellationToken cancellationToken,
        Func<Task<HttpResponseMessage>> continuation) {

        // We are here sure that the user is
        // authanticated and request can be kept executing
        // because the AuthorizeAttribute has  been invoked
        // before this filter's OnActionExecuting method.
        // Also, we are sure that the affiliate is
        // associated with the currently authanticated user
        // as the previous action filter has checked against this.
        IHttpRouteData routeData =
            actionContext.Request.GetRouteData();
        Uri requestUri =
            actionContext.Request.RequestUri;

        Guid affiliateKey =
            GetAffiliateKey(routeData);
        Guid shipmentKey =
            GetShipmentKey(routeData, requestUri);

        // Check if the affiliate really owns the shipment
        // whose key came from the request. We don't need
        // to check the existence of the affiliate as this
        // check has been already performed by
        // the AffiliateShipmentsDispatcher.
```

```csharp
        IShipmentService shipmentService =
            actionContext.Request.GetShipmentService();
        Shipment shipment =
            shipmentService.GetShipment(shipmentKey);

        // Check the shipment existance
        if (shipment == null) {

            return Task.FromResult(
                new HttpResponseMessage(HttpStatusCode.NotFound));
        }

        // Check the shipment ownership
        if (shipment.AffiliateKey != affiliateKey) {

            // You might want to return "404 NotFound"
            // response here if you don't want
            // to expose the existence of the shipment.
            return Task.FromResult(
                new HttpResponseMessage(
                    HttpStatusCode.Unauthorized));
        }

        // Stick the shipment inside the Properties
        // dictionary so that we won't need to have
        // another trip to database. The ShipmentParameterBinding
        // will bind the Shipment param if needed.
        actionContext.Request
            .Properties[ShipmentDictionaryKey] = shipment;

        // The request is legit, continue executing.
        return continuation();
    }

    private static Guid GetAffiliateKey(
        IHttpRouteData routeData) {

        var affiliateKey = routeData.Values["key"].ToString();
        return Guid.ParseExact(affiliateKey, "D");
    }

    private static Guid GetShipmentKey(
        IHttpRouteData routeData, Uri requestUri) {

        // We are sure at this point that the
        // shipmentKey value has been supplied
        // (either through route or quesry string)
        // because it wouldn't be possible for the
        // request to arrive here if it wasn't.
        object shipmentKeyString;
```

```
        if (routeData.Values.TryGetValue(
            "shipmentKey", out shipmentKeyString)) {

            return Guid.ParseExact(
                shipmentKeyString.ToString(), "D");
        }

        // It's now sure that query string has
        // the shipmentKey value.
        var quesryString = requestUri.ParseQueryString();
        return Guid.ParseExact(quesryString["shipmentKey"], "D");
    }

    public bool AllowMultiple {
        get { return false; }
    }
}
}
```

The EnsureShipmentOwnershipAttribute is itself an authorization filter, as you can see. So, it will run just after the controller level authorization filter. Briefly, you are retrieving the shipment inside the ExecuteAuthorizationFilterAsync method and first checking whether it exists. If not, it will return a *404 Not Found* response. If it exists, you will move on and compare the affiliate key of the shipment against the one that was retrieved through the route data object. When it sees that both are the same, it will put the found shipment record inside the request properties bag so that it can be retrieve later and reduce the trips that are made to the database. This is where BindShipmentAttribute comes into play, which we'll explain in the next section, but for now imagine you have the BindShipmentAttribute implementation and look at the retrieve process in action first.

Let's send a valid request to retrieve a single shipment record (see Figure 6-11).

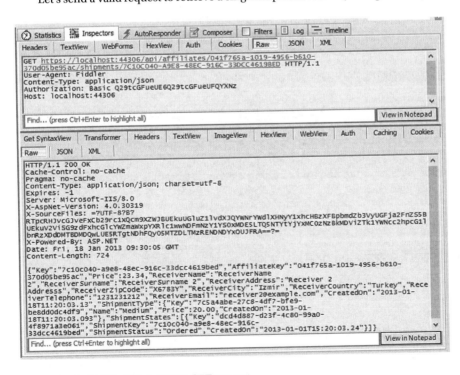

***Figure 6-11.** Valid affiliate HTTP GET request*

You will get the expected result back. Now, let's try to retrieve some other affiliate's shipment record and see what comes back this time (see Figure 6-12).

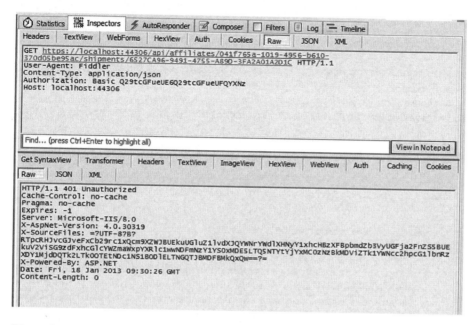

Figure 6-12. Invalid affiliate HTTP GET request

The *401 Unauthorized* response is returned this time. Again, you would want to return *404 Not Found* here instead for security reasons because you wouldn't be exposing the existence of that shipment.

Creating the ShipmentParameterBinding

Now that the shipment record has been retrieved for the request once inside the `EnsureShipmentOwnershipAttribute`, the same record for the `GetShipment` action method can be used to avoid another trip to the database for that same record.

The question is whether to retrieve this inside the action method. One way to do this is to directly retrieve it through the `Request.Properties` collection inside the action method. However, you can leverage one of the great features of ASP.NET Web API for this: parameter binding. You can apply a parameter binding attribute for an action parameter and that parameter will be bound by using the `HttpParameterBinding` instance supplied by the applied parameter binding attribute. For our case here, the `BindShipmentAttribute` implementation is shown in Listing 6-58.

Listing 6-58. The BindShipmentAttribute Implementation

```
public class BindShipmentAttribute : ParameterBindingAttribute {

    public override HttpParameterBinding GetBinding(
        HttpParameterDescriptor parameter) {

        return new ShipmentParameterBinding(parameter);
    }
}
```

The responsibility of the parameter binding attribute is to supply an HttpParameterBinding instance and BindShipmentAttribute returns the ShipmentParameterBinding for that. The ShipmentParameterBinding class is derived from HttpParameterBinding and is responsible for retrieving and binding the parameter value (see Listing 6-59).

Listing 6-59. The ShipmentParameterBinding Implementation

```
public class ShipmentParameterBinding : HttpParameterBinding {

    private readonly string _parameterName;
    private const string ShipmentDictionaryKey =
        "__AffiliateShipmentsController_Shipment";

    public ShipmentParameterBinding(
        HttpParameterDescriptor descriptor)
        : base(descriptor) {

        _parameterName = descriptor.ParameterName;
    }

    public override Task ExecuteBindingAsync(
        ModelMetadataProvider metadataProvider,
        HttpActionContext actionContext,
        CancellationToken cancellationToken) {

        // It is safe to assume that the Shipment
        // instance exists inside the
        // HttpRequestMessage.Properties dictionary
        // because we woulnd't be here if it doesn't.
        var shipment = actionContext.Request
            .Properties[ShipmentDictionaryKey] as Shipment;

        actionContext.ActionArguments.Add(
            _parameterName, shipment);

        return Task.FromResult(0);
    }
}
```

As you'll recall, the found Shipment object is inside the request properties bag. So, you are retrieving it through the HttpActionContext.Request.Properties collection and sticking it into HttpActionContex.ActionArguments collection for it to be passed inside the action method.

If you put a breakpoint on the GetShipment method in debug mode, you should see that the shipment parameter is supplied (see Figure 6-13).

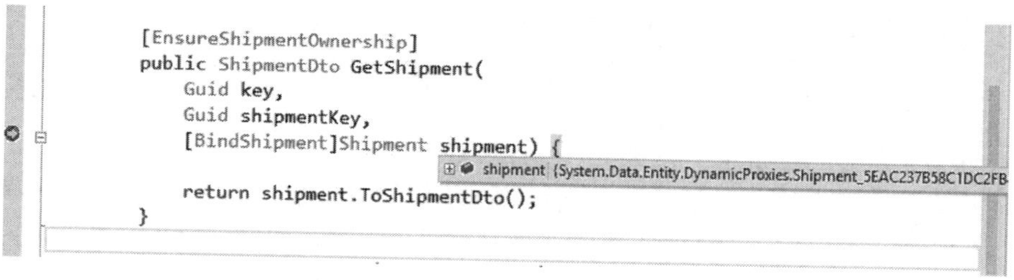

```
        [EnsureShipmentOwnership]
        public ShipmentDto GetShipment(
            Guid key,
            Guid shipmentKey,
            [BindShipment]Shipment shipment) {
                    ⊞ ● shipment {System.Data.Entity.DynamicProxies.Shipment_5EAC237B58C1DC2FB
            return shipment.ToShipmentDto();
        }
```

Figure 6-13. GetShipment method's shipment parameter is being bound

Creating Remaining Action Methods

There are a few other controller action methods that need to be implemented. One of them will handle the POST HTTP method for creating new shipment entries for an affiliate (see Listing 6-60).

Listing 6-60. The PostShipment Action Method

```
[EmptyParameterFilter("requestModel")]
public HttpResponseMessage PostShipment(
    Guid key,
    ShipmentByAffiliateRequestModel requestModel) {

    var createdShipmentResult =
        _shipmentService.AddShipment(
            requestModel.ToShipment(key));

    if (!createdShipmentResult.IsSuccess) {

        return new HttpResponseMessage(
            HttpStatusCode.Conflict);
    }

    var response = Request.CreateResponse(
        HttpStatusCode.Created,
        createdShipmentResult.Entity.ToShipmentDto());

    response.Headers.Location = new Uri(
        Url.Link(RouteName, new {
            key = createdShipmentResult.Entity.AffiliateKey,
            shipmentKey = createdShipmentResult.Entity.Key
        })
    );

    return response;
}
```

The PostShipment action method has a very straightforward implementation. Also, see the PutShipment action method shown in Listing 6-61 for updating an existing shipment record.

Listing 6-61. The PutShipment Action Method

```
[EnsureShipmentOwnership]
[EmptyParameterFilter("requestModel")]
public ShipmentDto PutShipment(
    Guid key,
    Guid shipmentKey,
    ShipmentByAffiliateUpdateRequestModel requestModel,
    [BindShipment]Shipment shipment) {

    var updatedShipment = _shipmentService.UpdateShipment(
        requestModel.ToShipment(shipment));

    return updatedShipment.ToShipmentDto();
}
```

Finally, there is the DeleteShipment action method for removing a shipment entry (see Listing 6-62).

Listing 6-62. The DeleteShipment Action Method

```
[EnsureShipmentOwnership]
public HttpResponseMessage DeleteShipment(
    Guid key,
    Guid shipmentKey,
    [BindShipment]Shipment shipment) {

    var operationResult =
        _shipmentService.RemoveShipment(shipment);

    if (!operationResult.IsSuccess) {

        return new HttpResponseMessage(HttpStatusCode.Conflict);
    }

    return new HttpResponseMessage(HttpStatusCode.NoContent);
}
```

Summary

This chapter looked at implementing the API layer by examining several parts of the ASP.NET Web API framework: message handlers, filters, route registrations, dependency resolver, controllers, and so forth. We also discussed how easy it is to write in-memory integration tests against the exposed API endpoints. You now have the API endpoints ready to be hit, so it is time to build a client application that will consume this API. The next chapter will explain how to build a reusable .NET client wrapper around the HTTP API to make it easy to consume. By using this client wrapper, you will have an ASP.NET MVC client application that an affiliate can use to manage its shipment records.

CHAPTER 7

■ ■ ■

Sample Application: Building the Wrapper and Web Client

So far, you have created your application's domain layer and the API application with ASP.NET Web API framework. Because you now have open endpoints, you can build clients around the HTTP API to consume and modify data.

In terms of HTTP APIs, there are lots of client options. You can build a Windows Phone client, a Windows Store App client, or a web client that directly consumes the HTTP API through Ajax requests. In this chapter, you'll create a .NET wrapper around the HTTP API, which will make it easy to consume with the HttpClient class. Afterward, you'll use that .NET wrapper library to create an ASP.NET MVC application for an affiliate to view, submit, and modify its shipment records.

■ **Note**   In a real-world scenario, you would also create an admin client to allow administrators to consume the HTTP API to do elevated operations such as create affiliates, changing the shipment state, and so forth.

Building a .NET Wrapper for the HTTP API

You have your HTTP API ready to be consumed and you want your consumers to have a first-class experience consuming your API. This is where you start considering building framework- or language-specific wrappers around your HTTP API. Depending on your consumers' portfolio, the platform you would like to invest in can vary. Also, one could argue that a well-designed HTTP API that follows the REST software architecture style doesn't need a specific client wrapper.

Nevertheless, in the next section, you'll design a .NET wrapper around your delivery company's HTTP API, which will make it easy for the clients on the .NET Framework to consume the API. Inside the wrapper library, the HttpClient class will be used to talk to HTTP endpoints, and you'll expose best practices to work with HttpClient throughout. Let's first have a look at the separate project that we have for this library.

PingYourPackage.API.Client Project

You'll have a separate class library project for the .NET wrapper of the HTTP API so that you can easily distribute the library as a separate assembly. You can even automate the process of this, distribute the library through NuGet if you want to, and allow you consumers to keep an eye on any library updates. The .NET library you are about to create will not have any dependency on the "Domain" (PingYourPackage.Domain) and "API" (PingYourPackage.API) projects.

However, it will have a dependency on the "Model" project (PingYourPackage.API.Model) here as you'll use the same .NET classes to represent the data transferred over the wire, which is going be a big code reuse for you. Also, the model classes will act as the contract here. You can see from Figure 7-1 that the PingYourPackage.API.Client project has a reference for the PingYourPackage.API.Model assembly.

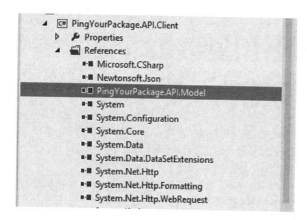

Figure 7-1. *The PingYourPackage.API.Model assembly reference*

Notice in Figure 7-1 that you have other types of references, such as System.Net.Http, which we'll explain in the next section.

Integrating with WebApiDoodle.Net.Http.Client NuGet Package

To be able to create a .NET wrapper around the HTTP API, you'll make use of the new HttpClient class. However, there are a few things you need to be concered with when using HttpClient, such as hitting the endpoint and deserializing the raw data asynchronously, which might be a bit tricky even if you use the C# 5.0 asynchronous language features. For instance, as we explained at the end of Chapter 2, you can easily make it possible for the consumers of your .NET API to introduce deadlocks. Besides that, there is a little bit of a performance effect to unnecessarily synchronize with current context. There is a NuGet package that makes all of this easy: WebApiDoodle.Net.Http.Client. This package integrates with the Microsoft.AspNet.WebApi.Client package. So, you can install only the WebApiDoodle.Net.Http.Client package and you'll be good to go (see Figure 7-2).

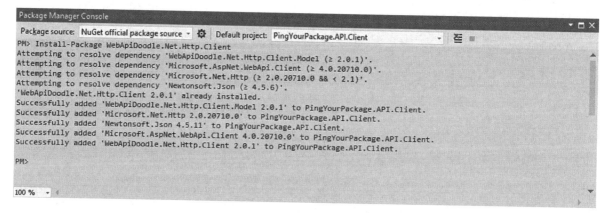

Figure 7-2. *Installing the WebApiDoodle.Net.Http.Client package*

The most important object this NuGet package provides is the `HttpApiClient<TResult>` generic abstract class, which is essentially the same as `HttpClient` but with a bit more functionality. This class is very opinionated about the way you are going to consume the HTTP endpoints but will fit very well with what we have in mind here. It has essentially the same methods as the `HttpClient` but with absolutely different signatures (see Figure 7-3).

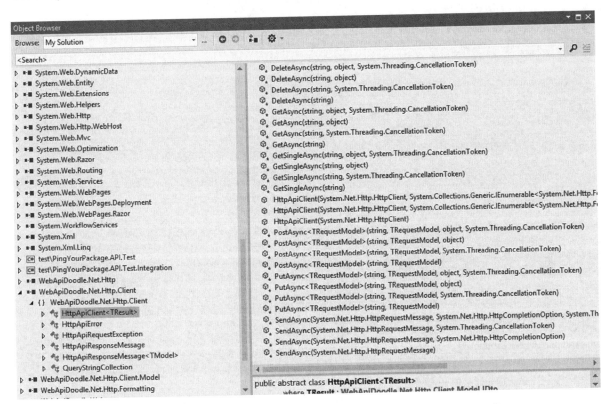

Figure 7-3. *The HttpApiClient<TResult> signature*

Depending on the operation type, the return types of these methods are either `Task<HttpApiResponseMessage <TResult>>` or `Task<HttpApiResponseMessage>`. The `HttpApiResponseMessage<TResult>` instance will save you from the serialization work, which will be done out of the box by the package. The next section will cover how to create the client classes (`ShipmentsClient` and `ShipmentTypesClient`), and this will give you more in-depth information about the library.

Creating the ShipmentsClient and ShipmentTypesClient

Adding, removing, and manipulating the shipment records through the HTTP API are the most important concepts for this client as you are writing this library for its affiliates. The `ShipmentsClient` class, which implements the `IShipmentsClient`, will be the client class for those operations. The signature of the `IShipmentsClient` interface is shown in Listing 7-1.

Listing 7-1. IShipmentsClient Interface

```
public interface IShipmentsClient {

    Task<PaginatedDto<ShipmentDto>> GetShipmentsAsync(
        PaginatedRequestCommand paginationCmd);

    Task<ShipmentDto> GetShipmentAsync(
        Guid shipmentKey);

    Task<ShipmentDto> AddShipmentAsync(
        ShipmentByAffiliateRequestModel requestModel);

    Task<ShipmentDto> UpdateShipmentAsync(
        Guid shipmentKey,
        ShipmentByAffiliateUpdateRequestModel requestModel);

    Task RemoveShipmentAsync(
        Guid shipmentKey);
}
```

This interface covers all the necessary information that will be used by an affiliate. The implementation class of the IShipmentsClient interface, ShipmentsClient, will be derived from the HttpApiClient<ShipmentDto> as all the return types can be either deserialized to ShipmentDto or PaginatedDto<ShipmentDto>, and this makes it easy to use HttpApiClient as the base class.

When you look at the constructors of the HttpApiClient class, you'll see that all of them accept a System.Net.Http.HttpClient instance to communicate through HTTP, and this enables you to share one instance of HttpClient across the client class implementations. Also, the specified HttpClient is not going to be disposed of by the HttpApiClient instance because an HttpClient instance can be used throughout the application lifecycle safely and its methods are thread safe:

- CancelPendingRequests

- DeleteAsync

- GetAsync

- GetByteArrayAsync

- GetStreamAsync

- GetStringAsync

- PostAsync

- PutAsync

- SendAsync

Optionally, the HttpApiClient class accepts the MediaTypeFormatter collection to deserialize the data and a MediaTypeFormatter instance to write (serialize) the data. Considering these options, our ShipmentsClient class's constructor looks like the code shown in Listing 7-2.

Listing 7-2. Initial Structure of the ShipmentsClient Class

```
public class ShipmentsClient :
    HttpApiClient<ShipmentDto>, IShipmentsClient {

    private const string BaseUriTemplate =
        "api/affiliates/{key}/shipments";

    private const string BaseUriTemplateForSingle =
        "api/affiliates/{key}/shipments/{shipmentKey}";

    private readonly string _affiliateKey;

    public ShipmentsClient(HttpClient httpClient, string affiliateKey)
        : base(httpClient, MediaTypeFormatterCollection.Instance) {

        if (string.IsNullOrEmpty(affiliateKey)) {

            throw new ArgumentException(
                "The argument 'affiliateKey' is null or empty.",
                "affiliateKey");
        }

        _affiliateKey = affiliateKey;
    }

    // Lines romoved for brevity
}
```

As you can see, the constructor of the ShipmentsClient class accepts an instance of the HttpClient object, and how this instance can be provided will be discussed in the next section. You also can see the singleton MediaTypeFormatterCollection class in Listing 7-3.

Listing 7-3. MediaTypeFormatterCollection Singleton Class

```
internal sealed class MediaTypeFormatterCollection :
    ReadOnlyCollection<MediaTypeFormatter> {

    private static readonly Lazy<MediaTypeFormatterCollection> lazy =
            new Lazy<MediaTypeFormatterCollection>(() =>
                new MediaTypeFormatterCollection());

    public static MediaTypeFormatterCollection Instance { get { return lazy.Value; } }

    private MediaTypeFormatterCollection()
        : base(new List<MediaTypeFormatter> { new JsonMediaTypeFormatter() }) {
    }
}
```

Inside the ShipmentClient class, you have a few private helper methods to help handle the response message properly (see Listing 7-4).

Listing 7-4. Private Helper Methods on ShipmentsClient

```
public class ShipmentsClient :
    HttpApiClient<ShipmentDto>, IShipmentsClient {

    // Lines romoved for brevity

    private async Task<TResult> HandleResponseAsync<TResult>(
        Task<HttpApiResponseMessage<TResult>> responseTask) {

        using (var apiResponse = await responseTask) {

            if (apiResponse.IsSuccess) {

                return apiResponse.Model;
            }

            throw GetHttpApiRequestException(apiResponse);
        }
    }

    private async Task HandleResponseAsync(
        Task<HttpApiResponseMessage> responseTask) {

        using (var apiResponse = await responseTask) {

            if (!apiResponse.IsSuccess) {

                throw GetHttpApiRequestException(apiResponse);
            }
        }
    }

    private HttpApiRequestException GetHttpApiRequestException(
        HttpApiResponseMessage apiResponse) {

        return new HttpApiRequestException(
            string.Format(ErrorMessages.HttpRequestErrorFormat,
                (int)apiResponse.Response.StatusCode,
                apiResponse.Response.ReasonPhrase),
                apiResponse.Response.StatusCode,
                apiResponse.HttpError);
    }
}
```

As you can see, there are two HandleResponseAsync methods and one of them is a generic method. These methods will be used for every HTTP request that you'll make and act on the response to either return the deserialized object or throw an HttpApiRequestException (which comes with the WebApiDoodle.Net.Http.Client NuGet package). In cases where there is no message body, it will just await the response and return the Task object.

Let's start looking at how the HTTP requests are being made. Listing 7-5 shows the GET request methods inside the ShipmentsClient.

Listing 7-5. GET Methods on ShipmentsClient

```
public class ShipmentsClient :
    HttpApiClient<ShipmentDto>, IShipmentsClient {

    // Lines romoved for brevity

    public async Task<PaginatedDto<ShipmentDto>> GetShipmentsAsync(
        PaginatedRequestCommand paginationCmd) {

        var parameters = new {
            key = _affiliateKey,
            page = paginationCmd.Page,
            take = paginationCmd.Take };

        var responseTask = base.GetAsync(
            BaseUriTemplate, parameters);

        var shipments = await HandleResponseAsync(responseTask);
        return shipments;
    }

    public async Task<ShipmentDto> GetShipmentAsync(
        Guid shipmentKey) {

        var parameters = new {
            key = _affiliateKey,
            shipmentKey = shipmentKey };

        var responseTask = base.GetSingleAsync(
            BaseUriTemplateForSingle, parameters);

        var shipment = await HandleResponseAsync(responseTask);
        return shipment;
    }

    // Lines romoved for brevity
}
```

One of the great features of the HttpApiClient class is that it allows you to generate the URI over a .NET object. In our case in Listing 7-5, we are creating anonymous types to hold the URI parameters and pass that variable into the HttpClientApi methods. Notice that you're retrieving the deserialized object through the HandleResponseAsync method, which will also handle the disposition of the HttpResponseMessage object.

Implementation of the ShipmentClient methods for POST, PUT, and DELETE HTTP operations will look very similar (see Listing 7-6).

Listing 7-6. Add, Update, and Remove Methods on ShipmentsClient

```
public class ShipmentsClient :
    HttpApiClient<ShipmentDto>, IShipmentsClient {

    // Lines romoved for brevity

    public async Task<ShipmentDto> AddShipmentAsync(
        ShipmentByAffiliateRequestModel requestModel) {

        var parameters = new { key = _affiliateKey };
        var responseTask = base.PostAsync(
            BaseUriTemplate, requestModel, parameters);

        var shipment = await HandleResponseAsync(responseTask);
        return shipment;
    }

    public async Task<ShipmentDto> UpdateShipmentAsync(
        Guid shipmentKey,
        ShipmentByAffiliateUpdateRequestModel requestModel) {

        var parameters = new { key = _affiliateKey, shipmentKey = shipmentKey };
        var responseTask = base.PutAsync(
            BaseUriTemplateForSingle, requestModel, parameters);

        var shipment = await HandleResponseAsync(responseTask);
        return shipment;
    }

    public async Task RemoveShipmentAsync(Guid shipmentKey) {

        var parameters = new { key = _affiliateKey, shipmentKey = shipmentKey };
        var responseTask = base.DeleteAsync(BaseUriTemplateForSingle, parameters);
        await HandleResponseAsync(responseTask);
    }

    // Lines romoved for brevity
}
```

■ **Note** Besides the ShipmentsClient class, there is also another client class: ShipmentTypesClient. Because it has the same structure as ShipmentsClient, we won't go into its detail here. However, you can see the implementation code inside the project's source code.

Now you have the client wrapper, but you still have to construct an instance properly. The following section is all about this topic.

Creating the ApiClientContext

In order to construct the client classes, you need an HttpClient instance that you can pass along safely. Also, you don't want to expose this client as a public member from the library as the library will be the only one using this. This is where the ApiClientContext class comes in handy. With the ApiClientContext class, you'll have a fluent API to construct your client instances. Let's look at the implementation of ApiClientContext first (see Listing 7-7) and then we'll explain it.

Listing 7-7. ApiClientContext Class

```
public sealed class ApiClientContext {

    private ApiClientContext() { }

    private static readonly Lazy<ConcurrentDictionary<Type, object>> _clients =
        new Lazy<ConcurrentDictionary<Type, object>>(() =>
            new ConcurrentDictionary<Type, object>(), isThreadSafe: true);

    private static readonly Lazy<HttpClient> _httpClient =
                new Lazy<HttpClient>(
                    () => {

                        Assembly assembly = Assembly.GetExecutingAssembly();
                        HttpClient httpClient = HttpClientFactory.Create(
                            innerHandler: new HttpClientHandler() {
                                AutomaticDecompression = DecompressionMethods.GZip });

                        httpClient.DefaultRequestHeaders.Accept.Add(
                            new MediaTypeWithQualityHeaderValue("application/json"));

                        httpClient.DefaultRequestHeaders.AcceptEncoding.Add(
                            new StringWithQualityHeaderValue("gzip"));

                        httpClient.DefaultRequestHeaders.Add(
                            "X-UserAgent",
                            string.Concat(
                                assembly.FullName,
                                "( ", FileVersionInfo.GetVersionInfo(
                                    assembly.Location).ProductVersion,
                                ")"
                            )
                        );

                        return httpClient;

                    }, isThreadSafe: true);

    internal ConcurrentDictionary<Type, object> Clients {

        get { return _clients.Value; }
    }
```

```
    internal Uri BaseUri { get; set; }
    internal string AuthorizationValue { get; set; }
    internal string AffiliateKey { get; set; }

    internal HttpClient HttpClient {

        get {

            if (!_httpClient.IsValueCreated) {

                InitializeHttpClient();
            }

            return _httpClient.Value;
        }
    }

    public static ApiClientContext Create(
        Action<ApiClientConfigurationExpression> action) {

        var apiClientContext = new ApiClientContext();
        var configurationExpression =
            new ApiClientConfigurationExpression(apiClientContext);

        action(configurationExpression);

        return apiClientContext;
    }

    private void InitializeHttpClient() {

        if (BaseUri == null) {
            throw new ArgumentNullException("BaseUri");
        }

        if (string.IsNullOrEmpty(AuthorizationValue)) {
            throw new ArgumentNullException("AuthorizationValue");
        }

        // Set BaseUri
        _httpClient.Value.BaseAddress = BaseUri;

        // Set default headers
        _httpClient.Value.DefaultRequestHeaders.Authorization =
            new AuthenticationHeaderValue("Basic", AuthorizationValue);
    }
}
```

What you have here is only a portion of the client API, but this class is the one on which you'll build your extensions. The Create method of ApiClientContext is the only public member that you are exposing, and it's responsible for constructing an ApiClientContext instance. The Create method accepts a parameter that is of type

Action<ApiClientConfigurationExpression>, and ApiClientConfigurationExpression has public methods to allow you to set the necessary values such as the base URI of the API. See Listing 7-8 for the implementation of the ApiClientConfigurationExpression class.

Listing 7-8. ApiClientConfigurationExpression Class

```
public class ApiClientConfigurationExpression {

    private readonly ApiClientContext _apiClientContext;

    internal ApiClientConfigurationExpression(
        ApiClientContext apiClientContext) {

        if (apiClientContext == null) {

            throw new ArgumentNullException("apiClientContext");
        }

        _apiClientContext = apiClientContext;
    }

    public ApiClientConfigurationExpression SetCredentialsFromAppSetting(
        string affiliateKeyAppSettingKey,
        string usernameAppSettingKey,
        string passwordAppSettingKey) {

        if (string.IsNullOrEmpty(affiliateKeyAppSettingKey)) {

            throw new ArgumentException(
                "The argument 'affiliateKeyAppSettingKey' is null or empty.",
                "affiliateKeyAppSettingKey");
        }

        if (string.IsNullOrEmpty(usernameAppSettingKey)) {

            throw new ArgumentException(
                "The argument 'usernameAppSettingKey' is null or empty.",
                "usernameAppSettingKey");
        }

        if (string.IsNullOrEmpty(passwordAppSettingKey)) {

            throw new ArgumentException(
                "The argument 'passwordAppSettingKey' is null or empty.",
                "passwordAppSettingKey");
        }

        string affiliateKey = ConfigurationManager.AppSettings[affiliateKeyAppSettingKey];
        string username = ConfigurationManager.AppSettings[usernameAppSettingKey];
        string password = ConfigurationManager.AppSettings[passwordAppSettingKey];
```

```csharp
        if (string.IsNullOrEmpty(affiliateKey)) {

            throw new ArgumentException(
                string.Format(
                    "The application setting '{0}' does not exist or its value is null.",
                    affiliateKeyAppSettingKey));
        }

        if (string.IsNullOrEmpty(username)) {

            throw new ArgumentException(
                string.Format(
                    "The application setting '{0}' does not exist or its value is null.",
                    usernameAppSettingKey));
        }

        if (string.IsNullOrEmpty(password)) {

            throw new ArgumentException(
                string.Format(
                    "The application setting '{0}' does not exist or its value is null.",
                    passwordAppSettingKey));
        }

        _apiClientContext.AffiliateKey = affiliateKey;
        _apiClientContext.AuthorizationValue =
            EncodeToBase64(string.Format("{0}:{1}", username, password));

        return this;
    }

    public ApiClientConfigurationExpression ConnectTo(string baseUri) {

        if (string.IsNullOrEmpty(baseUri)) {

            throw new ArgumentNullException("baseUri");
        }

        _apiClientContext.BaseUri = new Uri(baseUri);

        return this;
    }

    private static string EncodeToBase64(string value) {

        byte[] toEncodeAsBytes = Encoding.UTF8.GetBytes(value);
        return Convert.ToBase64String(toEncodeAsBytes);
    }
}
```

As you can see, there are not many methods exposed publicly, but if your API client needs any configuration points, this is the place where you can expose those. Also notice that all public methods return the class instance itself to expose a fluent API so you can chain method calls.

You have all the infrastructure for constructing your clients but you haven't had any implementation performing these operations. Let's perform these operations through extension methods on the ApiClientContext class (see Listing 7-9), which will retrieve the client instances through the internal ConcurrentDictionary that is on the ApiClientContext class.

Listing 7-9. ApiClientContext Extensions

```
public static class ApiClientContextExtensions {

    public static IShipmentsClient GetShipmentsClient(
        this ApiClientContext apiClientContext) {

        return apiClientContext.GetClient<IShipmentsClient>(() =>
            new ShipmentsClient(
                apiClientContext.HttpClient,
                apiClientContext.AffiliateKey));
    }

    public static IShipmentTypesClient GetShipmentTypesClient(
        this ApiClientContext apiClientContext) {

        return apiClientContext.GetClient<IShipmentTypesClient>(() =>
            new ShipmentTypesClient(apiClientContext.HttpClient));
    }

    internal static TClient GetClient<TClient>(
        this ApiClientContext apiClientContext, Func<TClient> valueFactory) {

        return (TClient)apiClientContext.Clients.GetOrAdd(
            typeof(TClient),
            k => valueFactory());
    }
}
```

Here you're taking advantage of the GetOrAdd method of the ConcurrentDictionary, which gives you the ability to retrieve the object if there is already one with the same key or add a new one if there is none. Because the client methods and the HttpClient methods are thread safe, there's nothing to prevent you from having single instances of the client classes.

Now the HTTP API's .NET wrapper is ready, so you can use it on your web application to consume the data through the HTTP API.

Building a Web Client with ASP.NET MVC

This section will use that .NET wrapper library you just created to create an ASP.NET MVC application for an affiliate to view, submit, and modify its shipment records. Note that this is a fairly simple web application and is not meant to be a guide on how to build your web applications with ASP.NET MVC. The only purpose of this web application is to show how to consume the HTTP API through the .NET wrapper library.

PingYourPackage.API.Client.Web Project

To create your client web application, you have to add a new ASP.NET MVC project named PingYourPackage.
API.Client.Web. We choose to use the default ASP.NET MVC template for this application as the UI design of the
application is not a big concern here. Besides the preinstalled NuGet packages on the ASP.NET MVC project template,
we have installed the following NuGet packages into our PingYourPackage.API.Client.Web:

- Autofac.Mvc4

- WebApiDoodle.Net.Http.Client

These packages have dependencies to other packages, and they got pulled into the project automatically.
In addition, we added the PingYourPackage.API.Client project reference in our web project.

Registering the Client Classes Through an IoC Container

In the ASP.Net MVC application, you'll leverage the ASP.NET MVC's dependency resolver extensibility as we did in our
Web API implementation. Both implementations are quite similar but registration points are obviously different.
Let's look at the code in Listing 7-10 for our ASP.NET MVC controller's constructor.

Listing 7-10. ASP.NET MVC Controller and Its Constructor

```
public class HomeController : Controller {

    private const int DefaultPageSize = 2;
    private readonly IShipmentsClient _shipmentsClient;
    private readonly IShipmentTypesClient _shipmentTypesClient;

    public HomeController(
        IShipmentsClient shipmentsClient,
        IShipmentTypesClient shipmentTypesClient) {

        _shipmentsClient = shipmentsClient;
        _shipmentTypesClient = shipmentTypesClient;
    }

    // Lines romoved for brevity
}
```

The controller's constructor accepts two parameters that are of type IShipmentsClient and
IShipmentTypesClient. By default, the ASP.NET MVC infrastructure cannot create this controller. However, you can
set a custom dependency resolver for ASP.NET MVC and set it through the static DependencyResolver.SetResolver
method. We used the Autofac ASP.NET MVC implementation (see Listing 7-11).

Listing 7-11. Internal AutofacMvc Class to Register Client Instances

```
internal static class AutofacMvc {

    internal static void Initialize() {

        var builder = new ContainerBuilder();
        DependencyResolver.SetResolver(
            new AutofacDependencyResolver(RegisterServices(builder)));
    }
```

```
private static IContainer RegisterServices(ContainerBuilder builder) {

    builder.RegisterControllers(typeof(MvcApplication).Assembly);

    ApiClientContext apiClientContex =
        ApiClientContext.Create(cfg =>
            cfg.SetCredentialsFromAppSetting(
                "Api:AffiliateKey", "Api:Username", "Api:Password")
                    .ConnectTo("https://localhost:44306"));

    // Register the clients
    builder.Register(c => apiClientContex.GetShipmentsClient())
        .As<IShipmentsClient>().InstancePerHttpRequest();

    builder.Register(c => apiClientContex.GetShipmentTypesClient())
        .As<IShipmentTypesClient>().InstancePerHttpRequest();

    return builder.Build();
    }
}
```

Looking at the AutofacMvc class, you can see that the RegisterServices method does the registration of the HTTP client wrappers. First, you create the ApiClientContext class through which you'll get the client instances. Then you use the SetCredentialsFromAppSetting method to set the credentials for the HTTP API, and these credentials are stored as appSettings inside the web.config file (see Listing 7-12).

Listing 7-12. AppSetting Values for API Credentials Inside Web.config

```
<appSettings>

    // Lines romoved for brevity

    <add key="Api:Username" value="CompanyA" />
    <add key="Api:Password" value="CompanyAPass" />
    <add key="Api:AffiliateKey" value="041f765a-1019-4956-b610-370d05be95ac" />
</appSettings>
```

Then, the clients are registered per request instance using the extension methods that were built for ApiClientContext. Finally, we called the static Initialize method of the AutofacMvc class during the application startup phase (see Listing 7-13).

Listing 7-13. Application_Start Method Inside Global.asax.cs

```
protected void Application_Start() {

    AutofacMvc.Initialize();
    FilterConfig.RegisterGlobalFilters(GlobalFilters.Filters);
    RouteConfig.RegisterRoutes(RouteTable.Routes);
    BundleConfig.RegisterBundles(BundleTable.Bundles);
}
```

The IoC container registration is now completed and we can move onto building the MVC controller to consume the HTTP API.

Implementing the MVC Controller

For this sample, we have one ASP.NET MVC controller named HomeController, and this controller will work with the IShipmentsClient and IShipmentTypesClient implementations, which will be provided through the dependency resolver that have been put in place. The other important part to mention is the asynchronous nature of our calls. Because the API wrappers are fully asynchronous, you'll make the network calls inside the ASP.NET MVC controller actions asynchronously thanks to MVC's support of the task-based asynchronous pattern. You can see the Index action method in Listing 7-14, which gets the paginated list of shipment records for the affiliate.

Listing 7-14. MVC Controller Index Method to Get Paginated Shipments Collection

```
public class HomeController : Controller {

    // Lines romoved for brevity

    public async Task<ViewResult> Index(int page = 1) {

        PaginatedDto<ShipmentDto> shipments =
            await _shipmentsClient.GetShipmentsAsync(
                new PaginatedRequestCommand(page, DefaultPageSize));

        return View(shipments);
    }

    // Lines romoved for brevity
}
```

Nearly all action methods are similar to the Index action method. You make a call to the HTTP API and get back the results. Then, you process the result in the ASP.NET MVC action. You can see a slightly different action method implementation for creating a new shipment record in Listing 7-15.

Listing 7-15. MVC Controller Create Action to Handle POST Request Against the HTTP API

```
public class HomeController : Controller {

    // Lines romoved for brevity

    [HttpGet]
    public async Task<ViewResult> Create() {

        await GetAndSetShipmentTypesAsync();
        return View();
    }

    [HttpPost]
    [ActionName("Create")]
    [ValidateAntiForgeryToken]
    public async Task<ActionResult> Create_Post(
        ShipmentByAffiliateRequestModel requestModel) {
```

```
    if (ModelState.IsValid) {

        ShipmentDto shipment =
            await _shipmentsClient.AddShipmentAsync(requestModel);

        return RedirectToAction("Details", new { id = shipment.Key });
    }

    await GetAndSetShipmentTypesAsync();
    return View(requestModel);
}

private async Task GetAndSetShipmentTypesAsync() {

    PaginatedDto<ShipmentTypeDto> shipmentTypes =
        await _shipmentTypesClient.GetShipmentTypesAsync(new PaginatedRequestCommand(1, 50));

    ViewBag.ShipmentTypes = shipmentTypes.Items.Select(x => new SelectListItem() {
        Text = x.Name,
        Value = x.Key.ToString()
    });
}

    // Lines romoved for brevity
}
```

We skipped other action method implementations here as they have nearly the same structure. However, you can find the implementation of those action methods inside the application's source code. With a bit more work on the ASP.NET MVC Razor views, you obtain the results as shown in Figure 7-4.

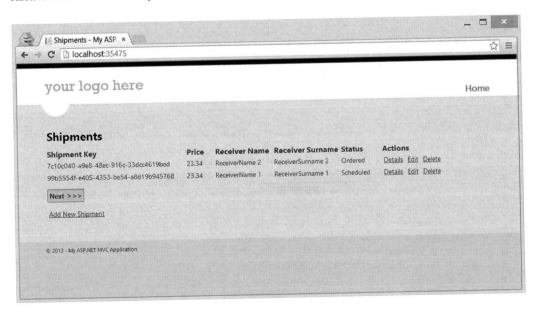

Figure 7-4. *Home page of the web client*

> ■ **Note** So far, we haven't shown how we host our Web API application because we have a dedicated chapter on this (Chapter 17). In that chapter, we'll show how you can host this application and get it up and running. For this demonstration, we used a simple ASP.NET host (also known as Web Host), which you can find the code for in the sample application.

Now you can see that we consumed the HTTP API successfully and got the paginated list of shipments data. You can also see the details of a shipment record by visiting the details page of a shipment (see Figure 7-5).

Figure 7-5. *Shipment details page of the web client*

When you run the application locally, you have the chance to create a new shipment record and edit or delete an existing one.

Summary

In the three sample application chapters, we wanted to dig through all the steps of building an ASP.NET Web API application. We explained how to design the application business layer and the API structure in Chapter 5. Then, in Chapter 6, we explored the details of implementing the ASP.NET Web API application itself. In this chapter, we focused on creating a client application that can consume the HTTP API with a custom-written wrapper. We hope that these three chapters have given you an idea on how to go ahead and build an API layer with ASP.NET Web API and that you are now ready to dive into each layer of ASP.NET Web API architecture in the following chapters.

CHAPTER 8

Routing

In our ASP.NET Web API applications, incoming HTTP requests are handled by controller action methods. When an incoming request is received, it is routed to a proper action method, and the routing system provides the fundamental layer for this movement.

The routing feature in ASP.NET Web API is one of the key components of the whole framework. The HTTP request is being retrieved by the routing system, and this routing system differs with the choice of the hosting environment (ASP.NET Host, Self-Host, etc.) There are a lot of implementation details involved in this process. We will go through them lightly rather than in depth, because one of this book's aims is to avoid too much talk about implementation details. Instead, we will look at the routing feature from the API standpoint, particularly at how that feature behaves and how to take control of it.

Understanding Routing Mechanism

Throughout the book, we generally try to avoid mentioning the framework's implementation details, but we think that going a little further inside the processing pipeline will help you understand how routing gets involved and where it is being used. The fundamental goal of this section is to show you that there is nothing magical about the routing mechanism by giving you a little bit of an inside scoop on its workings.

If you have ever played with ASP.NET MVC, the routing feature in ASP.NET Web API will seem very familiar because the concept is the same. ASP.NET routing was first introduced by ASP.NET MVC before .NET v4.0 in a separate, bin-deployable assembly named *System.Web.Routing.dll*. The main idea behind the routing mechanism was to enable request-dispatching by providing a certain URL with an HTTP handler that could process the requests made to that URL. These routes can be registered through the Add method of RouteTable.Routes static property, and this method accepts two parameters: the name of the route as a string and the route item as System.Web.Routing.RouteBase. In order to inject the routing mechanism into the request processing pipeline, an HTTP module named System.Web.Routing.UrlRoutingModule was introduced inside the same assembly. With the introduction of .NET v4.0, this module is registered by default when an application is run under *.NET Framework v4.0 Integrated Application Pool* in IIS.

You might be thinking that running an ASP.NET Web API application under IIS is not the only option and that we don't have a routing module in other hosting options, such as self-host. So what happens then? This is the key difference in the ASP.NET Web API routing system. The routing feature has been decoupled from the ASP.NET routing mechanism in ASP.NET Web API so that the same configuration model can be used regardless of the hosting choice.

Let's see a simple example of registering a route when an application is being hosted inside the IIS (Listing 8-1).

Listing 8-1. Route Registration in ASP.NET Web API with ASP.NET Hosting

```
protected void Application_Start(object sender, EventArgs e) {

    GlobalConfiguration.Configuration.Routes.MapHttpRoute(
        "DefaultHttpRoute",
```

```
        "api/{controller}/{id}",
        new { id = RouteParameter.Optional }
    );
}
```

When using the ASP.NET hosting option, routes are registered through the MapHttpRoute extension method of the static Routes property (a type of HttpRouteCollection) of the HttpConfiguration object, which can be reached through the GlobalConfiguration.Configuration property. If you are in a self-host environment, use the same MapHttpRoute extension method of HttpRouteCollection, but this time you will reach HttpRouteCollection through the Routes property of the HttpSelfHostConfiguration instance. Listing 8-2 shows how to register the route shown in Listing 8-1 but in a self-host environment. (Refer to Chapter 17 for more information about hosting options.)

Listing 8-2. Route Registration in ASP.NET Web API with Self-Host

```
class Program {

    static void Main(string[] args) {

        var config =
            new HttpSelfHostConfiguration(
                new Uri("http://localhost:5478"));

        config.Routes.MapHttpRoute(
            "DefaultHttpRoute",
            "api/{controller}/{id}",
            new { id = RouteParameter.Optional }
        );

        //Lines omitted for brevity
    }
}
```

In both scenarios, the MapHttpRoute extension method of HttpRouteCollection creates a System.Web.Http.Routing. IHttpRoute instance and adds it to the HttpRouteCollection. This IHttpRoute instance varies according to the hosting choice. For example, on the ASP.NET host, the System.Web.Http.WebHost.Routing.HostedHttpRoute internal class, which is one of the implementations of IHttpRoute, is being used. On the other side, in a self-host environment, System.Web.Http. Routing.HttpRoute, which is the route class for self-host (i.e., hosted outside of ASP.NET), is being used.

Finally, depending on the hosting choice, the routes are inspected and the proper actions take place if there are any matching routes. With ASP.NET hosting, a System.Web.Http.WebHost.HttpControllerRouteHandler instance is attached to every single route. This HttpControllerRouteHandler instance is an implementation of System.Web. Routing.IRouteHandler, which is responsible for returning a System.Web.IHttpHandler implementation to process the incoming request. In the case here, the handler is the System.Web.Http.WebHost.HttpControllerHandler, which processes the request by gluing together all the components of the ASP.NET Web API. In the case of self-host, the WCF channel stack and the service model layers are involved in receiving and processing the request.

The beauty here is that we don't have to concern ourselves about any of this when building Web API applications, but it never hurts to know what is going on under the hood or get a bit of a sense of how the system works. From now on, we will only talk about routing by giving samples with ASP.NET Web hosting. Except for the registration point, all the other features will work the same in a self-hosting environment.

Defining Web API Routes

In ASP.NET Web API, routes need to be defined on the System.Web.Http.GlobalConfiguration.Configuration. Routes property with the MapHttpRoute extension method, as shown in the previous section. Actually, there are other ways to register routes—the Add method of HttpRouteCollection class, for example. This method accepts two parameters: a string parameter for the name of the route and IHttpRoute implementation. Also, routes can be directly added into the System.Web.Routing.RouteTable.Routes static property with the MapHttpRoute extension method if the application is hosted under ASP.NET. We'll use the Routes static property on the GlobalConfiguration. Configuration object for registering routes, along with the MapHttpRoute extension method, throughout this chapter.

Listing 8-3 is an example of a registered route for ASP.NET Web API.

Listing 8-3. Sample Route Registration

```
protected void Application_Start(object sender, EventArgs e) {

    GlobalConfiguration.Configuration.Routes.MapHttpRoute(
        "DefaultHttpRoute",
        "api/{controller}/{id}",
        new { id = RouteParameter.Optional }
    );
}
```

Notice that the routes are registered inside the Application_Start method in the *Global.asax* file (actually, in full it's the *Global.asax.cs* file). Before explaining the route just defined, let's see the overloads of the MapHttpRoute extension method (Listing 8-4).

Listing 8-4. MapHttpRoute Extension Method Overloads

```
public static IHttpRoute MapHttpRoute(
    this HttpRouteCollection routes,
    string name,
    string routeTemplate);

public static IHttpRoute MapHttpRoute(
    this HttpRouteCollection routes,
    string name,
    string routeTemplate,
    object defaults);

public static IHttpRoute MapHttpRoute(
    this HttpRouteCollection routes,
    string name,
    string routeTemplate,
    object defaults,
    object constraints);

public static IHttpRoute MapHttpRoute(
    this HttpRouteCollection routes,
    string name,
    string routeTemplate,
    object defaults,
    object constraints,
    HttpMessageHandler handler);
```

In our example we used the first overload method shown in Listing 8-4. The first string parameter given here is the name of the route. The route name can be any arbitrary string, but if there are multiple routes, the name of each route should be unique. The second parameter passed is the route template, which will be compared with the URL of the incoming request. As a third parameter, an anonymous object for default values has been passed. If the Optional static property type of RouteParameter is passed for a route parameter, that route parameter can be omitted. As a fourth parameter, another anonymous object can be passed to specify the route constraints, which will be covered in the "Route Constraints" subsection. Finally, the last overload of the MapHttpRoute method accepts five parameters, and this overload is for per-route message handlers which we will see in Chapter 10.

> ■ **Note** If your ASP.NET Web API application is running under ASP.NET side by side with any other ASP.NET framework, such as ASP.NET MVC or ASP.NET Web Forms, all of your routes get collected inside the System.Web.Routing.RouteTable. Routes static property, regardless of the framework type. So each route needs a unique name. Otherwise you will get an error indicating that a route with the specified name is already in the route collection. For example, you cannot have both a Web API route and an MVC route named *MyRoute* inside the same application.

HTTP Methods and Routing

In routing with ASP.NET Web API, the HTTP methods that the incoming request is made through, virtually invisible at first glance, play a huge role in the selection of controller actions. Routing in ASP.NET Web API is inspired by ASP.NET MVC routing, but there is one missing part inside the example in Listing 8-3: the *action* route parameter. For those not familiar with ASP.NET MVC, the action parameter represents the ASP.NET MVC controller action method name and the action method inside the controller is selected on the basis of this parameter's value. In ASP.NET Web API, the actions selected depend upon the HTTP method the request is made through.

For example, there is a sample controller named CarsController, as shown in Listing 8-5.

Listing 8-5. Sample CarsController

```
public class CarsController : ApiController {

    public string[] Get() {

        return new string[] {
            "Car 1",
            "Car 2",
            "Car 3",
            "Car 4"
        };
    }

    public string Get(int id) {

        return string.Format("Car {0}", id);
    }

    public string[] GetCarsByType(string type) {

        return new string[] {
            "Car 2",
            "Car 4"
        };
    }
```

```
    public string[] GetCarsByMake(string make) {

        return new string[] {
            "Car 1",
            "Car 3",
            "Car 4"
        };
    }

    public string[] GetCarsByMakeByType(
        string make, string type) {

        return new string[] {
            "Car 4"
        };
    }
}
}
```

With the route registered in Listing 8-3, the first CarsController.Get method in Listing 8-5 will be invoked when there is a GET request to the /api/cars URL. Let's quickly go through the steps to understand how the Get method of CarsController is invoked.

The "api" part inside the URL is the static URL segment that was specified inside the route template. The second segment inside the URL is "cars". Because it was indicated inside the route template that the second segment would be the controller name, the system will look for a unique class that implements the IHttpController interface and has a prefix of "cars" (case insensitive) and "Controller" (again case insensitive), as concatenated on the prefix (CarsController). This action is performed by the registered implementation of the IHttpControllerSelector interface, which is the DefaultHttpControllerSelector class by default and the controller selector instance here is invoked by HttpControllerDispatcher. If any controller is found, the request goes up one level inside the pipeline. If no controller is found, the HttpControllerDispatcher sets up the "404 Not Found" response message and terminates the request. The example here has a controller named CarsController and this means that the request will be dispatched to a higher level inside the pipeline, where the execution of the ExecuteAsync method of the controller instance happens.

■ **Note** Until now, we have used ApiController in all examples in this book as a base controller class and the ApiController as the default implementation of IHttpController interface, which brings filters and a lot of useful functionality. The controller action selection logic that will be briefly explained in the next paragraphs is applicable only if the ApiController is used as the base controller class along with the ApiControllerActionSelector, which is the default implementation of IHttpActionSelector. If you want to replace the ApiController with another implementation of IHttpController, there won't be any default action methods. The controllers and action selection logic will be gone through in depth in Chapter 9, so that part will only be touched upon here.

In the example, when the ExecuteAsync method of the ApiController class is executed, the action method selection logic kicks in. (The details of how this logic is performed mostly belong to Chapter 9, where this will be covered in depth.) What you need to know here to make sense out of the current scenario is that the action method selection occurs on the basis of the HTTP method chosen. For example, here a GET request is being made to the api/cars URL, and it is dispatched to CarsController. As the request is made through the HTTP GET method, the controller will look for a method with a prefix of "Get" (case insensitive).

One question that may pop up right now might concern having two Get methods inside CarsController. As one of the Get methods accepts the parameter id and the request doesn't contain an id value (such as a route or a query string value), the system will select the method with no parameters. Trying to make a GET request to the URL api/cars/1 will invoke the second Get method because the third URL segment inside the route template represents the id value. This value is an optional parameter because its default value was defined as System.Web.Http.RouteParameter.Optional. Table 8-1 shows a list of request URLs and HTTP methods and their corresponding action methods.

Table 8-1. *Possible Request Options for the Sample in Listing 8-5 with the Route in Listing 8-3*

URL	HTTP Method	Corresponded Action Method
/api/cars	GET	Get()
/api/cars?foo = bar	GET	Get()
/api/cars/1	GET	Get(int id)
/api/cars?type = SUV	GET	GetCarsByType(string type)
/api/cars?make = make1	GET	GetCarsByMake(string make)
/api/cars?make = make1&type = SUV	GET	GetCarsByMakeByType(string make, string type)

This behavior is the same for other verbs as well (as indicated earlier, it will be explored in depth in Chapter 9). Another option with routing—also known as RPC, or Remote Procedure Call—enables the direct calling of an action method, for example, by issuing a GET request to /api/cars/ExpensiveCars and invoking the ExpensiveCars method inside the CarsController. This behavior mostly relates to the controller part of the framework, so it too will be thoroughly explored in Chapter 9.

Having Multiple Web API Routes

Depending on your needs, you might want to have multiple Web API routes in your application. This is a totally acceptable option in ASP.NET Web API, but there are a few important things to be aware of.

If you have multiple routes, the registration order of the routes matters. When a request comes to the routing level, the route collection is scanned to find a match. As soon as a match is found, the search stops, and the remaining routes get ignored. The first route registered will be looked at first, and so on. Let's see the example in Listing 8-6.

Listing 8-6. Multiple Routes Sample

```
protected void Application_Start(object sender, EventArgs e) {

    var routes = GlobalConfiguration.Configuration.Routes;

    routes.MapHttpRoute(
        "DefaultHttpRoute",
        "api/{controller}/{id}",
        new { id = RouteParameter.Optional }
    );
```

```
    routes.MapHttpRoute(
        "VehicleHttpRoute",
        "api/{vehicletype}/{controller}",
        defaults: new { },
        constraints: new { controller = "^vehicles$" }
    );
}
```

The first route is the route that has been used so far in this chapter, and the second one is a little different. Notice that a constraint was used for the controller parameter (don't worry, constraints will be explained later in this chapter). With this constraint in place, we are indicating the routing mechanism to match only if the controller parameter is "vehicles". To complete the sample, there are also two controllers: CarsController (Listing 8-7) and VehiclesController (Listing 8-8).

Listing 8-7. CarsController

```
public class CarsController : ApiController {

    public string[] Get() {

        return new string[] {
            "Car 1",
            "Car 2",
            "Car 3"
        };
    }
}
```

Listing 8-8. VehiclesController

```
public class VehiclesController : ApiController {

    public string[] Get(string vehicletype) {

        return new string[] {
            string.Format("Vehicle 1 ({0})", vehicletype),
            string.Format("Vehicle 2 ({0})", vehicletype),
            string.Format("Vehicle 3 ({0})", vehicletype),
        };
    }
}
```

In this case, if a request is sent against */api/SUV/vehicles* to invoke the action method inside VehiclesController, the second route will never be hit because the first one will be a match and "SUV" will be the value of the controller parameter for the first route template. So the response will be a *"404 Not Found"*, as shown in Figure 8-1.

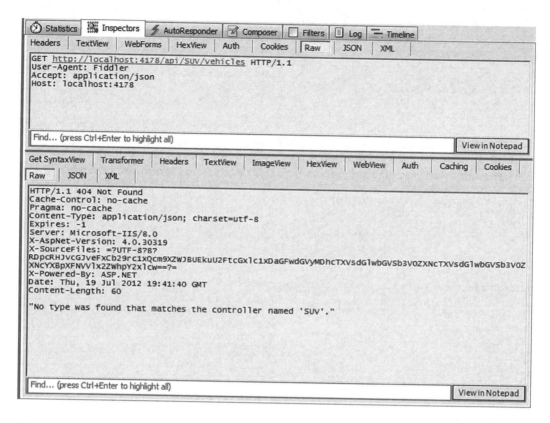

Figure 8-1. *GET request against /api/SUV/vehicles and 404 response*

If the routes are registered as Listing 8-9 shows, you will get the exact behavior desired here (Figure 8-2).

Listing 8-9. Multiple Routes Correct Sample

```
protected void Application_Start(object sender, EventArgs e) {

    var routes = GlobalConfiguration.Configuration.Routes;

    routes.MapHttpRoute(
        "VehicleHttpRoute",
        "api/{vehicletype}/{controller}",
        defaults: new { },
        constraints: new { controller = "^vehicles$" }
    );

    routes.MapHttpRoute(
        "DefaultHttpRoute",
        "api/{controller}/{id}",
        new { id = RouteParameter.Optional }
    );
}
```

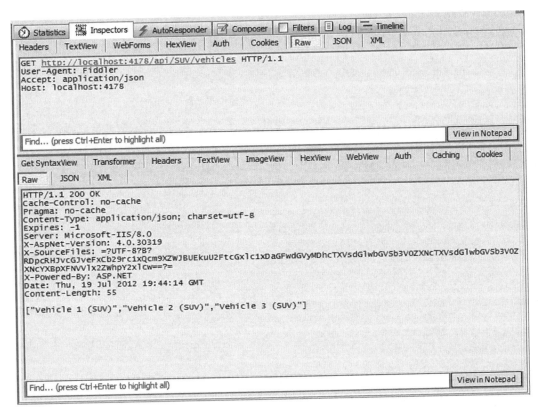

Figure 8-2. *GET request against /api/SUV/vehicles and 200 response*

Route Defaults

For a route to match a request, the first requirement is to supply all the parameter values. For example, if the route template consists of three parameters and only two of them are supplied, the route will be ignored unless the ignored parameters have a default value specified.

The route parameters can have default values and having them enables you to omit specifying parameters. Listing 8-10 shows a slightly different route from the one already used a lot in this chapter.

Listing 8-10. A Route Sample

```
protected void Application_Start(object sender, EventArgs e) {

    var routes = GlobalConfiguration.Configuration.Routes;

    routes.MapHttpRoute(
        "DefaultHttpRoute",
        "api/{controller}/{id}"
    );
}
```

A look at the route template will show that the URL for this route consists of three segments. The first one is the static value, and the remaining two are the parameters that can be changed. When a request is sent to */api/cars/15,* this route will be a match, and the request will get inside the ASP.NET Web API pipeline. Omit the `id` parameter and send a request against */api/cars*, however, and this route will never be a match.

There are two solutions to this issue.

- Specify another route, one that will be a match for the request.

- Provide a default value for the *id* parameter to omit the id segment inside the URL.

Let's take the second approach to solve the issue here. In order to provide default values for the parameters, let's provide an anonymous object for the `default` parameter of the `MapHttpRoute` extension method. The property names of the anonymous object should be the same as the parameter names. If a property name provided doesn't have a match among the route parameters, then that property will get ignored. Listing 8-11 is an example of a solution to the problem.

Listing 8-11. A Route Sample with Default Values

```
protected void Application_Start(object sender, EventArgs e) {

    var routes = GlobalConfiguration.Configuration.Routes;

    routes.MapHttpRoute(
        "DefaultHttpRoute",
        "api/{controller}/{id}",
        new { id = string.Empty }
    );
}
```

When a request is now sent to */api/cars*, this route will be a match, and the value of the id route parameter will be `String.Empty`, which is equivalent to " ". If a value is provided for the `id` segment, the default value will be overridden by the one provided. For example, if a request is sent to /api/cars/15, the value of the `id` route parameter will be *15*.

Optional Parameters

What is actually wanted in the above example is, not a default value for the `id` parameter, but an optional parameter. In the Web API framework, provide the `Optional` static property of the `System.Web.Http.RouteParameter` for a route parameter as the default value, and the route parameter will be omitted. Listing 8-12 is an example of this feature.

Listing 8-12. A Route with Optional Parameters

```
protected void Application_Start(object sender, EventArgs e) {

    var routes = GlobalConfiguration.Configuration.Routes;

    routes.MapHttpRoute(
        "DefaultHttpRoute",
        "api/{controller}/{id}",
        new { id = RouteParameter.Optional }
    );
}
```

When a request is sent to /api/cars, the route in Listing 8-12 will still be a match, but this time there will be no id parameter specified. Instead, the id parameter will be omitted.

Route Constraints

In some cases, you won't want a particular URL structure to match a route. In such cases, the route constraint feature allows you to restrict the requests that match a particular route. A route constraint can be applied to each route parameter and in order to specify a constraint for a route parameter, you will need to provide an anonymous object for the constraints parameter of the MapHttpRoute extension method. The property names of the anonymous object provided should be the same as the parameter names.

The route constraints can be applied either as regular expressions or as custom route constraints, and these options will be explained separately.

Regular Expression Route Constraints

If you provide a string value as a route constraint object property value, the system will assume that it is a regular expression route constraint and process the constraint that way. Let's assume that you'd like to receive id parameters as digits for a particular route. Listing 8-13 shows how to implement this using a regular expression route constraint.

Listing 8-13. Regular Expression Route Constraint Sample

```
protected void Application_Start(object sender, EventArgs e) {

    var routes = GlobalConfiguration.Configuration.Routes;

    routes.MapHttpRoute(
        "DefaultHttpRoute",
        routeTemplate: "api/{controller}/{id}",
        defaults: new { },
        constraints: new { id = @"\d+" }
    );
}
```

By sending a request to /api/cars/15, this route will be a match, because the id parameter value consists only of digits. If a request is sent to /api/cars/foo, the route will not be a match, because "foo" value doesn't match the digits-only regular expression specified.

Custom Route Constraints

In some cases, the route parameter value is not enough to see if the route should be a match or not, and custom route constraints come in handy in such cases. A custom route constraint is a class that implements the System.Web.Http.Routing.IHttpRouteConstraint interface. The IHttpRouteConstraint interface has only one method, called Match, which will return a Boolean value. If the return value is true, it means the route parameter is valid. If the return value is false, the route parameter is invalid.

Currently, the RouteParameter.Optional and regular expression route constraints don't get along very well. For example, in the example shown in Listing 8.13, RouteParameter.Optional couldn't be provided as the default value for the id parameter. Had we done that, all the requests that came to /api/cars would be rejected because the regular expression values would not match. Listing 8-14 shows a custom route constraint implementation which works around this problem.

Listing 8-14. A Custom Route Constraint Implementation

```
public class OptionalRegExConstraint : IHttpRouteConstraint {

    private readonly string _regEx;

    public OptionalRegExConstraint(string expression) {

        if (string.IsNullOrEmpty(expression)) {

            throw new ArgumentNullException("expression");
        }

        _regEx = expression;
    }

    public bool Match(
        HttpRequestMessage request,
        IHttpRoute route,
        string parameterName,
        IDictionary<string, object> values,
        HttpRouteDirection routeDirection) {

        if (values[parameterName] != RouteParameter.Optional) {

            object value;
            values.TryGetValue(parameterName, out value);
            string pattern = "^(" + _regEx + ")$";
            string input = Convert.ToString(
                value, CultureInfo.InvariantCulture);

            return Regex.IsMatch(
                input,
                pattern,
                RegexOptions.IgnoreCase |
                RegexOptions.CultureInvariant);
        }

        return true;
    }
}
```

As you can see, all the information you need is being provided inside the Match method. You have access to the whole HttpRequestMessage and necessary route information. The OptionalRegExConstraint mimics the regular expression constraint functionality of the underlying routing system. Additionally, this custom route constraint also examines the route parameter's value to see whether it is RouteParameter.Optional. If so, the route constraint just returns true indicating that a route parameter is a match.

Listing 8-15 shows the registration code for this custom constraint.

Listing 8-15. Custom Route Constraint Registration

```
protected void Application_Start(object sender, EventArgs e) {

    var routes = GlobalConfiguration.Configuration.Routes;

    routes.MapHttpRoute(
        "DefaultHttpRoute",
        "api/{controller}/{id}",
        new { id = RouteParameter.Optional },
        new { id = new OptionalRegExConstraint(@"\d+") }
    );
}
```

Now when a request comes for /api/cars, the request will pass through the routing successfully, as the id parameter is optional (Figure 8-3).

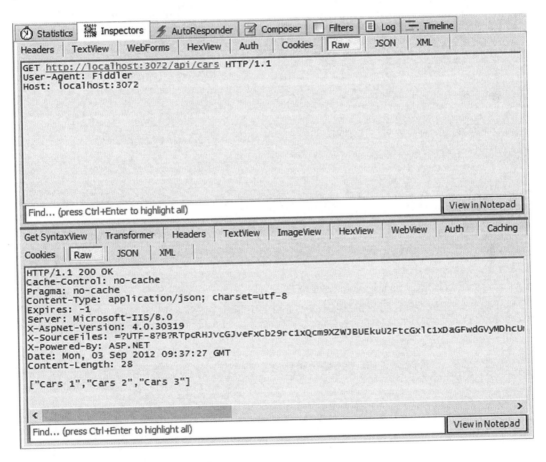

Figure 8-3. GET request against /api/cars

If a request is made to /api/cars/15, the route will still be a match, because the id segment of the URL consists only of digits (Figure 8-4).

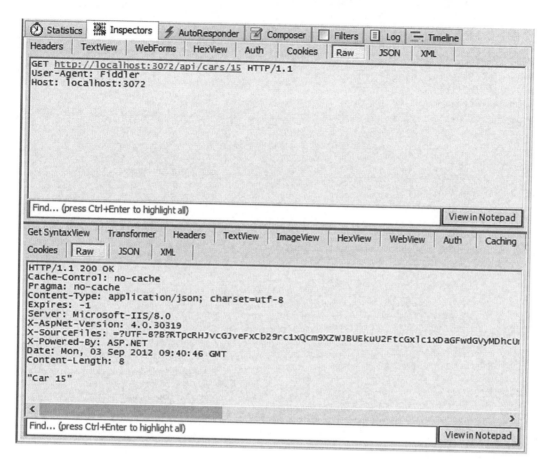

Figure 8-4. GET request against /api/cars/15

If we send a request to /api/cars/foo, the route won't be a match because the id segment of the URL doesn't consist of digits (Figure 8-5).

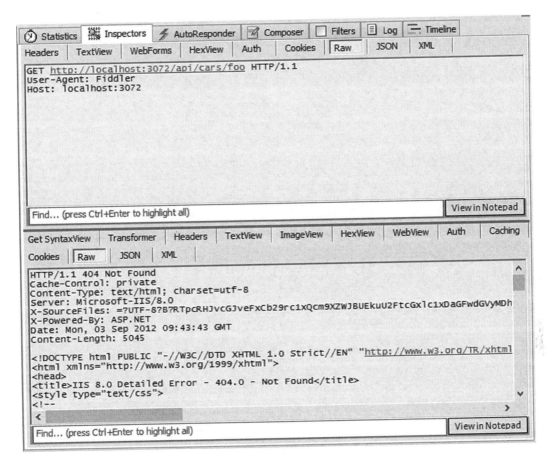

Figure 8-5. *GET request against /api/cars/foo*

Summary

Routing is one of the key components of the ASP.NET Web API framework and the first place where the actual request arrives. This chapter first looked at implementation details and then moved forward to the actual usage and features of the routing mechanism.

Routing has an important place inside the framework for several reasons. One is that default controller and action selection logics heavily rely on routing mechanism. Also, another key feature of routing allows us to produce REST-friendly URIs.

If you are familiar with ASP.NET routing mechanism, the routing feature in ASP.NET Web API will feel very familiar to you. Actually, the ASP.NET routing module is being used under the hood when you are hosting your Web API application on ASP.NET, but the framework abstracts the underlying infrastructure away to make its hosting layer agnostic.

CHAPTER 9

Controllers and Actions

If we think of the ASP.NET Web API framework as a human body, the controller and actions part is the heart of that body. Many components of the Web API framework are glued together by the `ApiController` class, which is the default controller implementation provided out of the box. Filters, model binding, formatters, action selection—these are all part of the controller execution process.

In this chapter, we will first explain how a request comes into a controller. Then we will take a different approach and get started with the hard way: implementing our own controller to understand what is really going on. Later on, we will look at `ApiController` to discover the possibilities and features it offers.

Overview

In ASP.NET Web API, the controller part is one of the components whose main responsibility is to process the business logic in view of request inputs and to return a proper result in the desired format. The controller class should be an implementation of the `System.Web.Http.IHttpController` interface, which has only one method, named `ExecuteAsync`, as shown in Listing 9-1.

Listing 9-1. System.Web.Http.IHttpController

```
public interface IHttpController {

    Task<HttpResponseMessage> ExecuteAsync(
        HttpControllerContext controllerContext,
        CancellationToken cancellationToken);
}
```

As was seen in Chapter 8, the first part of the processing pipeline, the part that deals with the request, is the routing component. If there is a route match, the request is taken to a higher level in the pipeline. This is the part where the message handlers are invoked (the responsibilities of the message handlers and how they fit inside the pipeline are explained in Chapter 10). If there is no message handler registered to run, then the request is directly taken to `HttpRoutingDispatcher`, which we explain in the next section.

Overview of HttpRoutingDispatcher

`HttpRoutingDispatcher` examines the matched route and chooses which message handler to call to process the request. `HttpRoutingDispatcher` is a message handler itself and is derived from the `HttpMessageHandler` abstract class.

The decision being made here is based on whether the matched route has a handler attached to it or not. We will see in Chapter 10 how to attach a custom handler to a route in some detail, including examples. Briefly, however, if `IHttpRoute.Handler` is null, then `HttpRoutingDispatcher` delegates it to the `HttpControllerDispatcher`, which is itself a message handler. If there is a handler attached to the matched route, the request will be processed by that message handler from that point on.

In terms of the controller component inside the framework, this is a life-altering decision, because if there is a handler attached to the matched route, the controller component will not be there unless the custom handler handles it specifically. So what we can take from this is that the HttpControllerDispatcher is the one that dispatches the request to an appropriate controller and processes the request accordingly.

The main responsibility of the HttpControllerDispatcher message handler is to select the appropriate controller type, activate the selected controller type, and invoke the ExecuteAsync method of the selected controller. The HttpControllerDispatcher is also the one that returns a "404 Not Found" HttpResponseMessage if there is no controller match.

The controller type selection is delegated to a controller selector service, which is an implementation of IHttpControllerSelector interface. Before moving forward, let's go through the controller type selection logic in the next subsection.

Controller Type Selection

The controller type selection is separated from the HttpControllerDispatcher implementation and performed by a service that is an implementation of the IHttpControllerSelector interface. The controller selector service is registered through the ServicesContainer, which was explained in the "Configuration" section in Chapter 1.

The IHttpControllerSelector interface has two working methods, as shown in Listing 9-2. We care only about the SelectController method in the present case.

Listing 9-2. IHttpControllerSelector Interface

```
public interface IHttpControllerSelector {

    HttpControllerDescriptor SelectController(HttpRequestMessage request);
    IDictionary<string, HttpControllerDescriptor> GetControllerMapping();
}
```

By default, the DefaultHttpControllerSelector is registered as a controller selector service. The controller selection will be performed by this class unless you replace it with a custom implementation, as was also explained in Chapter 1's discussion of how to replace an existing service (see the "Configuration" section). To find a controller, the DefaultHttpControllerSelector looks for some specific characteristics, as follows:

- Public classes that implement System.Web.Http.IHttpController interface.

- Public classes that have a suffix of Controller. This lookup is case insensitive.

- Public classes that have the same string value as the controller parameter of the matched route before the Controller suffix. For example, if the controller parameter of the matched route is Cars, the class name should be CarsController (case insensitive).

■ **Note**   The DefaultHttpControllerSelector class actually delegates some of the action to other services. These are assembly resolver (IAssembliesResolver) and controller type resolver (IHttpControllerTypeResolver) services. The default implementations of these services are also provided through ServicesContainer as DefaultAssembliesResolver and DefaultHttpControllerTypeResolver and can be replaced with your own implementations. However, we won't go through these services in this book because it is highly unlikely that you will want to replace these services with your own implementations.

According to these criteria, the DefaultHttpControllerSelector class also checks whether there are multiple matched controllers after the lookup is completed. If this is the case, the DefaultHttpControllerSelector throws an ambiguous controller exception, indicating that there are multiple matched controllers for the request. If there is only one matched controller type, the DefaultHttpControllerSelector will create an HttpControllerDescriptor instance and return it to its caller, which is the HttpControllerDispatcher.

From this point on, the HttpControllerDescriptor instance is responsable to construct the controller through its SelectController method. The activation of the controller type is also handled by a service: IHttpControllerActivator which has only one method named Create. By default, the DefaultHttpControllerActivator is registered as IHttpControllerActivator implementation. The DefaultHttpControllerActivator works with the dependency resolver, which we will dig into in Chapter 14, in order to construct the controller instance. If the dependency resolver is not able to create a controller instance, the DefaultHttpControllerActivator's Create method tries to perform this action itself assuming that the controller has a parameterless constructor. If the controller doesn't have a parameterless constructor and there is no custom dependency resolver registered, the DefaultHttpControllerActivator's Create method will throw an exception indicating this situation.

There are some words here which needs to be applied and I indicated them by putting suffix. Also, can we add the below one as note after this paragraph:

It's also worth pointing out here that unlike the message handlers, which we will see in Chapter 12, a controller instance is activated for each request and disposed at the end of the request.

Creating a Controller

As has been mentioned in previous sections of this chapter, the controller class needs to be an implementation of the IHttpController interface. Listing 9-1 shows that the IHttpController interface has only one method, named ExecuteAsync. The ExecuteAsync method is invoked by the HttpControllerDispatcher to process the request and return an HttpResponseMessage instance. The ExecuteAsync method actually returns a Task<HttpResponseMessage> instance. This means that the method is capable of asynchronous processing.

The ExecuteAsync method also takes two parameters. One is HttpControllerContext, and the other is a CancellationToken. The HttpControllerContext holds all the necessary information about the request and the controller, including the request message, route information, controller information, and the like, as shown in Table 9-1.

Table 9-1. *HttpControllerContext Class Properties*

Name	Type	Description
Configuration	HttpConfiguration	Holds the configuration information for the request.
Request	HttpRequestMessage	Represents the HttpRequestMessage of the request.
RouteData	IHttpRouteData	Holds the matched route information for the request.
ControllerDescriptor	HttpControllerDescriptor	Holds the description and configuration for a controller as HttpControllerDescriptor object.
Controller	IHttpController	Holds the controller instance itself.

These properties provide a controller enough information to have an idea about the request and return an appropriate response. In the next subsection, we will see an example of a simple controller.

IHttpController Interface and Your Own Controller

Creating a controller to handle the requests is a fairly easy task. All you need to do is create a class that implements IHttpController, handles the request inside the ExecuteAsync method, and then returns the response from there.

Listing 9-3 shows a sample controller that returns a list of cars for a GET request. As the controller class name is CarsController and assuming that the default route is used, any request that comes to */api/cars* will be dispatched to CarsController.

Listing 9-3. CarsController Sample

```
using System;
using System.Collections.Generic;
using System.Linq;
using System.Net;
using System.Net.Http;
using System.Threading;
using System.Threading.Tasks;
using System.Web;
using System.Web.Http.Controllers;

public class CarsController : IHttpController {

    public Task<HttpResponseMessage> ExecuteAsync(
        HttpControllerContext controllerContext,
        CancellationToken cancellationToken) {

        var request = controllerContext.Request;

        if (request.Method != HttpMethod.Get) {

            var notAllowedResponse =
                new HttpResponseMessage(
                    HttpStatusCode.MethodNotAllowed);

            return Task.FromResult(notAllowedResponse);
        }

        var cars = new[] {
            "Car 1",
            "Car 2",
            "Car 3"
        };

        var response =
            request.CreateResponse(HttpStatusCode.OK, cars);

        return Task.FromResult(response);
    }
}
```

Inside the ExecuteAsync method, we perform several operations.

- First, we check whether or not the request is a GET request.

- If the request is *not* a GET request, then we return a "405 Method Not Allowed" response.

- If the request *is* a GET request, we continue to the next step and return a list of Car instances. In order to return this list, we use the CreateResponse extension method of HttpRequestMessage, because we want to return the response in the format that best matches what the client has asked for. The CreateResponse method performs the content negotiation, as we will see in Chapter 12.

- In order to return the response message in either case, we use the FromResult method of the Task class to create a completed Task<HttpResponseMessage> object. Because we don't actually run anything asynchronously here, we want to avoid the cost of a thread switch, and the FromResult method gives us the ability to create a pre-completed Task object, as we have seen in Chapter 2.

Most of the operations just listed are not actually related to business logic. We are trying to adapt to the framework, which is not a very good programming model. Besides, the sample in Listing 9-3 deals only with GET requests. The experience would be worse if we were dealing with other types of HTTP requests.

In order to have a better programming model, the ASP.NET Web API framework includes an abstract controller base class, named ApiController, that implements the IHttpController interface. We will explain and use this abstract class for the rest of this chapter.

ApiControllers: Out of the Box IHttpController Implementation

The System.Web.Http.ApiController abstract controller class provides a very clean programming model and request-processing pipeline containing various types of components. When you use ApiController class as a base controller class, you will get actions, action selection logic, filters, and content negotiation, all of them free.

At the fundamental level, ApiController is no different from a typical controller. As was explained before, the HttpControllerDispatcher has no knowledge of the exact type of your controller class, nor is it concerned about it. The only thing it knows is that the controller class implements the IHttpController interface, and hence it will invoke the ExecuteAsync method of that controller. When you use the ApiController class as the base class of your controller, the same applies. However, under the hood, there are a few important operations that are triggered by the ExecuteAsync method of the ApiController. They include invoking the filters, processing the action selection logic, parameter binding, and invoking the selected action, among others.

■ **Note** In this chapter, we mention filters, which are one of the extensibility points of the framework. But we won't cover them in this chapter. Instead, we have dedicated Chapter 11 to filters.

Your First Controller Derived From ApiController

Let's try to implement a controller that holds the same logic as Listing 9-3 but uses ApiController as the base class this time. Listing 9-4 shows how it is implemented.

Listing 9-4. CarsController with ApiController

```
public class CarsController : ApiController {

    public string[] Get() {
```

```
        return new string[] {
            "Car 1",
            "Car 2",
            "Car 3"
        };
    }
}
```

When we send a GET request to /api/cars, we get the same result as in Listing 9-3 but obviously with a very clean programming model. Inside our CarsController in Listing 9-4, we didn't perform an HTTP method check, and we are returning just the object we care about. When a request comes to this CarsController controller class, the action selection logic is performed, at which we will look closely in the "Action Selection" section farther along in this chapter. The default convention here is that the action name should be the same name as the HTTP method name through which the request was made or with which it starts such as "GetCars." The lookup here is case insensitive.

Before moving forward, let's get to know the members of the ApiController abstract class first.

ApiController Members

ApiController exposes some properties and provides some methods that make it easy to work with the request. This subsection will list and explain those properties and methods. Table 9-2 lists public properties of the ApiController class.

Besides the properties listed in Table 9-2, there are three different public virtual methods of the ApiController class, as Listing 9-5 shows.

Table 9-2. *ApiController Properties*

Name	Type	Description
Configuration	HttpConfiguration	Holds the configuration information for the request.
ControllerContext	HttpControllerContext	Holds the context class that contains information for a single HTTP operation for the given controller.
ModelState	ModelStateDictionary	Holds the ModelStateDictionary dictionary object that carries the model state after the model binding process.
Request	HttpRequestMessage	Represents the HttpRequestMessage of the request.
Url	UrlHelper	A helper class to work generate URLs by providing route values.
User	IPrincipal	Holds the principal object that is set to Thread.CurrentPrincipal.

Listing 9-5. *ApiController Public Methods*

```
public abstract class ApiController : IHttpController, IDisposable {

    //Lines omitted for brevity

    protected virtual void Dispose(bool disposing);

    public virtual Task<HttpResponseMessage> ExecuteAsync(
        HttpControllerContext controllerContext, CancellationToken cancellationToken);

    protected virtual void Initialize(HttpControllerContext controllerContext);
}
```

The `Initialize` method sets up the proper public properties before the `ExecuteAsync` method logic is executed.

Controller Actions

One of the benefits of using the provided base controller class `ApiController` is the notion of action methods. Action methods are the public methods that we can provide in order to process the request and provide a response message. They are invoked on the basis of the action selection logic.

Controller action methods enable separation of the logic of each request. However, all actions under a controller can reach the context of that controller. For example, any private properties of the controller can be accessed by any action methods under the controller.

First of all, let's set up the infrastructure that we will use from now on in the chapter. We will have a `CarsContext` class, from which we will then be able to pull and manipulate our car gallery data (Listing 9-6).

Listing 9-6. CarsContext Class

```
public class Car {

    public int Id { get; set; }
    public string Make { get; set; }
    public string Model { get; set; }
    public int Year { get; set; }
    public float Price { get; set; }
}

public class CarsContext {

    private static int _nextId = 9;
    private static object _incLock = new object();

    // data store
    readonly static ConcurrentDictionary<int, Car> _carsDictionary =
        new ConcurrentDictionary<int, Car>(
          new HashSet<KeyValuePair<int, Car>> {
            new KeyValuePair<int, Car>(
                1,
                new Car {
                    Id = 1,
                    Make = "Make1",
                    Model = "Model1",
                    Year = 2010,
                    Price = 10732.2F
                }
            ),
            new KeyValuePair<int, Car>(
                2,
                new Car {
                    Id = 2,
                    Make = "Make2",
```

```
                       Model = "Model2",
                       Year = 2008,
                       Price = 27233.1F
                   }
               ),

               //Lines omitted for brevity . . .
        });

    public IEnumerable<Car> All {
        get {
            return _carsDictionary.Values;
        }
    }

    public IEnumerable<Car> Get(Func<Car, bool> predicate) {

        return _carsDictionary.Values.Where(predicate);
    }

    public Car GetSingle(Func<Car, bool> predicate) {

        return _carsDictionary.Values.FirstOrDefault(predicate);
    }

    public Car Add(Car car) {

        lock (_incLock) {

            car.Id = _nextId;
            _carsDictionary.TryAdd(car.Id, car);
            _nextId++;
        }

        return car;
    }
}
```

With our little data class in place, we can expose the data we have so that it can be consumed by our clients. Let's make it possible to retrieve the list of all cars first. Listing 9-7 shows the implementation.

Listing 9-7. CarsController with a Get Action

```
public class CarsController : ApiController {

    private readonly CarsContext _carsCtx = new CarsContext();

    public IEnumerable<Car> Get() {

        return _carsCtx.All;
    }
}
```

As you can see, by directly returning the IEnumerable<Car> object, we will get the content negotiation by default. This means that the list of cars will be sent to the client in the proper format. In addition, we have registered our default route, as Listing 9-8 shows.

Listing 9-8. Our Web API Route Registration

```
protected void Application_Start(object sender, EventArgs e) {

    var config = GlobalConfiguration.Configuration;
    var routes = config.Routes;

    routes.MapHttpRoute(
        "DefaultHttpRoute",
        "api/{controller}/{id}",
        new { id = RouteParameter.Optional }
    );
}
```

Figure 9-1 shows the sample GET request being made against this service and the response we get back.

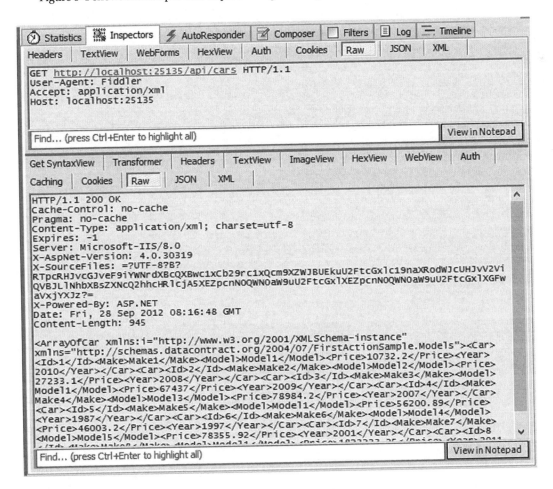

Figure 9-1. *GET request against /api/cars*

As the request is a GET request, the Get method of the CarsController has been invoked. In the request headers, we indicate that we want to get the response in XML format. The server honors the request and returns the response in that format.

Now, let's make a POST request to the same URI and see what happens (Figure 9-2).

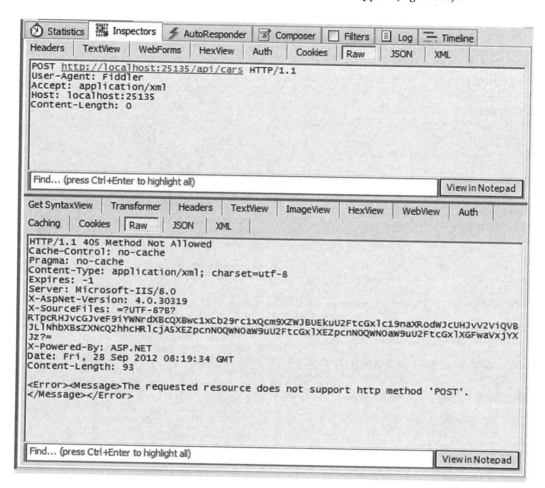

Figure 9-2. POST request against /api/cars

For this POST request, we got a response containing the "405 Method Not Allowed" status code because we haven't defined a method named POST or starting with Post in the CarsController class. Now we will create a method to process the POST requests to insert a new car object in the cars collection. Listing 9-9 shows the implementation of the PostCar action method.

Listing 9-9. CarsController with a Post Action

```
public class CarsController : ApiController {

    private readonly CarsContext _carsCtx =
        new CarsContext();

    //Lines omitted for brevity

    public HttpResponseMessage PostCar(Car car) {

        var createdCar = _carsCtx.Add(car);
        var response = Request.CreateResponse(
            HttpStatusCode.Created, createdCar);

        response.Headers.Location = new Uri(
            Url.Link("DefaultHttpRoute", new {
                id = createdCar.Id }));

        return response;
    }
}
```

This time, we have an action method with a parameter. This action parameter will be bound at runtime according to the request body (to be discussed in depth in Chapter 12). So if we want to add a new car, we need to include the car object in the message body of our POST request in the correct format. On the other hand, we also created an HttpResponseMessage instance through the CreateResponse extension method for the HttpRequestMessage. In this way, we can control the HTTP response message being sent. We also have set the status code of this response message as "201 Created," and the response will carry the created car object inside the response message body. You will see how this feature can be used in the section "Returning a Response Message" later in this chapter. Lastly, we have created the absolute URI of the created resource through the Url.Link helper method and send it inside the response as the location header value. The Url.Link method accepts the route name and the route values as a parameter to construct the proper URI.

Figure 9-3 shows a sample POST request made against the HTTP service.

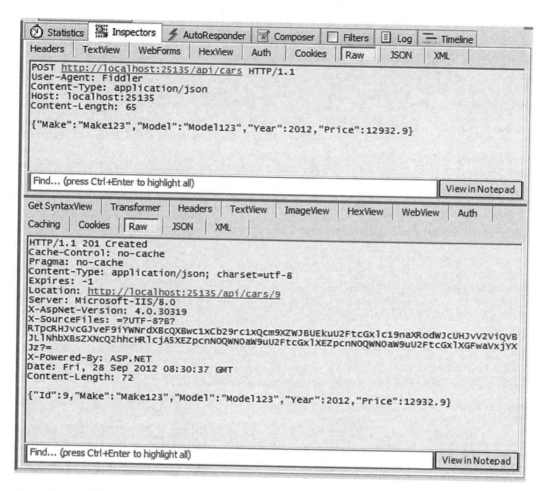

Figure 9-3. *POST request against /api/cars*

As the raw request pane in Figure 9-3 shows, the car object is sent in JSON format, and the content type header is set to *application/json*. The proper formatter binds the action method parameter accordingly on the basis of the request headers and request message body. Make a GET request to retrieve all cars, and you'll see that the new car object just added is also inside the list (Figure 9-4).

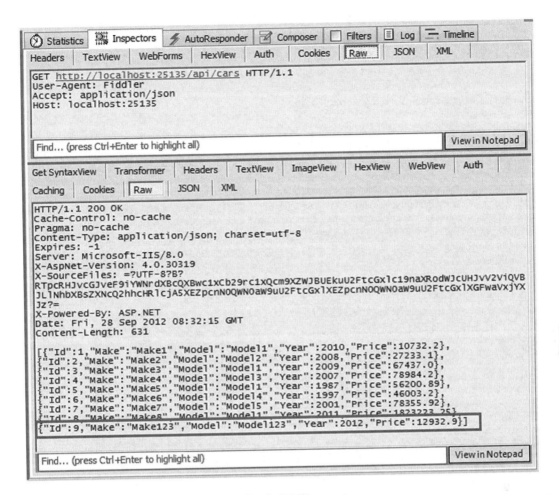

Figure 9-4. *GET request against /api/cars after the POST request*

Let's now enable the client to edit a car record on the server side. Since the most convenient HTTP method for modifications is the PUT method, we will name the controller action PutCar. Also, don't forget that we have an optional route parameter named *id*, which we have omitted so far. We'll take advantage of this parameter for an action to determine which record is requested for modification.

Listing 9-10 shows the implementation of the PutCar action method.

Listing 9-10. CarsController with a Put Action

```
public class CarsController : ApiController {

    private readonly CarsContext _carsCtx = new CarsContext();

    //Lines omitted for brevity

    public Car PutCar(int id, Car car) {

        car.Id = id;
```

```
        if (!_carsCtx.TryUpdate(car)) {

            var response =
                Request.CreateResponse(HttpStatusCode.NotFound);

            throw new HttpResponseException(response);
        }

        return car;
    }
}
```

First, let's try to update the record we got from the request. If the update is a success, then we'll return the updated record. If the update fails, we'll create a new instance of an HttpResponseMessage and throw an HttpResponseException that includes the HttpResponseMessage just created.

Let's make a PUT request against /api/cars/1 and try to update the car object whose Id is 9, which is the entry we just created (see Figure 9-5).

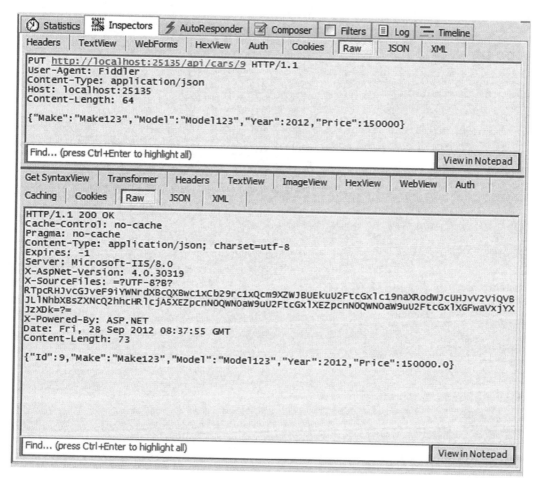

Figure 9-5. *PUT request against /api/cars/1*

As expected, we get a "200 OK" response, along with the updated car record in JSON format. Last of all, the DeleteCar action method is identical to the PutCar action method, as Listing 9-11 shows.

Listing 9-11. CarsController with a Delete Action Method

```
public class CarsController : ApiController {

    private readonly CarsContext _carsCtx = new CarsContext();

    //Lines omitted for brevity

    public HttpResponseMessage DeleteCar(int id) {

        if (!_carsCtx.TryRemove(id)) {

            var response =
                Request.CreateResponse(HttpStatusCode.NotFound);

            throw new HttpResponseException(response);
        }

        return Request.CreateResponse(HttpStatusCode.OK);
    }
}
```

Inside the DeleteCar action method, we are trying to delete the record, first of all, on the basis of the id parameter we got. If the car doesn't exist, the delete operation will fail. So, we do as we did in the PutCar method and get a response containing the "404 Not Found" status code. If the record requested for deletion does exist, we fire the DELETE operation and return a "200 OK" response, which indicates that the operation has been successful.

Figure 9-6 shows the details of the DELETE request against /api/cars/1.

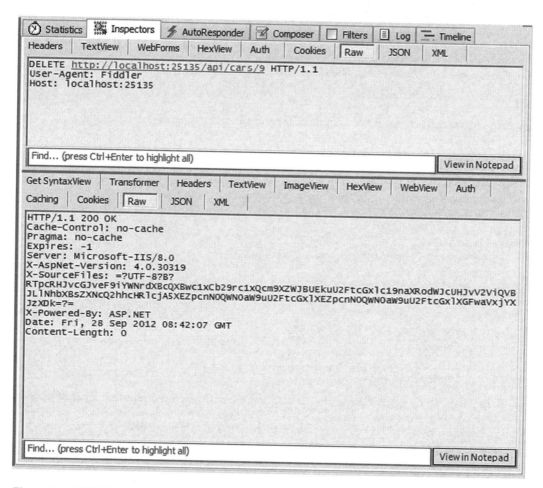

Figure 9-6. *DELETE request against /api/cars/1*

So far, controller action methods have really helped us separate the implementations of different operations, and we were able to set up the basics quickly. You may notice that we don't have any multiple action methods that serve for the same HTTP verb. For example, what if we need a way to get a single car record based on its id? Do we need to create another controller for this? Absolutely not. But in order to understand how this works, we'll have to step back and take a good look at the action selection logic.

Action Selection

The appropriate action inside a given controller is selected on the basis of the registered action selector service. This action selector service needs to implement the IHttpActionSelector interface, which has the signature shown in Listing 9-12.

Listing 9-12. IHttpActionSelector Interface

```
public interface IHttpActionSelector {

    HttpActionDescriptor SelectAction(
        HttpControllerContext controllerContext);

    ILookup<string, HttpActionDescriptor> GetActionMapping(
        HttpControllerDescriptor controllerDescriptor);
}
```

The SelectAction method of the IHttpActionSelector interface will be invoked to select the proper action. The responsibilities of the SelectAction method are as follows:

- finding the proper action method according to the HttpControllerContext object passed in as a parameter;

- throwing an HttpResponseException that holds the status code 404 if no proper action method is found;

- populating an instance of HttpActionDescriptor on the basis of the selected action method and the HttpControllerContext object passed in as a parameter and returning it.

The action selector service is registered through the ServicesContainer, which was explained in the "Configuration" section in Chapter 1. By default, ApiControllerActionSelector is registered as an action selector. It performs the action selection unless you replace it with your own implementation.

To explain its working roughly, the ApiControllerActionSelector does everything listed above as the core responsibilities of the action selection service. However, the most important point here is the logic behind the action selection rather than its responsibilities. This logic in ApiControllerActionSelector involves routing extensively. There are two key things that determine how the proper action method is selected. One of them is based on a route parameter named *action* and the HTTP method the request came through. The other one is based solely on the HTTP method the request came through. We decided to name them *Action-Based Routing* and *HTTP Method–Based Routing* for ease of reference. In the next two subsections we will look into both routings separately.

HTTP Method–Based Routing

HTTP method–based routing looks for the method names inside the controller and filters out the ones that have the exact name of the HTTP method or the prefix that equals the HTTP method name. This comparison is case insensitive.

Since we've been working with this approach in this section so far, we are familiar with it, but our car gallery API application has a problem we haven't found a solution for. We need to find two methods that will process the GET requests such that one of them will return a single car value based on the car's id. The ApiControllerActionSelector has a way of selecting the actions on the basis of their parameters. For example, if we have another Get method inside the CarsController, one that accepts a parameter named id, and the request contains either a route or a query string value named id, this Get method will be selected as the appropriate action method and invoked. Now, let's see this in action. Listing 9-13 shows the implementation of this second Get method.

Listing 9-13. CarsController with a Second Get Action

```
public class CarsController : ApiController {

    private readonly CarsContext _carsCtx =
        new CarsContext();

    //Lines omitted for brevity

    public Car GetCar(int id) {

        var carTuple = _carsCtx.GetSingle(id);

        if (!carTuple.Item1) {

            var response =
                Request.CreateResponse(HttpStatusCode.NotFound);

            throw new HttpResponseException(response);
        }

        return carTuple.Item2;
    }
}
```

When we send a request against /api/cars/1 (Figure 9-7), we'll be invoking the action method shown in Listing 9-13.

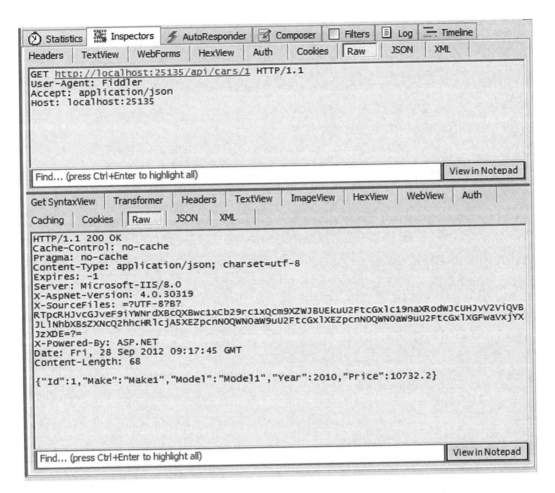

Figure 9-7. *GET request against /api/cars/1*

Also, we can get the same result by sending a request against /api/cars?id=1 (Figure 9-8).

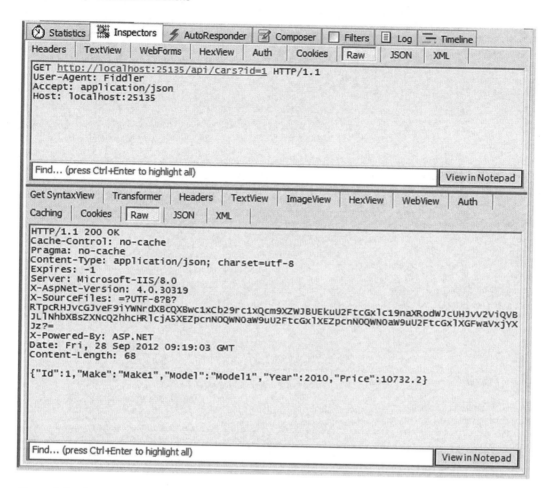

Figure 9-8. *GET request against /api/cars?id=1*

■ **Note** It's possible to use complex types as action parameters for GET requests and bind the route and query string values by marking the complex type parameters with `FromUriAttribute`. We explain this in Chapter 12. However, the default action selection logic only considers simple types (`String`, `DateTime`, `Decimal`, `Guid`, `DateTimeOffset`, `TimeSpan`), .NET Framework primitive types (`Boolean`, `Byte`, `SByte`, `Int16`, `UInt16`, `Int32`, `UInt32`, `Int64`, `UInt64`, `IntPtr`, `UIntPtr`, `Char`, `Double`, `Single`) and underlying simple types for the Nullable value types such as `Nullable<System.Int32>`. For example, if you have `GetCars(Foo foo)` and `GetCars(Bar bar)` methods in your controller, you will get the ambiguous action error as the complex types are completely ignored by the `ApiControllerActionSelector`. However, `WebAPIDoodle` NuGet package contains a custom action selector which we can use to support complex types for action selection. You may find more information about this from `http://www.tugberkugurlu.com/archive/complex-type-action-parameters-with-complextypeawareactionselector-in-asp-net-web-api-part-1` and `http://www.tugberkugurlu.com/archive/complex-type-action-parameters-with-complextypeawareaction selector-in-asp-net-web-api-part-2`.

Until this point, we've been telling you that the action method name needs to have the exact name of the HTTP method or the prefix that is the same as the HTTP method name. This is one way to proceed with the HTTP method–based routing. The other way is to provide an action HTTP method provider attribute for the action method.

HTTP Method Providers

An HTTP method provider is a .NET attribute that implements the IActionHttpMethodProvider interface and provides the supported HTTP methods for the controller action it is applied to. The IActionHttpMethodProvider interface is an internal interface. The seven available HTTP method providers are as follows:

- HttpGetAttribute
- HttpPostAttribute
- HttpPutAttribute
- HttpDeleteAttribute
- HttpHeadAttribute
- HttpPatchAttribute
- HttpOptionsAttribute

If a controller action method has one of these attributes applied, that action method will process the requests coming through the HTTP method in question. Listing 9-14 shows an example for the usage of HTTP method providers.

Listing 9-14. IActionHttpMethodProvider Interface

```
public class CarsController : ApiController {

    [HttpGet]
    public string[] Cars() {

        return new string[] {
            "Car 1",
            "Car 2",
            "Car 3"
        };
    }
}
```

As you can see in the sample in Listing 9-14, the action method does not follow the naming convention described earlier, but it has the HttpGetAttribute applied. So when you make a request against /api/cars, you should get back the list of cars (Figure 9-9).

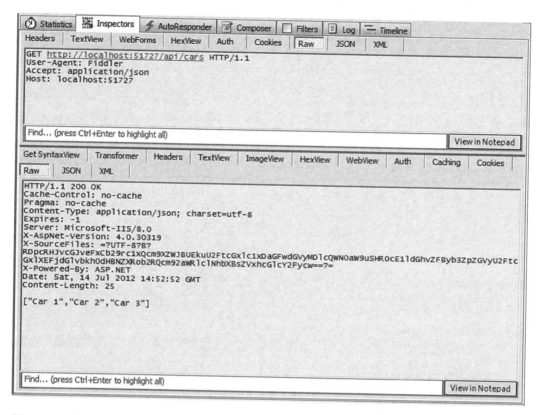

Figure 9-9. *GET request against /api/cars*

Action-Based Routing

Besides the HTTP method–based routing, there is also another routing feature that markedly affects the default action selection logic. If there is a route parameter named *action* for the chosen route, this parameter will look up the proper action. When using action-based routing, the HTTP method provider attribute needs to be set explicitly. Otherwise, the action method will never be selected.

Listing 9-15 shows a sample route definition that contains a parameter named *action*.

Listing 9-15. A Route for So-Called Action-Based Routing

```
protected void Application_Start(object sender, EventArgs e) {

    var config = GlobalConfiguration.Configuration;
    var routes = config.Routes;

    routes.MapHttpRoute(
        "DefaultHttpRoute",
        "api/{controller}/{action}/{id}",
        new { id = RouteParameter.Optional }
    );
}
```

There is also the CarsController class, which contains an action method named List (Listing 9-16).

Listing 9-16. CarsController with an Action Named List

```
public class CarsController : ApiController {

    [HttpGet]
    public string[] List() {

        return new string[] {
            "Car 1",
            "Car 2",
            "Car 3"
        };
    }
}
```

When you make a request against */api/cars/list*, you should get the cars list, as expected (Figure 9-10).

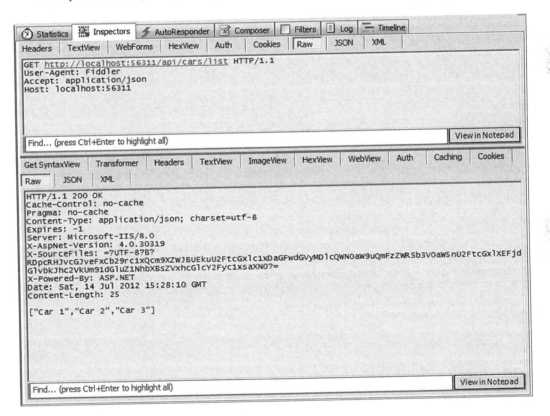

Figure 9-10. *GET request against /api/cars/list*

Action Method Selectors and NonActionAttribute

An action method selector is a .NET attribute that implements the IActionMethodSelector interface and allows interference in the action method selection process. The IActionMethodSelector is an internal interface. There is only one implementation of this interface: the NonActionAttribute.

■ **Note** If you replace the default action selector, which is the ApiControllerActionSelector, the action method selectors won't work unless you implement them manually. The ApiControllerActionSelector executes the defined action method selectors.

When you have a defined public method in your Web API controller and don't want it treated as a controller action method, you can apply the NonActionAttribute to that method. It won't then be available as an action method.

Listing 9-17 shows an example for this feature.

Listing 9-17. NonActionAttribute Usage Sample

```
public class CarsController : ApiController {

    public string[] Get() {

        return GetCars();
    }

    [NonAction]
    public string[] GetCars() {

        return new string[] {
            "Car 1",
            "Car 2",
            "Car 3"
        };
    }
}
```

We are using the default route for this example. If we make a GET request against /api/cars and don't use the NonActionAttribute for the GetCars method, we should get an HTTP 500 response, indicating that multiple actions were found that match the request. If the NonActionAttribute is applied to the GetCars method, the GetCars method will not be treated as an action method anymore.

Return Values

We can use anything as a return value of a Web API controller action. No matter what the return value type of the action method is, the return value will be converted into an HttpResponseMessage object.

Now let's go through the possible types of return values one by one.

Returning an Object

The most common occurrence is to return an object as a result. When an object instance is returned, the return value will be processed by the proper formatter according to the content negotiation process. Then the processed return value will be sent to the client, along with the response message. All these operations are done out of the box.

For instance, in nearly all of our examples so far, we've been returning a `string[]` object. We've seen that the response message carries the content in the proper format. Let's look at the example in Listing 9-18.

Listing 9-18. Returning string[] Object Inside an Action Method

```
public class CarsController : ApiController {

    public string[] Get() {

        return new string[] {
            "Car 1",
            "Car 2",
            "Car 3"
        };
    }
}
```

When we make a GET request against */api/cars*, we'll get the response message, along with the cars list in the proper format (Figure 9-11). The format differs on the basis of the request, the registered formatters, and the registered content negotiation service. (Chapter 12 is entirely dedicated to formatters and content negotiation. We'll see there how it matters.)

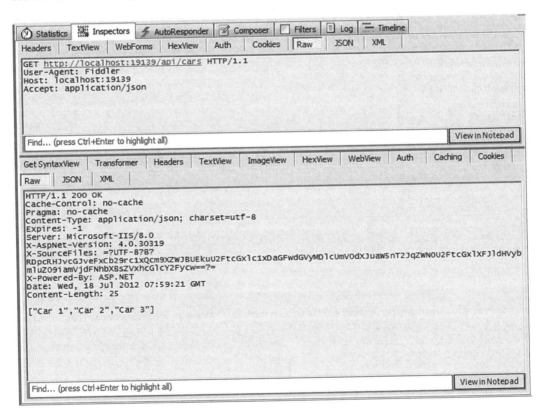

Figure 9-11. *GET request against /api/cars*

Except for the message body, we don't at the moment have any control over the returned response message inside the controller action, but we can solve this problem by explicitly creating and returning an HttpResponseMessage instance. Let's talk about that next.

■ **Note** Actually, you always have control over the response message when you are hosting your application on ASP.NET. The Properties collection on the HttpRequestMessage instance will always carry the current System.Web.HttpContext as HttpContextBase type under the key "*MS_HttpContext*"; the modifications you make in the response message here will be directly reflected in the response message sent over the wire. However, this is not the recommended way to alter the response message. The best practice here is to write an application in an agnostic way. This approach doesn't follow that pattern. The right way to alter the response message (headers, status code, etc.) inside a controller action method is to return an instance of the HttpResponseMessage class. We'll give some examples in the next section.

Returning a Response Message

When returning an instance of HttpResponseMessage, you have explicit control over the response message to be sent to the client. We can define the response headers and response status code in the case of HttpResponseMessage. Listing 9-19 shows an example of this procedure, with an action method for an HTTP DELETE request.

Listing 9-19. DeleteCar Controller Action That Returns an HttpResponseMessage Instance

```
public class CarsController : ApiController {

    public HttpResponseMessage DeleteCar(int id) {

        //Check here if the resource exists
        if (id != 1) {

            return new HttpResponseMessage(HttpStatusCode.NotFound);
        }

        //Delete the car object here

        var response = new HttpResponseMessage(HttpStatusCode.OK);
        return response;
    }
}
```

As usual with an HTTP DELETE request, the controller action first checks whether the resource exists according to the passed-in id parameter. If the resource exists, it deletes the associated object and returns a "200 OK" response (Figure 9-12). We're able to set the status code here because we're returning an HttpResponseMessage instance. We might go farther and alter the response headers as well if we want.

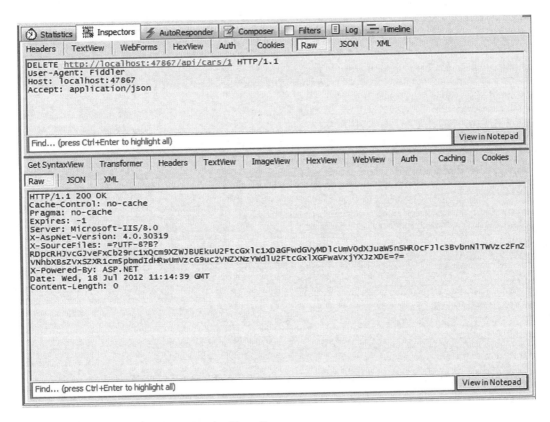

Figure 9-12. *DELETE request against /api/cars/1*

However, we might need to send a properly formatted object inside the response message body and alter the response message at the same time. As we learned in Chapter 4, HttpResponseMessage has a property named Content, which is a type of the abstract HttpContent class. We can pass the object we want here. Listing 9-20 shows an example for an action method that handles HTTP GET requests to return a list of cars.

Listing 9-20. *PostCar Controller Action That Returns an HttpResponseMessage Instance with an Object*

```
public class CarsController : ApiController {

    public HttpResponseMessage GetCars() {

        var cars = new string[] {
            "Car 1",
            "Car 2",
            "Car 3"
        };

        HttpResponseMessage response =
            Request.CreateResponse<string[]>(HttpStatusCode.OK, cars);
        response.Headers.Add("X-Foo", "Bar");
        return response;
    }
}
```

What we're returning here is an instance of HttpResponseMessage. We have a list of cars that we want to return as well. Also, we want to be able to handle the content negotiation automatically. All of our requirements can be fulfilled by the CreateResponse extension method for HttpRequestMessage class. Finally, we added a custom header to demonstrate that we have full control over the response.

When we make a GET request against /api/cars, we should get back a list of cars in a proper format and the custom response header we've set, too (Figure 9-13).

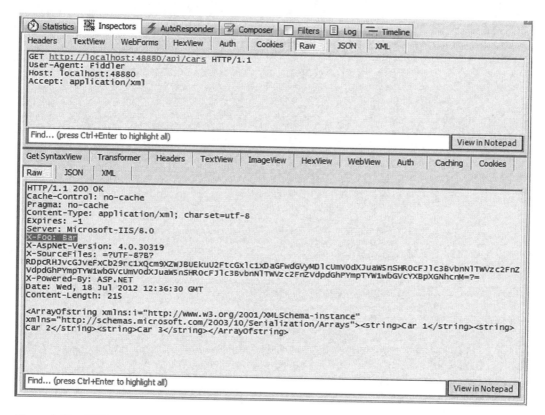

Figure 9-13. GET request against /api/cars

Also, notice that we want the response message in XML format, and the server gives us what we want.

Throwing HTTP Exceptions (HttpResponseException)

When an exception is thrown inside an action, the exception filters will be invoked to handle it (more about this in Chapter 11). If there is no exception filter or an exception filter didn't handle the exception, eventually the HttpControllerDispatcher will handle it and send back a proper HttpResponseMessage instance.

However, if the exception is a type of HttpResponseException, the exception will be handled by the ApiControllerActionInvoker immediately. The exception filters won't be invoked. This gives you the ability to stop processing immediately and return with a proper HTTP status code. Also, if you want to terminate the request inside a controller action and if the return expression type is not HttpResponseMessage, you can throw HttpResponseException to stop the processing of the action method.

Listing 9-21 is an example of throwing HttpResponseException inside a controller action.

Listing 9-21. A Sample Controller Action That Throws HttpResponseException

```
public class CarsController : ApiController {

    public string[] GetCars() {

        //stop processing and throw the HttpResponseException
        var response = new HttpResponseMessage(HttpStatusCode.BadRequest);
        throw new HttpResponseException(response);
    }
}
```

The return type of the action method is `string[]`. Note that we are still able to alter the response message. When we send a GET request against /api/cars, we will get a "400 Bad Request" response (Figure 9-14).

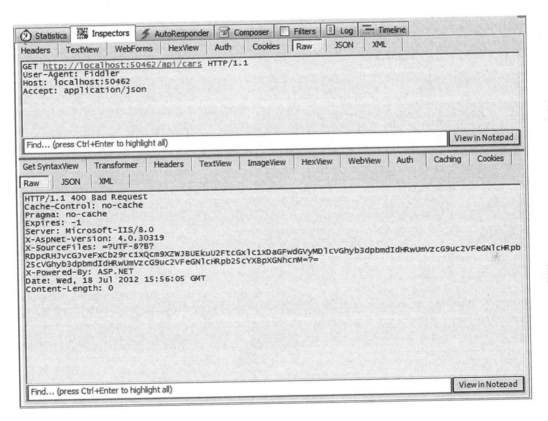

Figure 9-14. GET request against /api/cars

■ **Note**   There is also another special case, one where we can return a Task or Task<T> object to handle the operation inside the controller action asynchronously. Chapter 16 covers this feature in depth.

Returning Error Responses

The ASP.NET Web API framework has a built-in mechanism to handle errors efficiently and send user-friendly error messages to the consumer. This built-in error-handling mechanism also works well with validation and several other components of the framework, as will be seen in Chapter 13.

When an unhandled exception occurs at the controller level and the exception handler doesn't set any specific response message, the exception details are sent inside the message body with the "500 Internal Server Error" status code. Assuming the presence of the controller shown in Listing 9-22, the GetCars method will throw a DivideByZeroException.

Listing 9-22. The CarsController Class

```
public class CarsController : ApiController {

    public string[] GetCars() {

        int left = 10,
            right = 0;

        var result = left / right;

        return new[] {
            "Car 1",
            "Car 2",
            "Car 3"
        };
    }
}
```

When a request is sent to /api/cars, the response message body will carry the exception details (see Figure 9-15).

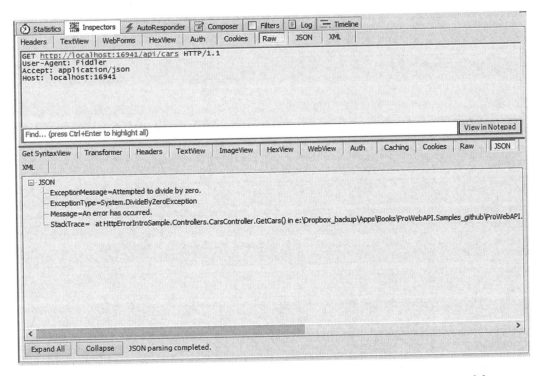

Figure 9-15. *A GET request against /api/cars with a "500 Internal Server Error" response and the response message body with the exception details*

If the request is sent by indicating acceptance of the XML format, the response body will be in XML format. Note, too, that this sample is being run locally; that is why you see the exception details. As Chapter 1's "Configuration" section shows, the IncludeErrorDetailPolicy is set by default to IncludeErrorDetailPolicy.LocalOnly, and the framework honors that setting here. Change this setting to Never, as shown in Listing 9-23, and you won't see the exception details (see Figure 9-16).

Listing 9-23. IncludeErrorDetailPolicy Set to Never

```
protected void Application_Start(object sender, EventArgs e) {

    var config = GlobalConfiguration.Configuration;

    //Lines omitted for brevity...

    config.IncludeErrorDetailPolicy = IncludeErrorDetailPolicy.Never;
}
```

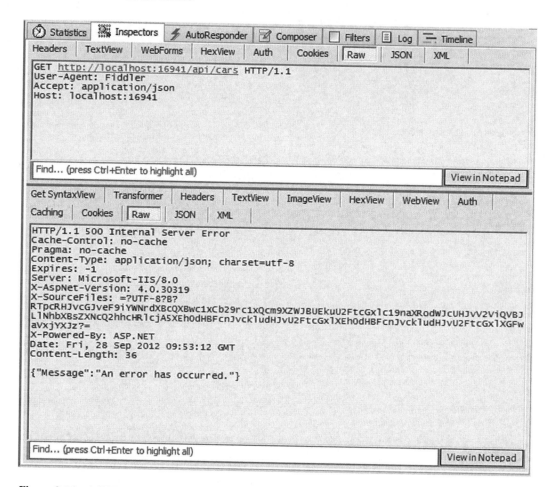

Figure 9-16. *A GET request against /api/cars with a "500 Internal Server Error" response and the response message body with limited exception details*

What you see here is the HttpError class in play. When an exception occurs inside a controller action, an instance of an HttpError is serialized to the wire by the proper formatter. The HttpError message is just a Dictionary<string, object> object that provides some helper methods for creating errors that contain error messages, exceptions, or invalid model states.

The HttpError class has four constructors, which accept parameters to create over the existing error stacks a new HttpError message, such as an Exception instance of a ModelStateDictionary instance. Listing 9-24 shows the signature of the HttpError class.

Listing 9-24. The Signature of the HttpError Class

```
[XmlRoot("Error")]
public sealed class HttpError : Dictionary<string, object>, IXmlSerializable {

    public HttpError();
    public HttpError(string message);
```

```
    public HttpError(Exception exception, bool includeErrorDetail);
    public HttpError(ModelStateDictionary modelState, bool includeErrorDetail);

    public string Message { get; set; }
}
```

If the framework didn't provide such a feature to return an exception message by default, the same result could be achieved via the process shown in Listing 9-25.

Listing 9-25. GetCars Action Method

```
public string[] GetCars() {

    try {

        int left = 10,
            right = 0;

        var result = left / right;

    }
    catch (DivideByZeroException ex) {

        var faultedResponse = Request.CreateResponse(
            HttpStatusCode.InternalServerError,
            new HttpError(ex, includeErrorDetail: true));

        throw new HttpResponseException(faultedResponse);
    }

    return new[] {
        "Car 1",
        "Car 2",
        "Car 3"
    };
}
```

A request now sent to /api/cars will generate the same result, shown in Figure 9-17, already seen in Figure 9-15.

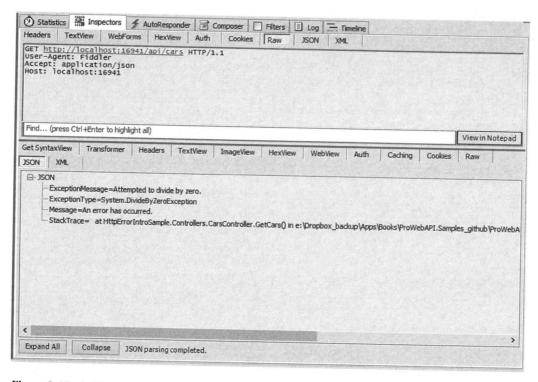

Figure 9-17. *A GET request against /api/cars with a "500 Internal Server Error" response and the response message body with the exception details*

Actually, the solution Listing 9-25 provides doesn't behave quite the same as the built-in default solution, because the `includeErrorDetail` parameter is directly set to true. This wouldn't honor the `IncludeErrorDetail` configuration settings. Of course, the value of the `IncludeErrorDetailPolicy` property could be retrieved from the controller's `Configuration` property, but there would then be a need to determine the cases where the error details had to be included and where they didn't.

To be able to honor the `IncludeErrorDetailPolicy` settings and make it easy to return error responses, there is an extension method for `HttpRequestMessage`. Called `CreateErrorResponse`, it has several overloads, as Listing 9-26 shows.

Listing 9-26. The CreateErrorResponse Extension Method for HttpRequestMessage and Its Overloads

```
public static class HttpRequestMessageExtensions {

    public static HttpResponseMessage CreateErrorResponse(
        this HttpRequestMessage request,
        HttpStatusCode statusCode, Exception exception);

    public static HttpResponseMessage CreateErrorResponse(
        this HttpRequestMessage request,
        HttpStatusCode statusCode, HttpError error);
```

```
public static HttpResponseMessage CreateErrorResponse(
    this HttpRequestMessage request,
    HttpStatusCode statusCode, ModelStateDictionary modelState);

public static HttpResponseMessage CreateErrorResponse(
    this HttpRequestMessage request,
    HttpStatusCode statusCode, string message);

public static HttpResponseMessage CreateErrorResponse(
    this HttpRequestMessage request,
    HttpStatusCode statusCode, string message, Exception exception);

//Other extension methods are omitted for brevity . . .
}
```

All overloads of the CreateErrorResponse extension method return an HttpResponseMessage instance. Just like the CreateResponse extension method, this extension method also runs the content negotiation behind the scenes to return the response in a proper format. The CreateErrorResponse can be used to create error responses anywhere inside the ASP.NET Web API pipeline, including message handlers, filters, and controllers.

Listing 9-27 shows the GetCars implementation by using the CreateErrorResponse method.

Listing 9-27. GetCars Action Method

```
public string[] GetCars() {

    try {

        int left = 10,
            right = 0;

        var result = left / right;

    }
    catch (DivideByZeroException ex) {

        var faultedResponse = Request.CreateErrorResponse(
            HttpStatusCode.InternalServerError, ex);

        throw new HttpResponseException(faultedResponse);
    }

    return new[] {
        "Car 1",
        "Car 2",
        "Car 3"
    };
}
```

A request now sent to /api/cars will again generate the same result as the one in Figure 9-15 (also shown in Figure 9-18) and will also honor the IncludeErrorDetailPolicy configuration settings.

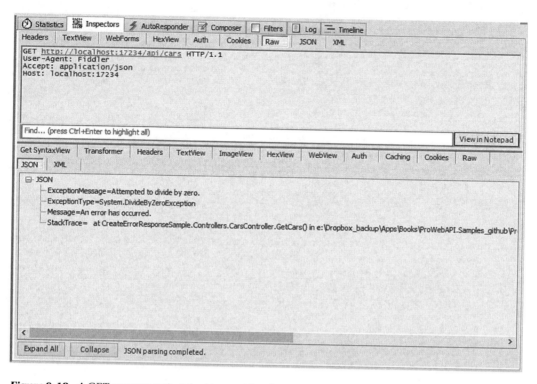

Figure 9-18. A GET request against /api/cars with a "500 Internal Server Error" response and the response message body with the exception details

The HttpError class can also be used for arbitrary error messages. As Listing 9-28 shows, one of the overloads of the CreateErrorResponse extension method accepts the HttpError instance. It's also possible to construct a new HttpError instance with custom error details and pass it into the CreateErrorResponse method.

The sample shown in Listing 9-28 demonstrates this usage. The GetCar controller action method accepts an integer for the id parameter, but we only allow even numbers. So if the number is odd, we will construct a new HttpError message, add the message for the error, and return a new HttpResponseMessage instance through the CreateErrorResponse extension method of the HttpRequestMessage.

Listing 9-28. GetCar Action Method

```
public HttpResponseMessage GetCar(int id) {

    if ((id % 2) != 0) {

        var httpError = new HttpError();
        httpError.Add("id",
            "Only \"even numbers\" are accepted as id.");

        return Request.CreateErrorResponse(
            HttpStatusCode.InternalServerError,
            httpError);
    }
```

```
    return Request.CreateResponse(
        HttpStatusCode.OK,
        string.Format("Car {0}", id));
}
```

When a request is sent against /api/cars/1, a "500 Internal Server Error" response is returned, because the id parameter supplied is not an even number (see Figure 9-19).

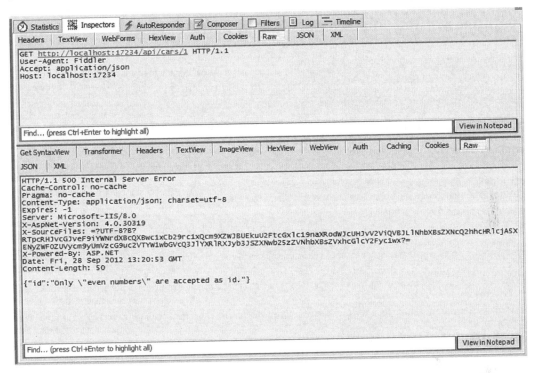

Figure 9-19. *A GET request against /api/cars/1 with a "500 Internal Server Error" response and the response message body with the exception details*

What will mostly be leveraged is the CreateErrorResponse extension method along with the validation. Chapter 13 is dedicated solely to the validation topic, and there you'll see samples showing how to efficiently use the CreateErrorResponse extension method to provide better validation error messages.

Per-Controller-Type Configuration

In some cases, we will want to have specific formatters or internal services for a controller type. For example, assume that we have two controllers, CarsController and VehiclesController, and for CarsController we want JSON to be the only supported return output and input media type. Also, as we want strong content negotiation, we explicitly require the client to specify the media type. In this and similar scenarios, the per-controller-type configuration feature of ASP.NET Web API comes in handy.

Per-controller-type configuration allows controllers to have a shadow copy of the global configuration, which can be modified as needed. The framework knows about per-controller-type configurations by examining the controller attributes to find an attribute that implements the System.Web.Http.Controllers IControllerConfiguration. The signature of the IControllerConfiguration interface is shown in Listing 9-29.

Listing 9-29. The IControllerConfiguration interface

```
public interface IControllerConfiguration {

    void Initialize(
        HttpControllerSettings controllerSettings,
        HttpControllerDescriptor controllerDescriptor);
}
```

The IControllerConfiguration has only one method, Initialize. Initialize accepts two parameters of the types HttpControllerSettings and HttpControllerDescriptor.

HttpControllerSettings provides the overrideable pieces of the configuration. The entire HttpConfiguration object is not passed here directly, because certain parts, including message handlers and routes, obviously cannot be customized. In terms of the processing pipeline, it would be too late to customize them per-controller type. Listing 9-30 shows the signature of the HttpControllerSettings class.

Listing 9-30. The HttpControllerSettings Class

```
public sealed class HttpControllerSettings {

    public MediaTypeFormatterCollection Formatters { get; }
    public ParameterBindingRulesCollection ParameterBindingRules { get; }
    public ServicesContainer Services { get; }
}
```

As can be predicted by looking at the HttpControllerSettings class, the Initialize method of the IControllerConfiguration implementation can change the internal services, formatters, and binding rules. After the Initialize method is run, the framework looks at the HttpControllerSettings instance and then creates a new shadow HttpConfiguration object and applies the changes. Parts that are unchanged will stay the same as the global configuration. Implementation of the necessary parts will make our CarsController and VehiclesController example (explained at the beginning of this section) work.

Listing 9-31 shows the OnlyJsonConfigAttribute class, which is the implementation of the IControllerConfiguration interface.

Listing 9-31. The OnlyJsonConfigAttribute Class, Which Implements the IControllerConfiguration Interface

```
public class OnlyJsonConfigAttribute :
    Attribute, IControllerConfiguration {

    public void Initialize(
        HttpControllerSettings controllerSettings,
        HttpControllerDescriptor controllerDescriptor) {

        var jqueryFormatter = controllerSettings.Formatters
            .FirstOrDefault(x =>
                x.GetType() == typeof(
                    JQueryMvcFormUrlEncodedFormatter));

        controllerSettings.Formatters.Remove(
            controllerSettings.Formatters.XmlFormatter);
```

```
        controllerSettings.Formatters.Remove(
            controllerSettings
            .Formatters
            .FormUrlEncodedFormatter);

        controllerSettings.Formatters.Remove(
            jqueryFormatter);

        controllerSettings.Services.Replace(
            typeof(IContentNegotiator),
            new DefaultContentNegotiator(
                excludeMatchOnTypeOnly: true));
    }
}
```

Here we remove all formatters except the JsonMediaTypeFormatter instance; also, we replace the IContentNegotiator service with a new DefaultContentNegotiator. To remove the flexibility from the content negotiation, the excludeMatchOnTypeOnly parameter needs to be passed as true. Also, note that the Initialize method will run only once when the controller is initialized first. The result produced here will be cached during the application's life cycle.

As for the controllers, Listing 9-32 shows the CarsController, which applies the OnlyJsonConfig attribute; Listing 9-33 shows the VehiclesController; it uses the global configuration and has no special configuration requirements.

Listing 9-32. The CarsController, Which Has Its Own Configuration

```
[OnlyJsonConfig]
public class CarsController : ApiController {

    public string[] GetCars() {

        var foo = this.ControllerContext;

        return new[] {
            "Car 1",
            "Car 2",
            "Car 3"
        };
    }
}
```

Listing 9-33. The VehiclesController, Which Uses the Global Configuration

```
public class VehiclesController : ApiController {

    public string[] GetVehicles() {

        return new[] {
            "Vehicle 1",
            "Vehicle 2",
            "Vehicle 3"
        };
    }
}
```

Furthermore, note that except for the route registration, there are no special requirements for the global configuration (see Listing 9-34).

Listing 9-34. The Route Registration Configuration

```
protected void Application_Start(object sender, EventArgs e) {

    var config = GlobalConfiguration.Configuration;
    var routes = config.Routes;

    routes.MapHttpRoute(
        "DefaultHttpRoute",
        "api/{controller}"
    );
}
```

As you will see, when a GET request is sent to /api/vehicles without Accept headers, the response message will be in the JSON format because JsonMediaTypeFormatter is the first formatter inside the collection. The globally registered DefaultContentNegotiator works this way by default (see Figure 9-20).

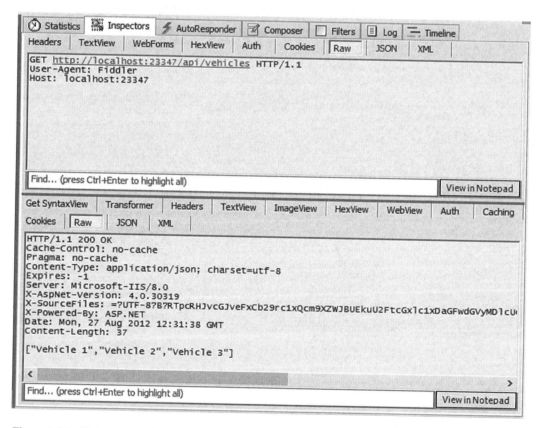

Figure 9-20. *GET request against /api/vehicles with no Accept header*

When a GET request is sent to /api/vehicles with the application/xml Accept header, the response comes in the expected XML format (see Figure 9-21).

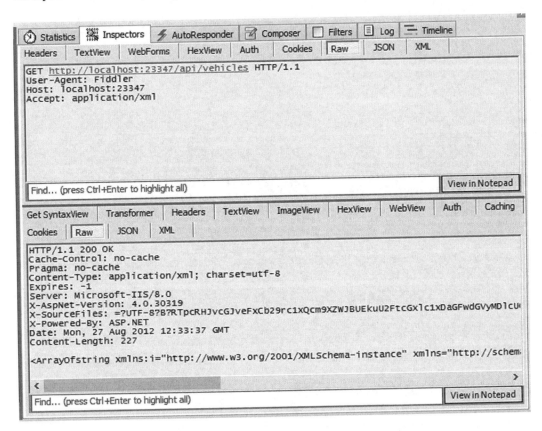

Figure 9-21. *GET request against /api/vehicles with an application/xml Accept header*

That is, VehiclesController works with the global configuration we have. Figure 9-22 shows a GET request sent to /api/cars with no Accept header. Let's see what we get.

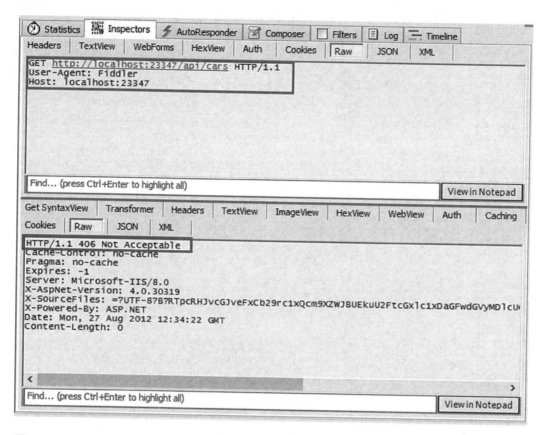

Figure 9-22. GET request against /api/cars with no Accept header

As intended, the response is "406 Not Acceptable", because the DefaultContentNegotiator was configured accordingly. If a GET request is sent to the same URI with an application/xml Accept header, the response will again be "406 Not Acceptable", as there is no formatter that can write to XML (see Figure 9-23).

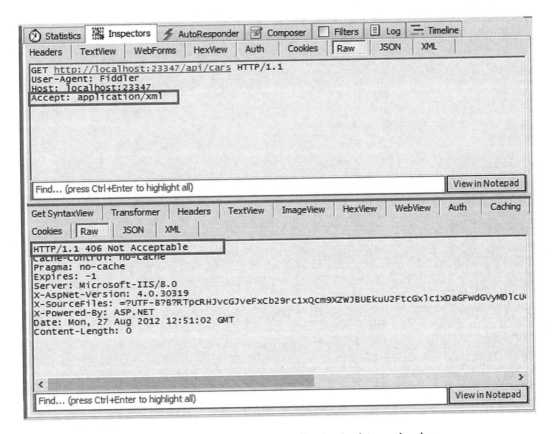

Figure 9-23. *GET request against /api/cars with an application/xml Accept header*

But when a GET request is sent with an application/json Accept header, the response is the healthy and expected "200 OK" (see Figure 9-24).

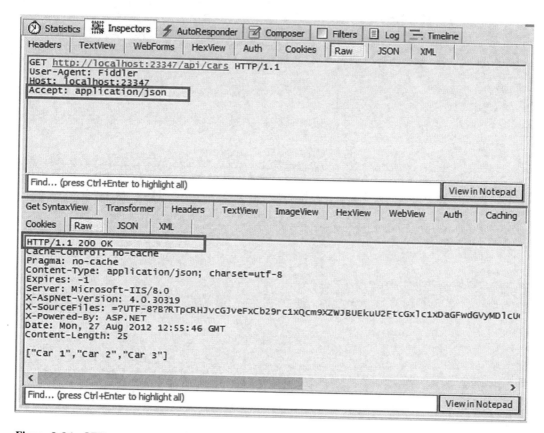

Figure 9-24. *GET request against /api/cars with an application/json Accept header*

The per-controller-type configuration feature provides really great flexibility. Multiple per-controller-type configurations and one global configuration can coexist within the context of a single application.

Summary

Controllers are among the main components of the ASP.NET Web API framework. They are supposed to be the place where the request message is processed and the main response message is generated. You saw, as we walked through this chapter, that the base controller type ApiController, which is provided out of the box, provides a nice programming model, and it covers nearly all of the different situations that you'll need to know to be able to handle action methods, filters, and the like.

CHAPTER 10

■ ■ ■

Message Handlers

When building an HTTP Application using ASP.NET Web API, you might face scenarios where the possibilities for processing and influencing the handling of requests and responses using the Routing module and the ApiController might not be enough. Furthermore there might be operations that you want to apply to more than one controller.

This chapter will give you an overview of how both—requests sent *from* the client and responses sent *to* the client—are processed in ASP.NET Web API on the server side. You'll also learn how to modify requests before they're routed to the controller and modify responses after they've left it.

Overview and Message Handler Mechanism

In ASP.NET Web API, HTTP requests and responses are processed in a pipeline on the server (to be honest, they're also processed on the way back to the client, as you'll see in the "Message Handlers and the Russian Doll Model" section). As mentioned in earlier chapters, requests in ASP.NET Web API are represented by the HttpRequestMessage class. Similarly, the code representation for responses is the HttpResponseMessage class.

HttpMessageHandler

As both HttpRequestMessage and HttpResponseMessage don't appear out of the blue, there must be something in the ASP.NET Web API framework that creates and handles them. That's where the HttpMessageHandler class enters the room. The HttpMessageHandler class is an abstract base class for HTTP message handlers that allow the processing of requests and sending of responses in an asynchronous manner.

HttpMessageHandler resides in the System.Net.Http namespace. The corresponding DLL is not part of the core ASP.NET Web API NuGet packages, but it is also available as a NuGet package (which, of course, is resolved as a dependency for ASP.NET Web API by NuGet): *System.Net.Http*.

The HttpMessageHandler implementation is pretty simple and straightforward, as shown in Listing 10-1.

Listing 10-1. HttpMessageHandler Abstract Base Class Implementation

```
namespace System.Net.Http
{
  public abstract class HttpMessageHandler : IDisposable
  {
    protected HttpMessageHandler()
    {
      if (Logging.On)
        Logging.Enter(Logging.Http, (object) this, ".ctor", (string) null);
      if (!Logging.On)
        return;
```

```
        Logging.Exit(Logging.Http, (object) this, ".ctor", (string) null);
    }

    protected internal abstract Task<HttpResponseMessage>
SendAsync(HttpRequestMessage request, CancellationToken cancellationToken);

    protected virtual void Dispose(bool disposing)
    {
    }

    public void Dispose()
    {
        this.Dispose(true);
        GC.SuppressFinalize((object) this);
    }
  }
}
```

The protected default constructor of HttpMessageHandler handles some Logging settings, which will be covered in Chapter 18. The Dispose methods implement a typical disposing behavior. The only method specific to HTTP message (that is to say, request and response) handling is the SendAsync method. It returns a Task<HttpResponseMessage> for an asynchronously created HttpResponseMessage. The first parameter being assigned to the SendAsync method is a HttpRequestMessage, which represents the request from the client. The second parameter is a CancellationToken, which propagates notification that operations should be aborted.

As we cannot process an HttpRequestMessage instance nor create an HttpResponseMessage instance without a concrete implementation of the SendAsync method, we need a class that derives from the base class. Of course, there's an implementation for that in the ASP.NET Web API framework. This is the DelegatingHandler class, which is explored in detail in the next section.

DelegatingHandler Class

The main purpose of the DelegatingHandler is to process the HttpRequestMessage or HttpResponseMessage and pass the work over to another DelegatingHandler. This creates a processing pipeline of DelegatingHandler instances. It is also possible for a DelegatingHandler implementation to stop the processing of the whole processing pipeline by creating an HttpResponseMessage and returning it instead of passing it to the next DelegatingHandler.

The abstract DelegatingHandler class is also located in the System.Net.Http namespace and its SendAsync method implementation is shown in Listing 10-2.

Listing 10-2. DelegatingHandler SendAsync Method Implemenation

```
protected internal override Task<HttpResponseMessage> SendAsync(HttpRequestMessage request,
CancellationToken cancellationToken)
{
  if (request == null)
      throw new ArgumentNullException("request",
SR.net_http_handler_norequest);
  this.SetOperationStarted();
  return this.innerHandler.SendAsync(request, cancellationToken);
}
```

As you can see, the SendAsync method implementation of the DelegatingHandler is pretty simple; it mainly passes the incoming HttpRequestMessage and the CancellationToken to the SendAsync method of InnerHandler, which is a private field of the DelegatingHandler itself. The InnerHandler gets populated from an overloaded constructor of DelegatingHandler, as shown in Listing 10-3.

Listing 10-3. DelegatingHandler Constructor Populating the InnerHandler Field

```
protected DelegatingHandler(HttpMessageHandler innerHandler)
{
  this.InnerHandler = innerHandler;
}

public HttpMessageHandler InnerHandler
{
  get
  {
      return this.innerHandler;
  }
  set
  {
      if (value == null)
        throw new ArgumentNullException("value");
      this.CheckDisposedOrStarted();
      if (Logging.On)
        Logging.Associate(Logging.Http, (object) this, (object) value);
      this.innerHandler = value;
  }
}
```

The just-shown mechanism of passing the work to a child DelegatingHandler (or even HttpMessageHandler) is also known as the *delegator pattern*, or *Russian Doll Model*; that's what will be explored inside the next section.

Message Handlers and the Russian Doll Model

The name *Russian Doll Model* comes from a Russian doll, a toy made of wood, wherein several hollow dolls of progressively smaller sizes are constructed so that the smallest nests inside the next smallest one and so on, till in the end what is seen is one big doll that contains all the others.

With the Russian Doll Model, the structure of the DelegatingHandler pipeline looks like Figure 10-1.

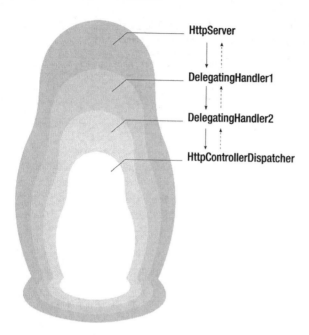

HttpServer

DelegatingHandler1

DelegatingHandler2

HttpControllerDispatcher

Figure 10-1. *Russian Doll Model of the DelegatingHandler pipeline*

As can be seen in Figure 10-1, the outermost doll (DelegatingHandler) is the HttpServer class, which itself just derives from DelegatingHandler.

The next DelegatingHandler implementation to be invoked is the DelegatingHandler1, which is a custom implementation of our own. It is assigned to the InnerHandler property of the HttpServer, which has been set up by the HttpControllerHandler if web hosting via Internet Information Services (IIS) is being used. If your ASP.NET Web API application is self-hosted, the plumbing gets done by the HttpSelfHostServer itself, which derives from HttpServer.

Regardless of the type of hosting chosen, the Innerhandler property of HttpServer is created by the HttpClientFactory, which creates the DelegatingHandler pipeline of your ASP.NET Web API application based on the collection of HttpMessageHandler instances in the configuration where your custom message handlers are registered (that'll be covered later in this chapter).

The next DelegatingHandler that gets to work in the pipeline shown in Figure 10-1 is the DelegatingHandler2, which just represents an arbitrary number of DelegatingHandler implementations that could be registered for your application.

The very last handler in the pipeline is always the HttpControllerDispatcher, which is passed as a parameter to the HttpServer constructor by the HttpControllerHandler based on the Dispatcher property of the GlobalConfiguration object of the ASP.NET Web API application.

As can also be seen in Figure 10-1 (by means of the dashed arrows) and as was mentioned earlier in this chapter, the pipeline not only runs from the outermost DelegatingHandler to the innermost one but also can run back from the formerly innermost DelegatingHandler to the formerly outermost one. These handlers are accessed again in reverse order if you defined a so-called continuation on the SendAsync method of the handlers' implementation, which is something you'll see later in this chapter, in the "Custom Message Handlers" section.

The following section shows an implementation of DelegatingHandler (see Listing 10-4) that allows you to inspect or even modify the request. Within the continuation, which is defined inside the ContinueWith method run on the result of the base.SendAsync method, you can do the same with the response when coming back from the controller.

When the response is inspected or modified, it is handled over to the next `DelegatingHandler` in the client's direction by returning it.

Now you know what `HttpMessageHandler` implementations are and what their purpose is in the context of an ASP.NET Web API application. Furthermore, you know how they are chained together in a pipeline that processes the instances of `HttpRequestMessage` and `HttpResponseMessage`. Now it's time to create your own custom message handlers and learn how to register them in the application configuration.

Custom Message Handlers

ASP.NET Web API is a powerful and well-designed framework with regard to the HTTP protocol. Nevertheless, it cannot cover all real-world HTTP application scenarios out of the box. Thanks to its sophisticated extensibility model, this is no problem, as it allows the tweaking of ASP.NET Web API if necessary.

One of the extensibility points of ASP.NET Web API is the `HttpMessageHandler` concept introduced earlier in this chapter. It allows not only modification of instances of `HttpRequestMessage` and `HttpResponseMessage` but also cancellation of the processing of the whole pipeline so that a request will be terminated and thus won't go to a higher level inside the pipeline.

In order to implement your own message handlers, you need to derive them from `DelegatingHandler`, as shown in Listing 10-4.

Listing 10-4. Basic Implementation of a Custom Message Handler

```
public class CustomMessageHandler : DelegatingHandler {

    protected override Task<HttpResponseMessage> SendAsync(HttpRequestMessage request, System.
Threading.CancellationToken cancellationToken) {

        // inspect or modify the request here

        return base.SendAsync(request, cancellationToken);
    }
}
```

As the implementation shown in Listing 10-4 does nothing with the request (or even the response), it is pretty useless. So let's head over to an implementation of `DelegatingHandler` that modifies the incoming request before it is passed to the controller.

MethodOverrideHandler

As explained in Chapter 3, in a RESTful application you make heavy use of different HTTP verbs like `GET`, `POST`, `PUT`, and `DELETE` among others. While that is no issue for the client if it is one that conforms to and implements the complete HTTP specification (like `HttpClient`, discussed in detail in Chapter 4), accessing all RESTful capabilities of a Web API via browsers often is problematic, as many (if not all) browsers only allow the sending of a form using the `GET` or `POST` verb. They don't allow for such other aforementioned HTTP methods as `HEAD`, `PUT`, and `DELETE`.

Google came up with a workaround for that problem. It involves adding a header to the HTTP request named `X-HTTP-Method-Override`, which has to be interpreted by the Web API, and to ignore the HTTP method (mostly `GET` or `POST`) being initially used by the web browser.

For example, to override the web browser's current method (more generally the client's), with the `PUT` method to be used instead, provide the header shown in Listing 10-5.

Listing 10-5. *Custom X-HTTP-Method-Override Header to Enforce the PUT HTTP Method*

```
X-HTTP-Method-Override: PUT
```

When it comes to the implementation of the requirements shown in Listing 10-6 and explained above, what actually has to be done is inspect the current request and check whether it contains an X-HTTP-Method-Override header. If that is the case, get the value of that header and replace the HTTP method of the request with the value of the X-HTTP-Method-Override header. That's pretty easy, thanks to the ASP.NET Web API HTTP abstraction implementation, as can be seen in Listing 10-6.

Listing 10-6. *DelegatingHandler That Overrides the HTTP Method from the Client Request*

```
public class XHttpMethodOverrideHandler : DelegatingHandler
{
    readonly string[] _methods = { "DELETE", "HEAD", "PUT" };
    const string XOVERRIDEHEADER = "X-HTTP-Method-Override";

    protected override Task<HttpResponseMessage> SendAsync(
        HttpRequestMessage request, CancellationToken cancellationToken)
    {
        // Check for HTTP POST with the X-HTTP-Method-Override header.
        if (HttpMethod.Post == request.Method && request.Headers.Contains(XOVERRIDEHEADER))
        {
            // Check if the header value is in our methods list.
            var overrideMethod = request.Headers.GetValues(XOVERRIDEHEADER).FirstOrDefault();
            if (_methods.Contains(overrideMethod, StringComparer.InvariantCultureIgnoreCase))
            {
                // Change the request method.
                request.Method = new HttpMethod(overrideMethod);
            }
        }
        return base.SendAsync(request, cancellationToken);
    }
}
```

Now, using Fiddler, let's issue a POST request to the API and override it to PUT by setting the X-HTTP-Method-Override header inside the request, as shown in Figure 10-2, and debug it. The breakpoint inside the PUT method of the controller is getting hit, as shown in Figure 10-3.

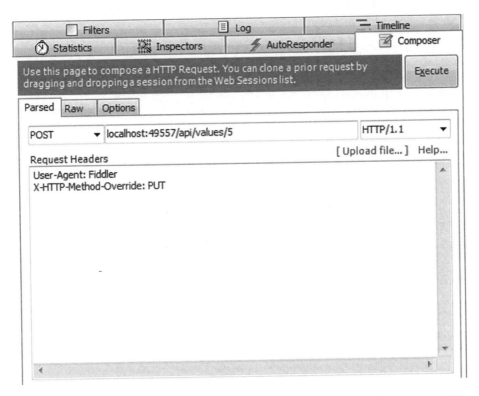

Figure 10-2. *Issuing a new POST request with X-HTTP-Method-Override header set to PUT*

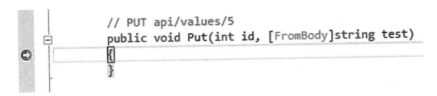

Figure 10-3. *Breakpoint being hit in the PUT method after rewriting the HTTP method*

Listing 10-6 shows how easy it is to access and modify information contained in the HTTP request from your clients, so you should be prepared for a slightly more difficult scenario, one where you're going to modify the outgoing response instead of the incoming request.

CustomResponseHeaderHandler

Now let's consider the opposite problem to the previous section's: adding your own custom response header instead of inspecting or modifying an existing one inside a request or response.

To do this, you have to access the response coming back from the controller. As was explained in the Russian Doll Model section earlier, this is done by using a continuation on the Task<HttpResponseMessage> return value of the base.SendAsync method inside the custom DelegatingHandler implementation, as shown in Listing 10-7.

Listing 10-7. Custom DelegatingHandler with Continuation

```
public class CustomMessageHandler : DelegatingHandler {

    protected override Task<HttpResponseMessage> SendAsync(HttpRequestMessage request, System.
Threading.CancellationToken cancellationToken) {

        //inspect request here

        return base.SendAsync(request, cancellationToken).ContinueWith(task => {

            //inspect the generated response
            var response = task.Result;

            return response;
        });
    }
}
```

Custom headers can be used to send some kinds of application- or server-wide information, as ASP.NET does with the X-Powered-By response header.

So let's add that X-Powered-By header to the response and set it to ASP.NET Web API. Listing 10-8 shows that implementation.

Listing 10-8. Adding a Custom Response Header

```
public class XPoweredByHeaderHandler : DelegatingHandler
{
    const string XPOWEREDBYHEADER = "X-Powered-By";
    const string XPOWEREDBYVALUE = "ASP.NET Web API";

    protected override Task<HttpResponseMessage> SendAsync(
        HttpRequestMessage request, CancellationToken cancellationToken)
    {
        return base.SendAsync(request, cancellationToken).ContinueWith(
            (task) =>
            {
                HttpResponseMessage response = task.Result;
                response.Headers.Add(XPOWEREDBYHEADER, XPOWEREDBYVALUE);
                return response;
            }
        );
    }
}
```

The response is the result of the Task<HttpResponseMessage> of the base DelegatingHandler class's SendAsync method from which the deriving is being done. By accessing that result inside the continuation of that SendAsync method, you can access the response on its way back from the controller and assign the new header and its value to the response.

When you're issuing a new request using Fiddler, your response now looks like that shown in Figure 10-4.

282

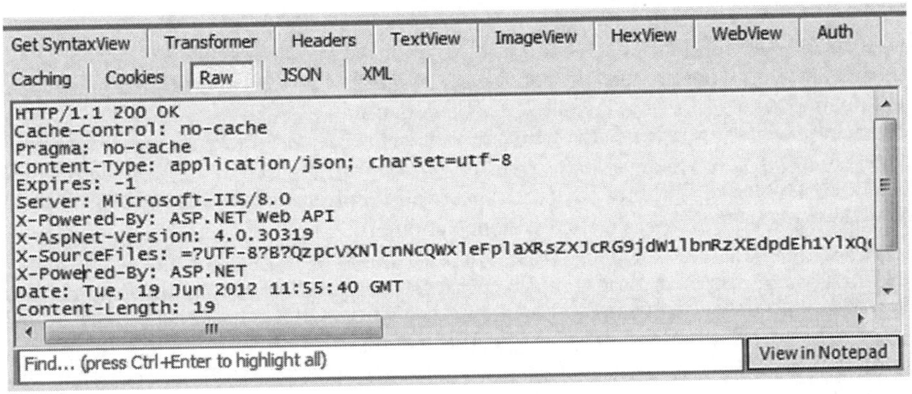

Figure 10-4. X-Power-By header in Web API response

As mentioned earlier in this chapter, the concept of the message handlers in ASP.NET Web API also allows you to cancel a request inside a `DelegatingHandler` so that the pipeline is not processed any longer and a response is sent immediately from within the current message handler. That's what will be implemented in the next section.

EmptyPostBodyMessageHandler

For the next implementation of a `DelegatingHandler`, please consider the following scenario: if a client is sending you a POST request, you would expect that the request also has a body containing data you should create a new entity from or start a new process on the server with. If you're assuming that this is true for all the controllers in your application, you could block all POST requests having an empty body by implementing a message handler that checks the body for its length. If it is empty, just cancel further processing of the request pipeline by returning a Bad Request status code. Listing 10-9 shows that implementation.

Listing 10-9. Aborting the Request Processing in a DelegatingHandler Implementation

```
public class EmptyPostBodyMessageHandler : DelegatingHandler
{
    protected override Task<HttpResponseMessage> SendAsync(
        HttpRequestMessage request, CancellationToken cancellationToken)
    {
        // Check for POST request and empty body.
        var content = request.Content.ReadAsStringAsync().Result;
        if (HttpMethod.Post == request.Method && 0 == content.Length)
        {
            TaskCompletionSource<HttpResponseMessage> tcs = new
TaskCompletionSource<HttpResponseMessage>();
            tcs.SetResult(new HttpResponseMessage(HttpStatusCode.BadRequest)
                { ReasonPhrase = "Empty body not allowed for POST."});
            return tcs.Task;
        }
        return base.SendAsync(request, cancellationToken);
    }
}
```

In ASP.NET Web API, the request body is contained in the Content property of the HttpRequestMessage; the framework provides some useful extensions methods that make it easy to handle that content in an asynchronous manner. To get the raw body of a request, you have to read the content as a string. The result of the asynchronous method ReadAsStringAsync contains that raw string representation of the request body.

If the check for a POST request is positive and the length of the raw body string is zero, a TaskCompletionSource of type HttpResponseMessage is created with a Bad Request status code. Furthermore, there is a reason phrase provided that tells the client why the request failed. The Task property of the TaskCompletionSource then contains the instantiated HttpResponseMessage, which will be returned to the client without further processing of the request.

Now that three custom message handlers have been implemented, you should have a rough overview of what's possible with message handlers. Of course, there are more complex operations possible, but you should be aware that they may slow down your Web API, as they eventually run on every request or response. Further HttpMessageHandler implementations are shown in Chapters 5-7, which cover the sample application .

You might have already asked yourself how ASP.NET Web API gets knowledge of the custom HttpMessageHandler implementations and runs them. That's part of the next and last section of this chapter.

Registering Custom Message Handlers

In the last two sections we've implemented custom message handlers, and you've seen the results of their work. But of course, to get a custom handler working, not only does it need to be implemented properly, but also ASP.NET Web API needs to get information that the handler(s) should be executed inside the request and response pipelines.

That mandatory registration process of custom message handlers is done using the code-based ASP.NET Web API configuration inside the Global.asax.cs (when choosing hosting in IIS). The GlobalConfiguration object, which encapsulates the whole ASP.NET application configuration, has a property Configuration type of HttpConfiguration, which itself represents the ASP.NET Web API configuration for the current application. The HttpConfiguration itself owns a property, MessageHandlers, which is a collection type of Collection<MessageHandler> from the System.Collections.ObjectModel namespace. Within this collection all custom message handlers can be added, removed or configured, as shown in Listing 10-10.

Listing 10-10. Registration of Two Custom Message Handlers in Global.asax.cs

```
public class WebApiApplication : System.Web.HttpApplication
{
    protected void Application_Start()
    {
        RouteConfig.RegisterRoutes(RouteTable.Routes);

        var config = GlobalConfiguration.Configuration;
        config.MessageHandlers.Add(new XHttpMethodOverrideHandler());
        config.MessageHandlers.Add(new XPoweredByHeaderHandler());
    }
}
```

Looking back at the Russian Doll Model is a reminder that there is one implicit question that's still not been covered: in which order does ASP.NET Web API process the HttpMessageHandler pipeline? You've learned that the pipeline is constructed by assigning one HttpMessageHandler to the InnerHandler property of the parent DelegatingHandler. That wiring must be done, not by hand, but by the HttpClientFactory when the HttpServer is initialized, as was discovered earlier.

In order to see how the `HttpMessageHandler` implementations are ordered, it's necessary to create two `DelegatingHandler` implementations that write some information to the Visual Studio Output Windows when debugging them. The information is split into two parts for each handler. The first part is the information that the request has just arrived at the handler; the second part goes for the response on the way back. The implementations are shown in Listings 10-11 and 10-12.

Listing 10-11. First Message Handler Logging Information About Request and Response

```
public class CustomMessageHandler1 : DelegatingHandler
{
    protected override System.Threading.Tasks.Task<HttpResponseMessage>
SendAsync(HttpRequestMessage request, System.Threading.CancellationToken cancellationToken)
    {
        Debug.WriteLine("CustomMessageHandler1 request invoked");
        return base.SendAsync(request, cancellationToken).ContinueWith((task) =>
        {
            Debug.WriteLine("CustomMessageHandler1 response invoked");
            var response = task.Result;
            return response;
        }
        );
    }
}
```

Listing 10-12. Second Message Handler Logging Information About Request and Response

```
public class CustomMessageHandler2 : DelegatingHandler
{
    protected override System.Threading.Tasks.Task<HttpResponseMessage> SendAsync(HttpRequestMessage
request, System.Threading.CancellationToken cancellationToken)
    {
        Debug.WriteLine("CustomMessageHandler2 request invoked");
        return base.SendAsync(request, cancellationToken).ContinueWith((task) =>
        {
            Debug.WriteLine("CustomMessageHandler2 response invoked");
            var response = task.Result;
            return response;
        });
    }
}
```

For consistency, both are registered in the order of their naming at the `Global.asax.cs`, as shown in Listing 10-13.

Listing 10-13. Registering Debugging Handlers in Order of Their Names

```
public class WebApiApplication : System.Web.HttpApplication
{
    protected void Application_Start()
    {
        RouteConfig.RegisterRoutes(RouteTable.Routes);
```

```
        var config = GlobalConfiguration.Configuration;
        config.MessageHandlers.Add(new CustomMessageHandler1());
        config.MessageHandlers.Add(new CustomMessageHandler2());
    }
}
```

When debugging the code from Listings 10-11 to 10-13 and looking at the output windows in Visual Studio, you get confirmation of the request and response pipeline processing order that you saw in the earlier "Message Handlers and the Russian Doll Model" section, as can be seen in Figure 10-5.

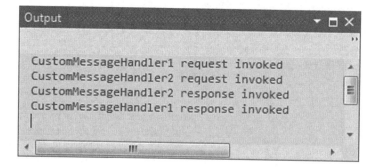

Figure 10-5. Output of the request and response pipeline order

So the understanding from Figure 10-5 is that the order of the registration of message handlers matters if there is a need to chain two custom message handlers, whereas one message handler depends on the result of another one.

As of now, we haven't covered self-hosting ASP.NET Web API with regard to message handlers. That's not a problem, as anything said in this chapter, except for the registration of the custom handler implementations, applies not only to web hosting ASP.NET Web API using IIS but also to self-hosting it—that's pretty nice, as you don't have to write different implementations of the handlers when your hosting environment changes. As was said, the only thing that's self-hosting specific is the registration of the handlers—or to be more specific, the creation of your configuration instance differs, whereas the registration of the handlers is almost the same, as you can see in Listing 10-14.

Listing 10-14. Registration of Custom Message Handlers in a Self-Hosting Scenario

```
class Program
{
    static void Main(string[] args)
    {
        var config = new HttpSelfHostConfiguration(new Uri("http://localhost:5478"));

        config.MessageHandlers.Add(new CustomMessageHandler1());
        config.MessageHandlers.Add(new CustomMessageHandler2());

        // routing code omitted for brevity

        using (var server = new HttpSelfHostServer(config))
        {
            server.OpenAsync().Wait();
            Console.ReadLine();
        }
    }
}
```

When debugging Listing 10-13 in your console, the output window will show the same result as it does for web hosting, as has already been shown in Figure 10-5.

Per-Route Message Handlers

The message handlers we registered in the samples in the previous sections were registered at application level. That means that every request gets handled by the registered message handlers. That might be good for a lot of scenarios, but there might also be other scenarios where it would be better to have message handlers that are invoked only for requests to specific routes. Such a scenario could be a protected part of a Web API application. Listing 10-15 shows an implementation of a message handler that checks for an API key by which access to the protected section of the application is allowed.

Listing 10-15. API Key Message Handler Implementation

```
public class ApiKeyProtectionMessageHandler : DelegatingHandler {
    protected override Task<HttpResponseMessage> SendAsync(HttpRequestMessage request,
CancellationToken cancellationToken) {
        IEnumerable<string> values;
        request.Headers.TryGetValues("apikey", out values);
        if (null != values && values.Count() == 1) {
            return base.SendAsync(request, cancellationToken);
        }

        var tcs = new TaskCompletionSource<HttpResponseMessage>();
        tcs.SetResult(new HttpResponseMessage(HttpStatusCode.Unauthorized) {
            ReasonPhrase = "API Key required."
        });
        return tcs.Task;

    }
}
```

In the overridden SendAsync method of the ApikeyProtectionMessageHandler, we're checking for a request header named "apikey". If that key has an arbitrary value (which you won't accept in a real-world application, of course), the request is redirected to the appropriate route by calling the SendAsync method of the DelegatingHandler from which we're deriving the ApikeyProtectionMessageHandler class.

If the "apikey" header is not set, we're returning a response with an HTTP status code 401 (i.e., unauthorized). In addition to that, we're providing a plain-text reason phrase indicating that the API key has been missing inside the request.

To get the ApiKeyProtectionMessageHandler working as a per-route message handler, it needs to be assigned to a route definition in the Web API application's route configuration. In addition to our existing Default API Route, we're defining a new route, one that will protect all resources behind the URI http://localhost:49557/secretapi/ using the API key. Listing 10-16 shows the definition of the route.

Listing 10-16. Route Definition for a Per-Route Message Handler

```
routes.MapHttpRoute(
    name: "Secret Api",
    routeTemplate: "secretapi/{controller}/{id}",
    defaults: new {id = RouteParameter.Optional},
    constraints: null,
```

```
handler: new ApiKeyProtectionMessageHandler() {
    InnerHandler =
        new HttpControllerDispatcher(GlobalConfiguration.Configuration)
});
```

As Listing 10-16 shows, the new route definition is akin to the Default API Route definition. The only differences are two parameters added to the new route. The first one is the `constraints` parameter, which is set to `null`. The second is the `handler` parameter, which expects a message handler implementation to be used for that particular route definition. We're creating a new instance of our `ApiKeyProtectionMessageHandler` class. Furthermore, we're assigning an instance of `HttpControllerDispatcher` (with the `GlobalConfiguration` as a parameter) to it. The reason for this assignment is that the per-route message handlers are invoked after the routing has been done.

As was seen earlier in the chapter, the message handler pipeline is built by assigning an inner message handler to the one external to it. As was also seen, the last message handler in the pipeline always has to be the `HttpControllerDispatcher`, in order to create an instance of the appropriate `ApiController`. If we didn't assign the `HttpControllerDispatcher` instance to the `InnerHandler` property of our `ApiKeyProtectionMessageHandler` instance, the pipeline would be broken, and an exception indicating that the `InnerHandler` property had not been set would be received.

If we explicitly want to stop the request from processing in our per-route message handler, we have to derive our implementation from the `HttpMessageHandler` base class. As we learned at the beginning of this chapter, in contrast to the more frequently used `DelegatingHandler` class, the `HttpMessageHandler` class has no `InnerHandler` property. The requests to that specific route never hit a controller.

With per-route message handlers, ASP.NET Web API allows you both to elegantly handle requests to particular routes in a way different from the usual one and to avoid executing code that's not necessary for certain requests.

Summary

ASP.NET Web API offers great and well-thought-out functionality out of the box. Nevertheless, there may occur requirements in your Web API implementation that are not covered by ASP.NET Web API features by default. As we've shown in this chapter, custom `HttpMessageHandler` implementations are an important extensibility point of ASP.NET Web API when it comes to inspecting or even modifying requests or responses.

Because of the Russian Doll Model, also explained in this chapter, it is possible to build a chain of dependent message handlers while still respecting the Separation of Concerns principle by having each handler's logic in its own class. With a consistent registration model for web hosting and self-hosting, you're able to switch from one to the other by simply changing the configuration without the need to reimplement the handlers themselves. Furthermore, you can register message handlers per route, which allows you to refine the usage of your message handlers.

CHAPTER 11

Filters

In our Web API applications, we might have some special logic that needs to run at specific points in the request processing stage, yet implementing this logic in every single place that we want to run it can lead to an undesirable result in our code base. In the first place, this action breaks our DRY (Don't Repeat Yourself) principle. Filters come into play at this point; they allow us to register our custom logic and have it run at specific points.

In this chapter, we will take a closer look at filters in ASP.NET Web API by discovering how they are implemented and registered and how they behave.

Overview and Filter Processing Model

In ASP.NET Web API, as we have seen in Chapter 9, `System.Web.Http.ApiController` is the default implementation of the `System.Web.Http.IHttpController`. Using `ApiController` provides many flexibilities in terms of application structure, and one of them is the ability to use filters. If we are working with `ApiController` as the base class of controllers, we can register different types of filters and inject custom logic at certain points of the request processing stage.

Filters are often .NET attributes that implement certain interfaces but they definitely don't have to be attributes. The reason why they are often attributes is to enable them to be easily applicable to individual controllers or even controller methods. There are three different types of filters inside the framework, as shown in Table 11-1.

Table 11-1. *Four Different Filter Types Inside the ASP.NET Web API Framework*

Filter Type	Interface	Description
Authorization	`IAuthorizationFilter`	The first filter; it runs before any other filters and is used for authorizing the request.
Action	`IActionFilter`	A type of filter that runs before the controller action is invoked.
Exception	`IExceptionFilter`	A type of filter that runs when an exception occurs.

In this chapter, the details of these filter types will be explained separately. When you look at the interfaces, you'll see that all of them implement the `IFilter` interface, which has only one public read-only property: `AllowMultiple`. This property determines whether a filter can be applied multiple times to a scope.

These three types of filters have their execution order inside the processing pipeline. The authorization filters run first, before any other filters and the controller action. Just before the controller action is invoked, action filters are aggregated and executed. At last, if any exception has occurred inside the controller or the filters, registered exceptions filters are invoked.

On the other hand, every filter has a scope behind the scenes depending on where it is registered; this scope information determines the order in which the same filter types run. The scope of a filter is indicated by the `FilterScope` enum (or enumeration) type, which has the implementation shown in Listing 11-1.

Listing 11-1. System.Web.Http.Filters.FilterScope

```
public enum FilterScope {
    Global = 0,
    Controller = 10,
    Action = 20
}
```

By looking at the FilterScope enum object, you can see that filters applied globally run before the others (lowest numbers first). Filters applied to controller classes run before the controller action level filters but after the global filters. Finally, action level filters run last, after all other filters.

■ **Note**   The scope of a filter doesn't change the filter type execution order. For example, if you have an authorization filter applied to your controller and an action filter applied globally, the authorization filter will run first. The filter scope determines only the execution order for the same types of filters.

Use Cases

In our sample application, we used all kinds of filters to make our application more compact and properly functional. Especially in cases where the same logic needs to be run multiple times, filters have their place. For example, let's assume that we need to write a trace information every time a controller action runs. Listing 11-2 shows a controller implementation without filters.

Listing 11-2. CarsController Without Filters

```
public class CarsController : ApiController {

    private readonly CarsContext _carsContext = new CarsContext();

    public IEnumerable<Car> GetCars() {

        log("GetCars");

        return _carsContext.All;
    }

    public Car GetCar(int id) {

        log("GetCar");

        return _carsContext.GetSingle(car => car.Id == id);
    }

    private void log(string actionName) {
```

```
        Trace.TraceInformation(
            string.Format(
                "Controller {0}, Action {1} is running...", "Cars", actionName
            )
        );
    }
}
```

CarsContext class here provides the data needed for our sample (Listing 11-3)

Listing 11-3. Car and CarsContext Classes

```
public class Car {

    public int Id { get; set; }
    public string Make { get; set; }
    public string Model { get; set; }
    public int Year { get; set; }
    public float Price { get; set; }
}

public class CarsContext {

    private static int _nextId = 9;
    private static object _incLock = new object();

    // data store
    readonly static ConcurrentDictionary<int, Car> _carsDictionary =
        new ConcurrentDictionary<int, Car>(
        new HashSet<KeyValuePair<int, Car>> {
            new KeyValuePair<int, Car>(
                1,
                new Car {
                    Id = 1,
                    Make = "Make1",
                    Model = "Model1",
                    Year = 2010,
                    Price = 10732.2F
                }
            ),
            new KeyValuePair<int, Car>(
                2,
                new Car {
                    Id = 2,
                    Make = "Make2",
                    Model = "Model2",
                    Year = 2008,
                    Price = 27233.1F
                }
            ),

            //Lines omitted for brevity . . .
    });
```

```
    public IEnumerable<Car> All {
        get {
            return _carsDictionary.Values;
        }
    }

    public IEnumerable<Car> Get(Func<Car, bool> predicate) {

        return _carsDictionary.Values.Where(predicate);
    }

    public Tuple<bool, Car> GetSingle(int id) {

        Car car;
        var doesExist = _carsDictionary.TryGetValue(id, out car);
        return new Tuple<bool, Car>(doesExist, car);
    }

    public Car GetSingle(Func<Car, bool> predicate) {

        return _carsDictionary.Values.FirstOrDefault(predicate);
    }

    public Car Add(Car car) {

        lock (_incLock) {

            car.Id = _nextId;
            _carsDictionary.TryAdd(car.Id, car);
            _nextId++;
        }

        return car;
    }

    public bool TryRemove(int id) {

        Car removedCar;
        return _carsDictionary.TryRemove(id, out removedCar);
    }

    public bool TryUpdate(Car car) {

        Car oldCar;
        if (_carsDictionary.TryGetValue(car.Id, out oldCar)) {

            return _carsDictionary.TryUpdate(car.Id, car, oldCar);
        }

        return false;
    }
}
}
```

Notice that we are running the same code for logging functionality inside every controller action by passing a relevant parameter to the private log method. Imagine that this needs to be done inside every single action of all application controllers. However, the same result can be achieved by using filters without repeating ourselves. Listing 11-4 shows a sample action filter implementation that generates the same logic.

Listing 11-4. CarsController with Filters

```
using System;
using System.Web.Http.Filters;
using System.Threading.Tasks;
using System.Net.Http;
using System.Web.Http.Controllers;
using System.Threading;
using System.Diagnostics;

namespace Overview.Filters {

    [AttributeUsage(
        AttributeTargets.Class | AttributeTargets.Method)]
    public class LoggerAttribute : Attribute, IActionFilter {

        public Task<HttpResponseMessage> ExecuteActionFilterAsync(
            HttpActionContext actionContext,
            CancellationToken cancellationToken,
            Func<Task<HttpResponseMessage>> continuation) {

            var controllerCtx = actionContext.ControllerContext;

            Trace.TraceInformation(
                "Controller {0}, Action {1} is running...",
                controllerCtx.ControllerDescriptor.ControllerName,
                actionContext.ActionDescriptor.ActionName
            );

            //the way of saying everything is OK
            return continuation();
        }

        public bool AllowMultiple {
            get {
                return false;
            }
        }
    }
}
```

When this filter is applied to CarsController, you should see the same result but with better implementation. However, if you need this filter to run for all controller actions, register the filter as a global filter inside the Global.asax file (see Listing 11-5).

Listing 11-5. Registering LoggerAttribute as a Global Filter

```
protected void Application_Start(object sender, EventArgs e) {

    //Lines omitted for brevity

    GlobalConfiguration.Configuration.Filters.Add(
        new LoggerAttribute());
}
```

■ **Note**   Filter registration will be explained in detail in the "Registering Filters" section.

The capabilities of filters are not limited to these types of scenarios. For example, you can intercept a request with filters and cancel the further execution inside the processing pipeline. Authorization filters are often used for types of scenarios where there is a need to validate the request according to the authorization logic and cancel further execution steps by returning a custom HttpResponseMessage instance.

THE DIFFERENCE BETWEEN FILTERS AND MESSAGE HANDLERS

At first glance, it might seem that filters and message handlers serve the same purpose. In some cases, they do; still, they have very distinct characteristics.

The message handlers are invoked very early inside the pipeline, even before the controller selector is invoked, and they are invoked for *every* request. Using a message handler is a great choice to run logics that have to be executed for every request, including authentication, as you'll see in Chapter 15. Also, by providing continuations inside the message handlers (as you saw in Chapter 10), you get a last chance to examine the response and perform some specific actions before the response goes out through the ASP.NET Web API pipeline.

The filters, on the other hand, have their own distinct purposes, as you might guess from their types. For example, exception filters are invoked only if an exception occurs inside the controller processing pipeline and authorization filters are invoked first, before any other filter types. In addition, filters can be invoked globally, per controller or per action. An excellent example of this is the AuthorizeAttribute, which is an authorization filter. AuthorizeAttribute checks against the Thread.CurrentPrincipal, on the basis of provided user names and roles, to decide whether or not the request is authorized. With AuthorizeAttribute, you can be very specific in deciding which controller or action allows access to which users or roles.

Default Filter Implementations

Besides filter interfaces, the Web API framework offers default implementation classes of those filters. These abstract classes are intended to make it easier to create custom filters, especially when we don't need to perform any asynchronous processing. Table 11-2 shows the three base classes we'll be using in the rest of this chapter.

Table 11-2. *Default Filter Implementations*

Interface	Implementation Class	Description
IAuthorizationFilter	AuthorizationFilterAttribute	Provides OnAuthorization method to authorize the request and handles returning generic Task object properly.
IactionFilter	ActionFilterAttribute	Unlike the IActionFilter interface, this class provides two methods: OnActionExecuting runs before the action is invoked, and OnActionExecuted runs just after the action is executed.
IExceptionFilter	ExceptionFilterAttribute	Provides the OnException method that will be invoked when an exception occurs.

All of those classes implement the relevant interfaces and are derived from the FilterAttribute class. FilterAttribute is an abstract class; it implements the IFilter interface and is derived from the Attribute class. FilterAttribute also properly sets the AllowMultiple property according to the AttributeUsage attribute's AllowMultiple property.

Filter Execution Order

As was mentioned earlier, filter types have an execution order relative to each other; but besides that, filter execution order depends on other factors. One of them is the scope of a filter. The filter types have an execution order depending on their scope. For example, if an action **Filter A** is registered at the controller level and action **Filter B** is registered at the action level, the Filter A OnActionExecuting method will always run before the Filter B OnActionExecuting method.

If you use the ActionFilterAttribute abstract class as your base class to create action filters, action filters have two methods, as seen in Table 11-2. One is the OnActionExecuting method; the other is OnActionExecuted. As you know, OnActionExecuting runs before the controller action is invoked, and OnActionExecuted runs just after the action method has been executed.

On the other side, when the system runs the filters, they are run in different orders, depending on which method is being executed. For example, IActionFilter.OnActionExecuting filters run in forward order, while IActionFilter.OnActionExecuted filters run in reverse. Let's look at an example to see these behaviors in action.

Here are two action filters: LoggerAttribute (Listing 11-6) and SecondaryLoggerAttribute (Listing 11-7).

Listing 11-6. LoggerAttribute Implementation

```
public class LoggerAttribute : ActionFilterAttribute {

    private const string _loggerName = "Logger";

    public override void OnActionExecuting(
        HttpActionContext actionContext) {

        var controllerCtx = actionContext.ControllerContext;

        LoggerUtil.WriteLog(
            _loggerName,
            "OnActionExecuting",
            controllerCtx.ControllerDescriptor.ControllerName,
```

```
                actionContext.ActionDescriptor.ActionName
        );
    }

    public override void OnActionExecuted(
        HttpActionExecutedContext actionExecutedContext) {

        var actionCtx = actionExecutedContext.ActionContext;
        var controllerCtx = actionCtx.ControllerContext;

        LoggerUtil.WriteLog(
            _loggerName,
            "OnActionExecuted",
            controllerCtx.ControllerDescriptor.ControllerName,
            actionCtx.ActionDescriptor.ActionName
        );
    }
}
```

Listing 11-7. SecondaryLoggerAttribute Implementation

```
public class SecondaryLoggerAttribute : ActionFilterAttribute {

    private const string _loggerName = "SecondaryLogger";

    public override void OnActionExecuting(
        HttpActionContext actionContext) {

        var controllerCtx = actionContext.ControllerContext;

        LoggerUtil.WriteLog(
            _loggerName,
            "OnActionExecuting",
            controllerCtx.ControllerDescriptor.ControllerName,
            actionContext.ActionDescriptor.ActionName
        );
    }

    public override void OnActionExecuted(
        HttpActionExecutedContext actionExecutedContext) {

        var actionCtx = actionExecutedContext.ActionContext;
        var controllerCtx = actionCtx.ControllerContext;

        LoggerUtil.WriteLog(
            _loggerName,
            "OnActionExecuted",
            controllerCtx.ControllerDescriptor.ControllerName,
            actionCtx.ActionDescriptor.ActionName
        );
    }
}
```

LoggerUtil here is a very simple class; it has only one static method to keep our Logger implementation clean (see Listing 11-8).

Listing 11-8. LoggerUtil Class

```
public class LoggerUtil {

    public static void WriteLog(
        string loggerName, string loggerMethodName,
        string controllerName, string actionName) {

        var logFormat =
            "{0}, {1} method for Controller {2}, Action {3} is running...";

        Trace.TraceInformation(
            logFormat,
            loggerName,
            loggerMethodName,
            actionName,
            controllerName);
    }
}
```

Inside our controller the action filters are registered, as shown in Listing 11-9.

Listing 11-9. CarsController

```
[Logger]
public class CarsController : ApiController {

    [SecondaryLogger]
    public string[] GetCars() {

        return new string[] {
            "Car 1",
            "Car 2",
            "Car 3",
            "Car 4"
        };
    }
}
```

The expected behavior here is to see the Logger action filter's OnActionExecuting method run first and then the SecondaryLogger's corresponding method run after it. However, the order should be reversed for the OnActionExecuted methods. When the application is run in debug mode, you should see the output result in the **Output** window (see Figure 11-1).

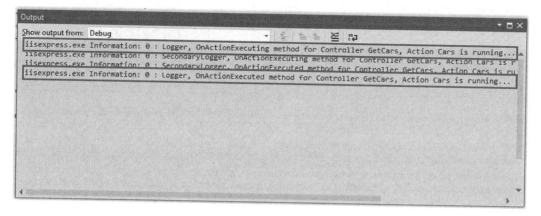

Figure 11-1. Action filters output result to Output window

Exception filters run in reverse order as well. For example, Filter A and Filter B are exception filters. Filter A is registered at the controller level, Filter B at the action level. Normally, Filter A should run before Filter B, but as these are exception filters, Filter B will always run before Filter A.

In addition to these filter behaviors, note that filters may be skipped in some situations. For instance, if the requested is terminated by an action filter, the upcoming action filters won't be run. At the same time, if there is any other action that has already been executed before the action filter that terminated the request, that action filter's OnActionExecuted method will be run, but the others won't.

Let's look at an example to see this behavior in action. There are now three Logger action filters with the same implementations as Listings 11-6 and 11-7. One of these three filters has a slightly different implementation (see Listing 11-10).

Listing 11-10. LoggerAttribute Action Filter That Will Terminate the Request

```
public class LoggerAttribute : ActionFilterAttribute {

    private const string _loggerName = "Logger";

    public override void OnActionExecuting(
        HttpActionContext actionContext) {

        //terminate the request by setting a new response
        //to actionContext.Response
        actionContext.Response = new HttpResponseMessage(
            HttpStatusCode.NotFound
        );
    }

    public override void OnActionExecuted(
        HttpActionExecutedContext actionExecutedContext) {

        var actionCtx = actionExecutedContext.ActionContext;
        var controllerCtx = actionCtx.ControllerContext;

        LoggerUtil.WriteLog(
            _loggerName,
```

```
                "OnActionExecuted",
                controllerCtx.ControllerDescriptor.ControllerName,
                actionCtx.ActionDescriptor.ActionName
            );
        }
    }
}
```

We have registered the Logger action filter at the controller level. At the same time, we have the GlobalLogger action filter registered as a global filter (see Listing 11-11) and the SecondaryLogger action filter applied at the controller action level (see Listing 11-12).

Listing 11-11. GlobalLogger Action Filter

```
public class GlobalLoggerAttribute : ActionFilterAttribute {

    private const string _loggerName = "GlobalLogger";

    public override void OnActionExecuting(
        HttpActionContext actionContext) {

        var controllerCtx = actionContext.ControllerContext;

        LoggerUtil.WriteLog(
            _loggerName,
            "OnActionExecuting",
            controllerCtx.ControllerDescriptor.ControllerName,
            actionContext.ActionDescriptor.ActionName
        );
    }

    public override void OnActionExecuted(
        HttpActionExecutedContext actionExecutedContext) {

        var actionCtx = actionExecutedContext.ActionContext;
        var controllerCtx = actionCtx.ControllerContext;

        LoggerUtil.WriteLog(
            _loggerName,
            "OnActionExecuted",
            controllerCtx.ControllerDescriptor.ControllerName,
            actionCtx.ActionDescriptor.ActionName
        );
    }
}
```

Listing 11-12. SecondaryLogger Action Filter

```
public class SecondaryLoggerAttribute : ActionFilterAttribute {

    private const string _loggerName = "SecondaryLogger";

    public override void OnActionExecuting(
        HttpActionContext actionContext) {
```

```
        var controllerCtx = actionContext.ControllerContext;

        LoggerUtil.WriteLog(
            _loggerName,
            "OnActionExecuting",
            controllerCtx.ControllerDescriptor.ControllerName,
            actionContext.ActionDescriptor.ActionName
        );
    }

    public override void OnActionExecuted(
        HttpActionExecutedContext actionExecutedContext) {

        var actionCtx = actionExecutedContext.ActionContext;
        var controllerCtx = actionCtx.ControllerContext;

        LoggerUtil.WriteLog(
            _loggerName,
            "OnActionExecuted",
            controllerCtx.ControllerDescriptor.ControllerName,
            actionCtx.ActionDescriptor.ActionName
        );
    }
}
```

So GlobalLogger filter should run first, and the Logger filter second. When the request is terminated by the Logger action filter's OnActionExecuting method, then the Logger filter's OnActionExecuted method shouldn't be run in addition to the SecondaryLogger action filter. Since the GlobalLogger filter's OnActionExecuting method has already been executed at this point, the system will run its OnActionExecuted method as well (see Figure 11-2).

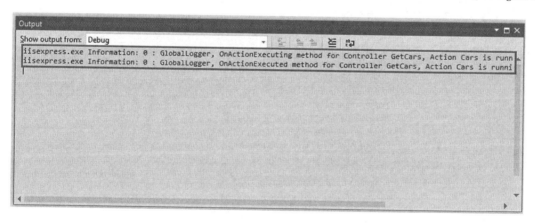

Figure 11-2. Action filter's output result to Output window

The same behavior can been seen if the Logger action filter throws an exception instead of terminating the request by setting a new response message.

Registering Filters

Filters can be registered in any of several different ways. This section of the chapter will look at those options.

Action and Controller-Based Filters

Filters can be registered at the controller or action level and this allows control of individual pieces of the framework in terms of filter execution. We generally implement filters as .NET attributes in order to attach them easily at the class and method level, the levels corresponding to controller and action in our case.

.NET ATTRIBUTES IN A NUTSHELL

In the .NET framework, attributes are special classes derived from the abstract `System.Attribute` class; they provide metadata about the objects, methods, properties, and fields. When an attribute is associated with a program entity, that attribute can be queried and read at runtime with the help of reflection. In C#, attributes are registered using square brackets, and their public properties can be used, as well (e.g., `[FooAttribute (FooBar = "Foo")]`). By convention, all attribute names end with the word "Attribute" to distinguish them from other items in the .NET Framework, but the Attribute suffix can be omitted when using attributes in code. For example, an attribute class named `FooAttribute` can be designated `[Foo]` when it's declared.

If a filter is registered at the controller level (as shown in Listing 11-13), the filter will be applied to all action methods under that controller.

Listing 11-13. Registering a Filter at the Controller Level

```
[MyFilter]
public class CarsController : ApiController {

    public string[] GetCars() {

        //Lines omitted for brevity
    }

    public string[] GetCar(int id) {

        //Lines omitted for brevity
    }
}
```

Doing the same thing for an individual action will ensure that the attached filter will be executed only for that action. For example, the `MyFilter` filter will be applied only to the `GetCars` action of `CarsController` (cf. Listing 11-14).

Listing 11-14. Registering a Filter at the Action Level

```
public class CarsController : ApiController {

    [MyFilter]
    public string[] GetCars() {

        //Lines omitted for brevity
    }
```

```
    public string[] GetCar(int id) {

        //Lines omitted for brevity
    }
}
```

Global Filters

Sometimes a filter—an exception filter, for example—might be a good fit for every controller action in an application. Luckily, you don't have to register it manually for every single controller. The system allow registration of global filters using GlobalConfiguration's static Configuration property inside Application_Start method in the Global.asax file.

Listing 11-15 shows MyFilter filter registered globally so that it will be applied to every controller action in our application.

Listing 11-15. Registering a Filter Globally

```
protected void Application_Start(object sender, EventArgs e) {

    //Lines omitted for brevity

    GlobalConfiguration.Configuration.Filters.Add(new MyFilter());
}
```

Types of Filters

In ASP.NET Web API framework, there are three different types of filters: action filters, authorization filters and exception filters. This section will explain each of them with samples.

Action Filters

Action filters allow you to inject code to run before the action is invoked and after it is executed. An action filter needs to implement the IActionFilter interface. We'll be working with the ActionFilterAttribute class (see Listing 11-16), the default implementation of IActionFilter.

Listing 11-16. ActionFilterAttribute Abstract Class

```
public abstract class ActionFilterAttribute :
    FilterAttribute, IActionFilter {

    public virtual void OnActionExecuted(
        HttpActionExecutedContext actionExecutedContext);

    public virtual void OnActionExecuting(
        HttpActionContext actionContext);
}
```

The OnActionExecuting method is the one that runs just before the action is invoked. Inside this method, the framework passes a context class named HttpActionContext, which carries the information related to the request, including controller descriptor, action descriptor, request message, and the like. This context class is used by other filter types as well. Table 11-3 shows the public properties of HttpActionContext class.

Table 11-3. *HttpActionContext Class Properties*

Name	Type	Description
ActionArguments	Dictionary<string, object>	Dictionary object; it holds the action method arguments.
ActionDescriptor	HttpActionDescriptor	Carries the action method details: action name, action method, binding details, etc.
ControllerContext	HttpControllerContext	Carries the controller information: controller type, controller name, controller instance, etc.
ModelState	ModelStateDictionary	Represents the model state, which has been populated by model binders.
Request	HttpRequestMessage	Represents the request message.
Response	HttpResponseMessage	Represents the response message of the request. If this property is set to an instance of an HttpResponseMessage, the further execution of the request will be canceled.

The OnActionExecuted method, which runs after the action is executed, is provided with a context class, HttpActionExecutedContext, which carries an HttpActionContext instance, response message details generated by the action, and exception details, if there are any. The HttpActionExecutedContext class is also provided inside the exception filters. Table 11-4 shows the public properties of the HttpActionExecutedContext class.

Table 11-4. *HttpActionExecutedContext Class Properties*

Name	Type	Description
HttpActionContext	HttpActionContext	Provides an instance of the HttpActionContext object.
Exception	Exception	Provides the exception details, if there are any.
Request	HttpRequestMessage	Represents the request message.
Response	HttpResponseMessage	Provides the response message instance that has been populated so far. The response message can be altered; doing so will cause the returned response message to hold the alterations.

Here's an example to show you how an action filter works.

Action Filter ModelState Validation Sample

Our applications often require us to validate incoming inputs according to our domain logic. For example, a data column inside our database system may not store a string value whose length is greater than 20. If this is the case and we receive an input for this object with a length greater than 20, we will most probably receive an error, depending on the database system, while trying to insert the value. To prevent these scenarios, some sort of validation logic is needed to respond properly if there is a validation error. Luckily, ASP.NET Web API supports validation with data annotation validation attributes along with action parameter binding.

■ **Note**   Don't worry! We will explain the details of validation in Chapter 13 and the action parameter binding feature of ASP.NET Web API in Chapter 12.

Let's assume that we handle POST requests in our Web API application to create new car entities in our car gallery database. Our Car POCO class is shown in Listing 11-17. As you may notice, some properties, such as Required, have validation attributes.

Listing 11-17. Car Class with Data Annotation Validation Attributes

```
public class Car {

    public int Id { get; set; }

    [Required]
    [StringLength(20)]
    public string Make { get; set; }

    [Required]
    [StringLength(20)]
    public string Model { get; set; }

    public int Year { get; set; }

    public float Price { get; set; }
}
```

For this example, we've created a class that acts like our data layer. What it does is manipulate a static collection (see Listing 11-18).

Listing 11-18. CarsContext Class

```
public class CarsContext {

    private static int _nextId = 9;
    private static object _incLock = new object();

    // data store
    readonly static ConcurrentDictionary<int, Car> _carsDictionary =
        new ConcurrentDictionary<int, Car>(
        new HashSet<KeyValuePair<int, Car>> {
            new KeyValuePair<int, Car>(
                1,
                new Car {
                    Id = 1,
                    Make = "Make1",
                    Model = "Model1",
                    Year = 2010,
                    Price = 10732.2F
                }
            ),
            new KeyValuePair<int, Car>(
                2,
                new Car {
                    Id = 2,
                    Make = "Make2",
```

```
                    Model = "Model2",
                    Year = 2008,
                    Price = 27233.1F
                }
            ),

            //Lines omitted for brevity . . .
    });

    public IEnumerable<Car> All {
        get {
            return _carsDictionary.Values;
        }
    }

    public IEnumerable<Car> Get(Func<Car, bool> predicate) {

        return _carsDictionary.Values.Where(predicate);
    }

    public Car GetSingle(Func<Car, bool> predicate) {

        return _carsDictionary.Values.FirstOrDefault(predicate);
    }

    public Car Add(Car car) {

        lock (_incLock) {

            car.Id = _nextId;
            _carsDictionary.TryAdd(car.Id, car);
            _nextId++;
        }

        return car;
    }
}
```

With this implementation, if the properties are not valid according to validation attributes and we try to add the object to the collection anyway, there's not going to be a problem, since it's just an in-memory store. However, we would be working with a database system in a real-world scenario to store the data, that can be problematic if we try to insert a null value inside a column that doesn't accept null values. So we need to be able to prevent this up front in our application.

Let's see our controller implementation first (Listing 11-19).

Listing 11-19. CarsController Implementation

```
public class CarsController : ApiController {

    private readonly CarsContext _carsContext = new CarsContext();

    public IEnumerable<Car> GetCars() {
```

```
        return _carsContext.All;
    }

    public Car GetCar(int id) {

        return _carsContext.GetSingle(car => car.Id == id);
    }

    public HttpResponseMessage PostCar(Car car) {

        _carsContext.Add(car);

        return new HttpResponseMessage(HttpStatusCode.Created);
    }
}
```

Inside the POST method, we will be receiving the Car object as a parameter and that Car will be populated by the proper HttpParameterBinding implementation. The FormatterParameterBinding, which is going to be selected for this case if the default configuration is in place, also validates the object according to validation attributes and populates the controller ModelState, which is a type of ModelStateDictionary, with error messages if there are any.

As has been seen earlier, we have access to a ModelStateDictionary instance through the HttpActionContext class, which is passed as a parameter to the OnActionExecuting method. So we can analyze the ModelState to see if it contains any validation errors. On the other hand, the OnActionExecuting method runs before the action is invoked. There is a chance to cancel the further execution of the request and set your own response message inside this method if you want to. This gives you the ability to cancel the request execution by setting your own response if there is any validation error that ModelState holds. To enable you to follow this approach, Listing 11-20 shows an action filter named ValidateModelStateAttribute.

Listing 11-20. ValidateModelStateAttribute Action Filter

```
[AttributeUsage(
    AttributeTargets.Class | AttributeTargets.Method,
    AllowMultiple = false, Inherited = true)]
public class ValidateModelStateAttribute : ActionFilterAttribute {

    public override void OnActionExecuting(
        HttpActionContext actionContext) {

        if (!actionContext.ModelState.IsValid) {

            actionContext.Response =
                actionContext.Request.CreateErrorResponse(
                    HttpStatusCode.BadRequest,
                    actionContext.ModelState);
        }
    }
}
```

The steps being taken inside the ValidateModelStateAttribute filter are fairly simple. First of all is to check whether the ModelState is valid or not by examining its IsValid property. If it is valid, it's left just as it is.

If the ModelState is not valid, you can create a new HttpResponseMessage by using the CreateErrorResponse extension method of HttpRequestMessage. One of the overloads of the CreateErrorResponse method accepts the ModelStateDictionary value as parameter and serializes it to the proper format, based on the content negotiation logic. This allows the server to process the content negotiation on your behalf. By doing it this way, you can send the response message with the format that the client wants—assuming the registered formatters are capable of doing it. Chapter 12 will cover formatters in detail.

If the ModelState is not valid, the ValidateModelStateAttribute will notify the framework not to continue processing the planned execution. The framework will do what you want here: return your response without executing the controller action method.

You now need to register this filter somehow. In our example that's done at the action level (recall that filter registration was covered in detail in an earlier section, "Registering Filters"). Listing 11-21 modifies the PostCar method from Listing 11-19.

Listing 11-21. Registering the ValidateModelStateAttribute Action Filter

```
//Lines omitted for brevity

[ValidateModelState]
public HttpResponseMessage PostCar(Car car) {

    _carsContext.Add(car);

    return new HttpResponseMessage(HttpStatusCode.Created);
}

//Lines omitted for brevity
```

To see it in action, use Fiddler to send a request to the API. First, let's see if it works when we send a valid request to our API (see Figure 11-3).

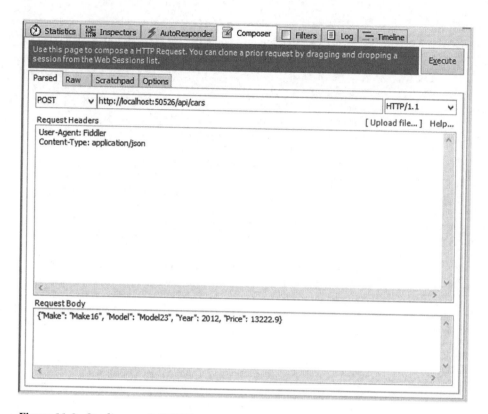

Figure 11-3. Sending a valid POST request using Fiddler

Once the request is sent, a 201 response should be returned. It indicates that the entry has been created successfully (see Figure 11-4).

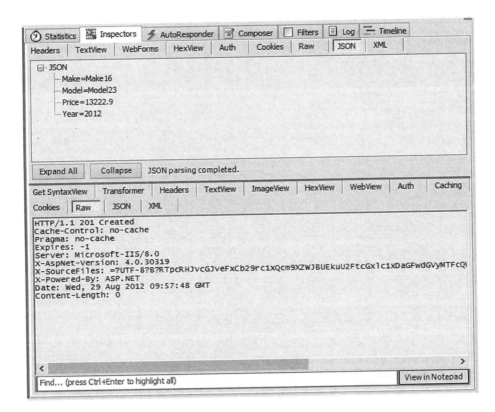

Figure 11-4. *Receiving the 201 response*

Let's send an invalid request to see if the validation filter functions properly. Remember that we have added the StringLengthAttribute to the Model property of our Car object, which specifies that this field requires a string value whose length should be a maximum of 20. So now let's test the logic (see Figure 11-5).

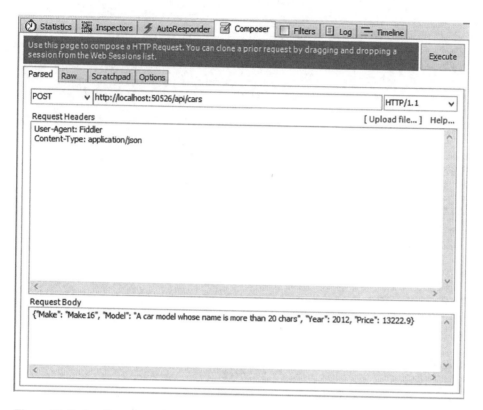

Figure 11-5. *Sending an invalid request using Fiddler*

After this POST request is sent, a 400 response should be returned, along with a validation error message (see Figure 11-6).

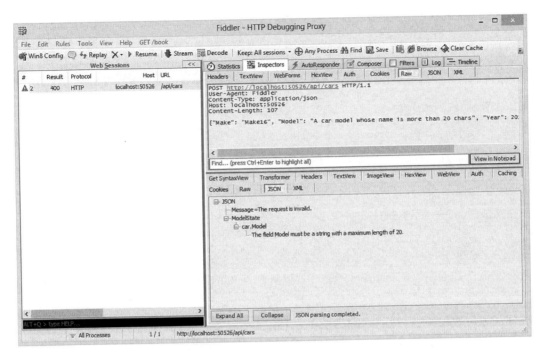

Figure 11-6. *Receiving the 400 response*

As you see, with a little extra implementation you have a nice model validation system. We've shown a commonly encountered example here, but action filters come in handy mostly for custom implementations specific to an application.

Authorization Filters

Authorization filters inside the Web API framework allow the authorization of the request just before the action filters and controller action are invoked. An authorization filter needs to implement the IAuthorizationFilter interface. We'll be working with the AuthorizationFilterAttribute class (see Listing 11-22), which is the default implementation of IAuthorizationFilter, which provides the synchronous OnAuthorization method.

Listing 11-22. AuthorizationFilterAttribute Abstract Class

```
public abstract class AuthorizationFilterAttribute :
    FilterAttribute, IAuthorizationFilter {

    public virtual void OnAuthorization(
        HttpActionContext actionContext);
}
```

As already noted several times, an authorization filter runs before any other filter, and its only method, OnAuthorization, is invoked by passing an instance of HttpActionContext class as a parameter. Inside the OnAuthorization method, the request is supposed to be analyzed to authorize the user according to the authorization logic. If the user cannot be authorized by the authorization logic, the request should be terminated. A new response message should be assigned to indicate the unauthorized request.

You'll see a sample use case, one where a custom authorization filter is implemented, later in this chapter. Before that, let's explain the use of the AuthorizeAttribute, which is provided inside the framework out of the box as an authorization filter to work with your custom and framework's built-in authentication features, including forms and windows authentication.

AuthorizeAttribute and Its Use

Use and logic of AuthorizeAttribute is fairly straightforward in ASP.NET Web API. It checks against the user IPrincipal returned via Thread.CurrentPrincipal. Authorization is denied if one of the following conditions is satisfied:

- The request is not associated with any user.

- The user is not authenticated.

- The user is not in the authorized group of Users.

- The user is authenticated but is not in the authorized group of Users (if defined) or is not in any of the authorized Roles (if defined).

This filter can be applied globally to secure our entire application, but this attribute can also be set at the controller or action level. Listing 11-23 shows how to register AuthorizeAttribute as a global filter.

Listing 11-23. AuthorizeAttribute as a Global Filter

```
protected void Application_Start(object sender, EventArgs e) {

    //Lines omitted for brevity

    GlobalConfiguration.Configuration.Filters.Add(
        new AuthorizeAttribute());
}
```

When AuthorizeAttribute is registered globally, authorization for every controller action in our application is required, even though you might want to give access to unauthorized users for some part of it. In order to deal with this kind of situation, there is an attribute class, AllowAnonymousAttribute. Actions and controllers marked with this attribute are skipped by AuthorizeAttribute. Listing 11-24 shows a sample use of AllowAnonymousAttribute. In this case, AuthController's POST action will be skipped by AuthorizeAttribute, and unauthorized users can have access to this endpoint.

Listing 11-24. *Sample Use of AllowAnonymousAttribute*

```
public class AuthController : ApiController {

    //Lines omitted for brevity

    [AllowAnonymous]
    public HttpResponseMessage Post(User user) {

        //Lines omitted for brevity
    }
}
```

In registering AuthorizeAttribute without any properties, access is given to every single user who is authorized in the application, regardless of the user name or role. You can specify authorized roles and users using two public properties of the AuthorizeAttribute class: Roles and Users. These two properties accept a string value. If there are multiple authorized users or roles in an instance, a comma-separated list for the properties can be provided. Listing 11-25 shows an example that gives access only to a user whose user name is *Alex* or *Tugberk*.

Listing 11-25. AuthorizeAttribute and Giving Access Only to Certain Users

```
[Authorize(Users = "Alex,Tugberk")]
public class CarsController : ApiController {

    //Lines omitted for brevity

    public IEnumerable<Car> Get() {

        //Lines omitted for brevity
    }
}
```

The same implementation applies to the Roles property, too.

To see the AuthorizeAttribute in action, we have created a small sample application that works with forms authentication. We use only ASP.NET Web API as a server-side component here and deal with communication between the browser and our API using AJAX requests.

■ **Note** To demonstrate the AuthorizeAttribute use here, we are working with ASP.NET forms authentication, which will work only if an application is hosted under IIS. (Chapter 15 will explain forms authentication.) So don't be overwhelmed by the sample application. For brevity, the full code for this sample application isn't provided here, but you can find the full code for the working application with the source code for this book.

The main idea of this application is to allow authorized users to retrieve the cars list inside the car gallery. As we are using forms authentication and the client application is under the same domain as our API, users need to authenticate themselves just once; then the encrypted authentication information will be stored inside the cookie.

Listing 11-26 implements the API controller through which the cars list can be gotten.

Listing 11-26. CarsController Implementation

```
public class CarsController : ApiController {

    private readonly CarsContext _carsContext = new CarsContext();

    public IEnumerable<Car> Get() {

        return _carsContext.All;
    }
}
```

CarsContext is just a class that deals with our data—in-memory data in this case. As we want to give access to the application only to authorized users, we have registered the AuthorizeAttribute as a global filter; the code used to register this filter globally is the same as the code in Listing 11-20.

The other logic needed here is to be able to authorize the users. We will deal with this through a POST request inside AuthController (see Listing 11-27).

Listing 11-27. AuthController Implementation

```
public class AuthController : ApiController {

    private readonly AuthorizationService authService =
        new AuthorizationService();

    private readonly FormsAuthenticationService formsAuthService =
        new FormsAuthenticationService();

    [AllowAnonymous]
    public HttpResponseMessage Post(User user) {

        var response = new HttpResponseMessage();

        if (user != null &&
            authService.Authorize(user.UserName, user.Password)) {

            //user has been authorized
            response.StatusCode = HttpStatusCode.OK;
            formsAuthService.SignIn(user.UserName, true);

            return response;
        }

        //if we have come this far, it means that
        //the user hasn't been authorized
        response.StatusCode = HttpStatusCode.Unauthorized;
        response.Content = new StringContent(
            "The user hasn't been authorized.");

        return response;
    }
}
```

The first thing to mention is the use of the AllowAnonymous attribute. As AuthorizeAttribute is already registered as a global filter, use the AllowAnonymous attribute here to give access to the POST action of AuthController. After all, we are using this action to authorize unauthorized users.

There are two service classes inside our controller to deal with authorization and authentication. Normally, they'd be accessed with dependency injection logic (discussed in Chapter 16), but let's just use them as they are to stick with the main topic here.

AuthorizationService here controls the authorization by checking the supplied credentials against an in-memory user list (see Listing 11-28). We use the Authorize method of this class to check that the supplied user credentials are valid.

Listing 11-28. AuthorizationService implementation

```
public class AuthorizationService {

    private static List<User> users = new List<User>() {
        new User {
            UserName = "tugberk",
            Email = "tugberk@example.com",
```

```
            Password = "12345678"
        },
        new User {
            UserName = "alex",
            Email = "alex@example.com",
            Password = "87654321"
        }
    };

    public bool Authorize(string userName, string password) {

        var user = users.FirstOrDefault(
            x => x.UserName == userName);

        if (user == null)
            return false;

        return string.Equals(password, user.Password);
    }
}
```

If the user is successfully authorized by AuthorizationService, the next step is to use FormsAuthenticationService (see Listing 11-29) to deal with ASP.NET forms authentication. The SignIn method of the FormsAuthenticationService is used here. It creates a persistent cookie for the authentication according to information supplied inside web.config, inside the **system.web > authentication > forms** element. (For more information about the forms element, check this MSDN reference: http://msdn.microsoft.com/en-us/library/1d3t3c61.aspx.

Listing 11-29. FormsAuthenticationService Implementation

```
public class FormsAuthenticationService {

    public void SignIn(
        string userName,
        bool createPersistentCookie) {

        if (String.IsNullOrEmpty(userName))
            throw new ArgumentNullException("userName");

        FormsAuthentication.SetAuthCookie(
            userName,
            createPersistentCookie);
    }

    public void SignOut() {

        FormsAuthentication.SignOut();
    }
}
```

If the user can't be authorized, a 401 unauthorized response gets returned, with a message indicating just that.

When visiting the web page to see the cars list, you should see a log-in dialog box first because you aren't authorized (see Figure 11-7).

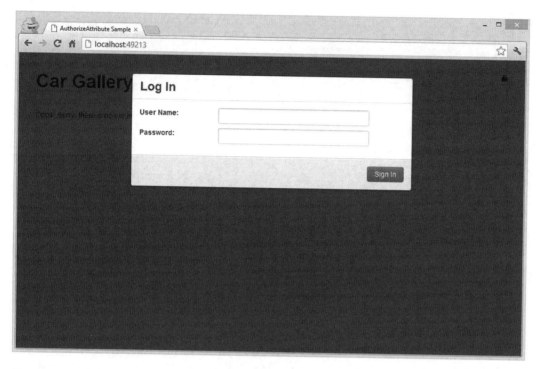

Figure 11-7. *The web page that shows authorized users the cars list*

This functionality is enabled with JavaScript code. A request is sent to our API to receive the cars list and show the dialog box if the request is unauthorized (see Listing 11-30).

Listing 11-30. jQuery Code That Makes an AJAX Request to Our API to Receive the Cars List

```
//Lines omitted for brevity

var apiBaseAddress = "/api/cars";

//Lines omitted for brevity

$.ajax({
    url: apiBaseAddress,
    type: "GET",
    contentType: "application/json; charset=utf-8",
    statusCode: {
        //OK
        200: function(result) {

            $.each(result, function(i, data) {
                vm.cars.push(buidCar(data));
            });
        },
        //Unauthorized
        401: function() {
```

```
                openAuthDialogBox();
        }
    }
});

//Lines omitted for brevity
```

Let's look at the code in Fiddler to see what happens when it runs (see Figure 11-8).

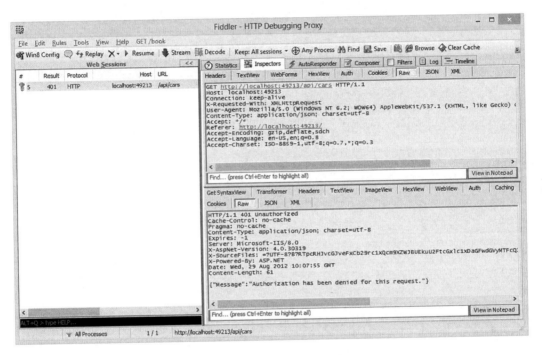

Figure 11-8. *Fiddler view of the unathorized GET request to /api/cars*

A 401 response, indicating the request is not authorized, is returned. Now let's try to log in with the wrong credentials and see the request and response in Fiddler (see Figure 11-9).

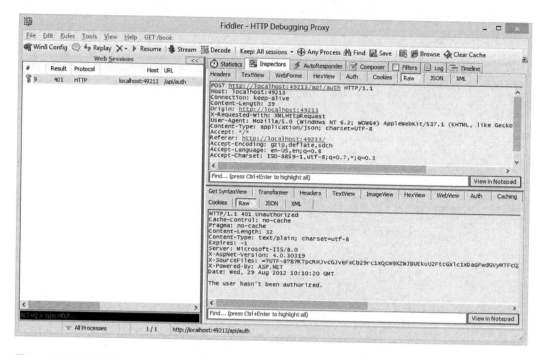

Figure 11-9. A Fiddler view of the unauthorized POST request to /api/auth

---

■ **Note** In the example, we sent the credentials as plain text (unencrypted); this is an insecure way of handling authorization. In a real-world application, you should use the Secure Transport Layer (SSL) to provide encryption.

As expected, the server again returns the 401 response. Now let's try to log in with valid credentials; this time we should get a 200 response, along with a Set-Cookie header (see Figure 11-10).

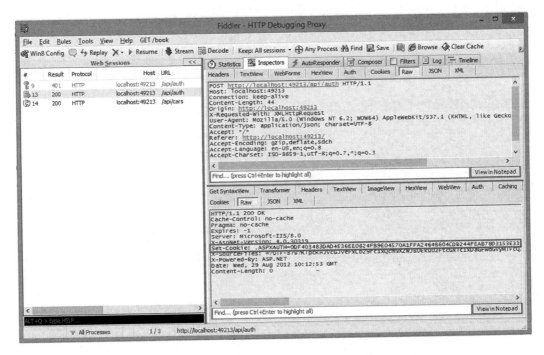

Figure 11-10. *A Fiddler view of the successful POST request to /api/auth*

Now that we're logged in, the cars list should be visible (see Figure 11-11).

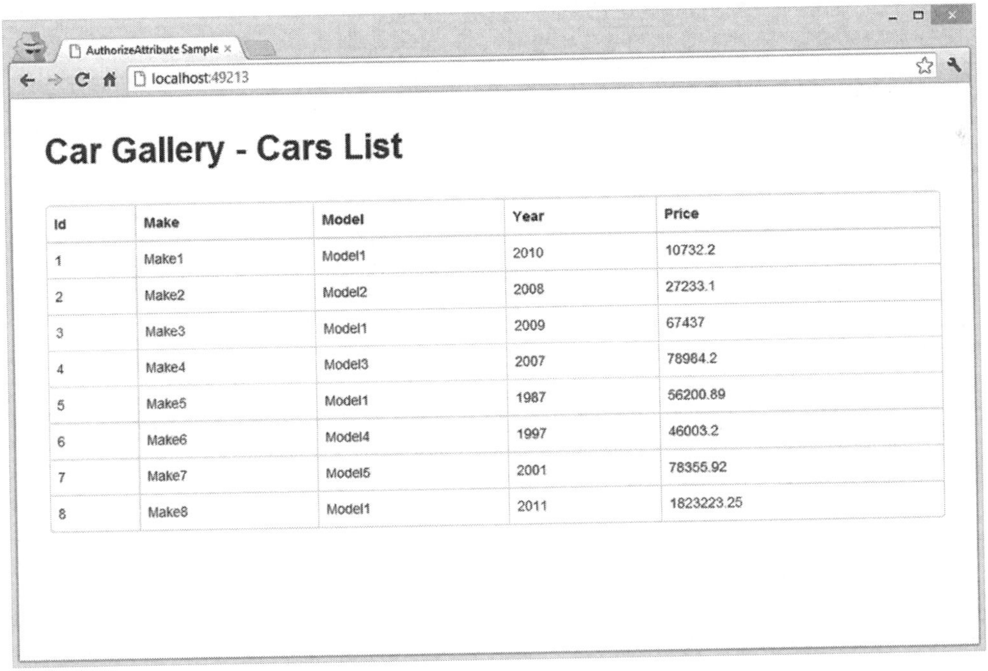

Car Gallery - Cars List

Id	Make	Model	Year	Price
1	Make1	Model1	2010	10732.2
2	Make2	Model2	2008	27233.1
3	Make3	Model1	2009	67437
4	Make4	Model3	2007	78984.2
5	Make5	Model1	1987	56200.89
6	Make6	Model4	1997	46003.2
7	Make7	Model5	2001	78355.92
8	Make8	Model1	2011	1823223.25

Figure 11-11. *View of the cars list inside the web page*

This example shows one way of dealing with forms authentication with ASP.NET Web API. On the other hand, if your Web API application is hosted in a project with an ASP.NET web application (ASP.NET MVC, ASP.NET Web Forms, etc.), you can deal with forms authentication using that web application. You should get the same result regardless of how you authenticate the user with forms authentication.

Require SSL Authorization Filter Sample

You might want to allow requests through HTTPS for your entire Web API application or only certain parts of it. To do this, you can create a custom authorization filter that will reject the request if it doesn't come through HTTPS. Listing 11-31 implements the RequireHttpsAttribute.

Listing 11-31. RequireHttpsAttribute

```
public override void OnAuthorization(
    HttpActionContext actionContext) {

    if (actionContext.Request.RequestUri.Scheme != Uri.UriSchemeHttps) {

        actionContext.Response = new
            HttpResponseMessage(HttpStatusCode.Forbidden) {
                Content = new StringContent("SSL required")
            };
    }
}
```

Since you've seen similar examples demonstrated already, what we're doing here should be familiar. The only logic here is for checking the schema of the request URI to see whether the request came through HTTPS. If it didn't, a new response message indicating the **403 Forbidden** status code should be set.

Finally, Listing 11-32 shows how to register our filter at the controller level.

Listing 11-32. Registering RequireHttpsFilter for CarsController

```
[RequireHttps]
public class CarsController : ApiController {

    public string[] GetCars() {

        return new string[] {
            "Car 1",
            "Car 2",
            "Car 3",
            "Car 4"
        };
    }
}
```

To demonstrate this properly, we have enabled SSL in IIS Express. If you'd like to enable SSL in your development environment, first open the Properties dialog box by clicking on the project and pressing F4. You should see the "Enable SSL" option (as in Figure 11-12). If it is set to true, your application will have two endpoints, one of them an HTTPS endpoint.

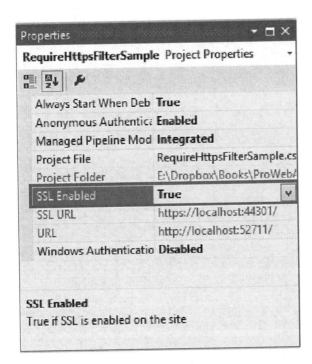

Figure 11-12. *Properties dialog box*

Visiting the two endpoints should generate a 403 response for the request made through HTTP (see Figure 11-13) but shouldn't pose problems for the request made through HTTPS (see Figure 11-14).

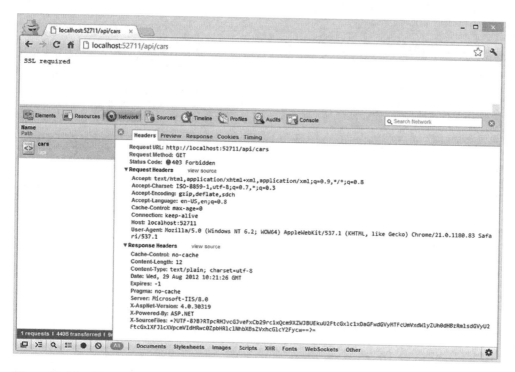

Figure 11-13. *403 response for the request made through HTTP*

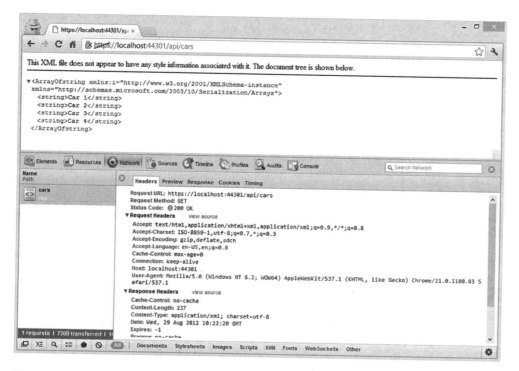

Figure 11-14. *200 response for the request made through HTTPS*

This is merely one sample use case for authorization filters. As you've seen, creating your own should be pretty easy.

Exception Filters

An exception filter is a special type of filter; it is invoked only when an exception occurs inside an action and its associated filters. An exception filter needs to implement the IExceptionFilter interface. We will be working with the ExceptionFilterAttribute class (see Listing 11-33), which is the default implementation of IExceptionFilter.

Listing 11-33. ExceptionFilterAttribute Abstract Class

```
public abstract class ExceptionFilterAttribute :
    FilterAttribute, IExceptionFilter {

    public virtual void OnException(
        HttpActionExecutedContext actionExecutedContext);
}
```

The OnException method of ExceptionFilterAttribute is executed when an exception occurs and an instance of an HttpActionExecutedContext class (already covered in Table 11-4) is passed as a parameter to this method. This lets us see exception details through the Exception property of HttpActionExecutedContext class and log the exception however we see fit.

To demonstrate use of this filter, Listing 11-34 shows a custom exception filter that writes the exception details to the trace.

Listing11-34. HandleErrorAttribute Exception Filter Implementation

```
public class HandleErrorAttribute : ExceptionFilterAttribute {

    public override void OnException(
        HttpActionExecutedContext actionExecutedContext) {

        var actionCtx = actionExecutedContext.ActionContext;
        var controllerCtx = actionCtx.ControllerContext;

        Trace.TraceInformation(
            "Exception occured. Controller: {0}, action: {1}. Exception message: {2}",
            controllerCtx.ControllerDescriptor.ControllerName,
            actionCtx.ActionDescriptor.ActionName,
            actionExecutedContext.Exception.Message);
    }
}
```

Listing 11-35 shows how this filter is registered at the controller level.

Listing 11-35. CarsController with HandleError Exception Filter

```
[HandleError]
public class CarsController : ApiController {

    public string[] GetCars() {

        throw new Exception();

        return new string[] {
            "Car 1",
            "Car 2",
            "Car 3",
            "Car 4"
        };
    }
}
```

Notice that we've thrown an exception on purpose inside our action method to test its functionality. So we should see the exception details being written to the Output window when the application is run under debug mode (see Figure 11-15).

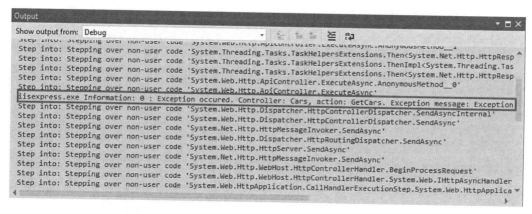

Figure 11-15. *The Output window showing the result*

You can use your favorite logging library to log exceptions (NLog, Elmah, etc.). It's pretty easy to wire them up with exception filters.

Summary

Filters are one of the richest extensibility points of ASP.NET Web API. You can inject your own logic into specific points to run and handle certain special operations: logging, error handling, authorization, and so on. This chapter has shown how filters behave and how they are implemented; it has also explained different types of filters. Also, to ensure that you can find a place for filters inside your application, sample use scenarios were provided.

■ ■ ■

CHAPTER 12

Media Type Formatters and Model Binding

As you learned in Chapter 3, one of the six REST constraints is the uniform interface constraint. Important parts of the uniform interface are representations of the URIs that identify our application entities or state. You also saw in Chapter 3 that the representation formats are identified by Internet media types (or MIME types, as they were called in the past). As ASP.NET Web API aims to ease the implementation of HTTP or even more RESTful applications, it obviously needs to provide a way to create and read from different Internet media types without a hassle. How this is done in ASP.NET Web API will be explained in the course of this chapter.

Overview

As ASP.NET Web API has been designed and developed with HTTP in mind, the result is an API that gives access to all elements of the HTTP specification in an elegant manner. Key parts of that specification for the ASP.NET Web API are Internet media types. They're even more important in a RESTful application when the aim is to follow the uniform interface constraint. If you want to embrace HATEOAS on top of the Internet media types, as shown in Chapter 3, you definitely need a framework that provides an easy way to handle the creation and parsing of different types of content.

Besides the Internet media types whose content is being sent to the server as part of the request or response body (see Listing 12-1), HTTP also allows sending requests containing parameters in the URI, as Listing 12-2 shows.

Listing 12-1. Response Body Containing a JSON Representation of a Contact

```
{
  "Name": "John Smith",
  "Age": 32,
  "Employed": true,
  "Address": {
    "Street": "701 First Ave.",
    "City": "Sunnyvale, CA 95125",
    "Country": "United States"
  }
}
```

Listing 12-2. URI Containing Parameters

```
http://localhost/api/customers/?firstname=bill&lastname=gates&company=microsoft
```

ASP.NET Web API supports both writing and reading content from and to the request or response body, as well as binding URI parameters against a code entity. The first one is implemented in ASP.NET Web API by the formatter processing model, and the latter one is done by model binding, which is similar to the model binding mechanism being introduced by ASP.NET MVC. In the following sections of this chapter, you'll see how the formatter processing model in ASP.NET Web API works and how you can implement your own formatters. After that you'll learn how the model binding mechanism works and how both play together in some scenarios.

Formatter Processing Model

As you've already learned in Chapter 3, the client tells the server in which media type the response should be represented using the HTTP Accept header. If the server is able to serve a requested entity in the required representation format, it sends the response with a body containing the entity in that representation format. That process, part of the HTTP specification, is referred to as "content negotiation," or just "conneg."

Content Negotiation Algorithm

The basics of conneg are pretty simple, as described above, but the Accept header is not the only header being used. You may ask, "What happens if the server is not able to serve the media type requested by the client?" Let's start with the headers that could be involved in conneg.

As we said, the HTTP header being used most is the Accept header. Please consider that our client is a processing tool for contact person images, and it can handle PNG besides other formats. So it wants to get a representation of a contact in the PNG image format—PNG supports transparency, which is useful for the integration of the processed contact image in web pages. The request using the Accept header would look like the one in Listing 12-3.

Listing 12-3. Requesting a PNG Image Representation of a Contact

```
GET http://localhost/api/contact/1/ HTTP/1.1
Host: localhost
Accept: image/PNG
```

Another criterion the conneg could be based on is the language the client prefers the representation to be formatted in. For example, a list of product criteria should be retrieved in the language a human being is able to read, when the response of the request is displayed in its UI—it may be a web site. The header being used to request a specific language is the Accept-Language header, as shown in Listing 12-4.

Listing 12-4. Requesting a List of Product Criteria in the German Language and JSON Format

```
GET http://localhost/api/product/1/criteria HTTP/1.1
Host: localhost
Accept: application/json
Accept-Language: de
```

Perhaps we are aware that the service from which we're requesting the representation of the product criteria list might not be able to serve the list in German. In that case, we would want to be able to read it in English while still having German as the preferred language whenever possible. These scenarios are also part of the HTTP specification, and HTTP provides an extension for the Accept headers to be used in these cases. The extension provides a so-called quality/priority decimal factor ranging from 0 to 1. The 0 value represents the lowest quality; that is to say, we would avoid that Accept type or Language type if better ones are available. The value 1, on the other hand, represents the highest quality and is thus the most preferred. The quality/priority extension is abbreviated by the character q (for "quality") followed by the decimal value depending on one's preference. The complete usage mode of the Accept-Language header for the aforementioned product property scenario can be seen in Listing 12-5.

Listing 12-5. Requesting Product Property, Preferably in German but Accepting English Also

```
GET http://localhost/api/product/1/criteria/ HTTP/1.1
Host: localhost
Accept: application/json
Accept-Language: de; q=1.0, en; q=0.5
```

Further Accept headers being considered for conneg are the Accept-Charset and the Accept-Encoding headers, as shown in Listings 12-6 and 12-7.

Listing 12-6. Requesting UTF-8 Charset

```
GET http://localhost/api/product/1/criteria/ HTTP/1.1
Host: localhost
Accept: application/json
Accept-Charset: UTF-8
```

Listing 12-7. Requesting Gzipped Content to Save Bandwith

```
GET http://localhost/api/product/1/criteria/ HTTP/1.1
Host: localhost
Accept: application/json
Accept-Encoding: application/x-gzip
```

As you see in these listings, the Accept headers can all be used in conjunction, and each one can also have its own quality/priority.

There is one scenario left which we haven't yet covered. What happens if the client does not provide an Accept header? A valid option is to check whether the client sent a content-type header in the event that he did send content to the server within the request. If this is the case, the server simply tries to send the response containing the requested representation using the same Internet media type as the client sent within the request. Listing 12-8 shows the request, and Listing 12-9 the response.

Listing 12-8. Request Without Accept Header but with Content-Type Header Set

```
POST http://localhost/api/products HTTP/1.1
Host: localhost
Content-Type: application/json

{
  "Name": "John Smith",
  "Age": 32,
  "Employed": true,
  "Address": {
    "Street": "701 First Ave.",
    "City": "Sunnyvale, CA 95125",
    "Country": "United States"
  }
}
```

Listing 12-9. Response to Request Without Accept Header but with Content-Type Header Set

```
HTTP/1.1 200 OK
Content-Type: application/json; charset=utf-8

{
  "Id": 1,
  "Name": "John Smith",
  "Age": 32,
  "Employed": true,
  "Address": {
    "Street": "701 First Ave.",
    "City": "Sunnyvale, CA 95125",
    "Country": "United States"
  }
}
```

Now that you've seen how content negotiation works at the HTTP level, we're ready to take a look at how ASP.NET Web API allows us handle conneg at the .NET CLR level. As you have already learned in this chapter's overview, ASP.NET Web API does this by providing a formatter processing model—but you haven't yet learned what that means exactly. Now it's time to look under the hood.

Media Type Formatters

ASP.NET Web API covers content negotiation, as described above, completely. Conneg mostly is about reading or creating representations of resources according to media type formats. In ASP.NET Web API, the basic functionality for that is encapsulated in the MediaTypeFormatter base class. During the next sections this class—and how to use it—will be described in detail.

ASP.NET Web API Content Negotiation in Practice

Before digging into the details of ASP.NET Web API conneg, let's take a step back and recall what was learned in Chapter 9. We can simply return a CLR type from the .NET Framework or even a .NET object we've implemented ourselves, like the Car class one shown in Listing 12-10.

Listing 12-10. A Car Class Implementation

```
public class Car {
    public int Id { get; set; }
    public string Make { get; set; }
    public string Model { get; set; }
    public int Year { get; set; }
    public float Price { get; set; }
}
```

In order to return an instance of this Car class, simply add a Get method to our CarController and return the instance being requested by its Id property, as shown in the simplified implementation of Listing 12-11.

Listing 12-11. Returning a Car Entity Instance Using an ASP.NET Web API Controller

```
public class CarController : ApiController {
    public Car Get(int id) {
        return new Car() {
            Id = id,
            Make = "Porsche",
            Model = "911",
            Price = 100000,
            Year = 2012
        };
    }
}
```

If that controller action is invoked by navigating to the URI http://localhost:1051/api/car/1 using our web browser, the XML representation shown in Listing 12-12 is returned.

Listing 12-12. XML Representation of the Cars Entity from Listing 12-11

```
<Car xmlns:i="http://www.w3.org/2001/XMLSchema-instance"
xmlns="http://schemas.datacontract.org/2004/07/WebApiConneg.Entities">
    <Id>1</Id>
    <Make>Porsche</Make>
    <Model>911</Model>
    <Price>100000</Price>
    <Year>2012</Year>
</Car>
```

Issuing a request, like the one in Listing 12-13, against the same URI using Fiddler but without specifying an Accept header produces a response returning a JSON representation, as Listing 12-14 confirms.

Listing 12-13. Request to the Cars API Without Specifying an Accept Header

```
GET http://localhost:1051/api/car/1 HTTP/1.1
User-Agent: Fiddler
Host: localhost:1051
```

Listing 12-14. Response Containing JSON Representation to the Cars API Request

```
HTTP/1.1 200 OK
Content-Type: application/json; charset=utf-8

{"Id":1,"Make":"Porsche","Model":"911","Year":2012,"Price":100000.0}
```

ASP.NET Web API Content Negotiation Demystified

What happened during the last two sample requests and responses? We didn't handle media types in our controller implementation, nor did we add a configuration with which we told our Web API how to handle requests for specific media types or how to generate XML or JSON. As was said earlier, ASP.NET Web API introduces a processing model where the requested media types are parsed or created transparently to our code. That is, there's no need to care about each Accept header we've learned about in the "Content Negotiation Algorithm" section to get the media type requested or to parse the content from the media type being specified in the content-type header in every request.

By implementing parsing the data from or writing to the content once, it can be reused throughout the whole API (or even many projects).

In ASP.NET Web API, classes handling this parsing and writing are called formatters, and the abstract base class all formatters derive from is called MediaTypeFormatter. It resides in the System.Net.Http.Formatting namespace beside some other classes related to formatting. Some of them will be covered later in this chapter.

MediaTypeFormatter Class

The most important members of the MediaTypeFormatter class are shown in Listing 12-15.

Listing 12-15. Members of the MediaTypeFormatter Base Class That Need to Be Overwritten or Set

```
public abstract class MediaTypeFormatter {
        public abstract bool CanReadType(Type type);
        public abstract bool CanWriteType(Type type);

        public virtual Task<object> ReadFromStreamAsync(Type type, Stream readStream,
HttpContent content, IFormatterLogger formatterLogger) {
                throw Error.NotSupported(Resources.MediaTypeFormatterCannotRead, new object[1] {
                        (object) this.GetType().Name
                });
        }

        public virtual Task WriteToStreamAsync(Type type, object value, Stream writeStream,
HttpContent content, TransportContext transportContext) {
                throw Error.NotSupported(Resources.MediaTypeFormatterCannotWrite, new object[1] {
                        (object) this.GetType().Name
                });
        }

        public Collection<Encoding> SupportedEncodings { get; private set; }
        public Collection<MediaTypeHeaderValue> SupportedMediaTypes { get; private set; }
}
```

In ASP.NET Web API, a formatter can always handle reading and writing within a given class. That's why there are methods to read and write to the content stream: reading from the content stream is done by the ReadFromStreamAsync method, and writing to it is done using the WriteToStreamAsync method. There are also two methods that allow indicating whether our formatter is able to read (CanReadType method) or write (CanWriteType method) a type. The SupportedMediaTypes collection contains the media types the formatter is able to read and/or write. The collection contains the items type MediaTypeHeaderValue. The encodings supported by our formatter are listed in the SupportedEncodings collection, which contains items of the type Encoding.

You might ask where the MediaTypeFormatter instances get invoked. When an incoming request occurs, the controller to be invoked is set up. When this is done, the ApiControllerActionSelector tries to determine the type of the ParameterBindings for the selected controller action. This information is held in the HttpActionBinding property of the DefaultActionValueBinder. If a ParameterBinding should read its content from the requests body, a FormatterParameterBinding instance is created for that parameter. When every ParameterBinding is executed later on in the pipeline using the ExecuteBindingAsync method for each binding, the ReadAsAsync method of HttpContentExtensions is executed. This code calls the FindReader method of a newly instantiated MediaTypeFormatterCollection, which gets the collection of formatters being registered in the Web API configuration passed as a constructor parameter. The FindReader method itself queries all passed formatters and tries to find the best matching MediaTypeFormatter by evaluating the CanReadType method result and the supported Internet media type of each formatter in the collection.

If it finds a match, the formatter is returned to the HttpContentExtensions instance, and the content is read from the request body executing the ReadFromStreamAsync method of the formatter found in the previous step.

If no match is found, an exception is thrown; it indicates that no formatter can be found that is able to read the request body content with the specified media type.

If the formatter correctly deserializes the media type sent to our controller action, our controller action gets the created CLR type as a parameter and can continue processing the code being defined inside the controller method. See Listing 12-11 for an example.

To stick with the example from Listing 12-11, after the method is executed, the JSON representation of the car being created is returned to the client.

Creating this representation from the CLR Car class instance is also done using the JsonMediaTypeFormatter. This time, the WriteToStreamAsync method of the JsonMediaTypeFormatter class (more generally, a class deriving from the MediaTypeFormatter base class) is executed. As WriteToStreamAsync isn't invoked by our own implementation inside the controller, there has to be automation similar to what we've seen for incoming requests. As you learned in Chapter 10, the last message handler for incoming requests in the Russian doll model is the HttpControllerDispatcher. As with all HttpMessageHandler implementations, the SendAsync method of the HttpControllerDispatcher is executed in the message handler chain (that is, the Russian doll model). Within the SendAsync method, the ExecuteAsync method of the controller (type ApiController) created using the HttpControllerDescriptor and the DefaultHttpControllerSelector is invoked.

From within this method, the InvokeActionAsync method of the ApiControllerActionInvoker is called. This in turn calls the Convert method of the ValueResultConverter, where the HttpRequestMessageExtensions.CreateResponse<T> method is invoked. This is the place where the Negotiate method of the DefaultContentNegotiator is called.

DefaultContentNegotiator: Finding a MediaTypeFormatter

The Negotiate method is the core of the conneg for response messages in ASP.NET Web API. The Negotiate method mainly uses two methods to do the conneg for a response message. The first one is the ComputeFormatterMatches method, as shown in Listing 12-16.

Listing 12-16. ComputeFormatterMatches Method of the DefaultContentNegotiator

```
protected virtual Collection<MediaTypeFormatterMatch> ComputeFormatterMatches(
    Type type, HttpRequestMessage request, IEnumerable<MediaTypeFormatter> formatters) {

    if (type == (Type)null)
        throw Error.ArgumentNull("type");
    if (request == null)
        throw Error.ArgumentNull("request");
    if (formatters == null)
        throw Error.ArgumentNull("formatters");

    IEnumerable<MediaTypeWithQualityHeaderValue> sortedAcceptValues =
        (IEnumerable<MediaTypeWithQualityHeaderValue>)null;

    Collection<MediaTypeFormatterMatch> collection =
        new Collection<MediaTypeFormatterMatch>();

    foreach (MediaTypeFormatter formatter in formatters) {
        if (formatter.CanWriteType(type)) {
            MediaTypeFormatterMatch typeFormatterMatch1;
            if ((typeFormatterMatch1 =
```

```
            this.MatchMediaTypeMapping(request, formatter)) != null) {
            collection.Add(typeFormatterMatch1);
        }
        else {
            if (sortedAcceptValues == null)
                sortedAcceptValues =
                    this.SortMediaTypeWithQualityHeaderValuesByQFactor((
                    ICollection<MediaTypeWithQualityHeaderValue>)request.Headers.Accept);

            MediaTypeFormatterMatch typeFormatterMatch2;

            if ((typeFormatterMatch2 =
                this.MatchAcceptHeader(sortedAcceptValues, formatter)) != null) {
                collection.Add(typeFormatterMatch2);
            }
            else {
                MediaTypeFormatterMatch typeFormatterMatch3;
                if ((typeFormatterMatch3 =
                    this.MatchRequestMediaType(request, formatter)) != null) {
                    collection.Add(typeFormatterMatch3);
                }
                else {
                    MediaTypeFormatterMatch typeFormatterMatch4;
                    if ((typeFormatterMatch4 =
                        this.MatchType(type, formatter)) != null)
                        collection.Add(typeFormatterMatch4);
                }
            }
        }
    }
    return collection;
}
```

The ComputeFormatterMatches method determines how well each formatter being registered in the ASP.NET Web API configuration matches an HTTP request. This is done by a multilevel evaluation of the various Accept headers, including their quality factors. The collection of MediaTypeFormatterMatch created in the ComputeFormatterMatches is passed as a parameter to the SelectResponseMediaTypeFormatter method (see Listing 12-17).

Listing 12-17. SelectResponseMediaTypeFormatter Method of DefaultContentNegotiator

```
protected virtual MediaTypeFormatterMatch
    SelectResponseMediaTypeFormatter(ICollection<MediaTypeFormatterMatch> matches) {
    if (matches == null)
        throw Error.ArgumentNull("matches");

    MediaTypeFormatterMatch typeFormatterMatch1 = (MediaTypeFormatterMatch)null;
    MediaTypeFormatterMatch typeFormatterMatch2 = (MediaTypeFormatterMatch)null;
    MediaTypeFormatterMatch typeFormatterMatch3 = (MediaTypeFormatterMatch)null;
    MediaTypeFormatterMatch typeFormatterMatch4 = (MediaTypeFormatterMatch)null;
    MediaTypeFormatterMatch current1 = (MediaTypeFormatterMatch)null;
    MediaTypeFormatterMatch typeFormatterMatch5 = (MediaTypeFormatterMatch)null;
```

```
foreach (MediaTypeFormatterMatch potentialReplacement
    in (IEnumerable<MediaTypeFormatterMatch>)matches) {

    switch (potentialReplacement.Ranking) {
        case MediaTypeFormatterMatchRanking.MatchOnCanWriteType:
            if (typeFormatterMatch1 == null) {
                typeFormatterMatch1 = potentialReplacement;
                continue;
            }
            else
                continue;
        case MediaTypeFormatterMatchRanking.MatchOnRequestAcceptHeaderLiteral:
            typeFormatterMatch2 =
                this.UpdateBestMatch(typeFormatterMatch2,
                    potentialReplacement);
            continue;

        case MediaTypeFormatterMatchRanking.MatchOnRequestAcceptHeaderSubtypeMediaRange:
            typeFormatterMatch3 =
                this.UpdateBestMatch(typeFormatterMatch3,
                    potentialReplacement);
            continue;

        case MediaTypeFormatterMatchRanking.MatchOnRequestAcceptHeaderAllMediaRange:
            typeFormatterMatch4 =
                this.UpdateBestMatch(typeFormatterMatch4,
                    potentialReplacement);
            continue;

        case MediaTypeFormatterMatchRanking.MatchOnRequestWithMediaTypeMapping:
            current1 = this.UpdateBestMatch(current1,
                    potentialReplacement);
            continue;

        case MediaTypeFormatterMatchRanking.MatchOnRequestMediaType:
            if (typeFormatterMatch5 == null) {
                typeFormatterMatch5 = potentialReplacement;
                continue;
            }
            else
                continue;
        default:
            continue;
    }
}

if (current1 != null &&
    this.UpdateBestMatch(
        this.UpdateBestMatch(
            this.UpdateBestMatch(current1, typeFormatterMatch2),
            typeFormatterMatch3),
        typeFormatterMatch4) != current1)
```

```
            current1 = (MediaTypeFormatterMatch)null;

    MediaTypeFormatterMatch current2 = (MediaTypeFormatterMatch)null;

    if (current1 != null)
        current2 = current1;
    else if (typeFormatterMatch2 != null
            || typeFormatterMatch3 != null
            || typeFormatterMatch4 != null)
        current2 = this.UpdateBestMatch(
            this.UpdateBestMatch(
                this.UpdateBestMatch(current2, typeFormatterMatch2),
                typeFormatterMatch3),
                typeFormatterMatch4);
    else if (typeFormatterMatch5 != null)
        current2 = typeFormatterMatch5;
    else if (typeFormatterMatch1 != null)
        current2 = typeFormatterMatch1;
    return current2;
}
```

The SelectResponseMediaTypeFormatter method selects the correct media type (or the most reasonable match) for the response message by processing the MediaTypeFormatterMatch collection from the ComputeFormatterMatches method of Listing 12-16 and negotiating the collection of possibly matching formatters and their quality factors.

After the correct MediaTypeFormatter has been found, the SelectResponseCharacterEncoding selects the encoding for the response by evaluating the Accept-Encoding header and its quality factor (see Listing 12-18).

Listing 12-18. SelectResponseCharacterEncoding Method of DefaultContentNegotiator

```
protected virtual Encoding SelectResponseCharacterEncoding(HttpRequestMessage request,
    MediaTypeFormatter formatter) {
        if (request == null)
            throw Error.ArgumentNull("request");
        if (formatter == null)
            throw Error.ArgumentNull("formatter");
        if (formatter.SupportedEncodings.Count <= 0)
            return (Encoding)null;

        foreach (StringWithQualityHeaderValue qualityHeaderValue in
            this.SortStringWithQualityHeaderValuesByQFactor(
                (ICollection<StringWithQualityHeaderValue>)request.Headers.AcceptCharset)) {
                    foreach (Encoding encoding in formatter.SupportedEncodings) {
                        if (encoding != null) {
                            double? quality = qualityHeaderValue.Quality;
                            if (
                                (quality.GetValueOrDefault() != 0.0
                                ? 1
                                : (!quality.HasValue ? 1 : 0)) != 0
                                && (qualityHeaderValue.Value.Equals(encoding.WebName,
                                    StringComparison.OrdinalIgnoreCase)
                                || qualityHeaderValue.Value.Equals("*",
```

```
                            StringComparison.OrdinalIgnoreCase)))
                        return encoding;
                }
            }
    }
    return formatter.SelectCharacterEncoding(
        request.Content != null ? request.Content.Headers : (HttpContentHeaders)null);
}
```

The SelectResponseCharacterEncoding method evaluates the incoming request's Accept-Encoding header, iterates over the list of SupportedEncodings of the passed-in MediaTypeFormatter instance, and either selects the encoding with the highest quality factor or assigns the highest quality factor for the best matching one. Then it returns the best matching response encoding.

After that, the selected MediaTypeFormatter instance is returned to the HttpRequestMessageExtensions.CreateResponse<T> method, where a new HttpRequestMessage instance is created. The Content property of that instance gets assigned a new instance of type ObjectContent, which is written to the output stream using the assigned formatter farther along the response pipeline.

The last two sections of this chapter have shown how the HTTP content negotiation works in theory and in ASP.NET Web API. Now that you've seen what the intention of the MediaTypeFormatter base class is in ASP.NET Web API, let's take a look at the MediaTypeFormatter implementations that are shipped with ASP.NET Web API by default.

Default Formatters

Over the years, the fact that a few media types in Web API development have proved to be available on many platforms has helped support interoperability. As it is likely that these media types might be requested by clients accessing Web APIs developed using ASP.NET Web API, a set of so-called default formatters is shipped with ASP.NET Web API, and so you don't have to implement them by yourself. The next sections will examine these default formatters and show how to modify their behavior when it's possible to do so.

JsonMediaTypeFormatter

The first MediaTypeFormatter implementation to discover is the JsonMediaTypeFormatter class. Residing in the System.Net.Http.Formatting namespace, it is able to read and write JSON body content from a request or to a response. Both operations are done using the **Json.NET** open source framework, which is a popular high-performance JSON framework for .NET.

During the early preview versions of ASP.NET Web API, Microsoft used its own DataContractJsonSerializer class, which was shipped as a part of the .NET Framework. As the DataContractJsonSerializer didn't support serialization or deserialization of Ilist and similar types or case-insensitive property deserialization and was in addition pretty slow, the ASP.NET Web API team decided to drop the DataContractJsonSerializer in favor of the faster and more flexible Json.NET implementation. This is a novelty in the history of the .NET Framework, as it was the first time that Microsoft shipped a part of the .NET Framework that included an open source third-party library.

Besides the methods and properties derived from the MediaTypeFormatter base class, the JsonMediaTypeFormatter class provides several properties and another method:

- Properties
  - SerializerSettings
  - UseDataContractJsonSerializer
  - Indent
  - MaxDepth

335

- Method

  - CreateDefaultSerializerSettings

The JsonSerializerSettings class's SerializerSettings property type allows you to modify the behavior of the JsonSerializer from the Json.NET framework. Since explaining all the possibilities of the JsonSerializer property and the JsonSerializerSettings class definitely goes beyond the scope of this chapter, we'll cover a real-world scenario to show how the flexibility of the JSON serialization/deserialization process is introduced to the ASP.NET Web API by use of the Json.NET framework.

Suppose that your Web API implementation is consumed by a JavaScript client. It's common to use camel case formatting for code written in JavaScript. As JSON is a sort of JavaScript code, you'd expect to use camel case for JSON also. By default, however, the JsonSerializer creates Pascal case–formatted JSON rather than camel case . To change that behavior, use the JsonSerializerSettings class.

The JsonSerializerSettings class provides a property, ContractResolver, that implements the IContractResolver interface. IContractResolver defines an interface for all its implementations, which are used by the JsonSerializer class to serialize/deserialize a .NET CLR type from or to JSON. Replacing the DefaultContractResolver implementation of IContractResolver can change the case style of the JSON returned by our JsonMediaTypeFormatter. Because camel case–formatted JSON occurs often with the Json.NET framework, Json.NET ships an implementation of a contract resolver that creates camel case JSON. That contract resolver is the CamelCasePropertyNamesContractResolver class, so we just need to create a new instance of JsonSerializerSettings and assign the camel case contract resolver instance to it, as shown in Listing 12-19.

Listing 12-19. Changing the Casing of a JsonMediaTypeFormatter to Camel Case

```
var jsonFormatter = new JsonMediaTypeFormatter() {
    SerializerSettings = new JsonSerializerSettings() {
        ContractResolver = new CamelCasePropertyNamesContractResolver()
    }
};
```

To learn more about using JsonSerializerSettings, we recommend that you read the Json.NET documentation (http://json.net).

Another property of the JsonMediaTypeFormatter class, UseDataContractJsonSerializer, a Boolean value, allows us to modify the behavior of the JSON media type formatter. The default value is false, but by setting it to true, the JsonMediaTypeFormatter can be forced to use the DataContractJsonSerializer, described at the beginning of this section.

The Indent property of the JsonMediaTypeFormatter class is another Boolean value; it allows us to create indented JSON, if needed, by setting the properties value to true (the default value is false).

The MaxDepth property of the JsonMediaTypeFormatter class allows us to define the level at which the JsonSerializer should stop deserializing nested child properties of the incoming JSON. If no value is specified, all nested child properties are deserialized.

The CreateDefaultSerializerSettings method of the JsonMediaTypeFormatter creates an instance of JsonSerializerSettings with the ContractResolver property set to the DefaultContractResolver, the MissingMemberHandling property set to MissingMemberHandling.Ignore, and the TypeNameHandling property set to TypeNameHandling.None. The created instance, used by the JsonMediaTypeFormatter itself, can also be used as a base for custom JsonSerializerSettings.

In the last section we saw how ASP.NET Web API allows us not only to create JSON out of the box but also to modify how JSON gets created using the default JsonMediaTypeFormatter and the underlying open source framework Json.NET.

XMLMediaTypeFormatter

Another important media type often used in Web APIs is XML. Like JSON, it is supported by default in ASP.NET Web API. XML in ASP.NET Web API is read and written by the XMLMediaTypeFormatter class, which resides in the same namespace as the JsonMediaTypeFormatter class.

The XMLMediaTypeFormatter by default uses the System.Runtime.Serialization.DataContractSerializer to serialize/deserialize XML in ASP.NET Web API. If you're setting the UseXmlSerializer to true, a System.Xml.Serialization.XmlSerializer instance is used instead. You can also register a specific XmlSerializer or XmlObjectSerializer instance to read or write a specific CLR type. This is done using the SetSerializer<T> and SetSerializer methods and both their overloads.

The XMLMediaTypeFormatter class provides the Indent and MaxDepth properties, as the JsonMediaTypeFormatter class does. Their behaviors are the same.

FormUrlEncodedMediaTypeFormatter

Another scenario where you can use MediaTypeFormatters is in parsing the content of HTML forms submitted normally by a web browser. The media type of a submitted form is application/x-www-form-urlencoded; in ASP.NET Web API it is handled by the FormUrlEncodedMediaTypeFormatter class. A sample HTML form to create a new car is shown in Listing 12-20.

Listing 12-20. A Sample HTML Form to Create a New Car

```
<form action="/api/cars" method="post">
<fieldset>
    <legend>New Car</legend>
    <label for="Make">Make:</label>
    <input type="text" name="Make" />
    <label for="Model">Model:</label>
    <input type="text" name="Model" />
    <label for="Year">Year:</label>
    <input type="text" name="Year" />
    <label for="Price">Price:</label>
    <input type="text" name="Price" />
    <input type="submit" />
</fieldset>
</form>
```

Figure 12-1 shows the filled HTML form.

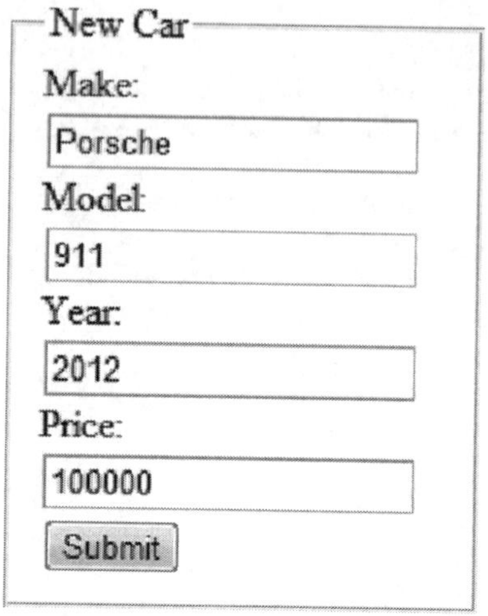

Figure 12-1. *The filled HTML form to create a new car using ASP.NET Web API*

The Post method of our CarsController, used to create a car from the form data, is shown in Listing 12-21.

Listing 12-21. Post Method of the CarsController to Create a Car

```
public Car Post(FormDataCollection carFormData) {
    var carFormKeyValues = carFormData.ReadAsNameValueCollection();
    var car = new Car() {
        Make = carFormKeyValues["Make"],
        Model = carFormKeyValues["Model"],
        Price = Convert.ToSingle(carFormKeyValues["Price"]),
        Year = Convert.ToInt32(carFormKeyValues["Year"])
    };
    return car;
}
```

If the form is submitted by clicking the Submit button, the request issued can be traced using Fiddler, as shown in Listing 12-22.

Listing 12-22. The Request of the Submitted HTML Form to Create a New Car Using ASP.NET Web API

```
POST http://localhost:1051/api/car HTTP/1.1
Host: localhost:1051
Connection: keep-alive
Content-Length: 45
Cache-Control: max-age=0
Origin: http://localhost:1051
User-Agent: Mozilla/5.0 (Windows NT 6.1; WOW64) AppleWebKit/536.11 (KHTML, like Gecko)
Chrome/20.0.1132.57 Safari/536.11
Content-Type: application/x-www-form-urlencoded
Accept: text/html,application/xhtml+xml,application/xml;q=0.9,*/*;q=0.8
Referer: http://localhost:1051/htmlform.html
Accept-Encoding: gzip,deflate,sdch
```

```
Accept-Language: en-US,en;q=0.8
Accept-Charset: ISO-8859-1,utf-8;q=0.7,*;q=0.3

Make=Porsche&Model=911&Year=2012&Price=100000
```

As Listing 12-22 shows, the form's fields and values are added to the content body as a string, which is the x-www-form-urlencoded representation of our form.

Our request body content is parsed by the FormUrlEncodedMediaTypeFormatter; as the content can be parsed as a FormDataCollection class instance, the Post method of our CarController from Listing 12-21 gets invoked, and the FormDataCollection instance is passed in as a parameter. If our Post method is being debugged, the FormDataCollection instance is created by the FormUrlEncodedMediaTypeFormatter, as expected. The debugging result is shown in Figure 12-2.

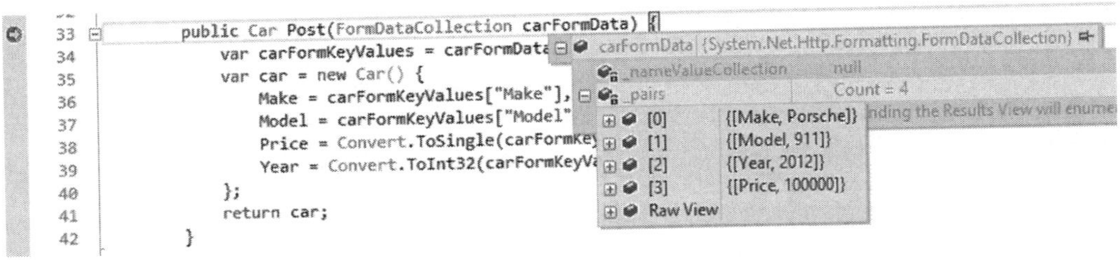

Figure 12-2. *Debugging output of the carFormData parameter passed to the Post method of the CarController*

Because the best matching Accept header value for the response created is application/xml;q=0.9, ASP. NET Web API then returns the new car representation as XML using the XMLMediaTypeFormatter, as the result in Listing 12-23 shows.

Listing 12-23. Response for the Request Issued by Sending the HTML Form of Listing 12-20

```
HTTP/1.1 200 OK
Cache-Control: no-cache
Pragma: no-cache
Content-Type: application/xml; charset=utf-8
Expires: -1
Server: Microsoft-IIS/8.0
X-AspNet-Version: 4.0.30319
X-SourceFiles: =?UTF-8?B?YzpcdXNlcnNcYXplaXRsZXJcZG9jdW1lbnRzXHZpc3VhbCBzdHVkaW8gMjAxMlxQcm9qZWN0c1x
XZWJBcGlDb25uZWdcV2ViQXBpQ29ubmVnXGFwaVxjYXI=?=
X-Powered-By: ASP.NET
Date: Mon, 16 Jul 2012 19:01:52 GMT
Content-Length: 219

<Car xmlns:i="http://www.w3.org/2001/XMLSchema-instance"
xmlns="http://schemas.datacontract.org/2004/07/WebApiConneg.Entities"><Id>1</Id><Make>Porsche</Make>
<Model>911</Model><Price>100000</Price><Year>2012</Year></Car>
```

As you see now, by providing support for the application/x-www-form-urlencoded media type, ASP.NET Web API also allows us to have plain HTML clients to create new content for a Web API–based application.

JQueryMvcFormUrlEncodedFormatter

In the previous section, you saw how to post form data from an HTML form to a Web API controller. Due to the FormUrlEncodedMediaTypeFormatter and use of the FormDataCollection type as a parameter for the Post method of our controller (see Listing 12-21), this works nicely. Nevertheless, for at least two reasons the solution shown is not perfect. First, the signature of the Post method does not show which type we're expecting to be passed in. Second, using the NameValueCollection returned by the ReadAsNameValueCollection method of the FormDataCollection instance is error-prone and not refactoring-safe. Furthermore, two Post methods might be needed if we want to allow HTML forms to post data to a Web API controller and also send XML or JSON to it.

A far more intuitive and refactoring-safe single-endpoint solution is shown in Listing 12-24.

Listing 12-24. Post Method of the CarController to Create a Car

```
public Car Post(Car car) {
    if(null != car) {
        car.Id = 1;
        return car;
    }
    throw new HttpResponseException(new HttpResponseMessage() {
        StatusCode = HttpStatusCode.BadRequest,
        ReasonPhrase = "Car data must contain at least one value."
    });
}
```

If you submit the form from Listing 12-20 by clicking the Submit button again, the response shown in Listing 12-25 is returned.

Listing 12-25. Response for the Request Issued by Sending the HTML Form of Listing 12-20

```
HTTP/1.1 200 OK
Cache-Control: no-cache
Pragma: no-cache
Content-Type: application/xml; charset=utf-8
Expires: -1
Server: Microsoft-IIS/8.0
X-AspNet-Version: 4.0.30319
X-SourceFiles: =?UTF-8?B?YzpcdXNlcnNcYXplaXRsZXJcZG9jdW1lbnRzXHZpc3VhbCBzdHVkaW8gMjAxMlxQcm9qZWN0c1x
XZWJBcGlDb25uZWdcV2ViQXBpQ29ubVnXGFwaVxjYXI=?=
X-Powered-By: ASP.NET
Date: Mon, 16 Jul 2012 19:01:52 GMT
Content-Length: 219

<Car xmlns:i="http://www.w3.org/2001/XMLSchema-instance"
xmlns="http://schemas.datacontract.org/2004/07/WebApiConneg.Entities"><Id>1</Id><Make>Porsche</Make>
<Model>911</Model><Price>100000</Price><Year>2012</Year></Car>
```

This works without further parsing inside the controller's action, because the request body content gets parsed by the JQueryMvcFormUrlEncodedFormatter. As the content can be parsed as a Car class instance, the Post method of our CarController from Listing 12-24 gets invoked, and the Car instance is passed in as a parameter. If we're debugging our Post method, we can see that the Car instance has been created by the FormUrlEncodedMediaTypeFormatter, as expected. The debugging result is shown in Figure 12-3.

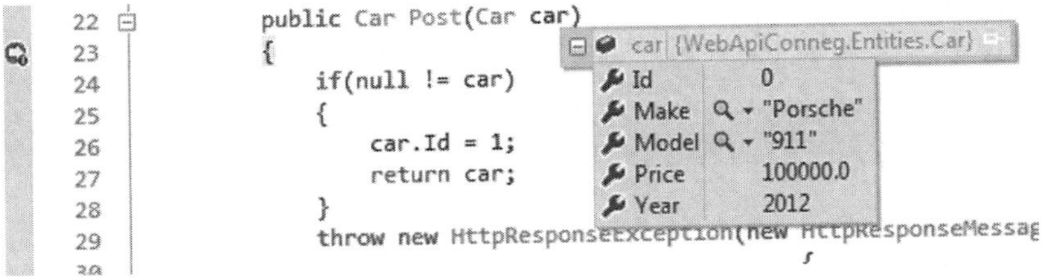

Figure 12-3. *Debugging Output of the Car Parameter Passed to the Post Method of the CarController*

As you see now, by providing support for the `application/x-www-form-urlencoded` media type, ASP.NET Web API also allows plain HTML clients to create new safe content for a Web API–based application.

BufferedMediaTypeFormatter

When you implement a media type formatter derived from the abstract `MediaTypeFormatter` class, the serialization/ deserialization inside the formatter should be handled by serializers supporting asynchronous serialization/ deserialization of CLR objects. If this is not the case, ASP.NET Web API provides the `BufferedMediaTypeFormatter` base class, which provides a convenient way to read and write small, synchronous pieces of data. Listing 12-26 shows an implementation of a `BufferedMediaTypeFormatter` that supports reading and writing plain text.

Listing 12-26. PlainTextMediaTypeFormatter to Handle a text/plain Media Type

```
public class PlainTextFormatter : BufferedMediaTypeFormatter {
    public PlainTextFormatter() {
        SupportedMediaTypes.Add(new MediaTypeHeaderValue("text/plain"));
        SupportedEncodings.Add(new UTF8Encoding());
        SupportedEncodings.Add(new UnicodeEncoding());
    }

    public override bool CanReadType(Type type) {
        return type == typeof(string);
    }

    public override bool CanWriteType(Type type) {
        return type == typeof(string);
    }
}

public class PlainTextFormatter : BufferedMediaTypeFormatter {
    public PlainTextFormatter() {
        SupportedMediaTypes.Add(new MediaTypeHeaderValue("text/plain"));
        SupportedEncodings.Add(new UTF8Encoding());
        SupportedEncodings.Add(new UnicodeEncoding());
    }

    public override bool CanReadType(Type type) {
        return type == typeof(string);
    }
}
```

```
    public override bool CanWriteType(Type type) {
        return type == typeof(string);
    }

    public override object ReadFromStream(Type type,
        Stream stream,
        HttpContent content,
        IFormatterLogger formatterLogger) {
            Encoding selectedEncoding = SelectCharacterEncoding(content.Headers);
            using (var reader = new StreamReader(stream, selectedEncoding)) {
            return reader.ReadToEnd();
        }
    }

    public override void WriteToStream(Type type,
        object value,
        Stream stream,
        HttpContent content) {
            Encoding selectedEncoding = SelectCharacterEncoding(content.Headers);
            using (var writer = new StreamWriter(stream, selectedEncoding)) {
                writer.Write(value);
        }
    }
}
}
```

You can see in Listing 12-26 that there's no call to the WriteToStreamAsync or ReadFromStreamAsync methods of the underlying MediaTypeFormatter base class, as these have been marked as sealed in the BufferedMediaTypeFormatter class we're deriving from. Instead, the implementation overrides the synchronous ReadFromStream and WriteToStream methods and uses a synchronous StreamReader or StreamWriter class to read content from and write it to.

Custom Formatters

As already mentioned, ASP.NET Web API allows you to add custom formatter implementations to your Web API project either by deriving from the abstract MediaTypeFormatter base class or by deriving from one of the five default formatters shown in the preceding sections. That's what we're doing when we implement our first custom MediaTypeFormatter.

JsonpMediaTypeFormatter

When it comes to consuming a Web API with jQuery, you'll want to use JSON; it's lightweight and easy to handle with jQuery. This works pretty nicely until you try to receive JSON from a foreign domain. If that happens, you'll face JavaScript browser security and won't be able to retrieve the JSON data without working around the security constraint. The custom MediaTypeFormatter we'll implement in this section will show you how to enable your public API to be consumed using JSON in a cross-domain scenario.

Let's assume your domain is http://localhost:34847, and you want to get a JSON representation from http://localhost:40553/api/car/1 using the jQuery code shown in Listing 12-27.

Listing 12-27. jQuery Cross-Domain Ajax Call

```
<script type="text/javascript">
    jQuery.getJSON("http://localhost:40553/api/car/1", function (car) {
        alert("Make: " + car.Make);
    });
</script>
```

If you run the code in Listing 12-27, you get back nothing—not even an error message. That's because jQuery.getJSON is a wrapper for jQuery.ajax. Instead of using this wrapper, the complete code to create the XmlHttpRequest, using the wrapped jQuery.ajax method instead, looks like what's shown in Listing 12-28.

Listing 12-28. Complete jQuery Cross-Domain Ajax Call with Error Handling

```
<script type="text/javascript">
    jQuery.ajax({
        type: "GET",
        url: 'http://localhost:40553/car/1',
        dataType: "json",
        success: function (results) {
            alert("Success!");
        },
        error: function (XMLHttpRequest, textStatus, errorThrown) {
            alert("error");
        }
    });
</script>
```

When executing the code from Listing 12-28, you'll get an alert with "error". This happens because you're trying to do cross-domain scripting, which is not allowed. To issue cross-domain jQuery Ajax calls receiving JSON representations, you have to use JSONP (that is, JSON with padding), which embeds a dynamically created <script> element containing the JSON representation into your document.

jQuery supports JSONP using jQuery.getJSON, as shown in Listing 12-29.

Listing 12-29. Issuing a Cross-Domain Ajax Call Using jQuery and JSONP

```
<script type="text/javascript">
    jQuery.getJSON("http://localhost:40553/car/1/?callback=?", function (car) {
                ("Make: " + car.Make);
        });
</script>
```

When it gets a URI like the one in Listing 12-29 as a parameter, jQuery replaces the last "?" with a dynamically created callback method name and embeds this method into the aforementioned script tag. Listing 12-30 shows a typical JSONP URI.

Listing 12-30. A Typical JSONP URI Created by jQuery.getJSON

```
http://localhost:40553/car/1?callback=jsonp1311664395075
```

The name of the dynamically created callback function has to be returned by your Web API controller method on the server; if it matches the name of the one that jQuery sent to it, you'll receive the JSON in your script for further handling. The JSONP response to the request looks like the one shown in Listing 12-31 (just the JSONP representation without the HTTP headers).

Listing 12-31. JSONP Representation Without HTTP Headers

```
jsonp1311664395075({"Make":"BMW"})
```

The task that our custom MediaTypeFormatter has to solve is to prefix the JSON output with the JSONP method name passed in as a request parameter. Listing 12-32 shows the implementation of the JsonpMediaTypeFormatter.

Listing 12-32. JsonpMediaTypeFormatter Implementation

```
using System;
using System.IO;
using System.Net;
using System.Net.Http;
using System.Net.Http.Formatting;
using System.Net.Http.Headers;
using System.Threading.Tasks;
using System.Web;

public class JsonpMediaTypeFormatter : JsonMediaTypeFormatter {
    private readonly HttpRequestMessage _request;
    private string _callbackQueryParameter;

    public JsonpMediaTypeFormatter() {
        SupportedMediaTypes.Add(DefaultMediaType);
        SupportedMediaTypes.Add(new MediaTypeHeaderValue("text/javascript"));

        MediaTypeMappings.Add(new UriPathExtensionMapping("jsonp", DefaultMediaType));
    }

    public JsonpMediaTypeFormatter(HttpRequestMessage request) : this() {
        this._request = request;
    }

    public string CallbackQueryParameter {
        get { return _callbackQueryParameter ?? "callback"; }
        set { _callbackQueryParameter = value; }
    }

    public override MediaTypeFormatter GetPerRequestFormatterInstance(Type type,
        HttpRequestMessage request,
        MediaTypeHeaderValue mediaType) {
            if (type == null)
                throw new ArgumentNullException("type");
            if (request == null)
                throw new ArgumentNullException("request");

            return new JsonpMediaTypeFormatter(request);
    }
```

```
public override Task WriteToStreamAsync(Type type,
    object value,
    Stream stream,
    HttpContent content,
    TransportContext transportContext) {
        string callback;
        if (IsJsonpRequest(_request, out callback)) {
            return Task.Factory.StartNew(() => {
                var writer = new StreamWriter(stream);
                writer.Write(callback + "(");
                writer.Flush();

                base.WriteToStreamAsync(type,
                    value, stream, content, transportContext)
                        .ContinueWith(_ => {
                            writer.Write(")");
                            writer.Flush();
                    });
            });
        }

    return base.WriteToStreamAsync(type,
        value, stream, content, transportContext);
}

private bool IsJsonpRequest(HttpRequestMessage request,
    out string callback) {
        callback = null;

        if (request == null || request.Method != HttpMethod.Get) {
            return false;
        }

        var query =
            HttpUtility.ParseQueryString(request.RequestUri.Query);

        callback = query[CallbackQueryParameter];

        return !string.IsNullOrEmpty(callback);
    }
}
```

The most relevant part of the code in Listing 12-32 is the WriteToStreamAsync method, which first checks whether the incoming request is a JSONP request. The incoming request is a JSONP request if it contains the URI parameter "callback". The name of that parameter is stored in the public property CallbackQueryParameter, which allows us to change this name when instantiating the formatter. If the request is a JSONP request, the already created JSON response content is written to a string and surrounded with the jQuery callback method name and opening and closing braces, so that it matches the format shown in Listing 12-31.

One thing not mentioned yet is a behavior specific to JSONP requests: they have an Accept header value of */*, which would break the conneg mechanism in general and Web API specifically, because the conneg would not be able to negotiate a valid response media type. The workaround for that issue is to have a distinct URI that returns only JSONP. So instead of using the URI in Listing 12-30, we need to provide a Web API URI like the one in Listing 12-33.

Listing 12-33. A Distinct URI Providing JSONP

```
http://localhost:40553/car/1/jsonp?callback=jsonp1311664395075
```

The problem now is how to tell the formatter that URIs containing the jsonp URI fragment should be treated as text/javascript media type. This is done by using a MediaTypeMapping property, which tells the Web API to set an Accept header value of text/javascript if the URI for an incoming request has the same jsonp fragment as the last one. That MediaTypeMapping is added in the last line of our JsonpMediaTypeFormatter's constructor. Media type mappings are discussed in more detail later in this chapter.

Another task to complete is updating our default route definition in our Web API configuration. The URI shown in Listing 12-33 would generate a 404 error response, as the default URI template does not contain a definition for the jsonp fragment. To solve the problem, add another optional RouteParameter called format—or you can choose any other distinct name (see Listing 12-34).

Listing 12-34. Enabling the Media Type Mapping Fragment in Web API Routing

```
routes.MapHttpRoute(
    name: "DefaultApi",
    routeTemplate: "api/{controller}/{id}/{format}",
    defaults: new {id = RouteParameter.Optional, format = RouteParameter.Optional }
);
```

If we now reissue our cross-domain jQuery Ajax call again, we get the data back from the Web API, as you can see in Figure 12-4.

Figure 12-4. JSONP result displayed for a cross-domain jQuery request

CSVMediaTypeFormatter

Another data exchange format, one still heavily used in the software industry, is CSV, an acronym for "comma-separated values." A sample CSV file's content—it lists some cars, to stick with our model—is shown in Listing 12-35.

Listing 12-35. Sample CSV File Content Listing Some Cars

```
17,VW, Golf,1999,1500
24,Porsche,911,2011,80000
30,Mercedes,A-Class,2007,10000
```

As Listing 12-35 shows, CSV has no column headers, and the order of the columns matters. Now let's consider a car reseller that needs a list of cars in the CSV format in order to import this file into Excel and do some further data processing. The described scenario can be easily expressed in ASP.NET Web API by adding a CarCsvMediaTypeFormatter class (this is a write-only media type formatter). As we're using the synchronous

StreamWriter class to serialize the Car class to CSV format, the derivation is from the BufferedMediaTypeFormatter class. The implementation is shown in Listing 12-36.

Listing 12-36. A CSV Media Type Formatter Implementation

```
public class CarCsvMediaTypeFormatter : BufferedMediaTypeFormatter {

    static readonly char[] SpecialChars = new char[] { ',', '\n', '\r', '"' };

    public CarCsvMediaTypeFormatter() {
        SupportedMediaTypes.Add(new MediaTypeHeaderValue("text/csv"));
    }

    public override bool CanReadType(Type type) {
        return false;
    }

    public override bool CanWriteType(Type type) {
        if (type == typeof(Car)) {
            return true;
        }
        else {
            var enumerableType = typeof(IEnumerable<Car>);
            return enumerableType.IsAssignableFrom(type);
        }
    }

    public override void WriteToStream(Type type,
        object value,
        Stream stream,
        HttpContent content) {
            using (var writer = new StreamWriter(stream)) {

                var cars = value as IEnumerable<Car>;
                if (cars != null) {
                    foreach (var car in cars) {
                        writeItem(car, writer);
                    }
                }
                else {
                    var car = value as Car;
                    if (car == null) {
                        throw new InvalidOperationException("Cannot serialize type");
                    }
                    writeItem(car, writer);
                }
            }
            stream.Close();
    }
```

```
private void writeItem(Car car, StreamWriter writer) {
    writer.WriteLine("{0},{1},{2},{3},{4}", Escape(car.Id),
        Escape(car.Make), Escape(car.Make), Escape(car.Year), Escape(car.Price));
}

private string Escape(object o) {
    if (o == null) {
        return "";
    }
    var field = o.ToString();
    return field.IndexOfAny(SpecialChars) != -1
        ? String.Format("\"{0}\"", field.Replace("\"", "\"\"")) : field;
}
}
```

The most relevant work in the CarCsvMediaTypeFormatter happens in the WriteToStream method, where the formatter first checks whether to serialize a collection of cars or a single car item and then starts serializing the corresponding instance. In the writeItem method the serialization of a single car item happens. The CSV format gets broken when a character like a comma or a line break is used inside the values. To avoid this, values containing commas or line breaks are eliminated using the Escape method before being serialized.

When invoking the request to the Get method of the CarsController (see Listing 12-37) and setting the Accept header to the text/csv media type, the response gotten is shown in Listing 12-38.

Listing 12-37. CarsController Implementation

```
public class CarsController : ApiController {
    public List<Car> Get() {
        return new List<Car>() {
                new Car() {
                    Id = 17,
                    Make = "VW",
                    Model = "Golf",
                    Year = 1999,
                    Price = 1500f
                },
                new Car() {
                    Id = 24,
                    Make = "Porsche",
                    Model = "911",
                    Year = 2011,
                    Price = 100000f
                },
                new Car() {
                    Id = 30,
                    Make = "Mercedes",
                    Model = "A-Class",
                    Year = 2007,
                    Price = 10000f
                }
            };
    }
}
```

Listing 12-38. CSV Formatted Response

```
HTTP/1.1 200 OK
Cache-Control: no-cache
Pragma: no-cache
Content-Type: text/csv
Expires: -1
Server: Microsoft-IIS/8.0
X-AspNet-Version: 4.0.30319
X-SourceFiles: =?UTF-8?B?RDpcRHJvcGJveFxQRE1MYWJcUHJvamVrdGVcMTAwMDU3ICOgV2ViIEFQSSBCdWNoXFByb1dlYkF
QSVxDYXJDc3ZNZWRpYVR5cGVGb3JtYXR0ZXJcQ2FyQ3N2N2TWVkaWFUeXBlRm9ybWF0dGVyXGFwaVxjYXJz?=
X-Powered-By: ASP.NET
Date: Tue, 17 Jul 2012 09:48:03 GMT
Content-Length: 82

17,VW,Golf,1999,1500
24,Porsche,911,2011,100000
30,Mercedes,A-Class,2007,10000
```

You've seen how formatters work and how to implement custom formatters, but there are still some things missing from the explanation: ASP.NET Web API needs to be told to use your formatter implementations at runtime—unless existing formatters are removed. That's what you'll discover in the next sections of this chapter.

Formatter Configuration

As for other extensibility points, like message handlers, ASP.NET Web API also offers the possibility to add, change, remove, or even reorder the default or custom formatters. Let's start with the modification of an existing formatter, one we've seen during this chapter's last few sections.

Modifying Existing Formatters

Implementing a new formatter for ASP.NET Web API is one option for modifying or extending the conneg behavior of ASP.NET Web API. Another option is modifying existing formatters in order to meet your needs. A good example of modifying existing formatters by configuration is the JsonMediaTypeFormatter, from this chapter's "Default Formatters" section, where we changed the SerializerSettings to output camel case JSON instead of Pascal case JSON. Back in that section we created a new instance of the default JsonMediaTypeFormatter using modified SerializerSettings, but we did not assign it to our Web API configuration. Instead of creating a new instance, we can modify the configuration of the already registered default JsonMediaTypeFormatter.

Registration of formatters occurs in the case of web hosting in the Application_Start method of the WebApiApplication class, which resides in the Global.asax.cs file. To modify the SerializerSettings of the default JsonMediaTypeFormatter, use the code shown in Listing 12-39.

Listing 12-39. Modifying the Behavior of the Default JsonMediaTypeFormatter

```
public class Global : HttpApplication {
    protected void Application_Start(object sender, EventArgs e) {
        var config = GlobalConfiguration.Configuration;
        config.Formatters.JsonFormatter.SerializerSettings =
            new JsonSerializerSettings() {
                ContractResolver = new CamelCasePropertyNamesContractResolver()
        };
```

```
        RouteConfig.RegisterRoutes(RouteTable.Routes);
    }
}
```

Issuing a new request to our Web API after that modification and requesting application/json as media type produces the result shown in Listing 12-40.

Listing 12-40. Camel Case JSON (Without HTTP Response Headers)

```
{"id":1,"make":"Porsche","model":"911","year":2012,"price":100000.0}
```

Registering a New Formatter

Implementing a new formatter for ASP.NET Web API is the first part of the work that has do be done to support Internet media beyond the defaults supported out of the box. The second part is to register the new formatter implementations in ASP.NET Web API configuration; this is done to tell ASP.NET Web API that there are more media types that it can handle.

As you saw in the last section, the default formatters are registered in the GlobalConfiguration.Configuration class. The same goes for custom formatters. Listing 12-41 shows how to register our implementation of a PlainTextFormatter from earlier in this chapter.

Listing 12-41. Registering a New Formatter in ASP.NET Web API Configuration

```
public class Global : HttpApplication {
    protected void Application_Start(object sender, EventArgs e) {
        var config = GlobalConfiguration.Configuration;
        config.Formatters.Add(new PlainTextFormatter());
        RouteConfig.RegisterRoutes(RouteTable.Routes);
    }
}
```

Listing 12-41 uses the Add method of the MediaTypeFormatterCollection to add a new MediaTypeFormatter implementation. The Add method allows us to add a new MediaTypeFormatter instance at the end of the formatter list. In contrast, the Insert method of the MediaTypeFormatterCollection adds a new MediaTypeFormatter instance at a specific index of the list (see Listing 12-42).

Listing 12-42. Adding a New Formatter at a Specific Position of the MediaTypeFormatterCollection

```
public class Global : HttpApplication {
    protected void Application_Start(object sender, EventArgs e) {
        var config = GlobalConfiguration.Configuration;
        config.Formatters.Insert(0, new JsonpMediaTypeFormatter());
        RouteConfig.RegisterRoutes(RouteTable.Routes);
    }
}
```

Removing a Formatter

In Listing 12-42 we added a new formatter at a specific index of our ASP.NET Web API media type formatter configuration. As was mentioned earlier, ASP.NET Web API has some default formatters, which are configured when you create a new ASP.NET Web API application. One of these, the JsonMediaTypeFormatter, is by default the formatter at index 0. We registered our JsonpMediaTypeFormatter in our configuration, and so we now have two formatters able to read and write JSON. One being enough for now, the default, `JsonMediaTypeFormatter`, can safely be removed, as we want to be able to create JSONP as well as JSON. Listing 12-43 shows updated code from Listing 12-42, including removal of the default `JsonMediaTypeFormatter`.

Listing 12-43. Replacing the Default JsonMediaTypeFormatter

```
public class Global : HttpApplication {
    protected void Application_Start(object sender, EventArgs e) {
        var config = GlobalConfiguration.Configuration;
        config.Formatters.Remove(config.Formatters.JsonFormatter);
        config.Formatters.Insert(0, new JsonpMediaTypeFormatter());
        RouteConfig.RegisterRoutes(RouteTable.Routes);
    }
}
```

Changing the Formatter Order

In this chapter's two previous sections, we inserted a new `MediaTypeFormatter` and removed an existing one. Instead of inserting the `JsonpMediaTypeFormatter` as we did there, we could have added it via the `Add` method, as shown before. If we had done this and issued a JSONP request to our Web API application, we would have gotten a script error during the execution of the JSONP request, because the request gets handled by the first `MediaTypeFormatter` able to handle a specific media type. In the case of the default ASP.NET Web API configuration this is the `JsonMediaTypeFormatter`. But for the `JsonpMediaTypeFormatter` to work, it needs to be registered before the `JsonMediaTypeFormatter`. This explains why inserting the `JsonpMediaTypeFormatter` at index 0 worked but adding it at the end of the list of formatters did not. So what we learn from this simple sample is that the registration order of `MediaTypeFormatter` instances matters. Keep that in mind when registering new `MediaTypeFormatters`!

As the last four sections have shown, modifying, adding, and removing `MediaTypeFormatter` instances in ASP.NET Web API is straightforward and quite simple. The only thing you must be aware of is the correct order of the formatter registration to avoid unwanted effects and get the correct `MediaTypeFormatter` instance invoked.

Media Type Mappings

In the earlier "JsonpMediaTypeFormatter" section, you saw that ASP.NET Web API offers a way to reroute a request to a specific formatter by mapping an incoming media type header to another media type. This technique, which ASP.NET Web API provides, is called `MediaTypeMappings`; we'll take a closer look at these mappings in the following sections.

Involving Content Negotiation with MediaTypeMapping

Every `MediaTypeFormatter` implementation has a property, `MediaTypeMappings`, which is a type of `Collection<MediaTypeMapping>`. `MediaTypeMapping` provides a way for developers to add some custom logic and decide whether they want the formatter to take part in writing the response. This differs from the default way of matching a media type value, like `application/json`, based on the request Accept and content-type headers and doing the content negotiation on the basis of that information.

Default Media Type Mappings

In the "JsonpMediaTypeFormatter" section we created a `UriPathExtensionMapping` instance and added it to the list of media type mappings of the `JsonpMediaFormatter` implementation. The `UriPathExtensionMapping` class is only one of three default MediaTypeMapping types being shipped with ASP.NET Web API by default. The three MediaTypeMapping types in ASP.NET Web API are

- UriPathExtensionMapping

- QueryStringMapping

- RequestHeaderMapping

In order to get an understanding of which MediaTypeMapping to use and how and when to use it, we'll take a closer look at each now.

UriPathExtensionMapping

The "JsonpMediaTypeFormatter" section already showed a UriPathExtensionMapping inside our JsonpMediaTypeFormatter constructor implementation. The UriPathExtensionMapping allows us to map a URI ending with a specific fragment to an arbitrary media type. This allows us to set the requested media type for the response using the URI instead of the Accept header. Again, as already shown in the "JsonpMediaTypeFormatter" section, this is useful for jQuery JSONP requests, as well as for scenarios where the client is a browser. As the user cannot modify the Accept header using the browser, providing a link with the media type in the URI enables the browser to request a specific media type.

QueryStringMapping

A QueryStringMapping can be used to add a media type based on a QueryString parameter. (We used a QueryString parameter in the "JsonpMediaTypeFormatter" section earlier when passing the jQuery method name to our JsonpMediaTypeFormatter instance.) The jQuery QueryString parameter is highlighted in Listing 12-44.

Listing 12-44. QueryString Parameter in jQuery Cross-Domain Ajax Call

http://localhost:40553/car/1?**callback=jsonp1311664395075**

As Listing 12-44 shows, the name of the QueryString parameter is callback, and its value is jsonp1311664395075. In the JsonpMediaTypeFormatter implementation, we've added a UriPathExtensionMapping to the URI fragment jsonp and to the application/json media type. Using a QueryStringMapping would have changed our URI format to look like Listing 12-45 for JSONP requests.

Listing 12-45. URI Using a QueryString Parameter to Define the Requested Media Type

http://localhost:40553/car/1?**format=jsonp&**callback=jsonp1311664395075

In order to get that URI working, we need to register the media type mapping in the JsonpMediaTypeFormatter constructor, as shown in Listing 12-46.

Listing 12-46. Registering a QueryStringMapping Instead of a UriPathExtensionMapping

```
public JsonpMediaTypeFormatter() {    SupportedMediaTypes.Add(DefaultMediaType);
    SupportedMediaTypes.Add(new MediaTypeHeaderValue("text/javascript"));
    MediaTypeMappings.Add(new QueryStringMapping("format", "jsonp", DefaultMediaType));
}
```

When running the cross-domain jQuery call using the URI from Listing 12-43 now, we get a return request for our JSONP representation of the Car instance, as expected.

RequestHeaderMapping

Another media type mapping that ASP.NET Web API provides to modify the conneg process is the RequestHeaderMapping class. As the name suggests, it allows us to change the media type being requested from a formatter by evaluating an arbitrary request header. For example, the default formatter is the JsonpMediaTypeFormatter; if the request comes from the same web site as the Web API is hosted on, it should forward the request to the text/xml media type in order to return XML instead of JSON. If the request is a cross-domain JSONP request, JSONP should be treated in the way shown before. This can be accomplished by using the configuration code in Listing 12-47.

Listing 12-47. Mapping the Media Type Based on the Referer Header Value Using ASP.NET Web API Configuration

```
public class Global : HttpApplication {
    protected void Application_Start(object sender, EventArgs e)        {
        var config = GlobalConfiguration.Configuration;
        config.Formatters.Remove(config.Formatters.JsonFormatter);
        config.Formatters.Insert(0, new JsonpMediaTypeFormatter());

        config.Formatters.JsonFormatter.MediaTypeMappings.Add(
            new RequestHeaderMapping(
                "Referer",
                "http://localhost:1501/",
                StringComparison.InvariantCultureIgnoreCase,
                false,
                "text/xml"));

        RouteConfig.RegisterRoutes(RouteTable.Routes);
    }
}
```

In contrast to the first two media type mapping types, the RequestHeaderMapping has not been added inside the MediaTypeFormatter implementation; instead, it has been applied at configuration level. This is also a valid option and allows us to add mappings without needing to modify a MediaTypeFormatter. The decision of which mapping (if any) to use can easily change from application to application.

As with other features discussed in this chapter, ASP.NET Web API allows us to customize the behavior in terms of media type mappings by implementing custom MediaTypeMapping classes—which are covered in the next section.

A Custom Media Type Mapping: RouteDataMapping

There may be scenarios where the aforementioned default MediaTypeMapping implementations might not suit your needs—as, for instance, when you want to include the mapping as part of your route definition. You'll want to provide URIs like the one shown in Listing 12-48.

Listing 12-48. URI Containing the Media Type Defined by a Route Template

```
http://localhost:1051/api/cars.json
```

The proper URI template for the URI shown in Listing 12-48 is the route definition shown in Listing 12-49.

Listing 12-49. Route Definition for URIs Containing the Media Type Selection

```
GlobalConfiguration.Configuration.Routes.MapHttpRoute(
    "defaultHttpRoute",
    routeTemplate: "api/{controller}.{extension}",
    defaults: new { },
    constraints: new { extension = "json|xml" }
);
```

The implementation of the RouteDataMapping looks like what is shown in Listing 12-50.

Listing 12-50. RouteDataMapping Implementation

```
public class RouteDataMapping : MediaTypeMapping {

    private readonly string _routeDataValueName;
    private readonly string _routeDataValueValue;

    public RouteDataMapping(
        string routeDataValueName,
        string routeDataValueValue,
        MediaTypeHeaderValue mediaType) : base(mediaType) {
            _routeDataValueName = routeDataValueName;
            _routeDataValueValue = routeDataValueValue;
    }

    public override double TryMatchMediaType(HttpRequestMessage request) {
        return (
            request.GetRouteData().
                Values[_routeDataValueName].ToString() == _routeDataValueValue)
                    ? 1.0 : 0.0;
    }
}
```

The name of the URI template parameter—it is extension here—and the value for the extension, as well as the matching media type, are passed as constructor parameters. At runtime, the TryMatchMediaType method evaluates whether the media type matches by comparing the extension value of the incoming request. If both are a match, the return value for the quality factor is 1.0 otherwise it is 0.0, which means it is not a match.

To get the RouteDataMapping working, we need to assign it to our JsonMediaTypeFormatter and the XMLMediaTypeFormatter in the Web API configuration (see Listing 12-51).

Listing 12-51. Applying the RouteDataMapping to the Default XML and JSON Formatters

```
protected void Application_Start(object sender, EventArgs e) {
    var config = GlobalConfiguration.Configuration;

    GlobalConfiguration.Configuration.Formatters.JsonFormatter.
        MediaTypeMappings.Add(
            new RouteDataMapping(
                "extension",
```

```
        "json",
        new MediaTypeHeaderValue("application/json")));

GlobalConfiguration.Configuration.Formatters.XmlFormatter.
    MediaTypeMappings.Add(
        new RouteDataMapping(
            "extension",
            "xml",
            new MediaTypeHeaderValue("application/xml")));

RouteConfig.RegisterRoutes(RouteTable.Routes);
```

As Listing 12-51 shows, the .json extension is mapped to the JsonFormatter, and the .xml extension is mapped to the XmlFormatter, with the appropriate media type assigned in each case.

■ **Tip** In order to avoid 404 errors when using this solution, you need to set `<modules runAllManagedModulesForAllRequests="true" />` in the `<system.webServer>` section in `web.config`.

When calling the URI http://localhost:1051/api/cars.json in our browser, we get the expected list of cars as a JSON representation, whereas the URI http://localhost:1051/api/cars.xml returns the list of cars as an XML document, as shown in Listings 12-52 and 12-53.

Listing 12-52. JSON Result for http://localhost:1051/api/cars.json

```
[{"Id":17,"Make":"VW","Model":"Golf","Year":1999,"Price":1500.0},
{"Id":24,"Make":"Porsche","Model":"911","Year":2011,"Price":100000.0},
{"Id":30,"Make":"Mercedes","Model":"A-Class","Year":2007,"Price":10000.0}]
```

Listing 12-53. XML Result for http://localhost:1051/api/cars.xml

```
<ArrayOfCar xmlns:i="http://www.w3.org/2001/XMLSchema-instance"
xmlns="http://schemas.datacontract.org/2004/07/WebApiConneg.Entities"><Car><Id>17</Id>
<Make>VW</Make><Model>Golf</Model><Price>1500</Price><Year>1999</Year></Car><Car><Id>24</Id>
<Make>Porsche</Make><Model>911</Model><Price>100000</Price><Year>2011</Year></Car><Car><Id>30</Id>
<Make>Mercedes</Make><Model>A-Class</Model><Price>10000</Price><Year>2007</Year></Car></ArrayOfCar>
```

To this point in the chapter, we have explained HTTP content negotiation in general and ASP.NET Web API conneg in particular. As you've learned, the conneg part is specific to request and response body content and is handled by MediaTypeFormatter instances and enhanced using MediaTypeMappings. As you also saw at the beginning of the chapter, ASP.NET Web API allows us to create ApiController method parameters not only from the request body but also from the URI. This part is covered by the model binding mechanism in ASP.NET Web API; we'll see what this means in the sections that follow.

Model Binding

ASP.NET Web API not only supports reading content from the request body or writing it to the response body; it also allows us to create simple types using QueryString parameters from incoming requests. This is possible for simple types like System.String or System.Int32, as well as for simple custom classes, like the Car class implementation used earlier in this chapter.

This process of mapping QueryString parameters to parameters for your controller's action methods is called model binding; it was introduced with ASP.NET MVC a few years ago. Model binding keeps your controller code clean from parsing QueryString parameters and allows you to do it in a generic, reusable way.

Model Binder Mechanism

Besides using body content like JSON or XML in requests (as seen in recent sections), we can also issue a request having QueryString parameters only (if it is a GET or DELETE request) or a content body and QueryString parameters (if we have a POST or PUT request). A sample GET request URI having two QueryString parameters is shown in Listing 12-54.

Listing 12-54. GET Request URI Having Two QueryString Parameters

```
http://localhost:1051/api/values/?param1=1&param2=2
```

In Listing 12-54, the QueryString parameters are param1, having a value of 1 and param2, having a value of 2. Without the model binding mechanism, your controller might look like Listing 12-55.

Listing 12-55. Manually Parsing QueryString Parameter Inside a Web API Controller

```
public class ValuesController : ApiController {
    public int Get() {
        var param1 = Request.RequestUri.ParseQueryString().Get("param1");
        var param2 = Request.RequestUri.ParseQueryString().Get("param2");

        if (!string.IsNullOrEmpty(param1) && !String.IsNullOrEmpty(param2)) {
            return Convert.ToInt32(param1) + Convert.ToInt32(param2);
        }

        throw new HttpResponseException(HttpStatusCode.BadRequest);
    }
}
```

The goal of the ValuesController in Listing 12-55 is simply to sum the values of the two incoming parameters and return the result. Because we have to parse the values (we aren't even validating them) from the params by ourselves, the code is bloated and hard to read—and we have only two numbers here!

As we said earlier, model binding was introduced with ASP.NET MVC a few years ago. It has been adopted in ASP.NET Web API for handling everything in a request save for media types (the request's body content).

The basic idea of model binding is to retrieve simple data ("simple" in the sense of structure), such as QueryString parameters and headers, from the request using Value Providers and then compose the data into a model using model binders.

This makes handling QueryString parameters much easier, as you can see in Listing 12-56. The ValuesController from the previous listing has now been reduced to the main goal: sum two incoming parameters and return that result.

Listing 12-56. An API Controller Accessing QueryString Parameters

```
public class ValuesController : ApiController {
    public int Get(int param1, int param2) {
        return param1 + param2;
    }
}
```

If you debug that request (see Figure 12-5), you will see that both parameters are assigned to our Get method as parameters.

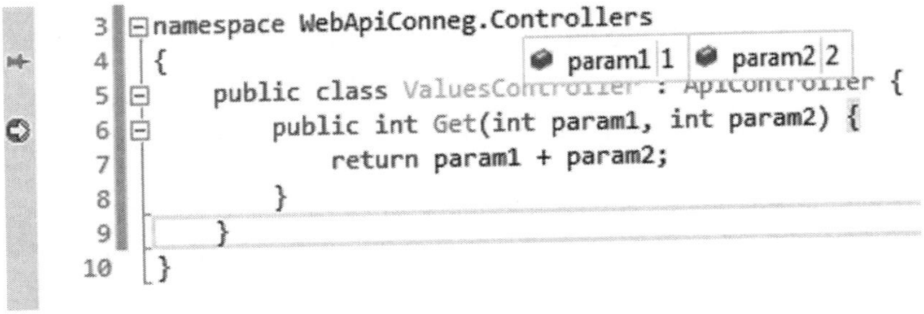

```
3  □namespace WebApiConneg.Controllers
4   |  {                          ● param1 1  ● param2 2
5   □      public class ValuesController : ApiController {
6   □          public int Get(int param1, int param2) {
7                  return param1 + param2;
8              }
9          }
10  └}
```

Figure 12-5. *QueryString parameters being assigned to a controller method*

Listing 12-56 works, because the model binding does the mapping between the QueryString parameters and the controller's action method parameters for us.

As mentioned earlier, ASP.NET Web API lets us bind QueryString parameters not only against simple CLR types but also to simple CLR objects. Listing 12-57 shows a Search class implementation having two properties to define a simple search and text to search for and the maximum number of results to be returned.

Listing 12-57. Search Class Implementation

```
public class Search {
    public string Text { get; set; }
    public int MaxResults { get; set; }
}
```

The Search class is used as a parameter for the SearchController shown in Listing 12-58.

Listing 12-58. SearchController to Perform a Search for Persons' Names

```
public class SearchController : ApiController {
    private readonly string[] _persons =
        new[] { "Bill", "Steve", "Scott", "Glenn", "Daniel" };

    public IEnumerable<string> Get([FromUri] Search search) {
        return _persons
        .Where(w => w.Contains(search.Text))
        .Take(search.MaxResults);
    }
}
```

To perform a search using the controller, browse the URI shown in Listing 12-59.

Listing 12-59. Performing a Search for Persons Based on QueryString Parameters

```
http://localhost:1051/api/search/?text=Bill&maxresults=2
```

If browsing the URI in Listing 12-59 is done with a web browser, we get back an XML document containing Bill as a search result.

In Listing 12-58, as you see, we aid the model binding by telling the controller that the Search parameter should be bound against parameters from the URI by assigning the [FromUri] attribute to the Search parameter type. There's also a [FromBody] attribute that is used by default, but you can also specify it explicitly; you can also mix both [FromUri] and [FromBody] within a single method signature.

In the introduction of this section we said that you can also mix body content and QueryString parameters; that's what we'll try in the next example.

In this example we'll use our Car class again; we'll perform a PUT operation where we explicitly pass the id of the Car resource to be updated as a QueryString parameter. The controller implementation is shown in Listing 12-60.

Listing 12-60. Mixing QueryString Parameters and Request Body Content

```
public class CarController : ApiController {
    public Car Put([FromUri]int id, Car car) {
        return car;
    }
}
```

Now let's issue a request like the one in Listing 12-61. When debugging this request, you can see that both id and car parameters are bound against the correct request QueryString and body content parameter, as seen in Figure 12-6.

Listing 12-61. A PUT Request Containing QueryString and Body Content Parameters

```
PUT http://localhost:1051/api/car?&id=1 HTTP/1.1
User-Agent: Fiddler
Host: localhost:1051
Content-Length: 70
Content-Type: application/json

{ "Id": 1, "Make":"VW", "Model":"Golf II", "Year":1995, "Price":1000 }
```

Figure 12-6. Debugging parameters from QueryString and request body content

Now that you've seen the ASP.NET Web API model binding in action, you might wonder how this works under the hood. That's the subject of the last section.

Default Model Binder

As we learned in this chapter's "MediaTypeFormatter Class" section, when the controller to be invoked is set up, the type of the ParameterBindings is determined. This is done by the ApiControllerActionSelector, by querying the HttpActionBinding from the DefaultActionValueBinder. If a ParameterBinding should read its content from the requests body, a FormatterParameterBinding instance is created for that parameter.

On the other hand, when a ParameterBinding reads the content from a QueryString parameter, a ModelBinderParameterBinding instance is created for that parameter. This binding is executed by invoking the

ExecuteBindingAsync method of the binding in the same way FormatterParameterBinding is. This is so because it has the same HttpParameterBinding base class.

Inside the ExecuteBindingAsync method, the GetValueProvider method of the CompositeValueProviderFactory is executed. This method tries to collect all IValueProvider instances from all ValueProviderFactory instances registered in the DefaultServices class for ASP.NET Web API. In the case of the QueryStringValueProviderFactory, this is the QueryStringValueProvider that itself derives from the NameValuePairsValueProvider base class, the one that allows a model binder to read values from a list of key/value pairs built from the QueryString parameters. The GetValue method of the IValueProvider is called later on from the model binder implementation's BindModel method and returns a ValueProviderResult instance. By default, the QueryStringValueProviderFactory and the RouteDataValueProviderFactory are registered in the DefaultServices class. The model binders are also registered in the DefaultServices class for the ASP.NET Web API and assigned to the HttpParameterBinding, which then calls the model binder's BindModel method inside the ExecuteBindingAsync method.

Customizing Model Binding

The process of model binding as described in the previous section might feel a bit complicated, so let's customize the model binding to get a better understanding of it.

In order to read a value from a request header, you could query the request headers collection, much as was done with the QueryString parameters shown in Listing 12-54. This would come at the same cost as described there.

IValueProvider

A more generic approach using model binding involves implementing your own IValueProvider. The IValueProvider interface has the signature shown in Listing 12-62.

Listing 12-62. IValueProvider Interface

```
public interface IValueProvider {
    bool ContainsPrefix(string prefix);
    ValueProviderResult GetValue(string key);
}
```

The ContainsPrefix method of the IValueProvider interface should return whether a prefix string is contained in the request (be it headers, QueryString, or anything else) and should be parsed. The GetValue method should return the value for a key being passed in to the method.

Our IValueProvider implementation should be able to read header information being passed in as nonstandard HTTP request headers, which start with the "X–" prefix. In our controller, we simply want to access a request header field name "X-Name" and return a string output, as shown in Listing 12-63.

Listing 12-63. HeaderHelloController to Return a String Based on a Request Header Field

```
public class HelloController : ApiController {
    public string Get(string name) {
    return "Hello, " + name;
    }
}
```

In order to pass the X-Name header field into the Get method of the HelloController, we now need to implement our IValueProvider. Listing 12-64 shows the XHeaderValueProvider implementation.

Listing 12-64. XHeaderValueProvider Implementation

```
public class XHeaderValueProvider : IValueProvider {
    private readonly HttpRequestHeaders _headers;
    private const string XHeaderPrefix = "X-";

    public XHeaderValueProvider(HttpActionContext actionContext) {
        _headers = actionContext.ControllerContext.Request.Headers;
    }

    public bool ContainsPrefix(string prefix) {
        return _headers.Any(header => header.Key.Contains(XHeaderPrefix + prefix));
    }

    public ValueProviderResult GetValue(string key) {
        IEnumerable<string> values;

        return _headers.TryGetValues(XHeaderPrefix + key, out values)
            ? new ValueProviderResult(
                values.First(),
                values.First(),
                CultureInfo.CurrentCulture)
            : null;
    }
}
```

The ContainsPrefix method implementation prefixes the incoming prefix (which is "Name" here because of the name controller method parameter) with an "X–" prefix, as we want to access only X-Header fields inside the request header collection. The header collection is created inside the constructor of our XHeaderValueProvider. Reading the content of the X-Name header field (if provided inside the request) is done using the GetValue method implementation. It queries the header field collection for the X-Name field and returns its value as a string.

In order to be able to make use of the XHeaderValueProvider, we also need—as described in the "Default Model Binder" section earlier—to implement a ValueProviderFactory. The implementation is pretty simple (see Listing 12-65), as it only returns a new instance of the XHeaderValueProvider when its GetValueProvider method is called.

Listing 12-65. XHeaderValueProviderFactory Implementation

```
public class XHeaderValueProviderFactory : ValueProviderFactory {
    public override IValueProvider GetValueProvider(HttpActionContext actionContext) {
        return new XHeaderValueProvider(actionContext);
    }
}
```

There's one small step left to get the X-Name field value passed as a string parameter to our controller's Get method. The update is highlighted in Listing 12-66.

Listing 12-66. Updated Version of HelloController

```
public class HelloController : ApiController {
    public string Get([ValueProvider(typeof(XHeaderValueProviderFactory))]string name) {
        return "Hello, " + name;
    }
}
```

The name parameter of the Get method is attributed now to the ValueProviderAttribute; it allows us to specify which ValueProviderFactory implementation (hence, which IValueProvider implementation) should try to provide that specific parameter.

When issuing a new request with Fiddler, providing an X-Name header field, as shown in Figure 12-7, we get the corresponding response.

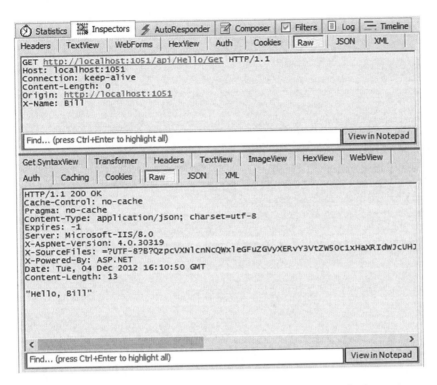

Figure 12-7. *Debugging parameters from QueryString and request body content*

As you now see how to implement a custom IValueProvider, let's move to the next step: implementing a custom model binder that allows us to compose a model based on QueryString parameters.

IModelBinder

For the custom model binder implementation, we'll reuse our scenario from Listings 12-57 to 12-59. Instead of decorating our Search parameter with the FromUri attribute inside our controller, we'll decorate our Search entity with a ModelBinder attribute, as shown in Listing 12-67.

Listing 12-67. Search Entity Decorated with the ModelBinder Attribute

```
[ModelBinder(typeof(SearchModelBinderProvider))]
public class Search {
    public string Text { get; set; }
    public int MaxResults { get; set; }
}
```

This tells the Web API model binding to look at the SearchModelBindingProvider implementation for which model binder to use to create an instance of the Search class from the requests parameters. Unfortunately, there is neither a SearchModelBinderProvider nor a corresponding model binder in ASP.NET Web API. But thanks to the IModelBinder interface, we can implement our custom model binder—it's SearchModelBinderProvider.

The IModelBinder interface requires us to implement a single method, named BindModel, as you can see in Listing 12-68.

Listing 12-68. IModelBinder Interface

```
public interface IModelBinder {    bool BindModel(HttpActionContext actionContext,
ModelBindingContext bindingContext);
}
```

The implementation of that interface is shown in Listing 12-68.

Listing 12-69. SearchModelBinder Implementation

```
public class SearchModelBinder : IModelBinder {
    public bool BindModel(HttpActionContext actionContext, ModelBindingContext bindingContext) {
        var model = (Search) bindingContext.Model ?? new Search();

        model.Text =
            bindingContext.ValueProvider.GetValue("Text").AttemptedValue;

        var maxResults = 0;
        if (int.TryParse(
            bindingContext
            .ValueProvider
            .GetValue("MaxResults").AttemptedValue, out maxResults)) {

            model.MaxResults = maxResults;
        }

        bindingContext.Model = model;

        return true;
    }
}
```

The SearchModelBinder implementation first checks whether the Model from the ModelBindingContext is null and creates a new Search instance if the model is null. Thereafter, the properties for the Search class instance are deserialized using the ValueProvider (it's the build in QueryStringValueProvider here) from the QueryString of the incoming request. The Search instance, with its assigned properties Text and MaxResults, then will be passed back to the incoming BindingContext instance; true is returned from the BindModel method to indicate that the model has been bound correctly. Of course, in a real-world implementation you would make the return value depend on some validation and/or a try/catch block.

When running the modified API and issuing a new request to the URI from Listing 12-59 again, we get the same result as before, but it's achieved this time using a different approach. The IModelBinder implementation shown has been quite simple; it's up to you to build model binders for more complex scenarios. But keep in mind that deserializing the body content of the request is, by convention, the sole responsibility of MediaTypeFormatters in ASP.NET Web API.

As you can see, the model binding in ASP.NET Web API offers a well-thought-out set of implementations to provide a mechanism that not only gives us the possibility to bind body content using the media type formatters from the previous sections of the chapter but also allows us to bind parameters from other sections of the requests, like the QueryString or header fields. The icing on the cake is that you can even combine them to mix request body content and QueryString parameters within the same controller method.

Summary

Content negotiation is a huge topic in implementing HTTP or even RESTful applications. ASP.NET Web API supports all parts of the HTTP specification regarding content negotiation and abstracts that complexity away in an easy-to-use way by providing media type formatters for body content and model binding for QueryString parameters. If necessary, ASP.NET Web API also provides extensibility points where you can tweak content negotiation. It thus allows you to read and write every type of content you want to consume or provide in your Web API application.

CHAPTER 13

Input Validation

Regardless of the application type, input validation is a very important topic if the application accepts user inputs. As developers, we tend to assume that every user input is evil and they should be validated before being processed. Checking whether an input field is empty or not, validating the length of an input value, and comparing two inputs against each other according to a specific logic—these are just some of the common validation checks.

This chapter will explain how ASP.NET Web API simplifies this process by offering out-of-the-box solutions and how its built-in implementations can be extended to customize the validation in accord with business logic. You will also see how to handle responses for invalid requests in view of the resource owner and the consumer.

Overview

The ASP.NET Web API validation model is very similar to ASP.NET MVC. Data annotation validation attributes are supported right out of the box, and discussion of these will take up most of this chapter.

Data Annotation Attributes were introduced in .NET 3.5 SP1 as a way to add validation to classes used by ASP.NET Dynamic Data applications. Since .NET 4.0, Data Annotation Attributes has been part of .NET Framework itself, and the library provides not only validation attributes but also others that give metadata information about the properties and fields in which they are applied.

The model validation system in ASP.NET Web API is not limited to data annotation validation attributes. Although validation with data annotations will be what you want most of the time, you'll have a chance to provide your own validation providers, too.

How Validation Works Through Parameter Binding

The built-in validation logic inside the ASP.NET Web API framework is triggered by the ExecuteAsync method of the ApiController. The ExecuteAsync method doesn't perform the validation itself. Instead, it invokes the proper HttpParameterBinding instances, some of which have the ability to perform validation.

■ **Note**   If you are using a custom base controller which is not derived from ApiController or overrides the default ApiController.ExecuteAsync method logic, you won't get validation for free.

As you saw in Chapter 12, there are two main types of HttpParameterBinding implementations provided by the framework: FormatterParameterBinding and ModelBinderParameterBinding. Depending on the action parameter types, registered parameter binding rules, and applied ParameterBinding attributes, an HttpParameterBinding instance is chosen to process the action parameter binding. Only these two parameter HttpParameterBinding implementations provide the action parameter validation.

However, they don't actually hold any information for the validation logic. They delegate this to other services. In the case of FormatterParameterBinding, the validation action is delegated to the registered IBodyModelValidator service. For ModelBinderParameterBinding, the provided System.Web.Http.Validation.ModelValidator implementations play the key role in performing the validation. The ModelValidator implementations are provided by the registered System.Web.Http.Validation.ModelValidatorProvider implementations, which are at the highest extensibility point for the validation system inside the framework.

There are three registered implementations of the ModelValidatorProvider:

- DataAnnotationsModelValidatorProvider

- DataMemberModelValidatorProvider

- InvalidModelValidatorProvider

The DataAnnotationsModelValidatorProvider provides the model validators for Data Annotation validation attributes (they will, as noted earlier, be covered in depth in this chapter). This ModelValidatorProvider also acts as a validator for types implementing System.ComponentModel.DataAnnotations.IValidatableObject (also covered in this chapter).

The DataMemberModelValidatorProvider provides a required ModelValidator for members marked [DataMember(IsRequired=true)]. The last implementation, the InvalidModelValidatorProvider, provides validators that throw exceptions when the model is invalid according to a specific logic which we are about to explain.

The InvalidModelValidatorProvider is not a model provider that you want in most cases because, in our opinion, it behaves too aggressively. It is meant to provide the functionality to throw an error if you have a value-type property marked with RequiredAttribute and not with [DataMember(IsRequired=true)]. Consider the example of the controller implementation shown in Listing 13-1.

Listing 13-1. CarsController and GetCar Action Method

```
[FromUri]
public class UriParameter {

    [Required]
    public int Id { get; set; }
}

public class CarsController : ApiController {

    // GET /api/cars/{id}
    public Car GetCar(UriParameter uriParameter) {

        //Lines omitted for brevity . . .
    }
}
```

Normally, when sending a GET request to /api/cars/10, one should hit the GetCar action method and process the request there. However, as Figure 13-1 shows, doing so will generate a complicated error message.

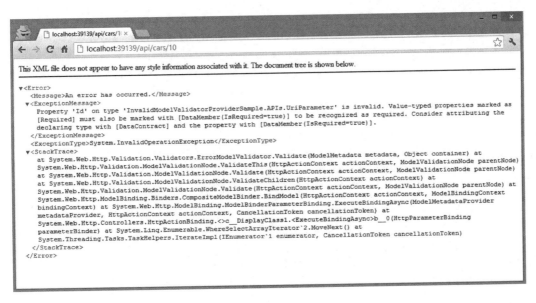

Figure 13-1. *A response message for the request against /api/cars/10*

If you don't require this kind of functionality, you can easily remove this validator provider (see Listing 13-2).

Listing 13-2. Removing InvalidModelValidatorProvider from the ModelValidatorProvider List

```
protected void Application_Start(object sender, EventArgs e) {

    var config = GlobalConfiguration.Configuration;

    //Lines omitted for brevity . . .

    config.Services.RemoveAll(
        typeof(ModelValidatorProvider),
        validator => validator is InvalidModelValidatorProvider);
}
```

Alternatively, you may want DataAnnotationsModelValidatorProvider solely registered. If such is the case, just remove all the validator providers except for DataAnnotationsModelValidatorProvider, as Listing 13-3 shows.

Listing 13-3. Removing All Validator Providers Except for DataAnnotationsModelValidatorProvider

```
protected void Application_Start(object sender, EventArgs e) {

    var config = GlobalConfiguration.Configuration;

    //Lines omitted for brevity . . .

    config.Services.RemoveAll(
        typeof(ModelValidatorProvider),
        validator => !(validator is DataAnnotationsModelValidatorProvider));
}
```

■ **Note**   Keep in mind that the validation providers and several other validation components for ASP.NET Web API live under the namespaces `System.Web.Http.Validation` and `System.Web.Http.Validation.Providers`. The fact that some of the class names also exist for the ASP.NET MVC and ASP.NET Web Forms may lead to confusion and possible conflicts.

Throughout this chapter, samples will be run with this implementation in place unless stated otherwise.

As already mentioned, the validation happens at the parameter binding level through certain `HttpParameterBinding` implementations. At this point, you might ask, "How will I be informed about the validation errors?" The next section answers that very question.

Model State

Right after the authorization filters are invoked, the proper `HttpParameterBinding` instances are invoked. If a validation is performed through any of the `HttpParameterBinding` instances, validation errors that occur during the parameter binding are propagated back to the `ApiController`'s `ExecuteAsync` method through the `ModelState` property of the `HttpActionContext`.

If these `HttpParameterBinding` instances perform without error, the `ModelState` property of the `ApiController` is set, and the action filters are invoked. The action filters are the first place where you can see and act on the `ModelState`. There you can inspect the `ModelState` property and terminate the request with an action filter if there are validation errors. Listing 13-4 shows an example of a filter that handles `ModelState` validation errors, which we also saw in Chapter 11.

Listing 13-4. InvalidModelStateFilterAttribute Class

```
[AttributeUsage(AttributeTargets.Class |
    AttributeTargets.Method, AllowMultiple = false, Inherited = true)]
public class InvalidModelStateFilterAttribute : ActionFilterAttribute {

    public override void OnActionExecuting(
        HttpActionContext actionContext) {

        if (!actionContext.ModelState.IsValid) {

            actionContext.Response =
                actionContext.Request.CreateErrorResponse(
                    HttpStatusCode.BadRequest, actionContext.ModelState);
        }
    }
}
```

The `CreateErrorResponse` extension method (explained in Chapter 9) is used here to create an error response over the `ModelState`. As you saw in Chapter 11, the request is terminated if the `Response` property of the `HttpActionContext` is set inside the `OnActionExecuting` method of our action filter. Throughout this chapter, this filter will be used to demonstrate the validations' behavior.

Data Annotation Validation Attributes

In most cases, validation will only be performed with data annotation validation attributes, which cover a huge part of the validation logic inside the ASP.NET Web API framework.

Data annotation validation attributes are based on the System.ComponentModel.DataAnnotations. ValidationAttribute abstract class, by means of which an attribute is recognized as a validation attribute. The ValidationAttribute class, which serves as the base class for all validation attributes, has the properties shown in Table 13-1.

Table 13-1. *Public Properties of the ValidationAttribute Class*

Name	Type	Description
ErrorMessage	String	Represents the error message to associate with a validation control if validation fails.
ErrorMessageResourceName	String	Represents the error message resource name to use to look up the ErrorMessageResourceType property value if validation fails.
ErrorMessageResourceType	Type	Represents the resource type to use for error-message lookup if validation fails.
ErrorMessageString	String	Represents the localized validation error message.
RequiresValidationContext	Boolean	Indicates whether the attribute requires validation context.

You can see that these are very basic properties, ones that every validation attribute will carry. Besides these common properties, every validation attribute can have its own properties.

.NET Framework provides several useful validation attributes out of the box. They cover most of the validation logic that our applications require. This section will explain them separately and show how to use them as well.

RequiredAttribute

The RequiredAttribute specifies that a field or property is required. As already explained, all validation attributes are derived from the ValidationAttribute abstract class. Besides the ValidationAttribute class's properties, the RequiredAttribute class holds one more property, AllowEmptyStrings. This property indicates whether an empty string is allowed or not. The default value for AllowEmptyStrings is false, and in most cases this is what is desired.

To demonstrate the RequiredAttribute in action, Listing 13-5 uses a simple car gallery API application scenario with a Car class.

Listing 13-5. Car Class

```
public class Car {

    public int Id { get; set; }

    [Required]
    public string Make { get; set; }

    [Required]
    public string Model { get; set; }
```

```
    public int Year { get; set; }

    public float Price { get; set; }
}
```

As you see, Make and Model properties are marked with RequiredAttribute. There is also a context class, which gets the car objects and adds them to the in-memory data store for demonstration purposes (see Listing 13-6).

Listing 13-6. CarsContext Class

```
public class CarsContext {

    private static int _nextId = 9;

    //data store
    readonly static ConcurrentDictionary<int, Car> _carsDictionary =
        new ConcurrentDictionary<int, Car>(
        new HashSet<KeyValuePair<int, Car>> {
            new KeyValuePair<int, Car>(
                1,
                new Car {
                    Id = 1,
                    Make = "Make1",
                    Model = "Model1",
                    Year = 2010,
                    Price = 10732.2F
                }
            ),
            new KeyValuePair<int, Car>(
                2,
                new Car {
                    Id = 2,
                    Make = "Make2",
                    Model = "Model2",
                    Year = 2008,
                    Price = 27233.1F
                }
            ),

            //Lines omitted for brevity . . .
    });

    public IEnumerable<Car> All {
        get {
            return _carsDictionary.Values;
        }
    }

    public IEnumerable<Car> Get(Func<Car, bool> predicate) {

        return _carsDictionary.Values.Where(predicate);
    }
```

```
public Tuple<bool, Car> GetSingle(int id) {

    Car car;
    var doesExist = _carsDictionary.TryGetValue(id, out car);
    return new Tuple<bool, Car>(doesExist, car);
}

public Car GetSingle(Func<Car, bool> predicate) {

    return _carsDictionary.Values.FirstOrDefault(predicate);
}

public Car Add(Car car) {

    car.Id = _nextId;
    _carsDictionary.TryAdd(car.Id, car);
    _nextId++;

    return car;
}

public bool TryRemove(int id) {

    Car removedCar;
    return _carsDictionary.TryRemove(id, out removedCar);
}

public bool TryUpdate(Car car) {

    Car oldCar;
    if (_carsDictionary.TryGetValue(car.Id, out oldCar)) {

        return _carsDictionary.TryUpdate(car.Id, car, oldCar);
    }

    return false;
}

}
```

Now, inside the controller, allow a GET request to retrieve all the cars, a POST request to add a new car, and a PUT request to edit an existing car entity. Listing 13-7 shows our controller implementation.

Listing 13-7. CarsController Implementation

```
[InvalidModelStateFilter]
public class CarsController : ApiController {

    private readonly CarsContext _carsCtx =
        new CarsContext();

    // GET /api/cars
    public IEnumerable<Car> Get() {

        return _carsCtx.All;
    }

    // POST /api/cars
    public HttpResponseMessage PostCar(Car car) {

        var createdCar = _carsCtx.Add(car);
        var response = Request.CreateResponse(
            HttpStatusCode.Created, createdCar);

        response.Headers.Location = new Uri(
            Url.Link("DefaultHttpRoute",
                new { id = createdCar.Id }));

        return response;
    }

    // PUT /api/cars/{id}
    public Car PutCar(int id, Car car) {

        car.Id = id;

        if (!_carsCtx.TryUpdate(car)) {

            var response = Request.CreateResponse(
                HttpStatusCode.NotFound);

            throw new HttpResponseException(response);
        }

        return car;
    }
}
```

The InvalidModelStateFilter, shown in Listing 13-4, is registered at the controller level to handle the validation errors and return an informative response to the client. When a valid POST request is sent against /api/cars, a "201 Created" response comes back, as shown in Figure 13-2.

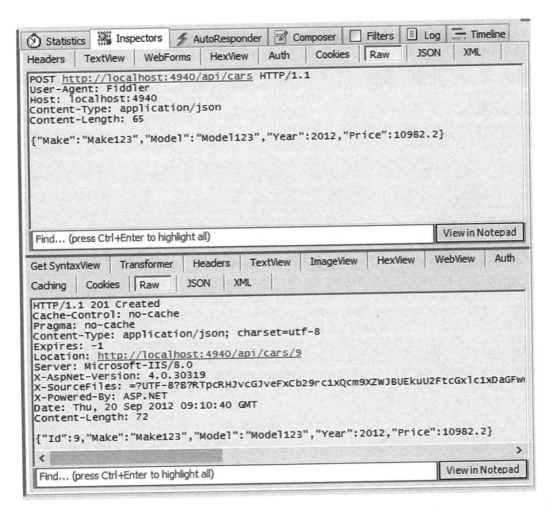

Figure 13-2. A POST request against /api/cars and the "201 Created" response

However, if the request is invalid according to our validation logic, the InvalidModelStateFilterAttribute action filter will kick in and terminate the request by setting a new "400 Bad Request" response, along with the Errors collection of the ModelState object (see Figure 13-3).

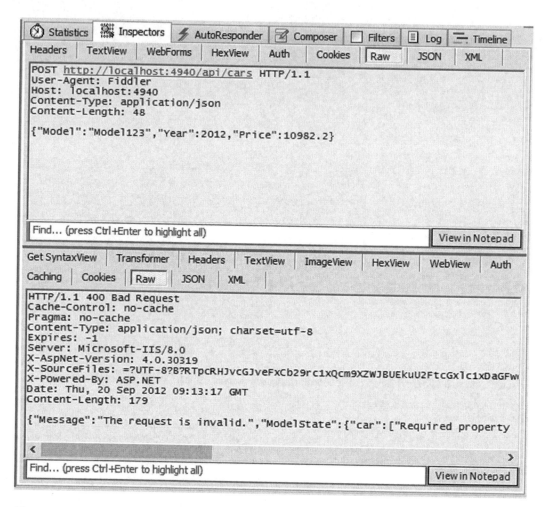

Figure 13-3. *Invalid POST request against /api/cars and the "400 Bad Request" response*

Figure 13-4 gives a formatted view of the message body that contains the validation errors.

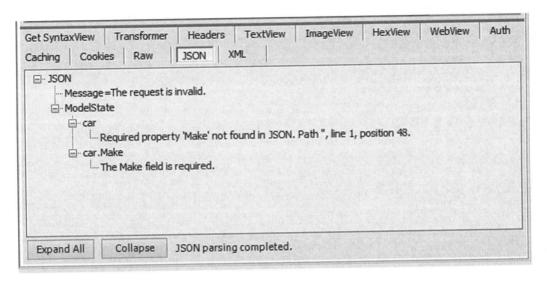

Figure 13-4. A "400 Bad Request" response body formatted in JSON view

As expected, the response message indicates that the Make property of the Car object is required. If you send the request by including the Make property but supplying an empty string value, you would still get the validation error because the RequiredAttribute doesn't allow empty strings. For the reverse to apply, the Car class should be changed to what is shown in Listing 13-8.

Listing 13-8. Car Class Reset to Allow Empty Strings for the Make Property

```
public class Car {

    public int Id { get; set; }

    [Required(AllowEmptyStrings = true)]
    public string Make { get; set; }

    [Required]
    public string Model { get; set; }

    public int Year { get; set; }

    public float Price { get; set; }
}
```

Notice that in the response body for the invalid request in Figure 13-4, there is one additional validation error message whose key is "car". This validation error message comes from the formatter itself. By default, formatters check required fields. If a required field is not supplied, the formatter throws an error that carries an error message similar to the one shown in Figure 13-4. Also by default, if a formatter error occurs during the formatting stage, the error message is put inside the Errors collection in the ModelState.

Some of the ways to suppress this behavior depend on the type of formatter. One way to suppress the behavior on every formatter is to create a custom IRequiredMemberSelector implementation to replace the default one. Listing 13-9 shows the proper IRequiredMemberSelector implementation for this behavior.

Listing 13-9. SuppressedRequiredMemberSelector Class

```
public class SuppressedRequiredMemberSelector
    : IRequiredMemberSelector {

    public bool IsRequiredMember(MemberInfo member) {

        return false;
    }
}
```

To replace the default IRequiredMemberSelector implementation on the formatters, iterate over all of them and replace the default on each formatter with our custom IRequiredMemberSelector implementation (see Listing 13-10).

Listing 13-10. Replacing the Default IRequiredMemberSelector Implementation

```
protected void Application_Start(object sender, EventArgs e) {

    var config = GlobalConfiguration.Configuration;

    // Lines omitted for brevity

    // Suppressing the IRequiredMemberSelector for all formatters
    foreach (var formatter in config.Formatters) {
        formatter.RequiredMemberSelector = new SuppressedRequiredMemberSelector();
    }
}
```

With this change in place, you won't see the additional duplicate error message if an invalid POST request is sent to /api/cars (see Figure 13-5).

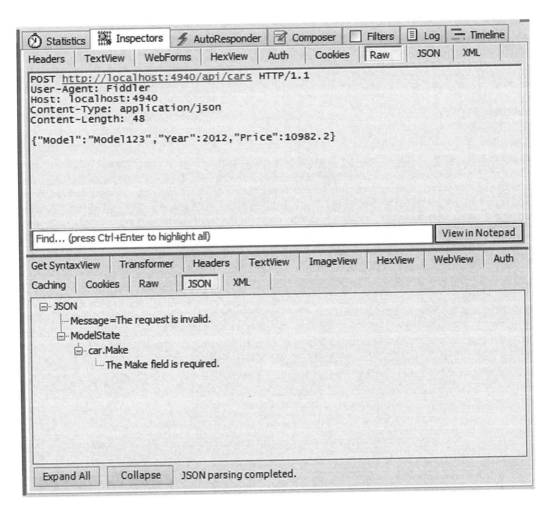

Figure 13-5. Invalid POST request against /api/cars and formatted response body

RequiredAttribute and Value Types

The RequiredAttribute doesn't validate the value types correctly. For example, when the RequiredAttribute is applied to a value-type field, you won't get an exception, but you will see that the validation isn't applied.

Let's have a look at the Car class shown in Listing 13-11.

Listing 13-11. Car Class with a Year Property Marked with RequiredAttribute

```
public class Car {

    public int Id { get; set; }

    [Required]
    public string Make { get; set; }
```

```
    [Required]
    public string Model { get; set; }

    [Required]
    public int Year { get; set; }

    public float Price { get; set; }
}
```

The one change made was to apply the RequiredAttribute to the Year property, an integer type (Int32 is a value type). With the changes applied in Listing 13-10, you won't get a "400 Bad Request" if a POST request containing a car entity with the missing Year field is sent. This is obviously not the behavior expected here. Instead, the request will be processed, and a new Car object added to the list, because the formatter or the model binding will assign a default value for the value type—which is 0 for Int32. What all of this produces is the response shown in Figure 13-6.

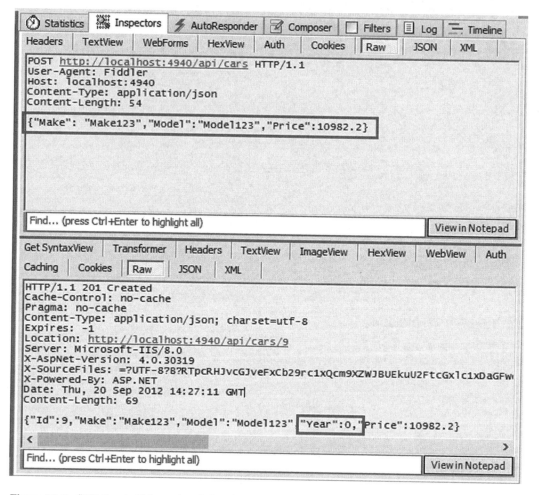

Figure 13-6. *"201 Created" for an invalid POST request against /api/cars*

One way to work around this issue is to use .NET Nullable types and apply `RequiredAttribute` to them. You can make a value type nullable either by adding the "?" sign as a suffix for the property name or using the `Nullable<T>` generic type. With this change, the `Car` class now looks like what is seen in Listing 13-12.

Listing 13-12. Car Class with a Nullable<int> Type of Year Property

```
public class Car {

    public int Id { get; set; }

    [Required]
    public string Make { get; set; }

    [Required]
    public string Model { get; set; }

    [Required]
    public Nullable<int> Year { get; set; }

    public float Price { get; set; }
}
```

If applied to your existing code and depending on your situation, this change may require additional changes. For example, consider an object that is a type of `Nullable<int>`. Integer values can be directly assigned to this object, but the object cannot be assigned to an `Int32` value type. To do that, the `Value` property of the `Nullable<T>` object needs to be used. The `Value` property will be a type of T. In the case here, no additional changes had to be made, and so if the request shown in Figure 13-6 was sent, the expected behavior would be what is seen in Figure 13-7.

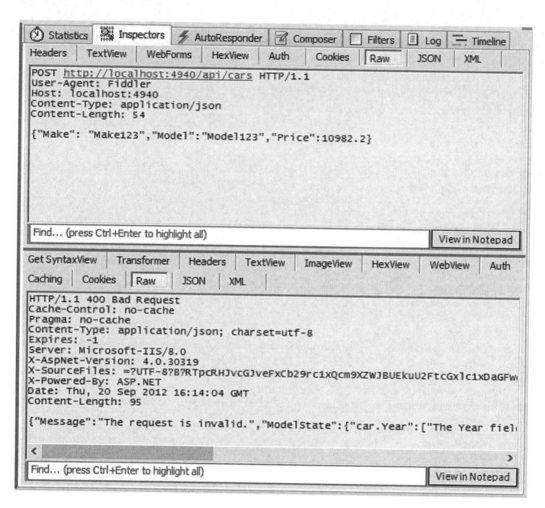

Figure 13-7. *Invalid POST request against /api/cars and the "400 Bad Request" response*

On the other hand, if the default IRequiredMemberSelector implementation on the formatters wasn't replaced, you'd get the ModelState error from the formatter even if you used RequiredAttribute on value types (see Figure 13-8).

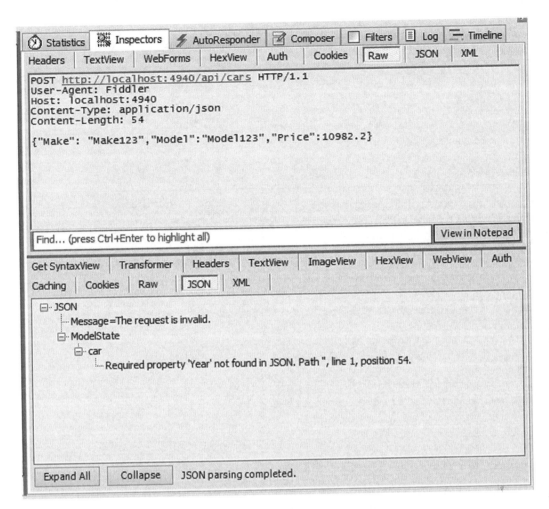

Figure 13-8. *Invalid POST request to /api/cars and the "400 Bad Request" response*

If you also support XML format with your API, the RequiredAttribute will not be enough by itself for the value-type fields. As indicated in earlier sections, our samples here are running with the configuration that has only DataAnnotationsModelValidatorProvider registered as ModelValidatorProvider. If a POST request is now sent against /api/cars in XML format with a missing Year field, assuming the Car class is as shown in Listing 13-11, there won't be any validation or runtime errors, and the object will be created with the default Int32 value for the Year field (see Figure 13-9).

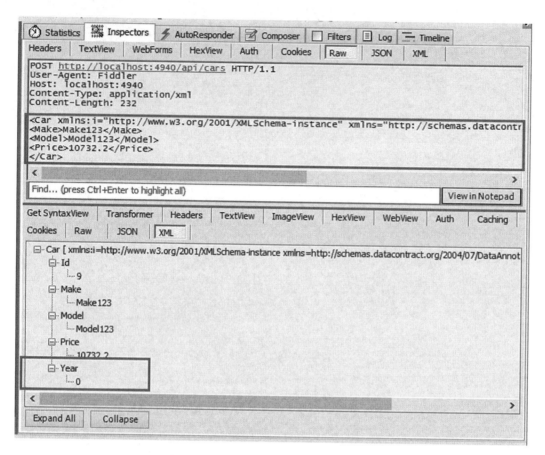

Figure 13-9. *Invalid POST request to /api/cars and "201 Created" response*

Let's change our configuration for this sample, leave all the registered ModelValidatorProvider instances by default as they are, and send the same request again. A runtime error similar to the one shown in Figure 13-10 should be returned.

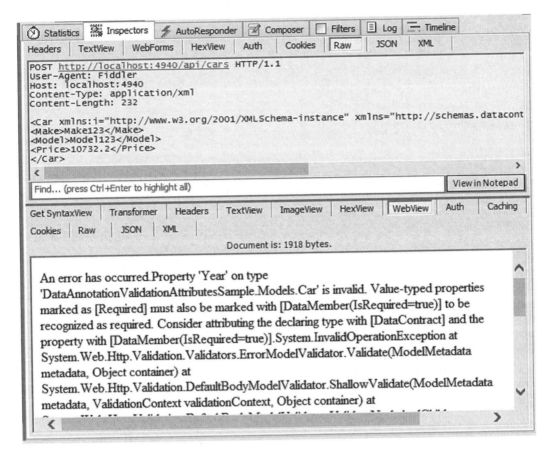

Figure 13-10. POST request to /api/cars and a "500 Internal Server Error" response

As was briefly explained earlier, this error is thrown by the InvalidModelValidatorProvider. For the value-typed properties to be recognized as required, they need to be marked with [DataMember(IsRequired=true)] if the property is marked with RequiredAttribute. Also, the Car class needs to be marked with DataContractAttribute, as Listing 13-13 shows. These attributes live under the System.Runtime.Serialization namespace. You need to add the System.Runtime.Serialization reference to your project to get hold of them.

■ **Note**   In the first RTW release of ASP.NET Web API, the InvalidModelValidatorProvider behaves overly aggressively and even throws runtime errors when the XmlMediaTypeFormatter is not registered. This issue—known but not yet solved at the time this book is being written (early 2013)—is also present in the FromUri attribute when using a class signature against the InvalidModelValidatorProvider. The issue is tracked on the official Codeplex page of the ASP.NET Web Stack project (http://aspnetwebstack.codeplex.com/workitem/270). According to team members' comments, the provider will be removed in the framework's next version, but to date there has been no official confirmation of this decision.

Listing 13-13. *The Car Class with DataContract and DataMember Attributes*

```
[DataContract]
public class Car {

    public int Id { get; set; }

    [Required]
    public string Make { get; set; }

    [Required]
    public string Model { get; set; }

    [Required]
    [DataMember(IsRequired = true)]
    public int Year { get; set; }

    public float Price { get; set; }
}
```

If we now send the same request, a "400 Bad Request" response should be returned (see Figure 13-11).

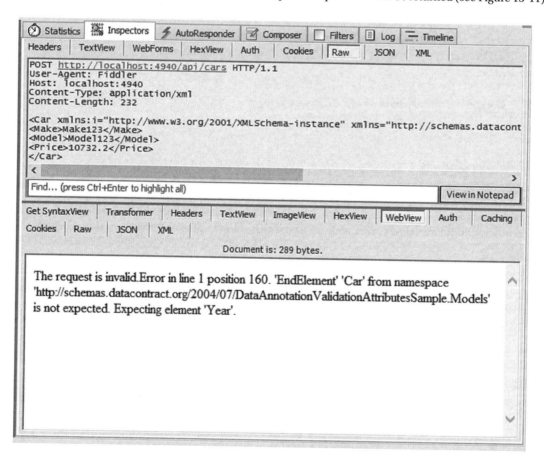

Figure 13-11. *Invalid POST request to /api/cars and a "400 Bad Request" response*

StringLengthAttribute

The StringLengthAttribute provides a way to specify minimum and maximum lengths of characters allowed in a string field. This validation attribute is most useful when you know that the field inside the database has a certain capacity and that you can apply the StringLengthAttribute to those class fields and properties to validate the member early—before the value gets to the database.

The Car class in Listing 13-14 shows an example of a class whose properties are marked with the StringLengthAttribute.

Listing 13-14. The Car Class That Contains Properties Marked with the StringLengthAttribute

```
public class Car {

    public int Id { get; set; }

    [Required]
    [StringLength(maximumLength: 20)]
    public string Make { get; set; }

    [Required]
    [StringLength(maximumLength: 20, MinimumLength = 5)]
    public string Model { get; set; }

    public int Year { get; set; }

    public float Price { get; set; }
}
```

The StringLengthAttribute accepts two custom inputs: one through the constructor that specifies the member's allowed maximum length value and the other through a property, named MinimumLength, that specifies the field's allowed minimum length value. In our Car class, the Make property is marked with a StringLengthAttribute indicating that the maximum length value allowed is 20. On the other hand, the Model property is forced to have a value whose length is a minimum of 5.

Let's use the sample set up, which is shown in the previous section, with the Car class implementation in Listing 13-14 and send an invalid POST request to /api/cars to create a new car entity. A "400 Bad Request" response will come back, as we have an action filter registered to handle the invalid ModelState (see Figure 13-12).

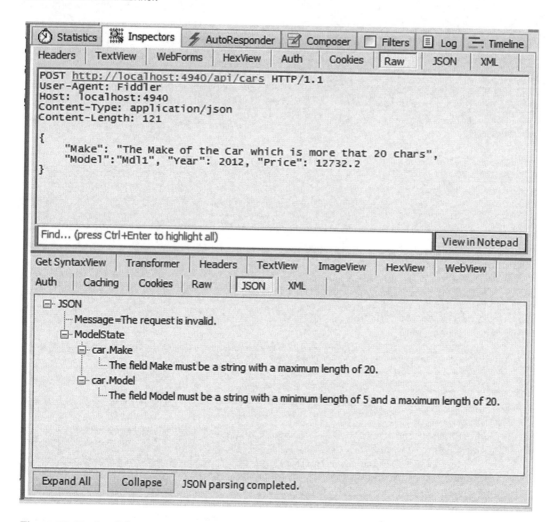

Figure 13-12. *Invalid POST request to /api/cars and a "400 Bad Request" response*

As you see, our request message body contains a JSON object with Model and Make properties whose values are invalid. The response message body states those validation errors clearly.

Although the validation error messages are pretty clear, you might also want to customize them. Remember that all validation attributes contain properties to customize the error messages. In addition, depending on the validation attribute type, error message formats that combine dynamic input values and static error messages can be supplied. Listing 13-15 shows an example of custom error messages for the Make and Model properties of the Car class.

Listing 13-15. *The Car class, which has properties marked with StringLengthAttribute, contains custom error messages*

```
public class Car {

    public int Id { get; set; }
```

```
    [Required]
    [StringLength(
        maximumLength: 20,
        ErrorMessage = "For {0} field, the maximum allowed length is {1}."
    )]
    public string Make { get; set; }

    [Required]
    [StringLength(
        maximumLength: 20, MinimumLength = 5,
        ErrorMessage = "For {0} field, the maximum allowed length is {1} and the minimum allowed
length is {2}."
    )]
    public string Model { get; set; }

    public int Year { get; set; }

    public float Price { get; set; }
}
```

The StringLengthAttribute accepts two different message formats depending on whether a MinimumLength was or wasn't supplied. If it was, you would get three arguments from the FormatErrorMessage of the ValidationAttribute class, which you will see in the "Custom Validation" section of this chapter. The first one will be the name of the field, the second will be the maximum allowed characters value, and the third will be the minimum allowed characters value. If a value for the MinimumLength property isn't supplied, you won't get the third argument.

Using the custom validation messages set in Listing 13-15, you'll now get different validation errors for invalid requests (see Figure 13-13).

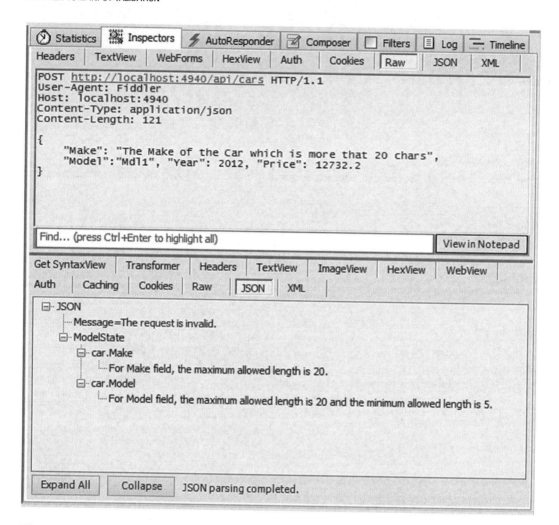

Figure 13-13. Invalid POST request to /api/cars and a "400 Bad Request" response with custom validation messages

Alternatively, you can put the error messages inside a resource file for any of several reasons (such as localization) and point the validation attribute to the message format inside that resource file. This example assumes that there is a resource file named ValidationErrors and that it has the same error message formats as in Listing 13-15 (see Figure 13-14).

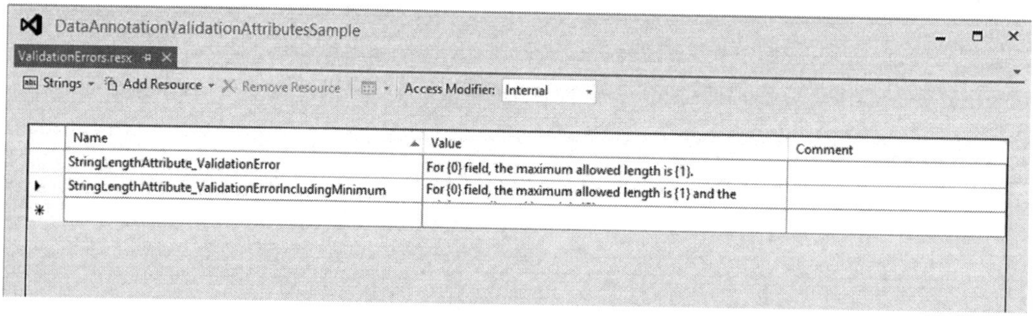

Figure 13-14. The ValidationErrors resource file view on Visual Studio

These string resources can now be used as validation message formats. As Table 13-1 briefly mentioned, the ErrorMessageResourceName and ErrorMessageResourceType properties of the ValidationAttribute class provide the ability to reference a resource inside a resource file (see Listing 13-16).

Listing 13-16. The Car Class, Which Contains Properties Marked with a StringLengthAttribute, Contains Custom Error Messages from a Resource File

```
public class Car {

    public int Id { get; set; }

    [Required]
    [StringLength(
        maximumLength: 20,
        ErrorMessageResourceName =
            "StringLengthAttribute_ValidationError",
        ErrorMessageResourceType =
            typeof(ValidationErrors)
    )]
    public string Make { get; set; }

    [Required]
    [StringLength(
        maximumLength: 20, MinimumLength = 5,
        ErrorMessageResourceName =
            "StringLengthAttribute_ValidationErrorIncludingMinimum",
        ErrorMessageResourceType =
            typeof(ValidationErrors)
    )]
    public string Model { get; set; }

    public int Year { get; set; }

    public float Price { get; set; }
}
```

The resource key has been set to the ErrorMessageResourceName property, and the type of the resource class through the ErrorMessageResourceType property has been specified. When an invalid request is now sent to the /api/cars URI, you will see the expected behavior (see Figure 13-15).

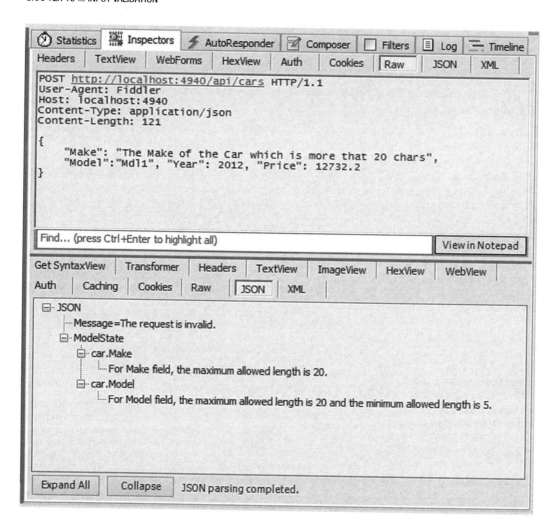

Figure 13-15. *Invalid POST request to /api/cars and a "400 Bad Request" response with custom validation messages stored inside a resource file*

As the `ErrorMessage`, `ErrorMessageResourceName`, and `ErrorMessageResourceType` properties are actually properties of the `ValidationAttribute` base class, they are available to all validation attributes and serve the same purpose in all of them. You'll recall that only the number of arguments supplied to create the complete error message will vary from one validation attribute type to another.

RangeAttribute

The RangeAttribute specifies the range constraints for the value of a field. There are three overloads of the RangeAttribute, and they commonly accept minimum and maximum values of the same type that are going to be compared.

Listing 13-17 shows an example of the RangeAttribute in use.

Listing 13-17. The Car Class Containing Properties Marked with the RangeAttribute

```
public class Car {

    public int Id { get; set; }

    [Required]
    [StringLength(maximumLength: 20)]
    public string Make { get; set; }

    [Required]
    [StringLength(maximumLength: 20)]
    public string Model { get; set; }

    public int Year { get; set; }

    [Range(minimum: 0F, maximum: 500000F)]
    public float Price { get; set; }
}
```

Here, the Price property is marked with the RangeAttribute, indicating that the value cannot be lower than 0 or higher than 500000. This is one of the overloads of the RangeAttribute, which accepts two Double-type parameters. Another one accepts Int32-type parameters for minimum and maximum values.

When a POST request against /api/cars containing an invalid value for the Price field according to our RangeAttribute is sent, a "400 Bad Request" response should come back, along with the message body displaying the validation error message (see Figure 13-16).

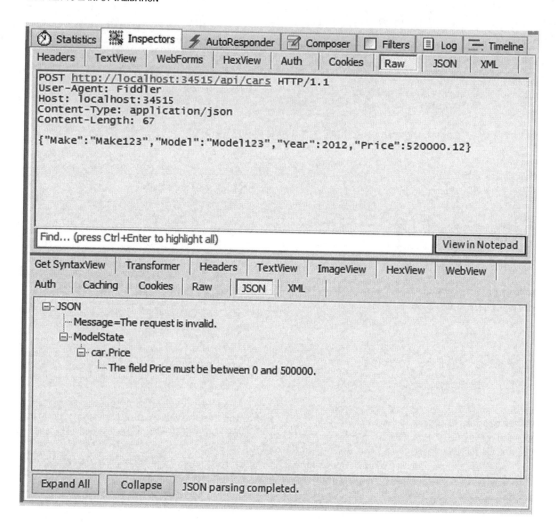

Figure 13-16. *Invalid POST request to /api/cars and a "400 Bad Request" response*

The RangeAttribute is applicable not only to Double and Int32 types. Any type that implements a System.IComparable interface can be used along with the RangeAttribute.

Listing 13-18 adds to Car class a new property, named PurchasedOn, which is of type DateTime. This property is also marked with RangeAttribute.

Listing 13-18. The Car Class Containing Properties Marked with RangeAttribute for a DateTime Field

```
public class Car {

    public int Id { get; set; }

    [Required]
    [StringLength(maximumLength: 20)]
    public string Make { get; set; }
```

```
[Required]
[StringLength(maximumLength: 20)]
public string Model { get; set; }

public int Year { get; set; }

[Range(minimum: OF, maximum: 500000F)]
public float Price { get; set; }

[Range(type: typeof(DateTime),
    minimum: "2010-01-01", maximum: "9999-12-31")]
public DateTime PurchasedOn { get; set; }
}
```

This overload of the RangeAttribute accepts three parameters. The first one is of the field type. The second and the third hold the minimum and maximum values. If the supplied value for the field is not within the specified range, a validation error message will be generated (see Figure 13-17).

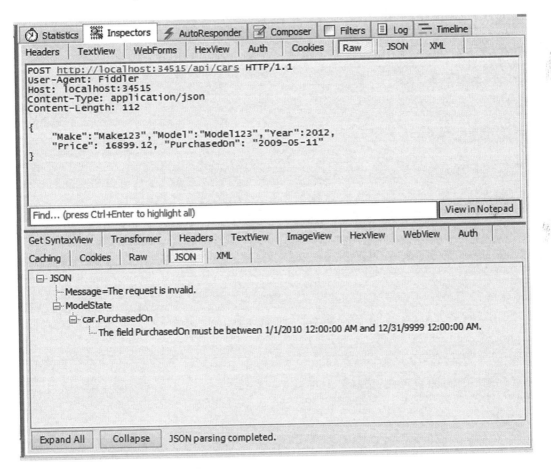

Figure 13-17. *Invalid POST request to /api/cars and a "400 Bad Request" response*

A DateTime type is used here to demonstrate this feature, but as was indicated before, you can use any type that implements the System.IComparable interface along with the RangeAttribute.

RegularExpressionAttribute

Sometimes a field value comes with specific and dynamic needs. In such cases, the built-in validation attributes are not going to work for those needs. One way to validate properties in those cases is to create a custom validation, which you will see in the "Custom Validation" section further along in this chapter. However, the .NET Framework provides a handy validation attribute for regular expressions.

The RegularExpressionAttribute provides a way to supply a regular expression so that a data field can validate according to that expression. Added to Listing 13-19 is a new property, ImageName, that indicates the image name for the Car entity. In accord with business logic, only file names that have a jpg, png, gif, or bmp extension are accepted. This property is marked with the RegularExpressionAttribute, by passing the regular expression for this logic.

Listing 13-19. The Car Class Containing a Property Marked with RegularExpressionAttribute

```
public class Car {

    public int Id { get; set; }

    [Required]
    [StringLength(20)]
    public string Make { get; set; }

    [Required]
    [StringLength(20)]
    public string Model { get; set; }

    public int Year { get; set; }

    [Range(0, 500000)]
    public float Price { get; set; }

    [RegularExpression("([^\\s]+(\\.(?i)(jpg|png|gif|bmp))$)")]
    public string ImageName { get; set; }
}
```

■ **Note** In a real-world scenario, this is not the best way to constrain the format of a file. This example has been chosen only as a sample-use case for the RegularExpressionAttribute.

Let's now send a POST request against /api/cars and use the "Make123.ico" value for the ImageName field. A "400 Bad Request" response should come back along with the validation error message (see Figure 13-18).

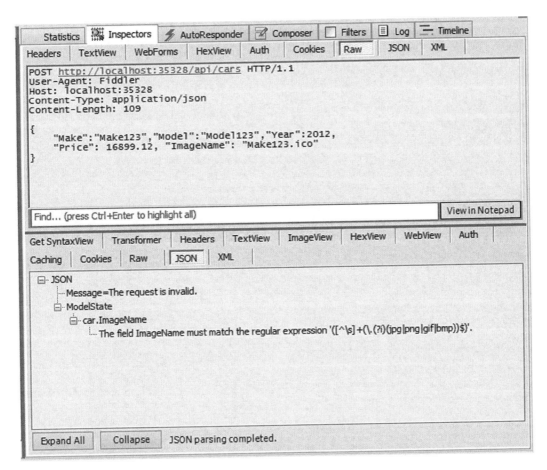

Figure 13-18. Invalid POST request to /api/cars and a "400 Bad Request" response

You can see that the regular expression is embedded in the error message. As was done in this chapter's "StringLengthAttribute" section, so too here it is probably better to customize the error message by making it friendlier.

If a POST request that meets our conditions is sent, there shouldn't be any validation issues, and a "201 Created" response should be returned (see Figure 13-19).

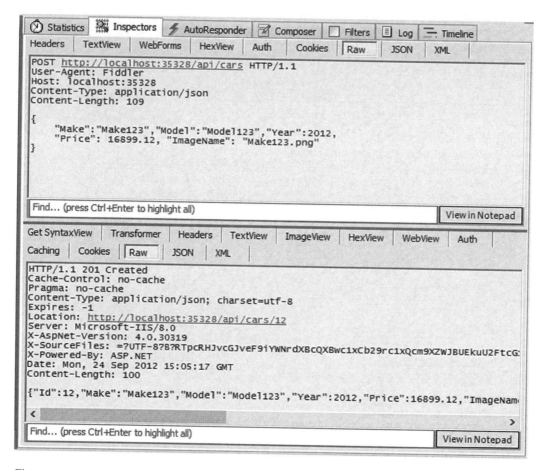

Figure 13-19. *Valid POST request to /api/cars and a "201 Created" response*

EmailAddressAttribute

The most common use case for the `RegularExpressionAttribute` is for validating an e-mail address format. Although this is not a strong validation of an e-mail address (i.e., as verifying its existence), the e-mail address format should be validated as early as possible.

The `EmailAddressAttribute` is one of the new validation attributes introduced with .NET Framework 4.5. Under the hood, this attribute uses a regular expression to validate an e-mail address, but it is abstracted away from the developer. Listing 13-20 shows the `Person` class, which has a property named `EmailAddress` and is marked with the `EmailAddressAttribute`.

Listing 13-20. The Person Class

```
public class Person {

    public int Id { get; set; }

    [Required]
    public string Name { get; set; }
```

```
    [Required]
    public string Surname { get; set; }

    [EmailAddress]
    public string EmailAddress { get; set; }
}
```

As has been done so far, InvalidModelStateFilterAttribute has again been registered. There is also a PeopleController this time (see Listing 13-21).

Listing 13-21. The PeopleController

```
[InvalidModelStateFilter]
public class PeopleController : ApiController {

    private readonly PeopleContext _peopleCtx = new PeopleContext();

    // GET /api/people
    public IEnumerable<Person> Get() {

        return _peopleCtx.All;
    }

    // POST /api/people
    public HttpResponseMessage PostPerson(Person person) {

        var createdPerson = _peopleCtx.Add(person);
        var response = Request.CreateResponse(HttpStatusCode.Created, createdPerson);
        response.Headers.Location = new Uri(
            Url.Link("DefaultHttpRoute", new { id = createdPerson.Id }));

        return response;
    }
}
```

The PeopleContext class here has the same implementation as the CarsContext class in Listing 13-6. When a GET request is sent to /api/people, the list of all existing people inside the collection is returned (see Figure 13-20).

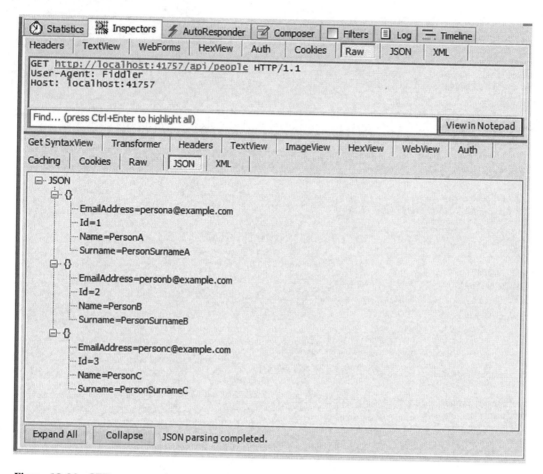

Figure 13-20. GET request to /api/people and a "200 OK" response along with the response body

Let's try to add a new Person entity to the collection by supplying an invalid e-mail address (see Figure 13-21).

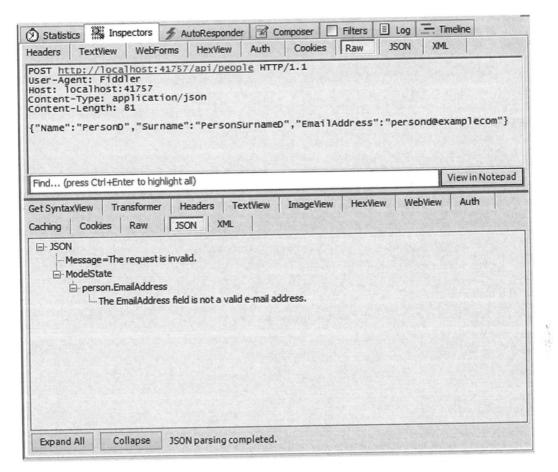

Figure 13-21. Invalid POST request to /api/people and a "400 Bad Request" response

Notice that the EmailAddress field value inside the request body doesn't contain a dot (.) before the com. This makes the value an invalid e-mail address. So a "400 Bad Request" came back along with the validation errors inside the response body. If a POST request is sent with a valid e-mail address, the entry should be created without any problem (see Figure 13-22).

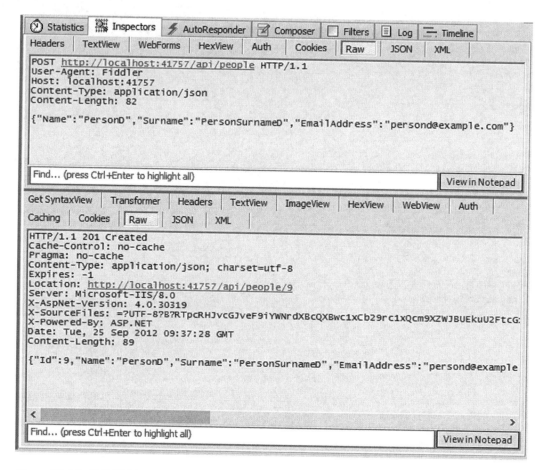

Figure 13-22. Valid POST request to /api/people and a "201 Created" response

MaxLengthAttribute and MinLengthAttribute

MaxLength and MinLength are individual validation attributes that have been introduced with .NET Framework 4.5. Respectively, they specify the maximum and the minimum length of an array or a data string that is allowed in a property. You will recall that there is already an attribute for validating the length of a string value. So for this function these attributes might have no appeal, but they really come in handy for constraining the length of an array field.

Listing 13-22 adds a string array property to the Car class we have been working with. That property represents the associated tags for the Car entity.

Listing 13-22. The Car Class

```
public class Car {

    public int Id { get; set; }

    [Required]
    [StringLength(20)]
    public string Make { get; set; }
```

```
[Required]
[StringLength(20)]
public string Model { get; set; }

public int Year { get; set; }

[Range(0, 500000)]
public float Price { get; set; }

[MinLength(1)]
[MaxLength(4)]
public string[] Tags { get; set; }
}
```

The Tags property has also been marked with two validation attributes: MinLength and MaxLength. These attributes specify that the minimum length allowed for this array is 1 and the maximum is 4.

When a GET request is sent to /api/cars, the cars list will come back along with the tags (see Figure 13-23).

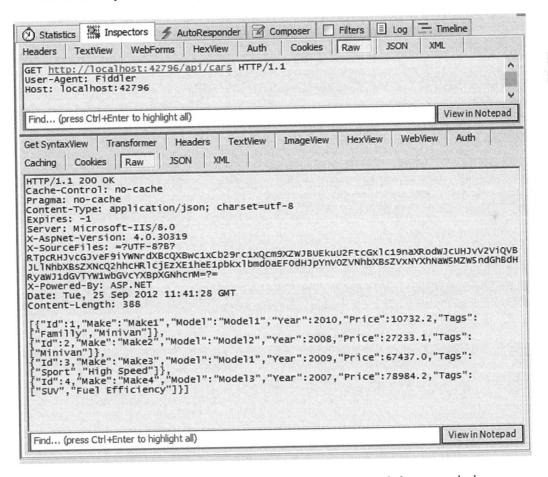

Figure 13-23. *GET request to /api/cars and a "200 OK" response along with the response body*

Let's now send a POST request to add a new Car entry containing no tag (see Figure 13-24).

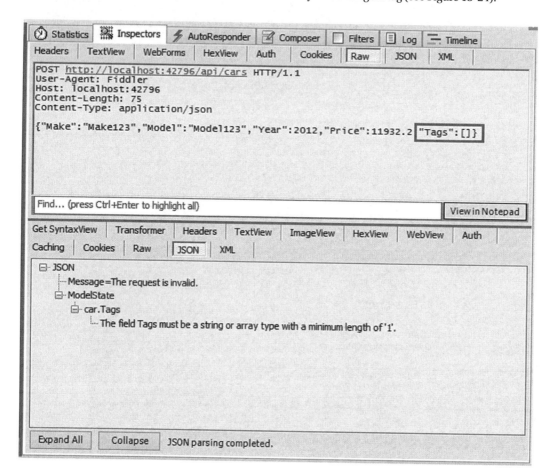

Figure 13-24. *Invalid POST request to /api/people and a "400 Bad Request" response*

As expected, MinLengthAttribute raised a validation error message because the minimum required tag length was set to 1. Let's now do the opposite: send a POST request to add a new Car entry containing five tags (see Figure 13-25).

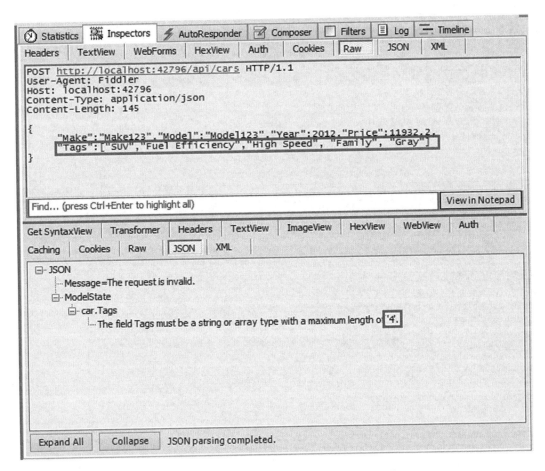

Figure 13-25. Invalid POST request to /api/people and a "400 Bad Request" response

This time, the MaxLengthAttribute complains because the maximum number of tags allowed is four (see Figure 13-26).

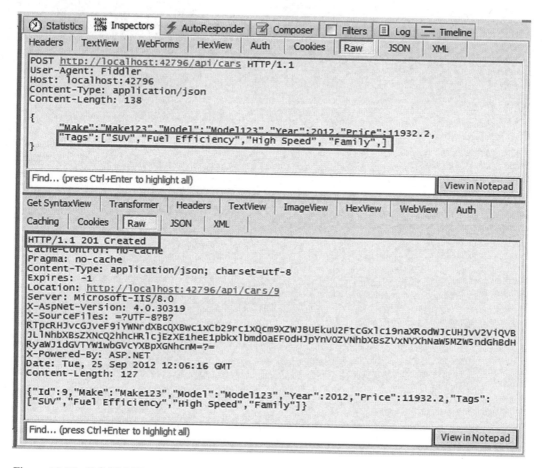

Figure 13-26. Valid POST request to /api/cars and a "201 Created" response

Custom Validation

.NET Framework provides a handful of validation attributes that are useful for most common use cases. Although these attributes will cover most needs, there will still be some custom validation needs. The existing validation system makes implementing your own custom validation logic elegant and fairly easy.

There are two ways of providing custom validation logic with this system. One is to create custom validation attributes, and the other is to implement the IValidatableObject interface. This section will look at these two options separately and offer examples for each.

Creating Custom Validation Attributes

At the beginning of the "Data Annotation Validation Attributes" section in this chapter, brief mention was made that all validation attributes are derived from the System.ComponentModel.DataAnnotations.ValidationAttribute abstract class. This class will be used as the base class for the custom validation attributes.

When you are working with the ValidationAttribute class, there are two methods you must override to perform the validation. One is the IsValid method that returns a Boolean value. The other is the IsValid method that returns a ValidationResult instance and accepts two parameters, one for the value of the object and one for the ValidationContext instance.

Another method generally used is the FormatErrorMessage method. It accepts a string parameter for the name of the field being validated and returns a string for the error message. This method is later called to format the error message.

The ValidationAttribute class also has three other methods, but they are not virtual methods (in other words, they cannot be overridden) and are called during the validation stage. Listing 13-23 shows all the methods that the ValidationAttribute abstract class holds.

Listing 13-23. Public Methods of the ValidationAttribute Class

```
public abstract class ValidationAttribute : Attribute {

    public virtual string FormatErrorMessage(string name);

    public ValidationResult GetValidationResult(
        object value, ValidationContext validationContext);

    public virtual bool IsValid(object value);

    protected virtual ValidationResult IsValid(
        object value, ValidationContext validationContext);

    public void Validate(object value, string name);

    public void Validate(
        object value, ValidationContext validationContext);
}
```

The ValidationAttribute properties carry the properties shown in Table 13-1. Only one of them, RequiresValidationContext, is virtual. RequiresValidationContext, a read-only, Boolean-type property, indicates whether the attribute requires a validation context, which gives a hint to validators that the object value alone is enough to validate or else that the ValidationContext is needed to perform the validation. The default value for this property is false.

Two other types—System.ComponentModel.DataAnnotations.ValidationContext and System.ComponentModel.DataAnnotations.ValidationResult—have been mentioned here. The ValidationContext class describes the context in which a validation check is performed and carries a lot of information necessary to perform the validation, including the type and the instance of the parent object. If you prefer to perform the validation by overriding the IsValid method that accepts a ValidationContext parameter, you will get access to all of this information. This method's return type is ValidationResult. ValidationResult is basically the carrier for the error message, which holds the message itself and the associated field names for the validation error message.

Let's create a custom validation attribute to get a better understanding of how it really works.

A Custom Validation Attribute Sample: GreaterThanAttribute

Some cases will require comparing two values, where one of them will be greater than the other. One canonical use case involves comparing the start date and end date for a particular instance. The end date always needs to be greater than the start date, and among the validation attributes that the .NET Framework offers, none performs such a validation. So this section will implement a general-purpose GreaterThanAttribute that works for all IComparable types.

Listing 13-24 shows the initial implementation of this GreaterThanAttribute.

Listing 13-24. Initial Implementation of the GreaterThanAttribute

```
[AttributeUsage(AttributeTargets.Property)]
public class GreaterThanAttribute : ValidationAttribute {

    public string OtherProperty { get; private set; }

    public override bool RequiresValidationContext {

        get {
            return true;
        }
    }

    public GreaterThanAttribute(string otherProperty) :
        base(errorMessage: "The {0} field must be greater than the {1} field.") {

        if (string.IsNullOrEmpty(otherProperty)) {

            throw new ArgumentNullException("otherProperty");
        }

        OtherProperty = otherProperty;
    }

    public override string FormatErrorMessage(string name) {

        return string.Format(
            CultureInfo.CurrentCulture,
            base.ErrorMessageString,
            name,
            OtherProperty);
    }

    protected override ValidationResult IsValid(
        object value, ValidationContext validationContext) {

        // Implementation comes here
    }
}
```

There are several things to note about this initial implementation.

- First of all, the GreaterThanAttribute is derived from the ValidationAttribute class. This is how our custom attribute will be recognized as a validation attribute.

- The RequiresValidationContext property has been overridden to return true because our validation logic requires the ValidationContext.

- A string property named OtherProperty has been added. It represents the name of the property that will be compared.

- Our single constructor has been set up. That constructor accepts a value for the OtherProperty string property. Also, the base keyword is set up to call the constructor of our base class to pass the error message structure.

- The FormatErrorMessage method to format the error message has been overridden. Notice that the ErrorMessageString property of the ValidationAttribute is used here because this property will ensure use of the right error message by inspecting any custom error message that is set or any resource key that is supplied.

Also overridden and left unimplemented is the IsValid method that returns ValidationResult. Listing 13-25 shows the implementation of the IsValid method.

Listing 13-25. Implementation of the IsValid Method

```
protected override ValidationResult IsValid(
    object value, ValidationContext validationContext) {

    IComparable firstValue = value as IComparable;
    IComparable secondValue = GetSecondValue(
        validationContext.ObjectType,
        validationContext.ObjectInstance);

    if (firstValue == null || secondValue == null) {

        throw new InvalidCastException(
            "The property types must implement System.IComparable");
    }

    if (firstValue.CompareTo(secondValue) < 1) {

        return new ValidationResult(
            this.FormatErrorMessage(
                validationContext.DisplayName));
    }

    return ValidationResult.Success;
}
```

The logic underlying this method is fairly simple. First of all, grab the values to be compared. Before performing the comparison, ensure that both objects implement the IComparable interface. Last, compare them. If the value that the validation attribute is applied to is not greater than the other, construct a new ValidationResult by passing the error message. If there are no validation issues, use the static Success field of the ValidationResult class to indicate that there are no errors. It also works if a null is returned (actually, that is basically what ValidationResult.Success is), but doing it as just described will make the code more readable.

Inside the IsValid method, a private method named GetSecondValue is used to get the value of the second instance. Listing 13-26 shows the implementation of the GetSecondValue method.

Listing 13-26. Implementation of the Private GetSecondValue Method

```
private IComparable GetSecondValue(Type type, object instance) {

    PropertyInfo propertyInfo =
        type.GetProperty(this.OtherProperty);

    if (propertyInfo == null) {

        throw new Exception(
            string.Format(
                "The property named {0} does not exist.",
                this.OtherProperty));
    }

    var value = propertyInfo.GetValue(instance, null);
    return value as IComparable;
}
```

To show the new custom method in action, two properties have been added to the Car class used so far. These properties will indicate the start and end dates of the sale for the particular Car, and the GreaterThanAttribute will be applied to the SalesEndsAt property (see Listing 13-27).

Listing 13-27. The Car Class

```
public class Car {

    public int Id { get; set; }

    [Required]
    public string Make { get; set; }

    [Required]
    public string Model { get; set; }

    public int Year { get; set; }

    public float Price { get; set; }

    public DateTime SalesStartsAt { get; set; }

    [GreaterThan("SalesStartsAt")]
    public DateTime SalesEndsAt { get; set; }
}
```

If a POST request is sent to /api/cars with a request body containing a Car entity along with invalid SalesStartsAt and SalesEndsAt properties, a "400 Bad Request" error will be returned (see Figure 13-27).

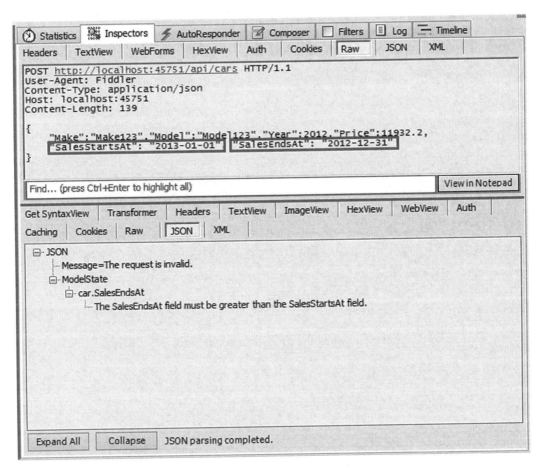

Figure 13-27. Invalid POST request to /api/people and a "400 Bad Request" response

If the request message body meets the set expectations, the request should go through, and a "201 Created" response will be returned (see Figure 13-28).

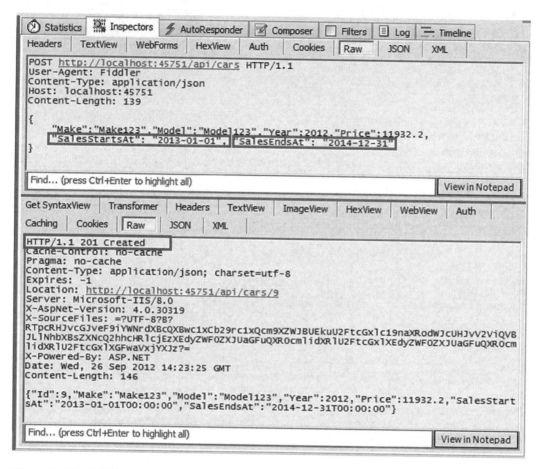

Figure 13-28. Valid POST request to /api/cars and a "201 Created" response

IValidatableObject Custom Validation

Sometimes you need a custom validation attribute, and you feel that the validation attribute to be implemented should be tightly coupled to a specific entity and not be used anywhere else. In such a case, the right solution is to implement the System.ComponentModel.DataAnnotations.IValidatableObject interface instead of providing a new validation attribute.

The IValidatableObject interface has only one method, named Validate, and its return type is IEnumerable<ValidationResult> (see Listing 13-28).

Listing 13-28. The IValidatableObject Interface

```
public interface IValidatableObject {

    IEnumerable<ValidationResult> Validate(ValidationContext validationContext);
}
```

ASP.NET Web API has built-in support for this validation type, and the Validate method will be called at the validation stage of the object. The Validate method accepts a parameter that is a type of ValidationContext.

As was seen earlier, this class carries all the necessary information for validating the object. Furthermore, inside the Validate method, the properties of the class can be directly accessed and validation performed according to them.

Let's assume that you won't accept any Car entities whose price is higher than 250000 and which was manufactured before 2010. This is a corner case issue, and if you try to solve this validation problem with a custom validation attribute, the attribute probably won't be used in any other place. Listing 13-29 shows a sample where the IValidatableObject interface is leveraged.

Listing 13-29. The Car Class Implementing the IValidatableObject

```
public class Car : IValidatableObject {

    public int Id { get; set; }

    [Required]
    public string Make { get; set; }

    [Required]
    public string Model { get; set; }

    public int Year { get; set; }

    public float Price { get; set; }

    public IEnumerable<ValidationResult> Validate(
        ValidationContext validationContext) {

        if (Year < 2010 && Price > 250000F) {

            yield return new ValidationResult(
                "The Price cannot be above 250000 if the Year value is lower than 2010.",
                new string[] { "Price" });
        }

        yield return ValidationResult.Success;
    }
}
```

In this implementation, the Validate method is no different from the IsValid method of the ValidateAttribute. As expected, if an invalid POST request is sent, the validation error should be as shown in Figure 13-29.

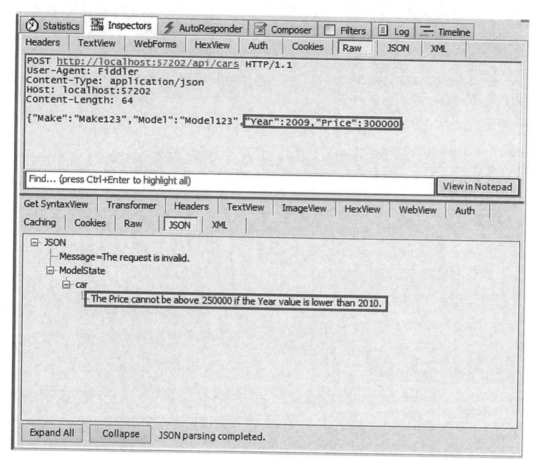

***Figure 13-29.** Invalid POST request to /api/people and a "400 Bad Request" response*

If the POST request is valid, there should be a "201 Created" response (see Figure 13-30).

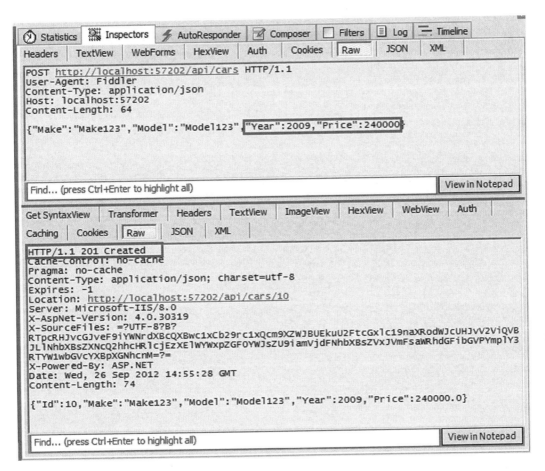

Figure 13-30. Valid POST request to /api/cars and a "201 Created" response

Summary

Input validation is a big deal for any application that requires user interaction with the back end. We developers tend to see every user input as evil and want to act on that input before processing it. ASP.NET Web API supports a great validation scenario out of the box. By embracing the .NET Data Annotation Validation, ASP.NET Web API already covers many validation cases, but it is also extremely easy to implement your own logic, as you have seen. On the other hand, validation components inside the framework are all pluggable, and you can extend the validation system of the framework by adding your own validation provider implementations or tweaking the existing ones.

Besides all of these great validation features and the system's extensible architecture, ASP.NET Web API also offers a very unobtrusive way of aggregating validation error messages inside the ModelStateDictionary. As this chapter has shown, you can return friendly validation error messages just by implementing a simple action filter.

CHAPTER 14

■ ■ ■

Dependency Resolution

Nowadays you could hardly find serious software that does not use one or another form of dependency injection. ASP.NET Web API has been built with this in mind, and in fact it uses a dependency resolution model similar to ASP.NET MVC to resolve its public dependencies. This model allows you to plug in your dependency injection framework of choice.

In this chapter we talk about dependency resolution and its model within ASP.NET Web API. Later on, we look into how to code against the ASP.NET Web API's dependency resolution model. At the end, we look into implementing dependency resolution model for popular dependency injection frameworks.

It is very likely that you have already used dependency injection (DI) in your projects and are familiar with it—and if you have not, no need to worry! After a brief introduction to DI and a few related terms, we move on to give you an understanding of how these concepts are used in ASP.NET Web API. Even if you have used DI before, this intro might still be useful, as there is a lot of confusion in the community as to exactly what each term means. However, if you think you have a good grasp of the concept, skip to the next topic, whose focus is ASP.NET Web API.

Key Inversion of Control Concepts

What is dependency injection (DI), and how is it different from Inversion of Control (IoC) or Service Location? Let's look briefly at these concepts.

Inversion of Control (IoC)

Inversion of Control (IoC), a computer science concept linked with Aspect Oriented Programming (AOP), is now mainly used in the context of dependency injection. However, what is Inversion of Control more generally?

Inversion of control is a general principle in software programming by which you change the flow of control in dependent components so that control of the dependencies is outside the dependent component rather than inside it. So if A is dependent on B, instead of A having full knowledge of B, you invert the control so that A has no knowledge of where B resides. This knowledge, which would sit inside an IoC container—in some ways similar to a repository—is responsible for providing dependencies based on the configuration defined by the application. Some frameworks also track the lifetime of the dependencies and manage the lifetime of dependencies they serve so that you do not have to.

Here's an example. Let's imagine you have just joined another development team, and the team is going out for lunch. You know neither the name or location of the restaurant nor the usual timing of the lunch (although you guess it is around midday!). So for lunch, you are fully dependent on the team. What would you do? Call up everyone, organize the lunch, and announce how you will get to the restaurant? Not at all! The team will tell you, "Don't worry, we will pick you up when we go there," because you are really the person least suited to organizing lunch. In the same way, a dependent component is the worst candidate to resolve its dependencies. Let's look at the patterns used for achieving IoC.

Dependency Injection

Dependency injection is a pattern (or a technique) to inject the dependencies of a software component into it. In line with the Single Responsibility principle (the first of five principles of software design usually referred to by the acronym **SOLID**), a software component (let's say a class) should not be worried about how to get hold of its dependencies to achieve its purpose since it will have too many responsibilities (resolving its dependencies as well as its main purpose). For example, a TaxCalculator class responsible for calculating the VAT (value-added tax) of a purchased item should not be responsible for reading the current value of the VAT percentage from the database (since to do so it would have to know the structure of the database, the technology to connect, etc.). Having to know so much would be having too many responsibilities. Instead it should depend on a TaxConfiguration class, which holds various tax rates. The former class uses the latter to get access to the current VAT rate.

■ **Note**   SOLID is the acronym for a set of five principles in software design presented by Robert C Martin (a.k.a Uncle Bob) in a paper in 1997. Its letters stand for **S**ingle responsibility, **O**pen-closed, **L**iskov substitution, **I**nterface segregation, and **D**ependency inversion. Along with DRY (**D**o not **R**epeat **Y**ourself) and YAGNI (**Y**ou **A**in't **G**onna **N**eed **I**t), the SOLID principles are some of the patterns and best practices software developers consider and go back to on a daily basis. If they are not familiar to you, time invested in fully understanding them is definitely time well spent.

Another aspect of the DI (the **D** in **SOLID**) is to design the types in a way that they depend on abstraction rather than concrete implementation. We normally design classes to depend on interfaces (or abstract classes) rather than actual implementation. This approach is extremely valuable in unit testing, as we can use mock (or stub) objects of the type being tested so that their behavior can be independently tested without the need to test in a real working environment.

There are two DI mechanisms available for classes: property injection and constructor injection. Property injection, the older approach, involves defining public properties of the abstract dependencies on the type. For example:

```
// a tax calculator implementing ITaxCalculator
// using property injection
public class TaxCalculator : ITaxCalculator
{
    public ITaxConfiguration Configuration {get; set;}

    // ... rest of the implementation
}
```

Here ITaxConfiguration is a service in DI terms since it requires resolving (note that ITaxCalculator can also be a service for other types).

There are several problems with this approach, one of which is that the property injection usually fails silently if it cannot find a matching type. You get null reference errors as soon as you want to use the dependency (as you know, null reference exceptions are hard to debug). Another problem is that these properties normally need to be defined as public read/write, which is not ideal.

A better (and currently standard) approach is to use constructor injection:

```
// a tax calculator implementing ITaxCalculator
// using constructor injection
public class TaxCalculator : ITaxCalculator
```

```
{
    private readonly ITaxConfiguration _configuration;

    public TaxCalculator(ITaxConfiguration configuration)
    {
        _configuration = configuration;
    }

    // ... rest of the implementation
}
```

Regardless of property injection or constructor injection, the job of resolving dependencies is with the IoC containers. An IoC container must have knowledge of how to resolve each dependency. There are many DI frameworks (providing IoC containers) to choose from—Castle Windsor, AutoFac, NInject, Unity—as well as other frameworks, such as StructureMap and Spring.NET and even Microsoft Extensibility Framework (MEF), which can be used for dependency injection. The first four are the most popular frameworks, and the coming sections review their use in ASP.NET Web API.

In dependency injection, you create the container and register the types against it. Then the dependencies are automatically resolved at the time of object creation. In the past registration was done through configuration files, but most recent frameworks provide fluent API.

Normally, registering "services" in the IoC container requires registering the abstract type against the container along with its concrete implementation. For example:

```
// registering ITaxCalculator in AutoFac
var builder = new ContainerBuilder();
builder.RegisterType<TaxCalculator>().As<ITaxCalculator>();
var container = builder.Build(); // 2-stage DI exclusive to AutoFac
```

The container object, which is the result of the Build() method, is the IoC container. In DI, the container is not directly used to resolve dependencies.

Service Locator

The Service Locator pattern is another pattern to achieve IoC. Unlike DI, where the components are oblivious of their construction and dependency resolution, in the Service Locator pattern, they proactively use the IoC container to resolve their dependencies. For example, we can use the container created above to resolve ITaxCalculator:

```
// Service Locator pattern in AutoFac
var taxCalculator = container.Resolve<ITaxCalculator>();
```

The Service Locator pattern is simple to understand but is generally considered inferior to dependency injection. First, it adds a new dependency to all classes: knowledge of the container. Another problem is that while IoC containers are responsible for resolving and possibly creating instance of services, they either track them and are responsible for their disposal (as in Castle Windsor) or provide a transient scope (in other assemblies) so that they are disposed of after use. This cannot happen in the Service Locator pattern unless each class becomes responsible for cleaning up its mess—if this is forgotten, bugs and memory leaks can result.

Having said that, each pattern has its own place, and each can be useful. As you will see, ASP.NET Web API uses the Service Locator pattern while allowing you to use the DI framework of your choice.

Factory Pattern

Another IoC technique is the Factory pattern. In this pattern, instead of taking dependency on the service itself, you take dependency on the Factory that can create the service. Factory generally is another type—or sometimes a Func<> in functional programming—that can create the service. IoC containers themselves are generally considered factories.

The Factory pattern is useful when you have to provide parameters to control various aspects of the object being returned from the factory. Factories are used heavily in ASP.NET Web API and ASP.NET MVC. Every class named with the postfix provider (such as ModelBinderProvider) is a factory.

Registration and Lifetime Scope in Dependency Injection

When registering services against the IoC container, you can register a type (which implements the abstract service), a factory to generate your service, or an instance.

If you register an instance, the instance is provided every time you resolve the service against the container. The instance as such can be seen as a singleton. This is an important concept, since ASP.NET Web API commonly uses this approach.

If you register a concrete type against your service, you normally get to choose a lifetime policy for instances of that service when they are resolved. Many DI frameworks provide different lifetime policies: transient, singleton, per HTTP request, and others. In a transient lifetime policy, you always get a new object from the IoC container. In a per-HTTP-request policy, you have one object per registration for the lifetime of the HTTP request. With a singleton policy, as the name implies, you always get the same object back for a given registration.

Service Location in ASP.NET Web API

ASP.NET Web API registers its services in its own container. It uses the Service Locator pattern to resolve these dependencies when it needs them. By using the container provided by the framework, you can change the default registration and register your own types.

Let's look at an example that will whet your appetite. Many services defined in the library can be replaced (we look at them later in the chapter), but now let's look at ITraceWriter, which is responsible for tracing (covered in Chapter 16). Imagine that we have written a trace writer called MyOwnTraceWriter and we need to replace the default trace writer with our own.

```
// assuming a web hosted service
var config = GlobalConfiguration.Configuration;
config.Services.Replace(typeof(ITraceWriter), new MyOwnTraceWriter()); // note that we registered an
instance against the dependency Resolver
```

Here we are replacing the registered ITraceWriter with our own instance of MyOwnTraceWriter. If you have enabled tracing in your ASP.NET Web API, it will use the type you provide.

The Services property, which sits on the HttpConfiguration class, is of the type ServicesContainer, and it can be looked at as a custom IoC container that implements the Service Locator pattern. Since we register the instance against the type, the registration will be singleton. To better understand these concepts, you'll need to take a closer look at ServicesContainer class.

This class is a special IoC container registration that you can use to register singleton instances against service types. Also, you may register more than one instance against a single service type. For example, for ModelBinderProvider, a number of ModelBinderProvider instances are registered, including instances of TypeConverterModelBinderProvider and TypeMatchModelBinderProvider.

Remember that this class is mainly designed to resolve dependencies of the framework itself. Registering a custom service against this class will not work.

```
// this will raise an error
config.Services.Add(typeof(ITaxCalculator), new TaxCalculator); // exception!
```

Table 14-1. *Important Services Registered in ServicesContainer Class*

Service Type	Description
IActionValueBinder	binds parameters of an action
IapiExplorer	responsible for gathering information about the API
IContentNegotiator	carries out content negotiation in the HTTP pipeline
ItraceWriter	responsible for outputting trace in the framework
IHttpControllerSelector	finds and selects the controller responsible for a request
IHttpControllerActivator	creates/activates an instance of the selected controller
IHttpActionSelector	selects the action responsible for serving the request
IHttpActionInvoker	invokes the selected action

The ability to replace default implementations provided by the framework is very powerful. For example, you would probably remember that IControllerActivator in ASP.NET MVC was important and could be replaced to hook in your dependency injection framework of choice. In the same fashion, IHttpControllerActivator is responsible for creating (or simply activating) the controller selected by the IHttpControllerSelector. However, ASP.NET Web API provides an easier means to hook in your dependency injection framework.

Dependency Resolution Model in ASP.NET Web API

ASP.NET Web API uses a service location pattern to resolve its public dependencies. The approach is very similar to the DependencyResolver model that has been part of ASP.NET MVC since version 3. However, the ASP.NET team has improved this approach for Web API, especially in terms of lifetime management. This section reviews the dependency resolution model in ASP.NET Web API.

A Typical Dependency Resolution Scenario

Let's say you use dependency injection in your project and use constructor injection for your classes. How does each relate to your ASP.NET Web API? Let's look at the controller below:

```
public class TaxController : ApiController
{
    private readonly ITaxCalculator _taxCalculator;

    public TaxController(ITaxCalculator taxCalculator)
    {
        _taxCalculator = taxCalculator;
    }
}
```

Your controller has a dependency to the ITaxCalculator, and you are relying on your DI framework to inject an instance of the concrete class that has been set up against ITaxCalculator to be passed to the constructor when ASP.NET Web API creates an instance of your controller. But if IHttpControllerActivator creates your controller, how would it know about your DI framework, and thus how could it use the framework to create an instance of your controller? This is where the DependencyResolver model comes into play.

HttpConfiguration class exposes the read/write property DependencyResolver, which is used to hook in the DI framework. This property is of the type IDependencyResolver, which means in order to plug in the DI frameworks, this interface needs to be implemented by you or the library provider. As you will see, there are already implementations available for all major DI libraries.

The IDependencyResolver interface itself is very simple:

```
public interface IDependencyResolver : IDependencyScope
{
    IDependencyScope BeginScope();
}
```

That is, IDependencyResolver implements IDependencyScope, which is itself simply a Service Locator interface:

```
public interface IDependencyScope : IDisposable
{
    object GetService(Type serviceType);
    IEnumerable<object> GetServices(Type serviceType);
}
```

So starting with IDependencyScope, you see that it contains two methods: one for resolving a single service and a second for resolving all services implementing a type. The latter is particularly important when using the strategy or visitor pattern.

To return to our TaxController example, DefaultHttpControllerActivator (which implements IHttpControllerActivator and is the default activator set up to create instances of your controllers) uses the dependency scope and calls the GetService method. If your DI Framework is hooked up, this will go to your IoC container, and all your types will have automatic resolution.

Depending on the case, internal implementation of ASP.NET Web API knows whether it needs to resolve a single service or multiple services and so calls either GetService() or GetServices(), respectively.

Look very closely at the IDependencyScope, and you will notice that it also implements IDisposable. To understand the disposal side of the dependency scope, you need to take a deeper look into the lifetime scope of the dependency scope.

Understanding the Lifetime of the IDependencyResolver and IDependencyScope

If you have used DI frameworks before, you are probably aware that the IoC container's lifetime normally is the same as that of the application AppDomain. In other words, you normally create the IoC container when the application is started and dispose of it only at the time the application is closed. Thus, you can think of it as singleton.

```
// configuration is an instance of HttpConfiguration class
Configuration.DependencyResolver = new MyCustomDependencyResolver(); // assuming
MyCustomDependencyResolver is an implementation of IDependencyResolver
```

So the IDependencyResolver interface is analogous to your IoC container: it is set once as a singleton on the HttpConfiguration (which itself can be thought of as a singleton, as you have one configuration for each ASP.NET Web API application) and used throughout the application. As you have already seen, IDependencyResolver implements IDisposable (indirectly through implementing IDependencyScope). The Dispose method on the dependency resolver is called only at the end of the application—that is, when AppDomain is being unloaded.

■ **Note**   If you have followed the ASP.NET Web API development since its early beta, you probably remember that the design of the DependencyResolver model underwent a few major changes. It initially used reflection to figure out the methods implementing GetService() and GetServices(). Also there was no BeginScope()—this was added later to complete the picture of creation and disposal of dependencies.

The lifetime of IDependencyScope, however, is the same as that of each request. At the start of each request, ASP.NET Web API calls BeginScope() method on the IDependencyResolver to create an instance of IDependencyScope (its implementation, rather) for the lifetime of the request. This dependency scope is responsible for keeping track of the dependencies resolved for the lifetime of the request and dispose of them when the request is disposed of. So the relationship between IDependencyScope and the request is one to one. Bear in mind that what we mean here by disposing of dependencies is not necessarily calling Dispose() on the objects implementing IDisposable. Some DI frameworks (Castle Windsor among them) keep track of objects created, so they need to know when to release them.

IDependencyScope and HttpRequestMessage

As already said, HttpRequestMessage and IDependencyScope have a one-to-one relationship. In fact, you can access an IDependencyScope instance for an HttpRequestMessage via its properties:

```
var dependencyScope = (IDependencyScope)
            request.Properties[HttpPropertyKeys.DependencyScope];
```

You can also use the extension GetDependencyScope() to achieve the same result, although calling this extension method gets hold of an IDependencyScope by calling BeginScope() if it is not already in the properties:

```
var dependencyScope = request.GetDependencyScope();
```

ASP.NET Web API breaks the long tradition (a pretty bad one) of storing the context in the HttpContext.Current. Instead, it stores its context directly inside the properties of the request. This is essential, since the HttpContext in some cases does not flow to other threads when a thread switch happens. Thread switching most commonly happens when using the Async model (explained in Chapter 2). When the context is stored in the properties of the request, it does not matter which thread processes the request. HttpContext.Current uses a thread's local storage area to store the context, while Properties is a plain (but thread-safe) dictionary for storing context.

As soon as an IDependencyScope is associated with an HttpRequestMessage, it is registered by the ASP.NET Web API for disposal. This is achieved using the RegisterForDispose() extension of the HttpRequestMessage. This in turn adds the IDependencyScope to a list stored in the Properties property of the request, later to be looped through, and Dispose() is called upon each object.

Using DependencyResolver Implementations Available for ASP.NET Web API

The ASP.NET Web API DependencyResolver model for common DI frameworks is implemented in the WebApiContrib project (available at GitHub, http://webapicontrib.github.io/), as well as other independent projects. NuGet packages are available that make the process of adding these libraries easier. Visit https://github.com/WebApiContrib to see the list of all projects.

For example, to add NInject DependencyResolver, type this command in the Package Manager console:

```
PM> Install-Package WebApiContrib.IoC.Ninject
```

This command will add the NInject library, as well as the DependencyResolver implementation. The next step is to create a NInject Kernel and use it to instantiate a NInject dependency resolver and set the DependencyResolver property against your configuration to your resolver instance:

```
var kernel = new StandardKernel();
// use kernel to register your dependencies
var dependencyResolver = new NInjectResolver(kernel);
config.DependencyResolver = dependencyResolver; // config is an instance of HttpConfiguration based
on your hosting scenario
```

For other DI frameworks the approach is very similar. To see the full list of available NuGet packages, search for WebApiContrib.IoC in the NuGet gallery.

Implementing DependencyResolver Model in DI Frameworks

Now we look into implementing the DependencyResolver model for some of the popular dependency injection frameworks. The reason you might want to look into implementing the DependencyResolver model yourself is that you might have a custom DI framework or a special requirement or limitation—or you might just be interested in knowing details of the interoperability of DI frameworks with the ASP.NET Web API. Implementation normally results in two classes, one implementing IDependencyResolver and the other IDependencyScope.

Implementing DependencyResolver for AutoFac

Implementing DependencyResolver model in the AutoFac framework is pretty straightforward. AutoFac has a concept of a LifetimeScope that fits the ASP.NET Web API's DependencyResolver model very well. Listing 14-1 shows this very concept used to implement IDependencyScope. This class expects ILifetimeScope as a constructor parameter.

Listing 14-1. Using LifetimeScope to Implement IDependencyScope

```
public class AutoFacDependencyScope : IDependencyScope
{
    private readonly ILifetimeScope _lifetimeScope;

    public AutoFacDependencyScope(ILifetimeScope lifetimeScope)
    {
        _lifetimeScope = lifetimeScope;
    }
```

```
    public void Dispose()
    {
        _lifetimeScope.Dispose();
    }

    public object GetService(Type serviceType)
    {
        object instance = null;
        _lifetimeScope.TryResolve(serviceType, out instance);
        return instance;
    }

    public IEnumerable<object> GetServices(Type serviceType)
    {
        object instance = null;
        var ienumerableType = typeof(IEnumerable<>).MakeGenericType(serviceType);
        _lifetimeScope.TryResolve(ienumerableType, out instance);
        return (IEnumerable<object>)instance;
    }
}
```

One thing to note is how AutoFac resolves multiple services. You need to ask for IEnumerable<> of the type you are interested in. Listing 14-1 made use of the MakeGenericType() method.

■ **Note**   Please note that when resolving dependencies, null should be returned if the container cannot resolve the dependency. The default behavior in most containers is to throw an exception that should be handled by returning null. The reason is that ASP.NET Web API initially uses DependencyResolver to resolve the dependency. If null is returned, it uses other methods to resolve the dependency. Throwing an exception breaks the work flow.

Listing 14-2 shows the implementation of the IDependencyResolver. In BeginScope() it calls BeginLifetimeScope() to create an ILifetimeScope.

Listing 14-2. Implementing the Dependency Resolver for AutoFac

```
public class AutoFacDependencyResolver : IDependencyResolver
{
    private readonly IContainer _container;

    public AutoFacDependencyResolver(IContainer container)
    {
        _container = container;
    }

    public void Dispose()
    {
        _container.Dispose();
    }
```

```
    public object GetService(Type serviceType)
    {
        object instance = null;
        _container.TryResolve(serviceType, out instance);
        return instance;
    }

    public IEnumerable<object> GetServices(Type serviceType)
    {
        object instance = null;
        var ienumerableType = typeof (IEnumerable<>).MakeGenericType(serviceType);
        _container.TryResolve(ienumerableType, out instance);
        return (IEnumerable<object>) instance;
    }

    public IDependencyScope BeginScope()
    {
        return new AutoFacDependencyScope(_container.BeginLifetimeScope());
    }
}
```

In order to use the AutoFacDependencyResolver with our Web API project, all we have to do is set it to the DependencyResolver property of the configuration, as shown in Listing 14-3 (normally in Application_Start of the global.asax).

Listing 14-3. Registering the AutoFac Dependency Resolver

```
var containerBuilder = new ContainerBuilder();
containerBuilder
    .RegisterType<TaxCalculator>()
    .As<ITaxCalculator>()
    .InstancePerLifetimeScope();

containerBuilder
    .RegisterType<ValuesController>()
    .As<ValuesController>();

GlobalConfiguration.Configuration.DependencyResolver =
    new AutoFacDependencyResolver(containerBuilder.Build());
```

Implementing DependencyResolver for Castle Windsor

Compared with other DI frameworks, Castle Windsor is unique. It differs from all others on a few levels. So if you decide to use it for your project and have used other frameworks, there are a few points to bear in mind.

First of all, it is the only framework that fully tracks your objects by default. If you are not careful, this can lead to memory leaks, and so it provides performance counters to help you identify such possibilities.

Because of the tracking, it also includes a concept that lets it release an object as well as resolve it. This is particularly useful if you have dependencies that implement IDisposable interface—for example, WCF client proxies. The Windsor container disposes of all disposable dependencies.

Another difference in the Castle Windsor framework is that by default, the lifetime of the registered components is singleton. Other frameworks have a default of transient. Yet another important matter is that the concept of a child container is completely different. In most other frameworks, a child container is one that has a shorter life span compared with the root container. In Castle Windsor, the child container does not display the same behavior, and so it is generally recommended not to be used.

In order to ensure that tracked components are released, we use a different technique: we keep track of the resolved dependencies and ask the container to release them at the time of disposing of the scope (see Listing 14-4).

Listing 14-4. Implementing the Dependency Scope for Castle Windsor

```
public class WindsorDependencyScope : IDependencyScope
{

    protected readonly IWindsorContainer _container;
    private ConcurrentBag<object> _toBeReleased = new ConcurrentBag<object>();

    public WindsorDependencyScope(IWindsorContainer container)
    {
        _container = container;
    }

    public void Dispose()
    {
        if (_toBeReleased != null)
        {
            foreach (var o in _toBeReleased)
            {
                _container.Release(o);
            }
        }
        _toBeReleased = null;
    }

    public object GetService(Type serviceType)
    {
        if (!_container.Kernel.HasComponent(serviceType))
            return null;

        var resolved = _container.Resolve(serviceType);
        if (resolved != null)
            _toBeReleased.Add(resolved);
        return resolved;

    }

    public IEnumerable<object> GetServices(Type serviceType)
    {
        if (!_container.Kernel.HasComponent(serviceType))
            return new object[0];

        var allResolved = _container.ResolveAll(serviceType).Cast<object>();
        if (allResolved != null)
```

```
        {
            allResolved.ToList()
                .ForEach(x => _toBeReleased.Add(x));
        }
        return allResolved;

    }
}
```

As Listing 14-4 shows, we make sure the container contains the dependency before trying to resolve it to avoid throwing an exception. On the other hand, we use a thread-safe bag (an instance of ConcurrentBag<T>) to keep track of resolved dependencies and release them at the end.

The WindsorDependencyResolver is simpler, as Listing 14-5 illustrates.

Listing 14-5. Implementing the Dependency Resolver for Castle Windsor

```
public class WindsorDependencyResolver : IDependencyResolver
{
    private readonly IWindsorContainer _container;

    public WindsorDependencyResolver(IWindsorContainer container)
    {
        _container = container;
    }

    public IDependencyScope BeginScope()
    {
        return new WindsorDependencyScope(_container);
    }

    public void Dispose()
    {
        _container.Dispose();
    }

    public object GetService(Type serviceType)
    {
        if (!_container.Kernel.HasComponent(serviceType))
            return null;

        return _container.Resolve(serviceType);
    }

    public IEnumerable<object> GetServices(Type serviceType)
    {
        if (!_container.Kernel.HasComponent(serviceType))
            return new object[0];

        return _container.ResolveAll(serviceType).Cast<object>();
    }
}
```

As you see, we have not used the child container. As we said earlier, the Castle Windsor library by default keeps track of the dependencies resolved, and if care isn't taken, this can lead to memory leaks, since the container will hang on to the resolved container until `Release()` gets called on the container.

Starting with version 3 of this library, a performance counter has been provided by the library to keep track of the unreleased components. This can be really handy to verify your implementation and make sure all is well and all tracked dependencies get released.

This performance counter is called "Instances tracked by the release policy". You find it under the "Castle Windsor" category. This is not on by default, so you need some code to enable it:

```
var counter = LifecycledComponentsReleasePolicy.GetTrackedComponentsPerformanceCounter(
    new PerformanceMetricsFactory());
var diagnostic =
    LifecycledComponentsReleasePolicy.GetTrackedComponentsDiagnostic(container.Kernel);
container.Kernel.ReleasePolicy = new LifecycledComponentsReleasePolicy(diagnostic, counter);
```

Once the counter can be published, you need to run the Windows Performance Monitoring tool (`perfmon.exe`) and add the counter underneath the Castle Windsor category for your ASP.NET Web API host, as Figure 14-1 shows.

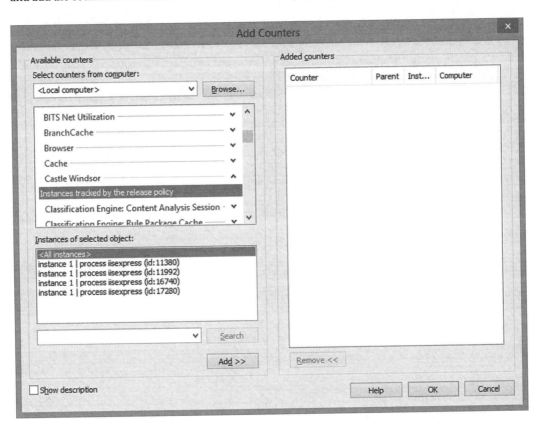

Figure 14-1. *Selecting the Castle Windsor performance counter in the Add Counter dialog*

From the list of instances, select the process running your application, and click Add. Then press OK to close the dialog. After running your application and hitting your endpoint, you must see the counter value (see Figure 14-2).

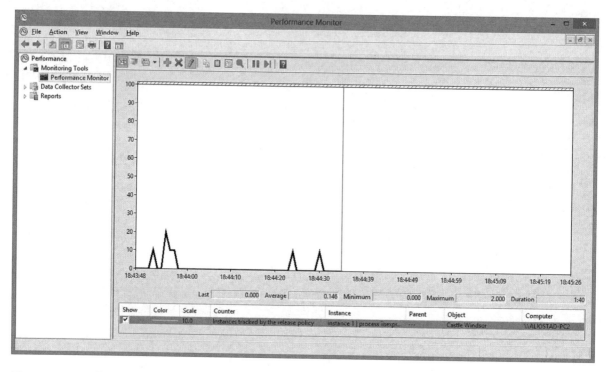

Figure 14-2. *The Castle Windsor counter showing dependencies being released*

As Figure 14-2 shows, there are occasional spikes of tracked dependencies, but the counter always returns to the baseline of 0. In other words, all tracked dependencies are released—and that is good news! There is more information on the library at the project's website, and the library's documentation is at http://docs.castleproject.org/Windsor.MainPage.ashx.

Implementing DependencyResolver for Unity

Unity, Microsoft's own DI framework, is lightweight but contains some of the advanced features of other frameworks. In Unity you can use the concept of the child container to implement lifetime scope, as Listing 14-6 shows.

Listing 14-6. Implementing the Dependency Scope for Unity

```
public class UnityDependencyScope : IDependencyScope
{
    protected readonly IUnityContainer _container;

    public UnityDependencyScope(IUnityContainer container)
    {
        _container = container;
    }

    public void Dispose()
    {
        _container.Dispose();
    }
```

```
    public object GetService(Type serviceType)
    {
        return _container.IsRegistered(serviceType) ?
            _container.Resolve(serviceType) :
            null;
    }

    public IEnumerable<object> GetServices(Type serviceType)
    {
        return _container.IsRegistered(serviceType) ?
            _container.ResolveAll(serviceType) :
            new object[0];
    }
}
```

Creating the dependency resolver is also straightforward. Just create a child container and return (see Listing 14-7).

Listing 14-7. Implementing the Dependency Resolver for Unity by Inheritance

```
public class UnityDependencyResolver : UnityDependencyScope, IDependencyResolver
{
    public UnityDependencyResolver(IUnityContainer container) : base(container)
    {
    }

    public IDependencyScope BeginScope()
    {
        return new UnityDependencyScope(_container.CreateChildContainer());
    }
}
```

Inheriting from the UnityDependencyScope helps to reuse much of the code you have.

Implementing DependencyResolver for NInject

Last but not least, we look into NInject. If you have read the previous codes, you probably have got the hang of implementing the DependencyResolver model. As with other frameworks, you need to start by implementing the dependency scope. Listing 14-8 shows how to take advantage of the fact that NInject always returns all resolvable types.

Listing 14-8. Implementing the Dependency Scope for NInject

```
public class NInjectDependencyScope : IDependencyScope
{
    private IResolutionRoot _resolutionRoot;

    public NInjectDependencyScope(IResolutionRoot resolutionRoot)
    {
        _resolutionRoot = resolutionRoot;
    }
```

```
    public void Dispose()
    {
        var disposable = _resolutionRoot as IDisposable;
        if(disposable!=null)
            disposable.Dispose();
        _resolutionRoot = null;
    }

    public object GetService(Type serviceType)
    {
        return GetServices(serviceType).FirstOrDefault();
    }

    public IEnumerable<object> GetServices(Type serviceType)
    {
        var request = _resolutionRoot.CreateRequest(serviceType, null,new IParameter[0], true,
true);
        return _resolutionRoot.Resolve(request);
    }
}
```

Listing 14-9 uses the BeginBlock() to create a block analogous to the child container in Unity.

Listing 14-9. Implementing the Dependency Resolver for Ninject Using Inheritance

```
public class NInjectDependencyResolver : NInjectDependencyScope, IDependencyResolver
{
    private IKernel _kernel;

    public NInjectDependencyResolver(IKernel kernel) : base(kernel)
    {
        _kernel = kernel;
    }

    public IDependencyScope BeginScope()
    {
        return new NInjectDependencyScope(_kernel.BeginBlock());
    }
}
```

Summary

In the journey we took in this chapter, you briefly got to see the difference between Inversion of Control (IoC), dependency injection (DI), and the Service Locator and Factory patterns. You also got to see how they are related.

You then looked at how these concepts and techniques are used in ASP.NET Web API and learned that it uses the Service Locator pattern to resolve dependencies. Then the DependencyResolver model and its two main interfaces, IDependencyScope and IDependencyResolver, were explored.

At the end, you were shown how to use existing libraries built on top of the ASP.NET Web API DependencyResolver model. Finally, this model was implemented for several popular frameworks: AutoFac, Castle Windsor, Unity, and NInject.

CHAPTER 15

■ ■ ■

Unit Testing and Integration Testing

It is very likely you have already written unit tests for your projects and thus are familiar with the concepts, frameworks, and steps involved in writing unit tests. This chapter therefore mainly deals with how to apply those skills to the effective writing of unit tests for your Web API. As you will see, unit testing is where you start, not where you finish.

As you know, industry is undergoing immense change at the moment. On one hand, Service Oriented Architecture (SOA) has resulted in big enterprise applications being broken into multiple independent or semi-independent services. On the other hand, recent trends in adoption of REST have led the API of those services to move from heavy, ceremony-rich SOAP toward lightweight HTTP APIs. That is, everyday more and more APIs are being built or are migrating to pure HTTP APIs, commonly referred to as RESTful (although not every HTTP API is actually RESTful, as you have already seen). Another side of the story is that the DevOps movement and adoption of automated deployment not only encourages automated integration tests but mandates it for its success. Many companies deploy new software into their production daily or even multiple times a day.

What does this mean for us? First of all, it means that while we will carry on writing unit tests for our API projects, we also need to cover our APIs with automated integration tests.

On the other hand, testing an HTTP endpoint poses new challenges. In SOAP, you could reduce the call to a remote procedure call (RPC), so that your test consisted of ensuring that the right output was returned for your inputs—although you still had to cover various aspects of SOAP headers. However, the behavior of an HTTP API is much richer. For example, an HTTP API implements content negotiation, which allows multiple formats to be returned per a client's request and preference. So not just the data but also the format needs to be tested when the data cross the wire. Other aspects include HTTP caching behavior, which can be complex to test.

This chapter looks at a few key concepts of testing and then moves to applying them in ASP.NET Web API.

Unit Testing in ASP.NET Web API

In unit testing, you test a unit of code. A unit of code usually maps to a method in a class. If you follow the single responsibility principle (the S in SOLID), your classes will have a single reason to change. So testing them will be easy, and you will have only a few tests per class.

In ASP.NET Web API, the main classes you will be writing are controllers and models. We focus on these classes first, and then move to handlers and filters.

Testing Frameworks

You could call the last few years the boom years of testing frameworks. Initially there was only NUnit, but gradually more and more frameworks came out. These include BDD frameworks, such as SpecFlow and SubSpec (we look at these in the section of this chapter called "Integration Testing and BDD"). At the end of the day, all of these frameworks help you define Arrange-Act-Assert within your unit tests and execute your tests interactively within Visual Studio as well as in your continuous integration environment.

> ■ **Note** Test-driven development (TDD) is a programming practice where writing code starts with writing tests first. These tests are initially broken (red). Then by implementing the functionality, you get the pass (green). At the end, you refactor the code while making sure the tests remain green.

Regardless of whether you practice TDD or write your tests after writing your implementation, unit testing is part and parcel of all but the most trivial projects. Given this, mastering unit testing techniques is essential for your project—as well as for your career.

As you saw in Chapter 5, xUnit is the testing framework of choice for this book. xUnit is a modern unit testing framework that has extended testing concepts and has been ported to .NET by Brad Wilson, one of the authors of ASP. NET Web API. For mocking dependencies, we use Moq library. You can add xUnit and Moq to your project using NuGet.

```
PM> Install-Package xUnit
PM> Install-Package Moq
PM> Install-Package xUnit.Extensions
```

For data-driven tests, you will need xUnit extensions as the last command.

Sample Application

In Chapter 5 you learned how to build a full-blown application. For the purpose of our tests, we use a small application to demonstrate unit testing in ASP.NET Web API. The source code is included with the samples for the rest of the book.

In this sample application we simulate a small pizza shop API, where a member of staff can take orders from customers over the phone. Also, orders can be updated or removed (canceled). We use the single-page application (SPA) approach using Knockout.js, which makes calls to our Web API for order's CRUD (Create-Read-Update-Delete) operations.

> ■ **Note** Single-page application (SPA) is a term referring to browser-based applications where the main page is loaded once and then the flow of the application is handled fully in the client side using JavaScript. (In conventional web applications pages are loaded by posting the state back to the server, which causes the whole page to be reloaded.) By providing a more natural and seamless experience for the user, it replicates some of the benefits of desktop applications while maintaining the power and interoperability of the Web.

For the UI theme, we use the home page theme of ASP.NET Web API samples available in the ASP.NET MVC 4 template (see Figure 15-1).

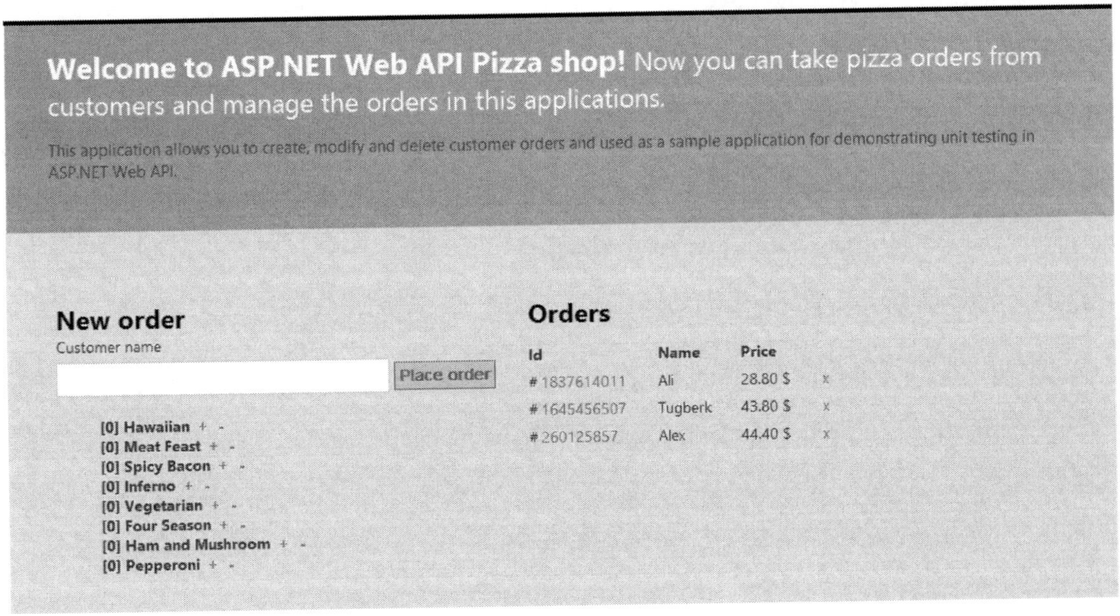

Figure 15-1. *Our sample pizza shop application with a single-page application user interface. Orders are created and edited on the left side, and the list of existing orders are displayed on the right side of the page*

Orders are stored in an in-memory repository. Our controller implements CRUD operations for orders, and these operations are called within our single-page application. New orders can be created by entering the name of the customer in the box and setting the number of each pizza in the order by clicking the plus (+) or minus (–) sign (see Figure 15-2). To delete an order, click the x sign, and to edit, click on the order number. The order Id is a random integer assigned on the server side.

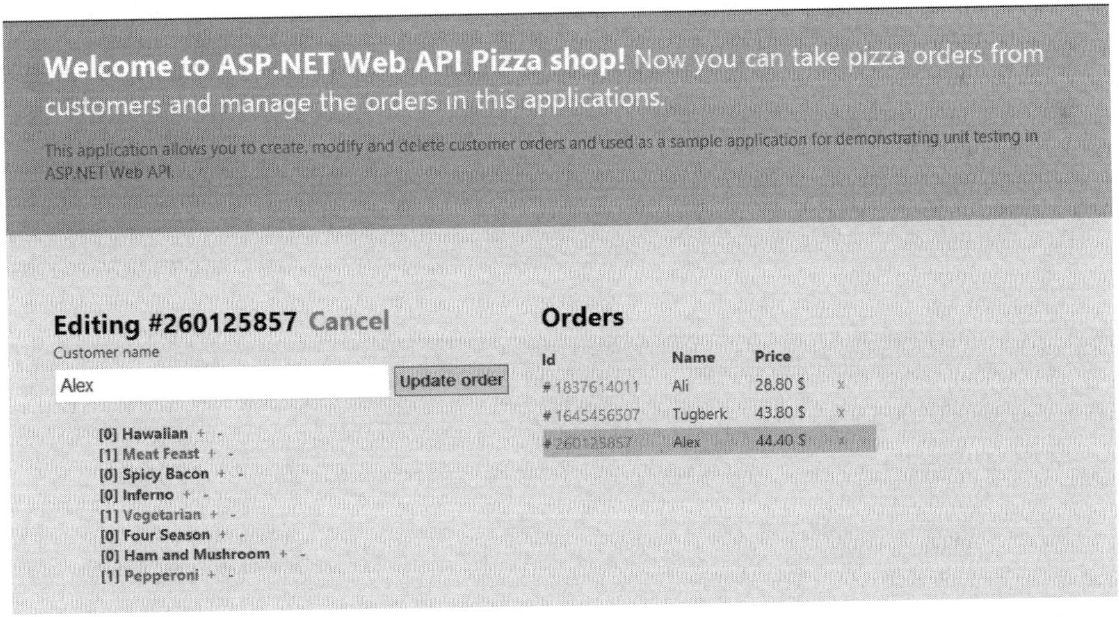

Figure 15-2. *Sample pizza shop user interface displayed while editing an item*

Our controller is a simple CRUD controller. It has a dependency on IOrderService (see Listing 15-1).

Listing 15-1. OrderController Implementing CRUD API

```
namespace PizzaApi.Api.Controllers
{
    public class OrderController : ApiController
    {
        private readonly IOrderService _orderService;

        public OrderController(IOrderService orderService)
        {
            _orderService = orderService;
        }

        public HttpResponseMessage Post(HttpRequestMessage request, Order order)
        {
            if (!order.Items.Any())
                return request.CreateErrorResponse(HttpStatusCode.BadRequest, "Order has no
                    items");

            if(_orderService.Exists(order.Id))
                return request.CreateErrorResponse(HttpStatusCode.BadRequest, "Order already
                    exists");

            _orderService.Save(order);
            var response = request.CreateResponse(HttpStatusCode.Created);
            response.Headers.Location = new Uri(Url.Link(null, new {id = order.Id}));
            return response;
        }

        public HttpResponseMessage Get(HttpRequestMessage request, int id)
        {
            if (!_orderService.Exists(id))
                return request.CreateErrorResponse(HttpStatusCode.NotFound, "Order does not
                    exist");

            return request.CreateResponse(HttpStatusCode.OK, _orderService.Get(id));
        }

        public IEnumerable<Order> Get()
        {
            return _orderService.GetAll();
        }

        public HttpResponseMessage Delete(HttpRequestMessage request, int id)
        {
            if (!_orderService.Exists(id))
                return request.CreateErrorResponse(HttpStatusCode.NotFound, "Order does not
                    exist");
```

```
        _orderService.Delete(id);
        return request.CreateResponse(HttpStatusCode.OK);
    }

    public HttpResponseMessage Put(HttpRequestMessage request, Order order)
    {
        if (!_orderService.Exists(order.Id))
            return request.CreateErrorResponse(HttpStatusCode.NotFound, "Order does not
                exist");

        _orderService.Update(order);
        return request.CreateResponse(HttpStatusCode.OK);
    }
  }
}
```

■ **Note**   As you have probably noticed, we pass the request as an input parameter to some of the actions. This is not necessary considering the current `HttpRequestMessage` is accessible using the `Request` property of the controller. However, by defining an input parameter of the type `HttpRequestMessage`, ASP.NET Web API automatically passes the request to action when calling it. This helps to make the action stateless and easier to test.

IOrderService is implemented in InMemoryOrderService class, which in turn has a dependency on IPricingService. For the sake of simplicity, InMemoryOrderService holds an in-memory repository (instead of a persistent one) for storing orders. IPricingService is implemented in SimplePricingService, which calculates the price of the order and adds the VAT (value-added tax), wherever it is applicable.

We use this simple application to demonstrate unit testing and integration testing in ASP.NET Web API. This application has a client-side code component requiring testing that is outside the scope of this book.

Testing Controllers

Since controllers are the mainstay of ASP.NET Web API, it is essential to test your controllers. In order to grasp controller unit testing, you need to ensure you understand the responsibility of the controller.

The controller in ASP.NET Web API is responsible for verifying the request (the last layer in the pipeline to have this responsibility), calling the business layer to complete the operation, and presenting the response. It is considered a best practice to keep the controllers free from any business logic. Most of the business logic of your application is to be implemented in your business classes or domain models—if, that is, you follow domain-driven design (DDD) guidelines.

■ **Note**   Domain-Driven Design is an approach to software design that involves modeling the business and dividing the domain into bounded contexts (see *Domain-Driven Design* by Eric Evans [Addison-Wesley, 2003]). "Bounded context" refers to a part of your domain that defines a ubiquitous vocabulary according to the models of your business in that context. For example, if your domain is pizza takeaway and delivery, "delivery" can be a bounded context containing these models: Driver, Address, DeliveryPackage, Bill, Vehicle, and so on. It probably does not contain Customer, Topping, or Pizza, as they belong to the "order taking" bounded context.

Let's look at this action:

```
public IEnumerable<Order> Get()
{
    return _orderService.GetAll();
}
```

This action, which returns all orders from the in-memory repository, has nothing Web API–specific in it. It could as easily belong to a repository or a service. On the other hand, the action uses controller context (see Listing 15-2).

Listing 15-2. Post Action in OrderController

```
public HttpResponseMessage Post(HttpRequestMessage request, Order order)
{
    if (!order.Items.Any())
        return request.CreateErrorResponse(HttpStatusCode.BadRequest, "Order has no items");

    _orderService.Save(order);
    var response = request.CreateResponse(HttpStatusCode.Created);
    response.Headers.Location = new Uri(Url.Link(null, new { id = order.Id }));
    return response;
}
```

This action uses Url, which is an instance of UrlHelper sitting on the base class ApiController. In this case, it cannot be treated as a simple method call since it relies on the controller context. Let's look at these tests separately.

Testing Actions Not Dependent on the Controller Context

In these tests, we test the action as we would any other method. Let's look at the action again:

```
public IEnumerable<Order> Get()
{
    return _orderService.GetAll();
}
```

You can see there is very little to test. Some might argue there is not a lot of value to test this method. At the end of the day, you need to make a judgment on the level of the testing required, but in order to test all you need do is make sure _orderService is called and returns GetAll as a result. Let's create a mock object and pass it to the constructor to supply the dependency (see Listing 15-3).

Listing 15-3. Testing GetAll()

```
[Fact]
public void GetAll_should_return_all_from_OrderService()
{
    // arrange
    var orders = new Order[0];
    var mockOrderService = new Mock<IOrderService>();
    mockOrderService.Setup(x => x.GetAll())
                .Returns(orders);
    var orderController = new OrderController(mockOrderService.Object);
```

```
    // act
    var result = orderController.Get();

    // assert
    Assert.Equal(orders, result);
}
```

> ■ **Note** You might have heard about the difference between mock and stub and the associated community discussion. Here we use a stub to return values to help test our code. We do not "verify" the mock at the end of the test (to ensure expectations are called) nor do we add checks for the inputs. On the other hand, for mocks (also known as strict mocks), we verify right input is passed to them from the system under test.

The difference here is black-box testing and white-box testing; in the first, we test the system as more or less a black-box (assuming little about its implementation), while in the second we test implementation. It is generally believed that using mocks leads to "brittle tests"—that is, the test breaks when you change the implementation even while maintaining the same behavior. This was one of the drivers behind the behavior-driven development (BDD) movement, which we look at later in the chapter. Brittle tests also make refactoring harder. Refactoring is one of the tenets of test-driven development (TDD): red-green-refactor. See Martin Fowler's article on the subject (`http://martinfowler.com/articles/mocksArentStubs.html`) for more information.

Testing Actions with Limited Dependency on the Context

Now let's look at the Get action, where the order Id is passed. You start by writing the test and then improve it step by step. In this case, the item is returned if it exists; otherwise HTTP status 404 (Not Found) is returned:

```
public HttpResponseMessage Get(HttpRequestMessage request, int id)
{
    if (!_orderService.Exists(id))
        return request.CreateErrorResponse(HttpStatusCode.NotFound, "Order does not exist");

    return request.CreateResponse(HttpStatusCode.OK, _orderService.Get(id));
}
```

Testing this action involves two tests: one where order exists, and one where it does not. So let's write the first test (shown in Listing 15-4).

Listing 15-4. Testing Getting an Existing Order Without Preparing the Request Context (Causes Exception)

```
[Fact]
public void Get_should_return_OK_if_order_exists()
{
    // arrange
    const int OrderId = 123;
    var order = new Order()
                {
                    Id = OrderId
                };
```

```
    var mockOrderService = new Mock<IOrderService>();
    mockOrderService.Setup(x => x.Exists(It.IsAny<int>()))
                .Returns(true);

    mockOrderService.Setup(x => x.Get(It.IsAny<int>()))
        .Returns(order);
    var orderController = new OrderController(mockOrderService.Object);

    // act
    var result = orderController.Get(new HttpRequestMessage(),  OrderId);

    // assert
    Assert.Equal(HttpStatusCode.OK, result.StatusCode);
}
```

This test looks all well and good, but when it is run, we get an error:

```
System.InvalidOperationException
The request does not have an associated configuration object or the provided configuration was null.
    at System.Net.Http.HttpRequestMessageExtensions.CreateResponse(HttpRequestMessage request,
HttpStatusCode statusCode, T value, HttpConfiguration configuration)
    at System.Net.Http.HttpRequestMessageExtensions.CreateResponse(HttpRequestMessage request,
HttpStatusCode statusCode, T value)
    at PizzaApi.Api.Controllers.OrderController.Get(HttpRequestMessage request, Int32 id) in
OrderController.cs: line 37
    at PizzaApi.Api.Tests.OrderControllerTests.Get_should_return_OK_if_exists() in
OrderControllerTests.cs: line 54
```

The test complains about the configuration object being null, but since HttpConfiguration was not used at all, where does it need to use the configuration? Remember from previous chapters that HttpRequestMessage contains a property bag, named Properties, that contains context-related properties of the request. This design has the benefit of not relying on the HttpContext.Current, but you need to supply the configuration when you create the request. So let's rewrite the test (see Listing 15-5).

Listing 15-5. Testing Getting an Existing Order with Setting the Request Property

```
[Fact]
public void Get_should_return_OK_if_order_exists()
{
    // arrange
    const int OrderId = 123;
    var order = new Order()
                    {
                        Id = OrderId
                    };

    var mockOrderService = new Mock<IOrderService>();
    mockOrderService.Setup(x => x.Exists(It.IsAny<int>()))
                .Returns(true);
```

```
    mockOrderService.Setup(x => x.Get(It.IsAny<int>()))
        .Returns(order);
    var orderController = new OrderController(mockOrderService.Object);
    var request = new HttpRequestMessage();
    request.Properties[HttpPropertyKeys.HttpConfigurationKey] = new HttpConfiguration();

    // act
    var result = orderController.Get(request,  OrderId);

    // assert
    Assert.Equal(HttpStatusCode.OK, result.StatusCode);
}
```

Now the test passes without an exception. So now you can write a test for the case where an Id does not exist (see Listing 15-6).

Listing 15-6. Testing Getting a Nonexisting Order

```
[Fact]
public void Get_should_return_NotFound_if_order_DoesNotExistS()
{
    // arrange
    const int OrderId = 123;
    var mockOrderService = new Mock<IOrderService>();
    mockOrderService.Setup(x => x.Exists(It.IsAny<int>()))
                .Returns(false);

    var orderController = new OrderController(mockOrderService.Object);
    var request = new HttpRequestMessage();
    request.Properties[HttpPropertyKeys.HttpConfigurationKey] = new HttpConfiguration();

    // act
    var result = orderController.Get(request, OrderId);

    // assert
    Assert.Equal(HttpStatusCode.NotFound, result.StatusCode);
}
```

Now let's look at the Delete action (see Listing 15-7). This action can be tested in a similar way, since it does not access controller context. Delete first checks to see whether the item exists. If it does, Delete deletes it and returns HTTP status 200 (OK); otherwise HTTP status 404 (Not Found) is returned.

Listing 15-7. Implementing Delete in OrderController

```
public HttpResponseMessage Delete(HttpRequestMessage request, int id)
{
    if (!_orderService.Exists(id))
        return request.CreateErrorResponse(HttpStatusCode.NotFound, "Order does not exist");

    _orderService.Delete(id);
    return Request.CreateResponse(HttpStatusCode.OK);
}
```

Writing tests for the PUT and DELETE methods is very similar to writing them for GET, and so there is no need to go into the matter here.

Testing Actions Dependent on Controller Context

Now let's look at the POST action. This method

1. Checks to make sure an order contains order items. If the order is invalid, the action returns a "Bad Request" error.

2. Checks to make sure an Id does not exist. If it does, a "Bad Request" error is returned.

3. Saves the order.

4. Creates a response with Created (201) HTTP status and creates an address for the new order in the Location header.

Step 3 is implemented by the IServiceOrder—since it is stubbed, it does not need to be tested, and hence three tests are needed for this method. The first two tests are easy to implement and very similar to previous tests. So let's look at testing the fourth step.

This is where things get interesting. Let us just create a test similar to those already done (see Listing 15-8).

Listing 15-8. Testing HTTP Status Code for a Valid Order Without Preparing Controller Context

```
[Fact]
public void Post_should_return_Created_if_order_good()
{
    // arrange
    const int OrderId = 123;
    var order = new Order(new OrderItem[]
                        {
                            new OrderItem()
                            {
                                Name = "Name",
                                Quantity = 1
                            }
                        })
    {
        Id = OrderId
    };
    var mockOrderService = new Mock<IOrderService>();
    mockOrderService.Setup(x => x.Exists(It.IsAny<int>()))
            .Returns(false);

    var orderController = new OrderController(mockOrderService.Object);
    var request = new HttpRequestMessage();
    request.Properties[HttpPropertyKeys.HttpConfigurationKey] = new HttpConfiguration();

    // act
    var result = orderController.Post(request, order);

    // assert
    Assert.Equal(HttpStatusCode.Created, result.StatusCode);
}
```

Running this test results in a null exception:

```
System.ArgumentNullException
Value cannot be null.
Parameter name: request
at System.Web.Http.ApiController.get_Url()
```

As you see, the problem is that the Url property of the controller is null since it has not been set up. It is time to set up the controller context, as our implementation depends upon it. For the Url property to work, the controller context must be set. The code in Listing 15-9 does exactly that.

Listing 15-9. Testing HTTP Status Code for a Valid Order Without Preparing Controller Context

```
[Fact]
public void Post_should_return_Created_if_order_good()
{
    // arrange
    const int OrderId = 123;
    var order = new Order(new OrderItem[]
                            {
                                new OrderItem()
                                    {
                                        Name = "Name",
                                        Quantity = 1
                                    }
                            })
    {
        Id = OrderId
    };
    var mockOrderService = new Mock<IOrderService>();
    mockOrderService.Setup(x => x.Exists(It.IsAny<int>()))
                .Returns(false);

    var orderController = new OrderController(mockOrderService.Object);
    var request = new HttpRequestMessage(HttpMethod.Post, "http://localhost:2345/api/Order/");
    var config = new HttpConfiguration();
    request.Properties[HttpPropertyKeys.HttpConfigurationKey] = config;
    orderController.Request = request;
    orderController.Configuration = config;
    config.Routes.MapHttpRoute("DefaultApi", "api/{controller}/{id}", _
        new {id = RouteParameter.Optional});
    var route = config.Routes["DefaultApi"];
    var httpRouteData = new HttpRouteData(route, new HttpRouteValueDictionary( _
        new {controller = "Order" }));
    orderController.Request.Properties[HttpPropertyKeys.HttpRouteDataKey] = httpRouteData;

    // act
    var result = orderController.Post(request, order);

    // assert
    Assert.Equal(HttpStatusCode.Created, result.StatusCode);
}
```

The code in Listing 15-9 works but is verbose, and setting up the context in each test, as we have done, will reduce readability. So to make the code more readable, let's devise a helper that can be used to create and set up the controller and its context. The ControllerContextSetup class has been created—you can find it in the book's samples—and it exposes a Fluent API for context setup. The test in Listing 15-10 uses the ControllerContextSetup class.

Listing 15-10. Using the Data Builder's Fluent API to Set Up the Controller Context

```
[Fact]
public void Post_should_return_Created_if_order_good_fluentApi()
{
    // arrange
    const int OrderId = 123;
    var order = new Order(new OrderItem[]
                        {
                            new OrderItem()
                            {
                                Name = "Name",
                                Quantity = 1
                            }
                        })
    {
        Id = OrderId
    };
    var mockOrderService = new Mock<IOrderService>();
    mockOrderService.Setup(x => x.Exists(It.IsAny<int>()))
                .Returns(false);

    var orderController = ControllerContextSetup
        .Of(() => new OrderController(mockOrderService.Object))
        .WithDefaultConfig()
        .WithDefaultRoute()
        .Requesting("http://localhost:2345/api/Order/")
        .WithRouteData(new {controller="Order"})
        .Build<OrderController>();

    // act
    var result = orderController.Post(orderController.Request, order);

    // assert
    Assert.Equal(HttpStatusCode.Created, result.StatusCode);
}
```

Great! You now have 100 percent coverage of the controller. Is there anything missing? Let's look at the test in Listing 15-10: does it cover all functionality of the SUT—that is, the system under test (the Post action here)? Not really. You have not yet checked the content or the location header.

■ **Tip** Be objective with the tests you write—do not write tests just to increase your test coverage. Test coverage is the percentage of your code that runs as part of one or more tests. When TDD started to get popular, test coverage became really important, and development teams set themselves to achieve higher and higher coverage. This led to more tests, but the quality and reliability of the code did not necessarily increase, as quality of the code has more to do with assertions than mere coverage. It became evident that test coverage was a poor indicator of code quality. Nowadays it is believed that you should not write a test to cover trivial code paths (getters and setters). Achieving 80 to 90 percent is a good coverage.

So more assertions are needed. However, it is generally accepted that every test needs to check only one piece of functionality. In effect, this means that you can have similar tests with only the assertions being different. This is also not ideal, but you will see later how to use SubSpec to overcome this problem. For now let's add more assertions to the test. After defining URL as a constant and adding more assertions, the code looks like Listing 15-11.

Listing 15-11. Adding more assertions

```
[Fact]
public void Post_should_return_Created_if_order_good_fluentApi()
{
    // arrange
    const string url = "http://localhost:2345/api/Order/";
    const int OrderId = 123;
    var order = new Order(new OrderItem[]
                    {
                        new OrderItem()
                        {
                            Name = "Name",
                            Quantity = 1
                        }
                    })
    {
        Id = OrderId
    };
    var mockOrderService = new Mock<IOrderService>();
    mockOrderService.Setup(x => x.Exists(It.IsAny<int>()))
            .Returns(false);

    var orderController = ControllerContextSetup
        .Of(() => new OrderController(mockOrderService.Object))
        .WithDefaultConfig()
        .WithDefaultRoute()
        .Requesting(url)
        .WithRouteData(new {controller="Order"})
        .Build<OrderController>();

    // act
    var result = orderController.Post(orderController.Request, order);
```

```
// assert
Assert.Equal(HttpStatusCode.Created, result.StatusCode);
Assert.NotNull(result.Headers.Location);
Assert.Equal(result.Headers.Location, new Uri(new Uri(url), order.Id.ToString()));
}
```

SubSpec helps to define each assertion by means of a separate test (this is examined later in the chapter).

Testing Routes

Routing in ASP.NET Web API is based on the IHttpRoute—a parallel to the IRoute in the ASP.NET MVC world.

```
public interface IHttpRoute
{
    string RouteTemplate { get; }
    IDictionary<string, object> Defaults { get; }
    IDictionary<string, object> Constraints { get; }
    IDictionary<string, object> DataTokens { get; }
    HttpMessageHandler Handler { get; }
    IHttpRouteData GetRouteData(string virtualPathRoot, HttpRequestMessage request);
    IHttpVirtualPathData GetVirtualPath(HttpRequestMessage request, IDictionary<string, object>
        values);
}
```

Testing routes in ASP.NET Web API is not very different from testing routes in ASP.NET MVC. So if you are familiar with testing routes in MVC, you should find them fairly straightforward.

Routing is a two-way concept: first comes the ability to break down the URL to its components and parameters, and second is being able to pass parameters and reconstruct links. These two concepts are modeled in the GetRouteData and GetVirtualPath methods. You need to test these two concepts separately. Remember that you want to test just the routes and not the Web API routing framework.

Currently there is only one route—the DefaultApi route. To make things a bit more interesting, let us add another route—for OrderItems. Then add a new controller, OrderItemController, its purpose being to return items of an order, and add the route shown in Listing 15-12.

Listing 15-12. Setting Up the Next Level of Routes

```
config.Routes.MapHttpRoute(
    name: "OrderItems",
    routeTemplate: "api/Order/{id}/{controller}/{name}",
    defaults: new { name = RouteParameter.Optional }
    );
```

Now let's test the two routes.

Testing `GetRouteData` and `GetVirtualPath`

As we said, GetRouteData matches URL to a route and extracts its parameters. To test it, create an instance of HttpConfiguration, and pass it to static Register method of WebApiConfig class (see Listing 15-13).

Listing 15-13. Data-Driven Cases for Testing Routing

```
[Theory]
[InlineData("http://localhost:12345/foo/route", "GET", false, null, null)]
[InlineData("http://localhost:12345/api/order/", "GET", true, "order", null)]
[InlineData("http://localhost:12345/api/order/123", "GET", true, "order", "123")]
public void DefaultRoute_Returns_Correct_RouteData(
    string url, string method, bool shouldfound, string controller, string id)
{
    // arrange
    var config = new HttpConfiguration();
    WebApiConfig.Register(config);
    var request = new HttpRequestMessage(new HttpMethod(method), url);

    // act
    var routeData = config.Routes.GetRouteData(request);

    // assert
    Assert.Equal(shouldfound, routeData!=null);
    if (shouldfound)
    {
        Assert.Equal(controller, routeData.Values["controller"]);
        Assert.Equal(id == null ? (object) RouteParameter.Optional : (object)id, routeData.
Values["id"]);
    }
}
```

To test the routing in Listing 15-13, call the Register method to initialize the configuration. Instead of using the Fact attribute, use the Theory attribute along with InlineData to create a data-driven test. Each InlineData attribute defines one test, and parameters defined in each InlineData attribute are passed to the test method. As Figure 15-3 shows, each InlineData case appears as a separate test. You can also add a parameter for the route name to ensure that the URL is mapped to the correct route name.

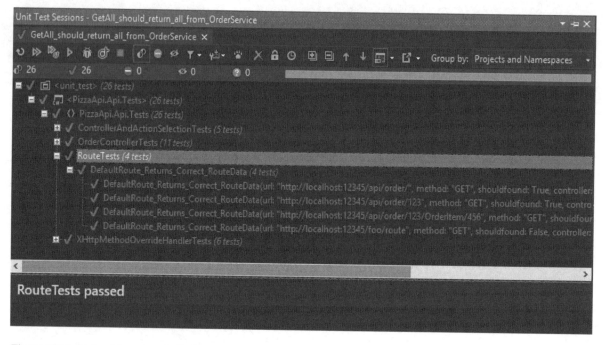

Figure 15-3. *Data-driven tests in Resharper unit testing window*

Now let's add a test for the OrderItems route:

```
[InlineData("http://localhost:12345/api/order/123/OrderItem/456",
"GET", true, "OrderItem", "123")]
```

This will ensure that the second added route works. Testing GetVirtualPath is also very similar, the difference being that the parameters are passed and the resultant path checked on the other side. Testing GetVirtualPath does not have a lot of value, and some exclude it from their coverage.

Testing Controller and Action Selection

Testing routes is very important, especially when you have many routes and the likelihood of route collision is high. But even checking that the correct route is selected and the correct route data are extracted does not ensure that the correct controller and action are selected. But not to worry! It is possible to test that, too.

As you learned in previous chapters, the controller selector (an implementation of IHttpControllerSelector) and the action selector (an implementation of IHttpActionSelector) are used by the framework to find the appropriate controller and action. It is not very difficult to run the same process in your tests so as to ensure correct selection of the controller and action—especially if you have replaced default services with your own. This test complements your routing tests, and so in a sense it is an integration test rather than a unit test. Either way, it is very important. You can write the tests in two ways:

- Relying on the routing result to be correct—hence, an integration test

- Providing your own route data to decouple the test from routing

The second option looks purer and more decoupled, but as it requires more setup, it can lead to less readable tests. We prefer the first option, since we prefer simplicity and readability and believe controller/action selection is an integration test anyway. We employ data-driven tests using the Theory attribute in Listing 15-14.

Listing 15-14. Data-Driven Cases for Checking Controller and Action Selection

```
[Theory]
[InlineData("http://localhost:12345/api/order/123", "GET", typeof(OrderController), "Get")]
[InlineData("http://localhost:12345/api/order", "POST", typeof(OrderController), "Post")]
[InlineData("http://localhost:12345/api/order/123", "PUT", typeof(OrderController), "Put")]
[InlineData("http://localhost:12345/api/order", "GET", typeof(OrderController), "Get")]
[InlineData("http://localhost:12345/api/order/123/OrderItem", "GET", typeof(OrderItemController),
"GetItems")]
public void Ensure_Correct_Controller_and_Action_Selected(
    string url,
    string method,
    Type controllerType,
    string actionName)
{
    // arrange
    var config = new HttpConfiguration();
    WebApiConfig.Register(config);
    var actionSelector = config.Services.GetActionSelector();
    var controllerSelector = config.Services.GetHttpControllerSelector();
    var request = new HttpRequestMessage(new HttpMethod(method), url);
    var routeData = config.Routes.GetRouteData(request);
    request.Properties[HttpPropertyKeys.HttpRouteDataKey] = routeData;
    request.Properties[HttpPropertyKeys.HttpConfigurationKey] = config;

    // act
    var controllerDescriptor = controllerSelector.SelectController(request);
    var context = new HttpControllerContext(config, routeData, request)
                        {
                            ControllerDescriptor = controllerDescriptor
                        };
    var actionDescriptor = actionSelector.SelectAction(context);

    // assert
    Assert.Equal(controllerType, controllerDescriptor.ControllerType);
    Assert.Equal(actionName, actionDescriptor.ActionName);
}
```

Testing Delegating Handlers (Message Handlers)

Delegating handlers are the backbone of the HTTP pipeline in ASP.NET Web API. As you saw in Chapter 10, they are very powerful elements of the pipeline and can be used for cross-cutting concerns such as security, tracing, and logging. Also, they are very useful if a special feature that applies globally to a request needs implementing. Delegating handlers can also be used on a particular route, but to keep things simple, let's test a global delegating handler. For the test's purposes, let's use the MethodOverrideHandler class (explored in Chapter 10).

Testing delegating handlers is straightforward, as there is mainly one method to be tested: SendAsync. One caveat is that the SendAsync method is protected; hence we cannot call it directly. However, the .NET Framework provides the HttpMessageInvoker class, which can be used to invoke the method. This is very useful, since the alternative would be calling the method through Reflection—this is possible, but it demands a bit more work.

■ **Tip** At times you may want to test a method without making it public. One solution is to declare the method internal but expose the method to the test project using the InternalVisibleTo attribute in the AssemblyInfo file of the project where the class is located. The ASP.NET Web API code base itself uses this technique in a number of places.

Delegating handlers are intermediary pipes in the HTTP pipeline. Hence they rely on their InnerHandler for the main processing of the request. Hence, too, you need to ensure that you populate the InnerHandler property. In this test a dummy inner handler class has been created to receive the request to verify whether the HTTP method was changed in the process. Note that data-driven tests are used again, since one test code can be written to run against various conditions. To improve readability, you could also implement this test as three different tests (see Listing 15-15).

Listing 15-15. Testing the XHttpMethodOverrideHandler DelegatingHandler

```
public class XHttpMethodOverrideHandlerTests
{
    [Theory]
    [InlineData("POST", "PUT", "PUT")]
    [InlineData("POST", "DELETE", "DELETE")]
    [InlineData("POST", "GET", "POST")]
    [InlineData("POST", "", "POST")]
    [InlineData("POST", "HEAD", "HEAD")]
    [InlineData("GET", "PUT", "GET")]
    public void XHttpMethodOverrideHandler_Should_Change_Method_correctly(
        string method, string xHttpMethodValue, string expectedMethod)
    {
        // arrange
        var innerHandler = new DummyInnerHandler();
        var handler = (HttpMessageHandler) new XHttpMethodOverrideHandler()
                        {
                            InnerHandler = innerHandler
                        };
        var request = new HttpRequestMessage(new HttpMethod(method),
            "http://localhost:12345/foo/bar");

        request.Headers.Add(XHttpMethodOverrideHandler.XOVERRIDEHEADER, xHttpMethodValue);
        var invoker = new HttpMessageInvoker(handler);

        // act
        var result = invoker.SendAsync(request, new CancellationToken());

        // assert
        Assert.Equal(expectedMethod, innerHandlder.Request.Method.Method);
    }
}
```

```
class DummyInnerHandler : HttpMessageHandler
{
    private HttpRequestMessage _request;

    public HttpRequestMessage Request
    {
        get { return _request; }
    }

    protected override Task<HttpResponseMessage> SendAsync(HttpRequestMessage request,
        CancellationToken cancellationToken)
    {
        _request = request;
        return null;
    }
}
}
```

Testing Filters

As Chapter 11 discussed filters, let's use one of its sample filters to test ValidateModelStateAttribute, which is responsible for returning BadRequest status if the ModelState is invalid (see Listing 15-16).

Listing 15-16. ValidateModelStateAttribute Filter

```
[AttributeUsage(
    AttributeTargets.Class | AttributeTargets.Method,
    AllowMultiple = false, Inherited = true)]
public class ValidateModelStateAttribute : ActionFilterAttribute {

    public override void OnActionExecuting(
        HttpActionContext actionContext) {

        if (!actionContext.ModelState.IsValid) {

            actionContext.Response =
                actionContext.Request.CreateErrorResponse(
                    HttpStatusCode.BadRequest,
                    actionContext.ModelState);
        }
    }
}
```

In this case the filter overrides only OnActionExecuting. Hence only this method is tested. All that we have to do is to create an instance of HttpActionContext with an invalid ModelState and then verify the response's status (see Listing 15-17).

Listing 15-17. Testing ValidateModelStateAttribute Filter

```
[Fact]
public void Should_Return_BadRequest_If_ModelState_Invalid()
{
    // arrange
    var filter = new ValidateModelStateAttribute();
    var context = new HttpActionContext(
        new HttpControllerContext(new HttpConfiguration(),
            new HttpRouteData(new HttpRoute("SomePattern")),
            new HttpRequestMessage()),
            new ReflectedHttpActionDescriptor());
    context.ModelState.AddModelError("foo", "some error");

    // act
    filter.OnActionExecuting(context);

    // assert
    Assert.NotNull(context.Response);
    Assert.Equal(HttpStatusCode.BadRequest, context.Response.StatusCode);
}
```

Here the context was not set up with any data since our controller did not use them, so we have passed only the defaults. In other filters you might have to populate the context with the appropriate data—configuration, routes, routes data, request properties, and the like—as you saw earlier in this chapter.

Integration Testing

You have now written unit tests and achieved a high coverage on your code with high-value unit tests. Is anything else needed?

The answer is yes: integration tests are needed. An integration test ensures that your code works not just on its own but in the framework it is going to run on. In other words, it prepares your code to meet codes that you do not own.

An example of integration testing is making sure the object returned by your controller is sent back in a format consumable by your clients. Another example is making sure your authentication message handler kicks in correctly, as the ordering of your message handlers could interfere with its functionality. Yet another is verifying that a request is handled by the controller and action it is meant to.

Before going into details of writing effective integration tests, let's review a few related subjects to better understand integration testing practices.

Integration Testing and Automation

Automated testing is one of the tenets of modern software development. If you need to deploy software multiple times a day, you cannot have exhaustive regression testing to make sure that, with all the changes since the previous release, everything still works. Instead you run automated tests to get assurance that all is well and that new software can be deployed.

Unit tests are very easy to automate and are normally part of the continuous integration cycle. Integration tests require a bit more setup since they will run in an environment. Automating the process of deployment can help in limiting the number of failing tests due to environmental issues.

When it comes to writing and automating tests, you need to keep the slanted pyramid shown in Figure 15-4 in mind. A system must have many unit tests, some integration tests, and very few UI tests. Also, the pyramid shows that most UI tests and a lot of integration tests can be defined by nontechnical stakeholders of the project—usually using BDD style tests.

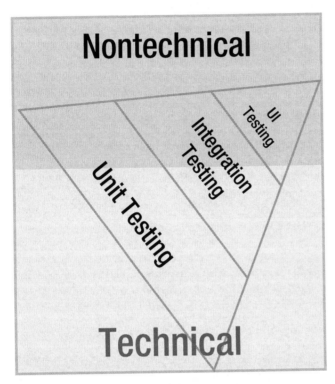

Figure 15-4. *A healthy testing pyramid. It shows the correct proportion of UI, integration, and unit testing. It also shows what proportion of each test category can be understood by nontechnical members of the team*

■ **Note**   User interface (UI) tests assess whether an application returns the right kinds of UI output for user actions. UI tests, often run using UI automation tools such as Selenium and Watin, have become very popular in the last few years. However, their effectiveness and cost have recently been questioned, since as soon as they get fairly complex, they become very hard to maintain. Another issue is a phenomenon known as "flickering tests"—that is, tests that should pass but occasionally fail for no code-related reason (they normally fail due to timing out). This reduces the reliability of the results and renders tests unuseful and unreliable.

The cost of writing, maintaining, and running these tests increases from unit tests to UI tests. As with unit tests, be objective with your integration tests, and choose the right granularity for writing tests.

Integration Testing and BDD

Behavior-driven development (BDD) is a testing paradigm that focuses on behavior instead of testing implementation. This methodology was developed to address the shortcomings of TDD. Nowadays it can be used alongside TDD.

One of the problems experienced in TDD was that as the tests grew more complex, refactoring the code sometimes led to breaking the tests. In other words, the red-green-refactor cycle would turn into a continuous loop: the refactor would lead to red, fixes would cause red to go green, and then any more refactoring reinforced the next round of the loop. This discouraged developers from refactoring—thus defeating the main objective of TDD. BDD solves this problem by focusing on behavior, which is independent of implementation.

Another problem was that unit tests tested implementation of the code, but there was no tangible relationship with the end business goal. While unit tests were meaningful for developers, nontechnical stakeholders of the project got no assurance from the unit-test coverage. In this sense, BDD is an "outside-in" process (it brings outsiders into the process) in that it tackles the problem by letting nontechnical stakeholders define the specification that is later wired to the code by the developers. This is an "executable specification," where BDD scenarios are written in a human-readable specification by stakeholders. The beauty of such tests is that they will break if the requirement changes.

The language of BDD specification is a domain-specific language (DSL) called Gherkin, which is very close to natural language. Each test is composed of a Given-When-Then scenario, similar to Arrange-Act-Assert of unit testing.

BDD-style tests can be used both for unit testing and integration testing. In fact BDD-style tests are more suitable for integration tests than traditional unit tests. BDD tools will thus be used for writing our integration tests.

SpecFlow

SpecFlow, a Visual Studio plug-in and library, implements Gherkin language and links its wiring to unit-testing frameworks. SpecFlow—not itself a testing framework—works with all popular unit-testing frameworks, including NUnit and xUnit.

In SpecFlow you start with the features of your system. Then stakeholders start to define one or more acceptance tests as scenario. Each scenario is composed of one or more Given statements, one When statement, and one or more Then statements. These are defined in a feature file (see Figure 15-5), and multiple statements are separated using And.

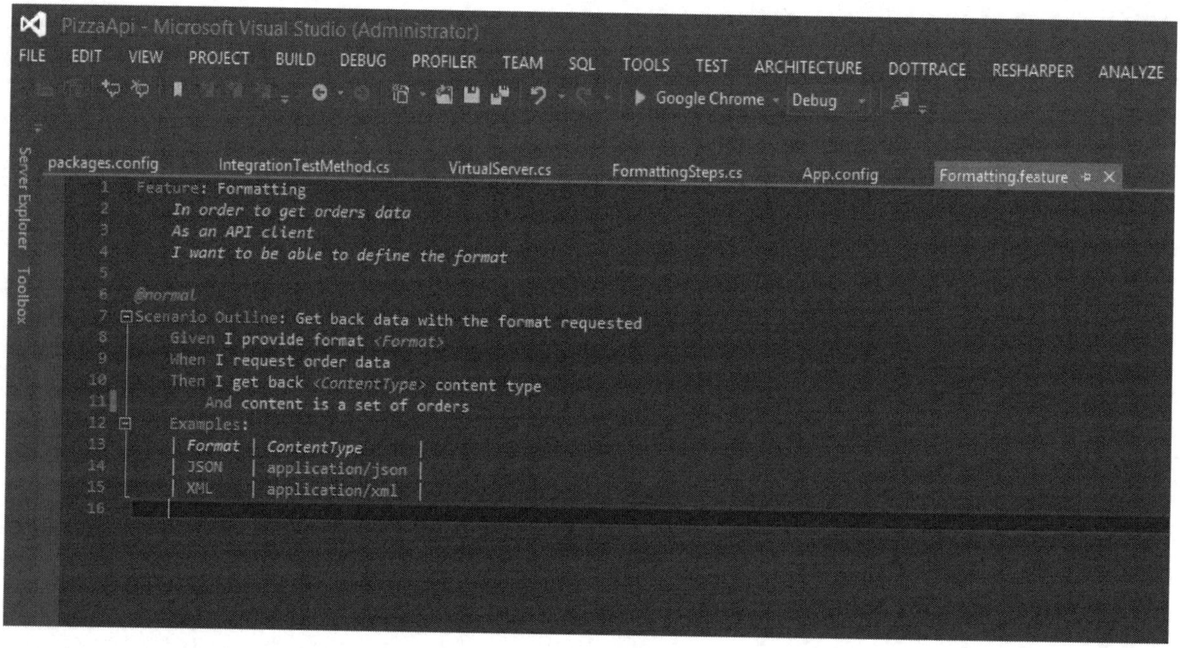

Figure 15-5. *Authoring a feature file in Visual Studio using SpecFlow*

Each Given/When/Then is mapped to a step. A step is the code implementation of the statement. These steps are methods in a class, methods that have Given, When and Then attributes defined against them. These attributes accept a string parameter that is the text of the statement. Let's look at SpecFlow in more detail and use it to write our integration tests.

SubSpec

SubSpec, an add-on to the xUnit framework, enables more readable BDD-style unit/integration tests. It defines Context, Do, and one or more Observation instances (analogous to Given, When, and Then) and helps define multiple assertions inside the test while making each one a separate test.

Since SubSpec tests use string extension methods, you can use strings (instead of comments) to define the requirement. Unlike typical xUnit tests, which are defined by [Fact] or [Theory] attributes, it uses a [Specification] attribute.

In order to use SubSpec, add it to your project using NuGet:

```
PM> Install-Package SubSpec
```

In order to demonstrate how to write unit/integration tests in SubSpec, let's rewrite GetAll_should_return_all_from_OrderService in SubSpec (see Listing 15-18).

Listing 15-18. Writing Multiple Assertions in SubSpec

```
[Specification]
public void GetAll_should_return_all_from_OrderService_Subspec()
{

    var orders = default(Order[]);
    var mockOrderService = default(Mock<IOrderService>);
    var orderController = default(OrderController);
    var result = default(IEnumerable<Order>);

    "Given order service contains no orders"
        .Context(() =>
                    {
                        orders = new Order[0];
                        mockOrderService = new Mock<IOrderService>();
                        orderController = new OrderController(mockOrderService.Object);
                        mockOrderService.Setup(x => x.GetAll())
                                    .Returns(orders);
                    });

    "When I ask for all orders from orderController"
        .Do(() =>
                {
                    result = orderController.Get();
                });
    "Then it must not be null"
        .Observation(() =>
                    {
                        Assert.NotNull(result);
                    });
```

```
"And it should contain no order"
    .Observation(() =>
                    {
                        Assert.Empty(result);
                    });
}
```

Tests of this style differ from tests with SpecFlow in that these tests are suited for writing (and reading) only by the developers. They are thus better suited for unit tests than integration tests.

Integration Testing in ASP.NET Web API

Now let us look into implementing integration tests for the Pizza API. There are two levels at which integration tests for an ASP.NET Web API application can be written: self-hosting and HttpServer. At the self-hosting level you would spin up an actual self-hosted server listening at a port and use HttpClient to connect to the server. In the HttpServer approach you come in at a level below the hosting, where HttpServer is invoked regardless of your hosting strategy. Our tests will be written so that you can toggle between them, but HttpServer is preferred since it is faster and does not require permission to listen on a port. Another problem is that some unit-testing tools run tests in parallel. Hence there could be a port collision between tests running concurrently unless you randomize the port number. There could be some benefit (not a huge one) in running your tests in a self-hosting solution since it is a more end-to-end process and might surface some configuration problems.

Let's use SpecFlow to write our integration tests. SpecFlow (like other testing frameworks) allows both normal and data-driven tests. Normal tests are created by a Scenario statement, and data-driven tests are created using Scenario Outline.

In order to use SpecFlow, use these steps to add it to the project:

1. Download SpecFlow Visual Studio plug-in from specflow.org.

2. Install the plug-in, and restart Visual Studio. Now you should see new item templates added to your Visual Studio.

3. Add SpecFlow library to the project by typing Install-Package SpecFlow in the NuGet Package Manager Console.

4. A testing framework still needs to be added. By default SpecFlow uses NUnit, but it's better to use xUnit with SpecFlow. So to use xUnit, type Install-Package SpecFlow.xUnit in the NuGet Package Manager Console.

5. Your environment is ready. From the "Add New Item" dialog, choose "SpecFlow Feature File" (see Figure 15-6).

Figure 15-6. *Adding a SpecFlow feature file*

Now you are ready to write your first scenario.

Integration Testing for Content Negotiation

We all rely on the framework to implement content negotiation and to return the correct format if it is requested by the client. Given that, we could be adding, removing, or replacing MediaTypeFormatters. Also, we could define ViewModel types that some formatters might have a problem serializing or deserializing. All in all, the importance of integration testing cannot be overemphasized.

OK, let's start with the first SpecFlow feature by adding the `Formatting.feature` file with the content shown in Listing 15-19.

Listing 15-19. Feature File Using Gherkin Syntax

```
Feature: Formatting
            In order to get orders data
            As an API client
            I want to be able to define the format


@normal
Scenario Outline: Get back data with the format requested
            Given I provide format <Format>
            When I request for all orders
```

```
        Then I get back <ContentType> content type
                        And content is a set of orders
    Examples:
    | Format | ContentType      |
    | JSON   | application/json |
    | XML    | application/xml  |
```

As you can see from the use of Scenario Outline, this is a data-driven test. In a Scenario Outline the data are defined in the Examples section using a table. Each row defines one test, with data of the row as the parameters passed to the test.

Now steps to map each statement to the code need to be created. An easy way to do this is to right-click on the feature file and select "Generate Step Definitions". A step is just a method in a class which has a [Binding] attribute. A [Binding] attribute tells SpecFlow to look for step definition methods.

Steps can be reused from one scenario to another if the statement is the same. So although the Gherkin syntax is very close to free text, be consistent in terms of the statement text. Keep them the same if they refer to the same action or condition.

Let's implement the steps. Listing 15-20 shows the step definitions. Note that parameters defined in statements using angle brackets—for example <Format>—are defined as regular expression statements.

Listing 15-20. Code for Steps Related to the Feature File in Listing 15-19

```csharp
[Binding]
public class FormattingSteps
{

    private const string Url = "http://localhost:12345/api/Order";
    private string _format = null;
    private HttpResponseMessage _response;

    [Given(@"I provide format (.+)")]
    public void GivenIProvideFormat(string format)
    {
        _format = format;
    }

    [When(@"When I request for all orders")]
    public void WhenIRequestOrderData()
    {
        var request = new HttpRequestMessage(HttpMethod.Get, Url);
        var server = new VirtualServer(WebApiConfig.Register,
            Convert.ToBoolean(ConfigurationManager.AppSettings["UseSelfHosting"]));
        request.Headers.Accept.Clear();
        request.Headers.Accept.Add( new MediaTypeWithQualityHeaderValue(
            _format == "JSON" ? "application/json" : "application/xml"));
        _response = server.Send(request);
    }

    [Then(@"I get back (.+) content type")]
    public void ThenIGetBackContentType(string contentType)
    {
        Assert.Equal(contentType, _response.Content.Headers.ContentType.MediaType);
    }
```

```
    [Then(@"content is a set of orders")]
    public void ThenContentIsASetOfOrders()
    {
        var content = _response.Content.ReadAsAsync<IEnumerable<Order>>().Result;
    }
}
```

Also note that we have defined the flag to use self-hosting or not as an appSettings key in the app.config file. You can flip the value to true or false depending on which one you prefer.

■ **Note**   There are several alternative ways to achieve this result in SpecFlow. One approach is to define two tags. @SelfHosted and @HttpServer, for the scenario and run the tests with the tag you prefer. Or you could run the tests twice, each time targeting one tag. However, implementing this requirement using tags and automating it using SpecRunner is outside the scope of this book.

The code in Listing 15-20 uses a class called VirtualServer (see Listing 15-21), which abstracts whether to use self-hosting or HttpServer.

Listing 15-21. Code for a VirtualServer class That Executes a Request Using a Self-Hosted or HttpServer

```
public class VirtualServer
{
    private readonly bool _useSelfHosting;
    private readonly Action<HttpConfiguration> _setupConfiguration;

    public VirtualServer(Action<HttpConfiguration> setupConfiguration, bool useSelfHosting = false)
    {
        _setupConfiguration = setupConfiguration;
        _useSelfHosting = useSelfHosting;
    }

    public HttpResponseMessage Send(HttpRequestMessage request)
    {
        return _useSelfHosting ? SendSelfHosted(request) : SendHttpServer(request);
    }

    private HttpResponseMessage SendHttpServer(HttpRequestMessage request)
    {
        var config = new HttpConfiguration();
        _setupConfiguration(config);
        var server = new HttpServer(config);
        var invoker = new HttpMessageInvoker(server);
        return invoker.SendAsync(request, new CancellationToken())
            .Result;
    }
}
```

```
    private HttpResponseMessage SendSelfHosted(HttpRequestMessage request)
    {
        var config = new HttpSelfHostConfiguration(new Uri("http://localhost:" +
            request.RequestUri.Port));
        _setupConfiguration(config);
        using (var host = new HttpSelfHostServer(config))
        {
            host.OpenAsync().Wait();
            var client = new HttpClient();
            var response = client.SendAsync(request).Result;
            host.CloseAsync().Wait();
            return response;
        }
    }
}
```

Once this is done, you can run or debug your integration tests by right-clicking the feature file and choosing the run/debug scenario. The tests also can be triggered using test-running tools (such as Resharper), and you may choose to run them there.

Our tests' current implementation works, but use of local member variables will prevent reuse of our steps. The next section introduces a technique to remove all member variables.

Integration Testing for Placing the Order

Now an integration test for placing the order would be great to have. Here we use Scenario instead of Scenario Outline. Also, this time we use the ScenarioContext.Current object rather than member variables for keeping the context. Using ScenarioContext is the preferred approach. In BDD terms, ScenarioContext is the "world"—that is, the context in which a test is running.

So let's add the PlaceOrder.feature file and write the feature and a scenario (see Listing 15-22).

Listing 15-22. PlaceOrders Feature File

```
Feature: PlaceOrders
                In order to inform kitchen of the customer orders
                As a pizza shop operator
                I want to be able to place customer orders


@normal
Scenario: Placing order
                Given I have an order for a mixture of pizzas
                                And it is for a particular customer
                When I place the order
                                And retrieve the order
                Then system must have priced the order
                                And system must have saved the order
                                And saved order must contain same pizzas
                                And saved order must have the name of the customer
```

Here we make sure that the order is saved and, when retrieved, contains the same data. We also check that the price is calculated. To do this, we need to make some changes in the VirtualServer class so that it keeps its state between requests (see Listing 15-23).

Listing 15-23. Updated VirtualServer

```
public class VirtualServer : IDisposable
{
    private readonly bool _useSelfHosting;
    private readonly Action<HttpConfiguration> _setupConfiguration;
    private Func<HttpRequestMessage, Task<HttpResponseMessage>> _invoker;
    private HttpSelfHostServer _server;

    public VirtualServer(Action<HttpConfiguration> setupConfiguration, bool useSelfHosting = false)
    {
        _setupConfiguration = setupConfiguration;
        _useSelfHosting = useSelfHosting;
        if (useSelfHosting)
        {
            var config = new HttpSelfHostConfiguration(new Uri(ConfigurationManager.
                AppSettings["BaseUrl"]));
            _setupConfiguration(config);
            _server = new HttpSelfHostServer(config);
            _server.OpenAsync().Wait();
            var client = new HttpClient();
            _invoker = client.SendAsync;
        }
        else
        {
            var config = new HttpConfiguration();
            _setupConfiguration(config);
            var server = new HttpServer(config);
            _invoker = (req) =>
                        {
                            return new HttpMessageInvoker(server).SendAsync(req,
                                new CancellationToken());
                        };
        }
    }

    public HttpResponseMessage Send(HttpRequestMessage request)
    {
        return _useSelfHosting ? SendSelfHosted(request) : SendHttpServer(request);
    }

    private HttpResponseMessage SendHttpServer(HttpRequestMessage request)
    {

        return _invoker(request)
            .Result;
    }

    private HttpResponseMessage SendSelfHosted(HttpRequestMessage request)
    {
        return _invoker(request)
                .Result;
    }
```

```
    public void Dispose()
    {
        if (_server != null)
        {
            _server.CloseAsync().Wait();
            _server.Dispose();
            _server = null;
        }
    }
}
```

Now we are ready to create our steps. But to make sure the server is created and destroyed at the right time, we need to use two SpecFlow hooks: BeforeScenario and AfterScenario. As the names imply, these hooks run, respectively, before and after the scenario steps (see Listing 15-24).

Listing 15-24. Steps for the PlaceOrder Feature

```
[Binding]
public class PlaceOrdersSteps
{

    [BeforeScenario]
    public void CreateVirtualServer()
    {
            var server = new VirtualServer(WebApiConfig.Register,
            Convert.ToBoolean(ConfigurationManager.AppSettings["UseSelfHosting"]));
            ScenarioContext.Current[TestContextKeys.VirtualServer] = server;
    }

    [AfterScenario]
    public void DisposeVirtualServer()
    {
        var server = ScenarioContext.Current.Get<VirtualServer>(TestContextKeys.VirtualServer);
        if (server != null)
        {
            server.Dispose();
        }

    }

    [Given(@"I have an order for a mixture of pizzas")]
    public void GivenIHaveAnOrderForAMixtureOfPizzas()
    {
        var order = new Order();
        order.Items = new[]
                        {
                            new OrderItem()
                                {
                                    Name = "Hawaiian",
                                    Quantity = 2
                                },
```

```
                              new OrderItem()
                                  {
                                      Name = "Meat Feast",
                                      Quantity = 1
                                  }
                      };
        ScenarioContext.Current[TestContextKeys.NewOrder] = order;
}

[Given(@"it is for a particular customer")]
public void GivenItIsForAParticularCustomer()
{
    const string CustomerName = "SomeCustomer";
    var order = ScenarioContext.Current.Get<Order>(TestContextKeys.NewOrder);
    ScenarioContext.Current[TestContextKeys.CustomerName] = CustomerName;
    order.CustomerName = CustomerName;
}

[When(@"I place the order")]
public void WhenIPlaceTheOrder()
{
    var request = new HttpRequestMessage(HttpMethod.Post,   _
            ConfigurationManager.AppSettings["BaseUrl"]
        + "api/Order");
    var server  = ScenarioContext.Current.Get<VirtualServer>(TestContextKeys.VirtualServer);
    var newOrder = ScenarioContext.Current.Get<Order>(TestContextKeys.NewOrder);
    request.Content = new ObjectContent<Order>(newOrder, new JsonMediaTypeFormatter());
    ScenarioContext.Current[TestContextKeys.Request] = request;
    var response = server.Send(request);
    ScenarioContext.Current[TestContextKeys.Response] = response;
    ScenarioContext.Current[TestContextKeys.OrderUrl] = response.Headers.Location;


}

[When(@"retrieve the order")]
public void WhenRetrieveTheOrder()
{
    var server = ScenarioContext.Current.Get<VirtualServer>(TestContextKeys.VirtualServer);
    var request = new HttpRequestMessage(HttpMethod.Get,
        ScenarioContext.Current.Get<Uri>(TestContextKeys.OrderUrl));
    var response = server.Send(request);
    var retrievedOrder = response.Content.ReadAsAsync<Order>().Result;
    ScenarioContext.Current[TestContextKeys.RetrievedOrder] = retrievedOrder;
}

[Then(@"system must have priced the order")]
public void ThenSystemMustHavePricedTheOrder()
{
    var retrievedOrder = ScenarioContext.Current.Get<Order>(TestContextKeys.RetrievedOrder);
    Assert.True(retrievedOrder.TotalPrice > 0);
}
```

```
[Then(@"system must have saved the order")]
public void ThenSystemMustHaveSavedTheOrder()
{
    var retrievedOrder = ScenarioContext.Current.Get<Order>(TestContextKeys.RetrievedOrder);
    Assert.True(retrievedOrder.Id != 0);
}

[Then(@"saved order must contain same pizzas")]
public void ThenSavedOrderMustContainSamePizzas()
{
    var retrievedOrder = ScenarioContext.Current.Get<Order>(TestContextKeys.RetrievedOrder);
    var newOrder = ScenarioContext.Current.Get<Order>(TestContextKeys.NewOrder);
    Assert.Equal(newOrder.Items.Count(), retrievedOrder.Items.Count());
    Assert.Equal(newOrder.Items.First().Name, retrievedOrder.Items.First().Name);
    Assert.Equal(newOrder.Items.First().Quantity, retrievedOrder.Items.First().Quantity);
}

[Then(@"saved order must have the name of the customer")]
public void ThenSavedOrderMustHaveTheNameOfTheCustomer()
{
    var retrievedOrder = ScenarioContext.Current.Get<Order>(TestContextKeys.RetrievedOrder);
    var customerName = ScenarioContext.Current.Get<string>(TestContextKeys.CustomerName);
    Assert.Equal(customerName, retrievedOrder.CustomerName);
}
}
```

OK, now our scenario is ready to run. Note that the use of ScenarioContext to avoid member variables will help to share steps, since the step relies on no context other than ScenarioContext.Current.

Creating other integration tests for other features of the system is more or less the same. As noted earlier, some common steps can be reused, such as the "retrieve the order" step which uses the order URL to retrieve the order from the server.

Summary

This chapter has shown how easy it is to test your ASP.NET Web API application. A sample project was created and used for testing. xUnit is a powerful unit-testing framework that can be used for writing normal unit tests as well as data-driven tests. Testing controllers can be tricky if the action relies on the controller context, but we built a class that helps prepare the context for the test.

Other elements of your API are equally testable, including filters, message handlers, and routing. It is also possible to test the controller and action.

Integration testing is an important part of your test suite. All tests need to be automated and run regularly so that failures occur in your development and integration environment, not in the live environment. BDD-style tests are ideal for writing unit tests, especially because they bridge the gap between requirements and code. SpecFlow is the tool of choice for writing BDD-style tests.

CHAPTER 16

∎ ∎ ∎

Optimization and Performance

Having a fully functional HTTP API is the main concern when transmitting data over HTTP, but once lots of traffic starts to come in, you should realize that there might be bottlenecks and they could affect the performance of an application. Most concerns are application-specific, but there are some common scenarios and best practices that ought to be taken into consideration when you are building an application.

This chapter will look at both server- and HTTP-level concerns to see what parts of the application can be optimized for high performance and how that optimization can be accomplished. After a first look at asynchronous processing inside the controller action methods, we will take a closer look at HTTP-level caching and how to apply it with ASP.NET Web API most efficiently.

ASP.NET Web API Asynchronous Actions

ASP.NET Web API supports asynchronous actions using the task-based asynchronous pattern, or TAP. As was mentioned in Chapter 2, TAP was introduced in .NET v4.0. The programming model was improved in .NET v4.5, and it is also supported by C# 5.0 language features using the new async and await keywords. The beauty of these new features is that we can take advantage of them in ASP.NET Web API with asynchronous controller actions.

When you have long-running I/O-intensive operations inside the controller actions, you will be blocking the thread that the operation is running on. To prevent this blocking, you can implement the controller actions asynchronously. Listing 16-1 shows a simple asynchronous Web API controller action.

Listing 16-1. Simple Web API Asynchronous Controller Action

```
public async Task<IEnumerable<Foo>> Get() {

    using(HttpClient httpClient = new HttpClient()) {

        var response = await httpClient.GetAsync("http://example.com/api");
        return await response.Content.ReadAsAsync<IEnumerable<Foo>>();
    }
}
```

The method, a standard asynchronous function, is marked with the async modifier and returns Task<T> for some T. In fact, Web API controller actions don't need to be marked with the async modifier. So using await expressions is not compulsory, but it simplifies the code structure a lot, as was discussed in Chapter 2. If the action method's return type is Task or Task<T> for some T, the Web API recognizes and processes the request asynchronously. Listing 16-1 exposes a collection of Foo entity, but one can also simply return HttpResponseMessage asynchronously (see Listing 16-2).

Listing 16-2. An Asynchronous Controller Action Returning Task<HttpResponseMessage>

```
public Task<HttpResponseMessage> GetContent(string topic) {

    //Implementation goes here
}
```

ASP.NET Web API has been designed asynchronously from top to bottom. This is a very important part of the framework. Knowing now how asynchronous actions can be implemented, we can move on and take advantage of some real-world use cases.

Scenarios and Use Cases

It was mentioned several times in Chapter 2 that trying to leverage asynchrony for every scenario is not a good idea, especially for server applications, such as any ASP.NET Web API application. This section of the chapter will guide you through some common scenarios suitable for asynchronous controller actions in an ASP.NET Web API application.

Asynchronous Database Calls

It is common to come across arguments about asynchronous database calls in ASP.NET web applications. Most of the time synchronous database calls work pretty well, but in some cases processing database queries asynchronously has a very important impact on the application's performance. One reason why asynchronous programming is not recommended for database queries is that it is extremely hard to get it right, even if TAP is adopted. However, with the new asynchronous language features of C# 5.0, it is easier but still complex.

Let's assume that we have an SQL Server database out there somewhere for our car gallery application and we want to query that database to get the cars list. The database has basically nothing inside it except for a table and a stored procedure. We will try to get the cars list inside the Cars table through the stored procedure, and we will wait for one second inside that stored procedure in order to simulate the long-running database call. Listing 16-3 shows the whole database script.

Listing 16-3. CarGallery SQL Server Database Script

```
CREATE TABLE dbo.[Cars] (
    Id INT IDENTITY(1000,1) NOT NULL,
    Model NVARCHAR(50) NULL,
    Make NVARCHAR(50) NULL,
    [Year] INT NOT NULL,
    Price REAL NOT NULL,
    CONSTRAINT [PK_Cars] PRIMARY KEY CLUSTERED (Id) ON [PRIMARY]
) ON [PRIMARY];
GO


CREATE PROCEDURE [dbo].[sp$GetCars]
AS
-- wait for 1 second
WAITFOR DELAY '00:00:01';
SELECT * FROM Cars;
GO
```

```sql
INSERT INTO dbo.Cars VALUES('Car1', 'Model1', 2006, 24950);
INSERT INTO dbo.Cars VALUES('Car2', 'Model1', 2003, 56829);
INSERT INTO dbo.Cars VALUES('Car3', 'Model2', 2006, 17382);
INSERT INTO dbo.Cars VALUES('Car4', 'Model3', 2002, 72733);
```

Before starting to implement the application to query this database, we have some additional configurations to make in order to write efficient asynchronous queries. First of all, ADO.NET does not process requests asynchronously by default even if code is written that way. Set the Asynchronous Processing property to true inside the connection string in order to allow the issuing of async requests through ADO.NET objects.

By default, the ADO.NET connection pool is also limited to 100 concurrent connections. In order to perform more asynchronous queries against the SQL Server instance, increase this number through the connection string by setting Max Pool Size value. Listing 16-4 shows the connection string we'll be using.

Listing 16-4. CarGallery Connection String Optimized for Asynchronous Processing

```xml
<connectionStrings>
    <add name="CarGalleryConnStr"
        connectionString="Data Source=.\SQLEXPRESS;initial catalog=CarGallery;Max Pool
Size=500;Integrated Security=true;Asynchronous Processing=True;"
        providerName="System.Data.SqlClient" />
</connectionStrings>
```

The configuration is now ready, and so let's create a class that will do the query operations and returns results as .NET CLR objects (see Listing 16-5).

Listing 16-5. GalleryContext Class That Does the Query Operations and Returns Results As C# CLR Objects

```csharp
using System;
using System.Collections.Generic;
using System.Linq;
using System.Data.SqlClient;
using System.Configuration;
using System.Data;
using System.Threading.Tasks;

public class GalleryContext {

    readonly string _spName = "sp$GetCars";

    readonly string _connectionString =

        ConfigurationManager.ConnectionStrings["CarGalleryConnStr"].ConnectionString;

    public IEnumerable<Car> GetCarsViaSP() {

        using (var conn = new SqlConnection(_connectionString)) {
            using (var cmd = new SqlCommand()) {

                cmd.Connection = conn;
                cmd.CommandText = _spName;
                cmd.CommandType = CommandType.StoredProcedure;
```

```
                conn.Open();

                using (var reader = cmd.ExecuteReader()) {

                    return reader.Select(r => carBuilder(r)).ToList();
                }
            }
        }
    }

    public async Task<IEnumerable<Car>> GetCarsViaSPAsync() {

        using (var conn = new SqlConnection(_connectionString)) {
            using (var cmd = new SqlCommand()) {

                cmd.Connection = conn;
                cmd.CommandText = _spName;
                cmd.CommandType = CommandType.StoredProcedure;

                conn.Open();

                using (var reader = await cmd.ExecuteReaderAsync()) {

                    return reader.Select(r => carBuilder(r)).ToList();
                }
            }
        }
    }

    //private helpers

    private Car carBuilder(SqlDataReader reader) {

        return new Car {

            Id = int.Parse(reader["Id"].ToString()),
            Make = reader["Make"] is DBNull ? null : reader["Make"].ToString(),
            Model = reader["Model"] is DBNull ? null : reader["Model"].ToString(),
            Year = int.Parse(reader["Year"].ToString()),
            Price = float.Parse(reader["Price"].ToString()),
        };
    }
}
```

The Car class is nothing but a simple POCO class (see Listing 16-6).

Listing 16-6. Car Entity Class

```
public class Car {

    public int Id { get; set; }
    public string Make { get; set; }
```

```
    public string Model { get; set; }
    public int Year { get; set; }
    public float Price { get; set; }
}
```

You may also notice that a Select method was used on the SqlDataReader, and it does not exist. It is a small extension method that makes the code look prettier (see Listing 16-7).

Listing 16-7. Select Extension Method for SqlDataReader

```
using System;
using System.Collections.Generic;
using System.Data.SqlClient;

public static class Extensions {

    public static IEnumerable<T> Select<T>(
        this SqlDataReader reader, Func<SqlDataReader, T> projection) {

        while (reader.Read()) {
            yield return projection(reader);
        }
    }
}
```

Look at the GalleryContext class, and you will see that there are two methods: GetCarsViaSP and GetCarsViaSPAsync. Both consume the same stored procedure and return the data. However, the GetCarsViaSPAsync method is an asynchronous version of this operation. Inside the GetCarsViaSPAsync method, the SqlCommand. ExecuteReaderAsync method is called instead of SqlCommand.ExecuteReader method, and ExecuteReaderAsync returns Task<SqlDataReader>, which represents an ongoing operation. As this is an asynchronous function, await it by using the await keyword in order to suspend the execution of the GetCarsViaSPAsync method till the operation is completed.

Now we should be able to query the SQL Server database inside the Web API controller actions. The implementation of our controller action is fairly simple for our sample (see Listing 16-8).

Listing 16-8. SPCarsAsyncController Controller

```
public class SPCarsAsyncController : ApiController {

    readonly GalleryContext galleryContext = new GalleryContext();

    public async Task<IEnumerable<Car>> Get() {

        return await galleryContext.GetCarsViaSPAsync();
    }
}
```

With this implementation, the database is now being queried (a long-running operation in this case) without blocking any ASP.NET threads. Also, we will create another controller that will have only one action method as SPCarsAsyncController, and that action method will return the same result—using the synchronous GetCarsViaSP method this time, however (see Listing 16-9).

Listing 16-9. SpCarsSyncController Controller

```
public class SPCarsSyncController : ApiController {

    readonly GalleryContext galleryContext = new GalleryContext();

    public IEnumerable<Car> Get() {

        return galleryContext.GetCarsViaSP();
    }
}
```

For this sample, the route shown in Listing 16-10 has been registered.

Listing 16-10. Default Route for the Sample

```
protected void Application_Start(object sender, EventArgs e) {

    var config = GlobalConfiguration.Configuration;
    config.Routes.MapHttpRoute(
        "DefaultHttpRoute",
        "api/{controller}/{id}",
        new { id = RouteParameter.Optional }
    );
}
```

When the project is run, we will hit one of the endpoints of the API to warm up the application. To measure the difference here, we will perform a small load test on two of the endpoints with the **Apache HTTP Server Benchmarking Tool**, also known as **ab.exe**. A hundred concurrent requests will be made to each endpoint, and ab.exe will give the results. First, let's hit /api/SPCarsSync, which makes a synchronous call to the database (see Figure 16-1).

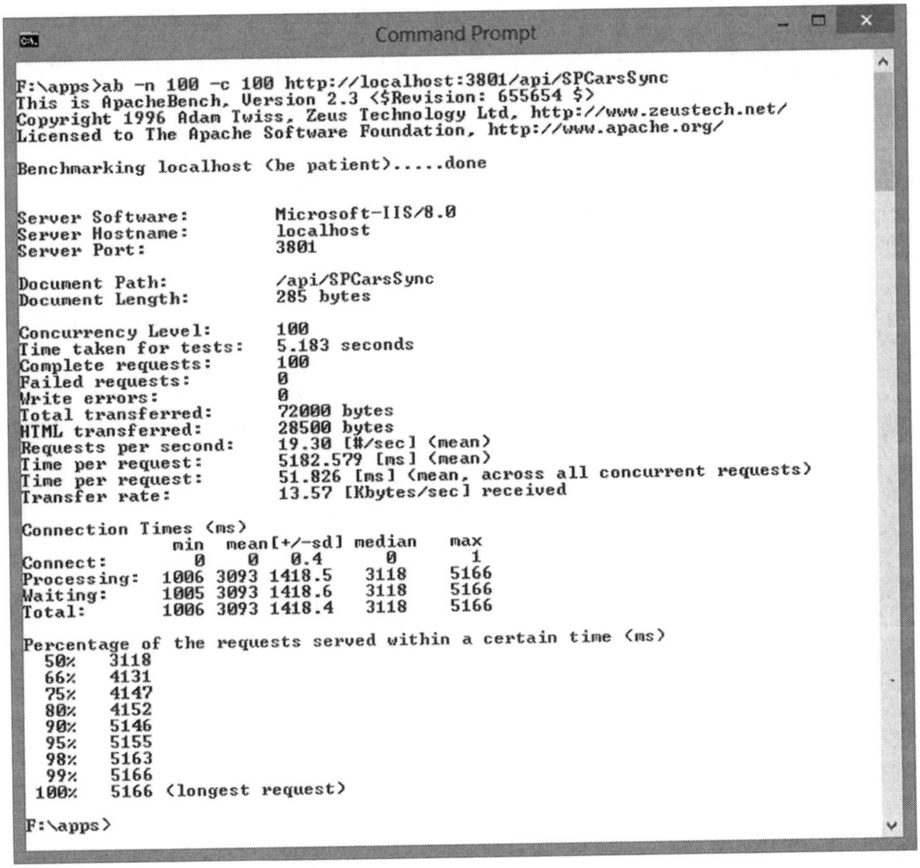

```
F:\apps>ab -n 100 -c 100 http://localhost:3801/api/SPCarsSync
This is ApacheBench, Version 2.3 <$Revision: 655654 $>
Copyright 1996 Adam Twiss, Zeus Technology Ltd, http://www.zeustech.net/
Licensed to The Apache Software Foundation, http://www.apache.org/

Benchmarking localhost (be patient).....done


Server Software:        Microsoft-IIS/8.0
Server Hostname:        localhost
Server Port:            3801

Document Path:          /api/SPCarsSync
Document Length:        285 bytes

Concurrency Level:      100
Time taken for tests:   5.183 seconds
Complete requests:      100
Failed requests:        0
Write errors:           0
Total transferred:      72000 bytes
HTML transferred:       28500 bytes
Requests per second:    19.30 [#/sec] (mean)
Time per request:       5182.579 [ms] (mean)
Time per request:       51.826 [ms] (mean, across all concurrent requests)
Transfer rate:          13.57 [Kbytes/sec] received

Connection Times (ms)
              min  mean[+/-sd] median   max
Connect:        0    0   0.4      0       1
Processing:  1006 3093 1418.5   3118    5166
Waiting:     1005 3093 1418.6   3118    5166
Total:       1006 3093 1418.4   3118    5166

Percentage of the requests served within a certain time (ms)
  50%   3118
  66%   4131
  75%   4147
  80%   4152
  90%   5146
  95%   5155
  98%   5163
  99%   5166
 100%   5166 (longest request)

F:\apps>
```

Figure 16-1. *100 concurrent requests to /api/SPCarsSync*

■ **Note** The Apache HTTP Server Benchmarking Tool is a tiny benchmarking utility that allows multiple concurrent requests to be made to an HTTP endpoint. While ab.exe comes with Apache server installation, you don't have to install Apache to get ab.exe. Download the zip file for Apache server, and you will find ab.exe there. It is a stand-alone executable file, one that can be used anywhere on your machine. (See http://httpd.apache.org/docs/2.2/programs/ab.html for more about ab.exe.) As an alternative, check out the Web Capacity Analysis Tool (WCAT), a lightweight HTTP load generation tool primarily designed to measure web server performance within a controlled environment (http://www.iis.net/downloads/community/2007/05/wcat-63-(x64)).

Let's do the same test on /api/SPCarsAsync, which makes an asynchronous call to the database (see Figure 16-2).

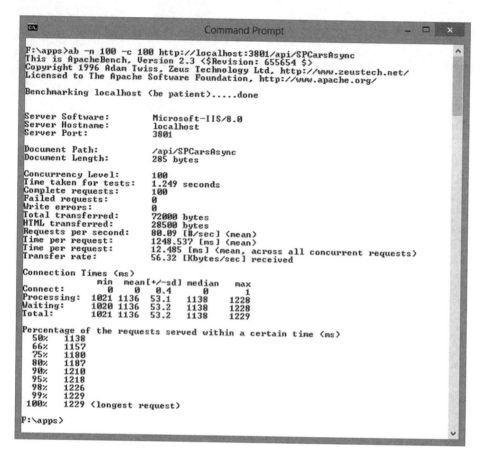

Figure 16-2. *100 concurrent requests to /api/SPCarsAsync*

■ **Note**   Depending on the computer's capabilities, numbers can change. This test was run on the Windows 8 operating system with Intel Core i5-2410M CPU @ 2.30GHz on an SATA drive.

Comparing the "Request per Seconds" field results shows that there is a major difference between the two. While the synchronous endpoint performs 19.30 requests per second, the asynchronous endpoint performs 80.09 requests per second—a huge performance increase.

However, querying an SQL Server database asynchronously may not be a good choice if the operation takes only a little time (for example, less than 40 milliseconds) and if your application has no high capacity requirements. In a real-world application, test your endpoints to see the performance results and adjust your application architecture accordingly.

Asynchronous HTTP Requests

Another scenario where asynchrony plays a key role involves HTTP requests, especially long-running HTTP requests. In Chapter 4, you saw a nice HTTP client API called HttpClient, which is under the System.Net.Http namespace and has no synchronous method making a network call. Use this API to consume an HTTP web service inside ASP.NET Web API controller actions. However, in this section we will use the System.Net.WebClient because new HttpClient has no synchronous methods to compare against. This section's main purpose is to emphasize the performance impact of the asynchronous operations.

If you are on .NET 4.0, you may need to make a few configuration changes to leverage asynchrony efficiently for TCP connections. If the ASP.NET application uses System.Net to communicate over HTTP, the maximum connection limit may need to be increased. For ASP.NET, this is limited by default to 12 times the number of CPUs by the autoConfig feature set in the ASP.NET process model settings. That is, on a quad-core processor, you can have at most 12 × 4, or 48, concurrent connections to an IP endpoint. The easiest way to increase maxconnection in an ASP.NET application is to set System.Net.ServicePointManager.DefaultConnectionLimit programmatically. In an ASP.NET Web API application, this can be done inside the Application_Start method in the Global.asax file (see Listing 16-11). The reason why this setting has been configured programmatically is that autoConfig also needs to be disabled if configuration is to be set inside the configuration file. If autoConfig is disabled, other properties tied to autoConfig, including maxWorkerThreads and maxIoThreads, need to be set as well. You can find more about this setting in the following knowledge base article: http://support.microsoft.com/kb/821268

However, under .NET 4.5, System.Net.ServicePointManager.DefaultConnectionLimit value is set to Int32.MaxValue by default under ASP.NET. On the other hand, regardless of the framework version, this number is set to 2 in other application platforms rather than ASP.NET (a console application, a WPF application, etc.) and as other application platforms don't have the autoConfig feature available, changing this value through the application configuration file should work out fine.

Listing 16-11. Increasing the connectionManagement/maxconnection Limit Inside the Application_Start Method

```
protected void Application_Start(object sender, EventArgs e) {

    //increases the connectionManagement/maxconnection limit
    System.Net.ServicePointManager.DefaultConnectionLimit = int.MaxValue;

    //Lines omitted for brevity . . .
}
```

The sample needs to employ an HTTP web service, which returns a cars list with details. What users will get are cars whose price value is greater than $30,000 (see Listing 16-12).

■ **Note** Don't worry about the implementation of this service. It is enough to know that the service, exposed through the http://localhost:11338/api/cars URI, will produce a list of cars. You'll find the code for this simple service inside the source code provided for this book.

Listing 16-12. Asynchronous HTTP Request Sample Inside a Controller Action

```
public class AsyncCarsController : ApiController {

    //HTTP service base address
    const string CountryAPIBaseAddress = "http://localhost:11338/api/cars";

    public async Task<IEnumerable<Car>> Get() {

        using (WebClient client = new WebClient()) {

            var content = await client.DownloadStringTaskAsync(CountryAPIBaseAddress);
            var cars = JsonConvert.DeserializeObject<List<Car>>(content);
            return cars.Where(x => x.Price > 30000.00F);
        }
    }
}
```

Listing 16-13 shows a synchronous version of the same action.

Listing 16-13. Synchronous HTTP Request Sample Inside a Controller Action

```
public class SyncCarsController : ApiController {

    const string CountryAPIBaseAddress = "http://localhost:11338/api/cars";

    public IEnumerable<Car> Get() {

        using (WebClient client = new WebClient()) {

            var content = client.DownloadString(CountryAPIBaseAddress);
            var cars = JsonConvert.DeserializeObject<List<Car>>(content);
            return cars.Where(x => x.Price > 30000.00F);
        }
    }
}
```

After warming the application up, let's generate a load test against each endpoint. We will send 500 requests this time and set the concurrency level to 100. Figure 16-3 shows the load test result for the synchronous endpoint.

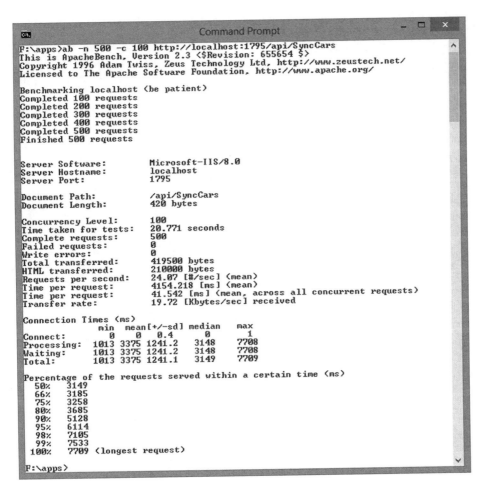

Figure 16-3. *500 requests with the concurrency level 100 to /api/SyncCars*

We can see that we get 24.07 requests per second. Let's do the same test on /api/AsyncCars which makes an asynchronous call to the web service (Figure 16-4).

```
                                    Command Prompt                        _   □   ✕
F:\apps>ab -n 500 -c 100 http://localhost:1795/api/AsyncCars
This is ApacheBench, Version 2.3 <$Revision: 655654 $>
Copyright 1996 Adam Twiss, Zeus Technology Ltd, http://www.zeustech.net/
Licensed to The Apache Software Foundation, http://www.apache.org/

Benchmarking localhost (be patient)
Completed 100 requests
Completed 200 requests
Completed 300 requests
Completed 400 requests
Completed 500 requests
Finished 500 requests


Server Software:        Microsoft-IIS/8.0
Server Hostname:        localhost
Server Port:            1795

Document Path:          /api/AsyncCars
Document Length:        420 bytes

Concurrency Level:      100
Time taken for tests:   10.132 seconds
Complete requests:      500
Failed requests:        0
Write errors:           0
Total transferred:      419500 bytes
HTML transferred:       210000 bytes
Requests per second:    49.35 [#/sec] (mean)
Time per request:       2026.402 [ms] (mean)
Time per request:       20.264 [ms] (mean, across all concurrent requests)
Transfer rate:          40.43 [Kbytes/sec] received

Connection Times (ms)
              min  mean[+/-sd] median   max
Connect:        0    0   0.4      0       1
Processing:  1003 1793 366.5    1988    2121
Waiting:     1003 1793 366.5    1988    2120
Total:       1003 1794 366.4    1988    2121

Percentage of the requests served within a certain time (ms)
  50%    1988
  66%    1997
  75%    2004
  80%    2008
  90%    2028
  95%    2078
  98%    2108
  99%    2115
 100%    2121 (longest request)

F:\apps>
```

Figure 16-4. 500 requests with a concurrency level of 100 to /api/AsyncCars

We get 49.35 requests per second this time—an overwhelming result and a huge performance increase. With network operations like these inside your Web API application, making network calls asynchronously could improve performance dramatically.

Asynchronous File Uploads

You probably upload several files daily from web sites via HTML form file upload and develop several applications that enable this functionality. However, in this section, we will look at how to handle form file uploads in ASP.NET Web API asynchronously.

ASP.NET Web API has APIs that can handle data encoded with MIME multipart. We will use it in our sample. So the request arriving at our server should be of the multipart/form-data type. Listing 16-14 shows the sample application's API controller.

Listing 16-14. UploadController, FileResult, and CustomMultipartFormDataStreamProvider Classes

```
Fpublic class FileResult {

    public IEnumerable<string> FileNames { get; set; }
    public string Submitter { get; set; }
}

public class UploadController : ApiController {

    public async Task<FileResult> Post() {

        //Check whether it is an HTML form file upload request
        if (!Request.Content.IsMimeMultipartContent("form-data"))
        {
            //return UnsupportedMediaType response back if not
            throw new HttpResponseException(
                new HttpResponseMessage(
                    HttpStatusCode.UnsupportedMediaType)
            );
        }

        //Determine the upload path
        var uploadPath =
            HttpContext.Current.Server.MapPath("~/Files");

        var multipartFormDataStreamProvider =
            new CustomMultipartFormDataStreamProvider(uploadPath);

        // Read the MIME multipart content asynchronously
        // using the stream provider just created.
        await Request.Content.ReadAsMultipartAsync(
            multipartFormDataStreamProvider);

        // Create response
        return new FileResult {

            FileNames =
                multipartFormDataStreamProvider
                .FileData.Select(
                    entry => entry.LocalFileName),

            Submitter =
                multipartFormDataStreamProvider
                .FormData["submitter"]
        };
    }
}

public class CustomMultipartFormDataStreamProvider
    : MultipartFormDataStreamProvider {

    public CustomMultipartFormDataStreamProvider(
        string rootPath) : base(rootPath) { }
```

```
    public override string GetLocalFileName(
        HttpContentHeaders headers) {

        if (headers != null &&
            headers.ContentDisposition != null) {

            return headers
                .ContentDisposition
                .FileName.TrimEnd('"').TrimStart('"');
        }

        return base.GetLocalFileName(headers);
    }
}
```

First, check whether the request is an HTML form file upload request or not. If not, an UnsupportedMediaType response is getting returned. Then create a new MultipartFormDataStreamProvider instance. This class is suited for use with HTML file uploads for writing file content to a System.IO.FileStream. The stream provider looks at the Content-Disposition header field and determines an output System.IO.Stream based on the presence of a file name parameter. This makes it convenient to process MIME Multipart HTML Form data, which combine form data and file content. Finally, invoke the ReadAsMultipartAsync extension method of HttpContent to actually read and save the file to the specified place.

In order to test the functionality of this sample, here's a console client that uploads the file to this HTTP service (see Figure 16-5).

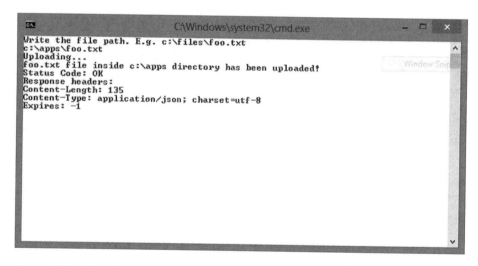

Figure 16-5. *File upload console client application after upload is completed*

After the upload is completed, the file can be seen inside the Files folder.

───

■ **Note**   You'll find the full source code of the file upload console client application inside the source code provided for this book.

───

Multiple Asynchronous Operations in One

Some situations may require you to run multiple asynchronous operations inside a controller action, each one of them to be executed separately. You can leverage WhenAll, one of the handy utilities of the Task class. The Task.WhenAll method receives a collection of tasks and creates another task that will complete when all the supplied tasks have completed (you have already seen this in Chapter 2).

In order to demonstrate a sample usage, we have created an API that exposes the cars list with two different resources. One resource returns the list of cheap cars, and the other, the list of expensive ones (see Listing 16-15). This API is the one that will be employed in our client application.

Listing 16-15. Cars API Controller

```
public class CarsController : ApiController {

    readonly CarsContext _carsContext = new CarsContext();

    [HttpGet]
    public IEnumerable<Car> Cheap() {

        Thread.Sleep(1000);

        return _carsContext.GetCars(car => car.Price < 50000);
    }

    [HttpGet]
    public IEnumerable<Car> Expensive() {

        Thread.Sleep(1000);

        return _carsContext.GetCars(car => car.Price >= 50000);
    }
}
```

The CarsContext class is a class that has the mock-up data and displays that data with a public method (see Listing 16-16). Also, as you can see, we are hanging the thread for one second in order to see the results clearly when testing against client implementation.

Listing 16-16. CarsContext Class

```
public class Car {

    public int Id { get; set; }
    public string Make { get; set; }
    public string Model { get; set; }
    public int Year { get; set; }
    public float Price { get; set; }
}
```

```
public class CarsContext {

    //data
    static List<Car> cars = new List<Car> {
        new Car {
            Id = 1,
            Make = "Make1",
            Model = "Model1",
            Year = 2010,
            Price = 10732.2F
        },
        new Car {
            Id = 2,
            Make = "Make2",
            Model = "Model2",
            Year = 2008,
            Price = 27233.1F
        },

        //Lines omitted for brevity
    };

    public IEnumerable<Car> GetCars(Func<Car, bool> predicate) {

        return cars.Where(predicate);
    }
}
```

The point in the client application is to get both the cheap and expensive cars and display them together at once. This goal will be achieved by consuming the APIs separately. Listing 16-17 shows the complete implementation for this.

Listing 16-17. Cars API Controller in the Client Application

```
public class Car {

    public int Id { get; set; }
    public string Make { get; set; }
    public string Model { get; set; }
    public int Year { get; set; }
    public float Price { get; set; }
}

public class CarsController : ApiController {

    readonly List<string> _payloadSources = new Liszt<string> {
        "http://localhost:2700/api/cars/cheap",
        "http://localhost:2700/api/cars/expensive"
    };

    readonly HttpClient _httpClient = new HttpClient();
```

```
[HttpGet]
public async Task<IEnumerable<Car>> AllCars() {

    var carsResult = new List<Car>();

    foreach (var uri in _payloadSources) {

        var cars = await getCars(uri);
        carsResult.AddRange(cars);
    }

    return carsResult;
}

//private helper which gets the payload and hands it back as IEnumerable<Car>
private async Task<IEnumerable<Car>> getCars(string uri) {

    var response = await _httpClient.GetAsync(uri);
    var content = await response.Content.ReadAsAsync<IEnumerable<Car>>();

    return content;
}
}
```

To make this example work, the so-called action-based route is used (you are familiar with it from Chapter 9) (see Listing 16-18).

Listing 16-18. Action-Based Route Used for the Sample in Listing 16-17

```
protected void Application_Start(object sender, EventArgs e) {

    GlobalConfiguration.Configuration.Routes.MapHttpRoute(
        "DefaultHttpRoute",
        "api/{controller}/{action}/{id}",
        new { id = RouteParameter.Optional }
    );
}
```

Inside the CarsController, there is a public method named AllCars, which will be our action. The AllCars method is, as usual, marked with the async modifier for all asynchronous Web API controller actions. Its return type is Task<IEnumerable<Car>>. Inside the AllCars action method, loop through the API source list, which has been defined as a List<string> object, and inside the foreach loop, get the cars list from the HTTP service asynchronously. Notice that the await keyword is used inside the foreach loop without any worries. This action was very hard to accomplish before, but the new C# asynchronous language features handle it now. When tested, this API should complete in roughly two seconds, because each HTTP call takes about one second. Figure 16-6 shows the benchmarking result issued with the Apache Benchmarking Tool.

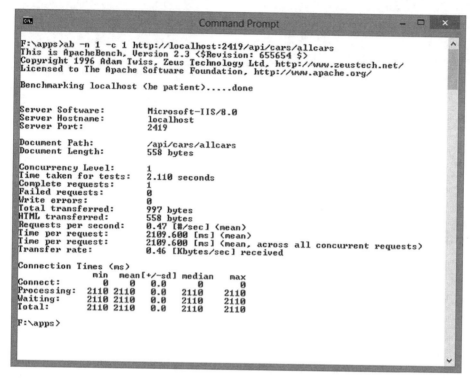

Figure 16-6. *Benchmarking result of Cars API AllCars controller action*

Let's see the implementation of the same operation with the help of Task.WhenAll (see Listing 16-19).

Listing 16-19. Cars API AllCarsInParallel Controller Action Using Task.WhenAll

```
[HttpGet]
public async Task<IEnumerable<Car>> AllCarsInParallel() {

    var allTasks = _payloadSources.Select(uri =>
        getCars(uri)
    );

    IEnumerable<Car>[] allResults = await Task.WhenAll(allTasks);

    return allResults.SelectMany(cars => cars);
}
```

First of all, get all of the tasks that are to be run in parallel. This is done here with the LINQ Select method and a lambda expression, and the type of allTasks variable is IEnumerable<Task<IEnumerable<Car>>>. As a second action, pass the collection of tasks into Task.WhenAll method to get a result of the type IEnumerable<Car> array. Actually, the Task.WhenAll method returns Task<IEnumerable<Car>[]> in this case, but as we "await" on this, we get the result as IEnumerable<Car> array. Task.WhenAll will run the supplied collection of tasks in parallel, and this will shorten the time for completion. Finally, we use another LINQ method, SelectMany, to return the result. SelectMany takes a series of collections and combines them all into one. Measure this action's completion time, and you'll see that it is reduced by half (see Figure 16-7).

480

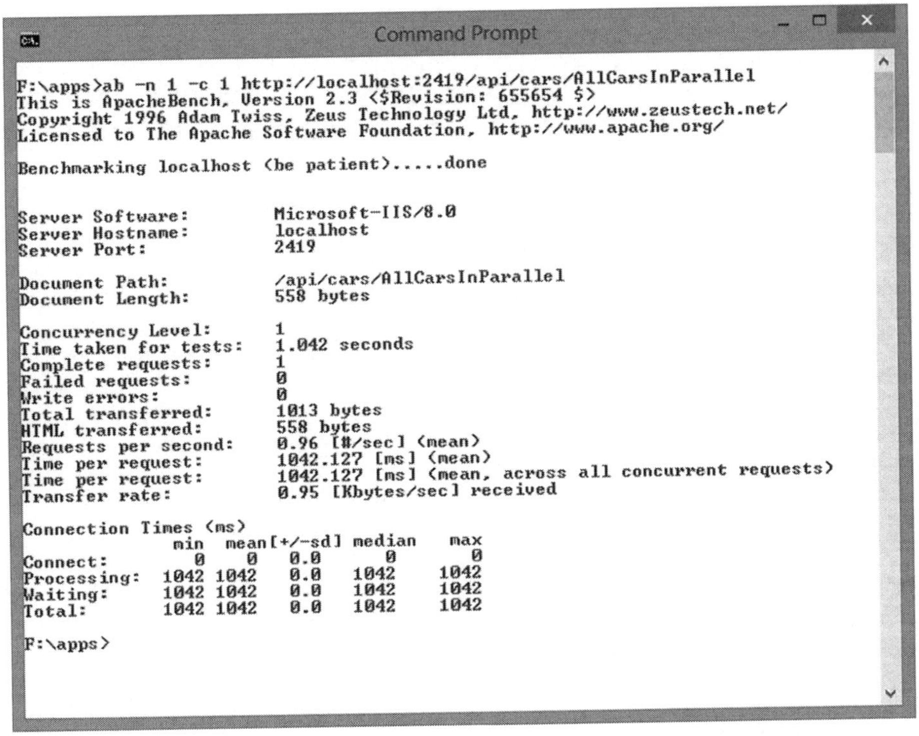

Figure 16-7. Benchmarking the result of Cars API AllCarsInParallel controller action

HTTP Caching

Caching, in general, is an optimization to improve performance and scalability by keeping a resource inside a fast-reachable store—a computer's random-access memory (RAM), for example. If you have resources that aren't likely to change over a given amount of time, making those resources cacheable provides huge performance benefits.

In the scope of ASP.NET Web API, the benefits of caching can be leveraged along with HTTP, a widely used and understood transport protocol with a very detailed specification. Inside this specification, HTTP caching plays a big part. It is controlled by the HTTP caching headers, which are sent by the web server to specify how long a resource is valid and when it last changed.

This section will take a close look at HTTP caching and how to implement this mechanism.

HTTP Specification for Caching

Caching's main purpose in HTTP/1.1[1] is to eliminate the need for sending requests in most cases and for sending full responses in most other cases. The HTTP caching mechanism can be divided into several parts:

- control of cachable resource by the origin server
- validation of a cached resource
- invalidation after updates and deletions

Let's look at each of these topics separately before implementing the logic with ASP.NET Web API.

---

[1] www.w3.org/Protocols/rfc2616/rfc2616.html

> ■ **Note** Although most parts of HTTP caching are covered in this section, there is more information about the HTTP caching specification (RFC 2616 Section 13, Caching in HTTP) at www.w3.org/Protocols/rfc2616/rfc2616-sec13.html.

Control of the Cachable Resource by the Origin Server

In order for caching to work with HTTP, the origin server of the resource must indicate that it supports caching. This action is performed by specific HTTP response headers. If the resource can be cached, the origin server also dictates by whom the content can be cached and for how long.

The main header that controls the cache for the server and the client is the Cache-Control[2] general header. The Cache-Control header dictates the cache behavior of the resource, which must be obeyed by all caching mechanisms along the request/response chain. Either the request or the response message may carry the Cache-Control header.

If the response message has the Cache-Control header, the Cache-Control header carries the cacheability information for the resource, including how long and by whom it can be cached. Figure 16-8 shows a sample GET request and its response message, which carries the Cache-Control header.

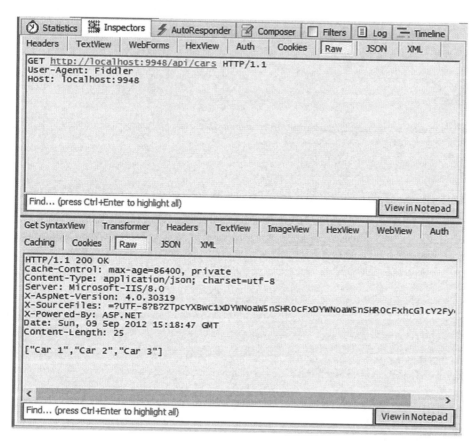

Figure 16-8. A GET request and its response message, which has the Cache-Control header

---

[2]www.w3.org/Protocols/rfc2616/rfc2616-sec14.html#sec14.9

In the response header, the origin server states that the resource can be cached for a day (in delta-seconds) with max-age directive, but it must not be cached by a shared cache, such as a proxy server. A client with this response message can cache the resource for a day and never needs to hit the origin server during that time.

Also, using the no-cache directive, the origin server can state that the response is noncacheable. Figure 16-9 shows a GET request and its response message, which carries the Cache-Control header with a no-cache directive.

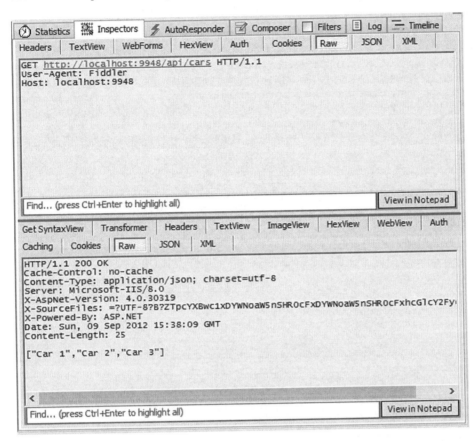

Figure 16-9. A GET Request and its response message, which has the Cache-Control header with a no-cache directive

As the content owners, we may state that the resource is cacheable for a day through the Cache-Control header so that the client can cache the response and serve it for a day. But what if the resource is changed during that cache period? The client would serve the stale resource (as indicated, the resource is cacheable only for a day). This is where cached resource validation—the next topic—enters the scene.

Validation of a Cached Resource

Consumers of our resource would prefer to have a fresh copy of the resource's representation. To ensure that they get what they want, consumers need to have some way of validating the resource with the origin server. Several HTTP headers enable them to do this.

Along with the response message, the origin server can append either the ETag or Last-Modified header (or both of them). The ETag (short for "entity tag")[3] is a response header that represents the state of a resource at a given point

---

[3] www.w3.org/Protocols/rfc2616/rfc2616-sec14.html#sec14.19

in time. An ETag is also just an opaque, server-generated string, one that the client shouldn't try to infer any meaning from. On the other hand, from the syntactic standpoint the ETag should, according to HTTP specification, always be in quotes.

The ETag is used for comparing two or more entities from the same requested resource, a resource identified by its unique URI, and one of the parts of the HTTP validation model. An entity tag has two main roles inside the HTTP specification. One is to validate the cached resource (the main subject of this section), and the other is to make concurrency checks.

When a consumer sends a request and receives a response that includes the ETag value, s/he can then send that ETag value in a conditional GET request to server. The server then looks at the received ETag value and decides whether the resource is up to date or stale. The way that the server informs the consumer of the result of this validation is determined via the HTTP response status code. If the origin server decides that the resource is still fresh, the server can send a "304 Not Modified" response with no message body. The ability to send a 304 response can save a lot of bandwidth and reduce response time. Besides, the origin server doesn't have to process the resource creation logic, which might involve a database lookup or a similar operation.

To see a sample showing this in action, let's send a GET request to a URI and respond with an ETag header (see Figure 16-10).

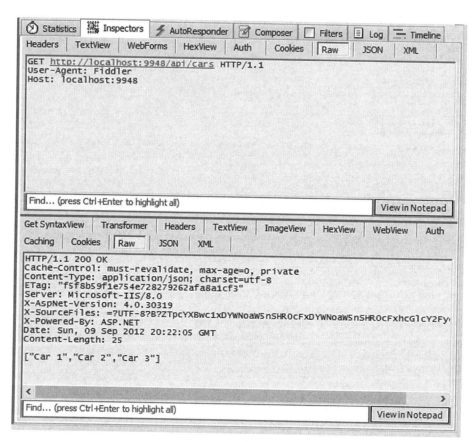

Figure 16-10. *A GET Request and its response message, which has the ETag header*

As you can see, the response has both Cache-Control and ETag headers. The Cache-Control header indicates that the resource must not be cached by a shared cache and that the resource can be cached for 0 seconds. The origin server stated that this resource representation can be cached for 0 seconds because the response also contains an

ETag key and the server wants the client to revalidate the resource when the cache expires—instantly, as it happens, since the max-age is 0.

Let's assume that we, as the client, cached the resource and need to send another request to the same URI. When we send a request this time, we will append the ETag header value, previously obtained from the server, to the request message with the If-None-Match[4] header. This means that we will send a conditional GET request to the origin server. The If-None-Match header will carry the entity tag and tell the server to return the full response only if this ETag is not fresh. If the resource is up to date, the server should respond with "304 Not Modified" response (see Figure 16-11).

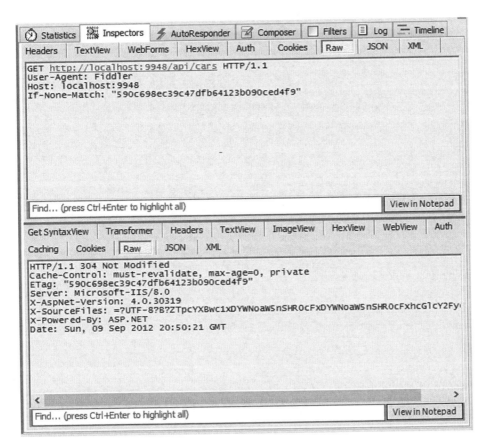

Figure 16-11. A conditional GET request and its "304 Not Modified" response

As you can see, the response status code is now "304 Not Modified," and the response body is empty. This response tells the client to go ahead and use the cached resource, as it is still up to date. Then the client will pull the resource out of the cache and use it.

Besides the ETag header, there is one more validation header that can be used: the Last-Modified[5] entity header. This header states the date and time at which the resource was last modified. The client can later use this value to check the state of the resource. Figure 16-12 shows a response that carries a Last-Modified header.

---

[4]www.w3.org/Protocols/rfc2616/rfc2616-sec14.html#sec14.26
[5]www.w3.org/Protocols/rfc2616/rfc2616-sec14.html#sec14.29

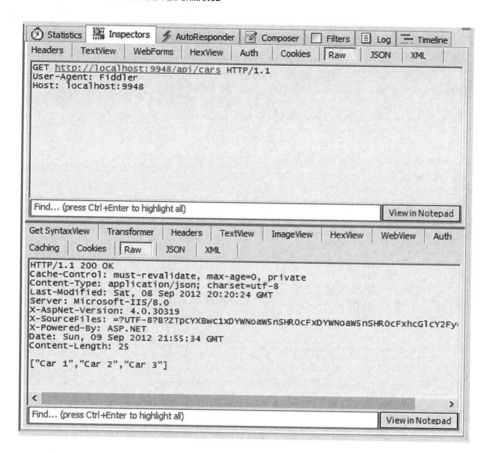

Figure 16-12. *A GET Request and its response message, which has the Last-Modified header*

With this header value in place, the client can now send a conditional GET request to the origin server with the Last-Modified header value with an If-Modified-Since[6] header. If the requested resource has not been modified since the time specified in the If-Modified-Since header, a full response will not be returned from the server. Instead, a "304 Not Modified" response will be returned without any message body (see Figure 16-13).

---

[6]www.w3.org/Protocols/rfc2616/rfc2616-sec14.html#sec14.25

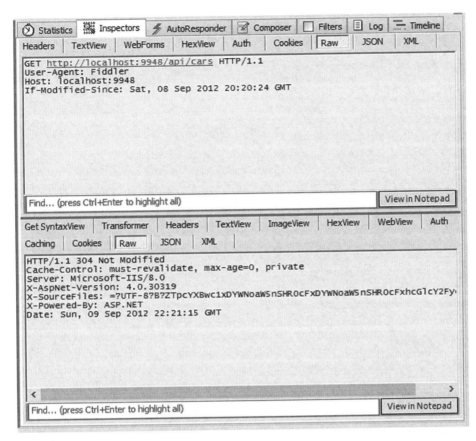

Figure 16-13. A conditional GET request with an If-Modified-Since header and its "304 Not Modified" response

You probably noticed that requests have been sent without an Accept header and responses have been returned in application/json format, the default format of the origin server. However, if a request were sent with an Accept header for application/xml, the XML representation of the resource would be returned. If the client has any validation header values from the response whose format is application/json, it will try to use the same validation value for a request whose Accept header states application/xml. If the server has an up-to-date copy of the resource, it will respond with a "304 Not Modified" status code. This is apperently not the desired behavior, because the resource format is different and they should be cached separately.

Another response header can be used to solve this problem. The Vary[7] header value indicates the set of request-header fields that determines whether a cache is permitted to use the response to reply to a subsequent request. Figure 16-14 shows a response message that carries the Vary header.

---

[7]www.w3.org/Protocols/rfc2616/rfc2616-sec14.html#sec14.44

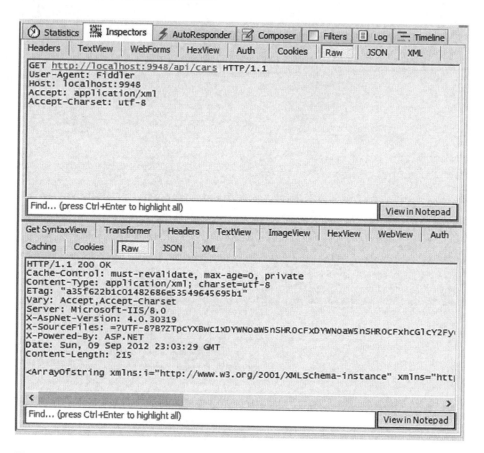

Figure 16-14. *A GET Request and its response message, which has the ETag and Vary headers*

The response message in this representation states that the Accept and the Accept-Charset header values are not changed. For example, if you try to send a conditional GET request with the ETag value obtained from this response and with the Accept header value of application/json, you should get a full "200 OK" response along with the response body, because the Accept header is different from that in the previous request (see Figure 16-15).

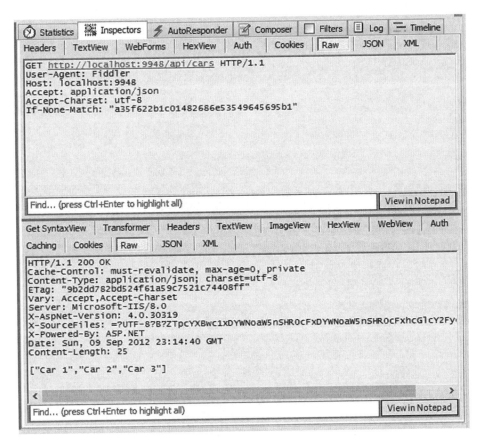

Figure 16-15. *A conditional GET request and its response message, which has the ETag and Vary headers*

You see that the ETag value is different in this representation of the resource. If you were to send a conditional GET request with this ETag value for a resource in `application/json` format, you would get "304 Not Modified" response if the resource is still up to date (see Figure 16-16).

Figure 16-16. *A conditional GET request and its "304 Not Modified" response message*

Invalidation After Updates and Deletions

As was explained in Chapter 3, POST, PUT, and DELETE are not recognized as safe verbs. They can change the state of a resource. If the origin server generates ETags by computing a hash value out of the resource content, then invalidating the cache would be easy, because if the content has changed, the hash value will be changed. However, as you will see, when implementing the HTTP caching in ASP.NET Web API, generating the ETag value by computing the hash of the content is unnecessary if the application's architecture is crafted correctly.

Assuming that /api/cars/1 URI represents the Car 1 object in our HTTP API, if we send a PUT or DELETE request to /api/cars/1, it is obvious that Car 1's state will change, and the previously created ETags can be invalidated. This requires storing the ETags in a separate place, such as memory collection, but this makes it much more efficient.

Applying HTTP Caching in ASP.NET Web API

ASP.NET Web API extensibility points make it easy to implement HTTP caching and to plug it into our application. With such rich HTTP API elements as strongly typed headers, it becomes even easier. What needs to be done now is to create a message handler to handle the caching and cache invalidation.

Let's look at a sample ASP.NET Web API application where we can retrieve a list of cars, get an individual car, update a car, and delete a car. Figure 16-17 shows the GET request against /api/cars and the corresponding response message with the headers.

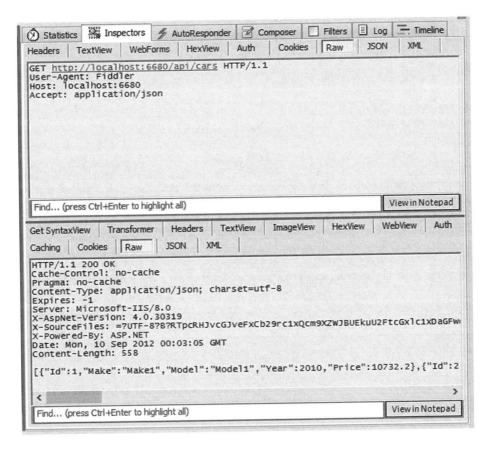

Figure 16-17. *A GET request against /api/cars*

Notice that the response contains neither the ETag nor the Last-Modified header, and the Cache-Control header states that this resource representation cannot be cached. Let's see how we can implement our HttpCachingHandler to enable caching for the application.

HTTP Caching Message Handler

First off, a separate class is needed to keep a record of the cached resource. For this purpose, we create a CacheableEntity class (see Listing 16-20).

Listing 16-20. The CacheableEntity Class

```
public class CacheableEntity {

    public CacheableEntity(string resourceKey) {

        ResourceKey = resourceKey;
    }
```

```
public string ResourceKey { get; private set; }
public EntityTagHeaderValue EntityTag { get; set; }
public DateTimeOffset LastModified { get; set; }

public bool IsValid(DateTimeOffset modifiedSince) {

    var lastModified = LastModified.UtcDateTime;
    return (lastModified.AddSeconds(-1) < modifiedSince.UtcDateTime);
}
}
```

The CacheableEntity class basically holds all the necessary information about a cacheable resource. The ResourceKey property of the CacheableEntity class will be the ID of the cached entity, against which others can be compared. The EntityTag and LastModified properties will hold corresponding header values. A method called IsValid will be used when drawing comparisons against the last-modified date and time of the resource.

■ **Note**   This section's main concern is, not to implement a fully functional and extensible caching handler, but to point you in the right direction. If you want a more flexible and robust caching handler, one you can plug into your ASP.NET Web API, Ali Kheyrollahi maintains an open source project called **CacheCow** on GitHub (https://github.com/aliostad/CacheCow). It allows you to extend the project-provided caching handler to fit your needs.

Let's have a look at the core structure of the HttpCachingHandler message handler (see Listing 16-21).

Listing 16-21. The Initial Structure of the HttpCachingHandler

```
public class HttpCachingHandler : DelegatingHandler {

    private readonly string[] _varyHeaders;

    public HttpCachingHandler(params string[] varyHeaders) {

        _varyHeaders = varyHeaders;
    }

    protected override Task<HttpResponseMessage> SendAsync(
        HttpRequestMessage request,
        CancellationToken cancellationToken) {

        return base.SendAsync(request, cancellationToken);
    }

    private string GetResourceKey(
        Uri uri,
        string[] varyHeaders,
        HttpRequestMessage request) {

        throw new NotImplementedException();
    }
```

```
    private string GetResourceKey(
        string trimedRequestUri,
        string[] varyHeaders,
        HttpRequestMessage request) {

        throw new NotImplementedException();
    }

    private EntityTagHeaderValue GenerateETag(string[] varyHeaders) {

        throw new NotImplementedException();
    }

    private string GetRequestUri(Uri requestUri) {

        throw new NotImplementedException();
    }
}
```

First of all, there is a constructor method that takes an array of strings as a parameter for Vary header values. There are also four private helper methods that are not yet implemented (we will implement them before moving further).

The GetRequestUri method will trim the RequestUri as the /api/cars URI, and the /api/cars/ URI will represent the same resource. So we will trim the "/" character at the end, if it is present. Listing 16-22 shows the implementation of the GetRequestUri method.

Listing 16-22. The Implementation of the GetRequestUri Method

```
private string GetRequestUri(Uri requestUri) {

    return string.Concat(
        requestUri.LocalPath.TrimEnd('/'),
        requestUri.Query).ToLower(CultureInfo.InvariantCulture);
}
```

The GenerateETag method is just a helper class where the ETag value is actually created. As Listing 16-23 shows, a Guid is used to generate the ETag.

Listing 16-23. The GenerateETag Method Implementation

```
private EntityTagHeaderValue GenerateETag() {

    var eTag = string.Concat(
        "\"", Guid.NewGuid().ToString("N"), "\"");

    return new EntityTagHeaderValue(eTag);
}
```

Notice that we put the ETag value in quotes. If this action wasn't performed, there would be a runtime error by the EntityTagHeaderValue class because it forces you to generate the ETag in quotes.

Last is the GetResourceKey method, which is a little bit more complicated than the others. Listing 16-24 shows the implementations of the GetResourceKey method and its only overload.

Listing 16-24. Implementation of the GetResourceKey Method

```
private string GetResourceKey(
    Uri uri,
    string[] varyHeaders,
    HttpRequestMessage request) {

    return GetResourceKey(GetRequestUri(uri), varyHeaders, request);
}

private string GetResourceKey(
    string trimedRequestUri,
    string[] varyHeaders,
    HttpRequestMessage request) {

    var requestedVaryHeaderValuePairs = request.Headers
        .Where(x => varyHeaders.Contains(x.Key))
        .Select(x => string.Format("{0}:{1}", x.Key, string.Join(";", x.Value)));

    return string.Format(
        "{0}:{1}",
        trimedRequestUri,
        string.Join("_", requestedVaryHeaderValuePairs)).ToLower(
            CultureInfo.InvariantCulture);
}
```

The difference between these two methods is that one accepts a Uri type as parameter and the other accepts a string as parameter for a trimmed URI. Actual implementation is inside the second method. Inside the second GetResourceKey method, first get all values of the headers whose keys will be passed through the constructor as Vary headers keys, and then join them to create a string value. Second, join those with the trimmed request URI to generate a unique key for our resource.

With our private helper methods in place, we can now go ahead and implement the actual logic inside a SendAsync method. But before moving further, let's create a static ConcurrentDictionary<string, CacheableEntity> instance inside the HttpCachingHandler class to keep track of the generated CacheableEntity instances (see Listing 16-25).

Listing 16-25. Static Dictionary Instance for the CacheEntity Values Inside the HttpCachingHandler Class

```
public class HttpCachingHandler : DelegatingHandler {

    private static ConcurrentDictionary<string, CacheableEntity> _eTagCacheDictionary =
            new ConcurrentDictionary<string, CacheableEntity>();

    //Lines omitted for brevity
}
```

First, you ought to be able to send "304 Not Modified" responses if the cache is still valid. To do that, follow this approach:

1. Inspect whether the request is a GET request or not.

2. Generate the ResourceKey according to the request URI and Vary headers.

3. If the request is a GET request, retrieve the If-None-Match, If-Modified-Since header values.

4. Inspect whether the request contains any ETag values or not.

5. If the request contains any ETag values, check whether there are any CacheableEntity instances for this request inside our CacheableEntity dictionary.

6. If there are any CacheableEntity instances for this request inside our CacheableEntity dictionary, go ahead and compare them with the ETag values obtained from the request.

7. If there is a match, return a "304 Not Modified" response.

8. If the request doesn't contain any ETag values, check whether the request contains the If-Modified-Since header.

9. If the request contains the If-Modified-Since header, check whether there are any CacheableEntity instances for this request inside our CacheableEntity dictionary.

10. If there are any CacheableEntity instances for this request inside our CacheableEntity dictionary, check the validity of the cache according to the If-Modified-Since header value.

11. If the cache is valid, return a "304 Not Modified" response.

12. If the request is not a GET request or if any of the cache validations doesn't pass, continue processing the request.

Listing 16-26 expresses these requirements with the code inside the SendAsync method.

Listing 16-26. Initial Implementation of the SendAsync Method

```
protected override async Task<HttpResponseMessage> SendAsync(
    HttpRequestMessage request,
    CancellationToken cancellationToken) {

    var resourceKey = GetResourceKey(request.RequestUri, _varyHeaders, request);
    CacheableEntity cacheableEntity = null;
    var cacheControlHeader = new CacheControlHeaderValue {
        Private = true,
        MustRevalidate = true,
        MaxAge = TimeSpan.FromSeconds(0)
    };

    if (request.Method == HttpMethod.Get) {

        var eTags = request.Headers.IfNoneMatch;
        var modifiedSince = request.Headers.IfModifiedSince;
        var anyEtagsFromTheClientExist = eTags.Any();
        var doWeHaveAnyCacheableEntityForTheRequest =
            _eTagCacheDictionary.TryGetValue(resourceKey, out cacheableEntity);

        if (anyEtagsFromTheClientExist) {
```

```
            if (doWeHaveAnyCacheableEntityForTheRequest) {
                if (eTags.Any(x => x.Tag == cacheableEntity.EntityTag.Tag)) {

                    var tempResp = new HttpResponseMessage(HttpStatusCode.NotModified);
                    tempResp.Headers.CacheControl = cacheControlHeader;
                    return tempResp;
                }
            }
        }
        else if (modifiedSince.HasValue) {

            if (doWeHaveAnyCacheableEntityForTheRequest) {
                if (cacheableEntity.IsValid(modifiedSince.Value)) {

                    var tempResp = new HttpResponseMessage(HttpStatusCode.NotModified);
                    tempResp.Headers.CacheControl = cacheControlHeader;
                    return tempResp;
                }
            }
        }
    }

    try {

        return await base.SendAsync(request, cancellationToken);
    }
    catch (Exception ex) {

        return request.CreateErrorResponse(
            HttpStatusCode.InternalServerError, ex);
    }
}
```

Everything done inside the SendAsync method here accords with the just-listed requirements, but there are a couple of parts worth pointing out. First of all, we have marked the method with an async modifier because the await operator will be used inside our method. Also, we put the base.SendAsync method inside a try/catch block because we want to catch the exception, which might occur inside the pipeline (e.g., inside another message handler), and return a formatted error message instead of just terminating the process.

So far, so good—but there's a problem. The logic to generate the cacheable entities and send them back as responses hasn't been implemented. The place to perform this action is where the response comes back through the pipeline—the last place where there's a chance to modify the response. We need to perform this action because we want to have the full response, which is ready to go out the door, to make the modifications (see Listing 16-27).

Listing 16-27. Implementation of the Generating Cacheable Response Messages

```
protected override async Task<HttpResponseMessage> SendAsync(
    HttpRequestMessage request,
    CancellationToken cancellationToken) {

    //Lines omitted for brevity
```

```
        HttpResponseMessage response;
        try {

            response = await base.SendAsync(request, cancellationToken);
        }
        catch (Exception ex) {

            response = request.CreateErrorResponse(
                HttpStatusCode.InternalServerError, ex);
        }

        if (response.IsSuccessStatusCode) {

            if (request.Method == HttpMethod.Get &&
                !_eTagCacheDictionary.TryGetValue(
                    resourceKey, out cacheableEntity)) {

                cacheableEntity = new CacheableEntity(resourceKey);
                cacheableEntity.EntityTag = GenerateETag();
                cacheableEntity.LastModified = DateTimeOffset.Now;

                _eTagCacheDictionary.AddOrUpdate(
                    resourceKey, cacheableEntity, (k, e) => cacheableEntity);
            }

            if (request.Method == HttpMethod.Get) {

                response.Headers.CacheControl = cacheControlHeader;
                response.Headers.ETag = cacheableEntity.EntityTag;
                response.Content.Headers.LastModified = cacheableEntity.LastModified;

                _varyHeaders.ForEach(
                    varyHeader => response.Headers.Vary.Add(varyHeader));
            }
        }

        return response;
    }
```

A little extension method called ForEach is used here. Listing 16-28 shows its implementation.

Listing 16-28. ForEach Extension Method

```
internal static class IEnumerableExtensions {

    public static void ForEach<T>(
        this IEnumerable<T> enumerable, Action<T> action) {

        foreach (var item in enumerable)
            action(item);
    }
}
```

The code stays the same before base.SendAsync is called, but the basic logic for creating the cacheable resource if the request is a GET request has been added. First, we check whether the response status code is a success status code. If it is, then we go ahead check whether there is a CacheableEntity for this request. If there isn't, we generate one. Last, if the request is a GET request, we make the response cacheable and return it.

Before trying this out, we need to register the message handler. Generally, we would want to register this caching handler as the first message handler because this handler should see the request first and the response last. Registering it as the first message handler will provide this ability (see Listing 16-29).

Listing 16-29. Registering the HttpCachingHandler

```
protected void Application_Start(object sender, EventArgs e) {

    HttpConfiguration config = GlobalConfiguration.Configuration;

    //Lines omitted for brevity

    config.MessageHandlers.Insert(0,
        new HttpCachingHandler("Accept", "Accept-Charset"));
}
```

■ **Note** If you have a message handler that performs the request authentication, you may want to register it before the caching handler, as you'd never want to deal with unauthenticated requests. Since everything depends on your scenario, consider the order while you are registering your message handlers.

You can see that Accept and Accept-Charset headers have to be passed in to be used as Vary header values. Let's give this a try with Fiddler. When a request is sent to /api/cars, the cacheable response should be returned (see Figure 16-18).

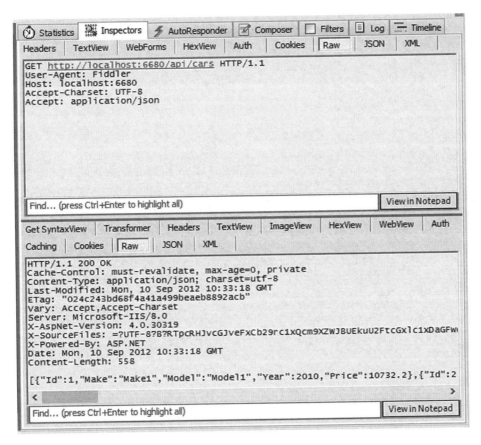

Figure 16-18. *A GET request to /api/cars and its cacheable response*

The cacheable response was returned. Now let's use the ETag to make a conditional GET request and see whether a "304 Not Modified" response comes back (see Figure 16-19).

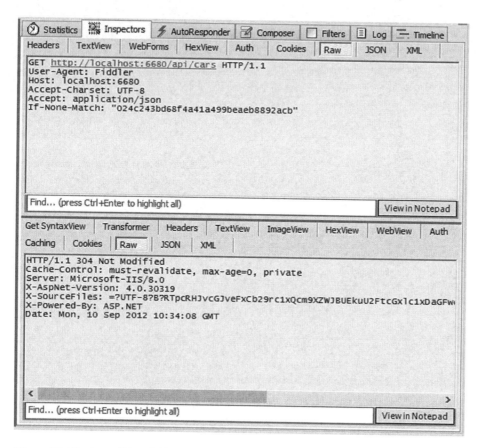

Figure 16-19. A conditional GET request and "304 Not Modified" response

It worked as expected! Now let's use the same ETag to make another conditional GET request, this time for the application/xml format. According to our requirement, there should be a full "200 OK" response and a new ETag (see Figure 16-20).

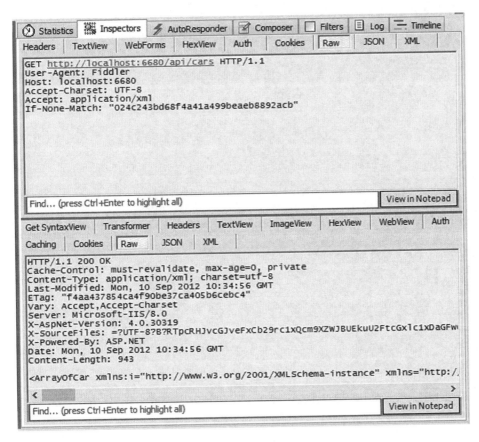

Figure 16-20. *A conditional GET request and full "200 OK" response*

Again, it worked as expected. This time, let's use the Last-Modified header value returned by the application/xml request to send a conditional GET request. A "304 Not Modified" response should come back (see Figure 16-21).

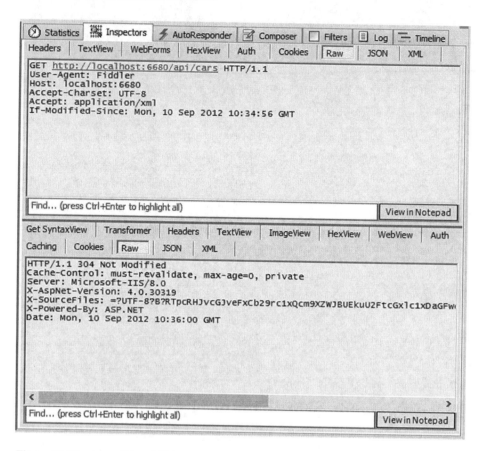

Figure 16-21. A conditional GET request with an If-Modified-Since header and a "304 Not Modified" response

Let's change the Accept-Charset value and send the same conditional GET request shown in Figure 16-21. Figure 16-22 shows the result.

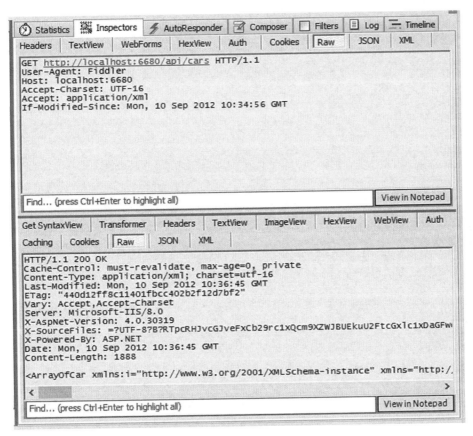

Figure 16-22. A conditional GET request with an If-Modified-Since header and a full "200 OK" response

A full "200 OK" response came back because the cache differs by the Accept-Charset header as well.

Our little handler works as expected, but it doesn't cover invalidation of a cached entity. For example, let's send a POST request to /api/cars to add a new car to the list (see Figure 16-23).

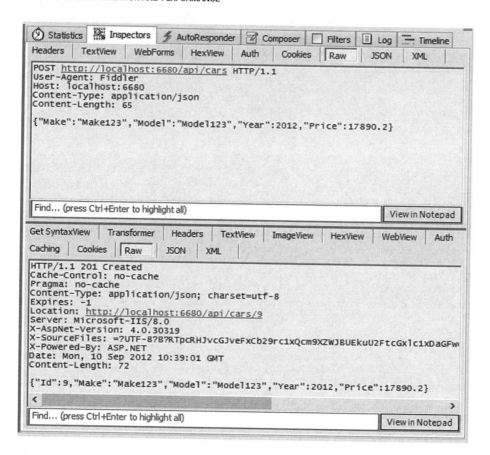

Figure 16-23. *A POST request to /api/cars*

Now the collection is changed. Let's send a conditional GET request to /api/cars with the previously obtained ETag value. Normally, a full "200 OK" response should come back, but because our handler doesn't invalidate the cache, "304 Not Modified", which wrongly states the freshness of the cache, will be returned (Figure 16-24).

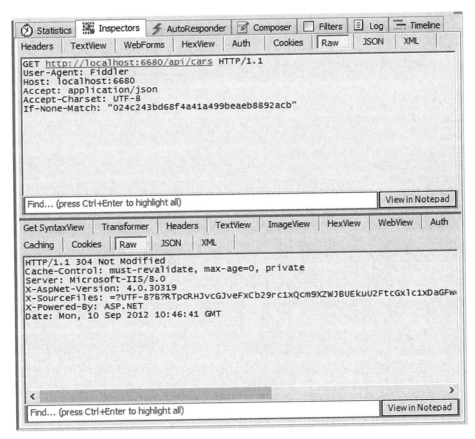

Figure 16-24. *A conditional GET request with an If-None-Match header and a "304 Not Modified" response*

The next section will show how to implement the invalidation scenario and also make it extensible, so that new invalidation logics can be plugged in.

Cache Invalidation with HttpCachingHandler

When we receive a POST, PUT or DELETE request to our resources, it is certain that our resource state has been changed if the response status code for the request is a success status code. In order to implement this functionality, we just need to make small changes to our previously implemented HttpCachingHandler class (Listing 16-30).

Listing 16-30. Implementation of Initial Cache Invalidation Logic

```
protected override async Task<HttpResponseMessage> SendAsync(
    HttpRequestMessage request,
    CancellationToken cancellationToken) {

    //Lines omitted for brevity
```

```
    HttpResponseMessage response;
    try {

        response = await base.SendAsync(request, cancellationToken);
    }
    catch (Exception ex) {

        response = request.CreateErrorResponse(
            HttpStatusCode.InternalServerError, ex);
    }

    if (response.IsSuccessStatusCode) {

        if (request.Method == HttpMethod.Get &&
            !_eTagCacheDictionary.TryGetValue(resourceKey, out cacheableEntity)) {

            cacheableEntity = new CacheableEntity(resourceKey);
            cacheableEntity.EntityTag = GenerateETag();
            cacheableEntity.LastModified = DateTimeOffset.Now;

            _eTagCacheDictionary.AddOrUpdate(
                resourceKey, cacheableEntity, (k, e) => cacheableEntity);
        }

        if (request.Method == HttpMethod.Put ||
            request.Method == HttpMethod.Post ||
            request.Method == HttpMethod.Delete) {

            var cacheEntityKey = _eTagCacheDictionary.Keys.FirstOrDefault(
                x => x.StartsWith(
                    string.Format("{0}:", invalidCacheUri),
                    StringComparison.InvariantCultureIgnoreCase));

            if (!string.IsNullOrEmpty(cacheEntityKey)) {

                CacheableEntity outVal = null;
                _eTagCacheDictionary.TryRemove(key, out outVal);
            }
        }
        else {

            response.Headers.CacheControl = cacheControlHeader;
            response.Headers.ETag = cacheableEntity.EntityTag;
            response.Content.Headers.LastModified = cacheableEntity.LastModified;

            _varyHeaders.ForEach(
                varyHeader => response.Headers.Vary.Add(varyHeader));
        }
    }

    return response;
}
```

But these changes still don't cover all the possibilities. For example, when there is a POST, PUT, or DELETE request to /api/cars/{id}, the /api/cars resource is also changed, but this code does not invalidate its cache. In order to be more flexible, let's open up a extensibility point for our message handler to invalidate the cache resources. Listing 16-31 shows the complete changes to HttpCachingHandler to enable this feature.

Listing 16-31. Final Implementation of the Cache Invalidation Logic

```
public class HttpCachingHandler : DelegatingHandler {

    private static ConcurrentDictionary<string, CacheableEntity> _eTagCacheDictionary =
            new ConcurrentDictionary<string, CacheableEntity>();

    public ICollection<Func<string, string[]>> CacheInvalidationStore =
        new Collection<Func<string, string[]>>();

    //Lines omitted for brevity

    protected override async Task<HttpResponseMessage> SendAsync(
        HttpRequestMessage request,
        CancellationToken cancellationToken) {

        HttpResponseMessage response;
        try {

            response = await base.SendAsync(request, cancellationToken);
        }
        catch (Exception ex) {

            response = request.CreateErrorResponse(
                HttpStatusCode.InternalServerError, ex);
        }

        if (response.IsSuccessStatusCode) {

            if ((!_eTagCacheDictionary.TryGetValue(resourceKey, out cacheableEntity) ||
                request.Method == HttpMethod.Put ||
                request.Method == HttpMethod.Post) &&
                request.Method != HttpMethod.Delete) {

                cacheableEntity = new CacheableEntity(resourceKey);
                cacheableEntity.EntityTag = GenerateETag();
                cacheableEntity.LastModified = DateTimeOffset.Now;

                _eTagCacheDictionary.AddOrUpdate(
                    resourceKey, cacheableEntity, (k, e) => cacheableEntity);
            }

            if (request.Method == HttpMethod.Put ||
                request.Method == HttpMethod.Post ||
                request.Method == HttpMethod.Delete) {
```

```
                HashSet<string> invalidCaches = new HashSet<string>();
                invalidCaches.Add(GetRequestUri(request.RequestUri));

                CacheInvalidationStore.ForEach(
                    func => func(GetRequestUri(request.RequestUri))
                        .ForEach(uri => invalidCaches.Add(uri)));

                invalidCaches.ForEach(invalidCacheUri => {

                    var cacheEntityKeys = _eTagCacheDictionary.Keys.Where(
                        x => x.StartsWith(
                            string.Format("{0}:", invalidCacheUri),
                            StringComparison.InvariantCultureIgnoreCase));

                    cacheEntityKeys.ForEach(key => {
                        if (!string.IsNullOrEmpty(key)) {

                            CacheableEntity outVal = null;
                            _eTagCacheDictionary.TryRemove(key, out outVal);
                        }
                    });
                });
            }
            else {

                response.Headers.CacheControl = cacheControlHeader;
                response.Headers.ETag = cacheableEntity.EntityTag;
                response.Content.Headers.LastModified = cacheableEntity.LastModified;

                _varyHeaders.ForEach(
                    varyHeader => response.Headers.Vary.Add(varyHeader));
            }
        }

        return response;
    }

    //Lines omitted for brevity
}
```

First of all, a public property which is of type ICollection<Func<string, string[]>> has been added to our handler. If there is a POST, PUT, or DELETE request to a resource, each Func object will be called by passing the request URI, and a string array value will be expected in return. This string array will carry the resource URIs whose cache is no longer valid. Finally, those URIs will be aggregated, and each corresponding cache will be removed.

Listing 16-32 shows how to register this message handler.

Listing 16-32. Registration of the HttpCachingHandler

```
protected void Application_Start(object sender, EventArgs e) {

    HttpConfiguration config = GlobalConfiguration.Configuration;
```

```
//Lines omitted for brevity

var eTagHandler = new HttpCachingHandler("Accept", "Accept-Charset");
eTagHandler.CacheInvalidationStore.Add(requestUri => {

    if (requestUri.StartsWith(
        "/api/cars/",
        StringComparison.InvariantCultureIgnoreCase)) {

        return new[] { "/api/cars" };
    }

    return new string[0];
});

config.MessageHandlers.Insert(0, eTagHandler);
}
```

One cache invalidation rule has been added here. It indicates that the /api/cars resource should be invalid if there is a POST, PUT, or DELETE request to a resource URI that starts with /api/cars. Let's give this a try. First, send a request to /api/cars to get back a cacheable resource (see Figure 16-25).

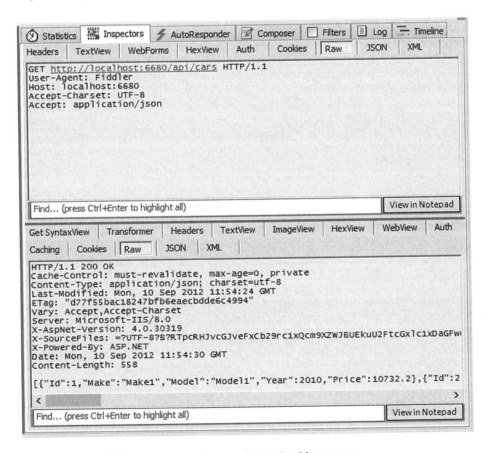

Figure 16-25. *A GET request to /api/cars and its cacheable response*

Then use the obtained ETag value to send a conditional GET request to /api/cars (see Figure 16-26).

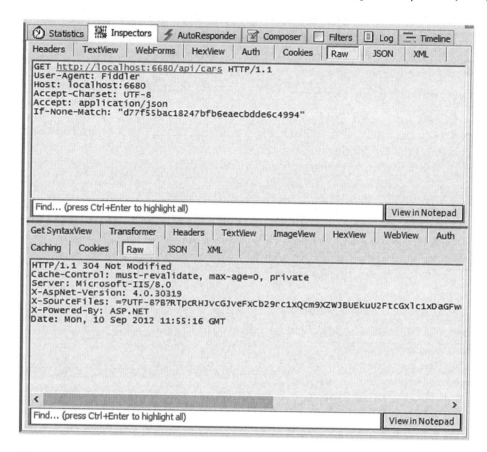

Figure 16-26. *A conditional GET request to /api/cars and its "304 Not Modified" response*

We got a "304 Not Modified" response as expected. Now let's send a POST request to /api/cars to add a new Car entity to the list (see Figure 16-27).

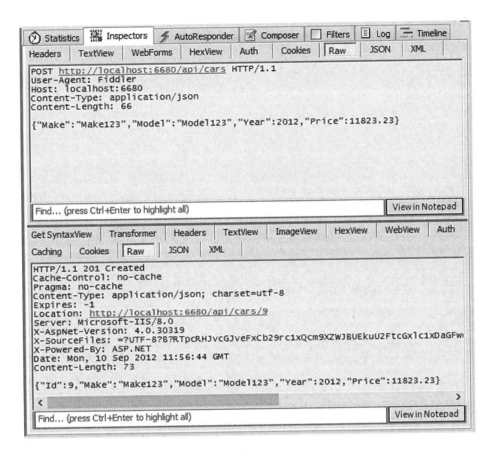

Figure 16-27. A POST request against /api/cars

The new Car entity is added successfully. Let's now try to send a conditional GET request to /api/cars with the previously obtained ETag value. This time there should be a "200 OK" response including the content, because the cars list in the cache should be stale now (see Figure 16-28).

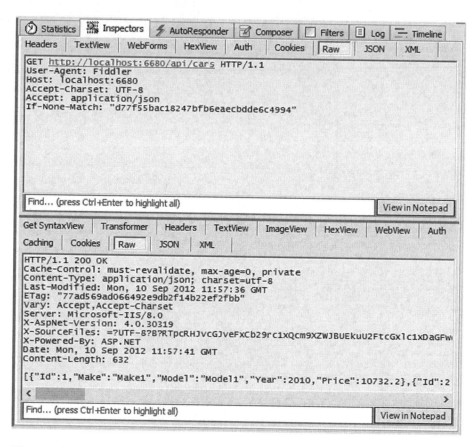

Figure 16-28. *A conditional GET request to /api/cars and its full "200 OK" response*

As expected, the previous cache has been invalidated, and a new ETag came back. Now let's send a GET request to /api/cars/2 to get the single Car entity (see Figure 16-29).

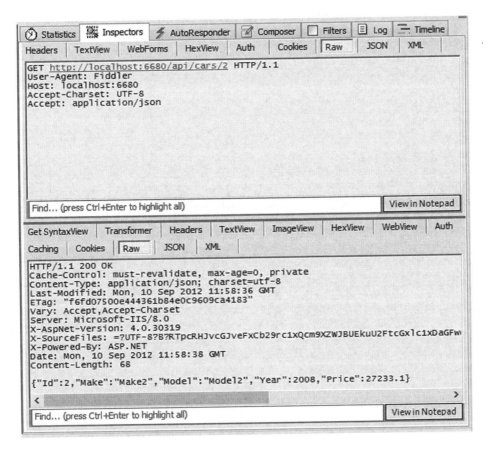

Figure 16-29. *A GET request against /api/cars/2*

Now let's send a PUT request against /api/cars/2 to update the entity (see Figure 16-30).

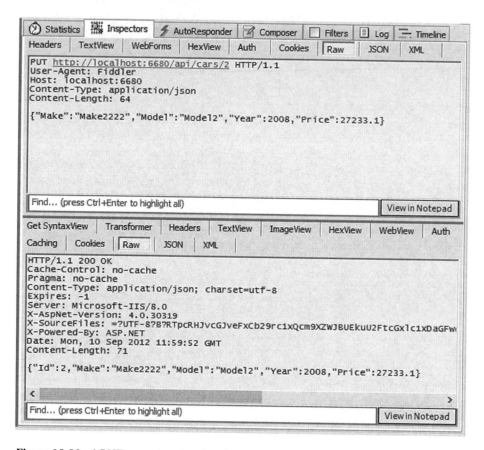

Figure 16-30. *A PUT request against /api/cars/2*

With one of the cars updated, the cars collection in the cache is now stale. If a conditional GET request were sent against /api/cars with the previously obtained ETag value, a "200 OK" response would come back because our custom invalidation logic has kicked in and invalidated the /api/cars cache when the PUT request occurred against /api/cars/2 (see Figure 16-31).

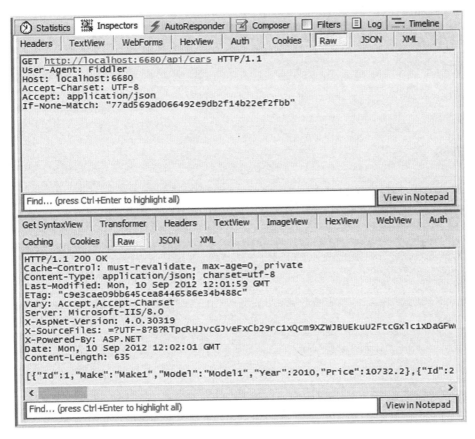

Figure 16-31. *A conditional GET request against /api/cars and its full "200 OK" response*

This handler covers most of the functionality you should ever need, but you can also extend it according to your needs. For example, you might want to use an external store for such CacheableEntity objects as an SQL Server database table, Windows Azure Table Store, and the like, instead of an in-memory dictionary. Keep in mind that if you prefer to use an in-memory dictionary in production, you will face inconsistencies in your application when you scale out through multiple servers.

Summary

Asynchrony is very important if your application aims at scalability when you are consuming long-running I/O-intensive operations. In this chapter, you have seen that it allows you to easily be part of this asynchronous infrastructure with TAP (task-based asynchronous patterns) and C# 5.0 asynchronous language features. In addition, HTTP has pretty robust caching standards, which were explained in detail. As the ASP.NET Web API embraces HTTP, plugging in our caching implementation was easy to do.

CHAPTER 17

Hosting

ASP.NET applications have historically used Internet Information Services (IIS) for their hosting, but during development, developers have used Visual Studio Development Server (also known as Cassini) or IIS Express. All in all, ASP.NET has been a web stack all the way and ASP.NET MVC did not change this.

However, with ASP.NET Web API, this pattern changed: there are now more options. ASP.NET Web API has been designed to support other hosting scenarios, because, as explained in Chapter 1, ASP.NET Web API comes from a line of server technologies, such as WCF, that can be hosted in IIS as well as other processes. Also the ability to host an HTTP service is really useful for non-web services and applications. The future of computing technologies is going to be heterogeneous and interconnected, so having the option to support alternative scenarios is crucial.

There are three main hosting options: web hosting (IIS, IIS Express, and Cassini), self-hosting, and OWIN (Open Web Interface for .NET). There are advantages and disadvantages with each of these, so you need to understand them and carefully weigh them against the requirements before deciding on any option.

Before we go into the details of each hosting scenario, we will explain the fundamentals of HTTP hosting under Windows and how it interacts with the ASP.NET Web API hosting model. The first section will explain HTTP.SYS, which sits at the core of Windows HTTP hosting. This section is designed to provide practical information about HTTP.SYS and its benefits. After this, we'll explain the hosting model in ASP.NET Web API and then cover the three hosting scenarios.

At the end of the day, it will be important for you to *develop your API in a hosting-agnostic fashion*. Most of your code can stay completely abstracted from your hosting, and you will need to try to achieve this separation whenever you can. Requirements of your application can change as well as your hosting needs, so bear in mind the advantage of ASP.NET Web API's hosting-agnostic programming model.

■ **Caution** One of the areas you need to be extremely careful about is the use of classic ASP.NET HttpContext object. Although use of HttpContext.Current provides an easy and convenient way to access the current request/response pair, it can lead to untestable and brittle code because there is no easy way to replace existing context. What's even worse, context might not be available during asynchronous task continuations. On the other hand, in the case of OWIN or self-hosting, HttpContext.Current will be null.

Hypertext Transfer Protocol Stack

HTTP hosting under Windows has been completely rearchitectured and improved since IIS 6.0. Instead of using Windows Sockets, which runs in user mode, Windows now uses a kernel-mode device driver to listen to HTTP requests. This kernel-mode driver is known as the Hypertext Transfer Protocol Stack or more commonly HTTP.SYS.

■ **Note**   Kernel mode and user mode are operating system concepts that basically refer to the priority and privilege of an operation in the runtime. Kernel-mode operations, which are normally operating system operations, have a higher priority and unrestricted access to system resources (such as memory or CPU), while all processes (except system) run in user mode. A bug in an application running in user mode will result in crashing the process but the operating system will continue. A bug or disruption in kernel-mode operations results in an operating system crash or "blue screen."

This change in architecture has made HTTP hosting in Windows very robust and secure because the HTTP.SYS is a hardened process and its security aspect has been carefully considered. As we'll explain later, in ASP.NET Web API, both web hosting and self-hosting take advantage of HTTP.SYS. Now let's look at how HTTP.SYS works.

HTTP.SYS Queuing

HTTP.SYS receives all HTTP requests and queues the requests. The requests are then picked up by the relevant application pool and are processed. After processing of the requests by the application pool, HTTP.SYS returns the response back to the client. If the application pool is unavailable or has been stopped, HTTP.SYS returns the 503 error stating "Service Unavailable" (see Figure 17-1).

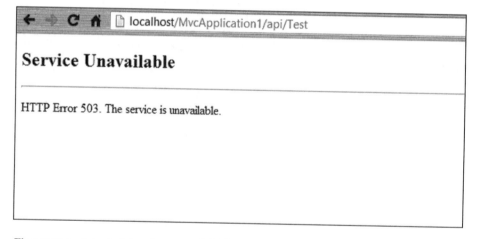

Figure 17-1.   *A typical "service unavailable" 503 HTTP error is returned from the HTTP.SYS when the application pool is stopped or is busy*

How Queuing Works

HTTP.SYS sets up a queue for each application pool. The queue length is defined by the application pool itself, and it is normally set to 1000 in IIS. This number can be set to a value in the range of 10 to 65,535. You can change this value in IIS using the Advanced Settings dialog of the application pool in IIS Manager (see Figure 17-2). If this queue gets full, HTTP.SYS will return an HTTP error 503 (service unavailable), similar to when the application pool is stopped.

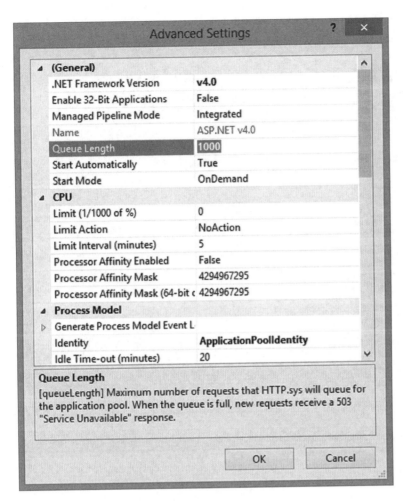

Figure 17-2. Setting the HTTP.SYS queue length for an application pool using the Advanced Settings dialog in IIS Manager; the default value is 1000

Demonstrating the Effect of HTTP.SYS Queuing

In this section, we'll explain how HTTP.SYS protects your service by providing request queueing. We'll reduce the queue length to remove the protective effect and, as a result, any request above the capacity of the queue will get rejected with a 503 error.

For the purposes of the test, you can use the ASP.NET Web API project templates that are registered in Visual Studio by installing ASP.NET MVC 4. This template contains a sample that will get you started quickly. To follow the example, first perform the steps to set up a new project and then to reduce the queue size.

Follow these steps to set up the project:

1. Open Visual Studio (we used Visual Studio 2012 here) and choose New Project.

2. From the center pane, choose Web ➤ ASP.NET MVC 4 Web Application (see Figure 17-3).
    For the name of the project, use HttpSysQueueing and click OK.

Figure 17-3. *From the New Project dialog, choose an ASP.NET MVC 4 Web Application*

3. After clicking OK, another dialog is shown for you to choose the type of the application. Choose "Web API" and let Visual Studio download the necessary NuGet packages, which will take a few seconds to finish.

4. Locate ValuesController class in the project and open it. This is the sample Web API controller in the project and you'll modify and use it to demonstrate queueing.

5. Now you need to add a delay to the action so that you get a chance to see the queue getting full and see the error 503 results. In order to achieve the delay, use Thread.Sleep. So modify this with this code:

```
// GET api/values/5
public string Get(int id)
{
    return "value";
}
```
to:
```
// GET api/values/5
public string Get(int id)
{
    Thread.Sleep(5 * 1000);
    return "value";
}
```

6. You have added a five-second delay to the GET action. Now you'll need to host the application in IIS. This is done by going to the project property and then the Web tab and changing the settings to match those in Figure 17-4.

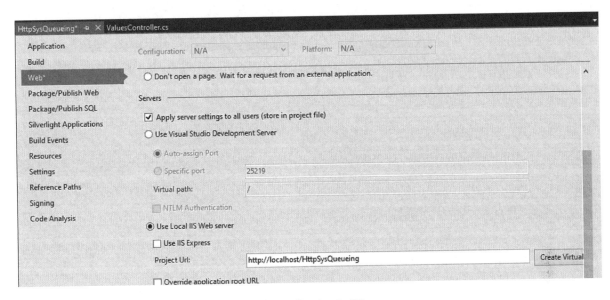

Figure 17-4. Changing project properties to host the application in IIS

7. Build the project and it should be ready.

8. Next, you need to reduce the queue size in IIS Manager: Open IIS Manager, locate the application pool running your application (normally "ASP.NET v4.0" application pool), and change the Queue Length from 1000 to 10 (refer to Figure 17-2).

9. Now you need to fire up more than ten concurrent requests. You can expect to see any request above ten to fail immediately with a 503 error. Fiddler is the right tool to fix this, so let's use it. Open Fiddler and in the composer dialog, type `http://localhost/HttpSysQueueing/api/values/1` in the URL with a GET verb and click Execute to run the action, which has a five-second delay. You should see a longer than five-second delay before the response is returned. Run an `iisreset` in an administrative command window to ensure the application is cold again.

10. Now in the left pane, select the request that you just executed and while pressing the Shift key, click the Replay button. You should now see Repeat Count dialog asking you for the number of times to repeat the replay (see Figure 17-5).

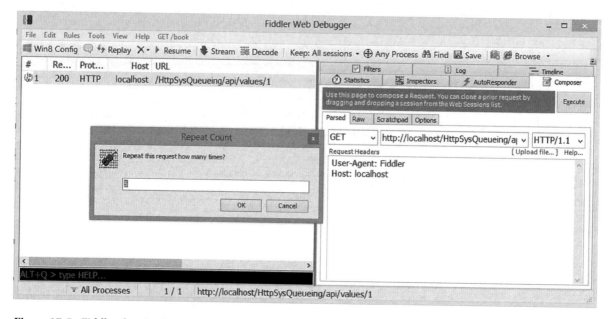

Figure 17-5. *Fiddler showing Repeat Count dialog for Replay. By holding the Shift key and clicking the Replay button, you can define the number of concurrent requests to be replayed*

11. Enter 12 and click OK. Now you should see 12 new concurrent requests, two of which immediately fail (see Figure 17-6).

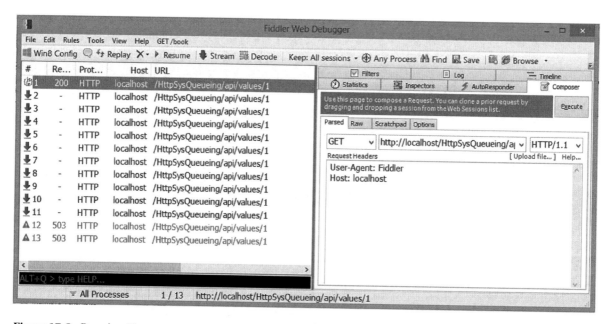

Figure 17-6. *Running 12 concurrent requests in Fiddler when the HTTP.SYS has been set to 10. As can be seen, the last two requests immediately fail with the 503 error because the HTTP.SYS queue gets full*

This simple test demonstrates the importance of HTTP.SYS queueing in application scalability. By queueing requests, HTTP.SYS acts as a buffer and allows temporary glitches and delays due to external web services to be absorbed without affecting the end user.

HTTP.SYS Caching

Another important feature of HTTP.SYS is the kernel-level caching of the static and dynamic content. This feature helps cached content to be served directly from HTTP.SYS without even hitting the application pool, which leads to improved scalability of the system. The HTTP.SYS cache is ON by default and all cacheable responses get cached by this highly performant kernel-mode cache.

As for static content (e.g., JavaScript, CSS, image and view files), all GET requests can be cached. However, by default, not all responses are cached. If static content is requested twice within ten seconds, it will be cached for 120 seconds. These interval values are stored in the registry and can be configured (see http://support.microsoft.com/kb/820129).

As for dynamic content, it is the responsibility of the application to tell HTTP.SYS whether a response is cacheable, but due to differences in integration, it might not always work. The application will mark the response as cacheable by setting these HTTP response headers:

- `Cache-Control: public`
- `Last-Modified: <date>`
- `Expires: <date>` (optional)

Kernel caching is very important for the scalability of your application, so make sure you take advantage of this feature. Under certain circumstances, the response cannot be cached, including the following situations (for the full list visit http://support.microsoft.com/kb/817445):

- Requests a URL that contains any query string
- Request is not anonymous or requires authentication
- Dynamic compression is enabled (make sure you enable only static compression)
- Response is too large; default limit is 256KB
- Cache is full
- `If-Range` or `Range` header is present in the request

The best way to test the HTTP.SYS caching is to use Windows performance counters. The HTTP.SYS cache entrees are under the "Web Service Cache" category and they all start with "`Kernel:`" (see Figure 17-7).

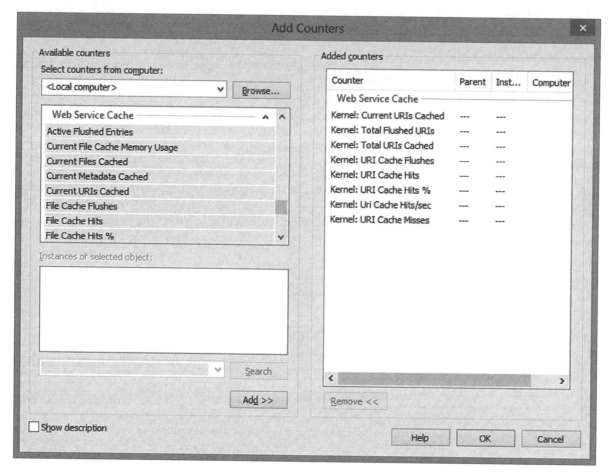

Figure 17-7. Performance counters for HTTP.SYS kernel-level caching

HTTP.SYS kernel-mode caching is by default enabled for static files. You can see the content of the kernel-mode cache by running the following command in the administrative command prompt:

```
C:\> netsh http show cachestate
```

ASP.NET Web API Hosting Model

The hosting model in ASP.NET Web API has two main concepts: *runtime configuration* and *runtime execution*. Runtime configuration is built on top of the HttpConfiguration class. Runtime execution, on the other hand, is based on the HttpServer class. In fact HttpServer constructors take an HttpConfiguration instance to configure their runtime. HttpConfiguration also usually sits inside HttpRequestMessage's Properties property so that the downstream components in the pipeline do not have to know about the execution runtime other than from the request they are processing.

Let's look at each in more detail.

HttpConfiguration

HttpConfiguration, as the name implies, is responsible for holding HTTP runtime configuration in ASP.NET Web API. These configuration elements are listed in Table 17-1.

Table 17-1. *Properties of HttpConfiguration Class*

Property	Type	Description
DependencyResolver	IDependencyResolver	Dependency resolver of the runtime providing service location resolution of dependencies.
Filters	HttpFilterCollection	A collection of global filters.
Formatters	MediaTypeFormatterCollection	This collection is also responsible for finding the correct formatter as part of content negotiation.
IncludeErrorDetailPolicy	IncludeErrorDetailPolicy	Sets the policy on error reporting because it could contain sensitive information. Possible values are Default, LocalOnly, Always, and Never.
Initializer	Action<HttpConfiguration>	Last step of the HttpConfiguration initialization and after being called, HttpConfiguration will be considered immutable.
MessageHandlers	Collection<DelegatingHandler>	Ordered list of message handlers. The first in the list will be triggered first for request and last for response.
ParameterBindingRules	ParameterBindingRulesCollection	Contains a list of HttpParameterBinding and implements a chain of responsibility pattern in LookupBinding method.
Properties	ConcurrentDictionary<Object, Object>	Can contain custom context. It is normally empty.
Routes	HttpRouteCollection	Contains Web API routes.
Services	ServicesContainer	Contains default services.
VirtualPathRoot	string	Root virtual path of the runtime. This is read-only and is set up in the constructors.

HttpConfiguration only needs to be set up at the startup and your request or responses are only meant to use the runtime configuration and not make any changes to it.

HttpServer

HttpServer is the head of the ASP.NET Web API HTTP processing pipeline and is designed to receive a request from the hosting platform and pass it to the pipeline and return the response it receives back. The tail of this pipeline is normally the ApiController's action.

HttpServer is designed to be hosting agnostic. It inherits from DelegatingHandler and, similar to all delegating handlers, has the important SendAsync method, which is called as a chain across the whole pipeline. Listing 17-1 is a snippet of the HttpServer's class.

Listing 17-1. HttpServer Class Constructors and SendAsync

```
public class HttpServer : DelegatingHandler
{
    public HttpServer()
            : this(new HttpConfiguration())
    {
    }

    public HttpServer(HttpConfiguration configuration)
            : this(configuration, new HttpRoutingDispatcher(configuration))
    {
    }

    public HttpServer(HttpMessageHandler dispatcher)
            : this(new HttpConfiguration(), dispatcher)
    {
    }

    public HttpServer(HttpConfiguration configuration, HttpMessageHandler dispatcher)
    {
        ...
    }
    protected override Task<HttpResponseMessage> SendAsync( _
            HttpRequestMessage request, CancellationToken cancellationToken)
            {
            ...
    }

    ...

}
```

As you can see in Listing 17-1, HttpServer is created by passing an instance of HttpConfiguration and a dispatcher of type HttpMessageHandler. The dispatcher represents the rest of the HTTP pipeline after the message handlers and by default is set to an instance of HttpRoutingDispatcher. In other words, HttpServer will be passing the request to the first handler in the MessageHandlers list on the HttpConfiguration. Each handler will pass the execution to the next until the last one, which passes the request to the HttpRoutingDispatcher.

HttpRoutingDispatcher is responsible for:

1. Calling GetRouteData to trigger the route selection:

    - If a route is not found, it returns a resource not found error (HTTP error 404).

    - If a route is found, it stores the IHttpRouteData returned in the request properties.

2.   Passing the execution to the next handler:

   - If the per-route message handlers are used, this will be the Handler property of
     IHttpRouteData, which will be non-null. In this case, handlers will be called in the same
     order they were defined. After these, an instance of HttpControllerDispatcher will be
     triggered.

   - In a case where there are no per-route handlers (which is usually the case), execution will
     be passed to an instance of HttpControllerDispatcher.

You can provide an alternative dispatcher instead of the default HttpRoutingDispatcher. This will bypass the routing and execution of requests by the controller actions and can be useful in testing scenarios where you need to test the succession of MessageHandlers and their interaction as a whole. The pipeline is shown in Figure 17-8.

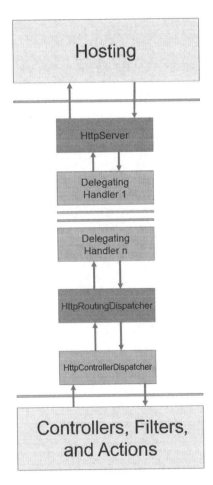

Figure 17-8. *HTTP procesing pipeline in ASP.NET*

Hosting is connected to controllers and actions via intermediaries, including HttpServer, delegating handlers, HttpRoutingDispatcher, and HttpRoutingDispatcher. Figure 17-8 does not show per-route message handlers. In the case of per-route handlers, they would be called between HttpRoutingDispatcher and HttpControllerDispatcher.

Web Hosting

Web hosting is where ASP.NET's web abstractions are implemented in the system.web.dll to host the API. The web server would normally be IIS, although using IIS Express or Visual Studio Development Server (Cassini) would also fall into this category.

Web hosting is the standard approach and arguably the most important hosting scenario of all. Taking advantage of the full power of IIS, *web hosting should be your default approach to ASP.NET Web API hosting whenever possible.* You get the full benefit of HTTP.SYS kernel-mode features, and it is the HTTP hosting platform most explored and best understood under Windows.

The next section will cover configuration and runtime features specific to web hosting.

Runtime Configuration

Runtime configuration in web hosting is based on the familiar class HttpConfiguration. But in order to set up a Web Host API, you need to configure the static instance sitting on GlobalConfiguration. As you've seen in different examples over the course of this book as well as in the ASP.NET Web API project template, configuration takes place in the Global.asax (see Listing 17-2).

Listing 17-2. Standard Approach to Configuring a Web Host API

```
public class WebApiApplication : System.Web.HttpApplication
{
    protected void Application_Start()
    {
        ...
        WebApiConfig.Register(GlobalConfiguration.Configuration);
        ...
    }
}

public static class WebApiConfig
{
    public static void Register(HttpConfiguration config)
    {
        config.Routes.MapHttpRoute(
            name: "DefaultApi",
            routeTemplate: "api/{controller}/{id}",
            defaults: new { id = RouteParameter.Optional }
        );
        ...
    }
}
```

As can be seen in Listing 17-2, GlobalConfiguration.Configuration is being used to configure the API. On the other hand, this static object is passed as the parameter to the WebApiConfig class. This simple separation has the benefit of allowing the configuration to be unit tested with no dependency to a global object. Not surprisingly, GlobalConfiguration.Configuration is the configuration used by HttpControllerHandler, which we'll look at next.

Runtime Execution

As mentioned earlier, in each scenario ASP.NET Web API's HTTP pipeline is triggered via a call to the HttpServer's SendAsync method. In the web host scenario, this is the responsibility of HttpControllerHandler. This class is the bridge between ASP.NET HTTP abstractions and ASP.NET Web API (HttpServer). HttpControllerHandler implements IHttpAsyncHandler, which was derived from IHttpHandler (see Listing 17-3).

Listing 17-3. HttpControllerHandler Implementing IHttpAsyncHandler and IHttpHandler

```
public class HttpControllerHandler : IHttpAsyncHandler
{
    ...
}

public interface IHttpAsyncHandler : IHttpHandler
{
    IAsyncResult BeginProcessRequest(HttpContext context, AsyncCallback cb, object extraData);
    void EndProcessRequest(IAsyncResult result);
}

public interface IHttpHandler
{
    bool IsReusable { get; }

    void ProcessRequest(HttpContext context);
}
```

As you can see from the signature of ProcessRequest in IHttpHandler, the HTTP processing model in ASP.NET is built on top of HttpContext. IHttpHandler and its async counterpart IHttpAsyncHandler are the components responsible for handling a request. Unlike modules that sit in the stream of incoming requests and outgoing responses and observe, intercept, or alter them, handlers are the endpoints capable of processing the request. Other examples of handlers are the Page class in Webforms, the MvcHandler class in MVC, and generic handlers (normally created as .ashx files).

HttpControllerHandler is responsible for converting the incoming HttpRequest (Request property of HttpContext) to an instance of ASP.NET Web API's HttpResponseMessage, and on the return of an instance of HttpResponseMessage, converting it into an instance of HttpResponse, which sits at the Response property of HttpContext. HttpControllerHandler is also responsible for extracting some hosting-related context and storing it in the Properties property of HttpRequestMessage. These include:

- Storing the HttpContext itself with the string key "MS_HttpContext". This is *very important* because using this stored context in the request properties is the only way to get to the current HttpContext if the context is not available in the asynchronous task continuations.

- Storing the current client certificate with the key HttpPropertyKeys. RetrieveClientCertificateDelegateKey. This entry's value will be null if there is no client certificate.

- Storing whether the request is local as a Boolean with the key HttpPropertyKeys.IsLocalKey.

- Storing whether a detailed error must be returned as a Boolean against the key HttpPropertyKeys.IncludeErrorDetailKey.

Web API web host shares many aspects of hosting ASP.NET Webforms or MVC, so it is important to have a solid understanding of IIS hosting (integrated vs. classic pipeline, HTTP modules, etc.), which is beyond the scope of this book.

Hosting *PingYourPackage* Sample

In Chapters 5 through 7, you developed a sample web application called `PingYourPackage`, and in Chapter 7, you chose web hosting to host it. To run the application successfully on your local environment, you need to perform a few steps first. This project requires Visual Studio 2012 or Visual Web Express 2012.

1. Open an elevated PowerShell command prompt.

2. Make sure that your ExecutionPolicy is set to Unrestricted. You can run the `Get-ExecutionPolicy` PowerShell command to see your execution policy. If it's not set to `Unrestricted`, run the following command:

   ```
   Set-ExecutionPolicy Unrestricted
   ```

3. After setting your execution policy properly, navigate to `PingYourPackage` solution's root folder and run the following command:

   ```
   .\AddIISExpressCertToTrustedStore.ps1
   ```

   This will add the IIS Express's development SSL (Secure Socket Layer) certificate into the Trusted Root Certificates store.

4. After these steps, open the solution on Visual Studio or Visual Web Developer Express. Click the solution and press ALT+ENTER to bring up the Solution Property Pages dialog window. From there, navigate to the Startup Project tab and set the following projects as the startup project (put them in the same order):

   ```
   PingYourPackage.API.WebHost
   PingYourPackage.API.Client.Web
   ```

You're done! Press F5 (or CTRL+F5) to get the application up and running.

Self-Hosting

As we covered in Chapter 1, self-hosting is a valuable scenario when you host an HTTP API inside a non-web server process. Some common use cases include:

- Providing an API to administer a Windows service

- Providing a web-based documentation, help, or administration console for a Windows application

- As a lightweight server for integration testing scenarios and development spikes

The option to host a service in an arbitrary process is not new. In fact, this could be done back in the days of WCF or even remoting. But what is new is the ability to serve a full-featured HTTP API with its extensible and reusable pipeline. Also self-hosting does not rely on user-mode socket programming, but as we'll explain, it takes advantage of kernel-mode HTTP.SYS, which offers better features and superior performance.

Let's look at two familiar aspects of hosting: configuration and execution. As you'll see, self-hosting uses HTTP.SYS through WCF; hence, you will notice the WCF-related configuration and set up.

Runtime Configuration

Self-host configuration is based on the HttpSelfHostConfiguration class, which inherits from HttpConfiguration. Extra properties are listed in Table 17-2.

Table 17-2. *Additional Properties of HttpSelfHostConfiguration (see Table 17-1 for Inherited Properties)*

Property	Type	Description
BaseAddress	Uri	Server's base address, a read-only property that gets initialized in the constructor
ClientCredentialType	HttpClientCredentialType	A WCF enumeration, used to define transport-level credentials the client must provide
HostNameComparisonMode	HostNameComparisonMode	A WCF enumeration; possible values are Exact, StrongWildcard, and WeakWildcard
MaxBufferSize	int	Maximum number of bytes in the buffer; default is 64KB
MaxConcurrentRequests	int	Maximum number of requests that can be processed concurrently; default is 100
MaxReceivedMessageSize	long	Maximum size of the message that is accepted by the host; default is 64KB
ReceiveTimeout	TimeSpan	WCF HttpBinding's receive timeout; default is ten minutes
SendTimeout	TimeSpan	WCF HttpBinding's send timeout; default is one minute
TransferMode	TransferMode	Another WCF enumeration; possible values are Buffered, Streamed, StreamedRequest, and StreamedResponse
UserNamePasswordValidator	UserNamePasswordValidator	A WCF identity concept responsible for validating a username and password in case of basic authentication
X509CertificateValidator	X509CertificateValidator	Verifies client X509 certificates; yet another WCF implementation

As you can see, self-host configuration "leaks" out many WCF-related properties. Properties of HttpSelfHostConfiguration will be used by HttpSelfHostServer to set up an HttpBinding, which can be modified by inheriting from HttpSelfHostConfiguration and overriding the protected OnConfigureBinding method. Let's look further into HttpSelfHostConfiguration properties in some code samples.

■ **Note** HttpBinding is not a standard WCF binding, but it is a custom binding (inherited from WCF's abstract Binding class) created purely for the self-host scenarios and it resides in System.Web.Http.SelfHost.dll.

Runtime Execution

HttpSelfHostServer is responsible for using the configuration and directs the incoming messages from HTTP.SYS to the ASP.NET Web API HTTP pipeline. HttpSelfHostServer is inherited from HttpServer and has two additional asynchronous methods—OpenAsync and CloseAsync—for starting and stopping accepting messages.

HttpSelfHostServer sets up an HttpBinding object and configures it via calling the internal method with ConfigureBinding on HttpSelfHostConfiguration and uses its properties to further configure the binding. This binding will then be used to create a WCF channel, which in turn communicates with HTTP.SYS.

Self-Hosting Example Scenarios

Let's look at several practical scenarios in self-hosting. These will be the scenarios you will most often come across in your projects, so this will help you gain a deeper understanding of ASP.NET Web API self-host.

Creating a Basic Self-Host Web API Application

Creating a self-host Web API server is very easy: create an instance of HttpSelfHostConfiguration, set up its properties, create an instance of HttpSelfHostServer by passing the configuration, and then call OpenAsync.

1. Open Visual Studio (make sure you open this in Administrative mode) and choose New Project ➤ Console Application. You can use .NET 4.0 or 4.5, although using .NET 4.5 has the benefit of using the async/await keywords.

2. Use the NuGet Package Manager Console to add the Web API self-host package:

    ```
    PM> Install-Package Microsoft.AspNet.WebApi.SelfHost
    ```

3. Change the static Main method:

    ```
    class Program
    {
        static void Main(string[] args)
        {
            var config = new HttpSelfHostConfiguration("http://localhost:18081");

            config.Routes.MapHttpRoute(
                "API Default", "api/{controller}/{id}",
                new { id = RouteParameter.Optional });

            using (var server = new HttpSelfHostServer(config))
            {
                server.OpenAsync().Wait();
                Console.WriteLine("Press Enter to quit.");
                Console.ReadLine();
            }
        }
    }
    ```

4. Now you can add a simple controller to test the application. This class does not have to reside in the `Controllers` namespace:

```
public class TestController : ApiController
{
    public string Get()
    {
        return DateTime.Now.ToString();
    }
}
```

5. Next, run the application. In your browser, point to `http://localhost:18081/api/Test`, and you should see the current date and time.

Although running Visual Studio in Administrative mode is useful, you cannot assume your Web API service will be running with administrative rights. In fact if you close Visual Studio and open it in nonadministrative mode and try to run it, you will get this error:

```
System.ServiceModel.AddressAccessDeniedException: HTTP could not register URL
http://+:18081/. Your process does not have access rights to this namespace
(see http://go.microsoft.com/fwlink/?LinkId=70353 for details).
```

This is because HTTP.SYS has been hardened so that every application that needs to listen to a port via HTTP.SYS either needs to have administrative rights or the URL would have to had been registered under a username. In order to register the URL, you would need to use the `netsh` Windows command line utility. The `netsh` command with the `http` parameter is used to view or modify HTTP.SYS configuration. To see all of the available parameter options, open a command prompt in administrative mode and enter this command:

```
netsh http
```

To register the URL, you'll need to use `netsh http add aclurl`:

```
netsh http add urlacl url=https://<ip address>:<port number>/ user=<username>
```

You need to provide values for these parameters:

- `ip address`: The IP address that you want to listen on. Provide the plus sign (+) to register against all addresses.

- `port number`: Port number you are listening on, in this case 18081.

- `username`: Username or the group name of the account that will be associated with this URL. This user (or group) will be allowed to create services that listen on this port.

There are other parameters that you do not need here, and you can learn about these by running the `netsh http add urlacl` command. So in order to register the URL against a users group, you need to enter the following command:

```
netsh http add urlacl url=http://+:18081/ user=users
```

After running this command, you should be able to run the application without a need to run with administrative privileges.

Secure a Self-Hosted Web API with an SSL Certificate

Let's look at what is needed to run our simple API with SSL security. The code we will use is the code in the previous sample and we will modify it to support SSL. As explained previously, the self-host model is based on HttpBinding. In order to host the API under the HTTPS scheme, you need to do the following:

1. Change the server's base address to https:// instead of http://.

2. Inherit from HttpSelfHostConfiguration and override OnConfigureBinding to set the security property of the binding. Create and pass an instance of this class to your HttpSelfHostServer instead of the standard HttpSelfHostConfiguration.

3. Register the URL using netsh http add urlacl and this time provide the new URL (which starts with https).

4. Register the SSL certificate using the netsh command line utility.

Step 1 is easy enough. In order to accomplish Step 2, you create the HttpsSelfHostConfiguration class (remember to add a reference to System.ServiceModel.dll):

```
public class HttpsSelfHostConfiguration : HttpSelfHostConfiguration
{
    public HttpsSelfHostConfiguration(string baseAddress) : base(baseAddress)
    {
    }

    public HttpsSelfHostConfiguration(Uri baseAddress) : base(baseAddress)
    {
    }

    protected override BindingParameterCollection OnConfigureBinding(HttpBinding httpBinding)
    {
        httpBinding.Security.Mode = HttpBindingSecurityMode.Transport;
        return base.OnConfigureBinding(httpBinding);
    }
}
```

Step 3 is very similar to what you did for the http scheme, but this time you change the URL to start with https. To achieve Step 4, you need to choose an SSL certificate. You can either create a self-signed certificate using makecert.exe (see http://msdn.microsoft.com/en-us/library/bfsktky3.aspx) or use an existing one. Here you will use the second approach. So in order to choose an existing certificate:

1. In the Run window, enter mmc.

2. From the File menu, choose Add or Remove Snap-ins.

3. Choose Certificates and click Add.

4. On the next dialog choose Computer Account and click Next.

5. On the next dialog keep the Local Computer selected and click Finish.

6. Click OK to close the dialog.

7. Now on the left pane, under Console Root, you'll see Certificates and under it a number of folders.

8. Expand the Personal folder and on the right pane choose a valid certificate that has not expired. Choose localhost certificate and double-click to open it.

Now on the Details tab find the Thumbprint, and you should see a screen similar to the one in Figure 17-9.

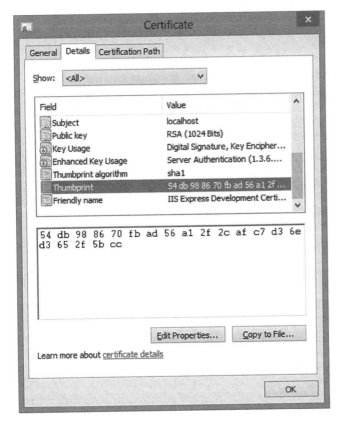

Figure 17-9. Obtaining the thumbprint for an SSL certificate

The hexadecimal code in the bottom pane is the thumbprint of the certificate. You need the thumbprint to register the SSL certificate. The command line for registering is:

```
netsh http add sslcert ipport=<ip>:<port> certhash=<thumbprint> appid=<guid>
```

The parameters are:

- ip: IP address of the server. Use 0.0.0.0 to register against all addresses.

- port: Port to be used by the service.

- thumbprint: 20-byte SHA1 hash of the certificate represented as hexadecimal code (as displayed above).

- appid: A guid representing the id of the application. It can be any guid.

So in this case, the command looks like:

```
netsh http add sslcert ipport=0.0.0.0:18081 certhash=1b7644dd
4ab5e5794f5696d9792d284d210e55dd appid={54F62034-D508-4738-88C0-3BA1C1617FA3}
```

After finishing these steps and rerunning the API, you should be able to browse to
`https://localhost:18081/api/Test`.

Adding Windows Authentication to a Self-Host API

A Web API usually needs an authentication and authorization mechanism. Although it is preferable to use web-friendly protocols such as basic authentication or OAuth to secure your Web API, you might be asked to provide Windows authentication in addition or instead of those protocols. This is more likely for an internal or hybrid API where single sign-on is a requirement.

In any case, providing this in a self-host Web API is simple. All you need to do is configure the HttpSelfHostConfiguration internal binding by inheriting and overriding it in a manner similar to the SSL case discussed previously. (Remember to add a reference to System.ServiceModel.dll.)

```
public class NtlmHttpSelfHostConfiguration : HttpSelfHostConfiguration
{
    public NtlmHttpSelfHostConfiguration(string baseAddress)
        : base(baseAddress)
    {
        this.ClientCredentialType = HttpClientCredentialType.Ntlm;
    }

    public NtlmHttpSelfHostConfiguration(Uri baseAddress)
        : base(baseAddress)
    {
        this.ClientCredentialType = HttpClientCredentialType.Ntlm;
    }

    protected override BindingParameterCollection OnConfigureBinding(HttpBinding httpBinding)
    {
        httpBinding.Security.Mode = HttpBindingSecurityMode.TransportCredentialOnly;
        return base.OnConfigureBinding(httpBinding);
    }
}
```

So if you use this configuration instead of HttpSelfHostConfiguration and then call the API using a browser such as Internet Explorer, there will be two requests. The first one is known as a 401 challenge, which sends NTLM (NT LAN Manager, the legacy Windows authentication) as the authentication method by the server (note the WWW-Authenticate header in the response in Figure 17-10).

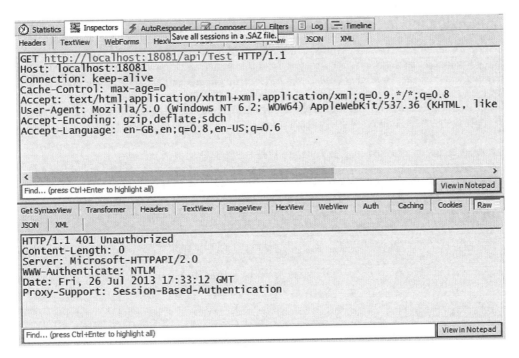

Figure 17-10. A "401 challenge" response requiring NTLM authentication

And the browser sends an NTLM token to the server, which results in a successful response, as can be seen below (note the Authorization header in the request in Figure 17-11).

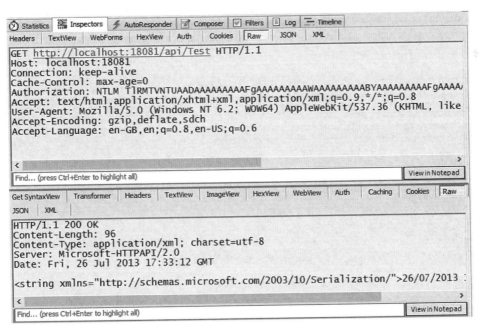

Figure 17-11. After a "401 challenge," the client contains an NTLM token and sends it in the Authorization header

Adding Basic Authentication to a Self-Host API

Basic authentication support can be added to your Web API by implementing a DelegatingHandler and adding it to the HTTP pipeline, but you can also use self-host's WCF features to implement basic authentication.

In order to add basic authentication for your self-host Web API, you first need to create another inherited configuration (similar to the example in preceding section) and then set the UserNamePasswordValidator property. We have combined these two in a single class as shown in the following code. (Remember to add a reference to System.ServiceModel.dll and System.IdentityModel.dll.)

```
public class BasicAuthenticationSelfHostConfiguration: HttpSelfHostConfiguration
{
    private readonly FunctionalUserNamePasswordValidator _functionalUserNamePasswordValidator;

    private class FunctionalUserNamePasswordValidator : UserNamePasswordValidator
    {
        private readonly Func<string, string, bool> _userNamePasswordValidator;

        public FunctionalUserNamePasswordValidator(Func<string, string, bool> _
            userNamePasswordValidator)
        {
            if(userNamePasswordValidator==null)
                throw new ArgumentNullException("userNamePasswordValidator");

            _userNamePasswordValidator = userNamePasswordValidator;
        }

        public override void Validate(string userName, string password)
        {
            if(!_userNamePasswordValidator(userName, password))
                throw new SecurityException("Invalid username/password pair.");
        }
    }

    public BasicAuthenticationSelfHostConfiguration(string baseAddress, Func<string, string,
        bool> userNamePasswordValidator) : base(baseAddress)
    {
        _functionalUserNamePasswordValidator = new _
            FunctionalUserNamePasswordValidator(userNamePasswordValidator);
    }

    public BasicAuthenticationSelfHostConfiguration(Uri baseAddress, Func<string, string, bool>
        userNamePasswordValidator)
        : base(baseAddress)
    {
        _functionalUserNamePasswordValidator = new _
            FunctionalUserNamePasswordValidator(userNamePasswordValidator);
    }
```

```
protected override BindingParameterCollection OnConfigureBinding(HttpBinding httpBinding)
{
    httpBinding.Security.Mode = HttpBindingSecurityMode.TransportCredentialOnly;
    httpBinding.Security.Transport.ClientCredentialType = HttpClientCredentialType.Basic;
    this.UserNamePasswordValidator = _functionalUserNamePasswordValidator;
    return base.OnConfigureBinding(httpBinding);
}
}
```

In order to use this class, you must create an instance by passing a username/password validator. For demonstration purposes, let's assume validation only checks whether username is "johndoe" and the password is "123456":

```
var config = new BasicAUthenticationSelfHostConfiguration("http://localhost:18081",
    (un, pwd) => un=="johndoe" && pwd=="123456");
```

Now upon starting the service, you can see that you get a 401 challenge requesting basic authentication, and then after entering the username and password, you see the response from the API (note the WWW-Authenticate header in the response in Figure 17-12).

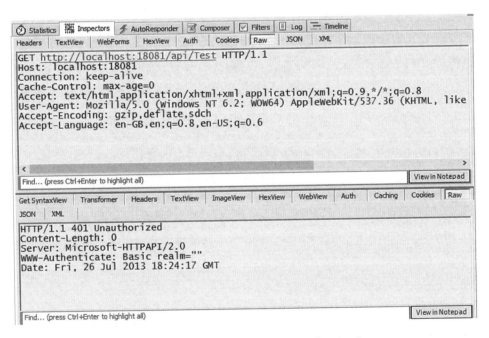

Figure 17-12. A "401 challenge" response requiring basic authentication

Then after entering the correct username and password, you get the resource in the response from the API (note the Authorization header in the request in Figure 17-13).

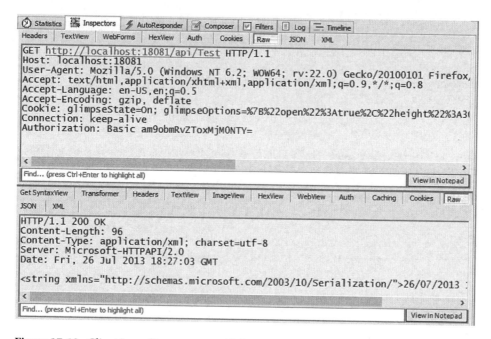

Figure 17-13. Client is sending a request with basic authentication (note Authorization header)

OWIN

OWIN is a published specification (`http://owin.org/spec/owin-1.0.0.html`) that abstracts communication between web servers and web applications and provides plumbing and pipeline for plugging various .NET web frameworks to .NET web servers. This abstraction allows application developers to focus on implementing the functionality without having to take a dependency on their hosting framework. Such a generic interface had been specified in other web platforms such as Ruby, Node.js, or Python but has been lacking in the .NET space.

The OWIN specification is the combined effort of Benjamin Vanderveen and Louis Dejardin and now has been widely implemented in the open source community. ASP.NET Web API implementations have not yet been finalized at the time of this writing, so our coverage of OWIN hosting will focus mainly on the concepts with some practical use cases.

Why Should I Learn About OWIN?

In late 2012, Microsoft announced that supporting OWIN will be a strategic goal and it has set up the Katana project to implement the interface for a variety of ASP.NET web frameworks. Future developments in the .NET space are likely to have OWIN-specific implementations and sooner or later you will be working on a project that has OWIN dependency. In fact, version 2.0 of the ASP.NET Web API, which is in development at the time of this writing, has been focused on delivering OWIN interoperability.

OWIN provides interoperability between web frameworks and makes it easy to write a single piece of code that can be reused in each and every framework. This is something that has been impossible so far.

The future of the .NET web technologies is going to be heterogenous with a heavy open source software presence. As such, it is important to be prepared for a shift in the .NET horizon.

OWIN Concepts and Runtime

OWIN is a web runtime that acts as a bridge (abstraction) between web hosts and web frameworks (see Figure 17-14). On the one hand, OWIN has defined interfaces for interaction of hosts and frameworks. On the other hand, each host or framework is connected to the OWIN runtime using its OWIN adapter.

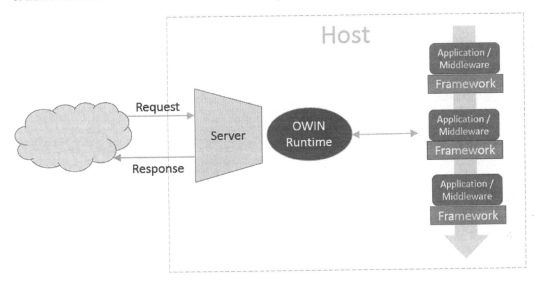

Figure 17-14. OWIN components

Concepts defined for an OWIN system are: **Host**, **Server**, **Framework**, **Application**, and **Middleware** (see http://owin.org/spec/owin-1.0.0.html#Definition for further information). **Host** in OWIN terms is a process that runs the initial set up and provides a runtime platform for incoming requests. **Server** is a linked concept and its responsibility is to route the incoming requests to the OWIN runtime. In the case of ASP.NET hosting, these two concepts are the same, while in self-host they could be different. OWIN runtime then passes a request to the **Application** stack and returns the response. The request processing system is composed of an ordered set of Middleware/Applications capable of handling the request. **Applications** are normally implemented in a **Framework** such as ASP.NET Web API, NancyFx, among others, and are responsible for the functionality of the web applications. Middlewares are normally pass-through components that enhance the functionality of the application and look after cross-cutting concerns such as security, tracing, caching, monitoring, and so forth. All communications are completely asynchronous (represented by TPL's Task) and requests and responses flow as part of a dictionary called **Environment**. Setup work at the startup is the responsibility of **AppBuilder**, which is represented by the IAppBuilder interface (see Listing 17-4). **AppBuilder** contains a dictionary called Properties, which represents Host's properties.

Listing 17-4. OWIN's IAppBuilder Interface

```
public interface IAppBuilder
{
  IDictionary<string, object> Properties { get; }

  IAppBuilder Use(object middleware, params object[] args);

  object Build(Type returnType);

  IAppBuilder New();
}
```

`IAppBuilder` is normally constructed by the **Host** and is passed to the startup code so that the application can configure itself. **Middlewares** are added by calling the `Use` method. These components are ordered and will be called in the order they are added.

A common interface within OWIN is a delegate called `AppFunc`, which is the entry point for the applications:

```
Func<IDictionary<string, object>, Task>
```

In this delegate, **Application** receives an **Environment** dictionary containing the request and response and returns a `Task`. **Application** is meant to complete the `Task` either by successfully processing the request or by faulting the `Task` (by throwing an exception).

OWIN projects are composed of the OWIN runtime core (which is in fact relatively small) and a set of adapter projects (see Figure 17-15). Each server or web framework requires an adapter to be able to communicate with OWIN components.

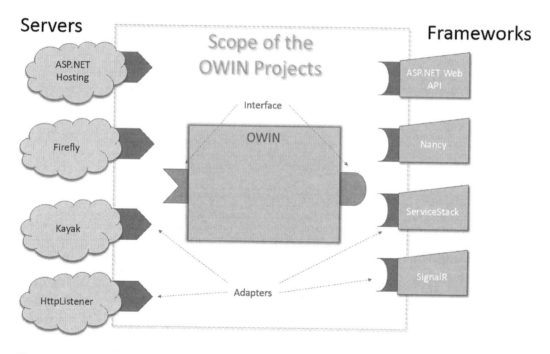

Figure 17-15. *OWIN working as a bridge between web hosting and web frameworks. Each framework or host needs to be plugged into OWIN using an adapter. OWIN runtime has a stack of middleware, which are in fact adapters connected to frameworks*

Example: Web Hosting ASP.NET Web API in OWIN

ASP.NET Web API in OWIN as a web host is pretty straightforward and that's what we'll show you now.

1. Open Visual Studio and create an empty Web Application. Install two NuGet packages by running the commands below in the Package Manager Console:

    ```
    PM> Install-Package microsoft.owin.host.systemweb
    PM> Install-Package Microsoft.AspNet.WebApi.Owin -pre -Version 0.21.0-pre
    ```

2. Add a simple controller:

```
public class TestController : ApiController
{
    public string Get()
    {
        return DateTime.Now.ToString();
    }
}
```

3. Create a class called Startup and add the following code:

```
public class Startup
{
    public void Configuration(IAppBuilder app)
    {
        var config = new HttpConfiguration();
        config.Routes.MapHttpRoute(
            name: "DefaultApi",
            routeTemplate: "api/{controller}/{id}",
            defaults: new { id = RouteParameter.Optional }
        );
        app.UseWebApi(config);
    }
}
```

As you can guess, the magic happens when you call .UseWebApi.

4. The last step is to add some appSetting configuration to your web.config to send all requests toward your OWIN application:

```
<appSettings>
  <!--Makes the OWIN module the default request handler-->
  <add key="owin:HandleAllRequests" value="true" />
  <!--Maps the current directory to the application's path-->
  <add key="owin:SetCurrentDirectory" value="true" />
</appSettings>
```

5. Now run the application and browse to http://localhost:<yourport>/api/Test. You should see the current date being returned.

Future of OWIN

As explained previously, ASP.NET Web API version 2.0, which is at the beta stage at the time of this writing, can work with OWIN. As far as the future of OWIN is concerned, you'll see more and more decoupling of the frameworks from hostings and further integration into abstractions of OWIN.

So it will be important to watch the developments of the Katana project and take advantage of its interoperability when it goes live.

Summary

This chapter reviewed three hosting options: web hosting, self-hosting, and OWIN. We started by talking about the benefits of using HTTP.SYS and described how its queuing and kernel-mode caching can improve the performance and scalability of your project.

Then we moved to ASP.NET Web API's hosting model and how it is based on a runtime configuration and a runtime execution, and provided explanation of these concepts' implementation in web hosting. We briefly looked at hosting the PingYourPackage sample in IIS Express.

We then looked at self-hosting and how it is based on WCF and looked at a few important practical use cases such as securing an API with SSL, supporting Windows authentication, and basic authentication. We also looked at the OWIN hosting concepts and explained how this can help you write applications decoupled from hosting scenarios.

The next chapter will explain additional features of ASP.NET Web API.

CHAPTER 18

■ ■ ■

Tracing, Logging, and API Documentation

When an application is being developed, there are two things everyone expects it to provide, but almost nobody likes doing the work that providing them entails. We're speaking of the implementation of tracing and logging features and the documentation of the application. Tracing and logging give the ability to write status or error logs or monitor the application state at runtime. Documentation of an application is mandatory, as the user needs guidance on how to work with an application. All these requirements exist independently of the type of application being developed. Documentation in the particular case of a public HTTP API is important, as nobody wants to explore the API by trial and error. This chapter will first focus on the tracing and logging features in ASP.NET Web API. The chapter's second part is dedicated to the API documentation features of ASP.NET Web API.

Tracing and Logging

There are several scenarios in developing a Web API that involve the need to trace and log information about the Web API at runtime. In one such scenario you might charge your Web API users per request, and so every request from your registered user needs to be logged to a database so you can bill him based on the use data. In another scenario your API misbehaves at runtime, and you want to inspect variable values at runtime without having to attach a debugger. ASP.NET Web API, which has been developed with such scenarios in mind, provides extensibility points for tracing and logging, so you don't have to do them on your own. The next three sections will explore how and where tracing in ASP.NET Web API works out of the box, how to make use of it in general, and how to use it with NLog. NLog is a popular logging framework for .NET, which was explained in Chapter 1.

The Tracing Mechanisms in ASP.NET Web API

In this section you'll see how ASP.NET Web API tracing works under the hood and how it allows you to trace the state of internals of the ASP.NET Web API framework. To set some context for tracing and logging with ASP.NET Web API, let's look up front at logging in general.

Logging

By default, tracing in ASP.NET Web API allows you to trace the state of the main services of ASP.NET Web API. As has been indicated everywhere in this book, these services are registered in the `Services` property of the `HttpConfiguration` class. If you don't explicitly activate tracing in ASP.NET, nothing gets logged. So if you don't activate it, no code being executed in ASP.NET Web API is even aware of tracing. First, let's take look at the code in Listing 18-1 which is the sort of logging code you might have seen already in some variations.

Listing 18-1. Typical Logging Source Code in .NET

```
internal class Program {
    private static string[] _args;

    private static void Main(string[] args) {
        _args = args;
        Trace.Listeners.Add(new ConsoleTraceListener());

        if (tracingEnabled()) {
            Trace.Write("Application started.\r\n");
        }

        Console.WriteLine("Press any key to exit.");
        Console.ReadLine();

        if (tracingEnabled()) {
            Trace.Write("Application stopped\r\n");
        }
    }

    private static bool tracingEnabled() {
        return _args.ToList().Contains("trace");
    }
}
```

First, the code in Listing 18-1 checks whether somebody enabled tracing. In our sample here, this check is done by providing the command line parameter "trace" when starting the sample program. Independent of that setting, a ConsoleTraceListener instance is added to the list of listeners to be used by the Trace class. The ConsoleTraceListener writes its output to the console window. If tracing is enabled, the Trace.Write method hands over the tracing information, which then is written by all registered trace listeners.

One of the first things that is apparent when reading the sample code is that the logging code creates a lot of overhead compared with the productive source code. Even though this is a constructed sample, there are many real-world scenarios where the source code looks pretty much the same. Besides the fact that the code is cluttered by the checks for enabled logging, thus making it hard to read, these checks slow down the code at runtime even if logging is not enabled.

Another drawback of the logging code shown in Listing 18-1 is that it is tied to a specific logging framework, which in that sample is the tracing from the System.Diagnostics namespace. If you need to replace the tracing framework being used, you have to touch each class containing your logging mechanism. This process can take a lot of effort and tends to be error-prone.

Furthermore, if you need tracing information from ASP.NET Web API itself, the logging framework being used for ASP.NET Web API logging might differ from the framework you want in your user code. Thus, you might end up with different kinds of event logs in different places.

To work around all of the above-named issues, the ASP.NET Web API team has chosen a different approach to support logging in. As was said before, if you don't enable tracing in the ASP.NET Web API configuration, there's no code being executed in ASP.NET Web API that is even aware of tracing. How could that be done? The ASP.NET Web API team solved this problem by creating wrapper classes for the main ASP.NET Web API services being registered in the Services collection property of the HttpConfiguration for your Web API application. These wrapper classes, being aware of tracing, can trace the beginning and the end of the service. Between the tracing events, they invoke the original service, which is wrapped in a try/catch block, so exceptions thrown inside the service can also be traced—indeed, that's why tracing's being done at all.

TraceManager

Most of the work in the ASP.NET Web API tracing mechanism, as described above, happens in a single class—TraceManager, in the System.Web.Http.Tracing namespace. TraceManager itself is registered as a service in the HttpConfiguration, as it implements the ITraceManager interface, which allows you to replace the instance being used inside the HttpConfiguration. The ITraceManager interface is pretty simple, as Listing 18-2 shows.

Listing 18-2. The ITraceManager Interface

```
public interface ITraceManager {
    void Initialize(HttpConfiguration configuration);
}
```

The only member that ITraceManager forces its derived types to implement is the Initialize method, which expects an HttpConfiguration instance as its parameter. The TraceManager instance, being registered as the default ITraceManager implementation for ASP.NET Web API, is initialized at the end of the static DefaultInitializer method of the HttpConfiguration class. The DefaultInitializer method creates the instance of the HttpConfiguration used in your ASP.NET Web API application.

With the TraceManager instance created and initialized, now is the perfect time to see what TraceManager itself actually does. Let's start with the Initialize method (see Listing 18-3).

Listing 18-3. Initialize Method of the TraceManager Class

```
public void Initialize(HttpConfiguration configuration) {
    ITraceWriter traceWriter = ServicesExtensions.GetTraceWriter(configuration.Services);
    if (traceWriter == null)
        return;
    TraceManager.CreateAllTracers(configuration, traceWriter);
}
```

First, the TraceManager requests an ITraceWriter instance from the list of registered services in the HttpConfiguration instance (what ITraceWriter is and how to use it will be covered a bit later in this chapter). If that instance is null, the Initialize method is exited, and no further code from the TraceManager class gets executed during the Web API application runtime. Otherwise, the CreateAllTracers method of the TraceManager class is executed with the current Web API application configuration and the recently read ITraceWriter instance as its parameters.

The logic being executed inside the just-described Initialize method actually is the single point where ASP.NET Web API decides whether tracing is enabled or not.

Having just whetted our appetite for tracing in ASP.NET Web API, let's assume that the returned ITraceWriter instance has not been null; thus, TraceManager.CreateAllTracers will be called (see Listing 18-4).

Listing 18-4. TraceManager.CreateAllTracers Method Implentation

```
private static void CreateAllTracers(HttpConfiguration configuration, ITraceWriter traceWriter) {
    TraceManager.CreateActionInvokerTracer(configuration, traceWriter);
    TraceManager.CreateActionSelectorTracer(configuration, traceWriter);
    TraceManager.CreateActionValueBinderTracer(configuration, traceWriter);
    TraceManager.CreateContentNegotiatorTracer(configuration, traceWriter);
    TraceManager.CreateControllerActivatorTracer(configuration, traceWriter);
    TraceManager.CreateControllerSelectorTracer(configuration, traceWriter);
    TraceManager.CreateMessageHandlerTracers(configuration, traceWriter);
    TraceManager.CreateMediaTypeFormatterTracers(configuration, traceWriter);
}
```

The `CreateAllTracers` method in Listing 18-4 contains no logic besides executing eight methods, all of whose names start with `Create` and end with `Tracer` or `Tracers`.

At the start of the introduction to the ASP.NET Web API tracing mechanism, we said that ASP.NET Web API creates wrapper classes around the service classes being registered in the Web API configuration if tracing is enabled. The tracers referenced in the names of the methods in Listings 18-3 and 18-4 are in fact these wrapper classes. Put simply, every method in Listing 18-4 creates one wrapper class around a particular service being registered in the configuration and replaces the original service with the corresponding wrapper.

As the implementations of the eight methods are very similar, only one of them needs explaining—namely, `CreateActionInvokerTracer` (see Listing 18-5), the first one invoked by the `CreateAllTracers` method.

Listing 18-5. CreateActionInvokerTracer Method

```
private static void CreateActionInvokerTracer(HttpConfiguration configuration,
ITraceWriter traceWriter) {
    IHttpActionInvoker service =
TraceManager.GetService<IHttpActionInvoker>(configuration.Services);
    if (service == null || service is HttpActionInvokerTracer)
        return;
    HttpActionInvokerTracer actionInvokerTracer = new HttpActionInvokerTracer(service, traceWriter);
    configuration.Services.Replace(typeof (IHttpActionInvoker), (object) actionInvokerTracer);
}
```

First, the `CreateActionInvokerTracer` method reads the `IHttpActionInvoker` instance from the configuration's list of registered services. If that instance is not null or is not already of the type `HttpActionInvokerTracer`, a new instance of `HttpActionInvokerTracer` is created, with the original `IHttpActionInvoker` service instance and the `ITraceWriter` instance parameter as constructor parameters. The original `IHttpActionInvoker` instance is then replaced by the `HttpActionInvokerTracer` in the configuration's services collection.

Listing 18-6 shows the signature of the `HttpActionInvokerTracer` class whose instance was created in Listing 18-5.

Listing 18-6. ActionInvokerTracer Class Signature

```
internal class HttpActionInvokerTracer : IHttpActionInvoker {

    public HttpActionInvokerTracer(
        IHttpActionInvoker innerInvoker,
        ITraceWriter traceWriter) {}

    Task<HttpResponseMessage> IHttpActionInvoker.InvokeActionAsync(
        HttpActionContext actionContext,
            CancellationToken cancellationToken) {
    }
}
```

The `HttpActionInvokerTracer` class implements the `IHttpActionInvoker` interface. It's necessary to do so to be able to replace the original `HttpActionInvoker` service (shown in Listing 18-5) that also implements this interface. Listing 18-6 also shows the signature of the constructor that expected the original `HttpActionInvoker` and the `ITraceWriter` implementation from the Web API application configuration. The `InvokeActionAsync` method is the implementation of the `InvokeActionAsync` method of the `IHttpActionInvoker` interface that is implemented by the `HttpActionInvokerTracer` class.

The constructor of the HttpActionInvokerTracer class passes its parameters only to private fields, so we won't explain that action in a dedicated listing.

The important part of the HttpActionInvokerTracer class happens in the InvokeActionAsync method, as Listing 18-7 shows.

Listing 18-7. InvokeActionAsync Method of the HttpActionInvokerTracer Class

```
Task<HttpResponseMessage> IHttpActionInvoker.InvokeActionAsync(HttpActionContext
actionContext, CancellationToken cancellationToken) {
    if (actionContext == null) {
        throw new ArgumentNullException("actionContext");
    }

    return _traceWriter.TraceBeginEndAsync<HttpResponseMessage>(
        actionContext.ControllerContext.Request,
        TraceCategories.ActionCategory,
        TraceLevel.Info,
        _innerInvoker.GetType().Name,
        InvokeActionAsyncMethodName,
        beginTrace: (tr) => {
            tr.Message = Error.Format(
                SRResources.TraceActionInvokeMessage,
                .FormattingUtilities
                    .ActionInvokeToString(actionContext));
        },
        execute:
            () => (Task<HttpResponseMessage>)
                _innerInvoker.InvokeActionAsync(actionContext,
                cancellationToken),
        endTrace: (tr, result) => {
            HttpResponseMessage response = result;
            if (response != null) {
                tr.Status = response.StatusCode;
            }
        },
        errorTrace: null);
}
```

The InvokeActionAsync method in Listing 18-7 consists of five steps that exist in similar form in each of the tracer wrapper instances created in Listing 18-4.

1. First, a call to the TraceBeginEndAsync<HttpResponseMessage> method is made. The following steps create the parameters for that method call itself.

2. The second step is to create the beginTrace Action delegate. This contains a TraceRecord instance, with its message set to the name of the controller's action and its parameters.

3. As a third step, the execute Func delegate is created. This gets assigned the InvokeActionAsync method of the original HttpActionInvoker instance that has been passed in as a parameter to the HttpActionInvokerTracer constructor.

4. The fourth step is similar to the second, but it creates the endTrace Action delegate. It gets assigned the StatusCode of the HttpResponseMessage returned from the controller's action.

5. The last step is pretty simple: it creates the errorTrace Action delegate, which is null. In another implementation, this delegate could contain the action to invoke if an error was encountered performing the operation.

The TraceBeginEndAsync<HttpResponseMessage> method from the first step is an extension of the ITraceWriterExtensions class. It is responsible for injecting the properties into the TraceRecord instances at runtime and invoking the concrete logger implementation with those instances. Furthermore, it wraps the execute Func delegate in a try/catch block and executes it.

As the method itself is a bit lengthy, we'll split it in sections to explain it, starting with the part that handles the beginTrace Action delegate being passed in as a parameter (see Listing 18-8).

Listing 18-8. Handling of the beginTrace Action Delegate in TraceBeginEndAsync Method

```
if (traceWriter == null)
    throw Error.ArgumentNull("traceWriter");

if (execute == null)
    throw Error.ArgumentNull("execute");

traceWriter.Trace(
    request,
    category,
    level,
    (TraceRecord traceRecord) => {
        traceRecord.Kind = TraceKind.Begin;
        traceRecord.Operator = operatorName;
        traceRecord.Operation = operationName;
        if (beginTrace != null) {
            beginTrace(traceRecord);
        }
    }
);
```

After checking the passed-in traceWriter and execute Func delegate against null, the method calls the trace writer's Trace method (to be covered in detail in the next section), injects the properties to the TraceRecord instance, and invokes the beginTrace method, with that instance as a parameter. This writes the begin-trace information to the selected trace log destination.

After writing the begin-trace information to the log, next is the execution of the execute Func delegate. As already explained, the delegate is wrapped in a try/catch block not only to log the begin- and end-trace information but also to log exceptions occurring during the execute operation.

First, let's look at the try block of the try/catch section (see Listing 18-9).

Listing 18-9. try Block of the TraceBeginEndAsync Method

```
Task<TResult> task = execute();
if (task == null) {
    return task;
}
```

```
return task
    .Then<TResult, TResult>((result) => {
        traceWriter.Trace(
            request,
            category,
            level,
            (TraceRecord traceRecord) => {
                traceRecord.Kind = TraceKind.End;
                traceRecord.Operator = operatorName;
                traceRecord.Operation = operationName;
                if (endTrace != null) {
                    endTrace(traceRecord, result);
                }
            });

        return result;
    })

    .Catch<TResult>((info) => {
        traceWriter.Trace(
            request,
            category,
            TraceLevel.Error,
            (TraceRecord traceRecord) => {
                traceRecord.Kind = TraceKind.End;
                traceRecord.Exception = info.Exception.GetBaseException();
                traceRecord.Operator = operatorName;
                traceRecord.Operation = operationName;
                if (errorTrace != null) {
                    errorTrace(traceRecord);
                }
            });

        return info.Throw();
    })

    .Finally(() => {
        if (task.IsCanceled) {
            traceWriter.Trace(
                request,
                category,
                TraceLevel.Warn,
                (TraceRecord traceRecord) => {
                    traceRecord.Kind = TraceKind.End;
                    traceRecord.Operator = operatorName;
                    traceRecord.Operation = operationName;
                    traceRecord.Message = SRResources.TraceCancelledMessage;
```

```
            if (errorTrace != null) {
                errorTrace(traceRecord);
            }
        });
    }
});
```

At the beginning of the try block, the execute Action delegate is invoked, and its returning Task object is then checked against null. If the Task instance is null, the tracing code is stopped, and everything behaves as if tracing were not enabled. If the Task instance is not null, it is returned with three continuations defined thus: Then, Catch, and Finally. Each invokes a call to the trace writer's Trace method, with the TraceRecord instance being created with the appropriate parameters. When the task is executed, the way the trace writer then writes the trace log depends on the result of the task operation.

Example: Microsoft.AspNet.WebApi.Tracing

Now that the theory of ASP.NET Web API tracing has been gone into and you know how it works under the hood, you might be interested to see it in action. By default, ASP.NET Web API doesn't provide trace writers, but the ASP.NET Web API Team has created a NuGet package named Microsoft.AspNet.WebApi.Tracing. You can install it by running Install-Package Microsoft.AspNet.WebApi.Tracing on the NuGet Package Manager Console.

■ **Note** At the time of writing, this NuGet package was in prerelease. If it is still in prerelease as you read this, you will need to use the –pre switch with the Install-Package command Microsoft.AspNet.WebApi.Tracing -pre.

After installing the package, you will see that a file named TraceConfig.cs has been added in your App_Start folder. Its content is shown in Listing 18-10.

Listing 18-10. TraceConfig.cs of the Microsoft.AspNet.WebApi.Tracing

```
public static class TraceConfig {
    public static void Register(HttpConfiguration configuration) {
        if (configuration == null) {
            throw new ArgumentNullException("configuration");
        }

        var traceWriter =
            new SystemDiagnosticsTraceWriter() {
                MinimumLevel = TraceLevel.Info,
                IsVerbose = false
            };

        configuration.Services.Replace(typeof (ITraceWriter), traceWriter);
    }
}
```

As Listing 18-10 shows, the created SystemDiagnosticsTraceWriter instance replaces the registered ITraceWriter instance (which is null at that moment) in the Services collection of the Web API configuration. Remember, that's the point that indicates to the TraceManager whether to enable tracing or not.

In order to get the tracing up and running, the `TraceConfig.Register` method needs to be invoked from the applications configuration (see Listing 18-11).

Listing 18-11. Registering the TraceConfig

```
public static class WebApiConfig {
    public static void Register(HttpConfiguration config) {
        RouteConfig.Register(config);
        TraceConfig.Register(config);
    }
}
```

If you hit F5 in Visual Studio now and point your browser to the URI `http://localhost:11850/api/values/5`, you'll get the output in the Output Window in Visual Studio.

```
iisexpress.exe Information: 0 : Request, Method=GET, Url=http://localhost:11850/api/values/5,
Message='http://localhost:11850/api/values/5'
iisexpress.exe Information: 0 : Message='Values',
Operation=DefaultHttpControllerSelector.SelectController
iisexpress.exe Information: 0 : Message='WebApiTracing.Controllers.ValuesController',
Operation=DefaultHttpControllerActivator.Create
iisexpress.exe Information: 0 : Message='WebApiTracing.Controllers.ValuesController',
Operation=HttpControllerDescriptor.CreateController
iisexpress.exe Information: 0 : Message='Selected action 'Get(Int32 id)'',
Operation=ApiControllerActionSelector.SelectAction
iisexpress.exe Information: 0 : Message='Parameter 'id' bound to the value '5'',
Operation=ModelBinderParameterBinding.ExecuteBindingAsync
iisexpress.exe Information: 0 : Message='Model state is valid. Values: id=5',
Operation=HttpActionBinding.ExecuteBindingAsync
iisexpress.exe Information: 0 : Message='Action returned 'value'',
Operation=ReflectedHttpActionDescriptor.ExecuteAsync
iisexpress.exe Information: 0 : Message='Will use same 'XmlMediaTypeFormatter' formatter',
Operation=XmlMediaTypeFormatter.GetPerRequestFormatterInstance
iisexpress.exe Information: 0 : Message='Selected formatter='XmlMediaTypeFormatter',
content-type='application/xml; charset=utf-8'', Operation=DefaultContentNegotiator.Negotiate
iisexpress.exe Information: 0 : Operation=ApiControllerActionInvoker.InvokeActionAsync,
Status=200 (OK)
iisexpress.exe Information: 0 : Operation=ValuesController.ExecuteAsync, Status=200 (OK)
iisexpress.exe Information: 0 : Response, Status=200 (OK), Method=GET,
Url=http://localhost:11850/api/values/5, Message='Content-type='application/xml;
charset=utf-8', content-length=unknown'
iisexpress.exe Information: 0 : Operation=XmlMediaTypeFormatter.WriteToStreamAsync
iisexpress.exe Information: 0 : Operation=ValuesController.Dispose
```

The log shows the output of all registered tracers. The output set in boldface shows the trace information being crafted in the `HttpControllerActionInvokerTracer`, which was dissected earlier in this chapter.

In this section, about the tracing mechanism in ASP.NET Web API, you have learned how the mechanism works under the hood and how it differs from classic tracing approaches—and you have seen it in action. One thing ignored until now—but already seen in a few places—is the piece of code that actually does the logging to a specific location, be it a log file or another form of event log. Let's head over to the `ITraceWriter` interface and change that.

ITraceWriter

In the last few paragraphs you have seen that you can get tracing up and running in an ASP.NET Web API application without knowing how it works or even implementing a trace writer when using the `Microsoft.AspNet.WebApi.Tracing` NuGet package. This is OK for fast results but not for most real-world scenarios, as you might want to log to other targets (like files or databases) as well, and that requires having more details about ASP.NET Web API tracing. We'll now create a trace writer that allows logging the trace output being created inside the already seen tracer wrapper class to the Windows console.

The core of each trace writer implementation is the `ITraceWriter` interface (see Listing 18-12), which has to be implemented by our trace writer.

Listing 18-12. The ITraceWriter Interface

```
public interface ITraceWriter {
    void Trace(HttpRequestMessage request, string category, TraceLevel level,
Action<TraceRecord> traceAction);
}
```

The interface defines only one method: Trace, which you've already seen in use (for example, in Listing 18-9). This method expects four parameters, of which the first is the current request made from the client. The category and the level parameters allow you to categorize the trace record and define its severity. The last parameter, traceAction delegate, allows you to pass in code that configures the TraceRecord being written to the trace log.

The TraceRecord has several properties you can use to create a comprehensive trace log. The implementation of TraceRecord is shown in Listing 18-13.

Listing 18-13. TraceRecord Implementation

```
public class TraceRecord {
    private Lazy<Dictionary<object, object>> _properties = new Lazy<Dictionary<object, object>>(
        () => new Dictionary<object, object>());

    public TraceRecord(HttpRequestMessage request, string category, TraceLevel level) {
        Timestamp = DateTime.UtcNow;
        Request = request;
        RequestId = request != null ? request.GetCorrelationId() : Guid.Empty;
        Category = category;
        Level = level;
    }

    public string Category { get; set; }
    public Exception Exception { get; set; }
    public TraceKind Kind { get; set; }
    public TraceLevel Level { get; set; }
    public string Message { get; set; }
    public string Operation { get; set; }
    public string Operator { get; set; }
    public Dictionary<object, object> Properties {
        get { return _properties.Value; }
    }
    public HttpRequestMessage Request { get; private set; }
    public Guid RequestId { get; private set; }
```

```
    public HttpStatusCode Status { get; set; }
    public DateTime Timestamp { get; private set; }
}
```

As you can see, some of the mandatory properties are created inside the constructor of TraceRecord. Properties are not available until after the instantiation of TraceRecord, like the Message or the Operation, are set from within the code that makes the call to the ITraceWriter instance later on.

Now there is a good foundation upon which to implement our console window trace writer. Listing 18-14 shows the implementation of the ConsoleTraceWriter class.

Listing 18-14. ConsoleTraceWriter Implementation

```
public class ConsoleTraceWriter : ITraceWriter {
    public void Trace(HttpRequestMessage request, string category,
                        TraceLevel level, Action<TraceRecord> traceAction) {
        var traceRecord = new TraceRecord(request, category, level);
        traceAction(traceRecord);
        traceToConsole(traceRecord);
    }

    private void traceToConsole(TraceRecord traceRecord) {
        Console.WriteLine(
            "{0} {1}: Category={2}, Level={3} {4} {5} {6} {7}",
            traceRecord.Request.Method,
            traceRecord.Request.RequestUri,
            traceRecord.Category,
            traceRecord.Level,
            traceRecord.Kind,
            traceRecord.Operator,
            traceRecord.Operation,
            traceRecord.Exception != null
                ? traceRecord.Exception.GetBaseException().Message
                : !string.IsNullOrEmpty(traceRecord.Message)
                    ? traceRecord.Message
                    : string.Empty
        );
    }
}
```

The Trace method implementation first creates a new TraceRecord instance and hands it over to the traceAction callback method. After that, it logs all available TraceRecord properties to the Windows console window.

As hosting in IIS does not allow showing a console window, let's instead create a self-host environment to see the ConsoleTraceWriter in action. The required code is shown in Listing 18-15.

Listing 18-15. A Console Application to Host ASP.NET Web API Using ConsoleTraceWriter

```
internal class Program {
    private static void Main(string[] args) {
        var config = new HttpSelfHostConfiguration("http://localhost:8080");

        config.Routes.MapHttpRoute(
            name: "DefaultApi",
```

```
            routeTemplate: "api/{controller}/{id}",
            defaults: new {id = RouteParameter.Optional}
            );

        var traceWriter = new ConsoleTraceWriter();
        config.Services.Replace(typeof (ITraceWriter), traceWriter);

        using (var server = new HttpSelfHostServer(config)) {
            server.OpenAsync().Wait();
            Console.WriteLine("Press Enter to quit.");
            Console.ReadLine();
        }
    }
}
```

After creating a new self-hosting configuration and assigning the default Web API route definition to it, the ConsoleTraceWriter is also added to the configuration. Running the self-host Web API server and pointing the browser to http://localhost:8080/api/values/ gives the output shown in Figure 18-1.

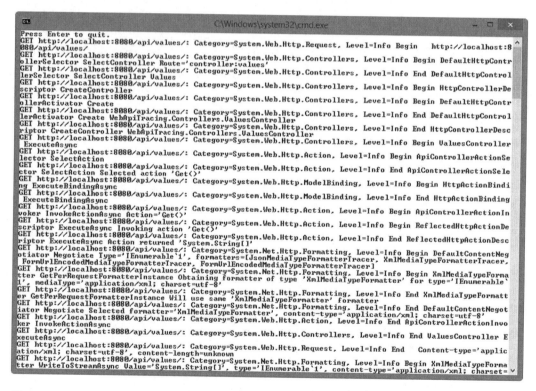

Figure 18-1. *Trace output in a self-host environment using ConsoleTraceWriter*

The output looks pretty much the same as that from the Microsoft.AspNet.WebApi.Tracing package despite its being shown inside a Windows console window instead of the Visual Studio output window.

Besides the Visual Studio output window and the Windows console window, there are many more options to which you might want to write your trace output. One drawback of the approaches taken in the last two samples is that, depending on the output target, the configuration of our Web API application had to be changed. To solve that problem, a generic ITraceWriter could be implemented. It would allow logging on to any arbitrary tracing target you might want to write the trace output to. That would imply writing implementations for each output target—quite an effort! To get rid of that complexity, let's consider taking another approach: reusing an existing tracing framework and wrapping it in an ITraceWriter implementation. Indeed, that's what the next section is about.

ITraceWrite Implementation Using NLog

Depending on the output target and the hosting environment chosen for your ASP.NET Web API application, the ITraceWriter implementation might vary. To have instead a generic implementation for all types of hosting scenarios and output targets, you'll need to wrap an existing tracing framework in an ITraceWriter implementation. The framework chosen here, NLog, is a popular open-source logging framework for the .NET platform. NLog allows you to write its output to the following targets:

- files
- event log
- database
- network
- e-mail
- Windows command window

Furthermore, you can add more output providers to write to other targets not listed here. NLog allows writing to custom targets by implementing a class that derives from the NLog.TargetWithLayout class and overrides its Write method. That custom target then has to be referenced as an extension inside the NLog configuration section in your application configuration file (web.config or app.config).

To use NLog for our ITraceWriter implementation, it has to be added to the current project using the NuGet command line: Install-Package NLog. Now let's head over to the implementation of our NLogTraceWriter class and explore it in sections, starting with the Trace method (see Listing 18-16).

Listing 18-16. The Trace Method of the NLogTraceWriter Class

```
public class NLogTraceWriter : ITraceWriter {
    public void Trace(
        HttpRequestMessage request,
        string category,
        TraceLevel level,
        Action<TraceRecord> traceAction) {
            if (level == TraceLevel.Off) return;
            var record = new TraceRecord(request, category, level);
            traceAction(record);
            logToNLog(record);
    }
}
```

The Trace method of the NLogTraceWriter implementation looks quite similar to the ones seen before. The main difference is the call to the logToNLog method, which is shown in Listing 18-17.

Listing 18-17. The logToNLog Method of the NLogTraceWriter Class

```
private void logToNLog(TraceRecord traceRecord) {
    var messageBuilder = new StringBuilder();

    if (traceRecord.Request != null) {
        if (traceRecord.Request.Method != null) {
            messageBuilder.Append(" " + traceRecord.Request.Method);
        }

        if (traceRecord.Request.RequestUri != null) {
            messageBuilder.Append(" " + traceRecord.Request.RequestUri);
        }
    }

    if (!string.IsNullOrWhiteSpace(traceRecord.Category)) {
        messageBuilder.Append(" " + traceRecord.Category);
    }

    if (!string.IsNullOrWhiteSpace(traceRecord.Operator)) {
        messageBuilder.Append(" " + traceRecord.Operator + " " + traceRecord.Operation);
    }

    if (!string.IsNullOrWhiteSpace(traceRecord.Message)) {
        messageBuilder.Append(" " + traceRecord.Message);
    }

    if (traceRecord.Exception != null) {
        messageBuilder.Append(traceRecord.Exception.GetBaseException().Message);
    }

    currentLogger[traceRecord.Level](messageBuilder.ToString());
}
```

The logToNLog method mainly joins all traceRecord properties into a single message string, which then gets handed over to the currentLogger method, which writes to the event log. The currentLogger method is a Dictionary<TraceLevel, Action<string>> that selects the method—Info(), Error(), or the like—to call on the current NLog logger instance based on the TraceRecord instance's Level property. The implementation is shown in Listing 18-18.

Listing 18-18. Mapping of TraceRecord Levels to NLog Logger Methods

```
private static readonly Lazy<Dictionary<TraceLevel, Action<string>>> Loggers =
    new Lazy<Dictionary<TraceLevel, Action<string>>>(() =>
        new Dictionary<TraceLevel, Action<string>> {
            { TraceLevel.Debug, LogManager.GetCurrentClassLogger().Debug },
            { TraceLevel.Error, LogManager.GetCurrentClassLogger().Error },
            { TraceLevel.Fatal, LogManager.GetCurrentClassLogger().Fatal },
```

```
                { TraceLevel.Info, LogManager.GetCurrentClassLogger().Info },
                { TraceLevel.Warn, LogManager.GetCurrentClassLogger().Warn }
        });

    private Dictionary<TraceLevel, Action<string>> currentLogger {
        get { return Loggers.Value; }
    }
}
```

The Loggers property, which is of the type Lazy<Dictionary<TraceLevel, Action<string>>>, maps the enumeration elements of the TraceLevel enum to the matching method of the Logger instance being returned from the LogManager.GetCurrentClassLogger() method. The currentLogger property then selects the appropriate value based on the TraceLevel being provided as key.

The registration of the NLogTraceWriter is very similar to others already seen. Listing 18-19 shows the registration inside the TraceConfig class.

Listing 18-19. Registering the NLogTraceWriter Using the TraceConfig Class

```
public static class TraceConfig {
    public static void Register(HttpConfiguration configuration) {
        if (configuration == null) {
            throw new ArgumentNullException("configuration");
        }

        var traceWriter =
            new NLogTraceWriter();

        configuration.Services.Replace(typeof (ITraceWriter), traceWriter);
    }
}
```

At the beginning of this section, it was noted that NLog allows logging against different log targets. You might wonder where to tell NLog which one to use for our sample application. NLog uses the application configuration to store that information. So before being able to log anything, you need to update web.config (or app.config if you're self-hosting) accordingly. NLog expects the application configuration file to have a section of the type NLog.Config.ConfigSectionHandler providing information about the targets to use and the rules being applied to the loggers. Listing 18-20 shows the relevant web.config fragments (they could also be used in an app.config file).

Listing 18-20. Configuration of the Logging Targets and Rules for NLog in web.config

```
<configuration>
  <configSections>
    <section name="nlog" type="NLog.Config.ConfigSectionHandler, NLog"/>
  </configSections>
  <nlog xmlns:xsi="http://www.w3.org/2001/XMLSchema-instance">
    <targets>
      <target name="logfile"
              xsi:type="File"
              fileName="${basedir}/${date:format=yyyy-MM-dd}.WebApiNLogTracing.log" />
      <target name="eventlog"
              xsi:type="EventLog"
              layout="${message}" log="Application" source="WebApiNLogTracing Application" />
    </targets>
```

```
    <rules>
      <logger name="*" minlevel="Trace" writeTo="logfile" />
      <logger name="*" minlevel="Trace" writeTo="eventlog" />
    </rules>
  </nlog>
</configuration>
```

First, the required NLog configuration section is created. Inside that section, two `targets`, `logfile` and `eventlog`, are created. The former logs to a file, and the latter logs to the Windows event log. The `logfile` is configured to name the file with the current date followed by the name of the application. The `eventlog` is configured to write, as is, the `Message` of the `Logger` to the Application section inside the Windows event log. The source of the event log entry identifies our application.

The `Rules` section of the NLog configuration applies two rules to all `Logger` instances and both targets and sets the minimum trace level in order to trace which one causes NLog to create a verbose log file or event log.

Since the `logfile` was defined to be written in the root of our applications directory, writing to that file works without any issues, as the user context is the same as that for the application. When trying to write to the event log using the credentials of your application, you might encounter the problem that no event log entry is created. This might occur because your application needs to be registered as an event source, and your credentials might not allow you to do that. Explaining how to create an event source would extend the scope of this book, but Microsoft provides a support document that describes how to write to an event log by creating an event source: `http://support.microsoft.com/kb/307024/en-us`. A quick workaround is to start Visual Studio as an administrator and run the application from within Visual Studio. Doing so creates the log file containing ASP.NET Web API trace messages, as well as the Windows event log entries. Figure 18-2 shows the log file in the root folder of the application, and Figure 18-3 shows the event log entries being created during the same requests.

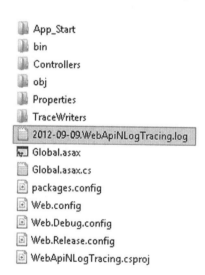

Figure 18-2. *Trace log file created by the NLogTraceWriter*

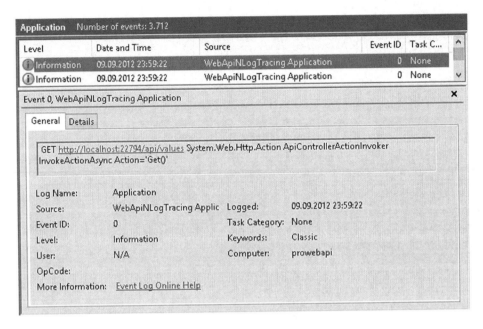

Figure 18-3. *Event log entry created by the NLogTraceWriter*

The NLogTraceWriter implementation in this section gives a way of tracing information to different targets (a way agnostic to a logging target) by registering the ITraceWriter implementation only once. Relevant changes can be made to the web.config or app.config without the need to change our code and recompile the application just for the purpose of changing the type of logging.

The last three sections have shown how to trace and log information from within the default services of ASP.NET Web API. Of course, the ITraceWriter implementation inside our own application code can also be used. How to do so will be the focus of the next section.

Using ITraceWriter in User Code

ASP.NET Web API traces information about the "infrastructure" of an ASP.NET Web API application when tracing is enabled. Many details can be read from that information but at times you may want to log even more details, especially about code specific to your own application.

Due to the way tracing works in ASP.NET Web API, you can also use the configured trace writer inside your own code. Listing 18-21 shows how to do so inside a controller action.

Listing 18-21. Using the ITraceWriter Instance Inside a Controllers Action

```
public IEnumerable<string> Get() {
    var traceWriter = Configuration.Services.GetTraceWriter();
    if(null != traceWriter) {
        traceWriter.Trace(Request, "WebApiNLogTracing.Controllers",
            TraceLevel.Info,
            (traceRecord) => {
                    traceRecord.Message = "Read all values.";
                });
    }
    return new string[] {"value1", "value2"};
}
```

After getting the ITraceWriter instance from the application configuration (when tracing is enabled, that is), a TraceRecord is wired up and written to the configured target. Listing 18-22 shows the log file entry being created by a request to the controller action from Listing 18-21.

Listing 18-22. Log File Entry Being Created Inside a Controllers Action

```
2012-09-10 00:29:21.8747|INFO|WebApiNLogTracing.TraceWriters.NLogTraceWriter| GET
http://localhost:22794/api/values WebApiNLogTracing.Controllers Read all values.
```

As it's cumbersome to constantly write traceWriter.Trace and then provide the TraceLevel parameter, the ASP.NET Web API team created the ITraceWriterExtensions class, which provides a few shorter methods with which to use the ITraceWriter. One example that uses the .Debug extension method is shown in Listing 18-23.

Listing 18-23. Using the .Debug Extension Method for ITraceWriter in a Controllers Action

```
public string Get(int id) {
    var traceWriter = Configuration.Services.GetTraceWriter();
    if (traceWriter != null) {
        traceWriter.Debug(Request, "WebApiNLogTracing.Controllers",
                        string.Format("Read value {0}", id));
    }
    return "value";
}
```

When pointing your browser to the URI http://localhost:22794/api/values/5, you find the corresponding entry in your log file. As said, the ITraceWriterExtensions class provides some more useful methods, which you can easily explorer using Visual Studio IntelliSense.

You have already seen that ASP.NET Web API provides a well-thought-out, unobtrusive, and extensible way to add tracing to your ASP.NET Web API application. If tracing is not enabled, the impact on performance is close to zero, as no code aware of tracing is executed after application configuration initialization. Furthermore, the tracing framework provided is reusable in the code inside your Web API application, and it can be used in conjunction with your preferred logging framework.

Now, as promised, let's continue with the documentation of ASP.NET Web API applications.

Documenting Your Web API

When creating a public HTTP API using ASP.NET Web API, in the end you are creating web services. People with backgrounds in classic .NET web services technologies like ASP.NET Web Services (ASMX) and Windows Communication Foundation (WCF) are used to having their public web services API-documented automatically by implementing those services. ASMX and WCF create a web page for each service, where the web service description language (WSDL) file is wrapped visually in an HTML page to provide information about the web service and its methods and parameters. The WSDL file is also available, and so the client proxy code can be created from that definition as well.

Due to the different approach in HTTP applications, wherein the server and client can evolve independently, it is not mandatory to provide a file on the server that describes methods and parameters for the client. Of course, the developer implementing the client needs that information anyway. A common practice here is to provide some static HTML pages describing the HTTP methods, URI templates, media types, and parameters supported by the API. Often these files are created by hand, a cumbersome and error-prone method.

When ASP.NET Web API first became publicly available in beta state, people who had an ASMX and WCF web services background started complaining about the additional work. The ASP.NET Web API team, which lent a sympathetic ear to the community from the framework's earliest days, came up with a solution for ASP.NET Web API, one that allows you to create documentation for your Web API in a simple and easy-to-modify way.

Before digging deeper into API documentation, let's first create a small API that allows creation, updating, and deletion of cars, one that's also able to get a specific car or a list of all cars. Then let's create the documentation for that API based on the mechanism ASP.NET Web API provides to do just that.

The Cars API

The API providing the typical CRUD functionality is pretty simple, as has earlier been stressed several times. The Car class in Listing 18-24 is the same one encountered in previous samples.

Listing 18-24. A Car Class Implementation

```
public class Car {
    public int Id { get; set; }
    public string Make { get; set; }
    public string Model { get; set; }
    public int Year { get; set; }
    public float Price { get; set; }
}
```

Listing 18-25 shows the CarsController implementation for which the documentation is to be created.

Listing 18-25. A Controller Handling Some Operations Using the Car Class

```
public class CarsController {
    private readonly List<Car> _cars;

    public CarsController() {
        _cars = new List<Car>() {
            new Car() {
                Id = 17,
                Make = "VW",
                Model = "Golf",
                Year = 1999,
                Price = 1500f
            },
            new Car() {
                Id = 30,
                Make = "Mercedes",
                Model = "A-Class",
                Year = 2007,
                Price = 10000f
            }
        };
    }

    public List<Car> Get() {
        return _cars;
    }
```

```
    public Car Post(Car car) {
        car.Id = _cars.Max(c => c.Id) + 1;
        _cars.Add(car);
        return car;
    }

    public Car Get(int id) {
        return _cars.FirstOrDefault(c => c.Id == id);
    }

    public Car Put([FromUri] int id, Car car) {
        _cars[_cars.FindIndex(c => c.Id == id)] = car;
        return car;
    }

    public HttpResponseMessage Delete(int id) {
        _cars.RemoveAt(_cars.FindIndex(c => c.Id == id));
        return new HttpResponseMessage(HttpStatusCode.NoContent);
    }
}
```

The implementation in Listing 18-25 is straightforward but, alas, not really useful in a real-world scenario. But it fits well and shows the "automatic" generation of API documentation in ASP.NET Web API as it implements several actions that provide return values and expect parameters to be passed in. Before generating an API documentation automatically, let's create it by hand to show what the ASP.NET Web API documentation mechanism is expected to create.

Documenting an HTTP API by Hand

It's common for a lot of developers of public HTTP applications to create the documentation by hand. As it's desirable to have some sort of a template for our automatically created documentation in this chapter's next section, let's first do documentation by hand for our `CarsController` and its operations. The requirements are to show

- the name of the resource being handled in the operations (here it's `Car`);
- the HTTP methods being supported and the URI templates for those operations;
- the URI and body parameters for those operations;
- a sample response for the supported media types;
- a plain-text description for each operation and its parameters.

The documentation shown in Listing 18-26 fulfills all these requirements.

Listing 18-26. A Complete, Handcrafted Documentation for the cars API

Cars
GET api/Cars
```
application/json Sample response body
[{"Id":17,"Make":"VW","Model":"Golf","Year":1999,"Price":1500.0},{"Id":24,"Make":"Porsche",
"Model":"911","Year":2011,"Price":100000.0}]
```

```
text/xml Sample response body
<ArrayOfCar xmlns:i="http://www.w3.org/2001/XMLSchema-instance"
xmlns="http://schemas.datacontract.org/2004/07/WebApiDocumentation.Entities"><Car><Id>17</Id>
<Make>VW</Make><Model>Golf</Model><Price>1500</Price><Year>1999</Year></Car><Car><Id>24</Id>
<Make>Porsche</Make><Model>911</Model><Price>100000</Price><Year>2011</Year></Car></ArrayOfCar>
```

GET api/Cars/{id}
Gets a car by its ID.

Parameter: id (FromUri): The ID of the car.

```
application/json Sample response body
{"Id":17,"Make":"VW","Model":"Golf","Year":1999,"Price":1500.0}
```

```
text/xml Sample response body
<Car xmlns:i="http://www.w3.org/2001/XMLSchema-instance"
xmlns="http://schemas.datacontract.org/2004/07/WebApiDocumentation.Entities"><Id>17</Id>
<Make>VW</Make><Model>Golf</Model><Price>1500</Price><Year>1999</Year></Car>
```

POST api/Cars
Parameter: car (FromBody):

```
application/json Sample response body
{"Id":17,"Make":"VW","Model":"Golf","Year":1999,"Price":1500.0}
```

```
text/xml Sample response body
<Car xmlns:i="http://www.w3.org/2001/XMLSchema-instance"
xmlns="http://schemas.datacontract.org/2004/07/WebApiDocumentation.Entities"><Id>17</Id>
<Make>VW</Make><Model>Golf</Model><Price>1500</Price><Year>1999</Year></Car>
```

PUT api/Cars/{id}
Parameter: id (FromUri):

Parameter: car (FromBody):

```
application/json Sample response body
{"Id":17,"Make":"VW","Model":"Golf","Year":1999,"Price":1500.0}
```

```
text/xml Sample response body
<Car xmlns:i="http://www.w3.org/2001/XMLSchema-instance"
xmlns="http://schemas.datacontract.org/2004/07/WebApiDocumentation.Entities"><Id>17</Id>
<Make>VW</Make><Model>Golf</Model><Price>1500</Price><Year>1999</Year></Car>
```

DELETE api/Cars/{id}
Parameter: id (FromUri):

Even though the operations and implementation of the controller are pretty simple, crafting and keeping its documentation can become a hard job—and might be error-prone as well. So let's get this job automated and keep our heads free for the implementations of APIs in the future.

Documenting an HTTP API Using ApiExplorer

Having created an API documentation by hand, let's see what ASP.NET Web API can do. The core of the ASP.NET Web API documentation mechanism is the ApiExplorer class, which implements the IApiExplorer interface. This interface, as Listing 18-27 shows, has only one property that has to be implemented by a derived type: the generic ApiDescriptions collection.

Listing 18-27. The IApiExplorer Interface

```
public interface IApiExplorer {
    Collection<ApiDescription> ApiDescriptions { get; }
}
```

The ApiDescription class itself contains the description for an API being defined by a relative URI and an HTTP method. The primary goal of an IApiExplorer implementation is to provide a collection of all API descriptions being implemented in an HTTP API application. The ApiExplorer class shipped with ASP.NET Web API is registered as the default IApiExplorer service in the application configuration. As with the other default services, ApiExplorer can be replaced by your own implementation. In order to provide the ApiDescription collection, the ApiExplorer, when instantiated, creates that collection and fills it with instances of ApiDescription. The ApiDescription instances are created by querying the ASP.NET Web API configuration and its default services. Some of the services and classes queried for the required information are

- HttpConfiguration.Routes
- HttpControllerSelector
- HttpControllerDescriptor
- HttpActionDescriptor
- HttpParameterDescriptor
- HttpActionBinding

As you might expect, this process is a lengthy one. Describing it in full detail would be beyond the scope of this book. Instead, let's focus on the results that ApiExplorer has created. At the end of this service-querying process inside its constructor, ApiExplorer has all ApiDescription instances available for use in documenting our API.

Although ASP.NET Web API is hosting layer agnostic, it is a part of the ASP.NET framework stack. So, we can use ASP.NET MVC and ASP.NET Web API inside the same project without any problems. This is pretty handy, as some web application framework that is able to render the output of our ApiExplorer to HTML code is needed. Of course, we choose ASP.NET MVC 4 for that. To create the HTML code, it's first necessary to create a model class that gets instantiated and assigned to the appropriate view in our ASP.NET MVC controllers action method. The model implementation, contained in the class ApiModel, is shown in Listing 18-28.

Listing 18-28. The ApiModel Class

```
public class ApiModel {
    private IApiExplorer _explorer;

    public ApiModel(IApiExplorer explorer) {
        if (explorer == null) {
            throw new ArgumentNullException("explorer");
        }
        _explorer = explorer;
    }
```

```
public ILookup<string, ApiDescription> GetApis() {
    return _explorer.ApiDescriptions.ToLookup(
        api => api.ActionDescriptor.ControllerDescriptor.ControllerName);
    }
}
```

The ApiModel class expects an IApiExplorer instance in its constructor, an instance that is assigned to a private field that is accessed in the GetApis method to return its ApiDescriptions collection items as ILookup<string, ApiDescription>. That collection is created using the ToLookup method, an extension method for IEnumerable<T> that resides in the System.Linq.Enumerable class. The ILookup interface itself defines the properties Count and Item and the method Contains, which can be applied to an IEnumerable<T>. The Item property gets the IEnumerable<T> sequence of values indexed by a specified key. So the ToLookup method applies an index on the ApiDescriptions property of the ApiExplorer instance. This allows use of the ControllerName string property of the ControllerDescriptor class as a key for that indexed collection. Thus, ApiDescriptions can now be accessed in a grouped manner based on the controller name. This may be a bit hard to grasp in theory, so let's take a look at the Index view for our HomeController (see Listing 18-29). The HomeController is an ASP.NET MVC 4 controller, a type we'll inspect soon.

Listing 18-29. The Index View for the ASP.NET MVC HomeController

```
@model WebApiDocumentation.Models.ApiModel

@{
    ViewBag.Title = "API Help";
}

@section Scripts
{
    @Scripts.Render("~/bundles/jqueryui")
    <script type="text/javascript">
        $(function() { $(".accordion").accordion(); });
    </script>
}

<div id="body" class="content-wrapper">
    <h2>API Help</h2>

    @foreach (var apiDescriptionGroup in Model.GetApis()) {
        <h3>@apiDescriptionGroup.Key</h3>

        <div class="accordion">
            @foreach (var api in apiDescriptionGroup) {
                <h4><a href="#">@api.HttpMethod @api.RelativePath</a></h4>
                <div>
                    @foreach (var param in api.ParameterDescriptions) {
                        <p>Parameter: <em>@param.Name</em> (@param.Source)</p>
                    }
                </div>
            }
        </div>
    }
</div>
```

The ApiModel class is referenced in the first line of the view using the @model directive, which allows access to its members inside the view. The model can be accessed using the view's Model property. Previously, when handcrafting our API documentation, we wanted to show the name of the resource as the title for the group of operations possible on the resource. Below the resource name, the list of operations appeared as URI templates, including their parameters and their source.

Look again at Listing 18-28. You'll see that the ILookup<string, ApiDescription> being returned from the Get Apis method of the ApiModel is used to iterate the groups of API descriptions. As you saw in Listing 18-29, the grouping key of that Lookup is the controller name, and so that name can be written to the HTML output stream using @apiDescriptionGroup.Key. Since the apiDescriptionGroup contains all ApiDescription instances for a particular controller, you can iterate over that collection to get the details for the operations of the controller, whose name was just used as the group title. To create an output similar to the handcrafted version, write out the HttpMethod and the relative URI for each operation. Each ApiDescription contains a list of parameters for each operation. So, iterating again, this time over the ParameterDescriptions collection, allows almost complete documentation for the cars API.

To get the code inside the view working, wire it up with the ApiModel instance inside our HomeController class (see Listing 18-30).

Listing 18-30. Wiring Up ApiModel and the Index View

```
public class HomeController : Controller {
    public ActionResult Index() {
        var config = GlobalConfiguration.Configuration;
        var explorer = config.Services.GetApiExplorer();
        return View(new ApiModel(explorer));
    }
}
```

The Index method on the HomeController, which derives from the System.Web.Mvc.Controller base class, gains access to the application configuration first. After querying the registered Services for the ApiExplorer instance, assign that result as the parameter to the ApiModel class, which is itself a parameter for the view to be rendered later on.

Pointing our browser to http://localhost:31438/ gives the API documentation created by the classes described previously. The result can be seen in Figure 18-4.

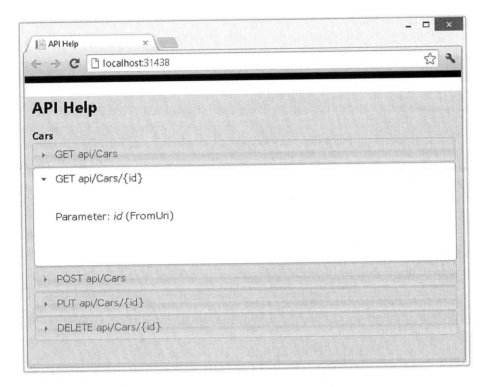

Figure 18-4. *Output of the API documentation created by ApiExplorer*

Again, when the result in Figure 18-4 is compared with our documentation created by hand, it still lacks two things: the description of the operation and its parameters, as well as the sample response bodies. Let's start with the latter. The ApiExplorer doesn't provide any help here, but as ASP.NET Web API already provides everything to create it by ourselves, that's no problem. One or more sample instances of our resource and its representation, like XML or JSON, are all that are needed. As a MediaTypeFormatter can be used anywhere, simply create the sample response output from the resource class instances in our ApiModel. That's what Listing 18-31 shows.

Listing 18-31. Creating the Sample Response Data

```
private static readonly List<Car> _cars = new List<Car>() {
    new Car() {
                Id = 17,
                Make = "VW",
                Model = "Golf",
                Year = 1999,
                Price = 1500f
            },
    new Car() {
                Id = 24,
                Make = "Porsche",
                Model = "911",
                Year = 2011,
                Price = 100000f
            }
};
```

```csharp
private Dictionary<Type, object> _sampleData =
    new Dictionary<Type, object>() {
    {typeof (Car), _cars[0]},
    {typeof (List<Car>), _cars}
};

public string GetSampleResponseBody(ApiDescription api, string mediaType) {
    string body = null;
    Type returnType = GetResponseType(api.ActionDescriptor);

    object o;
    if (returnType != null && _sampleData.TryGetValue(returnType, out o)) {
        var formatters = api.SupportedResponseFormatters;

        MediaTypeFormatter formatter = formatters.FirstOrDefault(
            f => f.SupportedMediaTypes.Any(m => m.MediaType == mediaType));

        if (formatter != null) {
            var content = new ObjectContent(returnType, o, formatter);
            body = content.ReadAsStringAsync().Result;
        }
    }
    return body;
}

private Type GetResponseType(HttpActionDescriptor action) {
    return action.ReturnType;
}
```

Listing 18-31 consists of three parts: creating a List<Car> named _cars, which contains the sample car resources. The _sampleData Dictionary maps the _cars list to the type of response the CarsController can be: List<Car> or Car. The work of creating the sample is done by the GetSampleResponseBody method, which first tries to find a matching response type for the currently selected operation (that is, the controllers action). If the return type can be determined from the API description and there is a match in the sample data dictionary, the ApiModel tries to find a matching MediaTypeFormatter for that particular return type. If this succeeds also, the MediaTypeFormatter is invoked to deserialize the return type to the requested media type—for example, application/json. To visualize that additional data, let's update our Index view now and add the code shown in Listing 18-32.

Listing 18-32. Visualizing the Sample Response Bodies

```csharp
@{
    string jsonResponse = @Model.GetSampleResponseBody(api, "application/json");
    string xmlResponse = @Model.GetSampleResponseBody(api, "text/xml");
}

@if (jsonResponse != null) {
    <h5>application/json Sample response body</h5>
    <p><code>@jsonResponse</code></p>
}
```

```
@if (xmlResponse != null) {
    <h5>text/xml Sample response body</h5>
    <p><code>@xmlResponse</code></p>
}
```

Our reference documentation contained sample response bodies for application/json as well as text/xml media types, so our automatically created documentation should be able to do the same. The code in Listing 18-33 is pretty straightforward in doing that by calling the GetSampleResponseBody method of the ApiModel twice—once for each media type. The results, if available, then are rendered to the HTML output stream.

The updated output of the Index view can be examined in Figure 18-5.

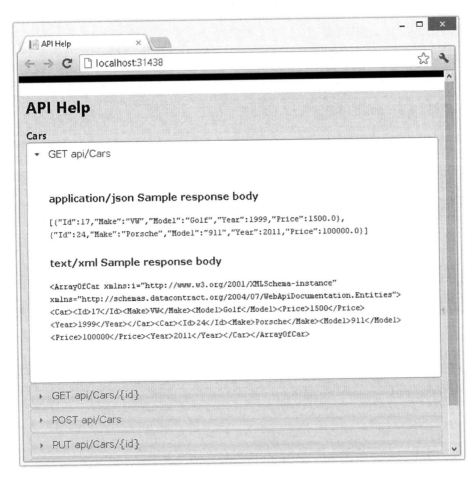

***Figure 18-5.** Sample response body for application/json and text/xml media types*

Although the code shown in the previous listings works fine, there's one drawback: If the return type of the controllers Action were of type HttpResponseMessage, no sample response output would be shown. But thanks to the ApiDescription class, there's a simple workaround for that problem. Listing 18-33 shows another mapping and updates our GetResponseType method introduced in Listing 18-31.

Listing 18-33. Improving the Sample Response Output Generation

```
private static readonly Dictionary<string, Type> _typeMappings =
    new Dictionary<string, Type>() {
        { @"GETapi/Cars/{id}", typeof (Car) }
};

private Type GetResponseType(ApiDescription api) {
    Type t;
    return _typeMappings.TryGetValue(api.ID, out t)
        ? t : api.ActionDescriptor.ReturnType;
}
```

The dictionary _typeMappings contains a list of elements for which the key is the ID of an API. That ID is available as a property on each ApiDescription instance and is a concatenation of the HTTP method and the relative URI path for that particular API. In our listing, that is GET api/Cars/{id}. The value for the key inside the _typeMappings dictionary is the returned HttpResponseMessage's value type, which in our sample is Car. The GetResponseType method now tries to get the sample response type from the mapping dictionary. If that fails, it falls back to its already known implementation. If you now change the implementation of the Get(int id) method of the CarsController class, as in Listing 18-34, the documentation will still be created including the sample response bodies already shown in Figure 18-5.

Listing 18-34. Returning an HttpResponseMessage Instead of a Car Instance

```
public HttpResponseMessage Get(int id) {
    return Request.CreateResponse(HttpStatusCode.OK,
        _cars.FirstOrDefault(c => c.Id == id));
}
```

Now there is only one thing missing from our API documentation: a text description of each operation and its parameters. As ASP.NET Web API is a sophisticated framework, there's also a solution available for that. Besides the others already used, the ApiDescription and the ApiParameterDescription classes provide a property named Documentation. These classes are designated to provide the plain-text description for an API or its parameter. This is perfect for our needs, but one question remains: how to populate that information with the description of the API or its parameters, especially since documentations haven't been defined until now? This problem is solvable with two classes and one interface. The classes are two attributes named ApiDocumentationAttribute and ApiParameterDocumentationAttribute. Both are shown in Listing 18-35.

Listing 18-35. ParameterDocAttribute and ApiParameterDocAttribute

```
[AttributeUsage(AttributeTargets.Method, AllowMultiple = false)]
public sealed class ApiDocumentationAttribute : Attribute {
    public ApiDocumentationAttribute(string description) {
        Description = description;
    }

    public string Description { get; private set; }
}

[AttributeUsage(AttributeTargets.Method, AllowMultiple = true)]
public sealed class ApiParameterDocumentationAttribute : Attribute {
    public ApiParameterDocumentationAttribute(string parameterName, string description) {
        ParameterName = parameterName;
```

```
        Description = description;
    }

    public string ParameterName { get; private set; }

    public string Description { get; private set; }
}
```

The ApiDocumentationAttribute contains only one property, Description, which is of type string. The ApiParameterDocumentationAttribute instead contains two properties: ParameterName and Description, both also of type string. The ParameterName property has to be provided, as an operation can have multiple parameters and the attribute then has to be applied multiple times to the method, once for each parameter.

The interface provided by ASP.NET Web API for API and parameter documentation purposes is the IDocumentationProvider interface. Its signature is shown in Listing 18-36.

Listing 18-36. The IDocumentationProvider Interface

```
public interface IDocumentationProvider {
    string GetDocumentation(HttpActionDescriptor actionDescriptor);
    string GetDocumentation(HttpParameterDescriptor parameterDescriptor);
}
```

The IDocumentationProvider interface defines two methods named GetDocumentation and expects a parameter of type HttpActionDescriptor or HttpParameterDescriptor. This makes sense, as providing documentation strings for APIs (which are the actions in this context) or their parameters is the goal. An implementation of IDocumentationProvider is the AttributeDocumentationProvider class, which can be seen in Listing 18-37.

Listing 18-37. The AttributeDocumentationProvider Implementation

```
public class AttributeDocumentationProvider : IDocumentationProvider {
    public string GetDocumentation(HttpActionDescriptor actionDescriptor) {
        var apiDocumentation =
            actionDescriptor
                .GetCustomAttributes<ApiDocumentationAttribute>()
                    .FirstOrDefault();
        if (apiDocumentation != null) {
            return apiDocumentation.Description;
        }

        return string.Empty;
    }

    public string GetDocumentation(HttpParameterDescriptor paramDescriptor) {
        var parameterDocumentation =
            paramDescriptor
                .ActionDescriptor
                    .GetCustomAttributes<ApiParameterDocumentationAttribute>().
                        FirstOrDefault(
                            param =>
                                param.ParameterName ==
                                    paramDescriptor.ParameterName);
```

```
        if (parameterDocumentation != null) {
            return parameterDocumentation.Description;
        }

        return string.Empty;
    }
}
```

The implementation of both GetDocumentation methods is pretty simple, although they are a bit lengthy and hard to read. The API's GetDocumentation method queries the HttpActionDescriptor for that particular action (the API) for each applied ApiDocumentationAttribute instance. If it succeeds, it returns the Description property string value from that attribute. The GetDocumentation implementation for the parameters is almost the same: it also queries the HttpActionDescriptor but, of course, for ApiParameterDocumentationAttribute instances. For each instance that matches the parameter's name—which we defined in the attribute definition on our controllers action method—the string value of the parameter's Description property is returned.

Although there is now an IDocumentationProvider implementation, our API documentation won't contain its output for two reasons: the AttributeDocumentationProvider is not registered in the Web API configuration, and the Index view doesn't use the Documentation properties of the ApiDescription and ApiParameterDescription classes. First, let's update the Index view, as shown in Listing 18-38.

Listing 18-38. Adding Api and Parameter Documentation to the Index View

```
<div>
    <p>@api.Documentation</p>
    @foreach (var param in api.ParameterDescriptions) {
        <p>Parameter: <em>@param.Name</em> (@param.Source): @param.Documentation</p>
    }

    @{
        string jsonResponse = @Model.GetSampleResponseBody(api, "application/json");
        string xmlResponse = @Model.GetSampleResponseBody(api, "text/xml");
    }

    @if (jsonResponse != null) {
        <h5>application/json Sample response body</h5>
        <p><code>@jsonResponse</code></p>
    }

    @if (xmlResponse != null) {
        <h5>text/xml Sample response body</h5>
        <p><code>@xmlResponse</code></p>
    }
</div>
```

As the changes are self-explanatory and have already been discussed in detail, let's give our documentation the final touch by registering the AttributeDocumentationProvider as an IDocumentationProvider instance in the Web API configuration shown in Listing 18-39.

Listing 18-39. Registration of the AttributeDocumentationProvider

```
public static class WebApiConfig {
    public static void Register(HttpConfiguration config) {
        config.Routes.MapHttpRoute(
            name: "DefaultApi",
            routeTemplate: "api/{controller}/{id}",
            defaults: new {id = RouteParameter.Optional}
            );

        config.Services.Replace(
            typeof(IDocumentationProvider),
            new AttributeDocumentationProvider());
    }
}
```

Reloading our API documentation in the browser for the last time, you see full-blown documentation according to the requirements set by the handcrafted version. Figure 18-6 shows the complete version.

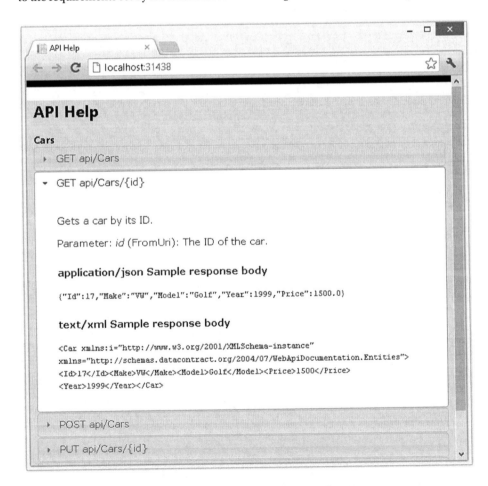

Figure 18-6. *A complete API documentation for ASP.NET Web API*

Now that all requirements for complete API documentation, once by hand and once automated, by use of ASP.NET Web API's mechanism have been fulfilled, you have a reusable solution for a tedious task in Web API development. Of course, you can modify the output to suit your needs, as you've seen, so that in the end everything sent to the browser is plain HTML. Even more, you can enrich your documentation with more information if it's required. An example would be minimum and maximum measurements if the return type is an image file.

Summary

As you saw in both the tracing and the documentation sections, ASP.NET Web API again proves to be a well-thought-out and sophisticated framework for Web API development. Even though it's in its first version, it provides mechanisms for tracing and logging and supports state-of-the-art software development by embracing concepts like dependency injection and easing test-driven development.

Index

■ I

Get the eBook for only $10!

> Now you can take the weightless companion with you anywhere, anytime. Your purchase of this book entitles you to 3 electronic versions for only $10.

This Apress title will prove so indispensible that you'll want to carry it with you everywhere, which is why we are offering the eBook in 3 formats for only $10 if you have already purchased the print book.

Convenient and fully searchable, the PDF version enables you to easily find and copy code—or perform examples by quickly toggling between instructions and applications. The MOBI format is ideal for your Kindle, while the ePUB can be utilized on a variety of mobile devices.

Go to www.apress.com/promo/tendollars to purchase your companion eBook.

Apress®
THE EXPERT'S VOICE™

Druck: KN Digital Printforce GmbH · Schockenriedstraße 37 · 70565 Stuttgart